Housing Act 2004

CHAPTER 34

Explanatory Notes are available separately

GRAN*GIS* UK Publishing

Adapted and published by GRANGIS (Grand Register Library).
Online: www.grangis.com
E-mail: contact@grangis.com

In this version:
ISBN: 979-8-88559-021-1

Note: This is the original version (as it was originally enacted). Title, sub-title and the generated date is as marked on the pages.

Housing Act 2004

CHAPTER 34

HOUSING ACT 2004

PART 1

HOUSING CONDITIONS

CHAPTER 1

ENFORCEMENT OF HOUSING STANDARDS: GENERAL

New system for assessing housing conditions

Procedure for assessing housing conditions

Enforcement of housing standards

CHAPTER 2

IMPROVEMENT NOTICES, PROHIBITION ORDERS AND HAZARD AWARENESS NOTICES

Improvement notices

Prohibition orders

Hazard awareness notices

Enforcement: improvement notices

Enforcement: prohibition orders

Enforcement: improvement notices and prohibition orders

Index

PART 2

LICENSING OF HOUSES IN MULTIPLE OCCUPATION

Introductory

Designation of additional licensing areas

HMOs required to be licensed

Grant or refusal of licences

Variation and revocation of licences

Procedure and appeals

Enforcement

Supplementary provisions

PART 3

SELECTIVE LICENSING OF OTHER RESIDENTIAL ACCOMMODATION

PART 4

ADDITIONAL CONTROL PROVISIONS IN RELATION TO RESIDENTIAL ACCOMMODATION

CHAPTER 1

INTERIM AND FINAL MANAGEMENT ORDERS

Introductory

Interim management orders: making and operation of orders

Interim management orders: variation and revocation

Final management orders: making and operation of orders

Final management orders: variation and revocation

Interim and final management orders: procedure and appeals

Interim and final management orders: other general provisions

Preliminary

Responsibility for marketing residential properties

Duties of a responsible person where a property is on the market

Other duties of person acting as estate agent

Exceptions from the duties

Contents of home information packs

Register of home condition reports

Enforcement

Supplementary

PART 6

OTHER PROVISIONS ABOUT HOUSING

CHAPTER 1

SECURE TENANCIES

Introductory tenancies

Right to buy: when exercisable

Right to buy: discounts

Right to buy: landlord's right of first refusal

Right to buy: information

Right to buy: termination of rent to mortgage scheme

Suspension of certain rights in connection with anti-social behaviour

CHAPTER 2

DISPOSALS ATTRACTING DISCOUNTS OTHER THAN UNDER RIGHT TO BUY

Disposals by local authorities

Enforcement

Authorisations

Documents

Other supplementary provisions

Meaning of "house in multiple occupation"

Other general interpretation provisions

Final provisions

SCHEDULES

Housing Act 2004

2004 CHAPTER 34

An Act to make provision about housing conditions; to regulate houses in multiple occupation and certain other residential accommodation; to make provision for home information packs in connection with the sale of residential properties; to make provision about secure tenants and the right to buy; to make provision about mobile homes and the accommodation needs of gypsies and travellers; to make other provision about housing; and for connected purposes. [18th November 2004]

BE IT ENACTED by the Queen's most Excellent Majesty, by and with the advice and consent of the Lords Spiritual and Temporal, and Commons, in this present Parliament assembled, and by the authority of the same, as follows:—

PART 1

HOUSING CONDITIONS

CHAPTER 1

ENFORCEMENT OF HOUSING STANDARDS: GENERAL

New system for assessing housing conditions

1 New system for assessing housing conditions and enforcing housing standards

(1) This Part provides—

(a) for a new system of assessing the condition of residential premises, and

(b) for that system to be used in the enforcement of housing standards in relation to such premises.

(2) The new system—

(a) operates by reference to the existence of category 1 or category 2 hazards on residential premises (see section 2), and

(b) replaces the existing system based on the test of fitness for human habitation contained in section 604 of the Housing Act 1985 (c. 68).

(3) The kinds of enforcement action which are to involve the use of the new system are—

(a) the new kinds of enforcement action contained in Chapter 2 (improvement notices, prohibition orders and hazard awareness notices),

(b) the new emergency measures contained in Chapter 3 (emergency remedial action and emergency prohibition orders), and

(c) the existing kinds of enforcement action dealt with in Chapter 4 (demolition orders and slum clearance declarations).

(4) In this Part "residential premises" means—

(a) a dwelling;

(b) an HMO;

(c) unoccupied HMO accommodation;

(d) any common parts of a building containing one or more flats.

(5) In this Part—

"building containing one or more flats" does not include an HMO;

"common parts", in relation to a building containing one or more flats, includes—

(a) the structure and exterior of the building, and

(b) common facilities provided (whether or not in the building) for persons who include the occupiers of one or more of the flats;

"dwelling" means a building or part of a building occupied or intended to be occupied as a separate dwelling;

"external common parts", in relation to a building containing one or more flats, means common parts of the building which are outside it;

"flat" means a separate set of premises (whether or not on the same floor)—

(a) which forms part of a building,

(b) which is constructed or adapted for use for the purposes of a dwelling, and

(c) either the whole or a material part of which lies above or below some other part of the building;

"HMO" means a house in multiple occupation as defined by sections 254 to 259, as they have effect for the purposes of this Part (that is, without the exclusions contained in Schedule 14);

"unoccupied HMO accommodation" means a building or part of a building constructed or adapted for use as a house in multiple occupation but for the time being either unoccupied or only occupied by persons who form a single household.

(6) In this Part any reference to a dwelling, an HMO or a building containing one or more flats includes (where the context permits) any yard, garden, outhouses and appurtenances belonging to, or usually enjoyed with, the dwelling, HMO or building (or any part of it).

(7) The following indicates how this Part applies to flats—

(a) references to a dwelling or an HMO include a dwelling or HMO which is a flat (as defined by subsection (5)); and

(b) subsection (6) applies in relation to such a dwelling or HMO as it applies in relation to other dwellings or HMOs (but it is not to be taken as referring to any common parts of the building containing the flat).

(8) This Part applies to unoccupied HMO accommodation as it applies to an HMO, and references to an HMO in subsections (6) and (7) and in the following provisions of this Part are to be read accordingly.

2 Meaning of "category 1 hazard" and "category 2 hazard"

(1) In this Act—

"category 1 hazard" means a hazard of a prescribed description which falls within a prescribed band as a result of achieving, under a prescribed method for calculating the seriousness of hazards of that description, a numerical score of or above a prescribed amount;

"category 2 hazard" means a hazard of a prescribed description which falls within a prescribed band as a result of achieving, under a prescribed method for calculating the seriousness of hazards of that description, a numerical score below the minimum amount prescribed for a category 1 hazard of that description; and

"hazard" means any risk of harm to the health or safety of an actual or potential occupier of a dwelling or HMO which arises from a deficiency in the dwelling or HMO or in any building or land in the vicinity (whether the deficiency arises as a result of the construction of any building, an absence of maintenance or repair, or otherwise).

(2) In subsection (1)—

"prescribed" means prescribed by regulations made by the appropriate national authority (see section 261(1)); and

"prescribed band" means a band so prescribed for a category 1 hazard or a category 2 hazard, as the case may be.

(3) Regulations under this section may, in particular, prescribe a method for calculating the seriousness of hazards which takes into account both the likelihood of the harm occurring and the severity of the harm if it were to occur.

(4) In this section—

"building" includes part of a building;

"harm" includes temporary harm.

(5) In this Act "health" includes mental health.

Procedure for assessing housing conditions

3 Local housing authorities to review housing conditions in their districts

(1) A local housing authority must keep the housing conditions in their area under review with a view to identifying any action that may need to be taken by them under any of the provisions mentioned in subsection (2).

(2) The provisions are—

(a) the following provisions of this Act—

(i) this Part,

(ii) Part 2 (licensing of HMOs),

(iii) Part 3 (selective licensing of other houses), and

(iv) Chapters 1 and 2 of Part 4 (management orders);

(b) Part 9 of the Housing Act 1985 (c. 68) (demolition orders and slum clearance);

(c) Part 7 of the Local Government and Housing Act 1989 (c. 42) (renewal areas); and

(d) article 3 of the Regulatory Reform (Housing Assistance) (England and Wales) Order 2002 (S.I. 2002/1860).

(3) For the purpose of carrying out their duty under subsection (1) a local housing authority and their officers must—

(a) comply with any directions that may be given by the appropriate national authority, and

(b) keep such records, and supply the appropriate national authority with such information, as that authority may specify.

4 Inspections by local housing authorities to see whether category 1 or 2 hazards exist

(1) If a local housing authority consider—

(a) as a result of any matters of which they have become aware in carrying out their duty under section 3, or

(b) for any other reason,

that it would be appropriate for any residential premises in their district to be inspected with a view to determining whether any category 1 or 2 hazard exists on those premises, the authority must arrange for such an inspection to be carried out.

(2) If an official complaint about the condition of any residential premises in the district of a local housing authority is made to the proper officer of the authority, and the circumstances complained of indicate—

(a) that any category 1 or category 2 hazard may exist on those premises, or

(b) that an area in the district should be dealt with as a clearance area,

the proper officer must inspect the premises or area.

(3) In this section "an official complaint" means a complaint in writing made by—

(a) a justice of the peace having jurisdiction in any part of the district, or

(b) the parish or community council for a parish or community within the district.

(4) An inspection of any premises under subsection (1) or (2)—

(a) is to be carried out in accordance with regulations made by the appropriate national authority; and

(b) is to extend to so much of the premises as the local housing authority or proper officer (as the case may be) consider appropriate in the circumstances having regard to any applicable provisions of the regulations.

(5) Regulations under subsection (4) may in particular make provision about—

(a) the manner in which, and the extent to which, premises are to be inspected under subsection (1) or (2), and

(b) the manner in which the assessment of hazards is to be carried out.

(6) Where an inspection under subsection (2) has been carried out and the proper officer of a local housing authority is of the opinion—

(a) that a category 1 or 2 hazard exists on any residential premises in the authority's district, or

(b) that an area in their district should be dealt with as a clearance area,

the officer must, without delay, make a report in writing to the authority which sets out his opinion together with the facts of the case.

(7) The authority must consider any report made to them under subsection (6) as soon as possible.

Enforcement of housing standards

5 Category 1 hazards: general duty to take enforcement action

(1) If a local housing authority consider that a category 1 hazard exists on any residential premises, they must take the appropriate enforcement action in relation to the hazard.

(2) In subsection (1) "the appropriate enforcement action" means whichever of the following courses of action is indicated by subsection (3) or (4)—

(a) serving an improvement notice under section 11;

(b) making a prohibition order under section 20;

(c) serving a hazard awareness notice under section 28;

(d) taking emergency remedial action under section 40;

(e) making an emergency prohibition order under section 43;

(f) making a demolition order under subsection (1) or (2) of section 265 of the Housing Act 1985 (c. 68);

(g) declaring the area in which the premises concerned are situated to be a clearance area by virtue of section 289(2) of that Act.

(3) If only one course of action within subsection (2) is available to the authority in relation to the hazard, they must take that course of action.

(4) If two or more courses of action within subsection (2) are available to the authority in relation to the hazard, they must take the course of action which they consider to be the most appropriate of those available to them.

(5) The taking by the authority of a course of action within subsection (2) does not prevent subsection (1) from requiring them to take in relation to the same hazard—

(a) either the same course of action again or another such course of action, if they consider that the action taken by them so far has not proved satisfactory, or

(b) another such course of action, where the first course of action is that mentioned in subsection (2)(g) and their eventual decision under section 289(2F) of the Housing Act 1985 means that the premises concerned are not to be included in a clearance area.

(6) To determine whether a course of action mentioned in any of paragraphs (a) to (g) of subsection (2) is "available" to the authority in relation to the hazard, see the provision mentioned in that paragraph.

(7) Section 6 applies for the purposes of this section.

6 Category 1 hazards: how duty under section 5 operates in certain cases

(1) This section explains the effect of provisions contained in subsection (2) of section 5.

(2) In the case of paragraph (b) or (f) of that subsection, the reference to making an order such as is mentioned in that paragraph is to be read as a reference to making instead a determination under section 300(1) or (2) of the Housing Act 1985 (c. 68) (power to purchase for temporary housing use) in a case where the authority consider the latter course of action to be the better alternative in the circumstances.

(3) In the case of paragraph (d) of that subsection, the authority may regard the taking of emergency remedial action under section 40 followed by the service of an improvement notice under section 11 as a single course of action.

(4) In the case of paragraph (e) of that subsection, the authority may regard the making of an emergency prohibition order under section 43 followed by the service of a prohibition order under section 20 as a single course of action.

(5) In the case of paragraph (g) of that subsection—

- (a) any duty to take the course of action mentioned in that paragraph is subject to the operation of subsections (2B) to (4) and (5B) of section 289 of the Housing Act 1985 (procedural and other restrictions relating to slum clearance declarations); and
- (b) that paragraph does not apply in a case where the authority have already declared the area in which the premises concerned are situated to be a clearance area in accordance with section 289, but the premises have been excluded by virtue of section 289(2F)(b).

7 Category 2 hazards: powers to take enforcement action

(1) The provisions mentioned in subsection (2) confer power on a local housing authority to take particular kinds of enforcement action in cases where they consider that a category 2 hazard exists on residential premises.

(2) The provisions are—

- (a) section 12 (power to serve an improvement notice),
- (b) section 21 (power to make a prohibition order),
- (c) section 29 (power to serve a hazard awareness notice),
- (d) section 265(3) and (4) of the Housing Act 1985 (power to make a demolition order), and
- (e) section 289(2ZB) of that Act (power to make a slum clearance declaration).

(3) The taking by the authority of one of those kinds of enforcement action in relation to a particular category 2 hazard does not prevent them from taking either—

- (a) the same kind of action again, or
- (b) a different kind of enforcement action,

in relation to the hazard, where they consider that the action taken by them so far has not proved satisfactory.

8 Reasons for decision to take enforcement action

(1) This section applies where a local housing authority decide to take one of the kinds of enforcement action mentioned in section 5(2) or 7(2) ("the relevant action").

(2) The authority must prepare a statement of the reasons for their decision to take the relevant action.

(3) Those reasons must include the reasons why the authority decided to take the relevant action rather than any other kind (or kinds) of enforcement action available to them under the provisions mentioned in section 5(2) or 7(2).

(4) A copy of the statement prepared under subsection (2) must accompany every notice, copy of a notice, or copy of an order which is served in accordance with—

(a) Part 1 of Schedule 1 to this Act (service of improvement notices etc.),

(b) Part 1 of Schedule 2 to this Act (service of copies of prohibition orders etc.), or

(c) section 268 of the Housing Act 1985 (service of copies of demolition orders),

in or in connection with the taking of the relevant action.

(5) In subsection (4)—

(a) the reference to Part 1 of Schedule 1 to this Act includes a reference to that Part as applied by section 28(7) or 29(7) (hazard awareness notices) or to section 40(7) (emergency remedial action); and

(b) the reference to Part 1 of Schedule 2 to this Act includes a reference to that Part as applied by section 43(4) (emergency prohibition orders).

(6) If the relevant action consists of declaring an area to be a clearance area, the statement prepared under subsection (2) must be published—

(a) as soon as possible after the relevant resolution is passed under section 289 of the Housing Act 1985, and

(b) in such manner as the authority consider appropriate.

9 Guidance about inspections and enforcement action

(1) The appropriate national authority may give guidance to local housing authorities about exercising—

(a) their functions under this Chapter in relation to the inspection of premises and the assessment of hazards,

(b) their functions under Chapter 2 of this Part in relation to improvement notices, prohibition orders or hazard awareness notices,

(c) their functions under Chapter 3 in relation to emergency remedial action and emergency prohibition orders, or

(d) their functions under Part 9 of the Housing Act 1985 (c. 68) in relation to demolition orders and slum clearance.

(2) A local housing authority must have regard to any guidance for the time being given under this section.

(3) The appropriate national authority may give different guidance for different cases or descriptions of case or different purposes (including different guidance to different descriptions of local housing authority or to local housing authorities in different areas).

(4) Before giving guidance under this section, or revising guidance already given, the Secretary of State must lay a draft of the proposed guidance or alterations before each House of Parliament.

(5) The Secretary of State must not give or revise the guidance before the end of the period of 40 days beginning with the day on which the draft is laid before each House of Parliament (or, if copies are laid before each House of Parliament on different days, the later of those days).

(6) The Secretary of State must not proceed with the proposed guidance or alterations if, within the period of 40 days mentioned in subsection (5), either House resolves that the guidance or alterations be withdrawn.

(7) Subsection (6) is without prejudice to the possibility of laying a further draft of the guidance or alterations before each House of Parliament.

(8) In calculating the period of 40 days mentioned in subsection (5), no account is to be taken of any time during which Parliament is dissolved or prorogued or during which both Houses are adjourned for more than four days.

10 Consultation with fire and rescue authorities in certain cases

(1) This section applies where a local housing authority—

(a) are satisfied that a prescribed fire hazard exists in an HMO or in any common parts of a building containing one or more flats, and

(b) intend to take in relation to the hazard one of the kinds of enforcement action mentioned in section 5(2) or section 7(2).

(2) Before taking the enforcement action in question, the authority must consult the fire and rescue authority for the area in which the HMO or building is situated.

(3) In the case of any proposed emergency measures, the authority's duty under subsection (2) is a duty to consult that fire and rescue authority so far as it is practicable to do so before taking those measures.

(4) In this section—

"emergency measures" means emergency remedial action under section 40 or an emergency prohibition order under section 43;

"fire and rescue authority" means a fire and rescue authority under the Fire and Rescue Services Act 2004 (c. 21);

"prescribed fire hazard" means a category 1 or 2 hazard which is prescribed as a fire hazard for the purposes of this section by regulations under section 2.

CHAPTER 2

IMPROVEMENT NOTICES, PROHIBITION ORDERS AND HAZARD AWARENESS NOTICES

Improvement notices

11 Improvement notices relating to category 1 hazards: duty of authority to serve notice

(1) If—

(a) the local housing authority are satisfied that a category 1 hazard exists on any residential premises, and

(b) no management order is in force in relation to the premises under Chapter 1 or 2 of Part 4,

serving an improvement notice under this section in respect of the hazard is a course of action available to the authority in relation to the hazard for the purposes of section 5 (category 1 hazards: general duty to take enforcement action).

(2) An improvement notice under this section is a notice requiring the person on whom it is served to take such remedial action in respect of the hazard concerned as is specified in the notice in accordance with subsections (3) to (5) and section 13.

(3) The notice may require remedial action to be taken in relation to the following premises—

(a) if the residential premises on which the hazard exists are a dwelling or HMO which is not a flat, it may require such action to be taken in relation to the dwelling or HMO;

(b) if those premises are one or more flats, it may require such action to be taken in relation to the building containing the flat or flats (or any part of the building) or any external common parts;

(c) if those premises are the common parts of a building containing one or more flats, it may require such action to be taken in relation to the building (or any part of the building) or any external common parts.

Paragraphs (b) and (c) are subject to subsection (4).

(4) The notice may not, by virtue of subsection (3)(b) or (c), require any remedial action to be taken in relation to any part of the building or its external common parts that is not included in any residential premises on which the hazard exists, unless the authority are satisfied—

(a) that the deficiency from which the hazard arises is situated there, and

(b) that it is necessary for the action to be so taken in order to protect the health or safety of any actual or potential occupiers of one or more of the flats.

(5) The remedial action required to be taken by the notice —

(a) must, as a minimum, be such as to ensure that the hazard ceases to be a category 1 hazard; but

(b) may extend beyond such action.

(6) An improvement notice under this section may relate to more than one category 1 hazard on the same premises or in the same building containing one or more flats.

(7) The operation of an improvement notice under this section may be suspended in accordance with section 14.

(8) In this Part "remedial action", in relation to a hazard, means action (whether in the form of carrying out works or otherwise) which, in the opinion of the local housing authority, will remove or reduce the hazard.

12 Improvement notices relating to category 2 hazards: power of authority to serve notice

(1) If—

(a) the local housing authority are satisfied that a category 2 hazard exists on any residential premises, and

(b) no management order is in force in relation to the premises under Chapter 1 or 2 of Part 4,

the authority may serve an improvement notice under this section in respect of the hazard.

(2) An improvement notice under this section is a notice requiring the person on whom it is served to take such remedial action in respect of the hazard concerned as is specified in the notice in accordance with subsection (3) and section 13.

(3) Subsections (3) and (4) of section 11 apply to an improvement notice under this section as they apply to one under that section.

(4) An improvement notice under this section may relate to more than one category 2 hazard on the same premises or in the same building containing one or more flats.

(5) An improvement notice under this section may be combined in one document with a notice under section 11 where they require remedial action to be taken in relation to the same premises.

(6) The operation of an improvement notice under this section may be suspended in accordance with section 14.

13 Contents of improvement notices

(1) An improvement notice under section 11 or 12 must comply with the following provisions of this section.

(2) The notice must specify, in relation to the hazard (or each of the hazards) to which it relates—

(a) whether the notice is served under section 11 or 12,

(b) the nature of the hazard and the residential premises on which it exists,

(c) the deficiency giving rise to the hazard,

(d) the premises in relation to which remedial action is to be taken in respect of the hazard and the nature of that remedial action,

(e) the date when the remedial action is to be started (see subsection (3)), and

(f) the period within which the remedial action is to be completed or the periods within which each part of it is to be completed.

(3) The notice may not require any remedial action to be started earlier than the 28th day after that on which the notice is served.

(4) The notice must contain information about—

(a) the right of appeal against the decision under Part 3 of Schedule 1, and

(b) the period within which an appeal may be made.

(5) In this Part of this Act "specified premises", in relation to an improvement notice, means premises specified in the notice, in accordance with subsection (2)(d), as premises in relation to which remedial action is to be taken in respect of the hazard.

14 Suspension of improvement notices

(1) An improvement notice may provide for the operation of the notice to be suspended until a time, or the occurrence of an event, specified in the notice.

(2) The time so specified may, in particular, be the time when a person of a particular description begins, or ceases, to occupy any premises.

(3) The event so specified may, in particular, be a notified breach of an undertaking accepted by the local housing authority for the purposes of this section from the person on whom the notice is served.

(4) In subsection (3) a "notified breach", in relation to such an undertaking, means an act or omission by the person on whom the notice is served—

(a) which the local housing authority consider to be a breach of the undertaking, and

(b) which is notified to that person in accordance with the terms of the undertaking.

(5) If an improvement notice does provide for the operation of the notice to be suspended under this section—

(a) any periods specified in the notice under section 13 are to be fixed by reference to the day when the suspension ends, and

(b) in subsection (3) of that section the reference to the 28th day after that on which the notice is served is to be read as referring to the 21st day after that on which the suspension ends.

15 Operation of improvement notices

(1) This section deals with the time when an improvement notice becomes operative.

(2) The general rule is that an improvement notice becomes operative at the end of the period of 21 days beginning with the day on which it is served under Part 1 of Schedule 1 (which is the period for appealing against the notice under Part 3 of that Schedule).

(3) The general rule is subject to subsection (4) (suspended notices) and subsection (5) (appeals).

(4) If the notice is suspended under section 14, the notice becomes operative at the time when the suspension ends.

This is subject to subsection (5).

(5) If an appeal against the notice is made under Part 3 of Schedule 1, the notice does not become operative until such time (if any) as is the operative time for the purposes of

this subsection under paragraph 19 of that Schedule (time when notice is confirmed on appeal, period for further appeal expires or suspension ends).

(6) If no appeal against an improvement notice is made under that Part of that Schedule within the period for appealing against it, the notice is final and conclusive as to matters which could have been raised on an appeal.

16 Revocation and variation of improvement notices

(1) The local housing authority must revoke an improvement notice if they are satisfied that the requirements of the notice have been complied with.

(2) The local housing authority may revoke an improvement notice if—

(a) in the case of a notice served under section 11, they consider that there are any special circumstances making it appropriate to revoke the notice; or

(b) in the case of a notice served under section 12, they consider that it is appropriate to revoke the notice.

(3) Where an improvement notice relates to a number of hazards—

(a) subsection (1) is to be read as applying separately in relation to each of those hazards, and

(b) if, as a result, the authority are required to revoke only part of the notice, they may vary the remainder as they consider appropriate.

(4) The local housing authority may vary an improvement notice—

(a) with the agreement of the person on whom the notice was served, or

(b) in the case of a notice whose operation is suspended, so as to alter the time or events by reference to which the suspension is to come to an end.

(5) A revocation under this section comes into force at the time when it is made.

(6) If it is made with the agreement of the person on whom the improvement notice was served, a variation under this section comes into force at the time when it is made.

(7) Otherwise a variation under this section does not come into force until such time (if any) as is the operative time for the purposes of this subsection under paragraph 20 of Schedule 1 (time when period for appealing expires without an appeal being made or when decision to vary is confirmed on appeal).

(8) The power to revoke or vary an improvement notice under this section is exercisable by the authority either—

(a) on an application made by the person on whom the improvement notice was served, or

(b) on the authority's own initiative.

17 Review of suspended improvement notices

(1) The local housing authority may at any time review an improvement notice whose operation is suspended.

(2) The local housing authority must review an improvement notice whose operation is suspended not later than one year after the date of service of the notice and at subsequent intervals of not more than one year.

(3) Copies of the authority's decision on a review under this section must be served—
(a) on the person on whom the improvement notice was served, and
(b) on every other person on whom a copy of the notice was required to be served.

18 Service of improvement notices etc. and related appeals

Schedule 1 (which deals with the service of improvement notices, and notices relating to their revocation or variation, and with related appeals) has effect.

19 Change in person liable to comply with improvement notice

(1) This section applies where—
(a) an improvement notice has been served on any person ("the original recipient") in respect of any premises, and
(b) at a later date ("the changeover date") that person ceases to be a person of the relevant category in respect of the premises.

(2) In subsection (1) the reference to a person ceasing to be a "person of the relevant category" is a reference to his ceasing to fall within the description of person (such as, for example, the holder of a licence under Part 2 or 3 or the person managing a dwelling) by reference to which the improvement notice was served on him.

(3) As from the changeover date, the liable person in respect of the premises is to be in the same position as if—
(a) the improvement notice had originally been served on him, and
(b) he had taken all steps relevant for the purposes of this Part which the original recipient had taken.

(4) The effect of subsection (3) is that, in particular, any period for compliance with the notice or for bringing any appeal is unaffected.

(5) But where the original recipient has become subject to any liability arising by virtue of this Part before the changeover date, subsection (3) does not have the effect of—
(a) relieving him of the liability, or
(b) making the new liable person subject to it.

(6) Subsection (3) applies with any necessary modifications where a person to whom it applies (by virtue of any provision of this section) ceases to be the liable person in respect of the premises.

(7) Unless subsection (8) or (9) applies, the person who is at any time the "liable person" in respect of any premises is the person having control of the premises.

(8) If—
(a) the original recipient was served as the person managing the premises, and
(b) there is a new person managing the premises as from the changeover date,
that new person is the "liable person".

(9) If the original recipient was served as an owner of the premises, the "liable person" is the owner's successor in title on the changeover date.

Prohibition orders

20 Prohibition orders relating to category 1 hazards: duty of authority to make order

(1) If—

(a) the local housing authority are satisfied that a category 1 hazard exists on any residential premises, and

(b) no management order is in force in relation to the premises under Chapter 1 or 2 of Part 4,

making a prohibition order under this section in respect of the hazard is a course of action available to the authority in relation to the hazard for the purposes of section 5 (category 1 hazards: general duty to take enforcement action).

(2) A prohibition order under this section is an order imposing such prohibition or prohibitions on the use of any premises as is or are specified in the order in accordance with subsections (3) and (4) and section 22.

(3) The order may prohibit use of the following premises—

(a) if the residential premises on which the hazard exists are a dwelling or HMO which is not a flat, it may prohibit use of the dwelling or HMO;

(b) if those premises are one or more flats, it may prohibit use of the building containing the flat or flats (or any part of the building) or any external common parts;

(c) if those premises are the common parts of a building containing one or more flats, it may prohibit use of the building (or any part of the building) or any external common parts.

Paragraphs (b) and (c) are subject to subsection (4).

(4) The notice may not, by virtue of subsection (3)(b) or (c), prohibit use of any part of the building or its external common parts that is not included in any residential premises on which the hazard exists, unless the authority are satisfied—

(a) that the deficiency from which the hazard arises is situated there, and

(b) that it is necessary for such use to be prohibited in order to protect the health or safety of any actual or potential occupiers of one or more of the flats.

(5) A prohibition order under this section may relate to more than one category 1 hazard on the same premises or in the same building containing one or more flats.

(6) The operation of a prohibition order under this section may be suspended in accordance with section 23.

21 Prohibition orders relating to category 2 hazards: power of authority to make order

(1) If—

(a) the local housing authority are satisfied that a category 2 hazard exists on any residential premises, and

(b) no management order is in force in relation to the premises under Chapter 1 or 2 of Part 4,

the authority may make a prohibition order under this section in respect of the hazard.

(2) A prohibition order under this section is an order imposing such prohibition or prohibitions on the use of any premises as is or are specified in the order in accordance with subsection (3) and section 22.

(3) Subsections (3) and (4) of section 20 apply to a prohibition order under this section as they apply to one under that section.

(4) A prohibition order under this section may relate to more than one category 2 hazard on the same premises or in the same building containing one or more flats.

(5) A prohibition order under this section may be combined in one document with an order under section 20 where they impose prohibitions on the use of the same premises or on the use of premises in the same building containing one or more flats.

(6) The operation of a prohibition order under this section may be suspended in accordance with section 23.

22 Contents of prohibition orders

(1) A prohibition order under section 20 or 21 must comply with the following provisions of this section.

(2) The order must specify, in relation to the hazard (or each of the hazards) to which it relates—

- (a) whether the order is made under section 20 or 21,
- (b) the nature of the hazard concerned and the residential premises on which it exists,
- (c) the deficiency giving rise to the hazard,
- (d) the premises in relation to which prohibitions are imposed by the order (see subsections (3) and (4)), and
- (e) any remedial action which the authority consider would, if taken in relation to the hazard, result in their revoking the order under section 25.

(3) The order may impose such prohibition or prohibitions on the use of any premises as—

- (a) comply with section 20(3) and (4), and
- (b) the local housing authority consider appropriate in view of the hazard or hazards in respect of which the order is made.

(4) Any such prohibition may prohibit use of any specified premises, or of any part of those premises, either—

- (a) for all purposes, or
- (b) for any particular purpose,

except (in either case) to the extent to which any use of the premises or part is approved by the authority.

(5) A prohibition imposed by virtue of subsection (4)(b) may, in particular, relate to—

- (a) occupation of the premises or part by more than a particular number of households or persons; or
- (b) occupation of the premises or part by particular descriptions of persons.

(6) The order must also contain information about—

- (a) the right under Part 3 of Schedule 2 to appeal against the order, and
- (b) the period within which an appeal may be made,

and specify the date on which the order is made.

(7) Any approval of the authority for the purposes of subsection (4) must not be unreasonably withheld.

(8) If the authority do refuse to give any such approval, they must notify the person applying for the approval of—

(a) their decision,

(b) the reasons for it and the date on which it was made,

(c) the right to appeal against the decision under subsection (9), and

(d) the period within which an appeal may be made,

within the period of seven days beginning with the day on which the decision was made.

(9) The person applying for the approval may appeal to a residential property tribunal against the decision within the period of 28 days beginning with the date specified in the notice as the date on which it was made.

(10) In this Part of this Act "specified premises", in relation to a prohibition order, means premises specified in the order, in accordance with subsection (2)(d), as premises in relation to which prohibitions are imposed by the order.

23 Suspension of prohibition orders

(1) A prohibition order may provide for the operation of the order to be suspended until a time, or the occurrence of an event, specified in the order.

(2) The time so specified may, in particular, be the time when a person of a particular description begins, or ceases, to occupy any premises.

(3) The event so specified may, in particular, be a notified breach of an undertaking accepted by the local housing authority for the purposes of this section from a person on whom a copy of the order is served.

(4) In subsection (3) a "notified breach", in relation to such an undertaking, means an act or omission by such a person—

(a) which the local housing authority consider to be a breach of the undertaking, and

(b) which is notified to that person in accordance with the terms of the undertaking.

24 Operation of prohibition orders

(1) This section deals with the time when a prohibition order becomes operative.

(2) The general rule is that a prohibition order becomes operative at the end of the period of 28 days beginning with the date specified in the notice as the date on which it is made.

(3) The general rule is subject to subsection (4) (suspended orders) and subsection (5) (appeals).

(4) If the order is suspended under section 23, the order becomes operative at the time when the suspension ends.

This is subject to subsection (5).

(5) If an appeal is brought against the order under Part 3 of Schedule 2, the order does not become operative until such time (if any) as is the operative time for the purposes of this subsection under paragraph 14 of that Schedule (time when order is confirmed on appeal, period for further appeal expires or suspension ends).

(6) If no appeal against a prohibition order is made under that Part of that Schedule within the period for appealing against it, the order is final and conclusive as to matters which could have been raised on an appeal.

(7) Sections 584A and 584B of the Housing Act 1985 (c. 68) provide for the payment of compensation where certain prohibition orders become operative, and for the repayment of such compensation in certain circumstances.

25 Revocation and variation of prohibition orders

(1) The local housing authority must revoke a prohibition order if at any time they are satisfied that the hazard in respect of which the order was made does not then exist on the residential premises specified in the order in accordance with section 22(2)(b).

(2) The local housing authority may revoke a prohibition order if—
- (a) in the case of an order made under section 20, they consider that there are any special circumstances making it appropriate to revoke the order; or
- (b) in the case of an order made under section 21, they consider that it is appropriate to do so.

(3) Where a prohibition order relates to a number of hazards—
- (a) subsection (1) is to be read as applying separately in relation to each of those hazards, and
- (b) if, as a result, the authority are required to revoke only part of the order, they may vary the remainder as they consider appropriate.

(4) The local housing authority may vary a prohibition order—
- (a) with the agreement of every person on whom copies of the notice were required to be served under Part 1 of Schedule 2, or
- (b) in the case of an order whose operation is suspended, so as to alter the time or events by reference to which the suspension is to come to an end.

(5) A revocation under this section comes into force at the time when it is made.

(6) If it is made with the agreement of every person within subsection (4)(a), a variation under this section comes into force at the time when it is made.

(7) Otherwise a variation under this section does not come into force until such time (if any) as is the operative time for the purposes of this subsection under paragraph 15 of Schedule 2 (time when period for appealing expires without an appeal being made or when decision to revoke or vary is confirmed on appeal).

(8) The power to revoke or vary a prohibition order under this section is exercisable by the authority either—
- (a) on an application made by a person on whom a copy of the order was required to be served under Part 1 of Schedule 2, or
- (b) on the authority's own initiative.

26 Review of suspended prohibition orders

(1) The local housing authority may at any time review a prohibition order whose operation is suspended.

(2) The local housing authority must review a prohibition order whose operation is suspended not later than one year after the date on which the order was made and at subsequent intervals of not more than one year.

(3) Copies of the authority's decision on a review under this section must be served on every person on whom a copy of the order was required to be served under Part 1 of Schedule 2.

27 Service of copies of prohibition orders etc. and related appeals

Schedule 2 (which deals with the service of copies of prohibition orders, and notices relating to their revocation or variation, and with related appeals) has effect.

Hazard awareness notices

28 Hazard awareness notices relating to category 1 hazards: duty of authority to serve notice

(1) If—

(a) the local housing authority are satisfied that a category 1 hazard exists on any residential premises, and

(b) no management order is in force in relation to the premises under Chapter 1 or 2 of Part 4,

serving a hazard awareness notice under this section in respect of the hazard is a course of action available to the authority in relation to the hazard for the purposes of section 5 (category 1 hazards: general duty to take enforcement action).

(2) A hazard awareness notice under this section is a notice advising the person on whom it is served of the existence of a category 1 hazard on the residential premises concerned which arises as a result of a deficiency on the premises in respect of which the notice is served.

(3) The notice may be served in respect of the following premises—

(a) if the residential premises on which the hazard exists are a dwelling or HMO which is not a flat, it may be served in respect of the dwelling or HMO;

(b) if those premises are one or more flats, it may be served in respect of the building containing the flat or flats (or any part of the building) or any external common parts;

(c) if those premises are the common parts of a building containing one or more flats, it may be served in respect of the building (or any part of the building) or any external common parts.

Paragraphs (b) and (c) are subject to subsection (4).

(4) The notice may not, by virtue of subsection (3)(b) or (c), be served in respect of any part of the building or its external common parts that is not included in any residential premises on which the hazard exists, unless the authority are satisfied—

(a) that the deficiency from which the hazard arises is situated there, and

(b) that it is desirable for the notice to be so served in the interests of the health or safety of any actual or potential occupiers of one or more of the flats.

(5) A notice under this section may relate to more than one category 1 hazard on the same premises or in the same building containing one or more flats.

(6) A notice under this section must specify, in relation to the hazard (or each of the hazards) to which it relates—

(a) the nature of the hazard and the residential premises on which it exists,

(b) the deficiency giving rise to the hazard,

(c) the premises on which the deficiency exists,

(d) the authority's reasons for deciding to serve the notice, including their reasons for deciding that serving the notice is the most appropriate course of action, and

(e) details of the remedial action (if any) which the authority consider that it would be practicable and appropriate to take in relation to the hazard.

(7) Part 1 of Schedule 1 (which relates to the service of improvement notices and copies of such notices) applies to a notice under this section as if it were an improvement notice.

(8) For that purpose, any reference in that Part of that Schedule to "the specified premises" is, in relation to a hazard awareness notice under this section, a reference to the premises specified under subsection (6)(c).

29 Hazard awareness notices relating to category 2 hazards: power of authority to serve notice

(1) If—

(a) the local housing authority are satisfied that a category 2 hazard exists on any residential premises, and

(b) no management order is in force in relation to the premises under Chapter 1 or 2 of Part 4,

the authority may serve a hazard awareness notice under this section in respect of the hazard.

(2) A hazard awareness notice under this section is a notice advising the person on whom it is served of the existence of a category 2 hazard on the residential premises concerned which arises as a result of a deficiency on the premises in respect of which the notice is served.

(3) Subsections (3) and (4) of section 28 apply to a hazard awareness notice under this section as they apply to one under that section.

(4) A notice under this section may relate to more than one category 2 hazard on the same premises or in the same building containing one or more flats.

(5) A notice under this section must specify, in relation to the hazard (or each of the hazards) to which it relates—

(a) the nature of the hazard and the residential premises on which it exists,

(b) the deficiency giving rise to the hazard,

(c) the premises on which the deficiency exists,

(d) the authority's reasons for deciding to serve the notice, including their reasons for deciding that serving the notice is the most appropriate course of action, and

(e) details of the remedial action (if any) which the authority consider that it would be practicable and appropriate to take in relation to the hazard.

(6) A notice under this section may be combined in one document with a notice under section 28 where they are served in respect of the same premises.

(7) Part 1 of Schedule 1 (which relates to the service of improvement notices and copies of such notices) applies to a notice under this section as if it were an improvement notice.

(8) For that purpose, any reference in that Part of that Schedule to "the specified premises" is, in relation to a hazard awareness notice under this section, a reference to the premises specified under subsection (5)(c).

Enforcement: improvement notices

30 Offence of failing to comply with improvement notice

(1) Where an improvement notice has become operative, the person on whom the notice was served commits an offence if he fails to comply with it.

(2) For the purposes of this Chapter compliance with an improvement notice means, in relation to each hazard, beginning and completing any remedial action specified in the notice—

(a) (if no appeal is brought against the notice) not later than the date specified under section 13(2)(e) and within the period specified under section 13(2)(f);

(b) (if an appeal is brought against the notice and is not withdrawn) not later than such date and within such period as may be fixed by the tribunal determining the appeal; and

(c) (if an appeal brought against the notice is withdrawn) not later than the 21st day after the date on which the notice becomes operative and within the period (beginning on that 21st day) specified in the notice under section 13(2)(f).

(3) A person who commits an offence under subsection (1) is liable on summary conviction to a fine not exceeding level 5 on the standard scale.

(4) In proceedings against a person for an offence under subsection (1) it is a defence that he had a reasonable excuse for failing to comply with the notice.

(5) The obligation to take any remedial action specified in the notice in relation to a hazard continues despite the fact that the period for completion of the action has expired.

(6) In this section any reference to any remedial action specified in a notice includes a reference to any part of any remedial action which is required to be completed within a particular period specified in the notice.

31 Enforcement action by local housing authorities

Schedule 3 (which enables enforcement action in respect of an improvement notice to be taken by local housing authorities either with or without agreement and which provides for the recovery of related expenses) has effect.

Enforcement: prohibition orders

32 Offence of failing to comply with prohibition order etc.

(1) A person commits an offence if, knowing that a prohibition order has become operative in relation to any specified premises, he—

(a) uses the premises in contravention of the order, or

(b) permits the premises to be so used.

(2) A person who commits an offence under subsection (1) is liable on summary conviction—

(a) to a fine not exceeding level 5 on the standard scale, and

(b) to a further fine not exceeding £20 for every day or part of a day on which he so uses the premises, or permits them to be so used, after conviction.

(3) In proceedings against a person for an offence under subsection (1) it is a defence that he had a reasonable excuse for using the premises, or (as the case may be) permitting them to be used, in contravention of the order.

33 Recovery of possession of premises in order to comply with order

Nothing in—

(a) the Rent Act 1977 (c. 42) or the Rent (Agriculture) Act 1976 (c. 80), or

(b) Part 1 of the Housing Act 1988 (c. 50),

prevents possession being obtained by the owner of any specified premises in relation to which a prohibition order is operative if possession of the premises is necessary for the purpose of complying with the order.

34 Power of tribunal to determine or vary lease

(1) Subsection (2) applies where—

(a) a prohibition order has become operative, and

(b) the whole or part of any specified premises form the whole or part of the subject matter of a lease.

(2) The lessor or the lessee may apply to a residential property tribunal for an order determining or varying the lease.

(3) On such an application the tribunal may make an order determining or varying the lease, if it considers it appropriate to do so.

(4) Before making such an order, the tribunal must give any sub-lessee an opportunity of being heard.

(5) An order under this section may be unconditional or subject to such terms and conditions as the tribunal considers appropriate.

(6) The conditions may, in particular, include conditions about the payment of money by one party to the proceedings to another by way of compensation, damages or otherwise.

(7) In deciding what is appropriate for the purposes of this section, the tribunal must have regard to the respective rights, obligations and liabilities of the parties under the lease and to all the other circumstances of the case.

(8) In this section "lessor" and "lessee" include a person deriving title under a lessor or lessee.

Enforcement: improvement notices and prohibition orders

35 Power of court to order occupier or owner to allow action to be taken on premises

(1) This section applies where an improvement notice or prohibition order has become operative.

(2) If the occupier of any specified premises—

(a) has received reasonable notice of any intended action in relation to the premises, but

(b) is preventing a relevant person, or any representative of a relevant person or of the local housing authority, from taking that action in relation to the premises,

a magistrates' court may order the occupier to permit to be done on the premises anything which the court considers is necessary or expedient for the purpose of enabling the intended action to be taken.

(3) If a relevant person—

(a) has received reasonable notice of any intended action in relation to any specified premises, but

(b) is preventing a representative of the local housing authority from taking that action in relation to the premises,

a magistrates' court may order the relevant person to permit to be done on the premises anything which the court considers is necessary or expedient for the purpose of enabling the intended action to be taken.

(4) A person who fails to comply with an order of the court under this section commits an offence.

(5) In proceedings for an offence under subsection (4) it is a defence that the person had a reasonable excuse for failing to comply with the order.

(6) A person who commits an offence under subsection (4) is liable on summary conviction to a fine not exceeding £20 in respect of each day or part of a day during which the failure continues.

(7) In this section "intended action", in relation to any specified premises, means—

(a) where an improvement notice has become operative, any action which the person on whom that notice has been served is required by the notice to take in relation to the premises and which—

(a) (in the context of subsection (2)) is proposed to be taken by or on behalf of that person or on behalf of the local housing authority in pursuance of Schedule 3, or

(b) (in the context of subsection (3)) is proposed to be taken on behalf of the local housing authority in pursuance of Schedule 3;

(b) where a prohibition order has become operative, any action which is proposed to be taken and which either is necessary for the purpose of giving effect to the order or is remedial action specified in the order in accordance with section 22(2)(e).

(8) In this section—

"relevant person", in relation to any premises, means a person who is an owner of the premises, a person having control of or managing the premises, or the holder of any licence under Part 2 or 3 in respect of the premises;

"representative" in relation to a relevant person or a local housing authority, means any officer, employee, agent or contractor of that person or authority.

36 Power of court to authorise action by one owner on behalf of another

(1) Where an improvement notice or prohibition order has become operative, an owner of any specified premises may apply to a magistrates' court for an order under subsection (2).

(2) A magistrates' court may, on an application under subsection (1), make an order enabling the applicant—

(a) immediately to enter on the premises, and

(b) to take any required action within a period fixed by the order.

(3) In this section "required action" means—

(a) in the case of an improvement notice, any remedial action which is required to be taken by the notice;

(b) in the case of a prohibition order, any action necessary for the purpose of complying with the order or any remedial action specified in the order in accordance with section 22(2)(e).

(4) No order may be made under subsection (2) unless the court is satisfied that the interests of the applicant will be prejudiced as a result of a failure by another person to take any required action.

(5) No order may be made under subsection (2) unless notice of the application has been given to the local housing authority.

(6) If it considers that it is appropriate to do so, the court may make an order in favour of any other owner of the premises which is similar to the order that it is making in relation to the premises under subsection (2).

Supplementary provisions

37 Effect of improvement notices and prohibition orders as local land charges

(1) An improvement notice or a prohibition order under this Chapter is a local land charge if subsection (2), (3) or (4) applies.

(2) This subsection applies if the notice or order has become operative.

(3) This subsection applies if—

(a) the notice or order is suspended under section 14 or 23, and

(b) the period for appealing against it under Part 3 of Schedule 1 or 2 has expired without an appeal having been brought.

(4) This subsection applies if—

(a) the notice or order is suspended under section 14 or 23,

(b) an appeal has been brought against it under Part 3 of Schedule 1 or 2, and

(c) were it not suspended—

(i) the notice would have become operative under section 15(5) by virtue of paragraph 19(2) of Schedule 1 (improvement notices: confirmation on appeal or expiry of period for further appeal), or

(ii) the order would have become operative under section 24(5) by virtue of paragraph 14(2) of Schedule 2 (prohibition orders: confirmation on appeal or expiry of period for further appeal).

38 Savings for rights arising from breach of covenant etc.

(1) Nothing in this Chapter affects any remedy of an owner for breach of any covenant or contract entered into by a tenant in connection with any premises which are specified premises in relation to an improvement notice or prohibition order.

(2) If an owner is obliged to take possession of any premises in order to comply with an improvement notice or prohibition order, the taking of possession does not affect his right to take advantage of any such breach which occurred before he took possession.

(3) No action taken under this Chapter affects any remedy available to the tenant of any premises against his landlord (whether at common law or otherwise).

39 Effect of Part 4 enforcement action and redevelopment proposals

(1) Subsection (2) applies if—

(a) an improvement notice or prohibition order has been served or made under this Chapter, and

(b) a management order under Chapter 1 or 2 of Part 4 comes into force in relation to the specified premises.

(2) The improvement notice or prohibition order—

(a) if operative at the time when the management order comes into force, ceases to have effect at that time, and

(b) otherwise is to be treated as from that time as if it had not been served or made.

(3) Subsection (2)(a) does not affect any right acquired or liability (civil or criminal) incurred before the improvement notice or prohibition order ceases to have effect.

(4) Subsection (5) applies where, under section 308 of the Housing Act 1985 (c. 68) (owner's re-development proposals), the local housing authority have approved proposals for the re-development of land.

(5) No action is to be taken under this Chapter in relation to the land if, and so long as, the re-development is being proceeded with (subject to any variation or extension approved by the authority)—

(a) in accordance with the proposals; and

(b) within the time limits specified by the local housing authority.

CHAPTER 3

EMERGENCY MEASURES

Emergency remedial action

40 Emergency remedial action

(1) If—

(a) the local housing authority are satisfied that a category 1 hazard exists on any residential premises, and

(b) they are further satisfied that the hazard involves an imminent risk of serious harm to the health or safety of any of the occupiers of those or any other residential premises, and

(c) no management order is in force under Chapter 1 or 2 of Part 4 in relation to the premises mentioned in paragraph (a),

the taking by the authority of emergency remedial action under this section in respect of the hazard is a course of action available to the authority in relation to the hazard for the purposes of section 5 (category 1 hazards: general duty to take enforcement action).

(2) "Emergency remedial action" means such remedial action in respect of the hazard concerned as the authority consider immediately necessary in order to remove the imminent risk of serious harm within subsection (1)(b).

(3) Emergency remedial action under this section may be taken by the authority in relation to any premises in relation to which remedial action could be required to be taken by an improvement notice under section 11 (see subsections (3) and (4) of that section).

(4) Emergency remedial action under this section may be taken by the authority in respect of more than one category 1 hazard on the same premises or in the same building containing one or more flats.

(5) Paragraphs 3 to 5 of Schedule 3 (improvement notices: enforcement action by local authorities) apply in connection with the taking of emergency remedial action under this section as they apply in connection with the taking of the remedial action required by an improvement notice which has become operative but has not been complied with.

But those paragraphs so apply with the modifications set out in subsection (6).

(6) The modifications are as follows—

(a) the right of entry conferred by paragraph 3(4) may be exercised at any time; and

(b) the notice required by paragraph 4 (notice before entering premises) must (instead of being served in accordance with that paragraph) be served on every person, who to the authority's knowledge—

(i) is an occupier of the premises in relation to which the authority propose to take emergency remedial action, or

(ii) if those premises are common parts of a building containing one or more flats, is an occupier of any part of the building; but

(c) that notice is to be regarded as so served if a copy of it is fixed to some conspicuous part of the premises or building.

(7) Within the period of seven days beginning with the date when the authority start taking emergency remedial action, the authority must serve—

(a) a notice under section 41, and

(b) copies of such a notice,

on the persons on whom the authority would be required under Part 1 of Schedule 1 to serve an improvement notice and copies of it.

(8) Section 240 (warrant to authorise entry) applies for the purpose of enabling a local housing authority to enter any premises to take emergency remedial action under this section in relation to the premises, as if—

(a) that purpose were mentioned in subsection (2) of that section, and

(b) the circumstances as to which the justice of the peace must be satisfied under subsection (4) were that there are reasonable grounds for believing that the authority will not be able to gain admission to the premises without a warrant.

(9) For the purposes of the operation of any provision relating to improvement notices as it applies by virtue of this section in connection with emergency remedial action or a notice under section 41, any reference in that provision to the specified premises is to be read as a reference to the premises specified, in accordance with section 41(2)(c), as those in relation to which emergency remedial action has been (or is to be) taken.

41 Notice of emergency remedial action

(1) The notice required by section 40(7) is a notice which complies with the following requirements of this section.

(2) The notice must specify, in relation to the hazard (or each of the hazards) to which it relates—

(a) the nature of the hazard and the residential premises on which it exists,

(b) the deficiency giving rise to the hazard,

(c) the premises in relation to which emergency remedial action has been (or is to be) taken by the authority under section 40 and the nature of that remedial action,

(d) the power under which that remedial action has been (or is to be) taken by the authority, and

(e) the date when that remedial action was (or is to be) started.

(3) The notice must contain information about—

(a) the right to appeal under section 45 against the decision of the authority to make the order, and

(b) the period within which an appeal may be made.

42 Recovery of expenses of taking emergency remedial action

(1) This section relates to the recovery by a local housing authority of expenses reasonably incurred in taking emergency remedial action under section 40 ("emergency expenses").

(2) Paragraphs 6 to 14 of Schedule 3 (improvement notices: enforcement action by local authorities) apply for the purpose of enabling alocal housing authority to recover emergency expenses as they apply for the purpose of enabling such an authority

to recover expenses incurred in taking remedial action under paragraph 3 of that Schedule.

But those paragraphs so apply with the modifications set out in subsection (3).

(3) The modifications are as follows—

(a) any reference to the improvement notice is to be read as a reference to the notice under section 41; and

(b) no amount is recoverable in respect of any emergency expenses until such time (if any) as is the operative time for the purposes of this subsection (see subsection (4)).

(4) This subsection gives the meaning of "the operative time" for the purposes of subsection (3)—

(a) if no appeal against the authority's decision to take the emergency remedial action is made under section 45 before the end of the period of 28 days mentioned in subsection (3)(a) of that section, "the operative time" is the end of that period;

(b) if an appeal is made under that section within that period and a decision is given on the appeal which confirms the authority's decision, "the operative time" is as follows—

(i) if the period within which an appeal to the Lands Tribunal may be brought expires without such an appeal having been brought, "the operative time" is the end of that period;

(ii) if an appeal to the Lands Tribunal is brought, "the operative time" is the time when a decision is given on the appeal which confirms the authority's decision.

(5) For the purposes of subsection (4)—

(a) the withdrawal of an appeal has the same effect as a decision which confirms the authority's decision, and

(b) references to a decision which confirms the authority's decision are to a decision which confirms it with or without variation.

Emergency prohibition orders

43 Emergency prohibition orders

(1) If—

(a) the local housing authority are satisfied that a category 1 hazard exists on any residential premises, and

(b) they are further satisfied that the hazard involves an imminent risk of serious harm to the health or safety of any of the occupiers of those or any other residential premises, and

(c) no management order is in force under Chapter 1 or 2 of Part 4 in relation to the premises mentioned in paragraph (a),

making an emergency prohibition order under this section in respect of the hazard is a course of action available to the authority in relation to the hazard for the purposes of section 5 (category 1 hazards: general duty to take enforcement action).

(2) An emergency prohibition order under this section is an order imposing, with immediate effect, such prohibition or prohibitions on the use of any premises as are specified in the order in accordance with subsection (3) and section 44.

(3) As regards the imposition of any such prohibition or prohibitions, the following provisions apply to an emergency prohibition order as they apply to a prohibition order under section 20—

(a) subsections (3) to (5) of that section, and

(b) subsections (3) to (5) and (7) to (9) of section 22.

(4) Part 1 of Schedule 2 (service of copies of prohibition orders) applies in relation to an emergency prohibition order as it applies to a prohibition order, but any requirement to serve copies within a specified period of seven days is to be read as a reference to serve them on the day on which the emergency prohibition order is made (or, if that is not possible, as soon after that day as is possible).

(5) The following provisions also apply to an emergency prohibition order as they apply to a prohibition order (or to a prohibition order which has become operative, as the case may be)—

(a) section 25 (revocation and variation);

(b) sections 32 to 36 (enforcement);

(c) sections 37 to 39 (supplementary provisions); and

(d) Part 2 of Schedule 2 (notices relating to revocation or variation);

(e) Part 3 of that Schedule (appeals) so far as it relates to any decision to vary, or to refuse to revoke or vary, a prohibition order; and

(f) sections 584A and 584B of the Housing Act 1985 (c. 68) (payment, and repayment, of compensation).

(6) For the purposes of the operation of any provision relating to prohibition orders as it applies in connection with emergency prohibition orders by virtue of this section or section 45, any reference in that provision to the specified premises is to be read as a reference to the premises specified, in accordance with section 44(2)(c), as the premises in relation to which prohibitions are imposed by the order.

44 Contents of emergency prohibition orders

(1) An emergency prohibition order under section 43 must comply with the following requirements of this section.

(2) The order must specify, in relation to the hazard (or each of the hazards) to which it relates—

(a) the nature of the hazard concerned and the residential premises on which it exists,

(b) the deficiency giving rise to the hazard,

(c) the premises in relation to which prohibitions are imposed by the order (see subsections (3) and (4) of section 22 as applied by section 43(3)), and

(d) any remedial action which the authority consider would, if taken in relation to the hazard, result in their revoking the order under section 25 (as applied by section 43(5)).

(3) The order must contain information about—

(a) the right to appeal under section 45 against the order, and

(b) the period within which an appeal may be made,

and specify the date on which the order is made.

Appeals

45 Appeals relating to emergency measures

(1) A person on whom a notice under section 41 has been served in connection with the taking of emergency remedial action under section 40 may appeal to a residential property tribunal against the decision of the local housing authority to take that action.

(2) A relevant person may appeal to a residential property tribunal against an emergency prohibition order.

(3) An appeal under subsection (1) or (2) must be made within the period of 28 days beginning with—

(a) the date specified in the notice under section 41 as the date when the emergency remedial action was (or was to be) started, or

(b) the date specified in the emergency prohibition order as the date on which the order was made,

as the case may be.

(4) A residential property tribunal may allow an appeal to be made to it after the end of that period if it is satisfied that there is a good reason for the failure to appeal before the end of that period (and for any delay since then in applying for permission to appeal out of time).

(5) An appeal under subsection (1) or (2)—

(a) is to be by way of a re-hearing, but

(b) may be determined having regard to matters of which the authority were unaware.

(6) The tribunal may—

(a) in the case of an appeal under subsection (1), confirm, reverse or vary the decision of the authority;

(b) in the case of an appeal under subsection (2), confirm or vary the emergency prohibition order or make an order revoking it as from a date specified in that order.

(7) Paragraph 16 of Schedule 2 applies for the purpose of identifying who is a relevant person for the purposes of subsection (2) in relation to an emergency prohibition order as it applies for the purpose of identifying who is a relevant person for the purposes of Part 3 of that Schedule in relation to a prohibition order.

CHAPTER 4

DEMOLITION ORDERS AND SLUM CLEARANCE DECLARATIONS

Demolition orders

46 Demolition orders

For section 265 of the Housing Act 1985 (c. 68) substitute—

"265 Demolition orders

(1) If—

(a) the local housing authority are satisfied that a category 1 hazard exists in a dwelling or HMO which is not a flat, and

(b) this subsection is not disapplied by subsection (5),

making a demolition order in respect of the dwelling or HMO is a course of action available to the authority in relation to the hazard for the purposes of section 5 of the Housing Act 2004 (category 1 hazards: general duty to take enforcement action).

(2) If, in the case of any building containing one or more flats—

(a) the local housing authority are satisfied that a category 1 hazard exists in one or more of the flats contained in the building or in any common parts of the building, and

(b) this subsection is not disapplied by subsection (5),

making a demolition order in respect of the building is a course of action available to the authority in relation to the hazard for the purposes of section 5 of the Housing Act 2004.

(3) The local housing authority may make a demolition order in respect of a dwelling or HMO which is not a flat if—

(a) they are satisfied that a category 2 hazard exists in the dwelling or HMO,

(b) this subsection is not disapplied by subsection (5), and

(c) the circumstances of the case are circumstances specified or described in an order made by the Secretary of State.

(4) The local housing authority may make a demolition order in respect of any building containing one or more flats if—

(a) they are satisfied that a category 2 hazard exists in one or more of the flats contained in the building or in any common parts of the building,

(b) this subsection is not disapplied by subsection (5), and

(c) the circumstances of the case are circumstances specified or described in an order made by the Secretary of State.

(5) None of subsections (1) to (4) applies if a management order under Chapter 1 or 2 of Part 4 is in force in relation to the premises concerned.

(6) This section also has effect subject to section 304(1) (no demolition order to be made in respect of listed building).

(7) In this section "HMO" means house in multiple occupation.

(8) An order made under subsection (3) or (4)—

(a) may make different provision for different cases or descriptions of case (including different provision for different areas);

(b) may contain such incidental, supplementary, consequential, transitory, transitional or saving provision as the Secretary of State considers appropriate; and

(c) shall be made by statutory instrument which shall be subject to annulment in pursuance of a resolution of either House of Parliament.

(9) Sections 584A and 584B provide for the payment of compensation where demolition orders are made under this section, and for the repayment of such compensation in certain circumstances."

Slum clearance declarations

47 Clearance areas

In section 289 of the Housing Act 1985 (c. 68) (declaration of clearance area) for subsections (2) and (2A) substitute—

"(2) If the local housing authority are satisfied, in relation to any area—

(a) that each of the residential buildings in the area contains a category 1 hazard, and

(b) that the other buildings (if any) in the area are dangerous or harmful to the health or safety of the inhabitants of the area,

declaring the area to be a clearance area is a course of action available to the authority in relation to the hazard or hazards for the purposes of section 5 of the Housing Act 2004 (category 1 hazards: general duty to take enforcement action).

(2ZA) The local housing authority may declare an area to be a clearance area if they are satisfied that—

(a) the residential buildings in the area are dangerous or harmful to the health or safety of the inhabitants of the area as a result of their bad arrangement or the narrowness or bad arrangement of the streets; and

(b) that the other buildings (if any) in the area are dangerous or harmful to the health or safety of the inhabitants of the area.

(2ZB) The local housing authority may declare an area to be a clearance area if they are satisfied that—

(a) that each of the residential buildings in the area contains a category 2 hazard,

(b) that the other buildings (if any) in the area are dangerous or harmful to the health or safety of the inhabitants of the area, and

(c) the circumstances of the case are circumstances specified or described in an order made by the Secretary of State.

Subsection (8) of section 265 applies in relation to an order under this subsection as it applies in relation to an order under subsection (3) or (4) of that section.

(2ZC) In this section "residential buildings" means buildings which are dwellings or houses in multiple occupation or contain one or more flats.

This is subject to subsection (2ZD).

(2ZD) For the purposes of subsection (2) or (2ZB)—

(a) subsection (2ZC) applies as if "two or more flats" were substituted for "one or more flats"; and

(b) a residential building containing two or more flats is only to be treated as containing a category 1 or 2 hazard if two or more of the flats within it contain such a hazard.

(2ZE) Subsections (2) to (2ZB) are subject to subsections (2B) to (4) and (5B)."

Appeals

48 Transfer of jurisdiction in respect of appeals relating to demolition orders etc.

(1) Part 9 of the Housing Act 1985 (c. 68) (slum clearance) is further amended as follows.

(2) In section 269 (right of appeal against demolition order etc.)—

(a) in subsection (1), for "the county court" substitute "a residential property tribunal";

(b) in subsection (3), for "court" substitute "tribunal"; and

(c) in subsection (6)(a) and (b), for "Court of Appeal" substitute "Lands Tribunal".

(3) In section 272 (demolition orders)—

(a) in subsection (2), for "the court" in the first place it appears substitute "a residential property tribunal", and in the second place it appears substitute "such a tribunal";

(b) in subsection (5), for the words from the beginning to "and has" substitute "A residential property tribunal has jurisdiction to hear and determine proceedings under subsection (1) (as well as those under subsection (2)), and a county court has"; and

(c) in subsection (6), for "the court" substitute "a tribunal or court".

(4) In section 317 (power of court to determine lease where premises demolished etc.)—

(a) in subsection (1), for "the county court" substitute "a residential property tribunal"; and

(b) in subsections (2) and (3), for "court" substitute "tribunal".

(5) In section 318 (power of court to authorise execution of works on unfit premises or for improvement)—

(a) in the sidenote, for "court" substitute "tribunal";

(b) in subsection (1), for "the court" in the first place it appears substitute "a residential property tribunal", and in the second place it appears substitute "the tribunal";

(c) in subsections (2) and (3), for "court" substitute "tribunal"; and

(d) omit subsection (4).

CHAPTER 5

GENERAL AND MISCELLANEOUS PROVISIONS RELATING TO ENFORCEMENT ACTION

Recovery of expenses relating to enforcement action

49 Power to charge for certain enforcement action

(1) A local housing authority may make such reasonable charge as they consider appropriate as a means of recovering certain administrative and other expenses incurred by them in—

(a) serving an improvement notice under section 11 or 12;

(b) making a prohibition order under section 20 or 21;

(c) serving a hazard awareness notice under section 28 or 29;

(d) taking emergency remedial action under section 40;

(e) making an emergency prohibition order under section 43; or

(f) making a demolition order under section 265 of the Housing Act 1985 (c. 68).

(2) The expenses are, in the case of the service of an improvement notice or a hazard awareness notice, the expenses incurred in—

(a) determining whether to serve the notice,

(b) identifying any action to be specified in the notice, and

(c) serving the notice.

(3) The expenses are, in the case of emergency remedial action under section 40, the expenses incurred in—

(a) determining whether to take such action, and

(b) serving the notice required by subsection (7) of that section.

(4) The expenses are, in the case of a prohibition order under section 20 or 21 of this Act, an emergency prohibition order under section 43 or a demolition order under section 265 of the Housing Act 1985, the expenses incurred in—

(a) determining whether to make the order, and

(b) serving copies of the order on persons as owners of premises.

(5) A local housing authority may make such reasonable charge as they consider appropriate as a means of recovering expenses incurred by them in—

(a) carrying out any review under section 17 or 26, or

(b) serving copies of the authority's decision on such a review.

(6) The amount of the charge may not exceed such amount as is specified by order of the appropriate national authority.

(7) Where a tribunal allows an appeal against the underlying notice or order mentioned in subsection (1), it may make such order as it considers appropriate reducing, quashing, or requiring the repayment of, any charge under this section made in respect of the notice or order.

50 Recovery of charge under section 49

(1) This section relates to the recovery by a local housing authority of a charge made by them under section 49.

(2) In the case of—

(a) an improvement notice under section 11 or 12, or

(b) a hazard awareness notice under section 28 or 29,

the charge may be recovered from the person on whom the notice is served.

(3) In the case of emergency remedial action under section 40, the charge may be recovered from the person served with the notice required by subsection (7) of that section.

(4) In the case of—

(a) a prohibition order under section 20 or 21,

(b) an emergency prohibition order under section 43, or

(c) a demolition order under section 265 of the Housing Act 1985 (c. 68),

the charge may be recovered from any person on whom a copy of the order is served as an owner of the premises.

(5) A demand for payment of the charge must be served on the person from whom the authority seek to recover it.

(6) The demand becomes operative, if no appeal is brought against the underlying notice or order, at the end of the period of 21 days beginning with the date of service of the demand.

(7) If such an appeal is brought and a decision is given on the appeal which confirms the underlying notice or order, the demand becomes operative at the time when—

(a) the period within which an appeal to the Lands Tribunal may be brought expires without such an appeal having been brought, or

(b) a decision is given on such an appeal which confirms the notice or order.

(8) For the purposes of subsection (7)—

(a) the withdrawal of an appeal has the same effect as a decision which confirms the notice or order, and

(b) references to a decision which confirms the notice or order are to a decision which confirms it with or without variation.

(9) As from the time when the demand becomes operative, the sum recoverable by the authority is, until recovered, a charge on the premises concerned.

(10) The charge takes effect at that time as a legal charge which is a local land charge.

(11) For the purpose of enforcing the charge the authority have the same powers and remedies under the Law of Property Act 1925 (c. 20) and otherwise as if they were mortgagees by deed having powers of sale and lease, of accepting surrenders of leases and of appointing a receiver.

(12) The power of appointing a receiver is exercisable at any time after the end of the period of one month beginning with the date on which the charge takes effect.

(13) The appropriate national authority may by regulations prescribe the form of, and the particulars to be contained in, a demand for payment of any charge under section 49.

Repeals

51 Repeal of power to improve existing enforcement procedures

Omit section 86 of the Housing Grants, Construction and Regeneration Act 1996 (c. 53) (power to improve existing enforcement procedures in relation to unfitness for human habitation etc.).

52 Repeal of provisions relating to demolition of obstructive buildings

Omit sections 283 to 288 of the Housing Act 1985 (c. 68) (demolition of obstructive buildings).

53 Miscellaneous repeals etc. in relation to fire hazards

(1) In the London Building Acts (Amendment) Act 1939 (c. xcvii)—

- (a) omit section 35(1)(c)(i) (protection against fire in certain old buildings let in flats or tenements);
- (b) in section 36(1) (projecting shops in which persons are employed or sleep) omit "or sleep"; and
- (c) in section 37(1) (means of access to roofs), in paragraph (b) for the words from "except" onwards substitute "except to the extent that it is occupied for residential purposes;".

(2) In the County of Merseyside Act 1980 (c. x) omit section 48 (means of escape from fire) and section 49(1) and (2) (maintenance of means of escape from fire).

(3) In the Building Act 1984 (c. 55) omit section 72(6)(a) (means of escape from fire in case of certain buildings let in flats or tenements).

(4) In the Leicestershire Act 1985 (c. xvii) omit section 54(6)(a) (means of escape from fire in case of certain buildings used as flats or tenements).

Index

54 Index of defined expressions: Part 1

The following table shows where expressions used in this Part are defined or otherwise explained.

Expression	*Provision of this Act*
Appropriate national authority	Section 261(1)
Building containing one or more flats	Section 1(5)
Category 1 hazard	Section 2(1)
Category 2 hazard	Section 2(1)
Common parts	Section 1(5)
Compliance with improvement notice	Section 30(2)
District of local housing authority	Section 261(6)

Expression	*Provision of this Act*
Dwelling	Section 1(5), (6)
External common parts	Section 1(5)
Flat	Section 1(5) to (7)
Hazard	Section 2(1)
Hazard awareness notice	Section 28(2) or 29(2)
Health	Section 2(5)
HMO	Section 1(5), (6) (and see also section 1(8))
Improvement notice	Section 11(2) or 12(2)
Lease, lessee etc.	Section 262(1) to (4)
Local housing authority	Section 261(2) to (5)
Occupier (and related expressions)	Section 262(6)
Owner	Section 262(7)
Person having control	Section 263(1) and (2)
Person managing	Section 263(3) and (4)
Prohibition order	Section 20(2) or 21(2)
Remedial action	Section 11(8)
Residential premises	Section 1(4)
Residential property tribunal	Section 229
Specified premises, in relation to an improvement notice	Section 13(5)
Specified premises, in relation to a prohibition order	Section 22(10)
Tenancy, tenant	Section 262(1) to (5)
Unoccupied HMO accommodation	Section 1(5) (and see also section 1(8)).

PART 2

LICENSING OF HOUSES IN MULTIPLE OCCUPATION

Introductory

55 Licensing of HMOs to which this Part applies

(1) This Part provides for HMOs to be licensed by local housing authorities where—

- (a) they are HMOs to which this Part applies (see subsection (2)), and
- (b) they are required to be licensed under this Part (see section 61(1)).

(2) This Part applies to the following HMOs in the case of each local housing authority—

(a) any HMO in the authority's district which falls within any prescribed description of HMO, and

(b) if an area is for the time being designated by the authority under section 56 as subject to additional licensing, any HMO in that area which falls within any description of HMO specified in the designation.

(3) The appropriate national authority may by order prescribe descriptions of HMOs for the purposes of subsection (2)(a).

(4) The power conferred by subsection (3) may be exercised in such a way that this Part applies to all HMOs in the district of a local housing authority.

(5) Every local housing authority have the following general duties—

(a) to make such arrangements as are necessary to secure the effective implementation in their district of the licensing regime provided for by this Part;

(b) to ensure that all applications for licences and other issues falling to be determined by them under this Part are determined within a reasonable time; and

(c) to satisfy themselves, as soon as is reasonably practicable, that there are no Part 1 functions that ought to be exercised by them in relation to the premises in respect of which such applications are made.

(6) For the purposes of subsection (5)(c)—

(a) "Part 1 function" means any duty under section 5 to take any course of action to which that section applies or any power to take any course of action to which section 7 applies; and

(b) the authority may take such steps as they consider appropriate (whether or not involving an inspection) to comply with their duty under subsection (5)(c) in relation to each of the premises in question, but they must in any event comply with it within the period of 5 years beginning with the date of the application for a licence.

Designation of additional licensing areas

56 Designation of areas subject to additional licensing

(1) A local housing authority may designate either—

(a) the area of their district, or

(b) an area in their district,

as subject to additional licensing in relation to a description of HMOs specified in the designation, if the requirements of this section are met.

(2) The authority must consider that a significant proportion of the HMOs of that description in the area are being managed sufficiently ineffectively as to give rise, or to be likely to give rise, to one or more particular problems either for those occupying the HMOs or for members of the public.

(3) Before making a designation the authority must—

(a) take reasonable steps to consult persons who are likely to be affected by the designation; and

(b) consider any representations made in accordance with the consultation and not withdrawn.

(4) The power to make a designation under this section may be exercised in such a way that this Part applies to all HMOs in the area in question.

(5) In forming an opinion as to the matter mentioned in subsection (2), the authority must have regard to any information regarding the extent to which any codes of practice approved under section 233 have been complied with by persons managing HMOs in the area in question.

(6) Section 57 applies for the purposes of this section.

57 Designations under section 56: further considerations

(1) This section applies to the power of a local housing authority to make designations under section 56.

(2) The authority must ensure that any exercise of the power is consistent with the authority's overall housing strategy.

(3) The authority must also seek to adopt a co-ordinated approach in connection with dealing with homelessness, empty properties and anti-social behaviour affecting the private rented sector, both—

(a) as regards combining licensing under this Part with other courses of action available to them, and

(b) as regards combining such licensing with measures taken by other persons.

(4) The authority must not make a particular designation under section 56 unless—

(a) they have considered whether there are any other courses of action available to them (of whatever nature) that might provide an effective method of dealing with the problem or problems in question, and

(b) they consider that making the designation will significantly assist them to deal with the problem or problems (whether or not they take any other course of action as well).

(5) In this Act "anti-social behaviour" means conduct on the part of occupiers of, or visitors to, residential premises—

(a) which causes or is likely to cause a nuisance or annoyance to persons residing, visiting or otherwise engaged in lawful activities in the vicinity of such premises, or

(b) which involves or is likely to involve the use of such premises for illegal purposes.

58 Designation needs confirmation or general approval to be effective

(1) A designation of an area as subject to additional licensing cannot come into force unless—

(a) it has been confirmed by the appropriate national authority; or

(b) it falls within a description of designations in relation to which that authority has given a general approval in accordance with subsection (6).

(2) The appropriate national authority may either confirm, or refuse to confirm, a designation as it considers appropriate.

(3) If the appropriate national authority confirms a designation, the designation comes into force on the date specified for this purpose by that authority.

(4) That date must be no earlier than three months after the date on which the designation is confirmed.

(5) A general approval may be given in relation to a description of designations framed by reference to any matters or circumstances.

(6) Accordingly a general approval may (in particular) be given in relation to—

(a) designations made by a specified local housing authority;

(b) designations made by a local housing authority falling within a specified description of such authorities;

(c) designations relating to HMOs of a specified description.

"Specified" means specified by the appropriate national authority in the approval.

(7) If, by virtue of a general approval, a designation does not need to be confirmed before it comes into force, the designation comes into force on the date specified for this purpose in the designation.

(8) That date must be no earlier than three months after the date on which the designation is made.

59 Notification requirements relating to designations

(1) This section applies to a designation—

(a) when it is confirmed under section 58, or

(b) (if it is not required to be so confirmed) when it is made by the local housing authority.

(2) As soon as the designation is confirmed or made, the authority must publish in the prescribed manner a notice stating—

(a) that the designation has been made,

(b) whether or not the designation was required to be confirmed and either that it has been confirmed or that a general approval under section 58 applied to it (giving details of the approval in question),

(c) the date on which the designation is to come into force, and

(d) any other information which may be prescribed.

(3) After publication of a notice under subsection (2), and for as long as the designation is in force, the local housing authority must make available to the public in accordance with any prescribed requirements—

(a) copies of the designation, and

(b) such information relating to the designation as is prescribed.

(4) In this section "prescribed" means prescribed by regulations made by the appropriate national authority.

60 Duration, review and revocation of designations

(1) Unless previously revoked under subsection (4), a designation ceases to have effect at the time that is specified for this purpose in the designation.

(2) That time must be no later than five years after the date on which the designation comes into force.

(3) A local housing authority must from time to time review the operation of any designation made by them.

(4) If following a review they consider it appropriate to do so, the authority may revoke the designation.

(5) If they do revoke the designation, the designation ceases to have effect at the time that is specified by the authority for this purpose.

(6) On revoking a designation the authority must publish notice of the revocation in such manner as is prescribed by regulations made by the appropriate national authority.

HMOs required to be licensed

61 Requirement for HMOs to be licensed

(1) Every HMO to which this Part applies must be licensed under this Part unless—

(a) a temporary exemption notice is in force in relation to it under section 62, or

(b) an interim or final management order is in force in relation to it under Chapter 1 of Part 4.

(2) A licence under this Part is a licence authorising occupation of the house concerned by not more than a maximum number of households or persons specified in the licence.

(3) Sections63 to 67 deal with applications for licences, the granting or refusal of licences and the imposition of licence conditions.

(4) The local housing authority must take all reasonable steps to secure that applications for licences are made to them in respect of HMOs in their area which are required to be licensed under this Part but are not.

(5) The appropriate national authority may by regulations provide for—

(a) any provision of this Part, or

(b) section 263 (in its operation for the purposes of any such provision),

to have effect in relation to a section 257 HMO with such modifications as are prescribed by the regulations.

A "section 257 HMO" is an HMO which is a converted block of flats to which section 257 applies.

(6) In this Part (unless the context otherwise requires)—

(a) references to a licence are to a licence under this Part,

(b) references to a licence holder are to be read accordingly, and

(c) references to an HMO being (or not being) licensed under this Part are to its being (or not being) an HMO in respect of which a licence is in force under this Part.

62 Temporary exemption from licensing requirement

(1) This section applies where a person having control of or managing an HMO which is required to be licensed under this Part (see section 61(1)) but is not so licensed, notifies the local housing authority of his intention to take particular steps with a view to securing that the house is no longer required to be licensed.

(2) The authority may, if they think fit, serve on that person a notice under this section ("a temporary exemption notice") in respect of the house.

(3) If a temporary exemption notice is served under this section, the house is (in accordance with sections 61(1) and 85(1)) not required to be licensed either under this Part or under Part 3 during the period for which the notice is in force.

(4) A temporary exemption notice under this section is in force—

- (a) for the period of 3 months beginning with the date on which it is served, or
- (b) (in the case of a notice served by virtue of subsection (5)) for the period of 3 months after the date when the first notice ceases to be in force.

(5) If the authority—

- (a) receive a further notification under subsection (1), and
- (b) consider that there are exceptional circumstances that justify the service of a second temporary exemption notice in respect of the house that would take effect from the end of the period of 3 months applying to the first notice,

the authority may serve a second such notice on the person having control of or managing the house (but no further notice may be served by virtue of this subsection).

(6) If the authority decide not to serve a temporary exemption notice in response to a notification under subsection (1), they must without delay serve on the person concerned a notice informing him of—

- (a) the decision,
- (b) the reasons for it and the date on which it was made,
- (c) the right to appeal against the decision under subsection (7), and
- (d) the period within which an appeal may be made under that subsection.

(7) The person concerned may appeal to a residential property tribunal against the decision within the period of 28 days beginning with the date specified under subsection (6) as the date on which it was made.

(8) Such an appeal—

- (a) is to be by way of a re-hearing, but
- (b) may be determined having regard to matters of which the authority were unaware.

(9) The tribunal—

- (a) may confirm or reverse the decision of the authority, and
- (b) if it reverses the decision, must direct the authority to serve a temporary exemption notice that comes into force on such date as the tribunal directs.

Grant or refusal of licences

63 Applications for licences

(1) An application for a licence must be made to the local housing authority.

(2) The application must be made in accordance with such requirements as the authority may specify.

(3) The authority may, in particular, require the application to be accompanied by a fee fixed by the authority.

(4) The power of the authority to specify requirements under this section is subject to any regulations made under subsection (5).

(5) The appropriate national authority may by regulations make provision about the making of applications under this section.

(6) Such regulations may, in particular—

(a) specify the manner and form in which applications are to be made;

(b) require the applicant to give copies of the application, or information about it, to particular persons;

(c) specify the information which is to be supplied in connection with applications;

(d) specify the maximum fees which are to be charged (whether by specifying amounts or methods for calculating amounts);

(e) specify cases in which no fees are to be charged or fees are to be refunded.

(7) When fixing fees under this section, the local housing authority may (subject to any regulations made under subsection (5)) take into account—

(a) all costs incurred by the authority in carrying out their functions under this Part, and

(b) all costs incurred by them in carrying out their functions under Chapter 1 of Part 4 in relation to HMOs (so far as they are not recoverable under or by virtue of any provision of that Chapter).

64 Grant or refusal of licence

(1) Where an application in respect of an HMO is made to the local housing authority under section 63, the authority must either—

(a) grant a licence in accordance with subsection (2), or

(b) refuse to grant a licence.

(2) If the authority are satisfied as to the matters mentioned in subsection (3), they may grant a licence either—

(a) to the applicant, or

(b) to some other person, if both he and the applicant agree.

(3) The matters are—

(a) that the house is reasonably suitable for occupation by not more than the maximum number of households or persons mentioned in subsection (4) or that it can be made so suitable by the imposition of conditions under section 67;

(b) that the proposed licence holder—
   (i) is a fit and proper person to be the licence holder, and
   (ii) is, out of all the persons reasonably available to be the licence holder in respect of the house, the most appropriate person to be the licence holder;

(c) that the proposed manager of the house is either—
   (i) the person having control of the house, or
   (ii) a person who is an agent or employee of the person having control of the house;

(d) that the proposed manager of the house is a fit and proper person to be the manager of the house; and

(e) that the proposed management arrangements for the house are otherwise satisfactory.

(4) The maximum number of households or persons referred to in subsection (3)(a) is—
   (a) the maximum number specified in the application, or
   (b) some other maximum number decided by the authority.

(5) Sections 65 and 66 apply for the purposes of this section.

65 Tests as to suitability for multiple occupation

(1) The local housing authority cannot be satisfied for the purposes of section 64(3)(a) that the house is reasonably suitable for occupation by a particular maximum number of households or persons if they consider that it fails to meet prescribed standards for occupation by that number of households or persons.

(2) But the authority may decide that the house is not reasonably suitable for occupation by a particular maximum number of households or persons even if it does meet prescribed standards for occupation by that number of households or persons.

(3) In this section "prescribed standards" means standards prescribed by regulations made by the appropriate national authority.

(4) The standards that may be so prescribed include—
   (a) standards as to the number, type and quality of—
      (i) bathrooms, toilets, washbasins and showers,
      (ii) areas for food storage, preparation and cooking, and
      (iii) laundry facilities,
   which should be available in particular circumstances; and
   (b) standards as to the number, type and quality of other facilities or equipment which should be available in particular circumstances.

66 Tests for fitness etc. and satisfactory management arrangements

(1) In deciding for the purposes of section 64(3)(b) or (d) whether a person ("P") is a fit and proper person to be the licence holder or (as the case may be) the manager of the house, the local housing authority must have regard (among other things) to any evidence within subsection (2) or (3).

(2) Evidence is within this subsection if it shows that P has—

(a) committed any offence involving fraud or other dishonesty, or violence or drugs, or any offence listed in Schedule 3 to the Sexual Offences Act 2003 (c. 42) (offences attracting notification requirements);

(b) practised unlawful discrimination on grounds of sex, colour, race, ethnic or national origins or disability in, or in connection with, the carrying on of any business;

(c) contravened any provision of the law relating to housing or of landlord and tenant law; or

(d) acted otherwise than in accordance with any applicable code of practice approved under section 233.

(3) Evidence is within this subsection if—

(a) it shows that any person associated or formerly associated with P (whether on a personal, work or other basis) has done any of the things set out in subsection (2)(a) to (d), and

(b) it appears to the authority that the evidence is relevant to the question whether P is a fit and proper person to be the licence holder or (as the case may be) the manager of the house.

(4) For the purposes of section 64(3)(b) the local housing authority must assume, unless the contrary is shown, that the person having control of the house is a more appropriate person to be the licence holder than a person not having control of it.

(5) In deciding for the purposes of section 64(3)(e) whether the proposed management arrangements for the house are otherwise satisfactory, the local housing authority must have regard (among other things) to the considerations mentioned in subsection (6).

(6) The considerations are—

(a) whether any person proposed to be involved in the management of the house has a sufficient level of competence to be so involved;

(b) whether any person proposed to be involved in the management of the house (other than the manager) is a fit and proper person to be so involved; and

(c) whether any proposed management structures and funding arrangements are suitable.

(7) Any reference in section 64(3)(c)(i) or (ii) or subsection (4) above to a person having control of the house, or to being a person of any other description, includes a reference to a person who is proposing to have control of the house, or (as the case may be) to be a person of that description, at the time when the licence would come into force.

67 Licence conditions

(1) A licence may include such conditions as the local housing authority consider appropriate for regulating all or any of the following—

(a) the management, use and occupation of the house concerned, and

(b) its condition and contents.

(2) Those conditions may, in particular, include (so far as appropriate in the circumstances)—

(a) conditions imposing restrictions or prohibitions on the use or occupation of particular parts of the house by persons occupying it;

(b) conditions requiring the taking of reasonable and practicable steps to prevent or reduce anti-social behaviour by persons occupying or visiting the house;

(c) conditions requiring facilities and equipment to be made available in the house for the purpose of meeting standards prescribed under section 65;

(d) conditions requiring such facilities and equipment to be kept in repair and proper working order;

(e) conditions requiring, in the case of any works needed in order for any such facilities or equipment to be made available or to meet any such standards, that the works are carried out within such period or periods as may be specified in, or determined under, the licence;

(f) conditions requiring the licence holder or the manager of the house to attend training courses in relation to any applicable code of practice approved under section 233.

(3) A licence must include the conditions required by Schedule 4.

(4) As regards the relationship between the authority's power to impose conditions under this section and functions exercisable by them under or for the purposes of Part 1 ("Part 1 functions")—

(a) the authority must proceed on the basis that, in general, they should seek to identify, remove or reduce category 1 or category 2 hazards in the house by the exercise of Part 1 functions and not by means of licence conditions;

(b) this does not, however, prevent the authority from imposing licence conditions relating to the installation or maintenance of facilities or equipment within subsection (2)(c) above, even if the same result could be achieved by the exercise of Part 1 functions;

(c) the fact that licence conditions are imposed for a particular purpose that could be achieved by the exercise of Part 1 functions does not affect the way in which Part 1 functions can be subsequently exercised by the authority.

(5) A licence may not include conditions imposing restrictions or obligations on a particular person other than the licence holder unless that person has consented to the imposition of the restrictions or obligations.

(6) A licence may not include conditions requiring (or intended to secure) any alteration in the terms of any tenancy or licence under which any person occupies the house.

68 Licences: general requirements and duration

(1) A licence may not relate to more than one HMO.

(2) A licence may be granted before the time when it is required by virtue of this Part but, if so, the licence cannot come into force until that time.

(3) A licence—

(a) comes into force at the time that is specified in or determined under the licence for this purpose, and

(b) unless previously terminated by subsection (7) or revoked under section 70, continues in force for the period that is so specified or determined.

(4) That period must not end more than 5 years after—

(a) the date on which the licence was granted, or

(b) if the licence was granted as mentioned in subsection (2), the date when the licence comes into force.

(5) Subsection (3)(b) applies even if, at any time during that period, the HMO concerned subsequently ceases to be one to which this Part applies.

(6) A licence may not be transferred to another person.

(7) If the holder of the licence dies while the licence is in force, the licence ceases to be in force on his death.

(8) However, during the period of 3 months beginning with the date of the licence holder's death, the house is to be treated for the purposes of this Part and Part 3 as if on that date a temporary exemption notice had been served in respect of the house under section 62.

(9) If, at any time during that period ("the initial period"), the personal representatives of the licence holder request the local housing authority to do so, the authority may serve on them a notice which, during the period of 3 months after the date on which the initial period ends, has the same effect as a temporary exemption notice under section 62.

(10) Subsections (6) to (8) of section 62 apply (with any necessary modifications) in relation to a decision by the authority not to serve such a notice as they apply in relation to a decision not to serve a temporary exemption notice.

Variation and revocation of licences

69 Variation of licences

(1) The local housing authority may vary a licence—

(a) if they do so with the agreement of the licence holder, or

(b) if they consider that there has been a change of circumstances since the time when the licence was granted.

For this purpose "change of circumstances" includes any discovery of new information.

(2) Subsection (3) applies where the authority—

(a) are considering whether to vary a licence under subsection (1)(b); and

(b) are considering—

(i) what number of households or persons is appropriate as the maximum number authorised to occupy the HMO to which the licence relates, or

(ii) the standards applicable to occupation by a particular number of households or persons.

(3) The authority must apply the same standards in relation to the circumstances existing at the time when they are considering whether to vary the licence as were applicable at the time when it was granted.

This is subject to subsection (4).

(4) If the standards—

(a) prescribed under section 65, and

(b) applicable at the time when the licence was granted,

have subsequently been revised or superseded by provisions of regulations under that section, the authority may apply the new standards.

(5) A variation made with the agreement of the licence holder takes effect at the time when it is made.

(6) Otherwise, a variation does not come into force until such time, if any, as is the operative time for the purposes of this subsection under paragraph 35 of Schedule 5 (time when period for appealing expires without an appeal being made or when decision to vary is confirmed on appeal).

(7) The power to vary a licence under this section is exercisable by the authority either—
- (a) on an application made by the licence holder or a relevant person, or
- (b) on the authority's own initiative.

(8) In subsection (7) "relevant person" means any person (other than the licence holder)—
- (a) who has an estate or interest in the HMO concerned (but is not a tenant under a lease with an unexpired term of 3 years or less), or
- (b) who is a person managing or having control of the house (and does not fall within paragraph (a)), or
- (c) on whom any restriction or obligation is imposed by the licence in accordance with section 67(5).

70 Revocation of licences

(1) The local housing authority may revoke a licence—
- (a) if they do so with the agreement of the licence holder;
- (b) in any of the cases mentioned in subsection (2) (circumstances relating to licence holder or other person);
- (c) in any of the cases mentioned in subsection (3) (circumstances relating to HMO concerned); or
- (d) in any other circumstances prescribed by regulations made by the appropriate national authority.

(2) The cases referred to in subsection (1)(b) are as follows—
- (a) where the authority consider that the licence holder or any other person has committed a serious breach of a condition of the licence or repeated breaches of such a condition;
- (b) where the authority no longer consider that the licence holder is a fit and proper person to be the licence holder; and
- (c) where the authority no longer consider that the management of the house is being carried on by persons who are in each case fit and proper persons to be involved in its management.

Section 66(1) applies in relation to paragraph (b) or (c) above as it applies in relation to section 64(3)(b) or (d).

(3) The cases referred to in subsection (1)(c) are as follows—
- (a) where the HMO to which the licence relates ceases to be an HMO to which this Part applies; and
- (b) where the authority consider at any time that, were the licence to expire at that time, they would, for a particular reason relating to the structure of the

HMO, refuse to grant a new licence to the licence holder on similar terms in respect of it.

(4) Subsection (5) applies where the authority are considering whether to revoke a licence by virtue of subsection (3)(b) on the grounds that the HMO is not reasonably suitable for the number of households or persons specified in the licence as the maximum number authorised to occupy the house.

(5) The authority must apply the same standards in relation to the circumstances existing at the time when they are considering whether to revoke the licence as were applicable at the time when it was granted.

This is subject to subsection (6).

(6) If the standards—

(a) prescribed under section 65, and

(b) applicable at the time when the licence was granted,

have subsequently been revised or superseded by provisions of regulations under that section, the authority may apply the new standards.

(7) A revocation made with the agreement of the licence holder takes effect at the time when it is made.

(8) Otherwise, a revocation does not come into force until such time, if any, as is the operative time for the purposes of this subsection under paragraph 35 of Schedule 5 (time when period for appealing expires without an appeal being made or when decision to vary is confirmed on appeal).

(9) The power to revoke a licence under this section is exercisable by the authority either—

(a) on an application made by the licence holder or a relevant person, or

(b) on the authority's own initiative.

(10) In subsection (9) "relevant person" means any person (other than the licence holder)—

(a) who has an estate or interest in the HMO concerned (but is not a tenant under a lease with an unexpired term of 3 years or less), or

(b) who is a person managing or having control of that house (and does not fall within paragraph (a)), or

(c) on whom any restriction or obligation is imposed by the licence in accordance with section 67(5).

Procedure and appeals

71 Procedural requirements and appeals against licence decisions

Schedule 5 (which deals with procedural requirements relating to the grant, refusal, variation or revocation of licences and with appeals against licence decisions) has effect for the purposes of this Part.

Enforcement

72 Offences in relation to licensing of HMOs

(1) A person commits an offence if he is a person having control of or managing an HMO which is required to be licensed under this Part (see section 61(1)) but is not so licensed.

(2) A person commits an offence if—
- (a) he is a person having control of or managing an HMO which is licensed under this Part,
- (b) he knowingly permits another person to occupy the house, and
- (c) the other person's occupation results in the house being occupied by more households or persons than is authorised by the licence.

(3) A person commits an offence if—
- (a) he is a licence holder or a person on whom restrictions or obligations under a licence are imposed in accordance with section 67(5), and
- (b) he fails to comply with any condition of the licence.

(4) In proceedings against a person for an offence under subsection (1) it is a defence that, at the material time—
- (a) a notification had been duly given in respect of the house under section 62(1), or
- (b) an application for a licence had been duly made in respect of the house under section 63,

and that notification or application was still effective (see subsection (8)).

(5) In proceedings against a person for an offence under subsection (1), (2) or (3) it is a defence that he had a reasonable excuse—
- (a) for having control of or managing the house in the circumstances mentioned in subsection (1), or
- (b) for permitting the person to occupy the house, or
- (c) for failing to comply with the condition,

as the case may be.

(6) A person who commits an offence under subsection (1) or (2) is liable on summary conviction to a fine not exceeding £20,000.

(7) A person who commits an offence under subsection (3) is liable on summary conviction to a fine not exceeding level 5 on the standard scale.

(8) For the purposes of subsection (4) a notification or application is "effective" at a particular time if at that time it has not been withdrawn, and either—
- (a) the authority have not decided whether to serve a temporary exemption notice, or (as the case may be) grant a licence, in pursuance of the notification or application, or
- (b) if they have decided not to do so, one of the conditions set out in subsection (9) is met.

(9) The conditions are—

(a) that the period for appealing against the decision of the authority not to serve or grant such a notice or licence (or against any relevant decision of a residential property tribunal) has not expired, or

(b) that an appeal has been brought against the authority's decision (or against any relevant decision of such a tribunal) and the appeal has not been determined or withdrawn.

(10) In subsection (9) "relevant decision" means a decision which is given on an appeal to the tribunal and confirms the authority's decision (with or without variation).

73 Other consequences of operating unlicensed HMOs: rent repayment orders

(1) For the purposes of this section an HMO is an "unlicensed HMO" if—

(a) it is required to be licensed under this Part but is not so licensed, and

(b) neither of the conditions in subsection (2) is satisfied.

(2) The conditions are—

(a) that a notification has been duly given in respect of the HMO under section 62(1) and that notification is still effective (as defined by section 72(8));

(b) that an application for a licence has been duly made in respect of the HMO under section 63 and that application is still effective (as so defined).

(3) No rule of law relating to the validity or enforceability of contracts in circumstances involving illegality is to affect the validity or enforceability of—

(a) any provision requiring the payment of rent or the making of any other periodical payment in connection with any tenancy or licence of a part of an unlicensed HMO, or

(b) any other provision of such a tenancy or licence.

(4) But amounts paid in respect of rent or other periodical payments payable in connection with such a tenancy or licence may be recovered in accordance with subsection (5) and section 74.

(5) If—

(a) an application in respect of an HMO is made to a residential property tribunal by the local housing authority or an occupier of a part of the HMO, and

(b) the tribunal is satisfied as to the matters mentioned in subsection (6) or (8),

the tribunal may make an order (a "rent repayment order") requiring the appropriate person to pay to the applicant such amount in respect of the housing benefit paid as mentioned in subsection (6)(b), or (as the case may be) the periodical payments paid as mentioned in subsection (8)(b), as is specified in the order (see section 74(2) to (8)).

(6) If the application is made by the local housing authority, the tribunal must be satisfied as to the following matters—

(a) that, at any time within the period of 12 months ending with the date of the notice of intended proceedings required by subsection (7), the appropriate person has committed an offence under section 72(1) in relation to the HMO (whether or not he has been charged or convicted),

(b) that housing benefit has been paid (to any person) in respect of periodical payments payable in connection with the occupation of a part or parts of the

HMO during any period during which it appears to the tribunal that such an offence was being committed, and

(c) that the requirements of subsection (7) have been complied with in relation to the application.

(7) Those requirements are as follows—

(a) the authority must have served on the appropriate person a notice (a "notice of intended proceedings")—

(i) informing him that the authority are proposing to make an application under subsection (5),

(ii) setting out the reasons why they propose to do so,

(iii) stating the amount that they will seek to recover under that subsection and how that amount is calculated, and

(iv) inviting him to make representations to them within a period specified in the notice of not less than 28 days;

(b) that period must have expired; and

(c) the authority must have considered any representations made to them within that period by the appropriate person.

(8) If the application is made by an occupier of a part of the HMO, the tribunal must be satisfied as to the following matters—

(a) that the appropriate person has been convicted of an offence under section 72(1) in relation to the HMO, or has been required by a rent repayment order to make a payment in respect of housing benefit paid in connection with occupation of a part or parts of the HMO,

(b) that the occupier paid, to a person having control of or managing the HMO, periodical payments in respect of occupation of part of the HMO during any period during which it appears to the tribunal that such an offence was being committed in relation to the HMO, and

(c) that the application is made within the period of 12 months beginning with—

(i) the date of the conviction or order, or

(ii) if such a conviction was followed by such an order (or vice versa), the date of the later of them.

(9) Where a local housing authority serve a notice of intended proceedings on any person under this section, they must ensure—

(a) that a copy of the notice is received by the department of the authority responsible for administering the housing benefit to which the proceedings would relate; and

(b) that that department is subsequently kept informed of any matters relating to the proceedings that are likely to be of interest to it in connection with the administration of housing benefit.

(10) In this section—

"the appropriate person", in relation to any payment of housing benefit or periodical payment payable in connection with occupation of a part of an HMO, means the person who at the time of the payment was entitled to receive on his own account periodical payments payable in connection with such occupation;

"housing benefit" means housing benefit provided by virtue of a scheme under section 123 of the Social Security Contributions and Benefits Act 1992 (c. 4);

"occupier", in relation to any periodical payment, means a person who was an occupier at the time of the payment, whether under a tenancy or licence or otherwise (and "occupation" has a corresponding meaning);

"periodical payments" means periodical payments in respect of which housing benefit may be paid by virtue of regulation 10 of the Housing Benefit (General) Regulations 1987 (S.I. 1987/1971) or any corresponding provision replacing that regulation.

(11) For the purposes of this section an amount which—

(a) is not actually paid by an occupier but is used by him to discharge the whole or part of his liability in respect of a periodical payment (for example, by offsetting the amount against any such liability), and

(b) is not an amount of housing benefit,

is to be regarded as an amount paid by the occupier in respect of that periodical payment.

74 Further provisions about rent repayment orders

(1) This section applies in relation to rent repayment orders made by residential property tribunals under section 73(5).

(2) Where, on an application by the local housing authority, the tribunal is satisfied—

(a) that a person has been convicted of an offence under section 72(1) in relation to the HMO, and

(b) that housing benefit was paid (whether or not to the appropriate person) in respect of periodical payments payable in connection with occupation of a part or parts of the HMO during any period during which it appears to the tribunal that such an offence was being committed in relation to the HMO,

the tribunal must make a rent repayment order requiring the appropriate person to pay to the authority an amount equal to the total amount of housing benefit paid as mentioned in paragraph (b).

This is subject to subsections (3), (4) and (8).

(3) If the total of the amounts received by the appropriate person in respect of periodical payments payable as mentioned in paragraph (b) of subsection (2) ("the rent total") is less than the total amount of housing benefit paid as mentioned in that paragraph, the amount required to be paid by virtue of a rent repayment order made in accordance with that subsection is limited to the rent total.

(4) A rent repayment order made in accordance with subsection (2) may not require the payment of any amount which the tribunal is satisfied that, by reason of any exceptional circumstances, it would be unreasonable for that person to be required to pay.

(5) In a case where subsection (2) does not apply, the amount required to be paid by virtue of a rent repayment order under section 73(5) is to be such amount as the tribunal considers reasonable in the circumstances.

This is subject to subsections (6) to (8).

(6) In such a case the tribunal must, in particular, take into account the following matters—

(a) the total amount of relevant payments paid in connection with occupation of the HMO during any period during which it appears to the tribunal that an offence was being committed by the appropriate person in relation to the HMO under section 72(1);

(b) the extent to which that total amount—

(i) consisted of, or derived from, payments of housing benefit, and

(ii) was actually received by the appropriate person;

(c) whether the appropriate person has at any time been convicted of an offence under section 72(1) in relation to the HMO;

(d) the conduct and financial circumstances of the appropriate person; and

(e) where the application is made by an occupier, the conduct of the occupier.

(7) In subsection (6) "relevant payments" means—

(a) in relation to an application by a local housing authority, payments of housing benefit or periodical payments payable by occupiers;

(b) in relation to an application by an occupier, periodical payments payable by the occupier, less any amount of housing benefit payable in respect of occupation of the part of the HMO occupied by him during the period in question.

(8) A rent repayment order may not require the payment of any amount which—

(a) (where the application is made by a local housing authority) is in respect of any time falling outside the period of 12 months mentioned in section 73(6)(a); or

(b) (where the application is made by an occupier) is in respect of any time falling outside the period of 12 months ending with the date of the occupier's application under section 73(5);

and the period to be taken into account under subsection (6)(a) above is restricted accordingly.

(9) Any amount payable to a local housing authority under a rent repayment order—

(a) does not, when recovered by the authority, constitute an amount of housing benefit recovered by them, and

(b) until recovered by them, is a legal charge on the HMO which is a local land charge.

(10) For the purpose of enforcing that charge the authority have the same powers and remedies under the Law of Property Act 1925 (c. 20) and otherwise as if they were mortgagees by deed having powers of sale and lease, and of accepting surrenders of leases and of appointing a receiver.

(11) The power of appointing a receiver is exercisable at any time after the end of the period of one month beginning with the date on which the charge takes effect.

(12) If the authority subsequently grant a licence under this Part or Part 3 in respect of the HMO to the appropriate person or any person acting on his behalf, the conditions contained in the licence may include a condition requiring the licence holder—

(a) to pay to the authority any amount payable to them under the rent repayment order and not so far recovered by them; and

(b) to do so in such instalments as are specified in the licence.

(13) If the authority subsequently make a management order under Chapter 1 of Part 4 in respect of the HMO, the order may contain such provisions as the authority consider appropriate for the recovery of any amount payable to them under the rent repayment order and not so far recovered by them.

(14) Any amount payable to an occupier by virtue of a rent repayment order is recoverable by the occupier as a debt due to him from the appropriate person.

(15) The appropriate national authority may by regulations make such provision as it considers appropriate for supplementing the provisions of this section and section 73, and in particular—

(a) for securing that persons are not unfairly prejudiced by rent repayment orders (whether in cases where there have been over-payments of housing benefit or otherwise);

(b) for requiring or authorising amounts received by local housing authorities by virtue of rent repayment orders to be dealt with in such manner as is specified in the regulations.

(16) Section 73(10) and (11) apply for the purposes of this section as they apply for the purposes of section 73.

75 Other consequences of operating unlicensed HMOs: restriction on terminating tenancies

(1) No section 21 notice may be given in relation to a shorthold tenancy of a part of an unlicensed HMO so long as it remains such an HMO.

(2) In this section—

a "section 21 notice" means a notice under section 21(1)(b) or (4)(a) of the Housing Act 1988 (c. 50) (recovery of possession on termination of shorthold tenancy);

a "shorthold tenancy" means an assured shorthold tenancy within the meaning of Chapter 2 of Part 1 of that Act;

"unlicensed HMO" has the same meaning as in section 73 of this Act.

Supplementary provisions

76 Transitional arrangements relating to introduction and termination of licensing

(1) Subsection (2) applies where—

(a) an order under section 55(3) which prescribes a particular description of HMOs comes into force; or

(b) a designation under section 56 comes into force in relation to HMOs of a particular description.

(2) This Part applies in relation to the occupation by persons or households of such HMOs on or after the coming into force of the order or designation even if their occupation began before, or in pursuance of a contract made before, it came into force.

This is subject to subsections (3) to (5).

(3) Subsection (4) applies where—

(a) an HMO which is licensed under this Part, or a part of such an HMO, is occupied by more households or persons than the number permitted by the licence; and
(b) the occupation of all or any of those households or persons began before, or in pursuance of a contract made before, the licence came into force.

(4) In proceedings against a person for an offence under section 72(2) it is a defence that at the material time he was taking all reasonable steps to try to reduce the number of households or persons occupying the house to the number permitted by the licence.

(5) Subsection (4) does not apply if the licence came into force immediately after a previous licence in respect of the same HMO unless the occupation in question began before, or in pursuance of a contract made before, the coming into force of the original licence.

(6) An order under section 270 may make provision as regards the licensing under this Part of HMOs—
(a) which are registered immediately before the appointed day under a scheme to which section 347 (schemes containing control provisions) or 348B (schemes containing special control provisions) of the Housing Act 1985 (c. 68) applies, or
(b) in respect of which applications for registration under such a scheme are then pending.

(7) In subsection (6) "the appointed day" means the day appointed for the coming into force of section 61.

77 Meaning of "HMO"

In this Part—
(a) "HMO" means a house in multiple occupation as defined by sections 254 to 259, and
(b) references to an HMO include (where the context permits) any yard, garden, outhouses and appurtenances belonging to, or usually enjoyed with, it (or any part of it).

78 Index of defined expressions: Part 2

The following table shows where expressions used in this Part are defined or otherwise explained.

Expression	*Provision of this Act*
Anti-social behaviour	Section 57(5)
Appropriate national authority	Section 261(1)
Category 1 hazard	Section 2(1)
Category 2 hazard	Section 2(1)
District of local housing authority	Section 261(6)
HMO	Section 77
HMO to which this Part applies	Section 55(2)

Expression	*Provision of this Act*
Licence and licence holder	Section 61(6)
Licence (to occupy premises)	Section 262(9)
Local housing authority	Section 261(2) to (5)
Modifications	Section 250(7)
Occupier (and related expressions)	Section 262(6)
Person having control	Section 263(1) and (2) (and see also section 66(7))
Person having estate or interest	Section 262(8)
Person managing	Section 263(3)
Person involved in management	Section 263(5)
Residential property tribunal	Section 229
Tenant	Section 262(1) to (5).

PART 3

SELECTIVE LICENSING OF OTHER RESIDENTIAL ACCOMMODATION

Introductory

79 Licensing of houses to which this Part applies

(1) This Part provides for houses to be licensed by local housing authorities where—

- (a) they are houses to which this Part applies (see subsection (2)), and
- (b) they are required to be licensed under this Part (see section 85(1)).

(2) This Part applies to a house if—

- (a) it is in an area that is for the time being designated under section 80 as subject to selective licensing, and
- (b) the whole of it is occupied either—
  - (i) under a single tenancy or licence that is not an exempt tenancy or licence under subsection (3) or (4), or
  - (ii) under two or more tenancies or licences in respect of different dwellings contained in it, none of which is an exempt tenancy or licence under subsection (3) or (4).

(3) A tenancy or licence is an exempt tenancy or licence if it is granted by a body which is registered as a social landlord under Part 1 of the Housing Act 1996 (c. 52).

(4) In addition, the appropriate national authority may by order provide for a tenancy or licence to be an exempt tenancy or licence—

- (a) if it falls within any description of tenancy or licence specified in the order; or
- (b) in any other circumstances so specified.

(5) Every local housing authority have the following general duties—

(a) to make such arrangements as are necessary to secure the effective implementation in their district of the licensing regime provided for by this Part; and

(b) to ensure that all applications for licences and other issues falling to be determined by them under this Part are determined within a reasonable time.

Designation of selective licensing areas

80 Designation of selective licensing areas

(1) A local housing authority may designate either—

(a) the area of their district, or

(b) an area in their district,

as subject to selective licensing, if the requirements of subsections (2) and (9) are met.

(2) The authority must consider that—

(a) the first or second set of general conditions mentioned in subsection (3) or (6), or

(b) any conditions specified in an order under subsection (7) as an additional set of conditions,

are satisfied in relation to the area.

(3) The first set of general conditions are—

(a) that the area is, or is likely to become, an area of low housing demand; and

(b) that making a designation will, when combined with other measures taken in the area by the local housing authority, or by other persons together with the local housing authority, contribute to the improvement of the social or economic conditions in the area.

(4) In deciding whether an area is, or is likely to become, an area of low housing demand a local housing authority must take into account (among other matters)—

(a) the value of residential premises in the area, in comparison to the value of similar premises in other areas which the authority consider to be comparable (whether in terms of types of housing, local amenities, availability of transport or otherwise);

(b) the turnover of occupiers of residential premises;

(c) the number of residential premises which are available to buy or rent and the length of time for which they remain unoccupied.

(5) The appropriate national authority may by order amend subsection (4) by adding new matters to those for the time being mentioned in that subsection.

(6) The second set of general conditions are—

(a) that the area is experiencing a significant and persistent problem caused by anti-social behaviour;

(b) that some or all of the private sector landlords who have let premises in the area (whether under leases or licences) are failing to take action to combat the problem that it would be appropriate for them to take; and

(c) that making a designation will, when combined with other measures taken in the area by the local housing authority, or by other persons together with the local housing authority, lead to a reduction in, or the elimination of, the problem.

"Private sector landlord" does not include a registered social landlord within the meaning of Part 1 of the Housing Act 1996 (c. 52).

(7) The appropriate national authority may by order provide for any conditions specified in the order to apply as an additional set of conditions for the purposes of subsection (2).

(8) The conditions that may be specified include, in particular, conditions intended to permit a local housing authority to make a designation for the purpose of dealing with one or more specified problems affecting persons occupying Part 3 houses in the area.

"Specified" means specified in an order under subsection (7).

(9) Before making a designation the local housing authority must—

(a) take reasonable steps to consult persons who are likely to be affected by the designation; and

(b) consider any representations made in accordance with the consultation and not withdrawn.

(10) Section 81 applies for the purposes of this section.

81 Designations under section 80: further considerations

(1) This section applies to the power of a local housing authority to make designations under section 80.

(2) The authority must ensure that any exercise of the power is consistent with the authority's overall housing strategy.

(3) The authority must also seek to adopt a co-ordinated approach in connection with dealing with homelessness, empty properties and anti-social behaviour, both—

(a) as regards combining licensing under this Part with other courses of action available to them, and

(b) as regards combining such licensing with measures taken by other persons.

(4) The authority must not make a particular designation under section 80 unless—

(a) they have considered whether there are any other courses of action available to them (of whatever nature) that might provide an effective method of achieving the objective or objectives that the designation would be intended to achieve, and

(b) they consider that making the designation will significantly assist them to achieve the objective or objectives (whether or not they take any other course of action as well).

82 Designation needs confirmation or general approval to be effective

(1) A designation of an area as subject to selective licensing cannot come into force unless—

(a) it has been confirmed by the appropriate national authority; or

(b) it falls within a description of designations in relation to which that authority has given a general approval in accordance with subsection (6).

(2) The appropriate national authority may either confirm, or refuse to confirm, a designation as it considers appropriate.

(3) If the appropriate national authority confirms a designation, the designation comes into force on a date specified for this purpose by that authority.

(4) That date must be no earlier than three months after the date on which the designation is confirmed.

(5) A general approval may be given in relation to a description of designations framed by reference to any matters or circumstances.

(6) Accordingly a general approval may (in particular) be given in relation to—

- (a) designations made by a specified local housing authority;
- (b) designations made by a local housing authority falling within a specified description of such authorities;
- (c) designations relating to Part 3 houses of a specified description.

"Specified" means specified by the appropriate national authority in the approval.

(7) If, by virtue of a general approval, a designation does not need to be confirmed before it comes into force, the designation comes into force on the date specified for this purpose in the designation.

(8) That date must be no earlier than three months after the date on which the designation is made.

(9) Where a designation comes into force, this Part applies in relation to the occupation by persons of houses in the area on or after the coming into force of the designation even if their occupation began before, or in pursuance of a contract made before, it came into force.

83 Notification requirements relating to designations

(1) This section applies to a designation—

- (a) when it is confirmed under section 82, or
- (b) (if it is not required to be so confirmed) when it is made by the local housing authority.

(2) As soon as the designation is confirmed or made, the authority must publish in the prescribed manner a notice stating—

- (a) that the designation has been made,
- (b) whether or not the designation was required to be confirmed and either that it has been confirmed or that a general approval under section 82 applied to it (giving details of the approval in question),
- (c) the date on which the designation is to come into force, and
- (d) any other information which may be prescribed.

(3) After publication of a notice under subsection (2), and for as long as the designation is in force, the local housing authority must make available to the public in accordance with any prescribed requirements—

- (a) copies of the designation, and
- (b) such information relating to the designation as is prescribed.

(4) In this section "prescribed" means prescribed by regulations made by the appropriate national authority.

84 Duration, review and revocation of designations

(1) Unless previously revoked under subsection (4), a designation ceases to have effect at the time that is specified for this purpose in the designation.

(2) That time must be no later than five years after the date on which the designation comes into force.

(3) A local housing authority must from time to time review the operation of any designation made by them.

(4) If following a review they consider it appropriate to do so, the authority may revoke the designation.

(5) If they do revoke the designation, the designation ceases to have effect on the date that is specified by the authority for this purpose.

(6) On revoking a designation, the authority must publish notice of the revocation in such manner as is prescribed by regulations made by the appropriate national authority.

Houses required to be licensed

85 Requirement for Part 3 houses to be licensed

(1) Every Part 3 house must be licensed under this Part unless—
- (a) it is an HMO to which Part 2 applies (see section 55(2)), or
- (b) a temporary exemption notice is in force in relation to it under section 86, or
- (c) a management order is in force in relation to it under Chapter 1 or 2 of Part 4.

(2) A licence under this Part is a licence authorising occupation of the house concerned under one or more tenancies or licences within section 79(2)(b).

(3) Sections 87 to 90 deal with applications for licences, the granting or refusal of licences and the imposition of licence conditions.

(4) The local housing authority must take all reasonable steps to secure that applications for licences are made to them in respect of houses in their area which are required to be licensed under this Part but are not so licensed.

(5) In this Part, unless the context otherwise requires—
- (a) references to a Part 3 house are to a house to which this Part applies (see section 79(2)),
- (b) references to a licence are to a licence under this Part,
- (c) references to a licence holder are to be read accordingly, and
- (d) references to a house being (or not being) licensed under this Part are to its being (or not being) a house in respect of which a licence is in force under this Part.

86 Temporary exemption from licensing requirement

(1) This section applies where a person having control of or managing a Part 3 house which is required to be licensed under this Part (see section 85(1)) but is not so licensed, notifies the local housing authority of his intention to take particular steps with a view to securing that the house is no longer required to be licensed.

(2) The authority may, if they think fit, serve on that person a notice under this section ("a temporary exemption notice") in respect of the house.

(3) If a temporary exemption notice is served under this section, the house is (in accordance with section 85(1)) not required to be licensed under this Part during the period for which the notice is in force.

(4) A temporary exemption notice under this section is in force—

- (a) for the period of 3 months beginning with the date on which it is served, or
- (b) (in the case of a notice served by virtue of subsection (5)) for the period of 3 months after the date when the first notice ceases to be in force.

(5) If the authority—

- (a) receive a further notification under subsection (1), and
- (b) consider that there are exceptional circumstances that justify the service of a second temporary exemption notice in respect of the house that would take effect from the end of the period of 3 months applying to the first notice,

the authority may serve a second such notice on the person having control of or managing the house (but no further notice may be served by virtue of this subsection).

(6) If the authority decide not to serve a temporary exemption notice in response to a notification under subsection (1), they must without delay serve on the person concerned a notice informing him of—

- (a) the decision,
- (b) the reasons for it and the date on which it was made,
- (c) the right to appeal against the decision under subsection (7), and
- (d) the period within which an appeal may be made under that subsection.

(7) The person concerned may appeal to a residential property tribunal against the decision within the period of 28 days beginning with the date specified under subsection (6) as the date on which it was made.

(8) Such an appeal—

- (a) is to be by way of a re-hearing, but
- (b) may be determined having regard to matters of which the authority were unaware.

(9) The tribunal—

- (a) may confirm or reverse the decision of the authority, and
- (b) if it reverses the decision, must direct the authority to issue a temporary exemption notice with effect from such date as the tribunal directs.

Grant or refusal of licences

87 Applications for licences

(1) An application for a licence must be made to the local housing authority.

(2) The application must be made in accordance with such requirements as the authority may specify.

(3) The authority may, in particular, require the application to be accompanied by a fee fixed by the authority.

(4) The power of the authority to specify requirements under this section is subject to any regulations made under subsection (5).

(5) The appropriate national authority may by regulations make provision about the making of applications under this section.

(6) Such regulations may, in particular—

- (a) specify the manner and form in which applications are to be made;
- (b) require the applicant to give copies of the application, or information about it, to particular persons;
- (c) specify the information which is to be supplied in connection with applications;
- (d) specify the maximum fees which may be charged (whether by specifying amounts or methods for calculating amounts);
- (e) specify cases in which no fees are to be charged or fees are to be refunded.

(7) When fixing fees under this section, the local housing authority may (subject to any regulations made under subsection (5)) take into account—

- (a) all costs incurred by the authority in carrying out their functions under this Part, and
- (b) all costs incurred by them in carrying out their functions under Chapter 1 of Part 4 in relation to Part 3 houses (so far as they are not recoverable under or by virtue of any provision of that Chapter).

88 Grant or refusal of licence

(1) Where an application in respect of a house is made to the local housing authority under section 87, the authority must either—

- (a) grant a licence in accordance with subsection (2), or
- (b) refuse to grant a licence.

(2) If the authority are satisfied as to the matters mentioned in subsection (3), they may grant a licence either—

- (a) to the applicant, or
- (b) to some other person, if both he and the applicant agree.

(3) The matters are—

- (a) that the proposed licence holder—
  - (i) is a fit and proper person to be the licence holder, and

(ii) is, out of all the persons reasonably available to be the licence holder in respect of the house, the most appropriate person to be the licence holder;

(b) that the proposed manager of the house is either—

(i) the person having control of the house, or

(ii) a person who is an agent or employee of the person having control of the house;

(c) that the proposed manager of the house is a fit and proper person to be the manager of the house; and

(d) that the proposed management arrangements for the house are otherwise satisfactory.

(4) Section 89 applies for the purposes of this section.

89 Tests for fitness etc. and satisfactory management arrangements

(1) In deciding for the purposes of section 88(3)(a) or (c) whether a person ("P") is a fit and proper person to be the licence holder or (as the case may be) the manager of the house, the local housing authority must have regard (among other things) to any evidence within subsection (2) or (3).

(2) Evidence is within this subsection if it shows that P has—

(a) committed any offence involving fraud or other dishonesty, or violence or drugs, or any offence listed in Schedule 3 to the Sexual Offences Act 2003 (c. 42) (offences attracting notification requirements);

(b) practised unlawful discrimination on grounds of sex, colour, race, ethnic or national origins or disability in, or in connection with, the carrying on of any business; or

(c) contravened any provision of the law relating to housing or of landlord and tenant law.

(3) Evidence is within this subsection if—

(a) it shows that any person associated or formerly associated with P (whether on a personal, work or other basis) has done any of the things set out in subsection (2)(a) to (c), and

(b) it appears to the authority that the evidence is relevant to the question whether P is a fit and proper person to be the licence holder or (as the case may be) the manager of the house.

(4) For the purposes of section 88(3)(a) the local housing authority must assume, unless the contrary is shown, that the person having control of the house is a more appropriate person to be the licence holder than a person not having control of it.

(5) In deciding for the purposes of section 88(3)(d) whether the proposed management arrangements for the house are otherwise satisfactory, the local housing authority must have regard (among other things) to the considerations mentioned in subsection (6).

(6) The considerations are—

(a) whether any person proposed to be involved in the management of the house has a sufficient level of competence to be so involved;

(b) whether any person proposed to be involved in the management of the house (other than the manager) is a fit and proper person to be so involved; and

(c) whether any proposed management structures and funding arrangements are suitable.

(7) Any reference in section 88(3)(b)(i) or (ii) or subsection (4) above to a person having control of the house, or to being a person of any other description, includes a reference to a person who is proposing to have control of the house, or (as the case may be) to be a person of that description, at the time when the licence would come into force.

90 Licence conditions

(1) A licence may include such conditions as the local housing authority consider appropriate for regulating the management, use or occupation of the house concerned.

(2) Those conditions may, in particular, include (so far as appropriate in the circumstances)—

(a) conditions imposing restrictions or prohibitions on the use or occupation of particular parts of the house by persons occupying it;

(b) conditions requiring the taking of reasonable and practicable steps to prevent or reduce anti-social behaviour by persons occupying or visiting the house.

(3) A licence may also include—

(a) conditions requiring facilities and equipment to be made available in the house for the purpose of meeting standards prescribed for the purposes of this section by regulations made by the appropriate national authority;

(b) conditions requiring such facilities and equipment to be kept in repair and proper working order;

(c) conditions requiring, in the case of any works needed in order for any such facilities or equipment to be made available or to meet any such standards, that the works are carried out within such period or periods as may be specified in, or determined under, the licence.

(4) A licence must include the conditions required by Schedule 4.

(5) As regards the relationship between the authority's power to impose conditions under this section and functions exercisable by them under or for the purposes of Part 1 ("Part 1 functions")—

(a) the authority must proceed on the basis that, in general, they should seek to identify, remove or reduce category 1 or category 2 hazards in the house by the exercise of Part 1 functions and not by means of licence conditions;

(b) this does not, however, prevent the authority from imposing (in accordance with subsection (3)) licence conditions relating to the installation or maintenance of facilities or equipment within subsection (3)(a) above, even if the same result could be achieved by the exercise of Part 1 functions;

(c) the fact that licence conditions are imposed for a particular purpose that could be achieved by the exercise of Part 1 functions does not affect the way in which Part 1 functions can be subsequently exercised by the authority.

(6) A licence may not include conditions imposing restrictions or obligations on a particular person other than the licence holder unless that person has consented to the imposition of the restrictions or obligations.

(7) A licence may not include conditions requiring (or intended to secure) any alteration in the terms of any tenancy or licence under which any person occupies the house.

91 Licences: general requirements and duration

(1) A licence may not relate to more than one Part 3 house.

(2) A licence may be granted before the time when it is required by virtue of this Part but, if so, the licence cannot come into force until that time.

(3) A licence—

(a) comes into force at the time that is specified in or determined under the licence for this purpose, and

(b) unless previously terminated by subsection (7) or revoked under section 93, continues in force for the period that is so specified or determined.

(4) That period must not end more than 5 years after—

(a) the date on which the licence was granted, or

(b) if the licence was granted as mentioned in subsection (2), the date when the licence comes into force.

(5) Subsection (3)(b) applies even if, at any time during that period, the house concerned subsequently ceases to be a Part 3 house or becomes an HMO to which Part 2 applies (see section 55(2)).

(6) A licence may not be transferred to another person.

(7) If the holder of the licence dies while the licence is in force, the licence ceases to be in force on his death.

(8) However, during the period of 3 months beginning with the date of the licence holder's death, the house is to be treated for the purposes of this Part as if on that date a temporary exemption notice had been served in respect of the house under section 86.

(9) If, at any time during that period ("the initial period"), the personal representatives of the licence holder request the local housing authority to do so, the authority may serve on them a notice which, during the period of 3 months after the date on which the initial period ends, has the same effect as a temporary exemption notice under section 86.

(10) Subsections (6) to (8) of section 86 apply (with any necessary modifications) in relation to a decision by the authority not to serve such a notice as they apply in relation to a decision not to serve a temporary exemption notice.

Variation and revocation of licences

92 Variation of licences

(1) The local housing authority may vary a licence—

(a) if they do so with the agreement of the licence holder, or

(b) if they consider that there has been a change of circumstances since the time when the licence was granted.

For this purpose "change of circumstances" includes any discovery of new information.

(2) A variation made with the agreement of the licence holder takes effect at the time when it is made.

(3) Otherwise, a variation does not come into force until such time, if any, as is the operative time for the purposes of this subsection under paragraph 35 of Schedule 5 (time when period for appealing expires without an appeal being made or when decision to vary is confirmed on appeal).

(4) The power to vary a licence under this section is exercisable by the authority either—

(a) on an application made by the licence holder or a relevant person, or

(b) on the authority's own initiative.

(5) In subsection (4) "relevant person" means any person (other than the licence holder)—

(a) who has an estate or interest in the house concerned (but is not a tenant under a lease with an unexpired term of 3 years or less), or

(b) who is a person managing or having control of the house (and does not fall within paragraph (a)), or

(c) on whom any restriction or obligation is imposed by the licence in accordance with section 90(6).

93 Revocation of licences

(1) The local housing authority may revoke a licence—

(a) if they do so with the agreement of the licence holder,

(b) in any of the cases mentioned in subsection (2) (circumstances relating to licence holder or other person),

(c) in any of the cases mentioned in subsection (3) (circumstances relating to house concerned), or

(d) in any other circumstances prescribed by regulations made by the appropriate national authority.

(2) The cases referred to in subsection (1)(b) are as follows—

(a) where the authority consider that the licence holder or any other person has committed a serious breach of a condition of the licence or repeated breaches of such a condition;

(b) where the authority no longer consider that the licence holder is a fit and proper person to be the licence holder; and

(c) where the authority no longer consider that the management of the house is being carried on by persons who are in each case fit and proper persons to be involved in its management.

Section 89(1) applies in relation to paragraph (b) or (c) above as it applies in relation to section 88(3)(a) or (c).

(3) The cases referred to in subsection (1)(c) are as follows—

(a) where the house to which the licence relates ceases to be a Part 3 house;

(b) where a licence has been granted under Part 2 in respect of the house;

(c) where the authority consider at any time that, were the licence to expire at that time, they would, for a particular reason relating to the structure of the house, refuse to grant a new licence to the licence holder on similar terms in respect of it.

(4) A revocation made with the agreement of the licence holder takes effect at the time when it is made.

(5) Otherwise, a revocation does not come into force until such time, if any, as is the operative time for the purposes of this subsection under paragraph 35 of Schedule 5 (time when period for appealing expires without an appeal being made or when decision to vary is confirmed on appeal).

This is subject to subsection (6).

(6) A revocation made in a case within subsection (3)(b) cannot come into force before such time as would be the operative time for the purposes of subsection (5) under paragraph 35 of Schedule 5 on the assumption that paragraph 35 applied—

(a) to an appeal against the Part 2 licence under paragraph 31 of the Schedule as it applies to an appeal under paragraph 32 of the Schedule, and

(b) to the period for appealing against the Part 2 licence mentioned in paragraph 33(1) of the Schedule as it applies to the period mentioned in paragraph 33(2) of the Schedule.

(7) The power to revoke a licence under this section is exercisable by the authority either—

(a) on an application made by the licence holder or a relevant person, or

(b) on the authority's own initiative.

(8) In subsection (7) "relevant person" means any person (other than the licence holder)—

(a) who has an estate or interest in the house concerned (but is not a tenant under a lease with an unexpired term of 3 years or less), or

(b) who is a person managing or having control of the house (and does not fall within paragraph (a)), or

(c) on whom any restriction or obligation is imposed by the licence in accordance with section 90(6).

Procedure and appeals

94 Procedural requirements and appeals against licence decisions

Schedule 5 (which deals with procedural requirements relating to the grant, refusal, variation or revocation of licences and with appeals against licence decisions) has effect for the purposes of this Part.

Enforcement

95 Offences in relation to licensing of houses under this Part

(1) A person commits an offence if he is a person having control of or managing a house which is required to be licensed under this Part (see section 85(1)) but is not so licensed.

(2) A person commits an offence if—

(a) he is a licence holder or a person on whom restrictions or obligations under a licence are imposed in accordance with section 90(6), and

(b) he fails to comply with any condition of the licence.

(3) In proceedings against a person for an offence under subsection (1) it is a defence that, at the material time—

(a) a notification had been duly given in respect of the house under section 62(1) or 86(1), or

(b) an application for a licence had been duly made in respect of the house under section 87,

and that notification or application was still effective (see subsection (7)).

(4) In proceedings against a person for an offence under subsection (1) or (2) it is a defence that he had a reasonable excuse—

(a) for having control of or managing the house in the circumstances mentioned in subsection (1), or

(b) for failing to comply with the condition,

as the case may be.

(5) A person who commits an offence under subsection (1) is liable on summary conviction to a fine not exceeding £20,000.

(6) A person who commits an offence under subsection (2) is liable on summary conviction to a fine not exceeding level 5 on the standard scale.

(7) For the purposes of subsection (3) a notification or application is "effective" at a particular time if at that time it has not been withdrawn, and either—

(a) the authority have not decided whether to serve a temporary exemption notice, or (as the case may be) grant a licence, in pursuance of the notification or application, or

(b) if they have decided not to do so, one of the conditions set out in subsection (8) is met.

(8) The conditions are—

(a) that the period for appealing against the decision of the authority not to serve or grant such a notice or licence (or against any relevant decision of a residential property tribunal) has not expired, or

(b) that an appeal has been brought against the authority's decision (or against any relevant decision of such a tribunal) and the appeal has not been determined or withdrawn.

(9) In subsection (8) "relevant decision" means a decision which is given on an appeal to the tribunal and confirms the authority's decision (with or without variation).

96 Other consequences of operating unlicensed houses: rent repayment orders

(1) For the purposes of this section a house is an "unlicensed house" if—

(a) it is required to be licensed under this Part but is not so licensed, and

(b) neither of the conditions in subsection (2) is satisfied.

(2) The conditions are—

(a) that a notification has been duly given in respect of the house under section 62(1) or 86(1) and that notification is still effective (as defined by section 95(7));

(b) that an application for a licence has been duly made in respect of the house under section 87 and that application is still effective (as so defined).

(3) No rule of law relating to the validity or enforceability of contracts in circumstances involving illegality is to affect the validity or enforceability of—

(a) any provision requiring the payment of rent or the making of any other periodical payment in connection with any tenancy or licence of the whole or a part of an unlicensed house, or

(b) any other provision of such a tenancy or licence.

(4) But amounts paid in respect of rent or other periodical payments payable in connection with such a tenancy or licence may be recovered in accordance with subsection (5) and section 97.

(5) If—

(a) an application in respect of a house is made to a residential property tribunal by the local housing authority or an occupier of the whole or part of the house, and

(b) the tribunal is satisfied as to the matters mentioned in subsection (6) or (8),

the tribunal may make an order (a "rent repayment order") requiring the appropriate person to pay to the applicant such amount in respect of the housing benefit paid as mentioned in subsection (6)(b), or (as the case may be) the periodical payments paid as mentioned in subsection (8)(b), as is specified in the order (see section 97(2) to (8)).

(6) If the application is made by the local housing authority, the tribunal must be satisfied as to the following matters—

(a) that, at any time within the period of 12 months ending with the date of the notice of intended proceedings required by subsection (7), the appropriate person has committed an offence under section 95(1) in relation to the house (whether or not he has been charged or convicted),

(b) that housing benefit has been paid (to any person) in respect of periodical payments payable in connection with the occupation of the whole or any part or parts of the house during any period during which it appears to the tribunal that such an offence was being committed, and

(c) that the requirements of subsection (7) have been complied with in relation to the application.

(7) Those requirements are as follows—

(a) the authority must have served on the appropriate person a notice (a "notice of intended proceedings")—

(i) informing him that the authority are proposing to make an application under subsection (5),

(ii) setting out the reasons why they propose to do so,

(iii) stating the amount that they will seek to recover under that subsection and how that amount is calculated, and

(iv) inviting him to make representations to them within a period specified in the notice of not less than 28 days;

(b) that period must have expired; and

(c) the authority must have considered any representations made to them within that period by the appropriate person.

(8) If the application is made by an occupier of the whole or part of the house, the tribunal must be satisfied as to the following matters—

(a) that the appropriate person has been convicted of an offence under section 95(1) in relation to the house, or has been required by a rent repayment order to make a payment in respect of housing benefit paid in connection with occupation of the whole or any part or parts of the house,

(b) that the occupier paid, to a person having control of or managing the house, periodical payments in respect of occupation of the whole or part of the house during any period during which it appears to the tribunal that such an offence was being committed in relation to the house, and

(c) that the application is made within the period of 12 months beginning with—

(i) the date of the conviction or order, or

(ii) if such a conviction was followed by such an order (or vice versa), the date of the later of them.

(9) Where a local housing authority serve a notice of intended proceedings on any person under this section, they must ensure—

(a) that a copy of the notice is received by the department of the authority responsible for administering the housing benefit to which the proceedings would relate; and

(b) that that department is subsequently kept informed of any matters relating to the proceedings that are likely to be of interest to it in connection with the administration of housing benefit.

(10) In this section—

"the appropriate person", in relation to any payment of housing benefit or periodical payment payable in connection with occupation of the whole or a part of a house, means the person who at the time of the payment was entitled to receive on his own account periodical payments payable in connection with such occupation;

"housing benefit" means housing benefit provided by virtue of a scheme under section 123 of the Social Security Contributions and Benefits Act 1992 (c. 4);

"occupier", in relation to any periodical payment, means a person who was an occupier at the time of the payment, whether under a tenancy or licence (and "occupation" has a corresponding meaning);

"periodical payments" means periodical payments in respect of which housing benefit may be paid by virtue of regulation 10 of the Housing Benefit (General) Regulations 1987 (S.I. 1987/1971) or any corresponding provision replacing that regulation.

(11) For the purposes of this section an amount which—

(a) is not actually paid by an occupier but is used by him to discharge the whole or part of his liability in respect of a periodical payment (for example, by offsetting the amount against any such liability), and

(b) is not an amount of housing benefit,

is to be regarded as an amount paid by the occupier in respect of that periodical payment.

97 Further provisions about rent repayment orders

(1) This section applies in relation to orders made by residential property tribunals under section 96(5).

(2) Where, on an application by the local housing authority, the tribunal is satisfied—
   (a) that a person has been convicted of an offence under section 95(1) in relation to the house, and
   (b) that housing benefit was paid (whether or not to the appropriate person) in respect of periodical payments payable in connection with occupation of the whole or any part or parts of the house during any period during which it appears to the tribunal that such an offence was being committed in relation to the house,

the tribunal must make a rent repayment order requiring the appropriate person to pay to the authority an amount equal to the total amount of housing benefit paid as mentioned in paragraph (b).

This is subject to subsections (3), (4) and (8).

(3) If the total of the amounts received by the appropriate person in respect of periodical payments payable as mentioned in paragraph (b) of subsection (2) ("the rent total") is less than the total amount of housing benefit paid as mentioned in that paragraph, the amount required to be paid by virtue of a rent repayment order made in accordance with that subsection is limited to the rent total.

(4) A rent repayment order made in accordance with subsection (2) may not require the payment of any amount which the tribunal is satisfied that, by reason of any exceptional circumstances, it would be unreasonable for that person to be required to pay.

(5) In a case where subsection (2) does not apply, the amount required to be paid by virtue of a rent repayment order under section 96(5) is to be such amount as the tribunal considers reasonable in the circumstances.

This is subject to subsections (6) to (8).

(6) In such a case the tribunal must, in particular, take into account the following matters—
   (a) the total amount of relevant payments paid in connection with occupation of the house during any period during which it appears to the tribunal that an offence was being committed by the appropriate person in relation to the house under section 95(1);
   (b) the extent to which that total amount—
      (i) consisted of, or derived from, payments of housing benefit, and
      (ii) was actually received by the appropriate person;
   (c) whether the appropriate person has at any time been convicted of an offence under section 95(1) in relation to the house;
   (d) the conduct and financial circumstances of the appropriate person; and
   (e) where the application is made by an occupier, the conduct of the occupier.

(7) In subsection (6) "relevant payments" means—
   (a) in relation to an application by a local housing authority, payments of housing benefit or periodical payments payable by occupiers;
   (b) in relation to an application by an occupier, periodical payments payable by the occupier, less any amount of housing benefit payable in respect of occupation of the house, or (as the case may be) the part of it occupied by him, during the period in question.

(8) A rent repayment order may not require the payment of an amount which—

(a) (where the application is made by a local housing authority) is in respect of any time falling outside the period of 12 months mentioned in section 96(6)(a); or

(b) (where the application is made by an occupier) is in respect of any time falling outside the period of 12 months ending with the date of the occupier's application under section 96(5);

and the period to be taken into account under subsection (6)(a) above is restricted accordingly.

(9) Any amount payable to a local housing authority under a rent repayment order—

(a) does not, when recovered by the authority, constitute an amount of housing benefit recovered by them, and

(b) is, until recovered by them, a legal charge on the house which is a local land charge.

(10) For the purpose of enforcing that charge the authority have the same powers and remedies under the Law of Property Act 1925 (c. 20) and otherwise as if they were mortgagees by deed having powers of sale and lease, and of accepting surrenders of leases and of appointing a receiver.

(11) The power of appointing a receiver is exercisable at any time after the end of the period of one month beginning with the date on which the charge takes effect.

(12) If the authority subsequently grant a licence under Part 2 or this Part in respect of the house to the appropriate person or any person acting on his behalf, the conditions contained in the licence may include a condition requiring the licence holder—

(a) to pay to the authority any amount payable to them under the rent repayment order and not so far recovered by them; and

(b) to do so in such instalments as are specified in the licence.

(13) If the authority subsequently make a management order under Chapter 1 of Part 4 in respect of the house, the order may contain such provisions as the authority consider appropriate for the recovery of any amount payable to them under the rent repayment order and not so far recovered by them.

(14) Any amount payable to an occupier by virtue of a rent repayment order is recoverable by the occupier as a debt due to him from the appropriate person.

(15) The appropriate national authority may by regulations make such provision as it considers appropriate for supplementing the provisions of this section and section 96, and in particular—

(a) for securing that persons are not unfairly prejudiced by rent repayment orders (whether in cases where there have been over-payments of housing benefit or otherwise);

(b) for requiring or authorising amounts received by local housing authorities by virtue of rent repayment orders to be dealt with in such manner as is specified in the regulations.

(16) Section 96(10) and (11) apply for the purposes of this section as they apply for the purposes of section 96.

98 Other consequences of operating unlicensed houses: restriction on terminating tenancies

(1) No section 21 notice may be given in relation to a shorthold tenancy of the whole or part of an unlicensed house so long as it remains such a house.

(2) In this section—

a "section 21 notice" means a notice under section 21(1)(b) or (4)(a) of the Housing Act 1988 (c. 50) (recovery of possession on termination of shorthold tenancy);

a "shorthold tenancy" means an assured shorthold tenancy within the meaning of Chapter 2 of Part 1 of that Act;

"unlicensed house" has the same meaning as in section 96 of this Act.

Supplementary provisions

99 Meaning of "house" etc.

In this Part—

"dwelling" means a building or part of a building occupied or intended to be occupied as a separate dwelling;

"house" means a building or part of a building consisting of one or more dwellings;

and references to a house include (where the context permits) any yard, garden, outhouses and appurtenances belonging to, or usually enjoyed with, it (or any part of it).

100 Index of defined expressions: Part 3

The following table shows where expressions used in this Part are defined or otherwise explained.

Expression	*Provision of this Act*
Anti-social behaviour	Section 57(5)
Appropriate national authority	Section 261(1)
Category 1 hazard	Section 2(1)
Category 2 hazard	Section 2(1)
District of local housing authority	Section 261(6)
Dwelling	Section 99
House	Section 99
Licence and licence holder	Section 85(5)
Licence (to occupy premises)	Section 262(9)
Local housing authority	Section 261(2) to (5)
Occupier (and related expressions)	Section 262(6)

Expression	*Provision of this Act*
Part 3 house	Section 85(5), together with section 79(2)
Person having control	Section 263(1) and (2) (and see also section 89(7))
Person having estate or interest	Section 262(8)
Person managing	Section 263(3)
Person involved in management	Section 263(5)
Residential property tribunal	Section 229
Tenant	Section 262(1) to (5).

PART 4

ADDITIONAL CONTROL PROVISIONS IN RELATION TO RESIDENTIAL ACCOMMODATION

CHAPTER 1

INTERIM AND FINAL MANAGEMENT ORDERS

Introductory

101 Interim and final management orders: introductory

(1) This Chapter deals with the making by a local housing authority of—

(a) an interim management order (see section 102), or

(b) a final management order (see section 113),

in respect of an HMO or a Part 3 house.

(2) Section 103 deals with the making of an interim management order in respect of a house to which that section applies.

(3) An interim management order is an order (expiring not more than 12 months after it is made) which is made for the purpose of securing that the following steps are taken in relation to the house—

(a) any immediate steps which the authority consider necessary to protect the health, safety or welfare of persons occupying the house, or persons occupying or having an estate or interest in any premises in the vicinity, and

(b) any other steps which the authority think appropriate with a view to the proper management of the house pending the grant of a licence under Part 2 or 3 in respect of the house or the making of a final management order in respect of it (or, if appropriate, the revocation of the interim management order).

(4) A final management order is an order (expiring not more than 5 years after it is made) which is made for the purpose of securing the proper management of the house on a long-term basis in accordance with a management scheme contained in the order.

(5) In this Chapter any reference to "the house", in relation to an interim or final management order (other than an order under section 102(7)), is a reference to the HMO or Part 3 house to which the order relates.

(6) Subsection (5) has effect subject to sections 102(8) and 113(7) (exclusion of part occupied by resident landlord).

(7) In this Chapter "third party", in relation to a house, means any person who has an estate or interest in the house (other than an immediate landlord and any person who is a tenant under a lease granted under section 107(3)(c) or 116(3)(c)).

Interim management orders: making and operation of orders

102 Making of interim management orders

(1) A local housing authority—

- (a) are under a duty to make an interim management order in respect of a house in a case within subsection (2) or (3), and
- (b) have power to make an interim management order in respect of a house in a case within subsection (4) or (7).

(2) The authority must make an interim management order in respect of a house if—

- (a) it is an HMO or a Part 3 house which is required to be licensed under Part 2 or Part 3 (see section 61(1) or 85(1)) but is not so licensed, and
- (b) they consider either—
  - (i) that there is no reasonable prospect of its being so licensed in the near future, or
  - (ii) that the health and safety condition is satisfied (see section 104).

(3) The authority must make an interim management order in respect of a house if—

- (a) it is an HMO or a Part 3 house which is required to be licensed under Part 2 or Part 3 and is so licensed,
- (b) they have revoked the licence concerned but the revocation is not yet in force, and
- (c) they consider either—
  - (i) that, on the revocation coming into force, there will be no reasonable prospect of the house being so licensed in the near future, or
  - (ii) that, on the revocation coming into force, the health and safety condition will be satisfied (see section 104).

(4) The authority may make an interim management order in respect of a house if—

- (a) it is an HMO other than one that is required to be licensed under Part 2, and
- (b) on an application by the authority to a residential property tribunal, the tribunal by order authorises them to make such an order, either in the terms of a draft order submitted by them or in those terms as varied by the tribunal;

and the authority may make such an order despite any pending appeal against the order of the tribunal (but this is without prejudice to any order that may be made on the disposal of any such appeal).

(5) The tribunal may only authorise the authority to make an interim management order under subsection (4) if it considers that the health and safety condition is satisfied (see section 104).

(6) In determining whether to authorise the authority to make an interim management order in respect of an HMO under subsection (4), the tribunal must have regard to the extent to which any applicable code of practice approved under section 233 has been complied with in respect of the HMO in the past.

(7) The authority may make an interim management order in respect of a house if—

(a) it is a house to which section 103 (special interim management orders) applies, and

(b) on an application by the authority to a residential property tribunal, the tribunal by order authorises them to make such an order, either in the terms of a draft order submitted by them or in those terms as varied by the tribunal;

and the authority may make such an order despite any pending appeal against the order of the tribunal (but this is without prejudice to any order that may be made on the disposal of any such appeal).

Subsections (2) to (6) of section 103 apply in relation to the power of a residential property tribunal to authorise the making of an interim management order under this subsection.

(8) The authority may make an interim management order which is expressed not to apply to a part of the house that is occupied by a person who has an estate or interest in the whole of the house.

In relation to such an order, a reference in this Chapter to "the house" does not include the part so excluded (unless the context requires otherwise, such as where the reference is to the house as an HMO or a Part 3 house).

(9) Nothing in this section requires or authorises the making of an interim management order in respect of a house if—

(a) an interim management order has been previously made in respect of it, and

(b) the authority have not exercised any relevant function in respect of the house at any time after the making of the interim management order.

(10) In subsection (9) "relevant function" means the function of—

(a) granting a licence under Part 2 or 3,

(b) serving a temporary exemption notice under section 62 or section 86, or

(c) making a final management order under section 113.

103 Special interim management orders

(1) This section applies to a house if the whole of it is occupied either—

(a) under a single tenancy or licence that is not an exempt tenancy or licence under section 79(3) or (4), or

(b) under two or more tenancies or licences in respect of different dwellings contained in it, none of which is an exempt tenancy or licence under section 79(3) or (4).

(2) A residential property tribunal may only authorise the authority to make an interim management order in respect of such a house under section 102(7) if it considers that both of the following conditions are satisfied.

(3) The first condition is that the circumstances relating to the house fall within any category of circumstances prescribed for the purposes of this subsection by an order under subsection (5).

(4) The second condition is that the making of the order is necessary for the purpose of protecting the health, safety or welfare of persons occupying, visiting or otherwise engaging in lawful activities in the vicinity of the house.

(5) The appropriate national authority may by order—

(a) prescribe categories of circumstances for the purposes of subsection (3),

(b) provide for any of the provisions of this Act to apply in relation to houses to which this section applies, or interim or final management orders made in respect of them, with any modifications specified in the order.

(6) The categories prescribed by an order under subsection (5) are to reflect one or more of the following—

(a) the first or second set of general conditions mentioned in subsection (3) or (6) of section 80, or

(b) any additional set of conditions specified under subsection (7) of that section,

but (in each case) with such modifications as the appropriate national authority considers appropriate to adapt them to the circumstances of a single house.

(7) In this section "house" has the same meaning as in Part 3 (see section 99).

(8) In this Chapter—

(a) any reference to "the house", in relation to an interim management order under section 102(7), is a reference to the house to which the order relates, and

(b) any such reference includes (where the context permits) a reference to any yard, garden, outhouses and appurtenances belonging to, or usually enjoyed with, it (or any part of it).

104 The health and safety condition

(1) This section explains what "the health and safety condition" is for the purposes of section 102.

(2) The health and safety condition is that the making of an interim management order is necessary for the purpose of protecting the health, safety or welfare of persons occupying the house, or persons occupying or having an estate or interest in any premises in the vicinity.

(3) A threat to evict persons occupying a house in order to avoid the house being required to be licensed under Part 2 may constitute a threat to the welfare of those persons for the purposes of subsection (2).

This does not affect the generality of that subsection.

(4) The health and safety condition is not to be regarded as satisfied for the purposes of section 102(2)(b)(ii) or (3)(c)(ii) where both of the conditions in subsections (5) and (6) are satisfied.

(5) The first condition is that the local housing authority either—

(a) (in a case within section 102(2)(b)(ii)) are required by section 5 (general duty to take enforcement action in respect of category 1 hazards) to take a course of action within subsection (2) of that section in relation to the house, or

(b) (in a case within section 102(3)(c)(ii)) consider that on the revocation coming into force they will be required to take such a course of action.

(6) The second condition is that the local housing authority consider that the health, safety or welfare of the persons in question would be adequately protected by taking that course of action.

105 Operation of interim management orders

(1) This section deals with the time when an interim management order comes into force or ceases to have effect.

(2) The order comes into force when it is made, unless it is made under section 102(3).

(3) If the order is made under section 102(3), it comes into force when the revocation of the licence comes into force.

(4) The order ceases to have effect at the end of the period of 12 months beginning with the date on which it is made, unless it ceases to have effect at some other time as mentioned below.

(5) If the order provides that it is to cease to have effect on a date falling before the end of that period, it accordingly ceases to have effect on that date.

(6) If the order is made under section 102(3)—

(a) it must include a provision for determining the date on which it will cease to have effect, and

(b) it accordingly ceases to have effect on the date so determined.

(7) That date must be no later than 12 months after the date on which the order comes into force.

(8) Subsections (9) and (10) apply where—

(a) a final management order ("the FMO") has been made under section 113 so as to replace the order ("the IMO"), but

(b) the FMO has not come into force because of an appeal to a residential property tribunal under paragraph 24 of Schedule 6 against the making of the FMO.

(9) If—

(a) the house would (but for the IMO being in force) be required to be licensed under Part 2 or 3 of this Act (see section 61(1) or 85(1)), and

(b) the date on which—

(i) the FMO,

(ii) any licence under Part 2 or 3, or

(iii) another interim management order,

comes into force in relation to the house (or part of it) following the disposal of the appeal is later than the date on which the IMO would cease to have effect apart from this subsection,

the IMO continues in force until that later date.

(10) If, on the application of the authority, the tribunal makes an order providing for the IMO to continue in force, pending the disposal of the appeal, until a date later than that on which the IMO would cease to have effect apart from this subsection, the IMO accordingly continues in force until that later date.

(11) This section has effect subject to sections 111 and 112 (variation or revocation of orders by authority) and to the power of revocation exercisable by a residential property tribunal on an appeal made under paragraph 24 or 28 of Schedule 6.

106 Local housing authority's duties once interim management order in force

(1) A local housing authority who have made an interim management order in respect of a house must comply with the following provisions as soon as practicable after the order has come into force.

(2) The authority must first take any immediate steps which they consider to be necessary for the purpose of protecting the health, safety or welfare of persons occupying the house, or persons occupying or having an estate or interest in any premises in the vicinity.

(3) The authority must also take such other steps as they consider appropriate with a view to the proper management of the house pending—

- (a) the grant of a licence or the making of a final management order in respect of the house as mentioned in subsection (4) or (5), or
- (b) the revocation of the interim management order as mentioned in subsection (5).

(4) If the house would (but for the order being in force) be required to be licensed under Part 2 or 3 of this Act (see section 61(1) or 85(1)), the authority must, after considering all the circumstances of the case, decide to take one of the following courses of action—

- (a) to grant a licence under that Part in respect of the house, or
- (b) to make a final management order in respect of it under section 113(1).

(5) If subsection (4) does not apply to the house, the authority must, after considering all the circumstances of the case, decide to take one of the following courses of action—

- (a) to make a final management order in respect of the house under section 113(3), or
- (b) to revoke the order under section 112 without taking any further action.

(6) In the following provisions, namely—

- (a) subsections (3) and (4), and
- (b) section 101(3)(b),

the reference to the grant of a licence under Part 2 or 3 in respect of the house includes a reference to serving a temporary exemption notice under section 62 or section 86 in respect of it (whether or not a notification is given under subsection (1) of that section).

(7) For the avoidance of doubt, the authority's duty under subsection (3) includes taking such steps as are necessary to ensure that, while the order is in force, reasonable provision is made for insurance of the house against destruction or damage by fire or other causes.

107 General effect of interim management orders

(1) This section applies while an interim management order is in force in relation to a house.

(2) The rights and powers conferred by subsection (3) are exercisable by the authority in performing their duties under section 106(1) to (3) in respect of the house.

(3) The authority—

(a) have the right to possession of the house (subject to the rights of existing occupiers preserved by section 124(3));

(b) have the right to do (and authorise a manager or other person to do) in relation to the house anything which a person having an estate or interest in the house would (but for the order) be entitled to do;

(c) may create one or more of the following—

(i) an interest in the house which, as far as possible, has all the incidents of a leasehold, or

(ii) a right in the nature of a licence to occupy part of the house.

(4) But the authority may not under subsection (3)(c) create any interest or right in the nature of a lease or licence unless consent in writing has been given by the person who (but for the order) would have power to create the lease or licence in question.

(5) The authority—

(a) do not under this section acquire any estate or interest in the house, and

(b) accordingly are not entitled by virtue of this section to sell, lease, charge or make any other disposition of any such estate or interest;

but, where the immediate landlord of the house or part of it (within the meaning of section 109) is a lessee under a lease of the house or part, the authority is to be treated (subject to paragraph (a)) as if they were the lessee instead.

(6) Any enactment or rule of law relating to landlords and tenants or leases applies in relation to—

(a) a lease in relation to which the authority are to be treated as the lessee under subsection (5), or

(b) a lease to which the authority become a party under section 124(4),

as if the authority were the legal owner of the premises (but this is subject to section 124(7) to (9)).

(7) None of the following, namely—

(a) the authority, or

(b) any person authorised under subsection (3)(b),

is liable to any person having an estate or interest in the house for anything done or omitted to be done in the performance (or intended performance) of the authority's duties under section 106(1) to (3) unless the act or omission is due to the negligence of the authority or any such person.

(8) References in any enactment to housing accommodation provided or managed by a local housing authority do not include a house in relation to which an interim management order is in force.

(9) An interim management order which has come into force is a local land charge.

(10) The authority may apply to the Chief Land Registrar for the entry of an appropriate restriction in the register of title in respect of such an order.

(11) In this section "enactment" includes an enactment comprised in subordinate legislation (within the meaning of the Interpretation Act 1978 (c. 30)).

108 General effect of interim management orders: leases and licences granted by authority

(1) This section applies in relation to any interest or right created by the authority under section 107(3)(c).

(2) For the purposes of any enactment or rule of law—

(a) any interest created by the authority under section 107(3)(c)(i) is to be treated as if it were a legal lease, and

(b) any right created by the authority under section 107(3)(c)(ii) is to be treated as if it were a licence to occupy granted by the legal owner of the premises,

despite the fact that the authority have no legal estate in the premises (see section 107(5)(a)).

(3) Any enactment or rule of law relating to landlords and tenants or leases accordingly applies in relation to any interest created by the authority under section 107(3)(c)(i) as if the authority were the legal owner of the premises.

(4) References to leases and licences—

(a) in this Chapter, and

(b) in any other enactment,

accordingly include (where the context permits) interests and rights created by the authority under section 107(3)(c).

(5) The preceding provisions of this section have effect subject to—

(a) section 124(7) to (9), and

(b) any provision to the contrary contained in an order made by the appropriate national authority.

(6) In section 107(5)(b) the reference to leasing does not include the creation of interests under section 107(3)(c)(i).

(7) In this section—

"enactment" has the meaning given by section 107(11);

"legal lease" means a term of years absolute (within section 1(1)(b) of the Law of Property Act 1925 (c. 20)).

109 General effect of interim management orders: immediate landlords, mortgagees etc.

(1) This section applies in relation to—

(a) immediate landlords, and

(b) other persons with an estate or interest in the house,

while an interim management order is in force in relation to a house.

(2) A person who is an immediate landlord of the house or a part of it—

(a) is not entitled to receive—
   (i) any rents or other payments from persons occupying the house or part which are payable to the local housing authority by virtue of section 124(4), or
   (ii) any rents or other payments from persons occupying the house or part which are payable to the authority by virtue of any leases or licences granted by them under section 107(3)(c);

(b) may not exercise any rights or powers with respect to the management of the house or part; and

(c) may not create any of the following—
   (i) any leasehold interest in the house or part (other than a lease of a reversion), or
   (ii) any licence or other right to occupy it.

(3) However (subject to subsection (2)(c)) nothing in section 107 or this section affects the ability of a person having an estate or interest in the house to make any disposition of that estate or interest.

(4) Nothing in section 107 or this section affects—
(a) the validity of any mortgage relating to the house or any rights or remedies available to the mortgagee under such a mortgage, or
(b) the validity of any lease of the house or part of it under which the immediate landlord is a lessee, or any superior lease, or (subject to section 107(5)) any rights or remedies available to the lessor under such a lease,

except to the extent that any of those rights or remedies would prevent the local housing authority from exercising their power under section 107(3)(c).

(5) In proceedings for the enforcement of any such rights or remedies the court may make such order as it thinks fit as regards the operation of the interim management order (including an order quashing it).

(6) For the purposes of this Chapter, as it applies in relation to an interim management order, a person is an "immediate landlord" of the house or a part of it if—
(a) he is an owner or lessee of the house or part, and
(b) (but for the order) he would be entitled to receive the rents or other payments from persons occupying the house or part which are payable to the local housing authority by virtue of section 124(4).

110 Financial arrangements while order is in force

(1) This section applies to relevant expenditure of a local housing authority who have made an interim management order.

(2) "Relevant expenditure" means expenditure reasonably incurred by the authority in connection with performing their duties under section 106(1) to (3) in respect of the house (including any premiums paid for insurance of the premises).

(3) Rent or other payments which the authority have collected or recovered, by virtue of this Chapter, from persons occupying the house may be used by the authority to meet—
(a) relevant expenditure, and
(b) any amounts of compensation payable to a third party by virtue of a decision of the authority under section 128.

(4) The authority must pay to such relevant landlord, or to such relevant landlords in such proportions, as they consider appropriate—

(a) any amount of rent or other payments collected or recovered as mentioned in subsection (3) that remains after deductions to meet relevant expenditure and any amounts of compensation payable as mentioned in that subsection, and

(b) (where appropriate) interest on that amount at a reasonable rate fixed by the authority,

and such payments are to be made at such intervals as the authority consider appropriate.

(5) The interim management order may provide for—

(a) the rate of interest which is to apply for the purposes of paragraph (b) of subsection (4); and

(b) the intervals at which payments are to be made under that subsection.

Paragraph 24(3) of Schedule 6 enables an appeal to be brought where the order does not provide for both of those matters.

(6) The authority must—

(a) keep full accounts of their income and expenditure in respect of the house; and

(b) afford to each relevant landlord, and to any other person who has an estate or interest in the house, all reasonable facilities for inspecting, taking copies of and verifying those accounts.

(7) A relevant landlord may apply to a residential property tribunal for an order—

(a) declaring that an amount shown in the accounts as expenditure of the authority does not constitute expenditure reasonably incurred by the authority as mentioned in subsection (2);

(b) requiring the authority to make such financial adjustments (in the accounts and otherwise) as are necessary to reflect the tribunal's declaration.

(8) In this section—

"expenditure" includes administrative costs;

"relevant landlord" means any person who is an immediate landlord of the house or part of it;

"rent or other payments" means rents or other payments payable under leases or licences or in respect of furniture within section 126(1).

Interim management orders: variation and revocation

111 Variation of interim management orders

(1) The local housing authority may vary an interim management order if they consider it appropriate to do so.

(2) A variation does not come into force until such time, if any, as is the operative time for the purposes of this subsection under paragraph 31 of Schedule 6 (time when period for appealing expires without an appeal being made or when decision to vary is confirmed on appeal).

(3) The power to vary an order under this section is exercisable by the authority either—

(a) on an application made by a relevant person, or

(b) on the authority's own initiative.

(4) In this section "relevant person" means—

(a) any person who has an estate or interest in the house or part of it (but is not a tenant under a lease with an unexpired term of 3 years or less), or

(b) any other person who (but for the order) would be a person managing or having control of the house or part of it.

112 Revocation of interim management orders

(1) The local housing authority may revoke an interim management order in the following cases—

(a) if the order was made under section 102(2) or (3) and the house has ceased to be an HMO to which Part 2 applies or a Part 3 house (as the case may be);

(b) if the order was made under section 102(2) or (3) and a licence granted by them in respect of the house is due to come into force under Part 2 or Part 3 on the revocation of the order;

(c) if a final management order has been made by them in respect of the house so as to replace the order;

(d) if in any other circumstances the authority consider it appropriate to revoke the order.

(2) A revocation does not come into force until such time, if any, as is the operative time for the purposes of this subsection under paragraph 31 of Schedule 6 (time when period for appealing expires without an appeal being made or when decision to revoke is confirmed on appeal).

(3) The power to revoke an order under this section is exercisable by the authority either—

(a) on an application made by a relevant person, or

(b) on the authority's own initiative.

(4) In this section "relevant person" means—

(a) any person who has an estate or interest in the house or part of it (but is not a tenant under a lease with an unexpired term of 3 years or less), or

(b) any other person who (but for the order) would be a person managing or having control of the house or part of it.

Final management orders: making and operation of orders

113 Making of final management orders

(1) A local housing authority who have made an interim management order in respect of a house under section 102 ("the IMO")—

(a) have a duty to make a final management order in respect of the house in a case within subsection (2), and

(b) have power to make such an order in a case within subsection (3).

(2) The authority must make a final management order so as to replace the IMO as from its expiry date if—

(a) on that date the house would be required to be licensed under Part 2 or 3 of this Act (see section 61(1) or 85(1)), and

(b) the authority consider that they are unable to grant a licence under Part 2 or 3 in respect of the house that would replace the IMO as from that date.

(3) The authority may make a final management order so as to replace the IMO as from its expiry date if—

(a) on that date the house will not be one that would be required to be licensed as mentioned in subsection (2)(a), and

(b) the authority consider that making the final management order is necessary for the purpose of protecting, on a long-term basis, the health, safety or welfare of persons occupying the house, or persons occupying or having an estate or interest in any premises in the vicinity.

(4) A local housing authority who have made a final management order in respect of a house under this section ("the existing order")—

(a) have a duty to make a final management order in respect of the house in a case within subsection (5), and

(b) have power to make such an order in a case within subsection (6).

(5) The authority must make a new final management order so as to replace the existing order as from its expiry date if—

(a) on that date the condition in subsection (2)(a) will be satisfied in relation to the house, and

(b) the authority consider that they are unable to grant a licence under Part 2 or 3 in respect of the house that would replace the existing order as from that date.

(6) The authority may make a new final management order so as to replace the existing order as from its expiry date if—

(a) on that date the condition in subsection (3)(a) will be satisfied in relation to the house, and

(b) the authority consider that making the new order is necessary for the purpose of protecting, on a long-term basis, the health, safety or welfare of persons within subsection (3)(b).

(7) The authority may make a final management order which is expressed not to apply to a part of the house that is occupied by a person who has an estate or interest in the whole of the house.

In relation to such an order, a reference in this Chapter to "the house" does not include the part so excluded (unless the context requires otherwise, such as where the reference is to the house as an HMO or a Part 3 house).

(8) In this section "expiry date", in relation to an interim or final management order, means—

(a) where the order is revoked, the date as from which it is revoked, and

(b) otherwise the date on which the order ceases to have effect under section 105 or 114;

and nothing in this section applies in relation to an interim or final management order which has been revoked on an appeal under Part 3 of Schedule 6.

114 Operation of final management orders

(1) This section deals with the time when a final management order comes into force or ceases to have effect.

(2) The order does not come into force until such time (if any) as is the operative time for the purposes of this subsection under paragraph 27 of Schedule 6 (time when period for appealing expires without an appeal being made or when order is confirmed on appeal).

(3) The order ceases to have effect at the end of the period of 5 years beginning with the date on which it comes into force, unless it ceases to have effect at some other time as mentioned below.

(4) If the order provides that it is to cease to have effect on a date falling before the end of that period, it accordingly ceases to have effect on that date.

(5) Subsections (6) and (7) apply where—

(a) a new final management order ("the new order") has been made so as to replace the order ("the existing order"), but

(b) the new order has not come into force because of an appeal to a residential property tribunal under paragraph 24 of Schedule 6 against the making of that order.

(6) If—

(a) the house would (but for the existing order being in force) be required to be licensed under Part 2 or 3 of this Act (see section 61(1) or 85(1)), and

(b) the date on which—

(i) the new order, or

(ii) any licence under Part 2 or 3, or

(iii) a temporary exemption notice under section 62 or 86,

comes into force in relation to the house (or part of it) following the disposal of the appeal is later than the date on which the existing order would cease to have effect apart from this subsection,

the existing order continues in force until that later date.

(7) If, on the application of the authority, the tribunal makes an order providing for the existing order to continue in force, pending the disposal of the appeal, until a date later than that on which it would cease to have effect apart from this subsection, the existing order accordingly continues in force until that later date.

(8) This section has effect subject to sections 121 and 122 (variation or revocation of orders) and to the power of revocation exercisable by a residential property tribunal on an appeal made under paragraph 24 or 28 of Schedule 6.

115 Local housing authority's duties once final management order in force

(1) A local housing authority who have made a final management order in respect of a house must comply with the following provisions once the order has come into force.

(2) The local housing authority must take such steps as they consider appropriate with a view to the proper management of the house in accordance with the management scheme contained in the order (see section 119).

(3) The local housing authority must from time to time review—

(a) the operation of the order and in particular the management scheme contained in it, and

(b) whether keeping the order in force in relation to the house (with or without making any variations under section 121) is the best alternative available to them.

(4) If on a review the authority consider that any variations should be made under section 121, they must proceed to make those variations.

(5) If on a review the authority consider that either—

(a) granting a licence under Part 2 or 3 in respect of the house, or

(b) revoking the order under section 122 and taking no further action,

is the best alternative available to them, the authority must grant such a licence or revoke the order (as the case may be).

(6) For the avoidance of doubt, the authority's duty under subsection (2) includes taking such steps as are necessary to ensure that, while the order is in force, reasonable provision is made for insurance of the house against destruction or damage by fire or other causes.

116 General effect of final management orders

(1) This section applies while a final management order is in force in relation to a house.

(2) The rights and powers conferred by subsection (3) are exercisable by the authority in performing their duty under section 115(2) in respect of the house.

(3) The authority—

(a) have the right to possession of the house (subject to the rights of existing and other occupiers preserved by section 124(3) and (6));

(b) have the right to do (and authorise a manager or other person to do) in relation to the house anything which a person having an estate or interest in the house would (but for the order) be entitled to do;

(c) may create one or more of the following—

(i) an interest in the house which, as far as possible, has all the incidents of a leasehold, or

(ii) a right in the nature of a licence to occupy part of the house.

(4) The powers of the authority under subsection (3)(c) are restricted as follows—

(a) they may not create any interest or right in the nature of a lease or licence—

(i) which is for a fixed term expiring after the date on which the order is due to expire, or

(ii) (subject to paragraph (b)) which is terminable by notice to quit, or an equivalent notice, of more than 4 weeks,

unless consent in writing has been given by the person who would (but for the order) have power to create the lease or licence in question;

(b) they may create an interest in the nature of an assured shorthold tenancy without any such consent so long as it is created before the beginning of the period of 6 months that ends with the date on which the order is due to expire.

(5) The authority—

(a) do not under this section acquire any estate or interest in the house, and

(b) accordingly are not entitled by virtue of this section to sell, lease, charge or make any other disposition of any such estate or interest;

but, where the immediate landlord of the house or part of it (within the meaning of section 118) is a lessee under a lease of the house or part, the authority is to be treated (subject to paragraph (a)) as if they were the lessee instead.

(6) Any enactment or rule of law relating to landlords and tenants or leases applies in relation to—

(a) a lease in relation to which the authority are to be treated as the lessee under subsection (5), or

(b) a lease to which the authority become a party under section 124(4),

as if the authority were the legal owner of the premises (but this is subject to section 124(7) to (9)).

(7) None of the following, namely—

(a) the authority, or

(b) any person authorised under subsection (3)(b),

is liable to any person having an estate or interest in the house for anything done or omitted to be done in the performance (or intended performance) of the authority's duty under section 115(2) unless the act or omission is due to the negligence of the authority or any such person.

(8) References in any enactment to housing accommodation provided or managed by a local housing authority do not include a house in relation to which a final management order is in force.

(9) A final management order which has come into force is a local land charge.

(10) The authority may apply to the Chief Land Registrar for the entry of an appropriate restriction in the register in respect of such an order.

(11) In this section "enactment" includes an enactment comprised in subordinate legislation (within the meaning of the Interpretation Act 1978 (c. 30)).

117 General effect of final management orders: leases and licences granted by authority

(1) This section applies in relation to any interest or right created by the authority under section 116(3)(c).

(2) For the purposes of any enactment or rule of law—

(a) any interest created by the authority under section 116(3)(c)(i) is to be treated as if it were a legal lease, and

(b) any right created by the authority under section 116(3)(c)(ii) is to be treated as if it were a licence to occupy granted by the legal owner of the premises,

despite the fact that the authority have no legal estate in the premises (see section 116(5)(a)).

(3) Any enactment or rule of law relating to landlords and tenants or leases accordingly applies in relation to any interest created by the authority under section 116(3)(c)(i) as if the authority were the legal owner of the premises.

(4) References to leases and licences—

(a) in this Chapter, and

(b) in any other enactment,

accordingly include (where the context permits) interests and rights created by the authority under section 116(3)(c).

(5) The preceding provisions of this section have effect subject to—

(a) section 124(7) to (9), and

(b) any provision to the contrary contained in an order made by the appropriate national authority.

(6) In section 116(5)(b) the reference to leasing does not include the creation of interests under section 116(3)(c)(i).

(7) In this section—

"enactment" has the meaning given by section 116(11);

"legal lease" means a term of years absolute (within section 1(1)(b) of the Law of Property Act 1925 (c. 20)).

118 General effect of final management orders: immediate landlords, mortgagees etc.

(1) This section applies in relation to—

(a) immediate landlords, and

(b) other persons with an estate or interest in the house,

while a final management order is in force in relation to a house.

(2) A person who is an immediate landlord of the house or a part of it—

(a) is not entitled to receive—

(i) any rents or other payments from persons occupying the house or part which are payable to the local housing authority by virtue of section 124(4), or

(ii) any rents or other payments from persons occupying the house or part which are payable to the authority by virtue of any leases or licences granted by them under section 107(3)(c) or 116(3)(c);

(b) may not exercise any rights or powers with respect to the management of the house or part; and

(c) may not create any of the following—

(i) any leasehold interest in the house or part (other than a lease of a reversion), or

(ii) any licence or other right to occupy it.

(3) However (subject to subsection (2)(c)) nothing in section 116 or this section affects the ability of a person having an estate or interest in the house to make any disposition of that estate or interest.

(4) Nothing in section 116 or this section affects—

(a) the validity of any mortgage relating to the house or any rights or remedies available to the mortgagee under such a mortgage, or

(b) the validity of any lease of the house or part of it under which the immediate landlord is a lessee, or any superior lease, or (subject to section 116(5)) any rights or remedies available to the lessor under such a lease,

except to the extent that any of those rights or remedies would prevent the local housing authority from exercising their power under section 116(3)(c).

(5) In proceedings for the enforcement of any such rights or remedies the court may make such order as it thinks fit as regards the operation of the final management order (including an order quashing it).

(6) For the purposes of this Chapter, as it applies in relation to a final management order, a person is an "immediate landlord" of the house or a part of it if—

(a) he is an owner or lessee of the house or part, and

(b) (but for the order) he would be entitled to receive the rents or other payments from persons occupying the house or part which are payable to the authority by virtue of section 124(4).

119 Management schemes and accounts

(1) A final management order must contain a management scheme.

(2) A "management scheme" is a scheme setting out how the local housing authority are to carry out their duty under section 115(2) as respects the management of the house.

(3) A management scheme is to be divided into two parts.

(4) Part 1 of the scheme is to contain a plan giving details of the way in which the authority propose to manage the house, which must (in particular) include—

(a) details of any works that the authority intend to carry out in connection with the house;

(b) an estimate of the capital and other expenditure to be incurred by the authority in respect of the house while the order is in force;

(c) the amount of rent or other payments that the authority will seek to obtain having regard to the condition or expected condition of the house at any time while the order is in force;

(d) the amount of any compensation that is payable to a third party by virtue of a decision of the authority under section 128 in respect of any interference in consequence of the final management order with the rights of that person;

(e) provision as to the payment of any such compensation;

(f) provision as to the payment by the authority to a relevant landlord, from time to time, of amounts of rent or other payments that remain after the deduction of—

(i) relevant expenditure, and

(ii) any amounts of compensation payable as mentioned in paragraph (d);

(g) provision as to the manner in which the authority are to pay to a relevant landlord, on the termination of the final management order, any amounts of rent or other payments that remain after the deduction of—

(i) relevant expenditure, and

(ii) any amounts of compensation payable as mentioned in paragraph (d);

(h) provision as to the manner in which the authority are to pay, on the termination of the final management order, any outstanding balance of compensation payable to a third party.

(5) Part 1 of the scheme may also state—

(a) the authority's intentions as regards the use of rent or other payments to meet relevant expenditure;

(b) the authority's intentions as regards the payment to a relevant landlord (where appropriate) of interest on amounts within subsection (4)(f) and (g);

(c) that section 129(2) or (4) is not to apply in relation to an interim or (as the case may be) final management order that immediately preceded the final management order, and that instead the authority intend to use any balance or amount such as is mentioned in that subsection to meet—

(i) relevant expenditure incurred during the currency of the final management order, and

(ii) any compensation that may become payable to a third party;

(d) that section 129(3) or (5) is not to apply in relation to an interim or (as the case may be) final management order that immediately preceded the final management order ("the order"), and that instead the authority intend to use rent or other payments collected during the currency of the order to reimburse the authority in respect of any deficit or amount such as is mentioned in that subsection;

(e) the authority's intentions as regards the recovery from a relevant landlord, with or without interest, of any amount of relevant expenditure that cannot be reimbursed out of the total amount of rent or other payments.

(6) Part 2 of the scheme is to describe in general terms how the authority intend to address the matters which caused them to make the final management order and may, for example, include—

(a) descriptions of any steps that the authority intend to take to require persons occupying the house to comply with their obligations under any lease or licence or under the general law;

(b) descriptions of any repairs that are needed to the property and an explanation as to why those repairs are necessary.

(7) The authority must—

(a) keep full accounts of their income and expenditure in respect of the house; and

(b) afford to each relevant landlord, and to any other person who has an estate or interest in the house, all reasonable facilities for inspecting, taking copies of and verifying those accounts.

(8) In this section—

"relevant expenditure" means expenditure reasonably incurred by the authority in connection with performing their duties under section 115(2) in respect of the house (including any reasonable administrative costs and any premiums paid for insurance of the premises);

"relevant landlord" means any person who is an immediate landlord of the house or part of it;

"rent or other payments" means rent or other payments—

(a) which are payable under leases or licences or in respect of furniture within section 126(1), and

(b) which the authority have collected or recovered by virtue of this Chapter.

(9) In the provisions of this Chapter relating to varying, revoking or appealing against decisions relating to a final management order, any reference to such an order includes (where the context permits) a reference to the management scheme contained in it.

120 Enforcement of management scheme by relevant landlord

(1) An affected person may apply to a residential property tribunal for an order requiring the local housing authority to manage the whole or part of a house in accordance with the management scheme contained in a final management order made in respect of the house.

(2) On such an application the tribunal may, if it considers it appropriate to do so, make an order—

(a) requiring the local housing authority to manage the whole or part of the house in accordance with the management scheme, or

(b) revoking the final management order as from a date specified in the tribunal's order.

(3) An order under subsection (2) may—

(a) specify the steps which the authority are to take to manage the whole or part of the house in accordance with the management scheme,

(b) include provision varying the final management order,

(c) require the payment of money to an affected person by way of damages.

(4) In this section "affected person" means—

(a) a relevant landlord (within the meaning of section 119), and

(b) any third party to whom compensation is payable by virtue of a decision of the authority under section 128.

Final management orders: variation and revocation

121 Variation of final management orders

(1) The local housing authority may vary a final management order if they consider it appropriate to do so.

(2) A variation does not come into force until such time, if any, as is the operative time for the purposes of this subsection under paragraph 31 of Schedule 6 (time when period for appealing expires without an appeal being made or when decision to vary is confirmed on appeal).

(3) The power to vary an order under this section is exercisable by the authority either—

(a) on an application made by a relevant person, or

(b) on the authority's own initiative.

(4) In this section "relevant person" means—

(a) any person who has an estate or interest in the house or part of it (but is not a tenant under a lease with an unexpired term of 3 years or less), or

(b) any other person who (but for the order) would be a person managing or having control of the house or part of it.

122 Revocation of final management orders

(1) The local housing authority may revoke a final management order in the following cases—

(a) if the order was made under section 113(2) or (5) and the house has ceased to be an HMO to which Part 2 applies or a Part 3 house (as the case may be);

(b) if the order was made under section 113(2) or (5) and a licence granted by them in respect of the house is due to come into force under Part 2 or Part 3 as from the revocation of the order;

(c) if a further final management order has been made by them in respect of the house so as to replace the order;

(d) if in any other circumstances the authority consider it appropriate to revoke the order.

(2) A revocation does not come into force until such time, if any, as is the operative time for the purposes of this subsection under paragraph 31 of Schedule 6 (time when period for appealing expires without an appeal being made or when decision to vary is confirmed on appeal).

(3) The power to revoke an order under this section is exercisable by the authority either—

(a) on an application made by a relevant person, or

(b) on the authority's own initiative.

(4) In this section "relevant person" means—

(a) any person who has an estate or interest in the house or part of it (but is not a tenant under a lease with an unexpired term of 3 years or less), or

(b) any other person who (but for the order) would be a person managing or having control of the house or part of it.

Interim and final management orders: procedure and appeals

123 Procedural requirements and appeals

Schedule 6 (which deals with procedural requirements relating to the making, variation or revocation of interim and final management orders and with appeals against decisions relating to such orders) has effect.

Interim and final management orders: other general provisions

124 Effect of management orders: occupiers

(1) This section applies to existing and new occupiers of a house in relation to which an interim or final management order is in force.

(2) In this section—

"existing occupier" means a person who, at the time when the order comes into force, either—

(a) (in the case of an HMO or a Part 3 house) is occupying part of the house and does not have an estate or interest in the whole of the house, or

(b) (in the case of a Part 3 house) is occupying the whole of the house,

but is not a new occupier within subsection (6);

"new occupier" means a person who, at a time when the order is in force, is occupying the whole or part of the house under a lease or licence granted under section 107(3)(c) or 116(3)(c).

(3) Sections 107 and 116 do not affect the rights or liabilities of an existing occupier under a lease or licence (whether in writing or not) under which he is occupying the whole or part of the house at the commencement date.

(4) Where the lessor or licensor under such a lease or licence—

(a) has an estate or interest in the house, and

(b) is not an existing occupier,

the lease or licence has effect while the order is in force as if the local housing authority were substituted in it for the lessor or licensor.

(5) Such a lease continues to have effect, as far as possible, as a lease despite the fact that the rights of the local housing authority, as substituted for the lessor, do not amount to an estate in law in the premises.

(6) Section 116 does not affect the rights or liabilities of a new occupier who, in the case of a final management order, is occupying the whole or part of the house at the time when the order comes into force.

(7) The provisions which exclude local authority lettings from the Rent Acts, namely—

(a) sections 14 to 16 of the Rent Act 1977 (c. 42), and

(b) those sections as applied by Schedule 2 to the Rent (Agriculture) Act 1976 (c. 80) and section 5(2) to (4) of that Act,

do not apply to a lease or agreement under which an existing or new occupier is occupying the whole or part of the house.

(8) Section 1(2) of, and paragraph 12 of Part 1 of Schedule 1 to, the Housing Act 1988 (c. 50) (which exclude local authority lettings from Part 1 of that Act) do not apply to a lease or agreement under which an existing or new occupier is occupying the whole or part of the house.

(9) Nothing in this Chapter has the result that the authority are to be treated as the legal owner of any premises for the purposes of—

(a) section 80 of the Housing Act 1985 (c. 68) (the landlord condition for secure tenancies); or

(b) section 124 of the Housing Act 1996 (c. 52) (introductory tenancies).

(10) If, immediately before the coming into force of an interim or final management order, an existing occupier was occupying the whole or part of the house under—

(a) a protected or statutory tenancy within the meaning of the Rent Act 1977 (c. 42),

(b) a protected or statutory tenancy within the meaning of the Rent (Agriculture) Act 1976 (c. 80), or

(c) an assured tenancy or assured agricultural occupancy within the meaning of Part 1 of the Housing Act 1988 (c. 50),

nothing in this Chapter prevents the continuance of that tenancy or occupancy or affects the continued operation of any of those Acts in relation to the tenancy or occupancy after the coming into force of the order.

(11) In this section "the commencement date" means the date on which the order came into force (or, if that order was preceded by one or more orders under this Chapter, the date when the first order came into force).

125 Effect of management orders: agreements and legal proceedings

(1) An agreement or instrument within subsection (2) has effect, while an interim or final management order is in force, as if any rights or liabilities of the immediate landlord under the agreement or instrument were instead rights or liabilities of the local housing authority.

(2) An agreement or instrument is within this subsection if—

(a) it is effective on the commencement date,

(b) one of the parties to it is a person who is the immediate landlord of the house or a part of the house ("the relevant premises"),

(c) it relates to the house, whether in connection with—

(i) any management activities with respect to the relevant premises, or

(ii) the provision of any services or facilities for persons occupying those premises,

or otherwise,

(d) it is specified for the purposes of this subsection in the order or falls within a description of agreements or instruments so specified, and

(e) the authority serve a notice in writing on all the parties to it stating that subsection (1) is to apply to it.

(3) An agreement or instrument is not within subsection (2) if—

(a) it is a lease within section 107(5) or 116(5), or

(b) it relates to any disposition by the immediate landlord which is not precluded by section 109(2) or 118(2), or

(c) it is within section 124(4).

(4) Proceedings in respect of any cause of action within subsection (5) may, while an interim or final management order is in force, be instituted or continued by or against the local housing authority instead of by or against the immediate landlord.

(5) A cause of action is within this subsection if—

(a) it is a cause of action (of any nature) which accrued to or against the immediate landlord of the house or a part of the house before the commencement date,

(b) it relates to the house as mentioned in subsection (2)(c),

(c) it is specified for the purposes of this subsection in the order or falls within a description of causes of action so specified, and

(d) the authority serve a notice in writing on all interested parties stating that subsection (4) is to apply to it.

(6) If, by virtue of this section, the authority become subject to any liability to pay damages in respect of anything done (or omitted to be done) before the commencement date by or on behalf of the immediate landlord of the house or a part of it, the immediate landlord is liable to reimburse to the authority an amount equal to the amount of the damages paid by them.

(7) In this section—

"agreement" includes arrangement;

"the commencement date" means the date on which the order comes into force (or, if that order was preceded by one or more orders under this Chapter, the date when the first order came into force);

"management activities" includes repair, maintenance, improvement and insurance.

126 Effect of management orders: furniture

(1) Subsection (2) applies where, on the date on which an interim or final management order comes into force, there is furniture in the house which a person occupying the house has the right to use in consideration of periodical payments to a person who is an immediate landlord of the house or a part of it (whether the payments are included in the rent payable by the occupier or not).

(2) The right to possession of the furniture against all persons other than the occupier vests in the local housing authority on that date and remains vested in the authority while the order is in force.

(3) The local housing authority may renounce the right to possession of the furniture conferred by subsection (2) if—

(a) an application in writing has been made to them for the purpose by the person owning the furniture, and

(b) they renounce the right by notice in writing served on that person not less than two weeks before the notice takes effect.

(4) If the authority's right to possession of furniture conferred by subsection (2) is a right exercisable against more than one person interested in the furniture, any of those persons may apply to a residential property tribunal for an adjustment of their respective rights and liabilities as regards the furniture.

(5) On such an application the tribunal may make an order for such an adjustment of rights and liabilities, either unconditionally or subject to such terms and conditions, as it considers appropriate.

(6) The terms and conditions may, in particular, include terms and conditions about the payment of money by a party to the proceedings to another party to the proceedings by way of compensation, damages or otherwise.

(7) In this section "furniture" includes fittings and other articles.

127 Management orders: power to supply furniture

(1) The local housing authority may supply the house to which an interim or final management order relates with such furniture as they consider to be required.

(2) For the purposes of section 110 or a management scheme under section 119, any expenditure incurred by the authority under this section constitutes expenditure incurred by the authority in connection with performing their duty under section 106(3) or 115(2).

(3) In this section "furniture" includes fittings and other articles.

128 Compensation payable to third parties

(1) If a third party requests them to do so at any time, the local housing authority must consider whether an amount by way of compensation should be paid to him in respect

of any interference with his rights in consequence of an interim or final management order.

(2) The authority must notify the third party of their decision as soon as practicable.

(3) Where the local housing authority decide under subsection (1) that compensation ought to be paid to a third party in consequence of a final management order, they must vary the management scheme contained in the order so as to specify the amount of the compensation to be paid and to make provision as to its payment.

129 Termination of management orders: financial arrangements

(1) This section applies where an interim or final management order ceases to have effect for any reason.

(2) If, on the termination date for an interim management order, the total amount of rent or other payments collected or recovered as mentioned in section 110(3) exceeds the total amount of—

(a) the local housing authority's relevant expenditure, and

(b) any amounts of compensation payable to third parties by virtue of decisions of the authority under section 128,

the authority must, as soon as practicable after the termination date, pay the balance to such relevant landlord, or to such relevant landlords in such proportions, as they consider appropriate.

(3) If, on the termination date for an interim management order, the total amount of rent or other payments collected or recovered as mentioned in section 110(3) is less than the total amount of—

(a) the authority's relevant expenditure, and

(b) any amounts of compensation payable as mentioned in subsection (2)(b),

the difference is recoverable by the authority from such relevant landlord, or such relevant landlords in such proportions, as they consider appropriate.

(4) If, on the termination date for a final management order, any amount is payable to—

(a) a third party, or

(b) any relevant landlord in accordance with the management scheme under section 119,

that amount must be paid to that person by the local housing authority in the manner provided by the scheme.

(5) If, on the termination date for a final management order, any amount is payable to the local housing authority in accordance with the management scheme, that amount is recoverable by the local housing authority—

(a) from such relevant landlord, or

(b) from such relevant landlords in such proportions,

as is provided by the scheme.

(6) The provisions of any of subsections (2) to (5) do not, however, apply in relation to the order if—

(a) the order is followed by a final management order, and

(b) the management scheme contained in that final management order provides for that subsection not to apply in relation to the order (see section 119(5)(c) and (d)).

(7) Any sum recoverable by the authority under subsection (3) or (5) is, until recovered, a charge on the house.

(8) The charge takes effect on the termination date for the order as a legal charge which is a local land charge.

(9) For the purpose of enforcing the charge the authority have the same powers and remedies under the Law of Property Act 1925 (c. 20) and otherwise as if they were mortgagees by deed having powers of sale and lease, of accepting surrenders of leases and of appointing a receiver.

(10) The power of appointing a receiver is exercisable at any time after the end of the period of one month beginning with the date on which the charge takes effect.

(11) If the order is to be followed by a licence granted under Part 2 or 3 in respect of the house, the conditions contained in the licence may include a condition requiring the licence holder—

(a) to repay to the authority any amount recoverable by them under subsection (3) or (5), and

(b) to do so in such instalments as are specified in the licence.

(12) In this section—

"relevant expenditure" has the same meaning as in section 110;

"relevant landlord" means a person who was the immediate landlord of the house or part of it immediately before the termination date or his successor in title for the time being;

"rent or other payments" means rents or other payments payable under leases or licences or in respect of furniture within section 126(1);

"the termination date" means the date on which the order ceases to have effect.

130 Termination of management orders: leases, agreements and proceedings

(1) This section applies where—

(a) an interim or final management order ceases to have effect for any reason, and

(b) the order is not immediately followed by a further order under this Chapter.

(2) As from the termination date—

(a) a lease or licence in which the local housing authority was substituted for another party by virtue of section 124(4) has effect with the substitution of the original party, or his successor in title, for the authority; and

(b) an agreement which (in accordance with section 108 or 117) has effect as a lease or licence granted by the authority under section 107 or 116 has effect with the substitution of the relevant landlord for the authority.

(3) If the relevant landlord is a lessee, nothing in a superior lease imposes liability on him or any superior lessee in respect of anything done before the termination date in pursuance of the terms of an agreement to which subsection (2)(b) applies.

(4) If the condition in subsection (5) is met, any other agreement entered into by the authority in the performance of their duties under section 106(1) to (3) or 115(2) in respect of the house has effect, as from the termination date, with the substitution of the relevant landlord for the authority.

(5) The condition is that the authority serve a notice on the other party or parties to the agreement stating that subsection (4) applies to the agreement.

(6) If the condition in subsection (7) is met—

(a) any rights or liabilities that were rights or liabilities of the authority immediately before the termination date by virtue of any provision of this Chapter or under any agreement to which subsection (4) applies are rights or liabilities of the relevant landlord instead, and

(b) any proceedings instituted or continued by or against the authority by virtue of any such provision or agreement may be continued by or against the relevant landlord instead,

as from the termination date.

(7) The condition is that the authority serve a notice on all interested parties stating that subsection (6) applies to the rights or liabilities or (as the case may be) the proceedings.

(8) If by virtue of this section a relevant landlord becomes subject to any liability to pay damages in respect of anything done (or omitted to be done) before the termination date by or on behalf of the authority, the authority are liable to reimburse to the relevant landlord an amount equal to the amount of the damages paid by him.

(9) Where two or more persons are relevant landlords in relation to different parts of the house, any reference in this section to "the relevant landlord" is to be taken to refer to such one or more of them as is determined by agreement between them or (in default of agreement) by a residential property tribunal on an application made by any of them.

(10) This section applies to instruments as it applies to agreements.

(11) In this section—

"agreement" includes arrangement;

"relevant landlord" means a person who was the immediate landlord of the house immediately before the termination date or his successor in title for the time being;

"the termination date" means the date on which the order ceases to have effect.

131 Management orders: power of entry to carry out work

(1) The right mentioned in subsection (2) is exercisable by the local housing authority, or any person authorised in writing by them, at any time when an interim or final management order is in force.

(2) That right is the right at all reasonable times to enter any part of the house for the purpose of carrying out works, and is exercisable as against any person having an estate or interest in the house.

(3) Where part of a house is excluded from the provisions of an interim or final management order under section 102(8) or 113(7), the right conferred by

subsection (1) is exercisable as respects that part so far as is reasonably required for the purpose of carrying out works in the part of the house which is subject to the order.

(4) If, after receiving reasonable notice of the intended action, any occupier of the whole or part of the house prevents any officer, employee, agent or contractor of the local housing authority from carrying out work in the house, a magistrates' court may order him to permit to be done on the premises anything which the authority consider to be necessary.

(5) A person who fails to comply with an order of the court under subsection (4) commits an offence.

(6) A person who commits an offence under subsection (5) is liable on summary conviction to a fine not exceeding level 5 on the standard scale.

CHAPTER 2

INTERIM AND FINAL EMPTY DWELLING MANAGEMENT ORDERS

Introductory

132 Empty dwelling management orders: introductory

(1) This Chapter deals with the making by a local housing authority of—
- (a) an interim empty dwelling management order (an "interim EDMO"), or
- (b) a final empty dwelling management order (a "final EDMO"),

in respect of a dwelling.

(2) An interim EDMO is an order made to enable a local housing authority, with the consent of the relevant proprietor, to take steps for the purpose of securing that a dwelling becomes and continues to be occupied.

(3) A final EDMO is an order made, in succession to an interim EDMO or a previous final EDMO, for the purpose of securing that a dwelling is occupied.

(4) In this Chapter—
- (a) "dwelling" means—
  - (i) a building intended to be occupied as a separate dwelling, or
  - (ii) a part of a building intended to be occupied as a separate dwelling which may be entered otherwise than through any non-residential accommodation in the building;
- (b) any reference to "the dwelling", in relation to an interim EDMO or a final EDMO, is a reference to the dwelling to which the order relates;
- (c) "relevant proprietor", in relation to a dwelling, means—
  - (i) if the dwelling is let under one or more leases with an unexpired term of 7 years or more, the lessee under whichever of those leases has the shortest unexpired term; or
  - (ii) in any other case, the person who has the freehold estate in the dwelling;
- (d) "third party", in relation to a dwelling, means any person who has an estate or interest in the dwelling (other than the relevant proprietor and any person

who is a tenant under a lease granted under paragraph 2(3)(c) or 10(3)(c) of Schedule 7); and

(e) any reference (however expressed) to rent or other payments in respect of occupation of a dwelling, includes any payments that the authority receive from persons in respect of unlawful occupation of the dwelling.

(5) In subsection (4)(c), the reference to an unexpired term of 7 years or more of a lease of a dwelling is—

(a) in relation to a dwelling in respect of which the local housing authority are considering making an interim EDMO, a reference to the unexpired term of the lease at the time the authority begin taking steps under section 133(3),

(b) in relation to a dwelling in respect of which an interim EDMO has been made, a reference to the unexpired term of the lease at the time the application for authorisation to make the interim EDMO was made under subsection (1) of that section, or

(c) in relation to a dwelling in respect of which a local housing authority are considering making or have made a final EDMO, a reference to the unexpired term of the lease at the time the application for authorisation to make the preceding interim EDMO was made under subsection (1) of that section.

"Preceding interim EDMO", in relation to a final EDMO, means the interim EDMO that immediately preceded the final EDMO or, where there has been a succession of final EDMOs, the interim EDMO that immediately preceded the first of them.

(6) Schedule 7 (which makes further provision regarding EDMOs) has effect.

Interim empty dwelling management orders

133 Making of interim EDMOs

(1) A local housing authority may make an interim EDMO in respect of a dwelling if—

(a) it is a dwelling to which this section applies, and

(b) on an application by the authority to a residential property tribunal, the tribunal by order authorises them under section 134 to make such an order, either in the terms of a draft order submitted by them or in those terms as varied by the tribunal.

(2) This section applies to a dwelling if—

(a) the dwelling is wholly unoccupied, and

(b) the relevant proprietor is not a public sector body.

"Wholly unoccupied" means that no part is occupied, whether lawfully or unlawfully.

(3) Before determining whether to make an application to a residential property tribunal for an authorisation under section 134, the authority must make reasonable efforts—

(a) to notify the relevant proprietor that they are considering making an interim EDMO in respect of the dwelling under this section, and

(b) to ascertain what steps (if any) he is taking, or is intending to take, to secure that the dwelling is occupied.

(4) In determining whether to make an application to a residential property tribunal for an authorisation under section 134, the authority must take into account the rights of the relevant proprietor of the dwelling and the interests of the wider community.

(5) The authority may make an interim EDMO in respect of the dwelling despite any pending appeal against the order of the tribunal (but this is without prejudice to any order that may be made on the disposal of any such appeal).

(6) An application to a residential property tribunal under this section for authorisation to make an interim EDMO in respect of a dwelling may include an application for an order under paragraph 22 of Schedule 7 determining a lease or licence of the dwelling.

(7) In this section "public sector body" means a body mentioned in any of paragraphs (a) to (f) of paragraph 2(1) of Schedule 14.

(8) Part 1 of Schedule 6 applies in relation to the making of an interim EDMO in respect of a dwelling as it applies in relation to the making of an interim management order in respect of a house, subject to the following modifications—

- (a) paragraph 7(2) does not apply;
- (b) paragraph 7(4)(c) is to be read as referring instead to the date on which the order is to cease to have effect in accordance with paragraph 1(3) and (4) or 9(3) to (5) of Schedule 7;
- (c) in paragraph 7(6)—
  - (i) paragraph (a) is to be read as referring instead to Part 4 of Schedule 7; and
  - (ii) paragraph (b) does not apply;
- (d) paragraph 8(4) is to be read as defining "relevant person" as any person who, to the knowledge of the local housing authority, is a person having an estate or interest in the dwelling (other than a person who is a tenant under a lease granted under paragraph 2(3)(c) of Schedule 7).

134 Authorisation to make interim EDMOs

(1) A residential property tribunal may authorise a local housing authority to make an interim EDMO in respect of a dwelling to which section 133 applies if the tribunal—

- (a) is satisfied as to the matters mentioned in subsection (2), and
- (b) is not satisfied that the case falls within one of the prescribed exceptions.

(2) The matters as to which the tribunal must be satisfied are—

- (a) that the dwelling has been wholly unoccupied for at least 6 months or such longer period as may be prescribed,
- (b) that there is no reasonable prospect that the dwelling will become occupied in the near future,
- (c) that, if an interim order is made, there is a reasonable prospect that the dwelling will become occupied,
- (d) that the authority have complied with section 133(3), and
- (e) that any prescribed requirements have been complied with.

(3) In deciding whether to authorise a local housing authority to make an interim EDMO in respect of a dwelling, the tribunal must take into account—

- (a) the interests of the community, and

(b) the effect that the order will have on the rights of the relevant proprietor and may have on the rights of third parties.

(4) On authorising a local housing authority to make an interim EDMO in respect of a dwelling, the tribunal may, if it thinks fit, make an order requiring the authority (if they make the EDMO) to pay to any third party specified in the order an amount of compensation in respect of any interference in consequence of the order with the rights of the third party.

(5) The appropriate national authority may by order—

(a) prescribe exceptions for the purposes of subsection (1)(b),

(b) prescribe a period of time for the purposes of subsection (2)(a), and

(c) prescribe requirements for the purposes of subsection (2)(e).

(6) An order under subsection (5)(a) may, in particular, include exceptions in relation to—

(a) dwellings that have been occupied solely or principally by the relevant proprietor who is at the material time temporarily resident elsewhere;

(b) dwellings that are holiday homes or that are otherwise occupied by the relevant proprietor or his guests on a temporary basis from time to time;

(c) dwellings undergoing repairs or renovation;

(d) dwellings in respect of which an application for planning permission or building control approval is outstanding;

(e) dwellings which are genuinely on the market for sale or letting;

(f) dwellings where the relevant proprietor has died not more than the prescribed number of months before the material time.

(7) In this section—

"building control approval" means approval for the carrying out of any works under building regulations;

"planning permission" has the meaning given by section 336(1) of the Town and Country Planning Act 1990 (c. 8);

"prescribed" means prescribed by an order under subsection (5);

"wholly unoccupied" means that no part is occupied, whether lawfully or unlawfully.

135 Local housing authority's duties once interim EDMO in force

(1) A local housing authority who have made an interim EDMO in respect of a dwelling must comply with the following provisions as soon as practicable after the order has come into force (see paragraph 1 of Schedule 7).

(2) The authority must take such steps as they consider appropriate for the purpose of securing that the dwelling becomes and continues to be occupied.

(3) The authority must also take such other steps as they consider appropriate with a view to the proper management of the dwelling pending—

(a) the making of a final EDMO in respect of the dwelling under section 136, or

(b) the revocation of the interim EDMO.

(4) If the local housing authority conclude that there are no steps which they could appropriately take under the order for the purpose of securing that the dwelling becomes occupied, the authority must either—

(a) make a final EDMO in respect of the dwelling under section 136, or

(b) revoke the order under paragraph 7 of Schedule 7 without taking any further action.

(5) For the avoidance of doubt, the authority's duty under subsection (3) includes taking such steps as are necessary to ensure that, while the order is in force, reasonable provision is made for insurance of the dwelling against destruction or damage by fire or other causes.

Final empty dwelling management orders

136 Making of final EDMOs

(1) A local housing authority may make a final EDMO to replace an interim EDMO made under section 133 if—

(a) they consider that, unless a final EDMO is made in respect of the dwelling, the dwelling is likely to become or remain unoccupied;

(b) where the dwelling is unoccupied, they have taken all such steps as it was appropriate for them to take under the interim EDMO with a view to securing the occupation of the dwelling.

(2) A local housing authority may make a new final EDMO so as to replace a final EDMO made under this section if—

(a) they consider that unless a new final EDMO is made in respect of the dwelling, the dwelling is likely to become or remain unoccupied; and

(b) where the dwelling is unoccupied, they have taken all such steps as it was appropriate for them to take under the existing final EDMO with a view to securing the occupation of the dwelling.

(3) In deciding whether to make a final EDMO in respect of a dwelling, the authority must take into account—

(a) the interests of the community, and

(b) the effect that the order will have on the rights of the relevant proprietor and may have on the rights of third parties.

(4) Before making a final EDMO under this section, the authority must consider whether compensation should be paid by them to any third party in respect of any interference in consequence of the order with the rights of the third party.

(5) Part 1 of Schedule 6 applies in relation to the making of a final EDMO in respect of a dwelling as it applies in relation to the making of a final management order in respect of a house, subject to the following modifications—

(a) paragraph 7(2) does not apply;

(b) paragraph 7(4)(c) is to be read as referring instead to the date on which the order is to cease to have effect in accordance with paragraph 1(3) and (4) or 9(3) to (5) of Schedule 7;

(c) in paragraph 7(6)—

(i) paragraph (a) is to be read as referring to Part 4 of Schedule 7, and

(ii) paragraph (b) is to be read as referring instead to paragraph 27(2) of Schedule 7;

(d) paragraph 7(6) in addition is to be read as requiring the notice under paragraph 7(5) also to contain—
   (i) the decision of the authority as to whether to pay compensation to any third party,
   (ii) the amount of any such compensation to be paid, and
   (iii) information about the right of appeal against the decision under paragraph 34 of Schedule 7;

(e) paragraph 8(4) is to be read as defining "relevant person" as any person who, to the knowledge of the local housing authority, is a person having an estate or interest in the dwelling (other than a person who is a tenant under a lease granted under paragraph 2(3)(c) or 10(3)(c) of Schedule 7).

137 Local housing authority's duties once final EDMO in force

(1) A local housing authority who have made a final EDMO in respect of a dwelling must comply with the following provisions once the order has come into force (see paragraph 9 of Schedule 7).

(2) The authority must take such steps as they consider appropriate for the purpose of securing that the dwelling is occupied.

(3) The authority must also take such other steps as they consider appropriate with a view to the proper management of the dwelling in accordance with the management scheme contained in the order (see paragraph 13 of Schedule 7).

(4) The authority must from time to time review—

(a) the operation of the order and in particular the management scheme contained in it,

(b) whether, if the dwelling is unoccupied, there are any steps which they could appropriately take under the order for the purpose of securing that the dwelling becomes occupied, and

(c) whether keeping the order in force in relation to the dwelling (with or without making any variations under paragraph 15 of Schedule 7) is necessary to secure that the dwelling becomes or remains occupied.

(5) If on a review the authority consider that any variations should be made under paragraph 15 of Schedule 7, they must proceed to make those variations.

(6) If the dwelling is unoccupied and on a review the authority conclude that either—

(a) there are no steps which they could appropriately take as mentioned in subsection (4)(b), or

(b) keeping the order in force is not necessary as mentioned in subsection (4)(c),

they must proceed to revoke the order.

(7) For the avoidance of doubt, the authority's duty under subsection (3) includes taking such steps as are necessary to ensure that, while the order is in force, reasonable provision is made for insurance of the dwelling against destruction or damage by fire or other causes.

Compensation

138 Compensation payable to third parties

(1) A third party may, while an interim EDMO is in force in respect of a dwelling, apply to a residential property tribunal for an order requiring the local housing authority to pay to him compensation in respect of any interference in consequence of the order with his rights in respect of the dwelling.

(2) On such an application, the tribunal may, if it thinks fit, make an order requiring the authority to pay to the third party an amount by way of compensation in respect of any such interference.

(3) If a third party requests them to do so at any time, the local housing authority must consider whether an amount by way of compensation should be paid to him in respect of any interference in consequence of a final EDMO with his rights.

(4) The authority must notify the third party of their decision as soon as practicable.

(5) Where the local housing authority decide under subsection (3) that compensation ought to be paid to a third party, they must vary the management scheme contained in the order so as to specify the amount of the compensation to be paid and to make provision as to its payment.

CHAPTER 3

OVERCROWDING NOTICES

139 Service of overcrowding notices

(1) This Chapter applies to any HMO—

- (a) in relation to which no interim or final management order is in force; and
- (b) which is not required to be licensed under Part 2.

(2) The local housing authority may serve an overcrowding notice on one or more relevant persons if, having regard to the rooms available, it considers that an excessive number of persons is being, or is likely to be, accommodated in the HMO concerned.

(3) The authority must, at least 7 days before serving an overcrowding notice—

- (a) inform in writing every relevant person (whether or not the person on whom the authority is to serve the notice) of their intention to serve the notice; and
- (b) ensure that, so far as is reasonably possible, every occupier of the HMO concerned is informed of the authority's intention.

(4) The authority must also give the persons informed under subsection (3) an opportunity of making representations about the proposal to serve an overcrowding notice.

(5) An overcrowding notice becomes operative, if no appeal is brought under section 143, at the end of the period of 21 days from the date of service of the notice.

(6) If no appeal is brought under section 143, an overcrowding notice is final and conclusive as to matters which could have been raised on such an appeal.

(7) A person who contravenes an overcrowding notice commits an offence and is liable on summary conviction to a fine not exceeding level 4 on the standard scale.

(8) In proceedings for an offence under subsection (7) it is a defence that the person had a reasonable excuse for contravening the notice.

(9) In this section "relevant person" means a person who is, to the knowledge of the local housing authority—

(a) a person having an estate or interest in the HMO concerned, or

(b) a person managing or having control of it.

140 Contents of overcrowding notices

(1) An overcrowding notice must state in relation to each room in the HMO concerned—

(a) what the local housing authority consider to be the maximum number of persons by whom the room is suitable to be occupied as sleeping accommodation at any one time; or

(b) that the local housing authority consider that the room is unsuitable to be occupied as sleeping accommodation.

(2) An overcrowding notice may specify special maxima applicable where some or all of the persons occupying a room are under such age as may be specified in the notice.

(3) An overcrowding notice must contain—

(a) the requirement prescribed by section 141 (not to permit excessive number of persons to sleep in the house in multiple occupation); or

(b) the requirement prescribed by section 142 (not to admit new residents if number of persons is excessive).

(4) The local housing authority may at any time—

(a) withdraw an overcrowding notice which has been served on any person and which contains the requirement prescribed by section 142, and

(b) serve on him instead an overcrowding notice containing the requirement prescribed by section 141.

141 Requirement as to overcrowding generally

(1) The requirement prescribed by this section is that the person on whom the notice is served must refrain from—

(a) permitting a room to be occupied as sleeping accommodation otherwise than in accordance with the notice; or

(b) permitting persons to occupy the HMO as sleeping accommodation in such numbers that it is not possible to avoid persons of opposite sexes who are not living together as husband and wife sleeping in the same room.

(2) For the purposes of subsection (1)(b)—

(a) children under the age of 10 are to be disregarded; and

(b) it must be assumed that the persons occupying the HMO as sleeping accommodation sleep only in rooms for which a maximum is set by the notice and that the maximum set for each room is not exceeded.

142 Requirement as to new residents

(1) The requirement prescribed by this section is that the person on whom the notice is served must refrain from—

(a) permitting a room to be occupied by a new resident as sleeping accommodation otherwise than in accordance with the notice; or

(b) permitting a new resident to occupy any part of the HMO as sleeping accommodation if that is not possible without persons of opposite sexes who are not living together as husband and wife sleeping in the same room.

(2) In subsection (1) "new resident" means a person who was not an occupier of the HMO immediately before the notice was served.

(3) For the purposes of subsection (1)(b)—

(a) children under the age of 10 are to be disregarded; and

(b) it must be assumed that the persons occupying any part of the HMO as sleeping accommodation sleep only in rooms for which a maximum is set by the notice and that the maximum set for each room is not exceeded.

143 Appeals against overcrowding notices

(1) A person aggrieved by an overcrowding notice may appeal to aresidential property tribunal within the period of 21 days beginning with the date of service of the notice.

(2) Such an appeal—

(a) is to be by way of a re-hearing, but

(b) may be determined having regard to matters of which the authority were unaware.

(3) On an appeal the tribunal may by order confirm, quash or vary the notice.

(4) If an appeal is brought, the notice does not become operative until—

(a) a decision is given on the appeal which confirms the notice and the period within which an appeal to the Lands Tribunal may be brought expires without any such appeal having been brought; or

(b) if an appeal is brought to the Lands Tribunal, a decision is given on the appeal which confirms the notice.

(5) For the purposes of subsection (4)—

(a) the withdrawal of an appeal has the same effect as a decision which confirms the notice appealed against; and

(b) references to a decision which confirms the notice are to a decision which confirms it with or without variation.

(6) A residential property tribunal may allow an appeal to be made to it after the end of the period mentioned in subsection (1) if it is satisfied that there is good reason for the failure to appeal before the end of that period (and for any delay since then in applying for permission to appeal out of time).

144 Revocation and variation of overcrowding notices

(1) The local housing authority may at any time, on the application of a relevant person—

(a) revoke an overcrowding notice; or

(b) vary it so as to allow more people to be accommodated in the HMO concerned.

(2) The applicant may appeal to a residential property tribunal if the local housing authority—

(a) refuse an application under subsection (1); or

(b) do not notify the applicant of their decision within the period of 35 days beginning with the making of the application (or within such further period as the applicant may in writing allow).

(3) An appeal under subsection (2) must be made within—

(a) the period of 21 days beginning with the date when the applicant is notified by the authority of their decision to refuse the application, or

(b) the period of 21 days immediately following the end of the period (or further period) applying for the purposes of paragraph (b) of that subsection,

as the case may be.

(4) Section 143(2) applies to such an appeal as it applies to an appeal under that section.

(5) On an appeal the tribunal may revoke the notice or vary it in any manner in which it might have been varied by the local housing authority.

(6) A residential property tribunal may allow an appeal to be made to it after the end of the 21-day period mentioned in subsection (3)(a) or (b) if it is satisfied that there is good reason for the failure to appeal before the end of that period (and for any delay since then in applying for permission to appeal).

(7) In this section "relevant person" means—

(a) any person who has an estate or interest in the HMO concerned, or

(b) any other person who is a person managing or having control of it.

CHAPTER 4

SUPPLEMENTARY PROVISIONS

145 Supplementary provisions

(1) The appropriate national authority may by regulations make such provision as it considers appropriate for supplementing the provisions of Chapter 1 or 2 in relation to cases where a local housing authority are to be treated as the lessee under a lease under—

(a) section 107(5) or 116(5), or

(b) paragraph 2(6) or 10(6) of Schedule 7.

(2) Regulations under this section may, in particular, make provision—

(a) as respects rights and liabilities in such cases of—

(i) the authority,

(ii) the person who (apart from the relevant provision mentioned in subsection (1)) is the lessee under the lease, or

(iii) other persons having an estate or interest in the premises demised under the lease;

(b) requiring the authority to give copies to the person mentioned in paragraph (a)(ii) of notices and other documents served on them in connection with the lease;

(c) for treating things done by or in relation to the authority as done by or in relation to that person, or vice versa.

146 Interpretation and modification of this Part

(1) In this Part—

"HMO" means a house in multiple occupation as defined by sections 254 to 259,

"Part 3 house" means a house to which Part 3 of this Act applies (see section 79(2)),

and any reference to an HMO or Part 3 house includes (where the context permits) a reference to any yard, garden, outhouses and appurtenances belonging to, or usually enjoyed with, it (or any part of it).

(2) For the purposes of this Part "mortgage" includes a charge or lien, and "mortgagee" is to be read accordingly.

(3) The appropriate national authority may by regulations provide for—

(a) any provision of this Part, or

(b) section 263 (in its operation for the purposes of any such provision),

to have effect in relation to a section 257 HMO with such modifications as are prescribed by the regulations.

(4) A "section 257 HMO" is an HMO which is a converted block of flats to which section 257 applies.

147 Index of defined expressions: Part 4

The following table shows where expressions used in this Part are defined or otherwise explained.

Expression	*Provision of this Act*
Appropriate national authority	Section 261(1)
Dwelling	Section 132(4)(a) and (b)
Final EDMO	Section 132(1)(b)
Final management order	Section 101(4)
Health	Section 2(5)
HMO	Section 146(1)
The house	Section 101(5) or 103(8)
Immediate landlord	Section 109(6) or 118(6)
Interim EDMO	Section 132(1)(a)
Interim management order	Section 101(3)
Landlord	Section 262(3)

Expression	*Provision of this Act*
Lease, lessee, etc.	Section 262(1) to (4)
Licence (to occupy premises)	Section 262(9)
Local housing authority	Section 261(2) to (5)
Modifications	Section 250(7)
Mortgage, mortgagee	Section 146(2)
Occupier (and related expressions)	Section 262(6)
Owner	Section 262(7)
Part 3 house	Section 146(1)
Person having control	Section 263(1) and (2)
Person having estate or interest	Section 262(8)
Person managing	Section 263(3)
Relevant proprietor	Section 132(4)(c) and (5)
Rent or other payments (in Chapter 2)	Section 132(4)(e)
Residential property tribunal	Section 229
Tenancy, tenant, etc.	Section 262(1) to (5)
Third party (in Chapter 1)	Section 101(7)
Third party (in Chapter 2)	Section 132(4)(d).

PART 5

HOME INFORMATION PACKS

Preliminary

148 Meaning of "residential property" and "home information pack"

(1) In this Part—

"residential property" means premises in England and Wales consisting of a single dwelling-house, including any ancillary land; and

"dwelling-house" means a building or part of a building occupied or intended to be occupied as a separate dwelling (and includes one that is being or is to be constructed).

(2) References in this Part to a home information pack, in relation to a residential property, are to a collection of documents relating to the property or the terms on which it is or may become available for sale.

149 Meaning of "on the market" and related expressions

(1) In this Part references to "the market" are to the residential property market in England and Wales.

(2) A residential property is put on the market when the fact that it is or may become available for sale is, with the intention of marketing the property, first made public in England and Wales by or on behalf of the seller.

(3) A residential property which has been put on the market is to be regarded as remaining on the market until it is taken off the market or sold.

(4) A fact is made public when it is advertised or otherwise communicated (in whatever form and by whatever means) to the public or to a section of the public.

150 Acting as estate agent

(1) A person acts as estate agent for the seller of a residential property if he does anything, in the course of a business in England and Wales, in pursuance of marketing instructions from the seller.

(2) For this purpose—

"business in England and Wales" means a business carried on (in whole or in part) from a place in England and Wales; and

"marketing instructions" means instructions to carry out any activities with a view to—

(a) effecting the introduction to the seller of a person wishing to buy the property; or

(b) selling the property by auction or tender.

(3) It is immaterial for the purposes of this section whether or not a person describes himself as an estate agent.

Responsibility for marketing residential properties

151 Responsibility for marketing: general

(1) References in this Part to a responsible person, in relation to a residential property, are to any person who is for the time being responsible for marketing the property.

(2) Sections 152 and 153 identify for the purposes of this Part—

(a) the person or persons who are responsible for marketing a residential property which is on the market ("the property"); and

(b) when the responsibility of any such person arises and ceases.

(3) Only the seller or a person acting as estate agent for the seller may be responsible for marketing the property.

(4) A person may be responsible for marketing the property on more than one occasion.

152 Responsibility of person acting as estate agent

(1) A person acting as estate agent becomes responsible for marketing the property when action taken by him or on his behalf—

(a) puts the property on the market; or

(b) makes public the fact that the property is on the market.

(2) That responsibility ceases when the following conditions are satisfied, namely—
   (a) his contract with the seller is terminated (whether by the withdrawal of his instructions or otherwise);
   (b) he has ceased to take any action which makes public the fact that the property is on the market; and
   (c) any such action being taken on his behalf has ceased.

(3) Any responsibility arising under this section also ceases when the property is taken off the market or sold.

153 Responsibility of the seller

(1) The seller becomes responsible for marketing the property when action taken by him or on his behalf—
   (a) puts the property on the market; or
   (b) makes public the fact that the property is on the market.

(2) That responsibility ceases when the following conditions are satisfied, namely—
   (a) there is at least one person acting as his estate agent who is responsible for marketing the property;
   (b) the seller has ceased to take any action which makes public the fact that the property is on the market; and
   (c) any such action being taken on the seller's behalf has ceased.

(3) In this section the references to action taken on behalf of the seller exclude action taken by or on behalf of a person acting as his estate agent.

(4) Any responsibility arising under this section also ceases when the property is taken off the market or sold.

Duties of a responsible person where a property is on the market

154 Application of sections 155 to 158

(1) Where a residential property is on the market, a person responsible for marketing the property is subject to the duties relating to home information packs that are imposed by sections 155 to 158 until his responsibility ceases.

(2) Each of those duties is subject to any exception relating to that duty which is provided for in those sections.

(3) The duty under section 156(1) is also subject to any condition imposed under section 157.

155 Duty to have a home information pack

(1) It is the duty of a responsible person to have in his possession or under his control a home information pack for the property which complies with the requirements of any regulations under section 163.

(2) That duty does not apply where the responsible person is the seller at any time when—

(a) there is another person who is responsible for marketing the property under section 152; and

(b) the seller believes on reasonable grounds that the other responsible person has a home information pack for the property in his possession or under his control which complies with the requirements of any regulations under section 163.

156 Duty to provide copy of home information pack on request

(1) Where a potential buyer makes a request to a responsible person for a copy of the home information pack, or of a document (or part of a document) which is or ought to be included in that pack, it is the duty of the responsible person to comply with that request within the permitted period.

(2) The responsible person does not comply with that duty unless—

(a) he provides the potential buyer with a document which is—

(i) a copy of the home information pack for the property as it stands at the time when the document is provided, or

(ii) a copy of a document (or part of a document) which is included in that pack,

as the case may be; and

(b) that pack or document complies with the requirements of any regulations under section 163 at that time.

(3) In subsection (2) "the home information pack" means the home information pack intended by the responsible person to be the one required by section 155.

(4) That duty does not apply if, before the end of the permitted period, the responsible person believes on reasonable grounds that the person making the request—

(a) is unlikely to have sufficient means to buy the property in question;

(b) is not genuinely interested in buying a property of a general description which applies to the property; or

(c) is not a person to whom the seller is likely to be prepared to sell the property.

Nothing in this subsection authorises the doing of anything which constitutes an unlawful act of discrimination.

(5) Subsection (4) does not apply if the responsible person knows or suspects that the person making the request is an officer of an enforcement authority.

(6) That duty does not apply where the responsible person is the seller if, when the request is made, the duty under section 155 does not (by virtue of subsection (2) of that section) apply to him.

(7) But where the duty under this section is excluded by subsection (6), it is the duty of the seller to take reasonable steps to inform the potential buyer that the request should be made to the other person.

(8) The responsible person may charge a sum not exceeding the reasonable cost of making and, if requested, sending a paper copy of the pack or document.

(9) The permitted period for the purposes of this section is (subject to section 157(5)) the period of 14 days beginning with the day on which the request is made.

(10) If the responsible person ceases to be responsible for marketing the property before the end of the permitted period (whether because the property has been taken off the market or sold or for any other reason), he ceases to be under any duty to comply with the request.

(11) A person does not comply with the duty under this section by providing a copy in electronic form unless the potential buyer consents to receiving it in that form.

157 Section 156 (1) duty: imposition of conditions

(1) A potential buyer who has made a request to which section 156(1) applies may be required to comply with either or both of the following conditions before any copy is provided.

(2) The potential buyer may be required to pay a charge authorised by section 156(8).

(3) The potential buyer may be required to accept any terms specified in writing which—

(a) are proposed by the seller or in pursuance of his instructions; and

(b) relate to the use or disclosure of the copy (or any information contained in or derived from it).

(4) A condition is only effective if it is notified to the potential buyer before the end of the period of 14 days beginning with the day on which the request is made.

(5) Where the potential buyer has been so notified of either or both of the conditions authorised by this section, the permitted period for the purposes of section 156 is the period of 14 days beginning with—

(a) where one condition is involved, the day on which the potential buyer complies with it by—

(i) making the payment demanded, or

(ii) accepting the terms proposed (or such other terms as may be agreed between the seller and the potential buyer in substitution for those proposed),

as the case may be; or

(b) where both conditions are involved, the day (or the later of the days) on which the potential buyer complies with them by taking the action mentioned in paragraph (a)(i) and (ii).

158 Duty to ensure authenticity of documents in other situations

(1) Where a responsible person provides a potential buyer with, or allows a potential buyer to inspect, any document purporting to be—

(a) a copy of the home information pack for the property, or

(b) a copy of a document (or part of a document) included in that pack,

the responsible person is under a duty to ensure that the document is authentic.

(2) A document is not authentic for the purposes of subsection (1) unless, at the time when it is provided or inspected—

(a) it is a copy of the home information pack for the property or a document (or part of a document) included in that pack, as the case may be; and

(b) that pack or document complies with the requirements of any regulations under section 163.

(3) In subsection (2) "the home information pack" means the pack intended by the responsible person to be the one required by section 155.

(4) The duty under this section does not apply to anything provided in pursuance of the duty under section 156.

Other duties of person acting as estate agent

159 Other duties of person acting as estate agent

(1) This section applies to a person acting as estate agent for the seller of a residential property where—

- (a) the property is not on the market; or
- (b) the property is on the market but the person so acting is not a person responsible for marketing the property.

(2) It is the duty of a person to whom this section applies to have in his possession or under his control, when any qualifying action is taken by him or on his behalf, a home information pack for the property which complies with the requirements of any regulations under section 163.

(3) In subsection (2) "qualifying action" means action taken with the intention of marketing the property which—

- (a) communicates to any person in England and Wales the fact that the property is or may become available for sale; but
- (b) does not put the property on the market or make public the fact that the property is on the market.

(4) Where a person to whom this section applies provides a potential buyer with, or allows a potential buyer to inspect, any document purporting to be—

- (a) a copy of the home information pack for the property; or
- (b) a copy of a document (or part of a document) included in that pack;

it is his duty to ensure that it is an authentic copy.

(5) A document is not authentic for the purposes of subsection (4) unless, at the time when it is provided or inspected—

- (a) it is a copy of the home information pack for the property or a document (or part of a document) included in that pack, as the case may be; and
- (b) that pack or document complies with the requirements of any regulations under section 163.

(6) In subsection (5) "the home information pack" means the home information pack intended by the person to whom this section applies to be the one required by subsection (2).

Exceptions from the duties

160 Residential properties not available with vacant possession

(1) The duties under sections 155 to 159 do not apply in relation to a residential property at any time when it is not available for sale with vacant possession.

(2) But for the purposes of this Part a residential property shall be presumed to be available with vacant possession, at any time when any of those duties would apply in relation to the property if it is so available, unless the contrary appears from the manner in which the property is being marketed at that time.

161 Power to provide for further exceptions

The Secretary of State may by regulations provide for other exceptions from any duty under sections 155 to 159 in such cases and circumstances, and to such extent, as may be specified in the regulations.

162 Suspension of duties under sections 155 to 159

(1) The Secretary of State may make an order suspending (or later reviving) the operation of any duty imposed by sections 155 to 159.

(2) An order under this section may provide for the suspension of a duty to take effect only for a period specified in the order.

(3) A duty which is (or is to any extent) revived after being suspended under this section is liable to be suspended again.

Contents of home information packs

163 Contents of home information packs

(1) The Secretary of State may make regulations prescribing—
- (a) the documents which are required or authorised to be included in the home information pack for a residential property; and
- (b) particular information which is required or authorised to be included in, or which is to be excluded from, any such document.

(2) A document prescribed under subsection (1) must be one that the Secretary of State considers would disclose relevant information.

(3) Any particular information required or authorised to be included in a prescribed document must be information that the Secretary of State considers to be relevant information.

(4) In this section "relevant information" means information about any matter connected with the property (or the sale of the property) that would be of interest to potential buyers.

(5) Without prejudice to the generality of subsection (4), the information which the Secretary of State may consider to be relevant information includes any information about—
- (a) the interest which is for sale and the terms on which it is proposed to sell it;
- (b) the title to the property;
- (c) anything relating to or affecting the property that is contained in—
  - (i) a register required to be kept by or under any enactment (whenever passed); or

(ii) records kept by a person who can reasonably be expected to give information derived from those records to the seller at his request (on payment, if required, of a reasonable charge);

(d) the physical condition of the property (including any particular characteristics or features of the property);

(e) the energy efficiency of the property;

(f) any warranties or guarantees subsisting in relation to the property;

(g) any taxes, service charges or other charges payable in relation to the property.

(6) The regulations may require or authorise the home information pack to include—

(a) replies the seller proposes to give to prescribed pre-contract enquiries; and

(b) documents or particular information indexing or otherwise explaining the contents of the pack.

(7) The regulations may require a prescribed document—

(a) to be in such form as may be prescribed; and

(b) to be prepared by a person of a prescribed description on such terms (if any) as may be prescribed.

(8) The terms mentioned in subsection (7)(b) may include terms which enable provisions of the contract under which the document is to be prepared to be enforced by—

(a) a potential or actual buyer;

(b) a mortgage lender; or

(c) any other person involved in the sale of the property who is not a party to that contract.

(9) The regulations may—

(a) provide for the time at which any document is to be included in or removed from the home information pack; and

(b) make different provision for different areas, for different descriptions of properties or for other different circumstances (including the manner in which a residential property is marketed).

(10) In this section "prescribed" means prescribed by regulations under this section.

164 Home condition reports

(1) Regulations under section 163 may make the provision mentioned in this section in relation to any description of document dealing with matters mentioned in section 163(5)(d) or (e) (reports on physical condition or energy efficiency) which is to be included in the home information pack.

(2) In this section "home condition report" means a document of that description.

(3) The regulations may require a home condition report to be made by an individual who is a member of an approved certification scheme following an inspection carried out by him in accordance with the provisions of the scheme.

(4) The regulations shall, if the provision mentioned in subsection (3) is made, make provision for the approval by the Secretary of State of one or more suitable certification schemes (and for the withdrawal by him of any such approval).

(5) The regulations shall require the Secretary of State to be satisfied, before approving a certification scheme, that the scheme contains appropriate provision—

(a) for ensuring that members of the scheme are fit and proper persons who are qualified (by their education, training and experience) to produce home condition reports;

(b) for ensuring that members of the scheme have in force suitable indemnity insurance;

(c) for facilitating the resolution of complaints against members of the scheme;

(d) for requiring home condition reports made by members of the scheme to be entered on the register mentioned in section 165;

(e) for the keeping of a public register of the members of the scheme; and

(f) for such other purposes as may be specified in the regulations.

(6) Subsection (5)(d) only applies where provision for a register of home condition reports is made under section 165.

(7) The regulations may require or authorise an approved certification scheme to contain provision about any matter relating to the home condition reports with which the scheme is concerned (including the terms on which members of the scheme may undertake to produce a home condition report).

(8) Nothing in this section limits the power under section 163 to make provision about home condition reports in the regulations.

Register of home condition reports

165 Register of home condition reports

(1) Where the provision mentioned in section 164(3) is made in relation to an approved certification scheme, regulations under section 163 may make provision for and in connection with a register of the home condition reports made by members of the scheme.

(2) The regulations may provide for the register to be kept—

(a) by (or on behalf of) the Secretary of State; or

(b) by such other person as the regulations may specify.

(3) The regulations may require a person wishing to enter a home condition report onto the register to pay such fee as may be prescribed.

(4) No person may disclose—

(a) the register or any document (or part of a document) contained in it; or

(b) any information contained in, or derived from, the register,

except in accordance with any provision of the regulations which authorises or requires such a disclosure to be made.

(5) The provision which may be made under subsection (1) includes (without prejudice to the generality of that subsection) provision as to circumstances in which or purposes for which a person or a person of a prescribed description—

(a) may (on payment of such fee, if any, as may be prescribed)—

(i) inspect the register or any document (or part of a document) contained in it;

(ii) take or be given copies of the register or any document (or part of a document) contained in it; or

(iii) be given information contained in, or derived from, the register; or

(b) may disclose anything obtained by virtue of provision made under paragraph (a).

(6) The purposes which may be so prescribed may be public purposes or purposes of private undertakings or other persons.

(7) A person who contravenes subsection (4) is guilty of an offence and liable on summary conviction to a fine not exceeding level 5 on the standard scale.

(8) Nothing in this section limits the power to make regulations under section 163.

Enforcement

166 Enforcement authorities

(1) Every local weights and measures authority is an enforcement authority for the purposes of this Part.

(2) It is the duty of each enforcement authority to enforce—

(a) the duties under sections 155 to 159 and 167(4), and

(b) any duty imposed under section 172(1),

in their area.

167 Power to require production of home information packs

(1) An authorised officer of an enforcement authority may require a person who appears to him to be or to have been subject to the duty under section 155 or 159(2), in relation to a residential property, to produce for inspection a copy of, or of any document included in, the home information pack for that property.

(2) The power conferred by subsection (1) includes power—

(a) to require the production in a visible and legible documentary form of any document included in the home information pack in question which is held in electronic form; and

(b) to take copies of any document produced for inspection.

(3) A requirement under this section may not be imposed more than six months after the last day on which the person concerned was subject to the duty under section 155 or 159(2) in relation to the property (as the case may be).

(4) Subject to subsection (5), it is the duty of a person subject to such a requirement to comply with it within the period of 7 days beginning with the day after that on which it is imposed.

(5) A person is not required to comply with such a requirement if he has a reasonable excuse for not complying with the requirement.

(6) In this section "the home information pack" means—

(a) where a requirement under this section is imposed on a person at a time when he is subject to the duty under section 155 or 159(2), the home information pack intended by him to be the one he is required to have at that time; or

(b) in any other case, the home information pack intended by the person concerned, when he was last subject to the duty under section 155 or 159(2), to be the one he was required to have at that time.

168 Penalty charge notices

(1) An authorised officer of an enforcement authority may, if he believes that a person has committed a breach of—

(a) any duty under sections 155 to 159 and 167(4), or

(b) any duty imposed under section 172(1),

give a penalty charge notice to that person.

(2) A penalty charge notice may not be given after the end of the period of six months beginning with the day (or in the case of a continuing breach the last day) on which the breach of duty was committed.

(3) Schedule 8 (which makes further provision about penalty charge notices) has effect.

169 Offences relating to enforcement officers

(1) A person who obstructs an officer of an enforcement authority acting in pursuance of section 167 is guilty of an offence.

(2) A person who, not being an authorised officer of an enforcement authority, purports to act as such in pursuance of section 167 or 168 is guilty of an offence.

(3) A person guilty of an offence under this section is liable on summary conviction to a fine not exceeding level 5 on the standard scale.

170 Right of private action

(1) This section applies where a person ("the responsible person") has committed a breach of duty under section 156 by failing to comply with a request from a potential buyer of a residential property for a copy of a prescribed document.

(2) If the potential buyer commissions his own version of the prescribed document at a time when both of the conditions mentioned below are satisfied, he is entitled to recover from the responsible person any reasonable fee paid by him in order to obtain the document.

(3) The first condition is that—

(a) the property is on the market; or

(b) the potential buyer and the seller are attempting to reach an agreement for the sale of the property.

(4) The second condition is that the potential buyer has not been provided with an authentic copy of the prescribed document.

(5) A copy of a prescribed document is not authentic for the purposes of subsection (4) unless—

(a) it is a copy of a document included in the home information pack for the property as it stands at the time the copy is provided to the potential buyer; and

(b) the document so included complies with the requirements of any regulations under section 163 at that time.

(6) In subsection (5) "the home information pack" means the home information pack intended by the responsible person to be the one required by section 155.

(7) In this section "prescribed document" means a document (being one required to be included in the home information pack by regulations under section 163) which is prescribed by regulations made by the Secretary of State for the purposes of this section.

(8) It is immaterial for the purposes of this section that the request in question did not specify the prescribed document but was for a copy of the home information pack or a part of the pack which included (or ought to have included) that document.

Supplementary

171 Application of Part to sub-divided buildings

(1) This section applies where—

(a) two or more dwelling-houses in a sub-divided building are marketed for sale (with any ancillary land) as a single property; and

(b) any one or more of those dwelling-houses—

(i) is not available for sale (with any ancillary land) as a separate residential property; but

(ii) is available with vacant possession.

(2) This Part applies to the dwelling-houses mentioned in subsection (1)(a) (with any ancillary land) as if—

(a) they were a residential property, and

(b) section 160 were omitted.

(3) Subsection (2) does not affect the application of this Part to any of those dwelling-houses which is available for sale (with any ancillary land) as a separate residential property.

(4) In this section "sub-divided building" means a building or part of a building originally constructed or adapted for use as a single dwelling which has been divided (on one or more occasions) into separate dwelling-houses.

172 Power to require estate agents to belong to a redress scheme

(1) The Secretary of State may by order require every estate agent to be a member of an approved redress scheme.

(2) Acting as estate agent for the seller of a residential property in contravention of such an order is a breach of duty under this Part.

(3) Before making such an order the Secretary of State must be satisfied that he has approved one or more redress schemes such that every estate agent who is (or will be) subject to the duty imposed by the order is eligible to join an approved redress scheme.

For this purpose "estate agent" does not include a person who is (by virtue of a prohibition imposed by or under the Estate Agents Act 1979 (c. 38)) unable lawfully to act as estate agent for the seller of a residential property.

(4) An order under this section may—

(a) exclude estate agents of a prescribed description from any duty imposed under subsection (1);

(b) limit any duty so imposed so that it applies only in relation to relevant complaints of a prescribed description.

(5) Nothing in this section is to be taken as preventing an approved redress scheme from providing—

(a) for membership to be open to persons who are not subject to any duty to belong to an approved redress scheme;

(b) for the investigation and determination of complaints, other than those in relation to which such a duty applies, made against members who have voluntarily accepted the jurisdiction of the scheme over such complaints;

(c) for the exclusion from investigation and determination under the scheme of any complaint in such cases or circumstances as may be specified in the scheme.

(6) In this section and sections 173 and 174—

"approved redress scheme" means a redress scheme that is for the time being approved under section 173;

"estate agent" means a person who acts as estate agent for sellers of residential properties for which a home information pack is (or will be) required under this Part;

"redress scheme" means a scheme under which certain relevant complaints may be investigated and determined by an independent person (referred to in those sections as "the ombudsman"); and

"relevant complaint" means a complaint against an estate agent which—

(a) is made by a person who at the material time is the seller or a potential buyer of a residential property; and

(b) relates to an act or omission affecting the complainant in the course of the estate agent's activities in relation to a home information pack that is (or will be) required for that property (including the giving of advice as to whether such a pack is required).

(7) For the purposes of the law relating to defamation, proceedings under an approved redress scheme in relation to the investigation and determination of a complaint which is subject to an order under this section are to be treated in the same way as proceedings before a court.

173 Approval of redress schemes

(1) If the Secretary of State considers that a redress scheme (including one made by him or in pursuance of arrangements made by him) is satisfactory for the purposes of section 172, he may approve it for those purposes.

(2) In determining whether a redress scheme is satisfactory the Secretary of State shall have regard to—

(a) the provisions of the scheme;

(b) the manner in which the scheme will be operated (so far as can be judged from the facts known to him); and

(c) the respective interests of members of the scheme and of sellers and potential buyers of residential properties.

(3) A redress scheme may not be approved unless it makes satisfactory provision about the following matters (among other things)—

(a) the matters about which complaints may be made (which may include non-compliance with the provisions of a code of practice or other document);

(b) the ombudsman's duties and powers in relation to the investigation and determination of complaints (which may include power to decide not to investigate or determine a complaint);

(c) the provision of information by the ombudsman to—

(i) persons exercising functions under other schemes providing a means of redress for consumers; and

(ii) the Secretary of State or any other person exercising regulatory functions in relation to the activities of estate agents.

(4) An application for approval of a redress scheme shall be made in such manner as the Secretary of State may determine, accompanied by such information as the Secretary of State may require.

(5) The person administering an approved redress scheme shall notify the Secretary of State of any change to the scheme as soon as practicable after the change is made.

174 Withdrawal of approval of redress schemes

(1) The Secretary of State may withdraw his approval of a redress scheme.

(2) But before withdrawing his approval, the Secretary of State shall serve on the person administering the scheme a notice stating—

(a) that he proposes to withdraw his approval;

(b) the grounds for the proposed withdrawal of approval; and

(c) that representations about the proposed withdrawal may be made within such period of not less than 14 days as is specified in the notice.

(3) The Secretary of State shall give notice of his decision on a proposal to withdraw approval, with his reasons, to the person administering the scheme.

(4) Withdrawal of approval has effect from such date as may be specified in that notice.

(5) The person administering the scheme shall give a copy of a notice under subsection (3) to every member of the scheme.

175 Office of Fair Trading

(1) An enforcement authority may notify the Office of Fair Trading of any breach of duty under this Part appearing to the authority to have been committed by a person acting as estate agent.

(2) An enforcement authority shall notify the Office of Fair Trading of—

(a) any penalty charge notice given by an officer of the authority under section 168;

(b) any notice given by the authority confirming or withdrawing a penalty charge notice; and

(c) the result of any appeal from the confirmation of a penalty charge notice.

(3) The Estate Agents Act 1979 (c. 38) applies in relation to a person who has committed a breach of duty under this Part in the course of estate agency work (within the meaning of that Act) as it applies in relation to a person who has engaged in a practice such as is mentioned in section 3(1)(d) of that Act in the course of such work.

176 Grants

(1) The Secretary of State may make grants towards expenditure incurred by any person in connection with—

(a) the development of proposals for any provision to be made by regulations under section 163;

(b) the development of schemes which are intended to be certification schemes for the purposes of any provision made or expected to be made in regulations under section 163 by virtue of section 164; or

(c) the development of a register for the purposes of any provision made or expected to be made in regulations under section 163 by virtue of section 165.

(2) A grant under this section may be made on conditions, which may include (among other things)—

(a) conditions as to the purposes for which the grant or any part of it may be used; and

(b) conditions requiring the repayment of the grant or any part of it in such circumstances as may be specified in the conditions.

177 Interpretation of Part 5

(1) In this Part—

"ancillary land", in relation to a dwelling-house or a sub-divided building, means any land intended to be occupied and enjoyed together with that dwelling-house or building;

"long lease" means—

(a) a lease granted for a term certain exceeding 21 years, whether or not it is (or may become) terminable before the end of that term by notice given by the tenant or by re-entry or forfeiture; or

(b) a lease for a term fixed by law under a grant with a covenant or obligation for perpetual renewal, other than a lease by sub-demise from one which is not a long lease;

and for this purpose "lease" does not include a mortgage term;

"potential buyer" means a person who claims that he is or may become interested in buying a residential property;

"sale", in relation to a residential property, means a disposal, or agreement to dispose, by way of sale of—

(a) the freehold interest;

(b) the interest under a long lease;

(c) an option to acquire the freehold interest or the interest under a long lease;

and "seller" means a person contemplating disposing of such an interest (and related expressions shall be construed accordingly).

(2) Any reference in the definition of "sale" to the disposal of an interest of a kind mentioned in that definition includes a reference to the creation of such an interest.

(3) A document which is not in electronic form is only to be regarded for the purposes of this Part as being under the control of a person while it is in the possession of another if he has the right to take immediate possession of the document on demand (and without payment).

(4) A document held in electronic form is only to be regarded for the purposes of this Part as being in a person's possession or under his control if he is readily able (using equipment available to him)—

(a) to view the document in a form that is visible and legible; and

(b) to produce copies of it in a visible and legible documentary form.

178 Index of defined expressions: Part 5

In this Part, the expressions listed in the left-hand column have the meaning given by, or are to be interpreted in accordance with, the provisions inserted in the right-hand column.

Expression	*Provision of this Act*
Acting as estate agent for the seller	Section 150
Ancillary land	Section 177(1)
Control of documents	Section 177(3) and (4)
Dwelling-house	Section 148(1)
Enforcement authority	Section 166
Home information pack	Section 148(2)
Long lease	Section 177(1)
Make public	Section 149(4)
Possession of electronic documents	Section 177(4)
Potential buyer	Section 177(1)
Putting on the market	Section 149(2)
Remaining on the market	Section 149(3)
Residential property	Section 148(1)
Responsible person	Section 151(1)
Sale (and related expressions)	Section 177(1)
Seller (and related expressions)	Section 177(1)
The market	Section 149(1).

PART 6

OTHER PROVISIONS ABOUT HOUSING

CHAPTER 1

SECURE TENANCIES

Introductory tenancies

179 Extension of introductory tenancies

(1) Part 5 of the Housing Act 1996 (c. 52) (conduct of tenants) is amended as follows.

(2) In section 125(2) (trial period for introductory tenancy to be one year) for "subject as follows" substitute "but this is subject to subsections (3) and (4) and to section 125A (extension of trial period by 6 months)."

(3) After section 125 insert—

"125A Extension of trial period by 6 months

(1) If both of the following conditions are met in relation to an introductory tenancy, the trial period is extended by 6 months.

(2) The first condition is that the landlord has served a notice of extension on the tenant at least 8 weeks before the original expiry date.

(3) The second condition is that either—

(a) the tenant has not requested a review under section 125B in accordance with subsection (1) of that section, or

(b) if he has, the decision on the review was to confirm the landlord's decision to extend the trial period.

(4) A notice of extension is a notice—

(a) stating that the landlord has decided that the period for which the tenancy is to be an introductory tenancy should be extended by 6 months, and

(b) complying with subsection (5).

(5) A notice of extension must—

(a) set out the reasons for the landlord's decision, and

(b) inform the tenant of his right to request a review of the landlord's decision and of the time within which such a request must be made.

(6) In this section and section 125B "the original expiry date" means the last day of the period of one year that would apply as the trial period apart from this section.

125B Review of decision to extend trial period

(1) A request for review of the landlord's decision that the trial period for an introductory tenancy should be extended under section 125A must be made before the end of the period of 14 days beginning with the day on which the notice of extension is served.

(2) On a request being duly made to it, the landlord shall review its decision.

(3) The Secretary of State may make provision by regulations as to the procedure to be followed in connection with a review under this section.

Nothing in the following provisions affects the generality of this power.

(4) Provision may be made by regulations—

(a) requiring the decision on review to be made by a person of appropriate seniority who was not involved in the original decision, and

(b) as to the circumstances in which the person concerned is entitled to an oral hearing, and whether and by whom he may be represented at such a hearing.

(5) The landlord shall notify the tenant of the decision on the review.

If the decision is to confirm the original decision, the landlord shall also notify him of the reasons for the decision.

(6) The review shall be carried out and the tenant notified before the original expiry date."

(4) The amendments made by this section do not apply in relation to any tenancy entered into before, or in pursuance of an agreement made before, the day on which this section comes into force.

Right to buy: when exercisable

180 Extension of qualifying period for right to buy

(1) In section 119(1) of the Housing Act 1985 (c. 68) (qualifying period for right to buy) for "two" substitute "five".

(2) In subsection (2)(a) of section 129 of that Act (discount)—

(a) for "two" substitute "five"; and

(b) for "32 per cent" substitute "35 per cent".

(3) In subsection (2)(b) of that section—

(a) for "two", where it appears for the second time, substitute "five"; and

(b) for "44 per cent" substitute "50 per cent".

(4) In subsection (2A)(b) of that section for "two" substitute "five".

(5) The amendments made by this section do not apply in relation to a secure tenancy—

(a) if the tenancy was entered into before, or in pursuance of an agreement made before, the day on which this section comes into force, or

(b) if paragraph (a) does not apply but the tenant is a public sector tenant on that day and does not cease to be such a tenant at any time before serving a notice in respect of the tenancy under section 122 of that Act.

(6) In subsection (5) "public sector tenant" has the same meaning as in Schedule 4 to that Act.

181 Exceptions to the right to buy: determination whether exception for dwelling-house suitable for elderly persons applies

(1) In Schedule 5 to the Housing Act 1985 (exceptions to the right to buy) paragraph 11 (single dwelling-house particularly suitable for elderly persons) is amended as follows.

(2) In sub-paragraph (4) (questions arising under paragraph 11 to be determined by the Secretary of State), for "the Secretary of State" (in both places) substitute "the appropriate tribunal or authority".

(3) After sub-paragraph (5) insert—

"(5A) In this paragraph "the appropriate tribunal or authority" means—

(a) in relation to England, a residential property tribunal; and

(b) in relation to Wales, the Secretary of State.

(5B) Section 231 of the Housing Act 2004 (appeals to Lands Tribunal) does not apply to any decision of a residential property tribunal under this paragraph."

(4) Subsections (5) and (6) apply to any application under paragraph 11(4) in respect of a dwelling-house in England which—

(a) has been made to the Secretary of State before the day on which this section comes into force, and

(b) has not been determined by him before that day.

(5) If the application was made more than 28 days before that day, it is to be determined by the Secretary of State as if the amendments made by this section had not come into force.

(6) Otherwise—

(a) the application is to be determined by a residential property tribunal, and

(b) the Secretary of State must make all such arrangements as he considers necessary for the purpose of, or in connection with, enabling it to be so determined.

182 Exceptions to the right to buy: houses due to be demolished

(1) In Schedule 5 to the Housing Act 1985 (c. 68) (exceptions to the right to buy) after paragraph 12 insert—

"13 Dwelling-house due to be demolished within 24 months

13 (1) The right to buy does not arise if a final demolition notice is in force in respect of the dwelling-house.

(2) A "final demolition notice" is a notice—

(a) stating that the landlord intends to demolish the dwelling-house or (as the case may be) the building containing it ("the relevant premises"),

(b) setting out the reasons why the landlord intends to demolish the relevant premises,

(c) specifying—

(i) the date by which he intends to demolish those premises ("the proposed demolition date"), and

(ii) the date when the notice will cease to be in force (unless extended under paragraph 15),

(d) stating that one of conditions A to C in paragraph 14 is satisfied in relation to the notice (specifying the condition concerned), and

(e) stating that the right to buy does not arise in respect of the dwelling-house while the notice is in force.

(3) If, at the time when the notice is served, there is an existing claim to exercise the right to buy in respect of the dwelling-house, the notice shall (instead of complying with sub-paragraph (2)(e)) state—

(a) that that claim ceases to be effective on the notice coming into force, but

(b) that section 138C confers a right to compensation in respect of certain expenditure,

and the notice shall also give details of that right to compensation and of how it may be exercised.

(4) The proposed demolition date must fall within the period of 24 months beginning with the date of service of the notice on the tenant.

(5) For the purposes of this paragraph a final demolition notice is in force in respect of the dwelling-house concerned during the period of 24 months mentioned in sub-paragraph (4), but this is subject to—

(a) compliance with the conditions in sub-paragraphs (6) and (7) (in a case to which they apply), and

(b) the provisions of paragraph 15(1) to (7).

(6) If—

(a) the dwelling-house is contained in a building which contains one or more other dwelling-houses, and

(b) the landlord intends to demolish the whole of the building,

the landlord must have served a final demolition notice on the occupier of each of the dwelling-houses contained in it (whether addressed to him by name or just as "the occupier").

An accidental omission to serve a final demolition notice on one or more occupiers does not prevent the condition in this sub-paragraph from being satisfied.

(7) A notice stating that the landlord intends to demolish the relevant premises must have appeared—

(a) in a local or other newspaper circulating in the locality in which those premises are situated (other than one published by the landlord), and
(b) in any newspaper published by the landlord, and
(c) on the landlord's website (if he has one).

(8) The notice mentioned in sub-paragraph (7) must contain the following information—
(a) sufficient information to enable identification of the premises that the landlord intends to demolish;
(b) the reasons why the landlord intends to demolish those premises;
(c) the proposed demolition date;
(d) the date when any final demolition notice or notices relating to those premises will cease to be in force, unless extended or revoked under paragraph 15;
(e) that the right to buy will not arise in respect of those premises or (as the case may be) in respect of any dwelling-house contained in them;
(f) that there may be a right to compensation under section 138C in respect of certain expenditure incurred in respect of any existing claim.

(9) In this paragraph and paragraphs 14 and 15 any reference to the landlord, in the context of a reference to an intention or decision on his part to demolish or not to demolish any premises, or of a reference to the acquisition or transfer of any premises, includes a reference to a superior landlord.

14 (1) A final demolition notice may only be served for the purposes of paragraph 13 if one of conditions A to C is satisfied in relation to the notice.

(2) Condition A is that the proposed demolition of the dwelling-house does not form part of a scheme involving the demolition of other premises.

(3) Condition B is that—
(a) the proposed demolition of the dwelling-house does form part of a scheme involving the demolition of other premises, but
(b) none of those other premises needs to be acquired by the landlord in order for the landlord to be able to demolish them.

(4) Condition C is that—
(a) the proposed demolition of the dwelling-house does form part of a scheme involving the demolition of other premises, and
(b) one or more of those premises need to be acquired by the landlord in order for the landlord to be able to demolish them, but
(c) in each case arrangements for their acquisition are in place.

(5) For the purposes of sub-paragraph (4) arrangements for the acquisition of any premises are in place if—
(a) an agreement under which the landlord is entitled to acquire the premises is in force, or

(b) a notice to treat has been given in respect of the premises under section 5 of the Compulsory Purchase Act 1965, or

(c) a vesting declaration has been made in respect of the premises under section 4 of the Compulsory Purchase (Vesting Declarations) Act 1981.

(6) In this paragraph—

"premises" means premises of any description;

"scheme" includes arrangements of any description.

15 (1) The Secretary of State may, on an application by the landlord, give a direction extending or further extending the period during which a final demolition notice is in force in respect of a dwelling-house.

(2) A direction under sub-paragraph (1) may provide that any extension of that period is not to have effect unless the landlord complies with such requirements relating to the service of further notices as are specified in the direction.

(3) A direction under sub-paragraph (1) may only be given at a time when the demolition notice is in force (whether by virtue of paragraph 13 or this paragraph).

(4) If, while a final demolition notice is in force, the landlord decides not to demolish the dwelling-house in question, he must, as soon as is reasonably practicable, serve a notice ("a revocation notice") on the tenant which informs him—

(a) of the landlord's decision, and

(b) that the demolition notice is revoked as from the date of service of the revocation notice.

(5) If, while a final demolition notice is in force, it appears to the Secretary of State that the landlord has no intention of demolishing the dwelling-house in question, he may serve a notice ("a revocation notice") on the tenant which informs him—

(a) of the Secretary of State's conclusion, and

(b) that the demolition notice is revoked as from the date of service of the revocation notice.

Section 169 applies in relation to the Secretary of State's power under this sub-paragraph as it applies in relation to his powers under the provisions mentioned in subsection (1) of that section.

(6) But the Secretary of State may not serve a revocation notice unless he has previously served a notice on the landlord which informs him of the Secretary of State's intention to serve the revocation notice.

(7) Where a revocation notice is served under sub-paragraph (4) or (5), the demolition notice ceases to be in force as from the date of service of the revocation notice.

(8) Once a final demolition notice has (for any reason) ceased to be in force in respect of a dwelling-house without it being demolished, no further final demolition notice may be served in respect of it during the period of 5 years following the time when the notice ceases to be in force, unless—

(a) it is served with the consent of the Secretary of State, and
(b) it states that it is so served.

(9) The Secretary of State's consent under sub-paragraph (8) may be given subject to compliance with such conditions as he may specify.

16 (1) Any notice under paragraph 13 or 15 may be served on a person—
(a) by delivering it to him, by leaving it at his proper address or by sending it by post to him at that address, or
(b) if the person is a body corporate, by serving it in accordance with paragraph (a) on the secretary of the body.

(2) For the purposes of this section and section 7 of the Interpretation Act 1978 (service of documents by post) the proper address of a person on whom a notice is to be served shall be—
(a) in the case of a body corporate or its secretary, that of the registered or principal office of the body, and
(b) in any other case, the last known address of that person."

(2) The amendment made by this section does not apply in any case where the tenant's notice under section 122 of that Act (notice claiming to exercise right to buy) was served before the day on which this section comes into force.

183 Right to buy: claim suspended or terminated by demolition notice

(1) In section 138 of the Housing Act 1985 (c. 68) (duty of landlord to convey freehold or grant lease), after the subsection (2D) inserted by section 193 of this Act, insert—

"(2E) Subsection (1) also has effect subject to—
(a) section 138A(2) (operation of subsection (1) suspended while initial demolition notice is in force), and
(b) section 138B(2) (subsection (1) disapplied where final demolition notice is served)."

(2) After section 138 of that Act insert—

"138A Effect of initial demolition notice served before completion

(1) This section applies where—
(a) an initial demolition notice is served on a secure tenant under Schedule 5A, and
(b) the notice is served on the tenant before the landlord has made to him such a grant as is required by section 138(1) in respect of a claim by the tenant to exercise the right to buy.

(2) In such a case the landlord is not bound to comply with section 138(1), in connection with any such claim by the tenant, so long as the initial demolition notice remains in force under Schedule 5A.

(3) Section 138C provides a right to compensation in certain cases where this section applies.

138B Effect of final demolition notice served before completion

(1) This section applies where—

(a) a secure tenant has claimed to exercise the right to buy, but

(b) before the landlord has made to the tenant such a grant as is required by section 138(1) in respect of the claim, a final demolition notice is served on the tenant under paragraph 13 of Schedule 5.

(2) In such a case—

(a) the tenant's claim ceases to be effective as from the time when the final demolition notice comes into force under that paragraph, and

(b) section 138(1) accordingly does not apply to the landlord, in connection with the tenant's claim, at any time after the notice comes into force.

(3) Section 138C provides a right to compensation in certain cases where this section applies.

138C Compensation where demolition notice served

(1) This section applies where—

(a) a secure tenant has claimed to exercise the right to buy,

(b) before the landlord has made to the tenant such a grant as is required by section 138(1) in respect of the claim, either an initial demolition notice is served on the tenant under Schedule 5A or a final demolition notice is served on him under paragraph 13 of Schedule 5, and

(c) the tenant's claim is established before that notice comes into force under Schedule 5A or paragraph 13 of Schedule 5 (as the case may be).

(2) If, within the period of three months beginning with the date when the notice comes into force ("the operative date"), the tenant serves on the landlord a written notice claiming an amount of compensation under subsection (3), the landlord shall pay that amount to the tenant.

(3) Compensation under this subsection is compensation in respect of expenditure reasonably incurred by the tenant before the operative date in respect of legal and other fees, and other professional costs and expenses, payable in connection with the exercise by him of the right to buy.

(4) A notice under subsection (2) must be accompanied by receipts or other documents showing that the tenant incurred the expenditure in question."

(3) After Schedule 5 to the Act insert, as Schedule 5A, the Schedule set out in Schedule 9 to this Act.

(4) The amendments made by this section do not apply in any case where the tenant's notice under section 122 of the Act (notice claim to exercise right to buy) was served before the day on which this section comes into force.

184 Landlord's notice to complete

(1) Section 140 of the Housing Act 1985 (c. 68) (landlord's first notice to complete) is amended as follows.

(2) In subsection (3) (notice not to be served earlier than twelve months after landlord's notice under section 125 or 146) for "twelve" substitute "three".

(3) The amendment made by this section does not apply in any case where the tenant's notice under section 122 of that Act (notice claiming right to buy) was served before the day on which this section comes into force.

Right to buy: discounts

185 Repayment of discount: periods and amounts applicable

(1) Section 155 of the Housing Act 1985 (repayment of discount on early disposal) is amended in accordance with subsections (2) and (3).

(2) For subsections (2) and (3) substitute—

"(2) In the case of a conveyance or grant in pursuance of the right to buy, the covenant shall be to pay the landlord such sum (if any) as the landlord may demand in accordance with section 155A on the occasion of the first relevant disposal (other than an exempted disposal) which takes place within the period of five years beginning with the conveyance or grant.

(3) In the case of a conveyance or grant in pursuance of the right to acquire on rent to mortgage terms, the covenant shall be to pay the landlord such sum (if any) as the landlord may demand in accordance with section 155B on the occasion of the first relevant disposal (other than an exempted disposal) which takes place within the period of five years beginning with the making of the initial payment."

(3) In subsection (3A) (modifications where tenant has served operative notice of delay) for "three years" substitute "five years".

(4) After section 155 insert—

"155A Amount of discount which may be demanded by landlord: right to buy

(1) For the purposes of the covenant mentioned in section 155(2), the landlord may demand such sum as he considers appropriate, up to and including the maximum amount specified in this section.

(2) The maximum amount which may be demanded by the landlord is a percentage of the price or premium paid for the first relevant disposal which is equal to the discount to which the secure tenant was entitled, where the discount is expressed as a percentage of the value which under section 127 was taken as the value of the dwelling-house at the relevant time.

(3) But for each complete year which has elapsed after the conveyance or grant and before the disposal the maximum amount which may be demanded by the landlord is reduced by one-fifth.

(4) This section is subject to section 155C.

155B Amount of discount which may be demanded by landlord: right to acquire on rent to mortgage terms

(1) For the purposes of the covenant mentioned in section 155(3), the landlord may demand such sum as he considers appropriate, up to and including the maximum amount specified in this section.

(2) The maximum amount which may be demanded by the landlord is the discount (if any) to which the tenant was entitled on the making of—

(a) the initial payment,

(b) any interim payment made before the disposal, or

(c) the final payment if so made,

reduced, in each case, by one-fifth for each complete year which has elapsed after the making of the initial payment and before the disposal."

(5) The amendments made by this section do not apply in any case where the tenant's notice under section 122 of the Act (notice claiming to exercise right to buy) was served before the day on which this section comes into force.

(6) Subsection (7), however, applies in any such case if the first relevant disposal to which the covenant for repayment of discount applies takes place on or after the day on which this section comes into force.

(7) In the following provisions—

(a) section 155(2) and (3) of the Housing Act 1985 (c. 68) (as it has effect without the amendments made by this section), and

(b) any covenant for repayment of discount,

any reference (however expressed) to a person being liable to pay an amount to the landlord on demand is to be read as a reference to his being liable to pay to the landlord so much of that amount (if any) as the landlord may demand.

(8) In subsections (6) and (7) "covenant for repayment of discount" means the covenant contained in a conveyance or grant in accordance with section 155 of that Act.

186 Repayment of discount: increase attributable to home improvements to be disregarded

(1) After section 155B of the Housing Act 1985 (c. 68) (inserted by section 185 of this Act) insert—

"155C Increase attributable to home improvements

(1) In calculating the maximum amount which may be demanded by the landlord under section 155A, such amount (if any) of the price or premium paid for the disposal which is attributable to improvements made to the dwelling-house—

(a) by the person by whom the disposal is, or is to be, made, and

(b) after the conveyance or grant and before the disposal,

shall be disregarded.

(2) The amount to be disregarded under this section shall be such amount as may be agreed between the parties or determined by the district valuer.

(3) The district valuer shall not be required by virtue of this section to make a determination for the purposes of this section unless—

(a) it is reasonably practicable for him to do so; and

(b) his reasonable costs in making the determination are paid by the person by whom the disposal is, or is to be, made.

(4) If the district valuer does not make a determination for the purposes of this section (and in default of an agreement), no amount is required to be disregarded under this section."

(2) In section 181 of that Act (jurisdiction of county court) for "and 158" substitute ", 155C and 158".

187 Deferred resale agreements

(1) After section 163 of the Housing Act 1985 insert—

"163A Treatment of deferred resale agreements for purposes of section 155

(1) If a secure tenant or his successor in title enters into an agreement within subsection (3), any liability arising under the covenant required by section 155 shall be determined as if a relevant disposal which is not an exempted disposal had occurred at the appropriate time.

(2) In subsection (1) "the appropriate time" means—

(a) the time when the agreement is entered into, or

(b) if it was made before the beginning of the discount repayment period, immediately after the beginning of that period.

(3) An agreement is within this subsection if it is an agreement between the secure tenant or his successor in title and any other person—

(a) which is made (expressly or impliedly) in contemplation of, or in connection with, the tenant exercising, or having exercised, the right to buy,

(b) which is made before the end of the discount repayment period, and

(c) under which a relevant disposal (other than an exempted disposal) is or may be required to be made to any person after the end of that period.

(4) Such an agreement is within subsection (3)—

(a) whether or not the date on which the disposal is to take place is specified in the agreement, and

(b) whether or not any requirement to make the disposal is or may be made subject to the fulfilment of any condition.

(5) The Secretary of State may by order provide—

(a) for subsection (1) to apply to agreements of any description specified in the order in addition to those within subsection (3);

(b) for subsection (1) not to apply to agreements of any description so specified to which it would otherwise apply.

(6) An order under subsection (5)—

(a) may make different provision with respect to different cases or descriptions of case; and

(b) shall be made by statutory instrument which shall be subject to annulment in pursuance of a resolution of either House of Parliament.

(7) In this section—

"agreement" includes arrangement;

"the discount repayment period" means the period of three or five years that applies for the purposes of section 155(2) or (3) (depending on whether the tenant's notice under section 122 was given before or on or after the date of the coming into force of section 185 of the Housing Act 2004)."

(2) The amendment made by this section does not apply in relation to any agreement or arrangement made before the day on which this section comes into force.

Right to buy: landlord's right of first refusal

188 Right of first refusal for landlord etc.

(1) After section 156 of the Housing Act 1985 (c. 68) insert—

"156A Right of first refusal for landlord etc.

(1) A conveyance of the freehold or grant of a lease in pursuance of this Part shall contain the following covenant, which shall be binding on the secure tenant and his successors in title.

This is subject to subsection (8).

(2) The covenant shall be to the effect that, until the end of the period of ten years beginning with the conveyance or grant, there will be no relevant disposal which is not an exempted disposal, unless the prescribed conditions have been satisfied in relation to that or a previous such disposal.

(3) In subsection (2) "the prescribed conditions" means such conditions as are prescribed by regulations under this section at the time when the conveyance or grant is made.

(4) The Secretary of State may by regulations prescribe such conditions as he considers appropriate for and in connection with conferring on—

(a) a landlord who has conveyed a freehold or granted a lease to a person ("the former tenant") in pursuance of this Part, or

(b) such other person as is determined in accordance with the regulations,

a right of first refusal to have a disposal within subsection (5) made to him for such consideration as is mentioned in section 158.

(5) The disposals within this subsection are—

(a) a reconveyance or conveyance of the dwelling-house; and

(b) a surrender or assignment of the lease.

(6) Regulations under this section may, in particular, make provision—

(a) for the former tenant to offer to make such a disposal to such person or persons as may be prescribed;

(b) for a prescribed recipient of such an offer to be able either to accept the offer or to nominate some other person as the person by whom the offer may be accepted;

(c) for the person who may be so nominated to be either a person of a prescribed description or a person whom the prescribed recipient considers, having regard to any prescribed matters, to be a more appropriate person to accept the offer;

(d) for a prescribed recipient making such a nomination to give a notification of the nomination to the person nominated, the former tenant and any other prescribed person;

(e) for authorising a nominated person to accept the offer and for determining which acceptance is to be effective where the offer is accepted by more than one person;

(f) for the period within which the offer may be accepted or within which any other prescribed step is to be, or may be, taken;

(g) for the circumstances in which the right of first refusal lapses (whether following the service of a notice to complete or otherwise) with the result that the former tenant is able to make a disposal on the open market;

(h) for the manner in which any offer, acceptance or notification is to be communicated.

(7) In subsection (6) any reference to the former tenant is a reference to the former tenant or his successor in title.

Nothing in that subsection affects the generality of subsection (4).

(8) In a case to which section 157(1) applies—

(a) the conveyance or grant may contain a covenant such as is mentioned in subsections (1) and (2) above instead of a covenant such as is mentioned in section 157(1), but

(b) it may do so only if the Secretary of State or, where the conveyance or grant is executed by a housing association within section 6A(3) or (4), the Relevant Authority consents.

(9) Consent may be given in relation to—

(a) a particular disposal, or

(b) disposals by a particular landlord or disposals by landlords generally,

and may, in any case, be given subject to conditions.

(10) Regulations under this section—

(a) may make different provision with respect to different cases or descriptions of case; and

(b) shall be made by statutory instrument which shall be subject to annulment in pursuance of a resolution of either House of Parliament.

(11) The limitation imposed by a covenant within subsection (2) (whether the covenant is imposed in pursuance of subsection (1) or (8)) is a local land charge.

(12) The Chief Land Registrar must enter in the register of title a restriction reflecting the limitation imposed by any such covenant."

(2) In section 157 of that Act (restriction on disposal of dwelling-houses in National Parks etc.)—

(a) in subsection (1), after "the conveyance or grant may" insert "(subject to section 156A(8)";

(b) in subsection (2), omit ", subject to subsection (4),"; and

(c) omit subsections (4) and (5) (which provide for a landlord's right of first refusal).

(3) In section 158 of that Act (consideration for conveyance or surrender under section 157)—

(a) in the sidenote, for "reconveyance or surrender under section 157" substitute "disposal under section 156A";

(b) for subsection (1) substitute—

"(1) The consideration for such a disposal as is mentioned in section 156A(4) shall be such amount as may be agreed between the parties, or determined by the district valuer, as being the amount which is to be taken to be the value of the dwelling-house at the time when the offer is made (as determined in accordance with regulations under that section).";

(c) in subsection (2), for "or surrendered" substitute ", conveyed, surrendered or assigned";

(d) in subsection (3), for "the landlord accepts the offer," substitute "the offer is accepted in accordance with regulations under section 156A,"; and

(e) in subsection (4), for "to reconvey or surrender" substitute "(as determined in accordance with regulations under section 156A)."

(4) In section 162 of that Act (exempted disposals which end liability under covenants), after paragraph (a) insert—

"(aa) the covenant required by section 156A (right of first refusal for landlord etc.) is not binding on the person to whom the disposal is made or any successor in title of his, and that covenant ceases to apply in relation to the property disposed of, and".

(5) The amendments made by this section do not apply in relation to a conveyance of the freehold or grant of a lease in pursuance of Part 5 of that Act if the notice under section 122 of the Act (tenant's notice claiming to exercise right to buy) was served before the day on which this section comes into force.

(6) Accordingly, nothing in this section affects—

(a) the operation of a limitation contained in such a conveyance or grant in accordance with section 157(4) of that Act, or

(b) the operation, in relation to such a limitation, of section 157(6) (so far as it renders a disposal in breach of covenant void) or section 158 (consideration payable) of that Act.

Right to buy: information

189 Information to help tenants decide whether to exercise right to buy etc.

(1) After section 121 of the Housing Act 1985 (c. 68) insert—

"121AA Information to help tenants decide whether to exercise right to buy etc.

(1) Every body which lets dwelling-houses under secure tenancies shall prepare a document that contains information for its secure tenants about such matters as are specified in an order made by the Secretary of State.

(2) The matters that may be so specified are matters which the Secretary of State considers that it would be desirable for secure tenants to have information about when considering whether to exercise the right to buy or the right to acquire on rent to mortgage terms.

(3) The information contained in the document shall be restricted to information about the specified matters, and the information about those matters—

(a) shall be such as the body concerned considers appropriate, but

(b) shall be in a form which the body considers best suited to explaining those matters in simple terms.

(4) Once a body has prepared the document required by subsection (1), it shall revise it as often as it considers necessary in order to ensure that the information contained in it—

(a) is kept up to date so far as is reasonably practicable, and

(b) reflects any changes in the matters for the time being specified in an order under this section.

(5) An order under this section shall be made by statutory instrument which shall be subject to annulment in pursuance of a resolution of either House of Parliament.

121B Provision of information

(1) This section sets out when the document prepared by a body under section 121AA is to be published or otherwise made available.

(2) The body shall—

(a) publish the document (whether in its original or a revised form), and

(b) supply copies of it to the body's secure tenants,

at such times as may be prescribed by, and otherwise in accordance with, an order made by the Secretary of State.

(3) The body shall make copies of the current version of the document available to be supplied, free of charge, to persons requesting them.

(4) The copies must be made available for that purpose—

(a) at the body's principal offices, and

(b) at such other places as it considers appropriate,

at reasonable hours.

(5) The body shall take such steps as it considers appropriate to bring to the attention of its secure tenants the fact that copies of the current version of the document can be obtained free of charge from the places where, and at the times when, they are made available in accordance with subsection (4).

(6) In this section any reference to the current version of the document is to the version of the document that was last published by the body in accordance with subsection (2)(a).

(7) An order under this section shall be made by statutory instrument which shall be subject to annulment in pursuance of a resolution of either House of Parliament."

(2) In section 104(1) of that Act (provision of information about tenancies), in paragraph (b) (information about Part 4 and Part 5), omit "and Part V (the right to buy)".

Right to buy: termination of rent to mortgage scheme

190 Termination of rent to mortgage scheme

(1) Before section 143 of the Housing Act 1985 (c. 68) insert—

"142A Termination of the right to acquire on rent to mortgage terms

(1) As from the termination date, the right to acquire on rent to mortgage terms is not exercisable except in pursuance of a notice served under section 144 before that date.

(2) In this section "the termination date" means the date falling 8 months after the date of the passing of the Housing Act 2004."

(2) In section 143(1) of that Act after "sections" insert "142A,".

(3) In section 144(1) of that Act for "A secure tenant" substitute "Subject to section 142A, a secure tenant".

Suspension of certain rights in connection with anti-social behaviour

191 Secure tenancies: withholding of consent to mutual exchange

(1) In Schedule 3 to the Housing Act 1985 (c. 68) (grounds for withholding consent to assignment by way of exchange) after Ground 2 insert—

"Ground 2A

Either—

(a) a relevant order or suspended Ground 2 or 14 possession order is in force, or

(b) an application is pending before any court for a relevant order, a demotion order or a Ground 2 or 14 possession order to be made,

in respect of the tenant or the proposed assignee or a person who is residing with either of them.

A "relevant order" means—

an injunction under section 152 of the Housing Act 1996 (injunctions against anti-social behaviour);

an injunction to which a power of arrest is attached by virtue of section 153 of that Act (other injunctions against anti-social behaviour);

an injunction under section 153A, 153B or 153D of that Act (injunctions against anti-social behaviour on application of certain social landlords);

an anti-social behaviour order under section 1 of the Crime and Disorder Act 1998; or

an injunction to which a power of arrest is attached by virtue of section 91 of the Anti-social Behaviour Act 2003.

A "demotion order" means a demotion order under section 82A of this Act or section 6A of the Housing Act 1988.

A "Ground 2 or 14 possession order" means an order for possession under Ground 2 in Schedule 2 to this Act or Ground 14 in Schedule 2 to the Housing Act 1988.

Where the tenancy of the tenant or the proposed assignee is a joint tenancy, any reference to that person includes (where the context permits) a reference to any of the joint tenants."

(2) The amendment made by this section applies in relation to applications for consent under section 92 of that Act (assignments by way of exchange) which are made on or after the day on which this section comes into force.

192 Right to buy: suspension by court order

(1) In section 121 of the Housing Act 1985 (circumstances in which right to buy cannot be exercised), after subsection (2) insert—

"(3) The right to buy cannot be exercised at any time during the suspension period under an order made under section 121A in respect of the secure tenancy."

(2) After section 121 of that Act insert—

"121A Order suspending right to buy because of anti-social behaviour

(1) The court may, on the application of the landlord under a secure tenancy, make a suspension order in respect of the tenancy.

(2) A suspension order is an order providing that the right to buy may not be exercised in relation to the dwelling-house during such period as is specified in the order ("the suspension period").

(3) The court must not make a suspension order unless it is satisfied—

(a) that the tenant, or a person residing in or visiting the dwelling-house, has engaged or threatened to engage in conduct to which section 153A or 153B of the Housing Act 1996 applies (anti-social behaviour or use of premises for unlawful purposes), and

(b) that it is reasonable to make the order.

(4) When deciding whether it is reasonable to make the order, the court must consider, in particular—

(a) whether it is desirable for the dwelling-house to be managed by the landlord during the suspension period; and

(b) where the conduct mentioned in subsection (3)(a) consists of conduct by a person which is capable of causing nuisance or annoyance, the effect that the conduct (or the threat of it) has had on other persons, or would have if repeated.

(5) Where a suspension order is made—

(a) any existing claim to exercise the right to buy in relation to the dwelling-house ceases to be effective as from the beginning of the suspension period, and

(b) section 138(1) shall not apply to the landlord, in connection with such a claim, at any time after the beginning of that period, but

(c) the order does not affect the computation of any period in accordance with Schedule 4.

(6) The court may, on the application of the landlord, make (on one or more occasions) a further order which extends the suspension period under the suspension order by such period as is specified in the further order.

(7) The court must not make such a further order unless it is satisfied—

(a) that, since the making of the suspension order (or the last order under subsection (6)), the tenant, or a person residing in or visiting the dwelling-house, has engaged or threatened to engage in conduct to which section 153A or 153B of the Housing Act 1996 applies, and

(b) that it is reasonable to make the further order.

(8) When deciding whether it is reasonable to make such a further order, the court must consider, in particular—

(a) whether it is desirable for the dwelling-house to be managed by the landlord during the further period of suspension; and

(b) where the conduct mentioned in subsection (7)(a) consists of conduct by a person which is capable of causing nuisance or annoyance, the effect that the conduct (or the threat of it) has had on other persons, or would have if repeated.

(9) In this section any reference to the tenant under a secure tenancy is, in relation to a joint tenancy, a reference to any of the joint tenants."

(3) Regulations under—

(a) section 171C of that Act (modifications of Part 5 in relation to preserved right to buy), or

(b) section 17 of the Housing Act 1996 (c. 52) (application of that Part in relation to right to acquire dwelling),

may make provision for continuing the effect of a suspension order where the secure tenancy in respect of which the order was made has been replaced by an assured tenancy.

193 Right to buy: suspension of landlord's obligation to complete

(1) In section 138 of the Housing Act 1985 (c. 68) (duty of landlord to convey freehold or grant lease) after subsection (2) insert—

"(2A) Subsection (2B) applies if an application is pending before any court—

(a) for a demotion order or Ground 2 possession order to be made in respect of the tenant, or

(b) for a suspension order to be made in respect of the tenancy.

(2B) The landlord is not bound to comply with subsection (1) until such time (if any) as the application is determined without—

(a) a demotion order or an operative Ground 2 possession order being made in respect of the tenant, or

(b) a suspension order being made in respect of the tenancy,

or the application is withdrawn.

(2C) For the purposes of subsection (2A) and (2B)—

"demotion order" means a demotion order under section 82A;

"Ground 2 possession order" means an order for possession under Ground 2 in Schedule 2;

"operative Ground 2 possession order" means an order made under that Ground which requires possession of the dwelling-house to be given up on a date specified in the order;

"suspension order" means a suspension order under section 121A.

(2D) Subsection (1) has effect subject to section 121A(5) (disapplication of subsection (1) where suspension order is made)."

(2) The amendment made by this section does not apply in any case where the tenant's notice under section 122 of that Act (notice claiming to exercise right to buy) was served before the day on which this section comes into force.

194 Disclosure of information as to orders etc. in respect of anti-social behaviour

(1) Any person may disclose relevant information to a landlord under a secure tenancy if the information is disclosed for the purpose of enabling the landlord—

(a) to decide whether either of the provisions of the Housing Act 1985 (c. 68) mentioned in subsection (2) can be invoked in relation to the tenant under the tenancy; or

(b) to take any appropriate action in relation to the tenant in reliance on either of those provisions.

(2) The provisions are—

(a) Ground 2A in Schedule 3 (withholding of consent to mutual exchange where order in force or application pending in connection with anti-social behaviour), and

(b) section 138(2B) (landlord's obligation to complete suspended while application pending in connection with such behaviour).

(3) In this section—

(a) "relevant information" means information relating to any order or application relevant for the purposes of either of the provisions mentioned in subsection (2), including (in particular) information identifying the person in respect of whom any such order or application has been made;

(b) "secure tenancy" has the meaning given by section 79 of the Housing Act 1985; and

(c) any reference to the tenant under a secure tenancy is, in relation to a joint tenancy, a reference to any of the joint tenants.

(4) Regulations under—

(a) section 171C of the Housing Act 1985 (modifications of Part 5 in relation to preserved right to buy), or

(b) section 17 of the Housing Act 1996 (c. 52) (application of that Part in relation to right to acquire dwelling),

may make provision corresponding to subsections (1) to (3) of this section so far as those subsections relate to section 138(2B) of the Housing Act 1985.

CHAPTER 2

DISPOSALS ATTRACTING DISCOUNTS OTHER THAN UNDER RIGHT TO BUY

Disposals by local authorities

195 Repayment of discount: periods and amounts applicable

(1) Section 35 of the Housing Act 1985 (repayment of discount on early disposal) is amended in accordance with subsections (2) and (3).

(2) In subsection (2) for the words from "to pay to the authority" to the end of the subsection substitute "to the following effect."

(3) After subsection (2) insert—

"(3) The covenant shall be to pay to the authority such sum (if any) as the authority may demand in accordance with subsection (4) on the occasion of the first relevant disposal (other than an exempted disposal) which takes place within the period of five years beginning with the conveyance, grant or assignment.

(4) The authority may demand such sum as they consider appropriate, up to and including the maximum amount specified in this section.

(5) The maximum amount which may be demanded by the authority is a percentage of the price or premium paid for the first relevant disposal which is equal to the percentage discount given to the purchaser in respect of the disposal of the house under section 32.

(6) But for each complete year which has elapsed after the conveyance, grant or assignment and before the first relevant disposal the maximum amount which may be demanded by the landlord is reduced by one-fifth.

(7) Subsections (4) to (6) are subject to section 35A."

(4) The amendments made by this section do not apply in any case where—

(a) the purchaser has accepted an offer for the disposal of the house from the authority, or

(b) the authority has accepted an offer for the disposal of the house from the purchaser,

before the day on which this section comes into force.

(5) Subsection (6), however, applies in any such case if the first relevant disposal by the purchaser to which the covenant for repayment of discount applies takes place on or after the day on which this section comes into force.

(6) In the following provisions—

(a) section 35(2) of the Housing Act 1985 (c. 68) (as it has effect without the amendments made by this section), and

(b) any covenant for repayment of discount,

any reference (however expressed) to a person being liable to pay an amount to the authority on demand is to be read as a reference to his being liable to pay to the authority so much of that amount (if any) as the authority may demand.

(7) In subsections (5) and (6) "covenant for repayment of discount" means the covenant contained in a conveyance, grant or assignment in accordance with section 35 of that Act.

196 Repayment of discount: increase attributable to home improvements to be disregarded

After section 35 of the Housing Act 1985 insert—

"35A Increase in value of house attributable to home improvements

(1) In calculating the maximum amount which may be demanded by the authority under section 35, such amount (if any) of the price or premium paid for the first relevant disposal which is attributable to improvements made to the house—

(a) by the person by whom the disposal is, or is to be, made, and

(b) after the conveyance, grant or assignment and before the disposal,

shall be disregarded.

(2) The amount to be disregarded under this section shall be such amount as may be agreed between the parties or determined by the district valuer.

(3) The district valuer shall not be required by virtue of this section to make a determination for the purposes of this section unless—

(a) it is reasonably practicable for him to do so; and

(b) his reasonable costs in making the determination are paid by the person by whom the disposal is, or is to be, made.

(4) If the district valuer does not make a determination for the purposes of this section (and in default of an agreement), no amount is required to be disregarded under this section."

197 Local authority's right of first refusal

(1) After section 36 of the Housing Act 1985 (c. 68) insert—

"36A Right of first refusal for local authority

(1) This section applies where, on a disposal of a house under section 32, a discount is given to the purchaser by the local authority in accordance with a consent given by the Secretary of State under subsection (2) of that section; but this section does not apply in any such case if the consent so provides.

(2) On the disposal the conveyance, grant or assignment shall contain the following covenant, which shall be binding on the purchaser and his successors in title.

(3) The covenant shall be to the effect that, until the end of the period of ten years beginning with the conveyance, grant or assignment, there will be no relevant disposal which is not an exempted disposal, unless the prescribed conditions have been satisfied in relation to that or a previous such disposal.

(4) In subsection (3) "the prescribed conditions" means such conditions as are prescribed by regulations under this section at the time when the conveyance, grant or assignment is made.

(5) The Secretary of State may by regulations prescribe such conditions as he considers appropriate for and in connection with conferring on—

- (a) a local authority which have made a disposal as mentioned in subsection (1), or
- (b) such other person as is determined in accordance with the regulations,

a right of first refusal to have a disposal within subsection (6) made to them or him for such consideration as is mentioned in section 36B.

(6) The disposals within this subsection are—

- (a) a reconveyance or conveyance of the house; and
- (b) a surrender or assignment of the lease.

(7) Regulations under this section may, in particular, make provision—

- (a) for the purchaser to offer to make such a disposal to such person or persons as may be prescribed;
- (b) for a prescribed recipient of such an offer to be able either to accept the offer or to nominate some other person as the person by whom the offer may be accepted;
- (c) for the person who may be so nominated to be either a person of a prescribed description or a person whom the prescribed recipient considers, having regard to any prescribed matters, to be a more appropriate person to accept the offer;
- (d) for a prescribed recipient making such a nomination to give a notification of the nomination to the person nominated, the purchaser and any other prescribed person;
- (e) for authorising a nominated person to accept the offer and for determining which acceptance is to be effective where the offer is accepted by more than one person;
- (f) for the period within which the offer may be accepted or within which any other prescribed step is to be, or may be, taken;

(g) for the circumstances in which the right of first refusal lapses (whether following the service of a notice to complete or otherwise) with the result that the purchaser is able to make a disposal on the open market;

(h) for the manner in which any offer, acceptance or notification is to be communicated.

(8) In subsection (7) any reference to the purchaser is a reference to the purchaser or his successor in title.

Nothing in that subsection affects the generality of subsection (5).

(9) Regulations under this section—

(a) may make different provision with respect to different cases or descriptions of case; and

(b) shall be made by statutory instrument which shall be subject to annulment in pursuance of a resolution of either House of Parliament.

(10) The limitation imposed by a covenant within subsection (3) is a local land charge.

(11) The Chief Land Registrar must enter in the register of title a restriction reflecting the limitation imposed by any such covenant.

36B Consideration payable for disposal under section 36A

(1) The consideration for a disposal made in respect of a right of first refusal as mentioned in section 36A(5) shall be such amount as may be agreed between the parties, or determined by the district valuer, as being the amount which is to be taken to be the value of the house at the time when the offer is made (as determined in accordance with regulations under that section).

(2) That value shall be taken to be the price which, at that time, the interest to be reconveyed, conveyed, surrendered or assigned would realise if sold on the open market by a willing vendor, on the assumption that any liability under the covenant required by section 35 (repayment of discount on early disposal) would be discharged by the vendor.

(3) If the offer is accepted in accordance with regulations under section 36A, no payment shall be required in pursuance of any such covenant as is mentioned in subsection (2), but the consideration shall be reduced, subject to subsection (4), by such amount (if any) as, on a disposal made at the time the offer was made, being a relevant disposal which is not an exempted disposal, would fall to be paid under that covenant.

(4) Where there is a charge on the house having priority over the charge to secure payment of the sum due under the covenant mentioned in subsection (2), the consideration shall not be reduced under subsection (3) below the amount necessary to discharge the outstanding sum secured by the first-mentioned charge at the date of the offer (as determined in accordance with regulations under section 36A)."

(2) In section 33(2) of the Housing Act 1985 (c. 68) (covenants and conditions which may be imposed), after "But" insert ", subject to sections 36A and 37,".

(3) In section 37(1) of that Act (restriction on disposal of dwelling-houses in National Parks etc.), after "restriction on assignment)" insert "or a covenant as mentioned in section 36A(3) (right of first refusal for local authority)".

(4) In section 41 of that Act (exempted disposals which end liability under covenants), after paragraph (a) insert—

"(aa) the covenant required by section 36A (right of first refusal for local authority) is not binding on the person to whom the disposal is made or any successor in title of his, and that covenant ceases to apply in relation to the property disposed of, and".

(5) The amendments made by this section do not apply in relation to a disposal under section 32 of that Act if—

(a) the purchaser has accepted an offer for the disposal of the house from the authority, or

(b) the authority has accepted an offer for the disposal of the house from the purchaser,

before the day on which this section comes into force.

198 Deferred resale agreements

(1) After section 39 of the Housing Act 1985 insert—

"39A Treatment of deferred resale agreements for purposes of section 35

(1) If a purchaser or his successor in title enters into an agreement within subsection (3), any liability arising under the covenant required by section 35 shall be determined as if a relevant disposal which is not an exempted disposal had occurred at the appropriate time.

(2) In subsection (1) "the appropriate time" means—

(a) the time when the agreement is entered into, or

(b) if it was made before the beginning of the discount repayment period, immediately after the beginning of that period.

(3) An agreement is within this subsection if it is an agreement between the purchaser or his successor in title and any other person—

(a) which is made (expressly or impliedly) in contemplation of, or in connection with, a disposal to be made, or made, under section 32,

(b) which is made before the end of the discount repayment period, and

(c) under which a relevant disposal (other than an exempted disposal) is or may be required to be made to any person after the end of that period.

(4) Such an agreement is within subsection (3)—

(a) whether or not the date on which the relevant disposal is to take place is specified in the agreement, and

(b) whether or not any requirement to make that disposal is or may be made subject to the fulfilment of any condition.

(5) The Secretary of State may by order provide—

(a) for subsection (1) to apply to agreements of any description specified in the order in addition to those within subsection (3);

(b) for subsection (1) not to apply to agreements of any description so specified to which it would otherwise apply.

(6) An order under subsection (5)—

(a) may make different provision with respect to different cases or descriptions of case; and

(b) shall be made by statutory instrument which shall be subject to annulment in pursuance of a resolution of either House of Parliament.

(7) In this section—

"agreement" includes arrangement;

"the discount repayment period" means the period of 3 years that applies for the purposes of section 35(2) or the period of five years that applies for the purposes of section 35(3) (depending on whether an offer such as is mentioned in section 195(4) of the Housing Act 2004 was made before or on or after the coming into force of that section)."

(2) The amendment made by this section does not apply in relation to any agreement or arrangement made before the day on which this section comes into force.

Disposals by registered social landlords

199 Repayment of discount: periods and amounts payable

(1) For section 11 of the Housing Act 1996 (c. 52) substitute—

"11 Covenant for repayment of discount on disposal

(1) Where on a disposal of a house by a registered social landlord, in accordance with a consent given by the Relevant Authority under section 9, a discount has been given to the purchaser, and the consent does not provide otherwise, the conveyance, grant or assignment shall contain a covenant binding on the purchaser and his successors in title to the following effect.

(2) The covenant shall be to pay to the landlord such sum (if any) as the landlord may demand in accordance with subsection (3) on the occasion of the first relevant disposal which is not an exempted disposal and which takes place within the period of five years beginning with the conveyance, grant or assignment.

(3) The landlord may demand such sum as he considers appropriate, up to and including the maximum amount specified in this section.

(4) The maximum amount which may be demanded by the landlord is a percentage of the price or premium paid for the first relevant disposal which is equal to the percentage discount given to the purchaser in respect of the disposal of the house by the landlord.

(5) But for each complete year which has elapsed after the conveyance, grant or assignment and before the first relevant disposal the maximum amount which may be demanded by the landlord is reduced by one-fifth.

(6) Subsections (3) to (5) are subject to section 11A.

11A Increase in value of house attributable to home improvements to be disregarded

(1) In calculating the maximum amount which may be demanded by the landlord under section 11, such amount (if any) of the price or premium paid for the first relevant disposal which is attributable to improvements made to the house—

(a) by the person by whom the disposal is, or is to be, made, and

(b) after the conveyance, grant or assignment and before the disposal,

shall be disregarded.

(2) The amount to be disregarded under this section shall be such amount as may be agreed between the parties or determined by the district valuer.

(3) The district valuer shall not be required by virtue of this section to make a determination for the purposes of this section unless—

(a) it is reasonably practicable for him to do so; and

(b) his reasonable costs in making the determination are paid by the person by whom the disposal is, or is to be, made.

(4) If the district valuer does not make a determination for the purposes of this section (and in default of an agreement), no amount is required to be disregarded under this section.

11B Liability to repay is a charge on the house

(1) The liability that may arise under the covenant required by section 11 is a charge on the house, taking effect as if it had been created by deed expressed to be by way of legal mortgage.

(2) Where there is a relevant disposal which is an exempted disposal by virtue of section 15(4)(d) or (e) (compulsory disposal or disposal of yard, garden, etc.)—

(a) the covenant required by section 11 is not binding on the person to whom the disposal is made or any successor in title of his, and

(b) the covenant and the charge taking effect by virtue of this section cease to apply in relation to the property disposed of."

(2) In section 12, for "section 11" in each place where it occurs substitute "section 11B".

(3) The amendments made by this section do not apply in any case where—

(a) the purchaser has accepted an offer for the disposal of the house from the landlord, or

(b) the landlord has accepted an offer for the disposal of the house from the purchaser,

before the day on which this section comes into force.

(4) Subsection (5), however, applies in any such case if the first relevant disposal by the purchaser to which the covenant for repayment of discount applies takes place on or after the day on which this section comes into force.

(5) In the following provisions—

(a) section 11(2) of the Housing Act 1996 (c. 52) (as it has effect without the amendments made by this section), and

(b) any covenant for repayment of discount,

any reference (however expressed) to a person being liable to pay an amount to the landlord on demand is to be read as a reference to his being liable to pay to the landlord so much of that amount (if any) as the landlord may demand.

(6) In subsections (4) and (5) "covenant for repayment of discount" means the covenant contained in a conveyance, grant or assignment in accordance with section 11 of that Act.

200 Registered social landlord's right of first refusal

(1) After section 12 of the Housing Act 1996 insert—

"12A Right of first refusal for registered social landlord

(1) Where on a disposal of a house by a registered social landlord, in accordance with a consent given by the Relevant Authority under section 9, a discount has been given to the purchaser, and the consent does not provide otherwise, the conveyance, grant or assignment shall contain the following covenant, which shall be binding on the purchaser and his successors in title.

(2) The covenant shall be to the effect that, until the end of the period of ten years beginning with the conveyance, grant or assignment, there will be no relevant disposal which is not an exempted disposal, unless the prescribed conditions have been satisfied in relation to that or a previous such disposal.

(3) In subsection (2) "the prescribed conditions" means such conditions as are prescribed by regulations under this section at the time when the conveyance, grant or assignment is made.

(4) The Secretary of State may by regulations prescribe such conditions as he considers appropriate for and in connection with conferring on—

(a) a registered social landlord which has made a disposal as mentioned in subsection (1), or

(b) such other person as is determined in accordance with the regulations,

a right of first refusal to have a disposal within subsection (5) made to him for such consideration as is mentioned in section 12B.

(5) The disposals within this subsection are—

(a) a reconveyance or conveyance of the house; and

(b) a surrender or assignment of the lease.

(6) Regulations under this section may, in particular, make provision—

(a) for the purchaser to offer to make such a disposal to such person or persons as may be prescribed;

(b) for a prescribed recipient of such an offer to be able either to accept the offer or to nominate some other person as the person by whom the offer may be accepted;

(c) for the person who may be so nominated to be either a person of a prescribed description or a person whom the prescribed recipient considers, having regard to any prescribed matters, to be a more appropriate person to accept the offer;

(d) for a prescribed recipient making such a nomination to give a notification of the nomination to the person nominated, the purchaser and any other prescribed person;

(e) for authorising a nominated person to accept the offer and for determining which acceptance is to be effective where the offer is accepted by more than one person;

(f) for the period within which the offer may be accepted or within which any other prescribed step is to be, or may be, taken;

(g) for the circumstances in which the right of first refusal lapses (whether following the service of a notice to complete or otherwise) with the result that the purchaser is able to make a disposal on the open market;

(h) for the manner in which any offer, acceptance or notification is to be communicated.

(7) In subsection (6) any reference to the purchaser is a reference to the purchaser or his successor in title.

Nothing in that subsection affects the generality of subsection (4).

(8) Regulations under this section—

(a) may make different provision with respect to different cases or descriptions of case; and

(b) shall be made by statutory instrument which shall be subject to annulment in pursuance of a resolution of either House of Parliament.

(9) The limitation imposed by a covenant within subsection (2) is a local land charge.

(10) The Chief Land Registrar must enter in the register of title a restriction reflecting the limitation imposed by any such covenant.

(11) Where there is a relevant disposal which is an exempted disposal by virtue of section 15(4)(d) or (e) (compulsory disposal or disposal of yard, garden, &c)—

(a) the covenant required by this section is not binding on the person to whom the disposal is made or any successor in title of his, and

(b) the covenant ceases to apply in relation to the property disposed of.

12B Consideration payable for disposal under section 12A

(1) The consideration for a disposal made in respect of a right of first refusal as mentioned in section 12A(4) shall be such amount as may be agreed between the parties, or determined by the district valuer, as being the amount which is to be taken to be the value of the house at the time when the offer is made (as determined in accordance with regulations under that section).

(2) That value shall be taken to be the price which, at that time, the interest to be reconveyed, conveyed, surrendered or assigned would realise if sold on the open market by a willing vendor, on the assumption that any liability under the covenant required by section 11 (repayment of discount on early disposal) would be discharged by the vendor.

(3) If the offer is accepted in accordance with regulations under section 12A, no payment shall be required in pursuance of any such covenant as is mentioned in subsection (2), but the consideration shall be reduced, subject to subsection (4), by such amount (if any) as, on a disposal made at the time the offer was made, being a relevant disposal which is not an exempted disposal, would fall to be paid under that covenant.

(4) Where there is a charge on the house having priority over the charge to secure payment of the sum due under the covenant mentioned in subsection (2), the consideration shall not be reduced under subsection (3) below the amount necessary to discharge the outstanding sum secured by the first-mentioned charge at the date of the offer (as determined in accordance with regulations under section 12A)."

(2) In section 13(1) of the Housing Act 1996 (c. 52) (restriction on disposal of houses in National Parks, &c), after "restriction on assignment)" insert "or a covenant as mentioned in section 12A(2) of this Act (right of first refusal for registered social landlord)".

(3) The amendments made by this section do not apply in relation to a disposal under section 8 of that Act if—

(a) the purchaser has accepted an offer for the disposal of the house from the landlord, or

(b) the landlord has accepted an offer for the disposal of the house from the purchaser,

before the day on which this section comes into force.

201 Deferred resale agreements

(1) After section 15 of the Housing Act 1996 insert—

"15A Treatment of deferred resale agreements for purposes of section 11

(1) If a purchaser or his successor in title enters into an agreement within subsection (3), any liability arising under the covenant required by section 11 shall be determined as if a relevant disposal which is not an exempted disposal had occurred at the appropriate time.

(2) In subsection (1) "the appropriate time" means—

(a) the time when the agreement is entered into, or

(b) if it was made before the beginning of the discount repayment period, immediately after the beginning of that period.

(3) An agreement is within this subsection if it is an agreement between the purchaser or his successor in title and any other person—

(a) which is made (expressly or impliedly) in contemplation of, or in connection with, a disposal to be made, or made, by virtue of section 8,

(b) which is made before the end of the discount repayment period, and

(c) under which a relevant disposal which is not an exempted disposal is or may be required to be made to any person after the end of that period.

(4) Such an agreement is within subsection (3)—

(a) whether or not the date on which the relevant disposal is to take place is specified in the agreement, and

(b) whether or not any requirement to make that disposal is or may be made subject to the fulfilment of any condition.

(5) The Secretary of State may by order provide—

(a) for subsection (1) to apply to agreements of any description specified in the order in addition to those within subsection (3);

(b) for subsection (1) not to apply to agreements of any description so specified to which it would otherwise apply.

(6) An order under subsection (5)—

(a) may make different provision with respect to different cases or descriptions of case; and

(b) shall be made by statutory instrument which shall be subject to annulment in pursuance of a resolution of either House of Parliament.

(7) In this section—

"agreement" includes arrangement;

"the discount repayment period" means the period of three or five years that applies for the purposes of section 11(2) (depending on whether an offer such as is mentioned in section 199(3) of the Housing Act 2004 was made before or on or after the coming into force of that section)."

(2) The amendment made by this section does not apply in relation to any agreement or arrangement made before the day on which this section comes into force.

202 Right of assured tenant to acquire dwelling not affected by collective enfranchisement

(1) Section 16 of the Housing Act 1996 (c. 52) (right of assured tenant of registered social landlord to acquire dwelling) is amended as follows.

(2) After subsection (3) insert—

"(3A) In subsection (3)(a) the reference to the freehold interest in the dwelling includes a reference to such an interest in the dwelling as is held by the landlord under a lease granted in pursuance of paragraph 3 of Schedule 9 to the Leasehold Reform, Housing and Urban Development Act 1993 (mandatory leaseback to former freeholder on collective enfranchisement)."

(3) The amendment made by subsection (2) applies in relation to the right conferred by section 16 as follows—

(a) it applies for the purposes of any exercise of that right on or after the day on which this section comes into force, and

(b) it so applies whether the lease granted in pursuance of paragraph 3 of Schedule 9 to the Leasehold Reform, Housing and Urban Development Act 1993 was granted on or after that day or before it.

Disposals by housing action trusts

203 Repayment of discount: periods and amounts payable

(1) Schedule 11 to the Housing Act 1988 (c. 50) (provisions applicable to certain disposals of houses) is amended as follows.

(2) In paragraph 1(2) for the words from "to pay to the housing action trust" to the end of the sub-paragraph substitute "to the following effect."

(3) After paragraph 1(2) insert—

"(3) The covenant shall be to pay to the housing action trust such sum (if any) as the trust may demand in accordance with sub-paragraph (4) on the occasion of the first relevant disposal (other than an exempted disposal) which takes place within the period of five years beginning with the conveyance, grant or assignment.

(4) The trust may demand such sum as it considers appropriate, up to and including the maximum amount specified in this paragraph.

(5) The maximum amount which may be demanded by the trust is a percentage of the price or premium paid for the first relevant disposal which is equal to the percentage discount given to the purchaser in respect of the disposal of the house under section 79.

(6) But for each complete year which has elapsed after the conveyance, grant or assignment and before the first relevant disposal the maximum amount which may be demanded by the trust is reduced by one-fifth.

(7) Sub-paragraphs (4) to (6) are subject to paragraph 1A.

1A Increase in value of house attributable to home improvements

1A (1) In calculating the maximum amount which may be demanded by the housing action trust under paragraph 1, such amount (if any) of the price or premium paid for the first relevant disposal which is attributable to improvements made to the house—

(a) by the person by whom the disposal is, or is to be, made, and

(b) after the conveyance, grant or assignment and before the disposal,

shall be disregarded.

(2) The amount to be disregarded under this paragraph shall be such amount as may be agreed between the parties or determined by the district valuer.

(3) The district valuer shall not be required by virtue of this paragraph to make a determination for the purposes of this paragraph unless—

(a) it is reasonably practicable for him to do so; and

(b) his reasonable costs in making the determination are paid by the person by whom the disposal is, or is to be, made.

(4) If the district valuer does not make a determination for the purposes of this paragraph (and in default of an agreement), no amount is required to be disregarded under this paragraph."

(4) The amendments made by this section do not apply in any case where—

(a) the purchaser has accepted an offer for the disposal of the house from the housing action trust, or

(b) the housing action trust has accepted an offer for the disposal of the house from the purchaser,

before the day on which this section comes into force.

(5) Subsection (6), however, applies in any such case if the first relevant disposal by the purchaser to which the covenant for repayment of discount applies takes place on or after the day on which this section comes into force.

(6) In the following provisions—

(a) paragraph 1(2) of Schedule 11 to the Housing Act 1988 (c. 50) (as it has effect without the amendments made by this section), and

(b) any covenant for repayment of discount,

any reference (however expressed) to a person being liable to pay an amount to the housing action trust on demand is to be read as a reference to his being liable to pay to the trust so much of that amount (if any) as the trust may demand.

(7) In subsections (5) and (6) "covenant for repayment of discount" means the covenant contained in a conveyance, grant or assignment in accordance with paragraph 1 of Schedule 11 to that Act.

204 Housing action trust's right of first refusal

(1) After paragraph 2 of Schedule 11 to the Housing Act 1988 insert—

"2A Right of first refusal for housing action trust

2A (1) This paragraph applies where, on the disposal of a house under section 79 of this Act, a discount is given to the purchaser by the housing action trust in accordance with a consent given by the Secretary of State under subsection (1) of that section and that consent does not exclude the application of this paragraph.

(2) On the disposal, the conveyance, grant or assignment shall contain the following covenant, which shall be binding on the purchaser and his successors in title.

(3) The covenant shall be to the effect that, until the end of the period of ten years beginning with the conveyance, grant or assignment, there will be no relevant disposal which is not an exempted disposal, unless the prescribed conditions have been satisfied in relation to that or a previous such disposal.

(4) In sub-paragraph (3) "the prescribed conditions" means such conditions as are prescribed by regulations under this section at the time when the conveyance, grant or assignment is made.

(5) The Secretary of State may by regulations prescribe such conditions as he considers appropriate for and in connection with conferring on—

(a) a housing action trust which has made a disposal as mentioned in sub-paragraph (1), or

(b) such other person as is determined in accordance with the regulations,

a right of first refusal to have a disposal within sub-paragraph (6) made to him for such consideration as is mentioned in paragraph 2B.

(6) The disposals within this sub-paragraph are—

(a) a reconveyance or conveyance of the house; and

(b) a surrender or assignment of the lease.

(7) Regulations under this paragraph may, in particular, make provision—

(a) for the purchaser to offer to make such a disposal to such person or persons as may be prescribed;

(b) for a prescribed recipient of such an offer to be able either to accept the offer or to nominate some other person as the person by whom the offer may be accepted;

(c) for the person who may be so nominated to be either a person of a prescribed description or a person whom the prescribed recipient considers, having regard to any prescribed matters, to be a more appropriate person to accept the offer;

(d) for a prescribed recipient making such a nomination to give a notification of the nomination to the person nominated, the purchaser and any other prescribed person;

(e) for authorising a nominated person to accept the offer and for determining which acceptance is to be effective where the offer is accepted by more than one person;

(f) for the period within which the offer may be accepted or within which any other prescribed step is to be, or may be, taken;

(g) for the circumstances in which the right of first refusal lapses (whether following the service of a notice to complete or otherwise) with the result that the purchaser is able to make a disposal on the open market;

(h) for the manner in which any offer, acceptance or notification is to be communicated.

(8) In sub-paragraph (7) any reference to the purchaser is a reference to the purchaser or his successor in title.

Nothing in that sub-paragraph affects the generality of sub-paragraph (5).

(9) Regulations under this paragraph—

(a) may make different provision with respect to different cases or descriptions of case; and

(b) shall be made by statutory instrument which shall be subject to annulment in pursuance of a resolution of either House of Parliament.

(10) The limitation imposed by a covenant within sub-paragraph (3) is a local land charge.

(11) The Chief Land Registrar must enter in the register of title a restriction reflecting the limitation imposed by any such covenant.

2B Consideration payable for disposal under paragraph 2A

2B (1) The consideration for a disposal made in respect of a right of first refusal as mentioned in paragraph 2A(5) shall be such amount as may be agreed between the parties, or determined by the district valuer, as being the amount which is to be taken to be the value of the house at the time when the offer is made (as determined in accordance with regulations under that paragraph).

(2) That value shall be taken to be the price which, at that time, the interest to be reconveyed, conveyed, surrendered or assigned would realise if sold on the open market by a willing vendor, on the assumption that any liability under the covenant required by paragraph 1 (repayment of discount on early disposal) would be discharged by the vendor.

(3) If the offer is accepted in accordance with regulations under paragraph 2A, no payment shall be required in pursuance of any such covenant as is mentioned in sub-paragraph (2), but the consideration shall be reduced, subject to sub-paragraph (4), by such amount (if any) as, on a disposal made at the time the offer was made, being a relevant disposal which is not an exempted disposal, would fall to be paid under that covenant.

(4) Where there is a charge on the house having priority over the charge to secure payment of the sum due under the covenant mentioned in sub-paragraph (2), the consideration shall not be reduced under sub-paragraph (3) below the amount necessary to discharge the outstanding sum secured by the first-mentioned charge at the date of the offer (as determined in accordance with regulations under paragraph 2A)."

(2) In paragraph 6 of Schedule 11 to that Act (exempted disposals ending obligation under covenants), at the end of paragraph (b) insert "and

(c) the covenant required by paragraph 2A above is not binding on the person to whom the disposal is made or any successor in title of his; and

(d) that covenant ceases to apply in relation to the property disposed of."

(3) The amendments made by this section do not apply in relation to a disposal under section 79 of that Act if—

(a) the purchaser has accepted an offer for the disposal of the house from the housing action trust, or

(b) the housing action trust has accepted an offer for the disposal of the house from the purchaser,

before the day on which this section comes into force.

205 Deferred resale agreements

(1) After paragraph 7 of Schedule 11 to the Housing Act 1988 (c. 50) insert—

"*8 Treatment of deferred resale agreements*

8 (1) If a purchaser or his successor in title enters into an agreement within sub-paragraph (3), any liability arising under the covenant required by paragraph 1 shall be determined as if a relevant disposal which is not an exempted disposal had occurred at the appropriate time.

(2) In sub-paragraph (1) "the appropriate time" means—

(a) the time when the agreement is entered into, or

(b) if it was made before the beginning of the discount repayment period, immediately after the beginning of that period.

(3) An agreement is within this sub-paragraph if it is an agreement between the purchaser or his successor in title and any other person—

(a) which is made (expressly or impliedly) in contemplation of, or in connection with, a disposal to be made, or made, under section 79,

(b) which is made before the end of the discount repayment period, and

(c) under which a relevant disposal (other than an exempted disposal) is or may be required to be made to any person after the end of that period.

(4) Such an agreement is within sub-paragraph (3)—

(a) whether or not the date on which the relevant disposal is to take place is specified in the agreement, and

(b) whether or not any requirement to make that disposal is or may be made subject to the fulfilment of any condition.

(5) The Secretary of State may by order provide—

(a) for sub-paragraph (1) to apply to agreements of any description specified in the order in addition to those within sub-paragraph (3);

(b) for sub-paragraph (1) not to apply to agreements of any description so specified to which it would otherwise apply.

(6) An order under sub-paragraph (5)—

(a) may make different provision with respect to different cases or descriptions of case; and

(b) shall be made by statutory instrument which shall be subject to annulment in pursuance of a resolution of either House of Parliament.

(7) In this paragraph—

"agreement" includes arrangement;

"the discount repayment period" means the period of 3 years that applies for the purposes of paragraph 1(2) or the period of five years that applies for the purposes of paragraph 1(3) (depending on whether an offer such as is mentioned in section 203(4) of the Housing Act 2004 was made before or on or after the coming into force of that section)."

(2) The amendment made by this section does not apply in relation to any agreement or arrangement made before the day on which this section comes into force.

CHAPTER 3

MOBILE HOMES

Site agreements

206 Particulars of site agreements to be given in advance

(1) For section 1 of the Mobile Homes Act 1983 (c. 34) (particulars of agreements between site owners and occupiers of mobile homes) substitute—

"1 Particulars of agreements

(1) This Act applies to any agreement under which a person ("the occupier") is entitled—

(a) to station a mobile home on land forming part of a protected site; and

(b) to occupy the mobile home as his only or main residence.

(2) Before making an agreement to which this Act applies, the owner of the protected site ("the owner") shall give to the proposed occupier under the agreement a written statement which—

(a) specifies the names and addresses of the parties;

(b) includes particulars of the land on which the proposed occupier is to be entitled to station the mobile home that are sufficient to identify that land;

(c) sets out the express terms to be contained in the agreement;

(d) sets out the terms to be implied by section 2(1) below; and

(e) complies with such other requirements as may be prescribed by regulations made by the appropriate national authority.

(3) The written statement required by subsection (2) above must be given—

(a) not later than 28 days before the date on which any agreement for the sale of the mobile home to the proposed occupier is made, or

(b) (if no such agreement is made before the making of the agreement to which this Act applies) not later than 28 days before the date on which the agreement to which this Act applies is made.

(4) But if the proposed occupier consents in writing to that statement being given to him by a date ("the chosen date") which is less than 28 days before the date mentioned in subsection (3)(a) or (b) above, the statement must be given to him not later than the chosen date.

(5) If any express term—

(a) is contained in an agreement to which this Act applies, but

(b) was not set out in a written statement given to the proposed occupier in accordance with subsections (2) to (4) above,

the term is unenforceable by the owner or any person within section 3(1) below.

This is subject to any order made by the court under section 2(3) below.

(6) If the owner has failed to give the occupier a written statement in accordance with subsections (2) to (4) above, the occupier may, at any time after the making of the agreement, apply to the court for an order requiring the owner—

(a) to give him a written statement which complies with paragraphs (a) to (e) of subsection (2) (read with any modifications necessary to reflect the fact that the agreement has been made), and

(b) to do so not later than such date as is specified in the order.

(7) A statement required to be given to a person under this section may be either delivered to him personally or sent to him by post.

(8) Any reference in this section to the making of an agreement to which this Act applies includes a reference to any variation of an agreement by virtue of which the agreement becomes one to which this Act applies.

(9) Regulations under this section—

(a) shall be made by statutory instrument;

(b) if made by the Secretary of State, shall be subject to annulment in pursuance of a resolution of either House of Parliament; and

(c) may make different provision with respect to different cases or descriptions of case, including different provision for different areas."

(2) Section 2 of that Act (terms of agreements) is amended as follows—

(a) in subsection (2), for "within six months of the giving of the statement under section 1(2) above" substitute "within the relevant period"; and

(b) for subsection (3) substitute—

"(3) The court may, on the application of either party made within the relevant period, make an order—

(a) varying or deleting any express term of the agreement;

(b) in the case of any express term to which section 1(6) above applies, provide for the term to have full effect or to have such effect subject to any variation specified in the order.

(3A) In subsections (2) and (3) above "the relevant period" means the period beginning with the date on which the agreement is made and ending—

(a) six months after that date, or

(b) where a written statement relating to the agreement is given to the occupier after that date (whether or not in compliance with an order under section 1(6) above), six months after the date on which the statement is given;

and section 1(8) above applies for the purposes of this subsection as it applies for the purposes of section 1."

(3) In section 5(1) of that Act (interpretation) insert at the appropriate place—

"""the appropriate national authority" means—

(a) in relation to England, the Secretary of State, and

(b) in relation to Wales, the National Assembly for Wales;".

(4) The amendments made by subsections (1) and (2) do not apply in relation to an agreement to which that Act applies where—

(a) the agreement, or

(b) (if it becomes one to which that Act applies as the result of any variation of it) the variation in question,

is made before the end of the period of 28 days beginning with the day on which those subsections come into force.

(5) The new section 1(9)(b) inserted by subsection (1) does not affect the continuing validity of any regulations made under section 1 of that Act before the passing of this Act.

207 Implied terms relating to termination of agreements or disposal of mobile homes

(1) Part 1 of Schedule 1 to the Mobile Homes Act 1983 (c. 34) (terms implied in site agreements) is amended as follows.

(2) In paragraph 6 (termination by owner on ground of detrimental effect resulting from age and condition of mobile home)—

(a) omit "age and"; and

(b) after sub-paragraph (2) insert—

"(3) Sub-paragraphs (4) and (5) below apply if, on an application under sub-paragraph (1) above—

(a) the court considers that, having regard to the present condition of the mobile home, paragraph (a) or (b) of that sub-paragraph applies to it, but

(b) it also considers that it would be reasonably practicable for particular repairs to be carried out on the mobile home that would result in neither of those paragraphs applying to it, and

(c) the occupier indicates that he intends to carry out those repairs.

(4) In such a case the court may make an order adjourning proceedings on the application for such period specified in the order as the court considers reasonable to allow the repairs to be carried out.

The repairs must be set out in the order.

(5) If the court makes such an order, the application shall not be further proceeded with unless the court is satisfied that the specified period has expired without the repairs having been carried out."

(3) In paragraph 8 (sale of mobile home to person approved by owner)—

(a) after sub-paragraph (1) insert—

"(1A) The occupier may serve on the owner a request for the owner to approve a person for the purposes of sub-paragraph (1) above.

(1B) Where the owner receives such a request, he must, within the period of 28 days beginning with the date on which he received the request—

(a) approve the person, unless it is reasonable for him not to do so, and

(b) serve on the occupier notice of his decision whether or not to approve the person.

(1C) A notice under sub-paragraph (1B) above must specify—

(a) if the approval is given subject to conditions, the conditions, and

(b) if the approval is withheld, the reasons for withholding it.

(1D) The giving of approval subject to any condition that is not a reasonable condition does not satisfy the requirement in sub-paragraph (1B)(a) above.

(1E) If the owner fails to notify the occupier as required by sub-paragraphs (1B) and (1C) above, the occupier may apply to the court for an order declaring that the person is approved for the purposes of sub-paragraph (1) above; and the court may make such an order if it thinks fit.

(1F) It is for the owner—

(a) if he served a notice as mentioned in sub-paragraphs (1B) and (1C) and the question arises whether he served the notice within the required period of 28 days, to show that he did;

(b) if he gave his approval subject to any condition and the question arises whether the condition was a reasonable condition, to show that it was;

(c) if he did not give his approval and the question arises whether it was reasonable for him not to do so, to show that it was reasonable.

(1G) A request or notice under this paragraph—

(a) must be in writing, and

(b) may be served by post.";

(b) in sub-paragraph (2) for "the Secretary of State" substitute "the appropriate national authority"; and

(c) in sub-paragraph (3)(a) after "which" insert "(if made by the Secretary of State)".

(4) After the existing provisions of paragraph 9 (gift of mobile home to person approved by owner), which become sub-paragraph (1), insert—

"(2) Sub-paragraphs (1A) to (1G) of paragraph 8 above shall apply in relation to the approval of a person for the purposes of sub-paragraph (1) above as they apply in relation to the approval of a person for the purposes of sub-paragraph (1) of that paragraph."

(5) After Part 2 of Schedule 1 to the Mobile Homes Act 1983 (c. 34) insert—

"PART 3

SUPPLEMENTARY PROVISIONS

1 (1) This paragraph applies to—

(a) a request by the occupier for the owner to approve a person for the purposes of paragraph 8(1) of Part 1 (see paragraph 8(1A)), or

(b) a request by the occupier for the owner to approve a person for the purposes of paragraph 9(1) of Part 1 (see paragraph 8(1A) as applied by paragraph 9(2)).

(2) If a person ("the recipient") receives such a request and he—

(a) though not the owner, has an estate or interest in the protected site, and

(b) believes that another person is the owner (and that the other person has not received such a request),

the recipient owes a duty to the occupier to take such steps as are reasonable to secure that the other person receives the request within the period of 28 days beginning with the date on which the recipient receives it.

(3) In paragraph 8(1B) of Part 1 of this Schedule (as it applies to any request within sub-paragraph (1) above) any reference to the owner receiving such a request includes a reference to his receiving it in accordance with sub-paragraph (2) above.

2 (1) A claim that a person has broken the duty under paragraph 1(2) above may be made the subject of civil proceedings in like manner as any other claim in tort for breach of statutory duty.

(2) The right conferred by sub-paragraph (1) is in addition to any right to bring proceedings, in respect of a breach of any implied term having effect by virtue of paragraph 8 or 9 of Part 1 of this Schedule, against a person bound by that term."

(6) The amendments made by this section apply in relation to an agreement to which the Mobile Homes Act 1983 applies that was made before the day on which this section comes into force ("the appointed day"), as well as in relation to one made on or after that day.

Any reference in this subsection to the making of an agreement to which that Act applies includes a reference to any variation of an agreement by virtue of which the agreement becomes one to which that Act applies.

(7) However—

(a) the amendments made by subsection (2) do not apply in relation to any application made before the appointed day for the purposes of paragraph 6 of Part 1 of Schedule 1 to that Act; and

(b) the amendments made by subsections (3)(a), (4) and (5) do not apply in relation to any request for approval made before the appointed day for the purposes of paragraph 8(1) or (as the case may be) 9(1) of that Part of that Schedule.

208 Power to amend terms implied in site agreements

(1) After section 2 of the Mobile Homes Act 1983 (c. 34) insert—

"2A Power to amend implied terms

(1) The appropriate national authority may by order make such amendments of Part 1 or 2 of Schedule 1 to this Act as the authority considers appropriate.

(2) An order under this section—

(a) shall be made by statutory instrument;

(b) may make different provision with respect to different cases or descriptions of case, including different provision for different areas;

(c) may contain such incidental, supplementary, consequential, transitional or saving provisions as the authority making the order considers appropriate.

(3) Without prejudice to the generality of subsections (1) and (2), an order under this section may—

(a) make provision for or in connection with the determination by the court of such questions, or the making by the court of such orders, as are specified in the order;

(b) make such amendments of any provision of this Act as the authority making the order considers appropriate in consequence of any amendment made by the order in Part 1 or 2 of Schedule 1.

(4) The first order made under this section in relation to England or Wales respectively may provide for all or any of its provisions to apply in relation to agreements to which this Act applies that were made at any time before the day on which the order comes into force (as well as in relation to such agreements made on or after that day).

(5) No order may be made by the appropriate national authority under this section unless the authority has consulted—

(a) such organisations as appear to it to be representative of interests substantially affected by the order; and

(b) such other persons as it considers appropriate.

(6) No order may be made by the Secretary of State under this section unless a draft of the order has been laid before, and approved by a resolution of, each House of Parliament."

(2) For the purposes of subsection (5) of the section 2A inserted by this section, consultation undertaken before the date of the passing of this Act constitutes as effective compliance with that subsection as if undertaken on or after that date.

Protection from eviction etc.

209 Protected sites to include sites for gypsies

(1) Section 1 of the Caravan Sites Act 1968 (c. 52) (application of provisions for protection of residential occupiers of caravan sites) is amended as follows.

(2) In subsection (2) (under which "protected site" includes certain local authority sites) for "paragraph 11 of Schedule 1 to that Act (exemption of land occupied by local authorities) substitute "paragraph 11 or 11A of Schedule 1 to that Act (exemption of gypsy and other local authority sites)".

(3) The amendment made by subsection (2) above does not affect the operation of—

(a) section 2 of the Act (minimum length of notice) in relation to any notice given before the day on which this section comes into force, or

(b) section 3 of the Act (protection from eviction) in relation to any conduct occurring before that day, or

(c) section 4 of the Act (suspension of eviction orders) in relation to any proceedings begun before that day.

(4) In subsection (3)(b) the reference to section 3 of the Act is to that section whether as amended by section 210 of this Act or otherwise.

210 Extension of protection from harassment for occupiers of mobile homes

(1) Section 3 of the Caravan Sites Act 1968 (protection of occupiers against eviction and harassment) is amended as follows.

(2) In subsection (1) (offence where person, with the specified intent, does acts calculated to interfere with the peace or comfort of the occupier etc.) for "calculated to interfere" substitute "likely to interfere".

(3) After subsection (1) insert—

"(1A) Subject to the provisions of this section, the owner of a protected site or his agent shall be guilty of an offence under this section if, whether during the subsistence or after the expiration or determination of a residential contract—

(a) he does acts likely to interfere with the peace or comfort of the occupier or persons residing with him, or

(b) he persistently withdraws or withholds services or facilities reasonably required for the occupation of the caravan as a residence on the site,

and (in either case) he knows, or has reasonable cause to believe, that that conduct is likely to cause the occupier to do any of the things mentioned in subsection (1)(c)(i) or (ii) of this section.

(1B) References in subsection (1A) of this section to the owner of a protected site include references to a person with an estate or interest in the site which is superior to that of the owner."

(4) In subsection (3) (penalties for offences), for the words from "be liable" onwards substitute "be liable—

(a) on summary conviction, to a fine not exceeding the statutory maximum or to imprisonment for a term not exceeding 12 months, or to both;

(b) on conviction on indictment, to a fine or to imprisonment for a term not exceeding 2 years, or to both."

(5) After subsection (4) insert—

"(4A) In proceedings for an offence under subsection (1A) of this section it shall be a defence to prove that the accused had reasonable grounds for doing the acts or withdrawing or withholding the services or facilities in question."

(6) The amendments made by this section do not apply in relation to any conduct occurring before the day on which this section comes into force.

(7) In the case of an offence committed before section 154(1) of the Criminal Justice Act 2003 (c. 44) comes into force, the amendment made by subsection (4) has effect as if for "12 months" there were substituted "6 months".

211 Suspension of eviction orders

(1) In section 4(6) of the Caravan Sites Act 1968 (c. 52) (provision for suspension of eviction orders) for the words from "in the following cases" to the end of paragraph (b) substitute "if—

(a) no site licence under Part 1 of that Act is in force in respect of the site, and

(b) paragraph 11 or 11A of Schedule 1 to the Caravan Sites and Control of Development Act 1960 (c. 2) does not apply;".

(2) The amendment made by subsection (1) does not apply in relation to proceedings begun before the day on which this section comes into force.

CHAPTER 4

TENANCY DEPOSIT SCHEMES

212 Tenancy deposit schemes

(1) The appropriate national authority must make arrangements for securing that one or more tenancy deposit schemes are available for the purpose of safeguarding tenancy deposits paid in connection with shorthold tenancies.

(2) For the purposes of this Chapter a "tenancy deposit scheme" is a scheme which—

(a) is made for the purpose of safeguarding tenancy deposits paid in connection with shorthold tenancies and facilitating the resolution of disputes arising in connection with such deposits, and

(b) complies with the requirements of Schedule 10.

(3) Arrangements under subsection (1) must be arrangements made with any body or person under which the body or person ("the scheme administrator") undertakes to establish and maintain a tenancy deposit scheme of a description specified in the arrangements.

(4) The appropriate national authority may—

(a) give financial assistance to the scheme administrator;

(b) make payments to the scheme administrator (otherwise than as financial assistance) in pursuance of arrangements under subsection (1).

(5) The appropriate national authority may, in such manner and on such terms as it thinks fit, guarantee the discharge of any financial obligation incurred by the scheme administrator in connection with arrangements under subsection (1).

(6) Arrangements under subsection (1) must require the scheme administrator to give the appropriate national authority, in such manner and at such times as it may specify, such information and facilities for obtaining information as it may specify.

(7) The appropriate national authority may make regulations conferring or imposing—

(a) on scheme administrators, or

(b) on scheme administrators of any description specified in the regulations,

such powers or duties in connection with arrangements under subsection (1) as are so specified.

(8) In this Chapter—

"authorised", in relation to a tenancy deposit scheme, means that the scheme is in force in accordance with arrangements under subsection (1);

"custodial scheme" and "insurance scheme" have the meaning given by paragraph 1(2) and (3) of Schedule 10);

"money" means money in the form of cash or otherwise;

"shorthold tenancy" means an assured shorthold tenancy within the meaning of Chapter 2 of Part 1 of the Housing Act 1988 (c. 50);

"tenancy deposit", in relation to a shorthold tenancy, means any money intended to be held (by the landlord or otherwise) as security for—

(a) the performance of any obligations of the tenant, or

(b) the discharge of any liability of his,

arising under or in connection with the tenancy.

(9) In this Chapter—

(a) references to a landlord or landlords in relation to any shorthold tenancy or tenancies include references to a person or persons acting on his or their behalf in relation to the tenancy or tenancies, and

(b) references to a tenancy deposit being held in accordance with a scheme include, in the case of a custodial scheme, references to an amount representing the deposit being held in accordance with the scheme.

213 Requirements relating to tenancy deposits

(1) Any tenancy deposit paid to a person in connection with a shorthold tenancy must, as from the time when it is received, be dealt with in accordance with an authorised scheme.

(2) No person may require the payment of a tenancy deposit in connection with a shorthold tenancy which is not to be subject to the requirement in subsection (1).

(3) Where a landlord receives a tenancy deposit in connection with a shorthold tenancy, the initial requirements of an authorised scheme must be complied with by the landlord

in relation to the deposit within the period of 14 days beginning with the date on which it is received.

(4) For the purposes of this section "the initial requirements" of an authorised scheme are such requirements imposed by the scheme as fall to be complied with by a landlord on receiving such a tenancy deposit.

(5) A landlord who has received such a tenancy deposit must give the tenant and any relevant person such information relating to—

(a) the authorised scheme applying to the deposit,

(b) compliance by the landlord with the initial requirements of the scheme in relation to the deposit, and

(c) the operation of provisions of this Chapter in relation to the deposit,

as may be prescribed.

(6) The information required by subsection (5) must be given to the tenant and any relevant person—

(a) in the prescribed form or in a form substantially to the same effect, and

(b) within the period of 14 days beginning with the date on which the deposit is received by the landlord.

(7) No person may, in connection with a shorthold tenancy, require a deposit which consists of property other than money.

(8) In subsection (7) "deposit" means a transfer of property intended to be held (by the landlord or otherwise) as security for—

(a) the performance of any obligations of the tenant, or

(b) the discharge of any liability of his,

arising under or in connection with the tenancy.

(9) The provisions of this section apply despite any agreement to the contrary.

(10) In this section—

"prescribed" means prescribed by an order made by the appropriate national authority;

"property" means moveable property;

"relevant person" means any person who, in accordance with arrangements made with the tenant, paid the deposit on behalf of the tenant.

214 Proceedings relating to tenancy deposits

(1) Where a tenancy deposit has been paid in connection with a shorthold tenancy, the tenant or any relevant person (as defined by section 213(10)) may make an application to a county court on the grounds—

(a) that the initial requirements of an authorised scheme (see section 213(4)) have not, or section 213(6)(a) has not, been complied with in relation to the deposit; or

(b) that he has been notified by the landlord that a particular authorised scheme applies to the deposit but has been unable to obtain confirmation from the scheme administrator that the deposit is being held in accordance with the scheme.

(2) Subsections (3) and (4) apply if on such an application the court—

(a) is satisfied that those requirements have not, or section 213(6)(a) has not, been complied with in relation to the deposit, or

(b) is not satisfied that the deposit is being held in accordance with an authorised scheme,

as the case may be.

(3) The court must, as it thinks fit, either—

(a) order the person who appears to the court to be holding the deposit to repay it to the applicant, or

(b) order that person to pay the deposit into the designated account held by the scheme administrator under an authorised custodial scheme,

within the period of 14 days beginning with the date of the making of the order.

(4) The court must also order the landlord to pay to the applicant a sum of money equal to three times the amount of the deposit within the period of 14 days beginning with the date of the making of the order.

(5) Where any deposit given in connection with a shorthold tenancy could not be lawfully required as a result of section 213(7), the property in question is recoverable from the person holding it by the person by whom it was given as a deposit.

(6) In subsection (5) "deposit" has the meaning given by section 213(8).

215 Sanctions for non-compliance

(1) If a tenancy deposit has been paid in connection with a shorthold tenancy, no section 21 notice may be given in relation to the tenancy at a time when—

(a) the deposit is not being held in accordance with an authorised scheme, or

(b) the initial requirements of such a scheme (see section 213(4)) have not been complied with in relation to the deposit.

(2) If section 213(6) is not complied with in relation to a deposit given in connection with a shorthold tenancy, no section 21 notice may be given in relation to the tenancy until such time as section 213(6)(a) is complied with.

(3) If any deposit given in connection with a shorthold tenancy could not be lawfully required as a result of section 213(7), no section 21 notice may be given in relation to the tenancy until such time as the property in question is returned to the person by whom it was given as a deposit.

(4) In subsection (3) "deposit" has the meaning given by section 213(8).

(5) In this section a "section 21 notice" means a notice under section 21(1)(b) or (4)(a) of the Housing Act 1988 (recovery of possession on termination of shorthold tenancy).

CHAPTER 5

MISCELLANEOUS

Overcrowding

216 Overcrowding

(1) The appropriate national authority may by order make such provision as it considers appropriate for and in connection with—
   (a) determining whether a dwelling is overcrowded for the purposes of Part 10 of the Housing Act 1985 (c. 68) (overcrowding);
   (b) introducing for the purposes of Chapter 3 of Part 4 of this Act a concept of overcrowding similar to that applying for the purposes of Part 10 (and accordingly removing the discretion of local housing authorities to decide particular issues arising under those sections);
   (c) securing that overcrowding in premises to which Chapter 3 of Part 4 of this Act would otherwise apply, or any description of such premises, is regulated only by provisions of Part 10.

(2) An order under this section may, in particular, make provision for regulating the making by local housing authorities of determinations as to whether premises are overcrowded, including provision prescribing—
   (a) factors that must be taken into account by such authorities when making such determinations;
   (b) the procedure that is to be followed by them in connection with making such determinations.

(3) An order under this section may modify any enactment (including this Act).

(4) In this section—
   (a) any reference to Part 10 of the Housing Act 1985 includes a reference to Part 10 as modified by an order under this section; and
   (b) "enactment" includes an enactment comprised in subordinate legislation (within the meaning of the Interpretation Act 1978 (c. 30)).

Energy efficiency

217 Energy efficiency of residential accommodation: England

(1) The Secretary of State must take reasonable steps to ensure that by 2010 the general level of energy efficiency of residential accommodation in England has increased by at least 20 per cent compared with the general level of such energy efficiency in 2000.

(2) Nothing in this section affects the duties of the Secretary of State under section 2 of the Sustainable Energy Act 2003 (c. 30) (energy efficiency aim in respect of residential accommodation in England).

(3) In this section "residential accommodation" has the meaning given by section 1 of the Home Energy Conservation Act 1995 (c. 10).

Registered social landlords

218 Amendments relating to registered social landlords

Schedule 11 (which makes amendments relating to registered social landlords) has effect.

219 Disclosure of information to registered social landlords for the purposes of section 1 of the Crime and Disorder Act 1998

In section 115(2) of the Crime and Disorder Act 1998 (c. 37) after paragraph (d) insert—

"(da) a person registered under section 1 of the Housing Act 1996 as a social landlord;".

Other provisions relating to social housing

220 Additional power to give grants for social housing

After section 27 of the Housing Act 1996 (c. 52) insert—

"Grants to bodies other than registered social landlords

27A Grants to bodies other than registered social landlords

(1) The Relevant Authority may make grants under this section to persons other than registered social landlords.

(2) Grants under this section are grants for any of the following purposes—

(a) acquiring, or repairing and improving, or creating by the conversion of houses or other property, houses to be disposed of—

(i) under equity percentage arrangements, or

(ii) on shared ownership terms;

(b) constructing houses to be disposed of—

(i) under equity percentage arrangements, or

(ii) on shared ownership terms;

(c) providing loans to be secured by mortgages to assist persons to acquire houses for their own occupation;

(d) providing, constructing or improving houses to be kept available for letting;

(e) providing, constructing or improving houses for letting that are to be managed by such registered social landlords, and under arrangements containing such terms, as are approved by the Relevant Authority;

(f) such other purposes as may be specified in an order under subsection (3).

(3) The Secretary of State may by order make such provision in connection with the making of grants under this section as he considers appropriate.

(4) An order under subsection (3) may, in particular, make provision—

(a) defining "equity percentage arrangements" for the purposes of this section;
(b) specifying or describing the bodies from whom loans may be obtained by persons wishing to acquire houses for their own occupation;
(c) dealing with the priority of mortgages entered into by such persons;
(d) specifying purposes additional to those mentioned in subsection (2)(a) to (e).

(5) As regards grants made by the Housing Corporation, an order under subsection (3) may also require the imposition of conditions in connection with such grants, and for this purpose may—
(a) prescribe conditions that are to be so imposed;
(b) prescribe matters about which conditions are to be so imposed and any particular effects that such conditions are to achieve.

(6) The Relevant Authority shall specify in relation to grants under this section—
(a) the procedure to be followed in relation to applications for grant,
(b) the circumstances in which grant is or is not to be payable,
(c) the method for calculating, and any limitations on, the amount of grant, and
(d) the manner in which, and the time or times at which, grant is to be paid.

(7) If, by virtue of subsection (5), an order under subsection (3) requires conditions to be imposed by the Housing Corporation in connection with a grant to a person under this section, the Corporation in making the grant—
(a) must provide that the grant is conditional on compliance by the person with such conditions as are required by the order; and
(b) if it exercises its power to impose conditions under subsection (8), must not impose any that are inconsistent with the requirements of the order.

(8) In making a grant to a person under this section the Relevant Authority may provide that the grant is conditional on compliance by the person with such conditions as the Authority may specify.

(9) The conditions that may be so specified include conditions requiring the payment to the Relevant Authority in specified circumstances of a sum determined by the Authority (with or without interest).

(10) An order under subsection (3) shall be made by statutory instrument which shall be subject to annulment in pursuance of a resolution of either House of Parliament.

(11) In this section—

"disposed of on shared ownership terms" has the meaning given by section 2(6);

"letting" includes the grant of a licence to occupy.

27B Transfer of property funded by grants under section 27A

(1) Where—
(a) any grant is paid or payable to any person under section 27A, and

(b) at any time property to which the grant relates becomes vested in, or is leased for a term of years to, or reverts to, another person who is not a registered social landlord,

this Part shall have effect, in relation to times falling after that time, as if the grant, or such proportion of it as is determined or specified under subsection (4), had been paid or (as the case may be) were payable to that other person under section 27A.

(2) Where—

(a) any amount is paid or payable to any person by way of grant under section 27A, and

(b) at any time property to which the grant relates becomes vested in, or is leased for a term of years to, or reverts to, a registered social landlord,

this Part shall have effect, in relation to times falling after that time, as if the grant, or such proportion of it as is determined or specified under subsection (4), had been paid or (as the case may be) were payable to that other person under section 18.

(3) In such a case, the relevant section 18 conditions accordingly apply to that grant or proportion of it, in relation to times falling after that time, in place of those specified under section 27A(8).

"The relevant section 18 conditions" means such conditions specified under section 18(3) as would have applied at the time of the making of the grant if it had been made under section 18 to a registered social landlord.

(4) The proportion mentioned in subsection (1) or (2) is that which, in the circumstances of the particular case—

(a) the Relevant Authority, acting in accordance with such principles as it may from time to time determine, may specify as being appropriate, or

(b) the Relevant Authority may determine to be appropriate."

221 Extension of right to acquire

After section 16 of the Housing Act 1996 (c. 52) insert—

"16A Extension of section 16 to dwellings funded by grants under section 27A

(1) Section 16 applies in relation to a dwelling ("a funded dwelling") provided or acquired wholly or in part by means of a grant under section 27A (grants to bodies other than registered social landlords) with the following modifications.

(2) In section 16(1) the reference to a registered social landlord includes a reference to any person to whom a grant has been paid under section 27A.

(3) In section 16(2) and (4) any reference to section 18 includes a reference to section 27A.

(4) For the purposes of section 16 a funded dwelling is to be regarded as having remained within the social rented sector in relation to any relevant time if, since it was acquired or provided as mentioned in subsection (1) above, it was used—

(a) by the recipient of the grant mentioned in that subsection, or

(b) if section 27B applies in relation to the grant, by each person to whom the grant was, or is treated as having been, paid,

exclusively for the purposes for which the grant was made or any other purposes agreed to by the Relevant Authority.

(5) In subsection (4) "relevant time" means a time when the dwelling would not be treated as being within the social rented sector by virtue of section 16(3)."

222 Rights of pre-emption in connection with assured tenancies

(1) Section 5 of the Housing Act 1988 (c. 50) (security of tenure for assured tenants) is amended as follows.

(2) After subsection (5) (certain obligations etc. of tenant to be unenforceable) insert—

"(5A) Nothing in subsection (5) affects any right of pre-emption—

(a) which is exercisable by the landlord under a tenancy in circumstances where the tenant indicates his intention to dispose of the whole of his interest under the tenancy, and

(b) in pursuance of which the landlord would be required to pay, in respect of the acquisition of that interest, an amount representing its market value.

"Dispose" means dispose by assignment or surrender, and "acquisition" has a corresponding meaning."

(3) The amendment made by subsection (2) does not apply in relation to any right of pre-emption granted before the day on which this section comes into force.

223 Allocation of housing accommodation by local authorities

In section 167(2)(d) of the Housing Act 1996 (c. 52) (people to whom preference is to be given in allocating housing accommodation) after "medical or welfare grounds" insert "(including grounds relating to a disability)".

Disabled facilities grant

224 Disabled facilities grant: caravans

(1) The Housing Grants, Construction and Regeneration Act 1996 (c. 53) is amended as follows.

(2) In section 1(1)(c)(i) (grants in relation to qualifying park homes) for "qualifying park homes" substitute "caravans".

(3) In section 19(1) (applications for grants) for paragraph (c) substitute—

"(c) that the applicant is an occupier (alone or jointly with others) of a qualifying houseboat or a caravan and, in the case of a caravan, that at the time the application was made the caravan was stationed on land within the authority's area."

(4) In section 22A (certificates required in case of occupier's application)—

(a) for "qualifying park home" in subsection (2)(b) and (3)(a) and (b) substitute "caravan", and

(b) for "pitch" in subsection (3)(a) substitute "land".

(5) In the following provisions for "qualifying park home" substitute "caravan"—

(a) section 23(1)(a)(i), (b)(i), (i) and (k) (purposes of grant);

(b) section 24(3)(b)(i) (approval of application);

(c) section 29(3) (restriction on grants for works already begun);

(d) section 41(1)(b) (change of circumstances).

(6) In section 57(2)(a) (power of authority to carry out works)—

(a) for "qualifying park home", in each place where it occurs, substitute "caravan", and

(b) for "pitch" in sub-paragraph (i) substitute "land".

(7) In section 58 (minor definitions for the purposes of Chapter 1 of Part 1)—

(a) before the definition of "common parts" insert—

""caravan"—

(a) means a caravan within the meaning of Part 1 of the Caravan Sites and Control of Development Act 1960 (disregarding the amendment made by section 13(2) of the Caravan Sites Act 1968); and

(b) includes any yard, garden, outhouses and appurtenances belonging to it or usually enjoyed with it;" and

(b) for "qualifying park home" in the definition of "premises" substitute "caravan", and

(c) omit the definition of "qualifying park home".

(8) In section 59 (index of defined expressions)—

(a) before the entry relating to "certified date" insert—

"caravan	section 58"; and

(b) omit the entry relating to "qualifying park home".

(9) The amendments made by this section do not apply in relation to any application for a disabled facilities grant under the Housing Grants, Construction and Regeneration Act 1996 (c. 53) that is made before the day on which this section comes into force.

Accommodation needs of gypsies and travellers

225 Duties of local housing authorities: accommodation needs of gypsies and travellers

(1) Every local housing authority must, when undertaking a review of housing needs in their district under section 8 of the Housing Act 1985 (c. 68), carry out an assessment of the accommodation needs of gypsies and travellers residing in or resorting to their district.

(2) Subsection (3) applies where a local housing authority are required under section 87 of the Local Government Act 2003 (c. 26) to prepare a strategy in respect of the meeting of such accommodation needs.

(3) The local authority who are that local housing authority must take the strategy into account in exercising their functions.

"Functions" includes functions exercisable otherwise than as a local housing authority.

(4) A local housing authority must have regard to any guidance issued under section 226 in—

(a) carrying out such an assessment as mentioned in subsection (1), and

(b) preparing any strategy that they are required to prepare as mentioned in subsection (2).

(5) In this section—

(a) "gypsies and travellers" has the meaning given by regulations made by the appropriate national authority;

(b) "accommodation needs" includes needs with respect to the provision of sites on which caravans can be stationed; and

(c) "caravan" has the same meaning as in Part 1 of the Caravan Sites and Control of Development Act 1960.

226 Guidance in relation to section 225

(1) The appropriate national authority may issue guidance to local housing authorities regarding—

(a) the carrying out of assessments under section 225(1), and

(b) the preparation of any strategies that local housing authorities are required to prepare as mentioned in section 225(2).

(2) Before giving guidance under this section, or revising guidance already given, the Secretary of State must lay a draft of the proposed guidance or alterations before each House of Parliament.

(3) The Secretary of State must not give or revise the guidance before the end of the period of 40 days beginning with the day on which the draft is laid before each House of Parliament (or, if copies are laid before each House of Parliament on different days, the later of those days).

(4) The Secretary of State must not proceed with the proposed guidance or alterations if, within the period of 40 days mentioned in subsection (3), either House resolves that the guidance or alterations be withdrawn.

(5) Subsection (4) is without prejudice to the possibility of laying a further draft of the guidance or alterations before each House of Parliament.

(6) In calculating the period of 40 days mentioned in subsection (3), no account is to be taken of any time during which Parliament is dissolved or prorogued or during which both Houses are adjourned for more than four days.

Annual reports by local housing authorities

227 Removal of duty on local housing authorities to send annual reports to tenants etc.

Omit section 167 of the Local Government and Housing Act 1989 (c. 42) (duty of local housing authorities to send annual reports to tenants).

Social Housing Ombudsman for Wales

228 Social Housing Ombudsman for Wales

(1) After subsection (6) of section 51 of the Housing Act 1996 (c. 52) (schemes for investigation of housing complaints) insert—

"(7) This section shall not apply in relation to social landlords in Wales (within the meaning given by section 51C)."

(2) After that section insert—

"51A Social Housing Ombudsman for Wales

(1) For the purpose of the investigation of complaints made about social landlords in Wales, there shall be an office of Social Housing Ombudsman for Wales or Ombwdsmon Tai Cymdeithasol Cymru.

(2) The person who is the Local Commissioner for Wales shall also be the Social Housing Ombudsman for Wales.

(3) If there is more than one person who is a Local Commissioner for Wales, the Commission for Local Administration in Wales shall designate one of them to be the Social Housing Ombudsman for Wales.

(4) If a person who is the Social Housing Ombudsman for Wales ceases to be a Local Commissioner for Wales, he shall cease to be the Social Housing Ombudsman for Wales.

(5) The power under section 23(6) of the Local Government Act 1974 to remove a Local Commissioner for Wales from office on grounds of incapacity or misbehaviour includes a power to remove him from that office on grounds of incapacity or misbehaviour which are exclusively or partly relevant to the office of Social Housing Ombudsman for Wales.

(6) "Local Commissioner for Wales" shall be construed in accordance with section 23 of the Local Government Act 1974.

(7) Schedule 2A (which contains further provision about the Social Housing Ombudsman for Wales) shall have effect.

51B Investigation of complaints

(1) The National Assembly for Wales may by regulations make provision about the investigation by the Social Housing Ombudsman for Wales of complaints made about social landlords in Wales.

(2) Regulations under subsection (1) may in particular make provision about—

(a) the matters about which complaints may be made;

(b) the grounds on which a matter may be excluded from investigation, including that the matter is the subject of court proceedings or was the subject of court proceedings where judgment on the merits was given;

(c) the description of individual who may make a complaint;

(d) a power of the Social Housing Ombudsman for Wales to investigate any complaint duly made (whether the complaint is subsequently withdrawn or not), and, where he investigates, the making of a determination;

(e) a power of the Social Housing Ombudsman for Wales to propose alternative methods of resolving a dispute;

(f) the powers of the Social Housing Ombudsman for Wales for the purposes of his investigations (including powers to consult and co-operate with other persons), and the procedure to be followed in the conduct of investigations;

(g) the powers of the Social Housing Ombudsman for Wales on making a determination, which may include power—

(i) to make recommendations as to action to be taken to remedy any injustice to the person aggrieved and to prevent any similar injustice being caused in the future,

(ii) to make orders with regard to the payment of compensation or to order that a person is not to exercise, or require the performance of, certain rights or obligations, and

(iii) to publish statements, or to make orders requiring the publication of statements, that a person has failed to comply with an order mentioned in sub-paragraph (ii);

(h) the manner in which determinations are to be—

(i) communicated to the complainant and the person against whom the complaint was made; and

(ii) published (with or without excisions).

(3) Regulations under this section may contain such supplementary, incidental, consequential or transitional provisions and savings as the National Assembly for Wales considers appropriate.

(4) Regulations under this section may make different provision for different cases or descriptions of case.

(5) Regulations under this section shall be made by statutory instrument.

51C Meaning of "social landlord in Wales"

(1) "Social landlord in Wales" means—

(a) a body which is registered as a social landlord in the register maintained by the National Assembly for Wales under section 1 of this Act;

(b) a body which was at any time registered as a social landlord in that register (or in the register previously maintained under that section by the Secretary of State or Housing for Wales); and

(c) any other body which was at any time registered with Housing for Wales, the Secretary of State or the National Assembly for Wales and which owns or manages publicly-funded dwellings.

(2) In subsection (1)(c) a "publicly-funded" dwelling means a dwelling which was—

(a) provided by means of a grant under—

(i) section 18 of this Act (social housing grant); or

(ii) section 50 of the Housing Act 1988, section 41 of the Housing Associations Act 1985, or section 29 or 29A of the Housing Act 1974 (housing association grant); or

(b) acquired on a disposal by a public sector landlord.

(3) The National Assembly for Wales may by order made by statutory instrument add to or amend the descriptions of landlords who are to be treated as social landlords in Wales.

(4) Before making any such order the National Assembly for Wales shall consult such persons as it considers appropriate.

(5) Any such order may contain such supplementary, incidental, consequential or transitional provisions and savings as the National Assembly for Wales considers appropriate."

(3) After Schedule 2 to that Act there is inserted, as Schedule 2A, the Schedule set out in Schedule 12 to this Act.

(4) In Schedule 4 to the Local Government Act 1974 (c. 7), in paragraph 1(3) (validity of acts despite disqualification for being appointed as, or for being, a Local Commissioner) after "office" there is inserted "or in the office of Social Housing Ombudsman for Wales".

PART 7

SUPPLEMENTARY AND FINAL PROVISIONS

Residential property tribunals

229 Residential property tribunals

(1) Any jurisdiction conferred on a residential property tribunal by or under any enactment is exercisable by a rent assessment committee constituted in accordance with Schedule 10 to the Rent Act 1977 (c. 42).

(2) When so constituted for exercising any such jurisdiction a rent assessment committee is known as a residential property tribunal.

(3) The appropriate national authority may by order make provision for and in connection with conferring on residential property tribunals, in relation to such matters as are specified in the order, such jurisdiction as is so specified.

(4) An order under subsection (3) may modify an enactment (including this Act).

(5) In this section "enactment" includes an enactment comprised in subordinate legislation (within the meaning of the Interpretation Act 1978 (c. 30)).

230 Powers and procedure of residential property tribunals

(1) A residential property tribunal exercising any jurisdiction by virtue of any enactment has, in addition to any specific powers exercisable by it in exercising that jurisdiction, the general power mentioned in subsection (2).

(2) The tribunal's general power is a power by order to give such directions as the tribunal considers necessary or desirable for securing the just, expeditious and economical disposal of the proceedings or any issue raised in or in connection with them.

(3) In deciding whether to give directions under its general power a tribunal must have regard to—

- (a) the matters falling to be determined in the proceedings,
- (b) any other circumstances appearing to the tribunal to be relevant, and
- (c) the provisions of the enactment by virtue of which it is exercising jurisdiction and of any other enactment appearing to it to be relevant.

(4) A tribunal may give directions under its general power whether or not they were originally sought by a party to the proceedings.

(5) When exercising jurisdiction under this Act, the directions which may be given by a tribunal under its general power include (where appropriate)—

- (a) directions requiring a licence to be granted under Part 2 or 3 of this Act;
- (b) directions requiring any licence so granted to contain such terms as are specified in the directions;
- (c) directions requiring any order made under Part 4 of this Act to contain such terms as are so specified;
- (d) directions that any building or part of a building so specified is to be treated as if an HMO declaration had been served in respect of it on such date as is so specified (without there being any right to appeal against it under section 255(9));
- (e) directions requiring the payment of money by one party to the proceedings to another by way of compensation, damages or otherwise.

(6) Nothing in any enactment conferring specific powers on a residential property tribunal is to be regarded as affecting the operation of the preceding provisions of this section.

(7) Schedule 13 (residential property tribunals: procedure) has effect.

(8) Section 229(5) applies also for the purposes of this section and Schedule 13.

231 Appeals from residential property tribunals

(1) A party to proceedings before a residential property tribunal may appeal to the Lands Tribunal from a decision of the residential property tribunal.

(2) But the appeal may only be made—

- (a) with the permission of the residential property tribunal or the Lands Tribunal, and

(b) within the time specified by rules under section 3(6) of the Lands Tribunal Act 1949 (c. 42).

(3) On the appeal—

(a) the Lands Tribunal may exercise any power which was available to the residential property tribunal, and

(b) a decision of the Lands Tribunal may be enforced in the same way as a decision of the residential property tribunal.

(4) Section 11(1) of the Tribunals and Inquiries Act 1992 (c. 53) (appeals from certain tribunals to High Court) does not apply to any decision of a residential property tribunal.

(5) For the purposes of section 3(4) of the Lands Tribunal Act 1949 (which enables a person aggrieved by a decision of the Lands Tribunal to appeal to the Court of Appeal) a residential property tribunal is not to be regarded as an aggrieved person.

Register of licences and management orders

232 Register of licences and management orders

(1) Every local housing authority must establish and maintain a register of—

(a) all licences granted by them under Part 2 or 3 which are in force;

(b) all temporary exemption notices served by them under section 62 or section 86 which are in force; and

(c) all management orders made by them under Chapter 1 or 2 of Part 4 which are in force.

(2) The register may, subject to any requirements that may be prescribed, be in such form as the authority consider appropriate.

(3) Each entry in the register is to contain such particulars as may be prescribed.

(4) The authority must ensure that the contents of the register are available at the authority's head office for inspection by members of the public at all reasonable times.

(5) If requested by a person to do so and subject to payment of such reasonable fee (if any) as the authority may determine, a local housing authority must supply the person with a copy (certified to be true) of the register or of an extract from it.

(6) A copy so certified is prima facie evidence of the matters mentioned in it.

(7) In this section "prescribed" means prescribed by regulations made by the appropriate national authority.

Codes of practice and management regulations relating to HMOs etc.

233 Approval of codes of practice with regard to the management of HMOs etc.

(1) The appropriate national authority may by order—

(a) approve a code of practice (whether prepared by that authority or another person) laying down standards of conduct and practice to be followed with

regard to the management of houses in multiple occupation or of excepted accommodation;
(b) approve a modification of such a code; or
(c) withdraw the authority's approval of such a code or modification.

(2) Before approving a code of practice or a modification of a code of practice under this section the appropriate national authority must take reasonable steps to consult—
(a) persons involved in the management of houses in multiple occupation or (as the case may be) excepted accommodation of the kind in question and persons occupying such houses or accommodation, or
(b) persons whom the authority considers to represent the interests of those persons.

(3) The appropriate national authority may only approve a code of practice or a modification of a code if satisfied that—
(a) the code or modification has been published (whether by the authority or by another person) in a manner that the authority considers appropriate for the purpose of bringing the code or modification to the attention of those likely to be affected by it; or
(b) arrangements have been made for the code or modification to be so published.

(4) The appropriate national authority may approve a code of practice which makes different provision in relation to different cases or descriptions of case (including different provision for different areas).

(5) A failure to comply with a code of practice for the time being approved under this section does not of itself make a person liable to any civil or criminal proceedings.

(6) In this section "excepted accommodation" means such description of living accommodation falling within any provision of Schedule 14 (buildings which are not HMOs for purposes of provisions other than Part 1) as is specified in an order under subsection (1).

234 Management regulations in respect of HMOs

(1) The appropriate national authority may by regulations make provision for the purpose of ensuring that, in respect of every house in multiple occupation of a description specified in the regulations—
(a) there are in place satisfactory management arrangements; and
(b) satisfactory standards of management are observed.

(2) The regulations may, in particular—
(a) impose duties on the person managing a house in respect of the repair, maintenance, cleanliness and good order of the house and facilities and equipment in it;
(b) impose duties on persons occupying a house for the purpose of ensuring that the person managing the house can effectively carry out any duty imposed on him by the regulations.

(3) A person commits an offence if he fails to comply with a regulation under this section.

(4) In proceedings against a person for an offence under subsection (3) it is a defence that he had a reasonable excuse for not complying with the regulation.

(5) A person who commits an offence under subsection (3) is liable on summary conviction to a fine not exceeding level 5 on the standard scale.

Information provisions

235 Power to require documents to be produced

(1) A person authorised in writing by a local housing authority may exercise the power conferred by subsection (2) in relation to documents reasonably required by the authority—

(a) for any purpose connected with the exercise of any of the authority's functions under any of Parts 1 to 4 in relation to any premises, or

(b) for the purpose of investigating whether any offence has been committed under any of those Parts in relation to any premises.

(2) A person so authorised may give a notice to a relevant person requiring him—

(a) to produce any documents which—

(i) are specified or described in the notice, or fall within a category of document which is specified or described in the notice, and

(ii) are in his custody or under his control, and

(b) to produce them at a time and place so specified and to a person so specified.

(3) The notice must include information about the possible consequences of not complying with the notice.

(4) The person to whom any document is produced in accordance with the notice may copy the document.

(5) No person may be required under this section to produce any document which he would be entitled to refuse to provide in proceedings in the High Court on grounds of legal professional privilege.

(6) In this section "document" includes information recorded otherwise than in legible form, and in relation to information so recorded, any reference to the production of a document is a reference to the production of a copy of the information in legible form.

(7) In this section "relevant person" means, in relation to any premises, a person within any of the following paragraphs—

(a) a person who is, or is proposed to be, the holder of a licence under Part 2 or 3 in respect of the premises, or a person on whom any obligation or restriction under such a licence is, or is proposed to be, imposed,

(b) a person who has an estate or interest in the premises,

(c) a person who is, or is proposing to be, managing or having control of the premises,

(d) a person who is, or is proposing to be, otherwise involved in the management of the premises,

(e) a person who occupies the premises.

236 Enforcement of powers to obtain information

(1) A person commits an offence if he fails to do anything required of him by a notice under section 235.

(2) In proceedings against a person for an offence under subsection (1) it is a defence that he had a reasonable excuse for failing to comply with the notice.

(3) A person who commits an offence under subsection (1) is liable on summary conviction to a fine not exceeding level 5 on the standard scale.

(4) A person commits an offence if he intentionally alters, suppresses or destroys any document which he has been required to produce by a notice under section 235.

(5) A person who commits an offence under subsection (4) is liable—
(a) on summary conviction, to a fine not exceeding the statutory maximum;
(b) on conviction on indictment, to a fine.

(6) In this section "document" includes information recorded otherwise than in legible form, and in relation to information so recorded—
(a) the reference to the production of a document is a reference to the production of a copy of the information in legible form, and
(b) the reference to suppressing a document includes a reference to destroying the means of reproducing the information.

237 Use of information obtained for certain other statutory purposes

(1) A local housing authority may use any information to which this section applies—
(a) for any purpose connected with the exercise of any of the authority's functions under any of Parts 1 to 4 in relation to any premises, or
(b) for the purpose of investigating whether any offence has been committed under any of those Parts in relation to any premises.

(2) This section applies to any information which has been obtained by the authority in the exercise of functions under—
(a) section 134 of the Social Security Administration Act 1992 (c. 5) (housing benefit), or
(b) Part 1 of the Local Government Finance Act 1992 (c. 14) (council tax).

238 False or misleading information

(1) A person commits an offence if—
(a) he supplies any information to a local housing authority in connection with any of their functions under any of Parts 1 to 4 or this Part,
(b) the information is false or misleading, and
(c) he knows that it is false or misleading or is reckless as to whether it is false or misleading.

(2) A person commits an offence if—
(a) he supplies any information to another person which is false or misleading,
(b) he knows that it is false or misleading or is reckless as to whether it is false or misleading, and

(c) he knows that the information is to be used for the purpose of supplying information to a local housing authority in connection with any of their functions under any of Parts 1 to 4 or this Part.

(3) A person who commits an offence under subsection (1) or (2) is liable on summary conviction to a fine not exceeding level 5 on the standard scale.

(4) In this section "false or misleading" means false or misleading in any material respect.

Enforcement

239 Powers of entry

(1) Subsection (3) applies where the local housing authority consider that a survey or examination of any premises is necessary and any of the following conditions is met—

(a) the authority consider that the survey or examination is necessary in order to carry out an inspection under section 4(1) or otherwise to determine whether any functions under any of Parts 1 to 4 or this Part should be exercised in relation to the premises;

(b) the premises are (within the meaning of Part 1) specified premises in relation to an improvement notice or prohibition order;

(c) a management order is in force under Chapter 1 or 2 of Part 4 in respect of the premises.

(2) Subsection (3) also applies where the proper officer of the local housing authority considers that a survey or examination of any premises is necessary in order to carry out an inspection under section 4(2).

(3) Where this subsection applies—

(a) a person authorised by the local housing authority (in a case within subsection (1)), or

(b) the proper officer (in a case within subsection (2)),

may enter the premises in question at any reasonable time for the purpose of carrying out a survey or examination of the premises.

(4) If—

(a) an interim or final management order is in force under Chapter 1 of Part 4 in respect of any premises consisting of part of a house ("the relevant premises"), and

(b) another part of the house is excluded from the order by virtue of section 102(8) or 113(7),

the power of entry conferred by subsection (3) is exercisable in relation to any premises comprised in that other part so far as is necessary for the purpose of carrying out a survey or examination of the relevant premises.

(5) Before entering any premises in exercise of the power conferred by subsection (3), the authorised person or proper officer must have given at least 24 hours' notice of his intention to do so—

(a) to the owner of the premises (if known), and

(b) to the occupier (if any).

(6) Subsection (7) applies where the local housing authority consider that any premises need to be entered for the purpose of ascertaining whether an offence has been committed under section 72, 95 or 234(3).

(7) A person authorised by the local housing authority may enter the premises for that purpose—
  (a) at any reasonable time, but
  (b) without giving any prior notice as mentioned in subsection (5).

(8) A person exercising the power of entry conferred by subsection (3) or (7) may do such of the following as he thinks necessary for the purpose for which the power is being exercised—
  (a) take other persons with him;
  (b) take equipment or materials with him;
  (c) take measurements or photographs or make recordings;
  (d) leave recording equipment on the premises for later collection;
  (e) take samples of any articles or substances found on the premises.

(9) An authorisation for the purposes of this section—
  (a) must be in writing; and
  (b) must state the particular purpose or purposes for which the entry is authorised.

(10) A person authorised for the purposes of this section must, if required to do so, produce his authorisation for inspection by the owner or any occupier of the premises or anyone acting on his behalf.

(11) If the premises are unoccupied or the occupier is temporarily absent, a person exercising the power of entry conferred by subsection (3) or (7) must leave the premises as effectively secured against trespassers as he found them.

(12) In this section "occupier", in relation to premises, means a person who occupies the premises, whether for residential or other purposes.

240 Warrant to authorise entry

(1) This section applies where a justice of the peace is satisfied, on a sworn information in writing, that admission to premises specified in the information is reasonably required for any of the purposes mentioned in subsection (2) by a person—
  (a) employed by, or
  (b) acting on the instructions of,

the local housing authority.

(2) The purposes are—
  (a) surveying or examining premises in order to carry out an inspection under section 4(1) or (2) or otherwise to determine whether any functions under any of Parts 1 to 4 or this Part should be exercised in relation to the premises;
  (b) surveying or examining premises—
    (i) which are (within the meaning of Part 1) specified premises in relation to an improvement notice or prohibition order, or
    (ii) in respect of which a management order is in force under Chapter 1 or 2 of Part 4;

(c) ascertaining whether an offence has been committed under section 72, 95 or 234(3).

(3) The justice may by warrant under his hand authorise the person mentioned in subsection (1) to enter on the premises for such of those purposes as may be specified in the warrant.

(4) But the justice must not grant the warrant unless he is satisfied—

(a) that admission to the premises has been sought in accordance with section 239(5) or (7) but has been refused;

(b) that the premises are unoccupied or that the occupier is temporarily absent and it might defeat the purpose of the entry to await his return; or

(c) that application for admission would defeat the purpose of the entry.

(5) The power of entry conferred by a warrant under this section includes power to enter by force (if necessary).

(6) Subsection (8) of section 239 applies to the person on whom that power is conferred as it applies to a person exercising the power of entry conferred by subsection (3) or (7) of that section.

(7) A warrant under this section must, if so required, be produced for inspection by the owner or any occupier of the premises or anyone acting on his behalf.

(8) If the premises are unoccupied or the occupier is temporarily absent, a person entering under the authority of a warrant under this section must leave the premises as effectively secured against trespassers as he found them.

(9) A warrant under this section continues in force until the purpose for which the entry is required is satisfied.

(10) In a case within section 239(4)(a) and (b), the powers conferred by this section are exercisable in relation to premises comprised in the excluded part of the house as well as in relation to the relevant premises.

(11) In this section "occupier", in relation to premises, means a person who occupies the premises, whether for residential or other purposes.

241 Penalty for obstruction

(1) A person who obstructs a relevant person in the performance of anything which, by virtue of any of Parts 1 to 4 or this Part, that person is required or authorised to do commits an offence.

(2) In proceedings against a person for an offence under subsection (1) it is a defence that he had a reasonable excuse for obstructing the relevant person.

(3) A person who commits an offence under subsection (1) is liable on summary conviction to a fine not exceeding level 4 on the standard scale.

(4) In this section "relevant person" means an officer of a local housing authority or any person authorised to enter premises by virtue of any of Parts 1 to 4 or section 239 or 240.

242 Additional notice requirements for protection of owners

(1) This section applies where an owner of premises gives a notice to the local housing authority for the purposes of this section informing them of his interest in the premises.

(2) The authority must give him notice of any action taken by them under any of Parts 1 to 4 or this Part in relation to the premises.

Authorisations

243 Authorisations for enforcement purposes etc.

(1) This section applies to any authorisation given for the purposes of any of the following provisions—

(a) section 131 (management orders: power of entry to carry out work),

(b) section 235 (power to require documents to be produced),

(c) section 239 (powers of entry),

(d) paragraph 3(4) of Schedule 3 (improvement notices: power to enter to carry out work), and

(e) paragraph 25 of Schedule 7 (EDMOs: power of entry to carry out work).

(2) Any such authorisation must be given by the appropriate officer of the local housing authority.

(3) For the purposes of this section a person is an "appropriate officer" of a local housing authority, in relation to an authorisation given by the authority, if either—

(a) he is a deputy chief officer of the authority (within the meaning of section 2 of the Local Government and Housing Act 1989 (c. 42)), and

(b) the duties of his post consist of or include duties relating to the exercise of the functions of the authority in connection with which the authorisation is given,

or he is an officer of the authority to whom such a deputy chief officer reports directly, or is directly accountable, as respects duties so relating.

Documents

244 Power to prescribe forms

(1) The appropriate national authority may by regulations prescribe the form of any notice, statement or other document which is required or authorised to be used under, or for the purposes of, this Act.

(2) The power conferred by this section is not exercisable where specific provision for prescribing the form of a document is made elsewhere in this Act.

245 Power to dispense with notices

(1) The appropriate national authority may dispense with the service of a notice which is required to be served by a local housing authority under this Act if satisfied that it is reasonable to do so.

(2) A dispensation may be given either before or after the time at which the notice is required to be served.

(3) A dispensation may be given either unconditionally or on such conditions (whether as to the service of other notices or otherwise) as the appropriate national authority considers appropriate.

(4) Before giving a dispensation under this section, the appropriate national authority shall, in particular, have regard to the need to ensure, so far as possible, that the interests of any person are not prejudiced by the dispensation.

246 Service of documents

(1) Subsection (2) applies where the local housing authority is, by virtue of any provision of Parts 1 to 4 or this Part, under a duty to serve a document on a person who, to the knowledge of the authority, is—

- (a) a person having control of premises,
- (b) a person managing premises, or
- (c) a person having an estate or interest in premises,

or a person who (but for an interim or final management order under Chapter 1 of Part 4) would fall within paragraph (a) or (b).

(2) The local housing authority must take reasonable steps to identify the person or persons falling within the description in that provision.

(3) A person having an estate or interest in premises may for the purposes of any provision to which subsections (1) and (2) apply give notice to the local housing authority of his interest in the premises.

(4) The local housing authority must enter a notice under subsection (3) in its records.

(5) A document required or authorised by any of Parts 1 to 4 or this Part to be served on a person as—

- (a) a person having control of premises,
- (b) a person managing premises,
- (c) a person having an estate or interest in premises, or
- (d) a person who (but for an interim or final management order under Chapter 1 of Part 4) would fall within paragraph (a) or (b),

may, if it is not practicable after reasonable enquiry to ascertain the name or address of that person, be served in accordance with subsection (6).

(6) A person having such a connection with any premises as is mentioned in subsection (5) (a) to (d) is served in accordance with this subsection if—

- (a) the document is addressed to him by describing his connection with the premises (naming them), and
- (b) delivering the document to some person on the premises or, if there is no person on the premises to whom it can be delivered, by fixing it, or a copy of it, to some conspicuous part of the premises.

(7) Subsection (1)(c) or (5)(c) applies whether the provision requiring or authorising service of the document refers in terms to a person having an estate or interest in premises or instead refers to a class of person having such an estate or interest (such as owners, lessees or mortgagees).

(8) Where under any provision of Parts 1 to 4 or this Part a document is to be served on—

(a) the person having control of premises,

(b) the person managing premises, or

(c) the owner of premises,

and more than one person comes within the description in the provision, the document may be served on more than one of those persons.

(9) Section 233 of the Local Government Act 1972 (c. 70) (service of notices by local authorities) applies in relation to the service of documents for any purposes of this Act by the authorities mentioned in section 261(2)(d) and (e) of this Act as if they were local authorities within the meaning of section 233.

(10) In this section—

(a) references to a person managing premises include references to a person authorised to permit persons to occupy premises; and

(b) references to serving include references to similar expressions (such as giving or sending).

(11) In this section—

"document" includes anything in writing;

"premises" means premises however defined.

247 Licences and other documents in electronic form

(1) A local housing authority may, subject to subsection (3), issue a licence to a person under Part 2 or 3 by transmitting the text of the licence to him by electronic means, provided the text—

(a) is received by him in legible form, and

(b) is capable of being used for subsequent reference.

(2) A local housing authority may, subject to subsection (3), serve a relevant document on a person by transmitting the text of the document to him in the way mentioned in subsection (1).

(3) The recipient, or the person on whose behalf the recipient receives the document, must have indicated to the local housing authority the recipient's willingness to receive documents transmitted in the form and manner used.

(4) An indication for the purposes of subsection (3)—

(a) must be given to the local housing authority in such manner as they may require;

(b) may be a general indication or one that is limited to documents of a particular description;

(c) must state the address to be used and must be accompanied by such other information as the local housing authority require for the making of the transmission; and

(d) may be modified or withdrawn at any time by a notice given to the local housing authority in such manner as they may require.

(5) In this section any reference to serving includes a reference to similar expressions (such as giving or sending).

(6) In this section—

"document" includes anything in writing; and

"relevant document" means any document which a local housing authority are, by virtue of any provision of Parts 1 to 4 or this Part, under a duty to serve on any person.

248 Timing and location of things done electronically

(1) The Secretary of State may by regulations make provision specifying, for the purposes of any of Parts 1 to 4 or this Part, the manner of determining—

(a) the times at which things done under any of Parts 1 to 4 or this Part by means of electronic communications networks are done;

(b) the places at which things done under any of Parts 1 to 4 or this Part by means of such networks are done; and

(c) the places at which things transmitted by means of such networks are received.

(2) The Secretary of State may by regulations make provision about the manner of proving in any legal proceedings—

(a) that something done by means of an electronic communications network satisfies any requirements of any of Parts 1 to 4 or this Part for the doing of that thing; and

(b) the matters mentioned in subsection (1)(a) to (c).

(3) Regulations under this section may provide for such presumptions to apply (whether conclusive or not) as the Secretary of State considers appropriate.

(4) In this section "electronic communications network" has the meaning given by section 32 of the Communications Act 2003 (c. 21).

249 Proof of designations

(1) This subsection applies in respect of a copy of—

(a) a designation under section 56 (designation of an area as subject to additional licensing), or

(b) a designation under section 80 (designation of an area as subject to selective licensing),

which purports to be made by a local housing authority.

(2) A certificate endorsed on such a copy and purporting to be signed by the proper officer of the authority stating the matters set out in subsection (3) is prima facie evidence of the facts so stated without proof of the handwriting or official position of the person by whom it purports to be signed.

(3) Those matters are—

(a) that the designation was made by the authority,

(b) that the copy is a true copy of the designation, and

(c) that the designation did not require confirmation by the confirming authority, or that on a specified date the designation was confirmed by the confirming authority.

Other supplementary provisions

250 Orders and regulations

(1) Any power of the Secretary of State or the National Assembly for Wales to make an order or regulations under this Act is exercisable by statutory instrument.

(2) Any power of the Secretary of State or the National Assembly for Wales to make an order or regulations under this Act—

(a) may be exercised so as to make different provision for different cases or descriptions of case or different purposes or areas; and

(b) includes power to make such incidental, supplementary, consequential, transitory, transitional or saving provision as the Secretary of State or (as the case may be) the National Assembly for Wales considers appropriate.

(3) The Secretary of State must consult the National Assembly for Wales before making any regulations under Part 5 which relate to residential properties in Wales.

(4) Subject to subsections (5) and (6), any order or regulations made by the Secretary of State under this Act are to be subject to annulment in pursuance of a resolution of either House of Parliament.

(5) Subsection (4) does not apply to any order under section 270 or paragraph 3 of Schedule 10.

(6) Subsection (4) also does not apply to—

(a) any order under section 55(3) which makes the provision authorised by section 55(4),

(b) any order under section 80(5) or (7),

(c) any order under section 216 or 229(3),

(d) any order under section 265(2) which modifies any provision of an Act,

(e) any regulations under section 254(6),

(f) any regulations under paragraph 3 of Schedule 4 or orders under paragraph 11 of Schedule 10, or

(g) any regulations made by virtue of paragraph 11(3)(b) or 12(3)(b) of Schedule 13;

and no such order or regulations may be made by the Secretary of State (whether alone or with other provisions) unless a draft of the statutory instrument containing the order or regulations has been laid before, and approved by a resolution of, each House of Parliament.

(7) In this Act "modify", in the context of a power to modify an enactment by order or regulations, includes repeal (and "modifications" has a corresponding meaning).

251 Offences by bodies corporate

(1) Where an offence under this Act committed by a body corporate is proved to have been committed with the consent or connivance of, or to be attributable to any neglect on the part of—

(a) a director, manager, secretary or other similar officer of the body corporate, or

(b) a person purporting to act in such a capacity,

he as well as the body corporate commits the offence and is liable to be proceeded against and punished accordingly.

(2) Where the affairs of a body corporate are managed by its members, subsection (1) applies in relation to the acts and defaults of a member in connection with his functions of management as if he were a director of the body corporate.

252 Power to up-rate level of fines for certain offences

(1) Subsection (2) applies if the Secretary of State considers that there has been a change in the value of money since the relevant date.

(2) The Secretary of State may by order substitute for the sum or sums for the time being specified in any provision mentioned in subsection (3) such other sum or sums as he considers to be justified by the change.

(3) The provisions are—

(a) section 32(2)(b);

(b) section 35(6);

(c) section 72(6); and

(d) section 95(5).

(4) In subsection (1) "the relevant date" means—

(a) the date of the passing of this Act; or

(b) where the sums specified in a provision mentioned in subsection (3) have been substituted by an order under subsection (2), the date of that order.

(5) Nothing in an order under subsection (2) affects the punishment for an offence committed before the order comes into force.

253 Local inquiries

The appropriate national authority may, for the purposes of the execution of any of the authority's functions under this Act, cause such local inquiries to be held as the authority considers appropriate.

Meaning of "house in multiple occupation"

254 Meaning of "house in multiple occupation"

(1) For the purposes of this Act a building or a part of a building is a "house in multiple occupation" if—

(a) it meets the conditions in subsection (2) ("the standard test");

(b) it meets the conditions in subsection (3) ("the self-contained flat test");

(c) it meets the conditions in subsection (4) ("the converted building test");

(d) an HMO declaration is in force in respect of it under section 255; or

(e) it is a converted block of flats to which section 257 applies.

(2) A building or a part of a building meets the standard test if—

(a) it consists of one or more units of living accommodation not consisting of a self-contained flat or flats;

(b) the living accommodation is occupied by persons who do not form a single household (see section 258);

(c) the living accommodation is occupied by those persons as their only or main residence or they are to be treated as so occupying it (see section 259);

(d) their occupation of the living accommodation constitutes the only use of that accommodation;

(e) rents are payable or other consideration is to be provided in respect of at least one of those persons' occupation of the living accommodation; and

(f) two or more of the households who occupy the living accommodation share one or more basic amenities or the living accommodation is lacking in one or more basic amenities.

(3) A part of a building meets the self-contained flat test if—

(a) it consists of a self-contained flat; and

(b) paragraphs (b) to (f) of subsection (2) apply (reading references to the living accommodation concerned as references to the flat).

(4) A building or a part of a building meets the converted building test if—

(a) it is a converted building;

(b) it contains one or more units of living accommodation that do not consist of a self-contained flat or flats (whether or not it also contains any such flat or flats);

(c) the living accommodation is occupied by persons who do not form a single household (see section 258);

(d) the living accommodation is occupied by those persons as their only or main residence or they are to be treated as so occupying it (see section 259);

(e) their occupation of the living accommodation constitutes the only use of that accommodation; and

(f) rents are payable or other consideration is to be provided in respect of at least one of those persons' occupation of the living accommodation.

(5) But for any purposes of this Act (other than those of Part 1) a building or part of a building within subsection (1) is not a house in multiple occupation if it is listed in Schedule 14.

(6) The appropriate national authority may by regulations—

(a) make such amendments of this section and sections 255 to 259 as the authority considers appropriate with a view to securing that any building or part of a building of a description specified in the regulations is or is not to be a house in multiple occupation for any specified purposes of this Act;

(b) provide for such amendments to have effect also for the purposes of definitions in other enactments that operate by reference to this Act;

(c) make such consequential amendments of any provision of this Act, or any other enactment, as the authority considers appropriate.

(7) Regulations under subsection (6) may frame any description by reference to any matters or circumstances whatever.

(8) In this section—

"basic amenities" means—

(a) a toilet,

(b) personal washing facilities, or

(c) cooking facilities;

"converted building" means a building or part of a building consisting of living accommodation in which one or more units of such accommodation have been created since the building or part was constructed;

"enactment" includes an enactment comprised in subordinate legislation (within the meaning of the Interpretation Act 1978 (c. 30);

"self-contained flat" means a separate set of premises (whether or not on the same floor)—

(a) which forms part of a building;
(b) either the whole or a material part of which lies above or below some other part of the building; and
(c) in which all three basic amenities are available for the exclusive use of its occupants.

255 HMO declarations

(1) If a local housing authority are satisfied that subsection (2) applies to a building or part of a building in their area, they may serve a notice under this section (an "HMO declaration") declaring the building or part to be a house in multiple occupation.

(2) This subsection applies to a building or part of a building if the building or part meets any of the following tests (as it applies without the sole use condition)—

(a) the standard test (see section 254(2)),
(b) the self-contained flat test (see section 254(3)), or
(c) the converted building test (see section 254(4)),

and the occupation, by persons who do not form a single household, of the living accommodation or flat referred to in the test in question constitutes a significant use of that accommodation or flat.

(3) In subsection (2) "the sole use condition" means the condition contained in—

(a) section 254(2)(d) (as it applies for the purposes of the standard test or the self-contained flat test), or
(b) section 254(4)(e),

as the case may be.

(4) The notice must—

(a) state the date of the authority's decision to serve the notice,
(b) be served on each relevant person within the period of seven days beginning with the date of that decision,
(c) state the day on which it will come into force if no appeal is made under subsection (9) against the authority's decision, and
(d) set out the right to appeal against the decision under subsection (9) and the period within which an appeal may be made.

(5) The day stated in the notice under subsection (4)(c) must be not less than 28 days after the date of the authority's decision to serve the notice.

(6) If no appeal is made under subsection (9) before the end of that period of 28 days, the notice comes into force on the day stated in the notice.

(7) If such an appeal is made before the end of that period of 28 days, the notice does not come into force unless and until a decision is given on the appeal which confirms the notice and either—

(a) the period within which an appeal to the Lands Tribunal may be brought expires without such an appeal having been brought, or

(b) if an appeal to the Lands Tribunal is brought, a decision is given on the appeal which confirms the notice.

(8) For the purposes of subsection (7), the withdrawal of an appeal has the same effect as a decision which confirms the notice appealed against.

(9) Any relevant person may appeal to a residential property tribunal against a decision of the local housing authority to serve an HMO declaration.

The appeal must be made within the period of 28 days beginning with the date of the authority's decision.

(10) Such an appeal—

(a) is to be by way of a re-hearing, but

(b) may be determined having regard to matters of which the authority were unaware.

(11) The tribunal may—

(a) confirm or reverse the decision of the authority, and

(b) if it reverses the decision, revoke the HMO declaration.

(12) In this section and section 256 "relevant person", in relation to an HMO declaration, means any person who, to the knowledge of the local housing authority, is—

(a) a person having an estate or interest in the building or part of the building concerned (but is not a tenant under a lease with an unexpired term of 3 years of less), or

(b) a person managing or having control of that building or part (and not falling within paragraph (a)).

256 Revocation of HMO declarations

(1) A local housing authority may revoke an HMO declaration served under section 255 at any time if they consider that subsection (2) of that section no longer applies to the building or part of the building in respect of which the declaration was served.

(2) The power to revoke an HMO declaration is exercisable by the authority either—

(a) on an application made by a relevant person, or

(b) on the authority's own initiative.

(3) If, on an application by such a person, the authority decide not to revoke the HMO declaration, they must without delay serve on him a notice informing him of—

(a) the decision,

(b) the reasons for it and the date on which it was made,

(c) the right to appeal against it under subsection (4), and

(d) the period within which an appeal may be made under that subsection.

(4) A person who applies to a local housing authority for the revocation of an HMO declaration under subsection (1) may appeal to a residential property tribunal against a decision of the authority to refuse to revoke the notice.

The appeal must be made within the period of 28 days beginning with the date specified under subsection (3) as the date on which the decision was made.

(5) Such an appeal—

(a) is to be by way of a re-hearing, but

(b) may be determined having regard to matters of which the authority were unaware.

(6) The tribunal may—

(a) confirm or reverse the decision of the authority, and

(b) if it reverses the decision, revoke the HMO declaration.

257 HMOs: certain converted blocks of flats

(1) For the purposes of this section a "converted block of flats" means a building or part of a building which—

(a) has been converted into, and

(b) consists of,

self-contained flats.

(2) This section applies to a converted block of flats if—

(a) building work undertaken in connection with the conversion did not comply with the appropriate building standards and still does not comply with them; and

(b) less than two-thirds of the self-contained flats are owner-occupied.

(3) In subsection (2) "appropriate building standards" means—

(a) in the case of a converted block of flats—

(i) on which building work was completed before 1st June 1992 or which is dealt with by regulation 20 of the Building Regulations 1991 (S.I. 1991/2768), and

(ii) which would not have been exempt under those Regulations,

building standards equivalent to those imposed, in relation to a building or part of a building to which those Regulations applied, by those Regulations as they had effect on 1st June 1992; and

(b) in the case of any other converted block of flats, the requirements imposed at the time in relation to it by regulations under section 1 of the Building Act 1984 (c. 55).

(4) For the purposes of subsection (2) a flat is "owner-occupied" if it is occupied—

(a) by a person who has a lease of the flat which has been granted for a term of more than 21 years,

(b) by a person who has the freehold estate in the converted block of flats, or

(c) by a member of the household of a person within paragraph (a) or (b).

(5) The fact that this section applies to a converted block of flats (with the result that it is a house in multiple occupation under section 254(1)(e)), does not affect the status of any flat in the block as a house in multiple occupation.

(6) In this section "self-contained flat" has the same meaning as in section 254.

258 HMOs: persons not forming a single household

(1) This section sets out when persons are to be regarded as not forming a single household for the purposes of section 254.

(2) Persons are to be regarded as not forming a single household unless—
- (a) they are all members of the same family, or
- (b) their circumstances are circumstances of a description specified for the purposes of this section in regulations made by the appropriate national authority.

(3) For the purposes of subsection (2)(a) a person is a member of the same family as another person if—
- (a) those persons are married to each other or live together as husband and wife (or in an equivalent relationship in the case of persons of the same sex);
- (b) one of them is a relative of the other; or
- (c) one of them is, or is a relative of, one member of a couple and the other is a relative of the other member of the couple.

(4) For those purposes—
- (a) a "couple" means two persons who are married to each other or otherwise fall within subsection (3)(a);
- (b) "relative" means parent, grandparent, child, grandchild, brother, sister, uncle, aunt, nephew, niece or cousin;
- (c) a relationship of the half-blood shall be treated as a relationship of the whole blood; and
- (d) the stepchild of a person shall be treated as his child.

(5) Regulations under subsection (2)(b) may, in particular, secure that a group of persons are to be regarded as forming a single household only where (as the regulations may require) each member of the group has a prescribed relationship, or at least one of a number of prescribed relationships, to any one or more of the others.

(6) In subsection (5) "prescribed relationship" means any relationship of a description specified in the regulations.

259 HMOs: persons treated as occupying premises as only or main residence

(1) This section sets out when persons are to be treated for the purposes of section 254 as occupying a building or part of a building as their only or main residence.

(2) A person is to be treated as so occupying a building or part of a building if it is occupied by the person—
- (a) as the person's residence for the purpose of undertaking a full-time course of further or higher education;
- (b) as a refuge, or

(c) in any other circumstances which are circumstances of a description specified for the purposes of this section in regulations made by the appropriate national authority.

(3) In subsection (2)(b) "refuge" means a building or part of a building managed by a voluntary organisation and used wholly or mainly for the temporary accommodation of persons who have left their homes as a result of—

(a) physical violence or mental abuse, or

(b) threats of such violence or abuse,

from persons to whom they are or were married or with whom they are or were co-habiting.

260 HMOs: presumption that sole use condition or significant use condition is met

(1) Where a question arises in any proceedings as to whether either of the following is met in respect of a building or part of a building—

(a) the sole use condition, or

(b) the significant use condition,

it shall be presumed, for the purposes of the proceedings, that the condition is met unless the contrary is shown.

(2) In this section—

(a) "the sole use condition" means the condition contained in—

(i) section 254(2)(d) (as it applies for the purposes of the standard test or the self-contained flat test), or

(ii) section 254(4)(e),

as the case may be; and

(b) "the significant use condition" means the condition contained in section 255(2) that the occupation of the living accommodation or flat referred to in that provision by persons who do not form a single household constitutes a significant use of that accommodation or flat.

Other general interpretation provisions

261 Meaning of "appropriate national authority", "local housing authority" etc.

(1) In this Act "the appropriate national authority" means—

(a) in relation to England, the Secretary of State; and

(b) in relation to Wales, the National Assembly for Wales.

(2) In this Act "local housing authority" means, in relation to England—

(a) a unitary authority;

(b) a district council so far as it is not a unitary authority;

(c) a London borough council;

(d) the Common Council of the City of London (in its capacity as a local authority);

(e) the Sub-Treasurer of the Inner Temple or the Under-Treasurer of the Middle Temple (in his capacity as a local authority); and

(f) the Council of the Isles of Scilly.

(3) In subsection (2) "unitary authority" means—
   (a) the council of a county so far as it is the council for an area for which there are no district councils;
   (b) the council of any district comprised in an area for which there is no county council.

(4) In this Act "local housing authority" means, in relation to Wales, a county council or a county borough council.

(5) References in this Act to "the local housing authority", in relation to land, are to the local housing authority in whose district the land is situated.

(6) References in this Act to the district of a local housing authority are to the area of the council concerned, that is to say—
   (a) in the case of a unitary authority, the area or district;
   (b) in the case of a district council so far as it is not a unitary authority, the district;
   (c) in the case of an authority within subsection (2)(c) to (f), the London borough, the City of London, the Inner or Middle Temple or the Isles of Scilly (as the case may be); and
   (d) in the case of a Welsh county council or a county borough council, the Welsh county or county borough.

(7) Section 618 of the Housing Act 1985 (c. 68) (committees and members of Common Council of City of London) applies in relation to this Act as it applies in relation to that Act.

262 Meaning of "lease", "tenancy", "occupier" and "owner" etc.

(1) In this Act "lease" and "tenancy" have the same meaning.

(2) Both expressions include—
   (a) a sub-lease or sub-tenancy; and
   (b) an agreement for a lease or tenancy (or sub-lease or sub-tenancy).

   And see sections 108 and 117 and paragraphs 3 and 11 of Schedule 7 (which also extend the meaning of references to leases).

(3) The expressions "lessor" and "lessee" and "landlord" and "tenant" and references to letting, to the grant of a lease or to covenants or terms, are to be construed accordingly.

(4) In this Act "lessee" includes a statutory tenant of the premises; and references to a lease or to a person to whom premises are let are to be construed accordingly.

(5) In this Act any reference to a person who is a tenant under a lease with an unexpired term of 3 years or less includes a statutory tenant as well as a tenant under a yearly or other periodic tenancy.

(6) In this Act "occupier", in relation to premises, means a person who—
   (a) occupies the premises as a residence, and
   (b) (subject to the context) so occupies them whether as a tenant or other person having an estate or interest in the premises or as a licensee;

   and related expressions are to be construed accordingly.

This subsection does not apply for the purposes of Part 5 and has effect subject to any other provision defining "occupier" for any purposes of this Act.

(7) In this Act "owner", in relation to premises—

(a) means a person (other than a mortgagee not in possession) who is for the time being entitled to dispose of the fee simple of the premises whether in possession or in reversion; and

(b) includes also a person holding or entitled to the rents and profits of the premises under a lease of which the unexpired term exceeds 3 years.

(8) In this Act "person having an estate or interest", in relation to premises, includes a statutory tenant of the premises.

(9) In this Act "licence", in the context of a licence to occupy premises—

(a) includes a licence which is not granted for a consideration, but

(b) excludes a licence granted as a temporary expedient to a person who entered the premises as a trespasser (whether or not, before the grant of the licence, another licence to occupy those or other premises had been granted to him);

and related expressions are to be construed accordingly.

And see sections 108 and 117 and paragraphs 3 and 11 of Schedule 7 (which also extend the meaning of references to licences).

263 Meaning of "person having control" and "person managing" etc.

(1) In this Act "person having control", in relation to premises, means (unless the context otherwise requires) the person who receives the rack-rent of the premises (whether on his own account or as agent or trustee of another person), or who would so receive it if the premises were let at a rack-rent.

(2) In subsection (1) "rack-rent" means a rent which is not less than two-thirds of the full net annual value of the premises.

(3) In this Act "person managing" means, in relation to premises, the person who, being an owner or lessee of the premises—

(a) receives (whether directly or through an agent or trustee) rents or other payments from—

(i) in the case of a house in multiple occupation, persons who are in occupation as tenants or licensees of parts of the premises; and

(ii) in the case of a house to which Part 3 applies (see section 79(2)), persons who are in occupation as tenants or licensees of parts of the premises, or of the whole of the premises; or

(b) would so receive those rents or other payments but for having entered into an arrangement (whether in pursuance of a court order or otherwise) with another person who is not an owner or lessee of the premises by virtue of which that other person receives the rents or other payments;

and includes, where those rents or other payments are received through another person as agent or trustee, that other person.

(4) In its application to Part 1, subsection (3) has effect with the omission of paragraph (a)(ii).

(5) References in this Act to any person involved in the management of a house in multiple occupation or a house to which Part 3 applies (see section 79(2)) include references to the person managing it.

264 Calculation of numbers of persons

(1) The appropriate national authority may prescribe rules with respect to the calculation of numbers of persons for the purposes of—

(a) any provision made by or under this Act which is specified in the rules, or

(b) any order or licence made or granted under this Act of any description which is so specified.

(2) The rules may provide—

(a) for persons under a particular age to be disregarded for the purposes of any such calculation;

(b) for persons under a particular age to be treated as constituting a fraction of a person for the purposes of any such calculation.

(3) The rules may be prescribed by order or regulations.

Final provisions

265 Minor and consequential amendments

(1) Schedule 15 (which contains minor and consequential amendments) has effect.

(2) The Secretary of State may by order make such supplementary, incidental or consequential provision as he considers appropriate—

(a) for the general purposes, or any particular purpose, of this Act; or

(b) in consequence of any provision made by or under this Act or for giving full effect to it.

(3) An order under subsection (2) may modify any enactment (including this Act).

"Enactment" includes an enactment comprised in subordinate legislation (within the meaning of the Interpretation Act 1978 (c. 30)).

(4) The power conferred by subsection (2) is also exercisable by the National Assembly for Wales in relation to provision dealing with matters with respect to which functions are exercisable by the Assembly.

(5) Nothing in this Act affects the generality of the power conferred by this section.

266 Repeals

Schedule 16 (which contains repeals) has effect.

267 Devolution: Wales

In Schedule 1 to the National Assembly for Wales (Transfer of Functions) Order 1999 (S.I. 1999/672) references to the following Acts are to be treated as references to those Acts as amended by virtue of this Act—

(a) the Housing Act 1985 (c. 68);

(b) the Housing Act 1988 (c. 50);
(c) the Housing Act 1996 (c. 52).

268 The Isles of Scilly

(1) This Secretary of State may by order provide that, in its application to the Isles of Scilly, this Act is have effect with such modifications as are specified in the order.

(2) Where a similar power is exercisable under another Act in relation to provisions of that Act which are amended by this Act, the power is exercisable in relation to those provisions as so amended.

269 Expenses

There shall be paid out of money provided by Parliament—

(a) any expenditure incurred by the Secretary of State by virtue of this Act;
(b) any increase attributable to this Act in the sums payable out of money so provided under any other enactment.

270 Short title, commencement and extent

(1) This Act may be cited as the Housing Act 2004.

(2) The following provisions come into force on the day on which this Act is passed—

(a) sections 2, 9, 161 to 164, 176, 190, 208, 216, 233, 234, 244, 248, 250, 252, 264, 265(2) to (5), 267 to 269 and this section, and
(b) any other provision of this Act so far as it confers any power to make an order or regulations which is exercisable by the Secretary of State or the National Assembly for Wales.

Subsections (3) to (7) have effect subject to paragraph (b).

(3) The following provisions come into force at the end of the period of two months beginning with the day on which this Act is passed—

(a) sections 180, 182 to 189, 195 to 207, 209 to 211, 217, 218, 219, 222, 224, 245 to 247, 249, 251 and 253 to 263,
(b) Schedule 9,
(c) Schedule 11, except paragraphs 15 and 16, and
(d) Schedule 14.

(4) The provisions listed in subsection (5) come into force—

(a) where they are to come into force in relation only to Wales, on such day as the National Assembly for Wales may by order appoint, and
(b) otherwise, on such day as the Secretary of State may by order appoint.

(5) The provisions referred to in subsection (4) are—

(a) Part 1 (other than sections 2 and 9),
(b) Parts 2 to 4,
(c) sections 179, 181, 191 to 194, 212 to 215, 220, 221, 223, 225, 226, 227, 229 to 232, 235 to 243, 265(1) and 266,
(d) Schedule 10,

(e) paragraphs 15 and 16 of Schedule 11, and
(f) Schedules 13, 15 and 16.

(6) Part 5 (other than sections 161 to 164 and 176) comes into force on such day as the Secretary of State may by order appoint.

(7) Section 228 and Schedule 12 come into force on such day as the National Assembly for Wales may by order appoint.

(8) Different days may be appointed for different purposes or different areas under subsection (4), (6) or (7).

(9) The Secretary of State may by order make such provision as he considers necessary or expedient for transitory, transitional or saving purposes in connection with the coming into force of any provision of this Act.

(10) The power conferred by subsection (9) is also exercisable by the National Assembly for Wales in relation to provision dealing with matters with respect to which functions are exercisable by the Assembly

(11) Subject to subsections (12) and (13), this Act extends to England and Wales only.

(12) Any amendment or repeal made by this Act has the same extent as the enactment to which it relates, except that any amendment or repeal in—

the Mobile Homes Act 1983 (c. 34), or

the Crime and Disorder Act 1998 (c. 37),

extends to England and Wales only.

(13) This section extends to the whole of the United Kingdom.

SCHEDULES

SCHEDULE 1

Section 18

PROCEDURE AND APPEALS RELATING TO IMPROVEMENT NOTICES

PART 1

SERVICE OF IMPROVEMENT NOTICES

Service of improvement notices: premises licensed under Part 2 or 3

1 (1) This paragraph applies where the specified premises in the case of an improvement notice are—

(a) a dwelling which is licensed under Part 3 of this Act, or

(b) an HMO which is licensed under Part 2 or 3 of this Act.

(2) The local housing authority must serve the notice on the holder of the licence under that Part.

Service of improvement notices: premises which are neither licensed under Part 2 or 3 nor flats

2 (1) This paragraph applies where the specified premises in the case of an improvement notice are—

(a) a dwelling which is not licensed under Part 3 of this Act, or

(b) an HMO which is not licensed under Part 2 or 3 of this Act,

and which (in either case) is not a flat.

(2) The local housing authority must serve the notice—

(a) (in the case of a dwelling) on the person having control of the dwelling;

(b) (in the case of an HMO) either on the person having control of the HMO or on the person managing it.

Service of improvement notices: flats which are not licensed under Part 2 or 3

3 (1) This paragraph applies where any specified premises in the case of an improvement notice are—

(a) a dwelling which is not licensed under Part 3 of this Act, or

(b) an HMO which is not licensed under Part 2 or 3 of this Act,

and which (in either case) is a flat.

(2) In the case of dwelling which is a flat, the local housing authority must serve the notice on a person who—

(a) is an owner of the flat, and

(b) in the authority's opinion ought to take the action specified in the notice.

(3) In the case of an HMO which is a flat, the local housing authority must serve the notice either on a person who—
(a) is an owner of the flat, and
(b) in the authority's opinion ought to take the action specified in the notice,
or on the person managing the flat.

Service of improvement notices: common parts

4 (1) This paragraph applies where any specified premises in the case of an improvement notice are—
(a) common parts of a building containing one or more flats; or
(b) any part of such a building which does not consist of residential premises.

(2) The local housing authority must serve the notice on a person who—
(a) is an owner of the specified premises concerned, and
(b) in the authority's opinion ought to take the action specified in the notice.

(3) For the purposes of this paragraph a person is an owner of any common parts of a building if he is an owner of the building or part of the building concerned, or (in the case of external common parts) of the particular premises in which the common parts are comprised.

Service of copies of improvement notices

5 (1) In addition to serving an improvement notice in accordance with any of paragraphs 1 to 4, the local housing authority must serve a copy of the notice on every other person who, to their knowledge—
(a) has a relevant interest in any specified premises, or
(b) is an occupier of any such premises.

(2) A "relevant interest" means an interest as freeholder, mortgagee or lessee.

(3) For the purposes of this paragraph a person has a relevant interest in any common parts of a building if he has a relevant interest in the building or part of the building concerned, or (in the case of external common parts) in the particular premises in which the common parts are comprised.

(4) The copies required to be served under sub-paragraph (1) must be served within the period of seven days beginning with the day on which the notice is served.

PART 2

SERVICE OF NOTICES RELATING TO REVOCATION OR VARIATION OF IMPROVEMENT NOTICES

Notice of revocation or variation

6 (1) This paragraph applies where the local housing authority decide to revoke or vary an improvement notice.

(2) The authority must serve—
(a) a notice under this paragraph, and

(b) copies of that notice,

on the persons on whom they would be required under Part 1 of this Schedule to serve an improvement notice and copies of it in respect of the specified premises.

(3) Sub-paragraph (4) applies if, in so doing, the authority serve a notice under this paragraph on a person who is not the person on whom the improvement notice was served ("the original recipient").

(4) The authority must serve a copy of the notice under this paragraph on the original recipient unless they consider that it would not be appropriate to do so.

(5) The documents required to be served under sub-paragraph (2) must be served within the period of seven days beginning with the day on which the decision is made.

7 A notice under paragraph 6 must set out—

(a) the authority's decision to revoke or vary the improvement notice;

(b) the reasons for the decision and the date on which it was made;

(c) if the decision is to vary the notice—

(i) the right of appeal against the decision under Part 3 of this Schedule, and

(ii) the period within which an appeal may be made (see paragraph 14(2)).

Notice of refusal to revoke or vary notice

8 (1) This paragraph applies where the local housing authority refuse to revoke or vary an improvement notice.

(2) The authority must serve—

(a) a notice under this paragraph, and

(b) copies of that notice,

on the persons on whom they would be required to serve an improvement notice and copies of it under Part 1 of this Schedule.

(3) Sub-paragraph (4) applies if, in so doing, the authority serve a notice under this paragraph on a person who is not the person on whom the improvement notice was served ("the original recipient").

(4) The authority must serve a copy of the notice under this paragraph on the original recipient unless they consider that it would not be appropriate to do so.

(5) The documents required to be served under sub-paragraph (2) must be served within the period of seven days beginning with the day on which the decision is made.

9 A notice under paragraph 8 must set out—

(a) the authority's decision not to revoke or vary the improvement notice;

(b) the reasons for the decision and the date on which it was made;

(c) the right of appeal against the decision under Part 3 of this Schedule; and

(d) the period within which an appeal may be made (see paragraph 14(2)).

PART 3

APPEALS RELATING TO IMPROVEMENT NOTICES

Appeal against improvement notice

10 (1) The person on whom an improvement notice is served may appeal to a residential property tribunal against the notice.

(2) Paragraphs 11 and 12 set out two specific grounds on which an appeal may be made under this paragraph, but they do not affect the generality of sub-paragraph (1).

11 (1) An appeal may be made by a person under paragraph 10 on the ground that one or more other persons, as an owner or owners of the specified premises, ought to—

(a) take the action concerned, or

(b) pay the whole or part of the cost of taking that action.

(2) Where the grounds on which an appeal is made under paragraph 10 consist of or include the ground mentioned in sub-paragraph (1), the appellant must serve a copy of his notice of appeal on the other person or persons concerned.

12 (1) An appeal may be made by a person under paragraph 10 on the ground that one of the courses of action mentioned in sub-paragraph (2) is the best course of action in relation to the hazard in respect of which the notice was served.

(2) The courses of action are—

(a) making a prohibition order under section 20 or 21 of this Act;

(b) serving a hazard awareness notice under section 28 or 29 of this Act; and

(c) making a demolition order under section 265 of the Housing Act 1985 (c. 68).

Appeal against decision relating to variation or revocation of improvement notice

13 (1) The relevant person may appeal to a residential property tribunal against—

(a) a decision by the local housing authority to vary an improvement notice, or

(b) a decision by the authority to refuse to revoke or vary an improvement notice.

(2) In sub-paragraph (1) "the relevant person" means—

(a) in relation to a decision within paragraph (a) of that provision, the person on whom the notice was served;

(b) in relation to a decision within paragraph (b) of that provision, the person who applied for the revocation or variation.

Time limit for appeal

14 (1) Any appeal under paragraph 10 must be made within the period of 21 days beginning with the date on which the improvement notice was served in accordance with Part 1 of this Schedule.

(2) Any appeal under paragraph 13 must be made within the period of 28 days beginning with the date specified in the notice under paragraph 6 or 8 as the date on which the decision concerned was made.

(3) A residential property tribunal may allow an appeal to be made to it after the end of the period mentioned in sub-paragraph (1) or (2) if it is satisfied that there is a good reason for the failure to appeal before the end of that period (and for any delay since then in applying for permission to appeal out of time).

Powers of residential property tribunal on appeal under paragraph 10

15 (1) This paragraph applies to an appeal to a residential property tribunal under paragraph 10.

(2) The appeal—

(a) is to be by way of a re-hearing, but

(b) may be determined having regard to matters of which the authority were unaware.

(3) The tribunal may by order confirm, quash or vary the improvement notice.

(4) Paragraphs 16 and 17 make special provision in connection with the grounds of appeal set out in paragraphs 11 and 12.

16 (1) This paragraph applies where the grounds of appeal consist of or include that set out in paragraph 11.

(2) On the hearing of the appeal the tribunal may—

(a) vary the improvement notice so as to require the action to be taken by any owner mentioned in the notice of appeal in accordance with paragraph 11; or

(b) make such order as it considers appropriate with respect to the payment to be made by any such owner to the appellant or, where the action is taken by the local housing authority, to the authority.

(3) In the exercise of its powers under sub-paragraph (2), the tribunal must take into account, as between the appellant and any such owner—

(a) their relative interests in the premises concerned (considering both the nature of the interests and the rights and obligations arising under or by virtue of them);

(b) their relative responsibility for the state of the premises which gives rise to the need for the taking of the action concerned; and

(c) the relative degree of benefit to be derived from the taking of the action concerned.

(4) Sub-paragraph (5) applies where, by virtue of the exercise of the tribunal's powers under sub-paragraph (2), a person other than the appellant is required to take the action specified in an improvement notice.

(5) So long as that other person remains an owner of the premises to which the notice relates, he is to be regarded for the purposes of this Part as the person on whom the notice was served (in place of any other person).

17 (1) This paragraph applies where the grounds of appeal consist of or include that set out in paragraph 12.

(2) When deciding whether one of the courses of action mentioned in paragraph 12(2) is the best course of action in relation to a particular hazard, the tribunal must have regard to any guidance given to the local housing authority under section 9.

(3) Sub-paragraph (4) applies where—

(a) an appeal under paragraph 10 is allowed against an improvement notice in respect of a particular hazard; and

(b) the reason, or one of the reasons, for allowing the appeal is that one of the courses of action mentioned in paragraph 12(2) is the best course of action in relation to that hazard.

(4) The tribunal must, if requested to do so by the appellant or the local housing authority, include in its decision a finding to that effect and identifying the course of action concerned.

Powers of residential property tribunal on appeal under paragraph 13

18 (1) This paragraph applies to an appeal to a residential property tribunal under paragraph 13.

(2) Paragraph 15(2) applies to such an appeal as it applies to an appeal under paragraph 10.

(3) The tribunal may by order confirm, reverse or vary the decision of the local housing authority.

(4) If the appeal is against a decision of the authority to refuse to revoke an improvement notice, the tribunal may make an order revoking the notice as from a date specified in the order.

"The operative time" for the purposes of section 15(5)

19 (1) This paragraph defines "the operative time" for the purposes of section 15(5) (operation of improvement notices).

(2) If an appeal is made under paragraph 10 against an improvement notice which is not suspended, and a decision on the appeal is given which confirms the notice, "the operative time" is as follows—

(a) if the period within which an appeal to the Lands Tribunal may be brought expires without such an appeal having been brought, "the operative time" is the end of that period;

(b) if an appeal to the Lands Tribunal is brought, "the operative time" is the time when a decision is given on the appeal which confirms the notice.

(3) If an appeal is made under paragraph 10 against an improvement notice which is suspended, and a decision is given on the appeal which confirms the notice, "the operative time" is as follows—

(a) the time that would be the operative time under sub-paragraph (2) if the notice were not suspended, or

(b) if later, the time when the suspension ends.

(4) For the purposes of sub-paragraph (2) or (3)—

(a) the withdrawal of an appeal has the same effect as a decision which confirms the notice, and

(b) references to a decision which confirms the notice are to a decision which confirms it with or without variation.

"The operative time" for the purposes of section 16(7)

20 (1) This paragraph defines "the operative time" for the purposes of section 16(7) (postponement of time when a variation of an improvement notice comes into force).

(2) If no appeal is made under paragraph 13 before the end of the period of 28 days mentioned in paragraph 14(2), "the operative time" is the end of that period.

(3) If an appeal is made under paragraph 13 before the end of that period and a decision is given on the appeal which confirms the variation, "the operative time" is as follows—

(a) if the period within which an appeal to the Lands Tribunal may be brought expires without such an appeal having been brought, "the operative time" is the end of that period;

(b) if an appeal to the Lands Tribunal is brought, "the operative time" is the time when a decision is given on the appeal which confirms the variation.

(4) For the purposes of sub-paragraph (3)—

(a) the withdrawal of an appeal has the same effect as a decision which confirms the variation, and

(b) references to a decision which confirms the variation are to a decision which confirms it with or without variation.

SCHEDULE 2

Section 27

PROCEDURE AND APPEALS RELATING TO PROHIBITION ORDERS

PART 1

SERVICE OF COPIES OF PROHIBITION ORDERS

Service on owners and occupiers of dwelling or HMO which is not a flat

1 (1) This paragraph applies to a prohibition order where the specified premises are a dwelling or HMO which is not a flat.

(2) The authority must serve copies of the order on every person who, to their knowledge, is—

(a) an owner or occupier of the whole or part of the specified premises;

(b) authorised to permit persons to occupy the whole or part of those premises; or

(c) a mortgagee of the whole or part of those premises.

(3) The copies required to be served under sub-paragraph (2) must be served within the period of seven days beginning with the day on which the order is made.

(4) A copy of the order is to be regarded as having been served on every occupier in accordance with sub-paragraphs (2)(a) and (3) if a copy of the order is fixed to some conspicuous part of the specified premises within the period of seven days mentioned in sub-paragraph (3).

Service on owners and occupiers of building containing flats etc.

2 (1) This paragraph applies to a prohibition order where the specified premises consist of or include the whole or any part of a building containing one or more flats or any common parts of such a building.

(2) The authority must serve copies of the order on every person who, to their knowledge, is—

(a) an owner or occupier of the whole or part of the building;

(b) authorised to permit persons to occupy the whole or part of the building; or

(c) a mortgagee of the whole or part of the building.

(3) Where the specified premises consist of or include any external common parts of such a building, the authority must, in addition to complying with sub-paragraph (2), serve copies of the order on every person who, to their knowledge, is an owner or mortgagee of the premises in which the common parts are comprised.

(4) The copies required to be served under sub-paragraph (2) or (3) must be served within the period of seven days beginning with the day on which the order is made.

(5) A copy of the order is to be regarded as having been served on every occupier in accordance with sub-paragraphs (2)(a) and (4) if a copy of the order is fixed to some conspicuous part of the building within the period of seven days mentioned in sub-paragraph (4).

PART 2

SERVICE OF NOTICES RELATING TO REVOCATION OR VARIATION OF PROHIBITION ORDERS

Notice of revocation or variation

3 (1) This paragraph applies where the local housing authority decide to revoke or vary a prohibition order.

(2) The authority must serve a notice under this paragraph on each of the persons on whom they would be required under Part 1 of this Schedule to serve copies of a prohibition order in respect of the specified premises.

(3) The notices required to be served under sub-paragraph (2) must be served within the period of seven days beginning with the day on which the decision is made.

(4) Paragraph 1(4) applies in relation to the service of notices on occupiers in accordance with sub-paragraphs (2) and (3) as it applies in relation to the service on them of copies of a prohibition order in accordance with paragraph 1(2)(a) and (3).

4 A notice under paragraph 3 must set out—

(a) the authority's decision to revoke or vary the order;

(b) the reasons for the decision and the date on which it was made;

(c) if the decision is to vary the order—

(i) the right of appeal against the decision under Part 3 of this Schedule; and

(ii) the period within which an appeal may be made (see paragraph 10(2)).

Notice of refusal to revoke or vary order

5 (1) This paragraph applies where the local housing authority refuse to revoke or vary a prohibition order.

(2) The authority must serve a notice under this paragraph on each of the persons on whom they would be required under Part 1 of this Schedule to serve copies of a prohibition order in respect of the specified premises.

(3) The notices required to be served under sub-paragraph (2) must be served within the period of seven days beginning with the day on which the decision is made.

(4) Paragraph 1(4) applies in relation to the service of notices on occupiers in accordance with sub-paragraphs (2) and (3) as it applies in relation to the service on them of copies of a prohibition order in accordance with paragraph 1(2)(a) and (3).

6 A notice under paragraph 5 must set out—

(a) the authority's decision not to revoke or vary the notice;

(b) the reasons for the decision and the date on which it was made;

(c) the right of appeal against the decision under Part 3 of this Schedule; and

(d) the period within which an appeal may be made (see paragraph 10(2)).

PART 3

APPEALS RELATING TO PROHIBITION ORDERS

Appeal against prohibition order

7 (1) A relevant person may appeal to a residential property tribunal against a prohibition order.

(2) Paragraph 8 sets out a specific ground on which an appeal may be made under this paragraph, but it does not affect the generality of sub-paragraph (1).

8 (1) An appeal may be made by a person under paragraph 7 on the ground that one of the courses of action mentioned in sub-paragraph (2) is the best course of action in relation to the hazard in respect of which the order was made.

(2) The courses of action are—

(a) serving an improvement notice under section 11 or 12 of this Act;

(b) serving a hazard awareness notice under section 28 or 29 of this Act;

(c) making a demolition order under section 265 of the Housing Act 1985 (c. 68).

Appeal against decision relating to revocation or variation of prohibition order

9 A relevant person may appeal to a residential property tribunal against—

(a) a decision by the local housing authority to vary a prohibition order, or

(b) a decision by the authority to refuse to revoke or vary a prohibition order.

Time limit for appeal

10 (1) Any appeal under paragraph 7 must be made within the period of 28 days beginning with the date specified in the prohibition order as the date on which the order was made.

(2) Any appeal under paragraph 9 must be made within the period of 28 days beginning with the date specified in the notice under paragraph 3 or 5 as the date on which the decision concerned was made.

(3) A residential property tribunal may allow an appeal to be made to it after the end of the period mentioned in sub-paragraph (1) or (2) if it is satisfied that there is a good reason for the failure to appeal before the end of that period (and for any delay since then in applying for permission to appeal out of time).

Powers of residential property tribunal on appeal under paragraph 7

11 (1) This paragraph applies to an appeal to a residential property tribunal under paragraph 7.

(2) The appeal—

(a) is to be by way of a re-hearing, but

(b) may be determined having regard to matters of which the authority were unaware.

(3) The tribunal may by order confirm, quash or vary the prohibition order.

(4) Paragraph 12 makes special provision in connection with the ground of appeal set out in paragraph 8.

12 (1) This paragraph applies where the grounds of appeal consist of or include that set out in paragraph 8.

(2) When deciding whether one of the courses of action mentioned in paragraph 8(2) is the best course of action in relation to a particular hazard, the tribunal must have regard to any guidance given to the local housing authority under section 9.

(3) Sub-paragraph (4) applies where—

(a) an appeal under paragraph 7 is allowed against a prohibition order made in respect of a particular hazard; and

(b) the reason, or one of the reasons, for allowing the appeal is that one of the courses of action mentioned in paragraph 8(2) is the best course of action in relation to that hazard.

(4) The tribunal must, if requested to do so by the appellant or the local housing authority, include in its decision a finding to that effect and identifying the course of action concerned.

Powers of residential property tribunal on appeal under paragraph 9

13 (1) This paragraph applies to an appeal to a residential property tribunal under paragraph 9.

(2) Paragraph 11(2) applies to such an appeal as it applies to an appeal under paragraph 7.

(3) The tribunal may by order confirm, reverse or vary the decision of the local housing authority.

(4) If the appeal is against a decision of the authority to refuse to revoke a prohibition order, the tribunal may make an order revoking the prohibition order as from a date specified in its order.

"The operative time" for the purposes of section 24(5)

14 (1) This paragraph defines "the operative time" for the purposes of section 24(5) (operation of prohibition orders).

(2) If an appeal is made under paragraph 7 against a prohibition order which is not suspended, and a decision on the appeal is given which confirms the order, "the operative time" is as follows—

(a) if the period within which an appeal to the Lands Tribunal may be brought expires without such an appeal having been brought, "the operative time" is the end of that period;

(b) if an appeal to the Lands Tribunal is brought, "the operative time" is the time when a decision is given on the appeal which confirms the order.

(3) If an appeal is made under paragraph 7 against a prohibition order which is suspended, and a decision is given on the appeal which confirms the order, "the operative time" is as follows—

(a) the time that would be the operative time under sub-paragraph (2) if the order were not suspended, or

(b) if later, the time when the suspension ends.

(4) For the purposes of sub-paragraph (2) or (3)—

(a) the withdrawal of an appeal has the same effect as a decision which confirms the notice, and

(b) references to a decision which confirms the order are to a decision which confirms it with or without variation.

"The operative time" for the purposes of section 25(7)

15 (1) This paragraph defines "the operative time" for the purposes of section 25(7) (revocation or variation of prohibition orders).

(2) If no appeal is made under paragraph 9 before the end of the period of 28 days mentioned in paragraph 10(2), "the operative time" is the end of that period.

(3) If an appeal is made under paragraph 10 within that period and a decision is given on the appeal which confirms the variation, "the operative time" is as follows—

(a) if the period within which an appeal to the Lands Tribunal may be brought expires without such an appeal having been brought, "the operative time" is the end of that period;

(b) if an appeal to the Lands Tribunal is brought, "the operative time" is the time when a decision is given on the appeal which confirms the variation.

(4) For the purposes of sub-paragraph (3)—

(a) the withdrawal of an appeal has the same effect as a decision which confirms the variation, and

(b) references to a decision which confirms the variation are to a decision which confirms it with or without variation.

Meaning of "relevant person"

16 (1) In this Part of this Schedule "relevant person", in relation to a prohibition order, means a person who is—

(a) an owner or occupier of the whole or part of the specified premises,

(b) authorised to permit persons to occupy the whole or part of those premises, or

(c) a mortgagee of the whole or part of those premises.

(2) If any specified premises are common parts of a building containing one or more flats, then in relation to those specified premises, "relevant person" means every person who is an owner or mortgagee of the premises in which the common parts are comprised.

SCHEDULE 3

Section 31

IMPROVEMENT NOTICES: ENFORCEMENT ACTION BY LOCAL HOUSING AUTHORITIES

PART 1

ACTION TAKEN BY AGREEMENT

Power to take action by agreement

1 (1) The local housing authority may, by agreement with the person on whom an improvement notice has been served, take any action which that person is required to take in relation to any premises in pursuance of the notice.

(2) For that purpose the authority have all the rights which that person would have against any occupying tenant of, and any other person having an interest in, the premises (or any part of the premises).

(3) In this paragraph—

"improvement notice" means an improvement notice which has become operative under Chapter 2 of Part 1 of this Act;

"occupying tenant", in relation to any premises, means a person (other than an owner-occupier) who—

(a) occupies or is entitled to occupy the premises as a lessee;

(b) is a statutory tenant of the premises;

(c) occupies the premises under a restricted contract;

(d) is a protected occupier within the meaning of the Rent (Agriculture) Act 1976 (c. 80); or

(e) is a licensee under an assured agricultural occupancy;

"owner-occupier", in relation to any premises, means the person who occupies or is entitled to occupy the premises as owner or lessee under a long tenancy (within the meaning of Part 1 of the Leasehold Reform Act 1967 (c. 88)).

Expenses of taking action by agreement

2 Any action taken by the local housing authority under paragraph 1 is to be taken at the expense of the person on whom the notice is served.

PART 2

POWER TO TAKE ACTION WITHOUT AGREEMENT

Power to take action without agreement

3 (1) The local housing authority may themselves take the action required to be taken in relation to a hazard by an improvement notice if sub-paragraph (2) or (3) applies.

(2) This sub-paragraph applies if the notice is not complied with in relation to that hazard.

(3) This sub-paragraph applies if, before the end of the period which under section 30(2) is appropriate for completion of the action specified in the notice in relation to the hazard, they consider that reasonable progress is not being made towards compliance with the notice in relation to the hazard.

(4) Any person authorised in writing by the authority may enter any part of the specified premises for the purposes of the taking of any action which the authority are authorised to take under this paragraph.

(5) The right of entry conferred by sub-paragraph (4) may be exercised at any reasonable time.

(6) Any reference in this Part of this Schedule (of whatever nature) to a local housing authority entering any premises under this paragraph is a reference to their doing so in accordance with sub-paragraph (4).

(7) In this paragraph "improvement notice" means an improvement notice which has become operative under Chapter 2 of Part 1 of this Act.

Notice requirements in relation to taking action without agreement

4 (1) The local housing authority must serve a notice under this paragraph before they enter any premises under paragraph 3 for the purpose of taking action in relation to a hazard.

(2) The notice must identify the improvement notice to which it relates and state—

(a) the premises and hazard concerned;

(b) that the authority intend to enter the premises;

(c) the action which the authority intend to take on the premises; and

(d) the power under which the authority intend to enter the premises and take the action.

(3) The notice must be served on the person on whom the improvement notice was served, and a copy of the notice must be served on any other person who is an occupier of the premises.

(4) The notice and any such copy must be served sufficiently in advance of the time when the authority intend to enter the premises as to give the recipients reasonable notice of the intended entry.

(5) A copy of the notice may also be served on any owner of the premises.

Obstruction of action taken without agreement

5 (1) If, at any relevant time—

(a) the person on whom the notice under paragraph 4 was served is on the premises for the purpose of carrying out any works, or

(b) any workman employed by that person, or by any contractor employed by that person, is on the premises for such a purpose,

that person is to be taken to have committed an offence under section 241(1).

(2) In proceedings for such an offence it is a defence that there was an urgent necessity to carry out the works in order to prevent danger to persons occupying the premises.

(3) In sub-paragraph (1) "relevant time" means any time—

(a) after the end of the period of 7 days beginning with the date of service of the notice under paragraph 4, and

(b) when any workman or contractor employed by the local housing authority is taking action on the premises which has been mentioned in the notice in accordance with paragraph 4(2)(c).

Expenses in relation to taking action without agreement

6 (1) Part 3 of this Schedule applies with respect to the recovery by the local housing authority of expenses incurred by them in taking action under paragraph 3.

(2) Sub-paragraph (3) applies where, after a local housing authority have given notice under paragraph 4 of their intention to enter premises and take action, the action is in fact taken by the person on whom the improvement notice is served.

(3) Any administrative and other expenses incurred by the authority with a view to themselves taking the action are to be treated for the purposes of Part 3 of this Schedule as expenses incurred by them in taking action under paragraph 3.

PART 3

RECOVERY OF CERTAIN EXPENSES

Introductory

7 This Part of this Schedule applies for the purpose of enabling a local housing authority to recover expenses reasonably incurred by them in taking action under paragraph 3.

Recovery of expenses

8 (1) The expenses are recoverable by the local housing authority from the person on whom the improvement notice was served ("the relevant person").

(2) Where the relevant person receives the rent of the premises as agent or trustee for another person, the expenses are also recoverable by the local housing authority from the other person, or partly from him and partly from the relevant person.

(3) Sub-paragraph (4) applies where the relevant person proves in connection with a demand under paragraph 9—

(a) that sub-paragraph (2) applies, and

(b) that he has not, and since the date of the service on him of the demand has not had, in his hands on behalf of the other person sufficient money to discharge the whole demand of the local housing authority.

(4) The liability of the relevant person is limited to the total amount of the money which he has, or has had, in his hands as mentioned in sub-paragraph (3)(b).

(5) Expenses are not recoverable under this paragraph so far as they are, by any direction given by a residential property tribunal on an appeal to the tribunal under paragraph 11, recoverable under an order of the tribunal.

Service of demand

9 (1) A demand for expenses recoverable under paragraph 8, together with interest in accordance with paragraph 10, must be served on each person from whom the local housing authority are seeking to recover them.

(2) If no appeal is brought, the demand becomes operative at the end of the period of 21 days beginning with the date of service of the demand.

(3) A demand which becomes operative under sub-paragraph (2) is final and conclusive as to matters which could have been raised on an appeal.

(4) Paragraph 11 deals with appeals against demands.

Interest

10 Expenses in respect of which a demand is served carry interest, at such reasonable rate as the local housing authority may determine, from the date of service until payment of all sums due under the demand.

Appeals

11 (1) A person on whom a demand for the recovery of expenses has been served may appeal to a residential property tribunal against the demand.

(2) An appeal must be made within the period of 21 days beginning with the date of service of the demand or copy of it under paragraph 9.

(3) A residential property tribunal may allow an appeal to be made to it after the end of the period mentioned in sub-paragraph (2) if it is satisfied that there is a good reason for the failure to appeal before the end of that period (and for any delay since then in applying for permission to appeal out of time).

(4) Where the demand relates to action taken by virtue of paragraph 3(3), an appeal may be brought on the ground that reasonable progress was being made towards compliance with the improvement notice when the local housing authority gave notice under paragraph 4 of their intention to enter and take the action.

This does not affect the generality of sub-paragraph (1).

(5) The tribunal may, on an appeal, make such order confirming, quashing or varying the demand as it considers appropriate.

(6) A demand against which an appeal is brought becomes operative as follows—

(a) if a decision is given on the appeal which confirms the demand and the period within which an appeal to the Lands Tribunal may be brought expires without such an appeal having been brought, the demand becomes operative at end of that period;

(b) if an appeal to the Lands Tribunal is brought and a decision is given on the appeal which confirms the demand, the demand becomes operative at the time of that decision.

(7) For the purposes of sub-paragraph (6)—

(a) the withdrawal of an appeal has the same effect as a decision which confirms the demand, and

(b) references to a decision which confirms the demand are to a decision which confirms it with or without variation.

(8) No question may be raised on appeal under this paragraph which might have been raised on an appeal against the improvement notice.

Expenses and interest recoverable from occupiers

12 (1) Where a demand becomes operative by virtue of paragraph 9(2) or 11(6), the local housing authority may serve a recovery notice on any person—

(a) who occupies the premises concerned, or part of those premises, as the tenant or licensee of the person on whom the demand was served under paragraph 9(1); and

(b) who, by virtue of his tenancy or licence, pays rent or any sum in the nature of rent to the person on whom the demand was served.

(2) A recovery notice is a notice—

(a) stating the amount of expenses recoverable by the local housing authority; and

(b) requiring all future payments by the tenant or licensee of rent or sums in the nature of rent (whether already accrued due or not) to be made direct to the authority until the expenses recoverable by the authority, together with any accrued interest on them, have been duly paid.

(3) In the case of a demand which was served on any person as agent or trustee for another person ("the principal"), sub-paragraph (1) has effect as if the references in paragraphs (a) and (b) to the person on whom the demand was served were references to that person or the principal.

(4) The effect of a recovery notice, once served under sub-paragraph (1), is to transfer to the local housing authority the right to recover, receive and give a discharge for the rent or sums in the nature of rent.

(5) This is subject to any direction to the contrary contained in a further notice served by the local housing authority on the tenant or licensee.

(6) In addition, the right to recover, receive and give a discharge for any rent or sums in the nature of rent is postponed to any right in respect of that rent or those sums

which may at any time be vested in a superior landlord by virtue of a notice under section 6 of the Law of Distress Amendment Act 1908 (c. 53).

Expenses and interest to be a charge on the premises

13 (1) Until recovered, the expenses recoverable by the local housing authority, together with any accrued interest on them, are a charge on the premises to which the improvement notice related.

(2) The charge takes effect when the demand for the expenses and interest becomes operative by virtue of paragraph 9(2) or 11(6).

(3) For the purpose of enforcing the charge, the local housing authority have the same powers and remedies, under the Law of Property Act 1925 (c. 20) and otherwise, as if they were mortgagees by deed having powers of sale and lease, of accepting surrenders of leases and of appointing a receiver.

(4) The power of appointing a receiver is exercisable at any time after the end of one month beginning with the date when the charge takes effect.

Recovery of expenses and interest from other persons profiting from taking of action

14 (1) Sub-paragraph (2) applies if, on an application to a residential property tribunal, the local housing authority satisfy the tribunal that—

(a) the expenses and interest have not been and are unlikely to be recovered; and

(b) a person is profiting by the taking of the action under paragraph 3 in respect of which the expenses were incurred in that he is obtaining rents or other payments which would not have been obtainable if the number of persons living in the premises was limited to that appropriate for the premises in their state before the action was taken.

(2) The tribunal may, if satisfied that the person concerned has had proper notice of the application, order him to make such payments to the local housing authority as the tribunal considers to be just.

SCHEDULE 4

Sections 67 and 90

LICENCES UNDER PARTS 2 AND 3: MANDATORY CONDITIONS

Conditions to be included in licences under Part 2 or 3

1 (1) A licence under Part 2 or 3 must include the following conditions.

(2) Conditions requiring the licence holder, if gas is supplied to the house, to produce to the local housing authority annually for their inspection a gas safety certificate obtained in respect of the house within the last 12 months.

(3) Conditions requiring the licence holder—

(a) to keep electrical appliances and furniture made available by him in the house in a safe condition;

(b) to supply the authority, on demand, with a declaration by him as to the safety of such appliances and furniture.

(4) Conditions requiring the licence holder—

(a) to ensure that smoke alarms are installed in the house and to keep them in proper working order;

(b) to supply the authority, on demand, with a declaration by him as to the condition and positioning of such alarms.

(5) Conditions requiring the licence holder to supply to the occupiers of the house a written statement of the terms on which they occupy it.

Additional conditions to be included in licences under Part 3

2 A licence under Part 3 must include conditions requiring the licence holder to demand references from persons who wish to occupy the house.

Power to prescribe conditions

3 The appropriate national authority may by regulations amend this Schedule so as to alter (by the addition or removal of conditions) the conditions which must be included—

(a) in a licence under Part 2 or 3, or

(b) only in a licence under one of those Parts.

Interpretation

4 In this Schedule "the house" means the HMO or Part 3 house in respect of which the licence is granted.

SCHEDULE 5

Sections 71 and 94

LICENCES UNDER PARTS 2 AND 3: PROCEDURE AND APPEALS

PART 1

PROCEDURE RELATING TO GRANT OR REFUSAL OF LICENCES

Requirements before grant of licence

1 Before granting a licence, the local housing authority must—

(a) serve a notice under this paragraph, together with a copy of the proposed licence, on the applicant for the licence and each relevant person, and

(b) consider any representations made in accordance with the notice and not withdrawn.

2 The notice under paragraph 1 must state that the authority are proposing to grant the licence and set out—

(a) the reasons for granting the licence,

(b) the main terms of the licence, and

(c) the end of the consultation period.

3 (1) This paragraph applies if, having considered representations made in accordance with a notice under paragraph 1 or this paragraph, the local housing authority propose to grant a licence with modifications.

(2) Before granting the licence the authority must—

(a) serve a notice under this paragraph on the applicant for the licence and each relevant person, and

(b) consider any representations made in accordance with the notice and not withdrawn.

4 The notice under paragraph 3 must set out—

(a) the proposed modifications,

(b) the reasons for them, and

(c) the end of the consultation period.

Requirements before refusal to grant licence

5 Before refusing to grant a licence, the local housing authority must—

(a) serve a notice under this paragraph on the applicant for the licence and each relevant person, and

(b) consider any representations made in accordance with the notice and not withdrawn.

6 The notice under paragraph 5 must state that the local housing authority are proposing to refuse to grant the licence and set out—

(a) the reasons for refusing to grant the licence, and

(b) the end of the consultation period.

Requirements following grant or refusal of licence

7 (1) This paragraph applies where the local housing authority decide to grant a licence.

(2) The local housing authority must serve on the applicant for the licence (and, if different, the licence holder) and each relevant person—

(a) a copy of the licence, and

(b) a notice setting out—

(i) the reasons for deciding to grant the licence and the date on which the decision was made,

(ii) the right of appeal against the decision under Part 3 of this Schedule, and

(iii) the period within which an appeal may be made (see paragraph 33(1)).

(3) The documents required to be served under sub-paragraph (2) must be served within the period of seven days beginning with the day on which the decision is made.

8 (1) This paragraph applies where the local housing authority refuse to grant a licence.

(2) The local housing authority must serve on the applicant for the licence and each relevant person a notice setting out—

(a) the authority's decision not to grant the licence,

(b) the reasons for the decision and the date on which it was made,

(c) the right of appeal against the decision under Part 3 of this Schedule, and

(d) the period within which an appeal may be made (see paragraph 33(1)).

(3) The notices required to be served under sub-paragraph (2) must be served within the period of seven days beginning with the day on which the decision is made.

Exceptions from requirements in relation to grant or refusal of licences

9 The requirements of paragraph 3 (and those of paragraph 1) do not apply if the local housing authority—

(a) have already served a notice under paragraph 1 but not paragraph 3 in relation to the proposed licence, and

(b) consider that the modifications which are now being proposed are not material in any respect.

10 The requirements of paragraph 3 (and those of paragraph 1) do not apply if the local housing authority—

(a) have already served notices under paragraphs 1 and 3 in relation to the matter concerned, and

(b) consider that the further modifications which are now being proposed do not differ in any material respect from the modifications in relation to which a notice was last served under paragraph 3.

11 Paragraphs 5, 6 and 8 do not apply to a refusal to grant a licence on particular terms if the local housing authority are proposing to grant the licence on different terms.

Meaning of "the end of the consultation period"

12 (1) In this Part of this Schedule "the end of the consultation period" means the last day for making representations in respect of the matter in question.

(2) The end of the consultation period must be—

(a) in the case of a notice under paragraph 1 or 5, a day which is at least 14 days after the date of service of the notice; and

(b) in the case of a notice under paragraph 3, a day which is at least 7 days after the date of service of the notice.

(3) In sub-paragraph (2) "the date of service" of a notice means, in a case where more than one notice is served, the date on which the last of the notices is served.

Meaning of "licence" and "relevant person"

13 (1) In this Part of this Schedule "licence" means a licence under Part 2 or 3 of this Act.

(2) In this Part of this Schedule "relevant person", in relation to a licence under Part 2 or 3 of this Act, means any person (other than a person excluded by sub-paragraph (3))—

(a) who, to the knowledge of the local housing authority concerned, is—

(i) a person having an estate or interest in the HMO or Part 3 house in question, or

(ii) a person managing or having control of that HMO or Part 3 house (and not falling within sub-paragraph (i)), or

(b) on whom any restriction or obligation is or is to be imposed by the licence in accordance with section 67(5) or 90(6).

(3) The persons excluded by this sub-paragraph are—

(a) the applicant for the licence and (if different) the licence holder, and
(b) any tenant under a lease with an unexpired term of 3 years or less.

PART 2

PROCEDURE RELATING TO VARIATION OR REVOCATION OF LICENCES

Variation of licences

14 Before varying a licence, the local housing authority must—
(a) serve a notice under this paragraph on the licence holder and each relevant person, and
(b) consider any representations made in accordance with the notice and not withdrawn.

15 The notice under paragraph 14 must state that the local housing authority are proposing to make the variation and set out—
(a) the effect of the variation,
(b) the reasons for the variation, and
(c) the end of the consultation period.

16 (1) This paragraph applies where the local housing authority decide to vary a licence.

(2) The local housing authority must serve on the licence holder and each relevant person—
(a) a copy of the authority's decision to vary the licence, and
(b) a notice setting out—
(i) the reasons for the decision and the date on which it was made,
(ii) the right of appeal against the decision under Part 3 of this Schedule, and
(iii) the period within which an appeal may be made (see paragraph 33(2)).

(3) The documents required to be served under sub-paragraph (2) must be served within the period of seven days beginning with the day on which the decision is made.

Exceptions from requirements of paragraph 14

17 The requirements of paragraph 14 do not apply if—
(a) the local housing authority consider that the variation is not material, or
(b) the variation is agreed by the licence holder and the local housing authority consider that it would not be appropriate to comply with the requirements of that paragraph.

18 The requirements of paragraph 14 do not apply if the local housing authority—
(a) have already served a notice under that paragraph in relation to a proposed variation, and
(b) consider that the variation which is now being proposed is not materially different from the previous proposed variation.

Refusal to vary a licence

19 Before refusing to vary a licence, the local housing authority must—

(a) serve a notice under this paragraph on the licence holder and each relevant person, and

(b) consider any representations made in accordance with the notice and not withdrawn.

20 The notice under paragraph 19 must state that the authority are proposing to refuse to vary the licence and set out—

(a) the reasons for refusing to vary the licence, and

(b) the end of the consultation period.

21 (1) This paragraph applies where the local housing authority refuse to vary a licence.

(2) The authority must serve on the licence holder and each relevant person a notice setting out—

(a) the authority's decision not to vary the licence,

(b) the reasons for the decision and the date on which it was made,

(c) the right of appeal against the decision under Part 3 of this Schedule, and

(d) the period within which an appeal may be made (see paragraph 33(2)).

(3) The documents required to be served under sub-paragraph (2) must be served within the period of seven days beginning with the day on which the decision is made.

Revocation of licences

22 Before revoking a licence, the local housing authority must—

(a) serve a notice on the licence holder under this paragraph and each relevant person, and

(b) consider any representations made in accordance with the notice and not withdrawn.

23 The notice under paragraph 22 must state that the authority are proposing to revoke the licence and set out—

(a) the reasons for the revocation, and

(b) the end of the consultation period.

24 (1) This paragraph applies where the local housing authority decide to revoke a licence.

(2) The authority must serve on the licence holder and each relevant person—

(a) a copy of the authority's decision to revoke the licence, and

(b) a notice setting out—

(i) the reasons for the decision and the date on which it was made,

(ii) the right of appeal against the decision under Part 3 of this Schedule, and

(iii) the period within which an appeal may be made (see paragraph 33(2)).

(3) The documents required to be served under sub-paragraph (2) must be served within the period of seven days beginning with the day on which the decision is made.

Exception from requirements of paragraph 22

25 The requirements of paragraph 22 do not apply if the revocation is agreed by the licence holder and the local housing authority consider that it would not be appropriate to comply with the requirements of that paragraph.

Refusal to revoke a licence

26 Before refusing to revoke a licence, the local housing authority must—

(a) serve a notice under this paragraph on the licence holder and each relevant person, and

(b) consider any representations made in accordance with the notice and not withdrawn.

27 The notice under paragraph 26 must state that the authority are proposing to refuse to revoke the licence and set out—

(a) the reasons for refusing to revoke the licence, and

(b) the end of the consultation period.

28 (1) This paragraph applies where the local housing authority refuse to revoke a licence.

(2) The authority must serve on the licence holder and each relevant person a notice setting out—

(a) the authority's decision not to revoke the licence,

(b) the reasons for the decision and the date on which it was made,

(c) the right of appeal against the decision under Part 3 of this Schedule, and

(d) the period within which an appeal may be made (see paragraph 33(2)).

(3) The notices required to be served under sub-paragraph (2) must be served within the period of seven days beginning with the day on which the decision is made.

Meaning of "the end of the consultation period"

29 (1) In this Part of this Schedule "the end of the consultation period" means the last day on which representations may be made in respect of the matter in question.

(2) That date must be at least 14 days after the date of service of the notice in question.

(3) In sub-paragraph (2) "the date of service" of a notice means, in a case where more than one notice is served, the date on which the last of the notices is served.

Meaning of "licence" and "relevant person"

30 (1) In this Part of this Schedule "licence" means a licence under Part 2 or 3 of this Act.

(2) In this Part of this Schedule "relevant person", in relation to a licence under Part 2 or 3 of this Act, means any person (other than a person excluded by sub-paragraph (3))—

(a) who, to the knowledge of the local housing authority concerned, is—

(i) a person having an estate or interest in the HMO or Part 3 house in question, or

(ii) a person managing or having control of that HMO or Part 3 house (and not falling within sub-paragraph (i)), or

(b) on whom any restriction or obligation is or is to be imposed by the licence in accordance with section 67(5) or 90(6).

(3) The persons excluded by this sub-paragraph are—

(a) the licence holder, and

(b) any tenant under a lease with an unexpired term of 3 years or less.

PART 3

APPEALS AGAINST LICENCE DECISIONS

Right to appeal against refusal or grant of licence

31 (1) The applicant or any relevant person may appeal to a residential property tribunal against a decision by the local housing authority on an application for a licence—

(a) to refuse to grant the licence, or

(b) to grant the licence.

(2) An appeal under sub-paragraph (1)(b) may, in particular, relate to any of the terms of the licence.

Right to appeal against decision or refusal to vary or revoke licence

32 (1) The licence holder or any relevant person may appeal to a residential property tribunal against a decision by the local housing authority—

(a) to vary or revoke a licence, or

(b) to refuse to vary or revoke a licence.

(2) But this does not apply to the licence holder in a case where the decision to vary or revoke the licence was made with his agreement.

Time limits for appeals

33 (1) Any appeal under paragraph 31 against a decision to grant, or (as the case may be) to refuse to grant, a licence must be made within the period of 28 days beginning with the date specified in the notice under paragraph 7 or 8 as the date on which the decision was made.

(2) Any appeal under paragraph 32 against a decision to vary or revoke, or (as the case may be) to refuse to vary or revoke, a licence must be made within the period of 28 days beginning with the date specified in the notice under paragraph 16, 21, 24 or 28 as the date on which the decision was made.

(3) A residential property tribunal may allow an appeal to be made to it after the end of the period mentioned in sub-paragraph (1) or (2) if it is satisfied that there is a good reason for the failure to appeal before the end of that period (and for any delay since then in applying for permission to appeal out of time).

Powers of residential property tribunal hearing appeal

34 (1) This paragraph applies to appeals to a residential property tribunal under paragraph 31 or 32.

(2) An appeal—

(a) is to be by way of a re-hearing, but

(b) may be determined having regard to matters of which the authority were unaware.

(3) The tribunal may confirm, reverse or vary the decision of the local housing authority.

(4) On an appeal under paragraph 31 the tribunal may direct the authority to grant a licence to the applicant for the licence on such terms as the tribunal may direct.

"The operative time" for the purposes of section 69(6), 70(8), 92(3) or 93(5)

35 (1) This paragraph defines "the operative time" for the purposes of—

(a) section 69(6) or 70(8) (variation or revocation of licence under Part 2 of this Act), or

(b) section 92(3) or 93(5) (variation or revocation of licence under Part 3 of this Act).

(2) If the period of 28 days mentioned in paragraph 33(2) has expired without an appeal having been made under paragraph 32, "the operative time" is the end of that period.

(3) If an appeal is made under paragraph 32 within that period and a decision is given on the appeal which confirms the variation or revocation, "the operative time" is as follows—

(a) if the period within which an appeal to the Lands Tribunal may be brought expires without such an appeal having been brought, "the operative time" is the end of that period;

(b) if an appeal to the Lands Tribunal is brought, "the operative time" is the time when a decision is given on the appeal which confirms the variation or revocation.

(4) For the purposes of sub-paragraph (3)—

(a) the withdrawal of an appeal has the same effect as a decision confirming the variation or revocation appealed against; and

(b) references to a decision which confirms a variation are to a decision which confirms it with or without variation.

Meaning of "licence" and "relevant person"

36 (1) In this Part of this Schedule "licence" means a licence under Part 2 or 3 of this Act.

(2) In this Part of this Schedule "relevant person", in relation to a licence under Part 2 or 3 of this Act, means any person (other than a person excluded by sub-paragraph (3))—

(a) who is—

(i) a person having an estate or interest in the HMO or Part 3 house concerned, or

(ii) a person managing or having control of that HMO or Part 3 house (and not falling within sub-paragraph (i)), or

(b) on whom any restriction or obligation is or is to be imposed by the licence in accordance with section 67(5) or 90(6).

(3) The persons excluded by this sub-paragraph are—

(a) the applicant for the licence and (if different) the licence holder, and

(b) any tenant under a lease with an unexpired term of 3 years or less.

SCHEDULE 6

Section 123

MANAGEMENT ORDERS: PROCEDURE AND APPEALS

PART 1

PROCEDURE RELATING TO MAKING OF MANAGEMENT ORDERS

Requirements before making final management order

1 Before making a final management order, the local housing authority must—

(a) serve a copy of the proposed order, together with a notice under this paragraph, on each relevant person; and

(b) consider any representations made in accordance with the notice and not withdrawn.

2 The notice under paragraph 1 must state that the authority are proposing to make a final management order and set out—

(a) the reasons for making the order;

(b) the main terms of the proposed order (including those of the management scheme to be contained in it); and

(c) the end of the consultation period.

3 (1) This paragraph applies if, having considered representations made in accordance with a notice under paragraph 1 or this paragraph, the local housing authority propose to make a final management order with modifications.

(2) Before making the order, the authority must—

(a) serve a notice under this paragraph on each relevant person; and

(b) consider any representations made in accordance with the notice and not withdrawn.

4 The notice under paragraph 3 must set out—

(a) the proposed modifications;

(b) the reasons for them; and

(c) the end of the consultation period.

Exceptions from requirements relating to making of final management order

5 The requirements of paragraph 3 (and those of paragraph 1) do not apply if the local housing authority—

(a) have already served notice under paragraph 1 but not paragraph 3 in relation to the proposed final management order; and

(b) consider that the modifications which are now being proposed are not material in any respect.

6 The requirements of paragraph 3 (and those of paragraph 1) do not apply if the local housing authority—

(a) have already served notices under paragraphs 1 and 3 in relation to the matter concerned; and

(b) consider that the further modifications which are now being proposed do not differ in any material respect from the modifications in relation to which a notice was last served under paragraph 3.

Requirements following making of interim or final management order

7 (1) This paragraph applies where the local housing authority make an interim management order or a final management order.

(2) As soon as practicable after the order is made, the authority must serve on the occupiers of the house—

(a) a copy of the order, and

(b) a notice under this sub-paragraph.

(3) Those documents are to be regarded as having been served on the occupiers if they are fixed to a conspicuous part of the house.

(4) The notice under sub-paragraph (2) must set out—

(a) the reasons for making the order and the date on which it was made,

(b) the general effect of the order, and

(c) the date on which the order is to cease to have effect in accordance with section 105(4) and (5) or 114(3) and (4) (or, if applicable, how the date mentioned in section 105(6) is to be determined),

and (if it is a final management order) give a general description of the way in which the house is to be managed by the authority in accordance with the management scheme contained in the order.

(5) The authority must also serve a copy of the order, together with a notice under this sub-paragraph, on each relevant person.

(6) The notice under sub-paragraph (5) must comply with sub-paragraph (4) and also contain information about—

(a) the right of appeal against the order under Part 3 of this Schedule, and

(b) the period within which any such appeal may be made (see paragraph 25(2)).

(7) The documents required to be served on each relevant person under sub-paragraph (5) must be served within the period of seven days beginning with the day on which the order is made.

Meaning of "the end of the consultation period" and "relevant person"

8 (1) In this Part of this Schedule "the end of the consultation period" means the last day for making representations in respect of the matter in question.

(2) The end of the consultation period must be—

(a) in the case of a notice under paragraph 1, a day which is at least 14 days after the date of service of the notice; and

(b) in the case of a notice under paragraph 3, a day which is at least 7 days after the date of service of the notice.

(3) In sub-paragraph (2) "the date of service" of a notice means, in a case where more than one notice is served, the date on which the last of the notices is served.

(4) In this Part of this Schedule "relevant person" means any person who, to the knowledge of the local housing authority, is—
(a) a person having an estate or interest in the house or part of it (but who is not a tenant under a lease with an unexpired term of 3 years or less), or
(b) any other person who (but for the order) would be a person managing or having control of the house or part of it.

PART 2

PROCEDURE RELATING TO VARIATION OR REVOCATION OF MANAGEMENT ORDERS

Variation of management orders

9 Before varying an interim or final management order, the local housing authority must—
(a) serve a notice under this paragraph on each relevant person, and
(b) consider any representations made in accordance with the notice and not withdrawn.

10 The notice under paragraph 9 must state that the authority are proposing to make the variation and specify—
(a) the effect of the variation,
(b) the reasons for the variation, and
(c) the end of the consultation period.

11 (1) This paragraph applies where the local housing authority decide to vary an interim or final management order.
(2) The local housing authority must serve on each relevant person—
(a) a copy of the authority's decision to vary the order, and
(b) a notice setting out—
(i) the reasons for the decision and the date on which it was made,
(ii) the right of appeal against the decision under Part 3 of this Schedule, and
(iii) the period within which an appeal may be made (see paragraph 29(2)).
(3) The documents required to be served on each relevant person under sub-paragraph (2) must be served within the period of seven days beginning with the day on which the decision is made.

Exceptions from requirements of paragraph 9

12 The requirements of paragraph 9 do not apply if the local housing authority consider that the variation is not material.

13 The requirements of paragraph9 do not apply if the local housing authority—
(a) have already served a notice under that paragraph in relation to a proposed variation; and
(b) consider that the variation which is now being proposed is not materially different from the previous proposed variation.

Refusal to vary interim or final management order

14 Before refusing to vary an interim or final management order, the local housing authority must—

(a) serve a notice under this paragraph on each relevant person, and

(b) consider any representations made in accordance with the notice and not withdrawn.

15 The notice under paragraph 14 must state that the authority are proposing to refuse to make the variation and set out—

(a) the reasons for refusing to make the variation, and

(b) the end of the consultation period.

16 (1) This paragraph applies where the local housing authority refuse to vary an interim or final management order.

(2) The authority must serve on each relevant person a notice setting out—

(a) the authority's decision not to vary the order;

(b) the reasons for the decision and the date on which it was made;

(c) the right of appeal against the decision under Part 3 of this Schedule; and

(d) the period within which an appeal may be made (see paragraph 29(2)).

(3) The notices required to be served on each relevant person under sub-paragraph (2) must be served within the period of seven days beginning with the day on which the decision is made.

Revocation of management orders

17 Before revoking an interim or final management order, the local housing authority must—

(a) serve a notice under this paragraph on each relevant person, and

(b) consider any representations made in accordance with the notice and not withdrawn.

18 The notice under paragraph 17 must state that the authority are proposing to revoke the order and specify—

(a) the reasons for the revocation, and

(b) the end of the consultation period.

19 (1) This paragraph applies where the local housing authority decide to revoke an interim or final management order.

(2) The authority must serve on each relevant person—

(a) a copy of the authority's decision to revoke the order; and

(b) a notice setting out—

(i) the reasons for the decision and the date on which it was made;

(ii) the right of appeal against the decision under Part 3 of this Schedule; and

(iii) the period within which an appeal may be made (see paragraph 29(2)).

(3) The documents required to be served on each relevant person under sub-paragraph (2) must be served within the period of seven days beginning with the day on which the decision is made.

Refusal to revoke management order

20 Before refusing to revoke an interim or final management order, the local housing authority must—

(a) serve a notice under this paragraph on each relevant person; and

(b) consider any representations made in accordance with the notice and not withdrawn.

21 The notice under paragraph 20 must state that the authority are proposing to refuse to revoke the order and set out—

(a) the reasons for refusing to revoke the order, and

(b) the end of the consultation period.

22 (1) This paragraph applies where the local housing authority refuse to revoke an interim or final management order.

(2) The authority must serve on each relevant person a notice setting out—

(a) the authority's decision not to revoke the order;

(b) the reasons for the decision and the date on which it was made;

(c) the right of appeal against the decision under Part 3 of this Schedule; and

(d) the period within which an appeal may be made (see paragraph 29(2)).

(3) The notices required to be served on each relevant person under sub-paragraph (2) must be served within the period of seven days beginning with the day on which the decision is made.

Meaning of "the end of the consultation period" and "relevant person"

23 (1) In this Part of this Schedule "the end of the consultation period" means the last day for making representations in respect of the matter in question.

(2) The end of the consultation period must be a day which is at least 14 days after the date of service of the notice.

(3) In sub-paragraph (2) "the date of service" of a notice means, in a case where more than one notice is served, the date on which the last of the notices is served.

(4) In this Part of this Schedule "relevant person" means any person who, to the knowledge of the local housing authority, is—

(a) a person having an estate or interest in the house or part of it (but who is not a tenant under a lease with an unexpired term of 3 years or less), or

(b) any other person who (but for the order) would be a person managing or having control of the house or part of it.

PART 3

APPEALS AGAINST DECISIONS RELATING TO MANAGEMENT ORDERS

Right to appeal against making of order etc.

24 (1) A relevant person may appeal to a residential property tribunal against—

(a) a decision of the local housing authority to make an interim or final management order, or

(b) the terms of such an order (including, if it is a final management order, those of the management scheme contained in it).

(2) Except to the extent that an appeal may be made in accordance with sub-paragraphs (3) and (4), sub-paragraph (1) does not apply to an interim management order made under section 102(4) or (7) or in accordance with a direction given under paragraph 26(5).

(3) An appeal may be made under sub-paragraph (1)(b) on the grounds that the terms of an interim management order do not provide for one or both of the matters mentioned in section 110(5)(a) and (b) (which relate to payments of surplus rent etc.).

(4) Where an appeal is made under sub-paragraph (1)(b) only on those grounds—

(a) the appeal may be brought at any time while the order is in force (with the result that nothing in sub-paragraph (5) or paragraph 25 applies in relation to the appeal); and

(b) the powers of the residential property tribunal under paragraph 26 are limited to determining whether the order should be varied by the tribunal so as to include a term providing for the matter or matters in question, and (if so) what provision should be made by the term.

(5) If no appeal is brought against an interim or final management order under this paragraph within the time allowed by paragraph 25 for making such an appeal, the order is final and conclusive as to the matters which could have been raised on appeal.

Time limits for appeals under paragraph 24

25 (1) This paragraph applies in relation to an appeal under paragraph 24 in respect of an interim or final management order.

(2) Any such appeal must be made within the period of 28 days beginning with the date specified in the notice under paragraph 7(5) as the date on which the order was made.

(3) A residential property tribunal may allow an appeal to be made to it after the end of the period mentioned in sub-paragraph (2) if it is satisfied that there is a good reason for the failure to appeal before the end of that period (and for any delay since then in applying for permission to appeal out of time).

Powers of residential property tribunal on appeal under paragraph 24

26 (1) This paragraph applies to an appeal to a residential property tribunal under paragraph 24 in respect of an interim or final management order.

(2) The appeal—

(a) is to be by way of a re-hearing, but

(b) may be determined having regard to matters of which the authority were unaware.

(3) The tribunal may confirm or vary the order or revoke it —

(a) (in the case of an interim management order) as from a date specified in the tribunal's order, or

(b) (in the case of a final management order) as from the date of the tribunal's order.

(4) If —

(a) the tribunal revokes an interim or final management order,

(b) it appears to the tribunal that, on the revocation of the order, the house will be required to be licensed under Part 2 or 3 of this Act, and

(c) the tribunal does not give a direction under sub-paragraph (5) or (6),

the tribunal must direct the local housing authority to grant such a licence to such person and on such terms as the tribunal may direct.

(5) If the tribunal revokes a final management order, the tribunal may direct the local housing authority to make an interim management order in respect of the house or part of it on such terms as the tribunal may direct.

This applies despite section 102(9).

(6) If the tribunal revokes a final management order, the tribunal may direct the local housing authority to serve a temporary exemption notice under section 62 or 86 in respect of the house that comes into force on such date as the tribunal directs.

(7) The revocation of an interimmanagement order by the tribunal does not affect the validity of anything previously done in pursuance of the order.

"The operative time" for the purposes of section 114(2)

27 (1) This paragraph defines "the operative time" for the purposes of section 114(2).

(2) If no appeal is made under paragraph 24 before the end of the period of 28 days mentioned in paragraph 25(2), "the operative time" is the end of that period.

(3) If an appeal is made under paragraph 24 before the end of that period, and a decision is given on the appeal which confirms the order, "the operative time" is as follows—

(a) if the period within which an appeal to the Lands Tribunal may be brought expires without such an appeal having been brought, "the operative time" is the end of that period;

(b) if an appeal to the Lands Tribunal is brought, "the operative time" is the time when a decision is given on the appeal which confirms the order.

(4) For the purposes of sub-paragraph (3)—

(a) the withdrawal of an appeal has the same effect as a decision which confirms the order, and

(b) references to a decision which confirms the order are to a decision which confirms it with or without variation.

Right to appeal against decision or refusal to vary or revoke interim management order

28 A relevant person may appeal to a residential property tribunal against—

(a) a decision of a local housing authority to vary or revoke an interim or final management order, or

(b) a refusal of a local housing authority to vary or revoke an interim or final management order.

Time limits for appeals under paragraph 28

29 (1) This paragraph applies in relation to an appeal under paragraph 28 against a decision to vary or revoke, or (as the case may be) to refuse to vary or revoke, an interim or final management order.

(2) Any such appeal must be made before the end of the period of 28 days beginning with the date specified in the notice under paragraph 11, 16, 19 or 22 as the date on which the decision concerned was made.

(3) A residential property tribunal may allow an appeal to be made to it after the end of the period mentioned in sub-paragraph (2) if it is satisfied that there is a good reason for the failure to appeal before the end of that period (and for any delay since then in applying for permission to appeal out of time).

Powers of residential property tribunal on appeal under paragraph 28

30 (1) This paragraph applies to an appeal to a residential property tribunal under paragraph 28 against a decision to vary or revoke, or (as the case may be) to refuse to vary or revoke, an interim or final management order.

(2) Paragraph 26(2) applies to such an appeal as it applies to an appeal under paragraph 24.

(3) The tribunal may confirm, reverse or vary the decision of the local housing authority.

(4) If the appeal is against a decision of the authority to refuse to revoke the order, the tribunal may make an order revoking the order as from a date specified in its order.

"The operative time" for the purposes of section 111(2), 112(2), 121(2) or 122(2)

31 (1) This paragraph defines "the operative time" for the purposes of—

(a) section 111(2) or 112(2) (variation or revocation of interim management order), or

(b) section 121(2) or 122(2) (variation or revocation of final management order).

(2) If no appeal is made under paragraph 28 before the end of the period of 28 days mentioned in paragraph 29(2), "the operative time" is the end of that period.

(3) If an appeal is made under paragraph 28 within that period, and a decision is given on the appeal which confirms the variation or revocation, "the operative time" is as follows—

(a) if the period within which an appeal to the Lands Tribunal may be brought expires without such an appeal having been brought, "the operative time" is the end of that period;

(b) if an appeal to the Lands Tribunal is brought, "the operative time" is the time when a decision is given on the appeal which confirms the variation or revocation.

(4) For the purposes of sub-paragraph (3)—

(a) the withdrawal of an appeal has the same effect as a decision which confirms the variation or revocation appealed against; and

(b) references to a decision which confirms a variation are to a decision which confirms it with or without variation.

Right to appeal against decision in respect of compensation payable to third parties

32 (1) This paragraph applies where a local housing authority have made a decision under section 128 as to whether compensation should be paid to a third party in respect of any interference with his rights in consequence of an interim or final management order.

(2) The third party may appeal to a residential property tribunal against—

(a) a decision by the authority not to pay compensation to him, or

(b) a decision of the authority so far as relating to the amount of compensation that should be paid.

Time limits for appeals under paragraph 32

33 (1) This paragraph applies in relation to an appeal under paragraph 32 against a decision of a local housing authority not to pay compensation to a third party or as to the amount of compensation to be paid.

(2) Any such appeal must be made within the period of 28 days beginning with the date the authority notifies the third party under section 128(2).

(3) A residential property tribunal may allow an appeal to be made to it after the end of the period mentioned in sub-paragraph (2) if it is satisfied that there is good reason for the failure to appeal before the end of that period (and for any delay since then in applying for permission to appeal out of time).

Powers of residential property tribunal on appeal under paragraph 32

34 (1) This paragraph applies in relation to an appeal under paragraph 32 against a decision of a local housing authority not to pay compensation to a third party or as to the amount of compensation to be paid.

(2) The appeal—

(a) is to be by way of re-hearing, but

(b) may be determined having regard to matters of which the authority were unaware.

(3) The tribunal may confirm, reverse or vary the decision of the local housing authority.

(4) Where the tribunal reverses or varies a decision of the authority in respect of a final management order, it must make an order varying the management scheme contained in the final management order accordingly.

Meaning of "relevant person"

35 In this Part of this Schedule "relevant person" means—

(a) any person who has an estate or interest in the house or part of it (but is not a tenant under a lease with an unexpired term of 3 years or less), or

(b) any other person who (but for the order) would be a person managing or having control of the house or part of it.

SCHEDULE 7

Section 132

FURTHER PROVISIONS REGARDING EMPTY DWELLING MANAGEMENT ORDERS

PART 1

INTERIM EDMOS

Operation of interim EDMOs

1 (1) This paragraph deals with the time when an interim EDMO comes into force or ceases to have effect.

(2) The order comes into force when it is made.

(3) The order ceases to have effect at the end of the period of 12 months beginning with the date on which it is made, unless it ceases to have effect at some other time as mentioned below.

(4) If the order provides that it is to cease to have effect on a date falling before the end of that period, it accordingly ceases to have effect on that date.

(5) Sub-paragraphs (6) and (7) apply where—

(a) a final EDMO ("the final EDMO") has been made under section 136 so as to replace the order ("the interim EDMO"), but

(b) the final EDMO has not come into force because of an appeal to a residential property tribunal under paragraph 26 against the making of the final EDMO.

(6) If the date on which the final EDMO comes into force in relation to the dwelling following the disposal of the appeal is later than the date on which the interim EDMO would cease to have effect apart from this sub-paragraph, the interim EDMO continues in force until that later date.

(7) If, on the application of the authority, the tribunal makes an order providing for the interim EDMO to continue in force, pending the disposal of the appeal, until a date later than that on which the interim EDMO would cease to have effect apart from this sub-paragraph, the interim EDMO accordingly continues in force until that later date.

(8) This paragraph has effect subject to paragraphs 6 and 7 (variation or revocation of orders by authority) and to the power of revocation exercisable by a residential property tribunal on an appeal made under paragraph 30.

General effect of interim EDMOs

2 (1) This paragraph applies while an interim EDMO is in force in relation to a dwelling.

(2) The rights and powers conferred by sub-paragraph (3) are exercisable by the authority in performing their duties under section 135(1) to (3) in respect of the dwelling.

(3) The authority—

(a) have the right to possession of the dwelling (subject to the rights of existing occupiers preserved by paragraph 18(3));

(b) have the right to do (and authorise a manager or other person to do) in relation to the dwelling anything which the relevant proprietor of the dwelling would (but for the order) be entitled to do;

(c) may create one or more of the following—

(i) an interest in the dwelling which, as far as possible, has all the incidents of a leasehold, or

(ii) a right in the nature of a licence to occupy part of the dwelling;

(d) may apply to a residential property tribunal for an order under paragraph 22 determining a lease or licence of the dwelling.

(4) But the authority may not under sub-paragraph (3)(c) create any interest or right in the nature of a lease or licence unless—

(a) consent in writing has been given by the relevant proprietor of the dwelling, and

(b) where the relevant proprietor is a lessee under a lease of the dwelling, the interest or right is created for a term that is less than the term of that lease.

(5) The authority—

(a) do not under this paragraph acquire any estate or interest in the dwelling, and

(b) accordingly are not entitled by virtue of this paragraph to sell, lease, charge or make any other disposition of any such estate or interest.

(6) But, where the relevant proprietor of the dwelling is a lessee under a lease of the dwelling, the authority are to be treated (subject to sub-paragraph (5)(a)) as if they were the lessee instead.

(7) Any enactment or rule of law relating to landlords and tenants or leases applies in relation to—

(a) a lease in relation to which the authority are to be treated as the lessee under sub-paragraph (6), or

(b) a lease to which the authority become a party under paragraph 4(2),

as if the authority were the legal owner of the premises (but this is subject to paragraph 4(4) to (6)).

(8) None of the following, namely—

(a) the authority, or

(b) any person authorised under sub-paragraph (3)(b),

is liable to any person having an estate or interest in the dwelling for anything done or omitted to be done in the performance (or intended performance) of the authority's duties under section 135(1) to (3) unless the act or omission is due to negligence of the authority or any such person.

(9) An interim EDMO which has come into force is a local land charge.

(10) The authority may apply to the Chief Land Registrar for the entry of an appropriate restriction in the register of title in respect of such an order.

(11) In this paragraph "enactment" includes an enactment comprised in subordinate legislation (within the meaning of the Interpretation Act 1978 (c. 30)).

General effect of interim EDMOs: leases and licences granted by authority

3 (1) This paragraph applies in relation to any interest or right created by the authority under paragraph 2(3)(c).

(2) For the purposes of any enactment or rule of law—

(a) any interest created by the authority under paragraph 2(3)(c)(i) is to be treated as if it were a legal lease, and

(b) any right created by the authority under paragraph 2(3)(c)(ii) is to be treated as if it were a licence to occupy granted by the legal owner of the dwelling,

despite the fact that the authority have no legal estate in the dwelling (see paragraph 2(5)(a)).

(3) Any enactment or rule of law relating to landlords and tenants or leases accordingly applies in relation to any interest created by the authority under paragraph 2(3)(c)(i) as if the authority were the legal owner of the dwelling.

(4) References to leases and licences—

(a) in this Chapter, and

(b) in any other enactment,

accordingly include (where the context permits) interests and rights created by the authority under paragraph 2(3)(c).

(5) The preceding provisions of this paragraph have effect subject to—

(a) paragraph 4(4) to (6), and

(b) any provision to the contrary contained in an order made by the appropriate national authority.

(6) In paragraph 2(5)(b) the reference to leasing does not include the creation of interests under paragraph 2(3)(c)(i).

(7) In this paragraph—

"enactment" has the meaning given by paragraph 2(11);

"legal lease" means a term of years absolute (within section 1(1)(b) of the Law of Property Act 1925 (c. 20)).

General effect of interim EDMOs: relevant proprietor, mortgagees etc.

4 (1) This paragraph applies in relation to—

(a) the relevant proprietor, and

(b) other persons with an estate or interest in the dwelling,

while an interim EDMO is in force in relation to a dwelling.

(2) Where the relevant proprietor is a lessor or licensor under a lease or licence of the dwelling, the lease or licence has effect while the order is in force as if the local housing authority were substituted in it for the lessor or licensor.

(3) Such a lease continues to have effect, as far as possible, as a lease despite the fact that the rights of the local housing authority, as substituted for the lessor, do not amount to an estate in law in the dwelling.

(4) The provisions mentioned in sub-paragraph (5) do not apply to a lease or licence within sub-paragraph (2).

(5) The provisions are—

(a) the provisions which exclude local authority lettings from the Rent Acts, namely—

(i) sections 14 to 16 of the Rent Act 1977 (c. 42), and

(ii) those sections as applied by Schedule 2 to the Rent (Agriculture) Act 1976 (c. 80) and section 5(2) to (4) of that Act; and

(b) section 1(2) of, and paragraph 12 of Part 1 of Schedule 1 to, the Housing Act 1988 (c. 50) (which exclude local authority lettings from Part 1 of that Act).

(6) Nothing in this Chapter has the result that the authority are to be treated as the legal owner of any premises for the purposes of—

(a) section 80 of the Housing Act 1985 (c. 68) (the landlord condition for secure tenancies); or

(b) section 124 of the Housing Act 1996 (c. 52) (introductory tenancies).

(7) The relevant proprietor of the dwelling—

(a) is not entitled to receive any rents or other payments made in respect of occupation of the dwelling;

(b) may not exercise any rights or powers with respect to the management of the dwelling; and

(c) may not create any of the following—

(i) any leasehold interest in the dwelling or a part of it (other than a lease of a reversion), or

(ii) any licence or other right to occupy it.

(8) However (subject to sub-paragraph (7)(c)) nothing in paragraph 2 or this paragraph affects the ability of a person having an estate or interest in the dwelling to make any disposition of that estate or interest.

(9) Nothing in paragraph 2 or this paragraph affects—

(a) the validity of any mortgage relating to the dwelling or any rights or remedies available to the mortgagee under such a mortgage, or

(b) the validity of any lease of the dwelling under which the relevant proprietor is a lessee, or any superior lease, or (subject to paragraph 2(6)) any rights or remedies available to the lessor under such a lease,

except to the extent that any of those rights or remedies would prevent the local housing authority from exercising their power under paragraph 2(3)(c).

(10) In proceedings for the enforcement of any such rights or remedies the court may make such order as it thinks fit as regards the operation of the interim EDMO (including an order quashing it).

Financial arrangements while order is in force

5 (1) This paragraph applies to relevant expenditure of a local housing authority who have made an interim EDMO.

(2) "Relevant expenditure" means—

(a) expenditure incurred by the authority with the consent of the relevant proprietor, or

(b) any other expenditure reasonably incurred by the authority, in connection with performing their duties under section 135(1) to (3) in respect of the dwelling (including any premiums paid for insurance of the premises).

(3) Rent or other payments which the authority have collected or recovered, by virtue of this Chapter, from persons occupying or having the right to occupy the dwelling may be used by the authority to meet—

(a) relevant expenditure, and

(b) any amounts of compensation payable to a third party by virtue of an order under section 134(4) or 138(2) or to a dispossessed landlord or tenant by virtue of an order under paragraph 22(5).

(4) The authority must pay to the relevant proprietor—

(a) any amount of rent or other payments collected or recovered as mentioned in sub-paragraph (3) that remains after deductions to meet relevant expenditure and any amounts of compensation payable as mentioned in that sub-paragraph, and

(b) (where appropriate) interest on that amount at a reasonable rate fixed by the authority,

and such payments are to be made at such intervals as the authority consider appropriate.

(5) The interim EDMO may provide for—

(a) the rate of interest which is to apply for the purposes of paragraph (b) of sub-paragraph (4); and

(b) the intervals at which payments are to be made under that sub-paragraph.

Paragraph 26(1)(c) enables an appeal to be brought where the order does not provide for both of those matters.

(6) The authority must—

(a) keep full accounts of their income and expenditure in respect of the dwelling; and

(b) afford to the relevant proprietor, and to any other person who has an estate or interest in the dwelling, all reasonable facilities for inspecting, taking copies of and verifying those accounts.

(7) The relevant proprietor may apply to a residential property tribunal for an order—

(a) declaring that an amount shown in the accounts as expenditure of the authority does not constitute relevant expenditure (see sub-paragraph (2));

(b) requiring the authority to make such financial adjustments (in the accounts and otherwise) as are necessary to reflect the tribunal's declaration.

(8) In this paragraph—

"dispossessed landlord or tenant" means a person who was a lessor, lessee, licensor or licensee under a lease or licence determined by an order under paragraph 22;

"expenditure" includes administrative costs.

Variation or revocation of interim EDMOs

6 (1) The local housing authority may vary an interim EDMO if they consider it appropriate to do so.

(2) A variation does not come into force until such time, if any, as is the operative time for the purposes of this sub-paragraph under paragraph 33 (time when period for appealing expires without an appeal being made or when decision to vary is confirmed on appeal).

(3) The power to vary an order under this paragraph is exercisable by the authority either—

(a) on an application made by a relevant person, or

(b) on the authority's own initiative.

(4) In this paragraph "relevant person" means any person who has an estate or interest in the dwelling (other than a person who is a tenant under a lease granted under paragraph 2(3)(c)).

7 (1) The local housing authority may revoke an interim EDMO in the following cases—

(a) where the authority conclude that there are no steps which they could appropriately take for the purpose of securing that the dwelling is occupied (see section 135(4));

(b) where the authority are satisfied that—

(i) the dwelling will either become or continue to be occupied, despite the order being revoked, or

(ii) that the dwelling is to be sold;

(c) where a final EDMO has been made by the authority in respect of the dwelling so as to replace the order;

(d) where the authority conclude that it would be appropriate to revoke the order in order to prevent or stop interference with the rights of a third party in consequence of the order; and

(e) where in any other circumstances the authority consider it appropriate to revoke the order.

(2) But, in a case where the dwelling is occupied, the local housing authority may not revoke an interim EDMO under sub-paragraph (1)(b), (d) or (e) unless the relevant proprietor consents.

(3) A revocation does not come into force until such time, if any, as is the operative time for the purposes of this sub-paragraph under paragraph 33 (time when period for appealing expires without an appeal being made or when decision to revoke is confirmed on appeal).

(4) The power to revoke an order under this paragraph is exercisable by the authority either—

(a) on an application made by a relevant person, or

(b) on the authority's own initiative.

(5) Where a relevant person applies to the authority for the revocation of an order under this paragraph, the authority may refuse to revoke the order unless the relevant proprietor (or some other person) agrees to pay to the authority any deficit such as is mentioned in paragraph 23(4).

(6) In this paragraph "relevant person" means any person who has an estate or interest in the dwelling (other than a person who is a tenant under a lease granted under paragraph 2(3)(c)).

8 (1) Part 2 of Schedule 6 applies in relation to the variation or revocation of an interim EDMO as it applies in relation to the variation or revocation of an interim management order.

(2) But Part 2 of that Schedule so applies as if—

(a) references to the right of appeal under Part 3 of the Schedule and to paragraph 29(2) were to the right of appeal under Part 4 of this Schedule and to paragraph 31(2) of this Schedule, and

(b) paragraph 23(4) defined "relevant person" as any person who, to the knowledge of the local housing authority, is a person having an estate or interest in the dwelling (other than a person who is a tenant under a lease granted under paragraph 2(3)(c) of this Schedule).

PART 2

FINAL EDMOS

Operation of final EDMOs

9 (1) This paragraph deals with the time when a final EDMO comes into force or ceases to have effect.

(2) The order does not come into force until such time (if any) as is the operative time for the purposes of this sub-paragraph under paragraph 29 (time when period for appealing expires without an appeal being made or when order is confirmed on appeal).

(3) The order ceases to have effect at the end of the period of 7 years beginning with the date on which it comes into force, unless it ceases to have effect at some other time as mentioned below.

(4) If the order provides that it is to cease to have effect on a date falling before the end of that period, it accordingly ceases to have effect on that date.

(5) If—

(a) the order provides that it is to cease to have effect on a date falling after the end of that period, and

(b) the relevant proprietor of the dwelling has consented to that provision,

the order accordingly ceases to have effect on that date.

(6) Sub-paragraphs (7) and (8) apply where—

(a) a new final EDMO ("the new order") has been made so as to replace the order ("the existing order"), but

(b) the new order has not come into force because of an appeal to a residential property tribunal under paragraph 26 against the making of that order.

(7) If the date on which the new order comes into force in relation to the dwelling following the disposal of the appeal is later than the date on which the existing order would cease to have effect apart from this sub-paragraph, the existing order continues in force until that later date.

(8) If, on the application of the authority, the tribunal makes an order providing for the existing order to continue in force, pending the disposal of the appeal, until a date

later than that on which it would cease to have effect apart from this sub-paragraph, the existing order accordingly continues in force until that later date.

(9) This paragraph has effect subject to paragraphs 15 and 16 (variation or revocation of orders) and to the power of revocation exercisable by a residential property tribunal on an appeal made under paragraph 26 or 30.

General effect of final EDMOs

10 (1) This paragraph applies while a final EDMO is in force in relation to a dwelling.

(2) The rights and powers conferred by sub-paragraph (3) are exercisable by the authority in performing their duties under section 137(1) to (3) in respect of the dwelling.

(3) The authority—

(a) have the right to possession of the dwelling (subject to the rights of existing and other occupiers preserved by paragraph 18(3) and (4));

(b) have the right to do (and authorise a manager or other person to do) in relation to the dwelling anything which the relevant proprietor of the dwelling would (but for the order) be entitled to do;

(c) may create one or more of the following—

(i) an interest in the dwelling which, as far as possible, has all the incidents of a leasehold, or

(ii) a right in the nature of a licence to occupy part of the dwelling;

(d) may apply to a residential property tribunal for an order under paragraph 22 determining a lease or licence of the dwelling.

(4) The powers of the authority under sub-paragraph (3)(c) are restricted as follows—

(a) they may not create any interest or right in the nature of a lease or licence—

(i) which is for a fixed term expiring after the date on which the order is due to expire, or

(ii) (subject to paragraph (b)) which is terminable by notice to quit, or an equivalent notice, of more than 4 weeks,

unless consent in writing has been given by the relevant proprietor;

(b) they may create an interest in the nature of an assured shorthold tenancy without any such consent so long as it is created before the beginning of the period of 6 months that ends with the date on which the order is due to expire.

(5) The authority—

(a) do not under this paragraph acquire any estate or interest in the dwelling, and

(b) accordingly are not entitled by virtue of this paragraph to sell, lease, charge or make any other disposition of any such estate or interest.

(6) But, where the relevant proprietor of the dwelling is a lessee under a lease of the dwelling, the authority are to be treated (subject to sub-paragraph (5)(a)) as if they were the lessee instead.

(7) Any enactment or rule of law relating to landlords and tenants or leases applies in relation to—

(a) a lease in relation to which the authority are to be treated as the lessee under sub-paragraph (6), or

(b) a lease to which the authority become a party under paragraph 12(2), as if the authority were the legal owner of the premises (but this is subject to paragraph 12(4) to (6)).

(8) None of the following, namely—

(a) the authority, or

(b) any person authorised under sub-paragraph (3)(b),

is liable to any person having an estate or interest in the dwelling for anything done or omitted to be done in the performance (or intended performance) of the authority's duties under section 137(1) to (3) unless the act or omission is due to negligence of the authority or any such person.

(9) A final EDMO which has come into force is a local land charge.

(10) The authority may apply to the Chief Land Registrar for the entry of an appropriate restriction in the register in respect of such an order.

(11) In this paragraph "enactment" includes an enactment comprised in subordinate legislation (within the meaning of the Interpretation Act 1978 (c. 30)).

General effect of final EDMOs: leases and licences granted by authority

11 (1) This paragraph applies in relation to any interest or right created by the authority under paragraph 10(3)(c).

(2) For the purposes of any enactment or rule of law—

(a) any interest created by the authority under paragraph 10(3)(c)(i) is to be treated as if it were a legal lease, and

(b) any right created by the authority under paragraph 10(3)(c)(ii) is to be treated as if it were a licence to occupy granted by the legal owner of the dwelling,

despite the fact that the authority have no legal estate in the dwelling (see paragraph 10(5)(a)).

(3) Any enactment or rule of law relating to landlords and tenants or leases accordingly applies in relation to any interest created by the authority under paragraph 10(3)(c)(i) as if the authority were the legal owner of the dwelling.

(4) References to leases and licences—

(a) in this Chapter, and

(b) in any other enactment,

accordingly include (where the context permits) interests and rights created by the authority under paragraph 10(3)(c).

(5) The preceding provisions of this paragraph have effect subject to—

(a) paragraph 12(4) to (6), and

(b) any provision to the contrary contained in an order made by the appropriate national authority.

(6) In paragraph 10(5)(b) the reference to leasing does not include the creation of interests under paragraph 10(3)(c)(i).

(7) In this paragraph—

"enactment" has the meaning given by paragraph 10(11);

"legal lease" means a term of years absolute (within section 1(1)(b) of the Law of Property Act 1925 (c. 20)).

General effect of final EDMOs: relevant proprietor, mortgagees etc.

12 (1) This paragraph applies in relation to—

(a) the relevant proprietor, and

(b) other persons with an estate or interest in the dwelling,

while a final EDMO is in force in relation to a dwelling.

(2) Where the relevant proprietor is a lessor or licensor under a lease or licence of the dwelling, the lease or licence has effect while the order is in force as if the local housing authority were substituted in it for the lessor or licensor.

(3) Such a lease continues to have effect, as far as possible, as a lease despite the fact that the rights of the local housing authority, as substituted for the lessor, do not amount to an estate in law in the dwelling.

(4) The provisions mentioned in sub-paragraph (5) do not apply to a lease or licence within sub-paragraph (2).

(5) The provisions are—

(a) the provisions which exclude local authority lettings from the Rent Acts, namely—

(i) sections 14 to 16 of the Rent Act 1977 (c. 42), and

(ii) those sections as applied by Schedule 2 to the Rent (Agriculture) Act 1976 (c. 80) and section 5(2) to (4) of that Act; and

(b) section 1(2) of, and paragraph 12 of Part 1 of Schedule 1 to, the Housing Act 1988 (c. 50) (which exclude local authority lettings from Part 1 of that Act).

(6) Nothing in this Chapter has the result that the authority are to be treated as the legal owner of any premises for the purposes of—

(a) section 80 of the Housing Act 1985 (c. 68) (the landlord condition for secure tenancies); or

(b) section 124 of the Housing Act 1996 (c. 52) (introductory tenancies).

(7) The relevant proprietor of the dwelling—

(a) is not entitled to receive any rents or other payments made in respect of occupation of the dwelling;

(b) may not exercise any rights or powers with respect to the management of the dwelling; and

(c) may not create any of the following—

(i) any leasehold interest in the dwelling or a part of it (other than a lease of a reversion), or

(ii) any licence or other right to occupy it.

(8) However (subject to sub-paragraph (7)(c)) nothing in paragraph 10 or this paragraph affects the ability of a person having an estate or interest in the dwelling to make any disposition of that estate or interest.

(9) Nothing in paragraph 10 or this paragraph affects—

(a) the validity of any mortgage relating to the dwelling or any rights or remedies available to the mortgagee under such a mortgage, or

(b) the validity of any lease of the dwelling under which the relevant proprietor is a lessee, or any superior lease, or (subject to paragraph 10(6)) any rights or remedies available to the lessor under such a lease;

except to the extent that any of those rights or remedies would prevent the local housing authority from exercising their power under paragraph 10(3)(c).

(10) In proceedings for the enforcement of any such rights or remedies the court may make such order as it thinks fit as regards the operation of the final EDMO (including an order quashing it).

Management scheme and accounts

13 (1) A final EDMO must contain a management scheme.

(2) A "management scheme" is a scheme setting out how the local housing authority are to carry out their duties under section 137(1) to (3) as respects the dwelling.

(3) The scheme is to contain a plan giving details of the way in which the authority propose to manage the dwelling, which must (in particular) include—

(a) details of any works that the authority intend to carry out in connection with the dwelling;

(b) an estimate of the capital and other expenditure to be incurred by the authority in respect of the dwelling while the order is in force;

(c) the amount of rent which, in the opinion of the authority, the dwelling might reasonably be expected to fetch on the open market at the time the management scheme is made;

(d) the amount of rent or other payments that the authority will seek to obtain;

(e) the amount of any compensation that is payable to a third party by virtue of a decision of the authority under section 136(4) or 138(3) in respect of any interference in consequence of the final EDMO with the rights of that person;

(f) provision as to the payment of any such compensation and of any compensation payable to a dispossessed landlord or tenant by virtue of an order under paragraph 22(5);

(g) where the amount of rent payable to the authority in respect of the dwelling for a period is less than the amount of rent mentioned in paragraph (c) in respect of a period of the same length, provision as to the following—

(i) the deduction from the difference of relevant expenditure and any amounts of compensation payable to a third party or dispossessed landlord or tenant;

(ii) the payment of any remaining amount to the relevant proprietor;

(iii) the deduction from time to time of any remaining amount from any amount that the authority are entitled to recover from the proprietor under paragraph 23(5) or (6);

(h) provision as to the payment by the authority to the relevant proprietor from time to time of amounts of rent or other payments that remain after the deduction of—

(i) relevant expenditure, and

(ii) any amount of compensation payable to a third party or dispossessed landlord or tenant;

(i) provision as to the manner in which the authority are to pay to the relevant proprietor, on the termination of the final EDMO, the balance of any amounts of rent or other payments that remain after the deduction of relevant expenditure and any amounts of compensation payable to a third party or dispossessed landlord or tenant;

(j) provision as to the manner in which the authority are to pay, on the termination of the final EDMO, any outstanding amount of compensation payable to a third party or dispossessed landlord or tenant.

(4) The scheme may also state—

(a) the authority's intentions as regards the use of rent or other payments to meet relevant expenditure;

(b) the authority's intentions as regards the payment to the relevant proprietor (where appropriate) of interest on amounts within sub-paragraph (3)(h) and (i);

(c) that paragraph 23(2) or, where the relevant proprietor consents, paragraph 23(3)(c) is not to apply in relation to an interim EDMO or (as the case may be) final EDMO that immediately preceded the final EDMO, and that instead the authority intend to use any balance such as is mentioned in that sub-paragraph to meet—

(i) relevant expenditure incurred during the currency of that final EDMO, and

(ii) any compensation that may become payable to a third party or a dispossessed landlord or tenant;

(d) that paragraph 23(4) to (6) are not to apply in relation to an interim EDMO or, where the relevant proprietor consents, a final EDMO that immediately preceded the final EDMO, and that instead the authority intend to use rent or other payments collected during the currency of that final EDMO to reimburse the authority in respect of any deficit such as is mentioned in paragraph 23(4);

(e) the authority's intentions as regards the recovery from the relevant proprietor, with or without interest, of any amount of relevant expenditure incurred under a previous interim EDMO or final EDMO that the authority are entitled to recover from the proprietor under paragraph 23(5) or (6).

(5) The authority must—

(a) keep full accounts of their income and expenditure in respect of the dwelling; and

(b) afford to the relevant proprietor, and to any other person who has an estate or interest in the dwelling, all reasonable facilities for inspecting, taking copies of and verifying those accounts.

(6) In this paragraph—

"dispossessed landlord or tenant" means a person who was a lessor, lessee, licensor or licensee under a lease or licence determined by an order under paragraph 22;

"relevant expenditure" means—

(a) expenditure incurred by the authority with the consent of the relevant proprietor, or

(b) any other expenditure reasonably incurred by the authority, in connection with performing their duties under section 135(1) to (3) or 137(1) to (3) in respect of the dwelling (including any reasonable administrative costs and any premiums paid for insurance of the premises);

"rent or other payments" means rent or other payments collected or recovered, by virtue of this Chapter, from persons occupying or having the right to occupy the dwelling.

(7) In any provision of this Chapter relating to varying, revoking or appealing against decisions relating to a final EDMO, any reference to such an order includes (where the context permits) a reference to the management scheme contained in it.

Application to residential property tribunal in respect of breach of management scheme

14 (1) An affected person may apply to a residential property tribunal for an order requiring the local housing authority to manage a dwelling in accordance with the management scheme contained in a final EDMO made in respect of the dwelling.

(2) On such an application the tribunal may, if it considers it appropriate to do so, make an order—

(a) requiring the authority to manage the dwelling in accordance with the management scheme, or

(b) revoking the final EDMO as from a date specified in the tribunal's order.

(3) An order under sub-paragraph (2) may—

(a) set out the steps which the authority are to take to manage the dwelling in accordance with the management scheme,

(b) include provision varying the final EDMO, and

(c) require the payment of money to an affected person by way of damages.

(4) In this paragraph "affected person" means—

(a) the relevant proprietor, and

(b) any third party to whom compensation is payable by virtue of an order under section 134(4) or 138(2) or a decision of the authority under section 136(4) or 138(3) or who was a lessor, lessee, licensor or licensee under a lease or licence determined by an order of the residential property tribunal under paragraph 22 and to whom compensation is payable by virtue of an order under sub-paragraph (5) of that paragraph.

Variation or revocation of final EDMOs

15 (1) The local housing authority may vary a final EDMO if they consider it appropriate to do so.

(2) A variation does not come into force until such time, if any, as is the operative time for the purposes of this sub-paragraph under paragraph 33 (time when period for appealing expires without an appeal being made or when decision to vary is confirmed on appeal).

(3) The power to vary an order under this paragraph is exercisable by the authority either—

(a) on an application made by a relevant person, or

(b) on the authority's own initiative.

(4) In this paragraph "relevant person" means any person who has an estate or interest in the dwelling (other than a person who is a tenant under a lease granted under paragraph 2(3)(c) or 10(3)(c)).

16 (1) The local housing authority may revoke a final EDMO in the following cases—

(a) where the authority conclude that there are no steps which they could appropriately take as mentioned in section 137(4)(b) or that keeping the order in force is not necessary as mentioned in section 137(4)(c);

(b) where the authority are satisfied that—

(i) the dwelling will either become or continue to be occupied, despite the order being revoked, or

(ii) that the dwelling is to be sold;

(c) where a further final EDMO has been made by the authority in respect of the dwelling so as to replace the order;

(d) where the authority conclude that it would be appropriate to revoke the order in order to prevent or stop interference with the rights of a third party in consequence of the order; and

(e) where in any other circumstances the authority consider it appropriate to revoke the order.

(2) But, in a case where the dwelling is occupied, the local housing authority may not revoke a final EDMO under sub-paragraph (1)(b), (d) or (e) unless the relevant proprietor consents.

(3) A revocation does not come into force until such time, if any, as is the operative time for the purposes of this sub-paragraph under paragraph 33 (time when period for appealing expires without an appeal being made or when decision to revoke is confirmed on appeal).

(4) The power to revoke an order under this paragraph is exercisable by the authority either—

(a) on an application made by a relevant person, or

(b) on the authority's own initiative.

(5) Where a relevant person applies to the authority for the revocation of an order under this paragraph, the authority may refuse to revoke the order unless the relevant proprietor (or some other person) agrees to pay to the authority any deficit such as is mentioned in paragraph 23(4).

(6) In this paragraph "relevant person" means any person who has an estate or interest in the dwelling (other than a person who is a tenant under a lease granted under paragraph 2(3)(c) or 10(3)(c)).

17 (1) Part 2 of Schedule 6 applies in relation to the variation or revocation of a final EDMO as it applies in relation to the variation or revocation of a final management order.

(2) But Part 2 of that Schedule so applies as if—

(a) references to the right of appeal under Part 3 of the Schedule and to paragraph 29(2) were to the right of appeal under Part 4 of this Schedule and to paragraph 31(2) of this Schedule, and

(b) paragraph 23(4) defined "relevant person" as any person who, to the knowledge of the local housing authority, is a person having an estate or interest in the dwelling (other than a person who is a tenant under a lease granted under paragraph 2(3)(c) or 10(3)(c) of this Schedule).

PART 3

INTERIM AND FINAL EDMOS: GENERAL PROVISIONS (OTHER THAN PROVISIONS RELATING TO APPEALS)

Effect of EDMOs: persons occupying or having a right to occupy the dwelling

18 (1) This paragraph applies to existing and new occupiers of a dwelling in relation to which an interim EDMO or final EDMO is in force.

(2) In this paragraph—

"existing occupier" means a person other than the relevant proprietor who, at the time when the order comes into force—

(a) has the right to occupy the dwelling, but

(b) is not a new occupier within sub-paragraph (4);

"new occupier" means a person who, at a time when the order is in force, is occupying the dwelling under a lease or licence granted under paragraph 2(3)(c) or 10(3)(c).

(3) Paragraphs 2 and 10 do not affect the rights or liabilities of an existing occupier under a lease or licence (whether in writing or not) under which he has the right to occupy the dwelling at the commencement date.

(4) Paragraph 10 does not affect the rights and liabilities of a new occupier who, in the case of a final EDMO, is occupying the dwelling at the time when the order comes into force.

(5) The provisions mentioned in sub-paragraph (6) do not apply to a lease or agreement under which a new occupier has the right to occupy or is occupying the dwelling.

(6) The provisions are—

(a) the provisions which exclude local authority lettings from the Rent Acts, namely—

(i) sections 14 to 16 of the Rent Act 1977 (c. 42), and

(ii) those sections as applied by Schedule 2 to the Rent (Agriculture) Act 1976 (c. 80) and section 5(2) to (4) of that Act; and

(b) section 1(2) of, and paragraph 12 of Part 1 of Schedule 1 to, the Housing Act 1988 (c. 50) (which exclude local authority lettings from Part 1 of that Act).

(7) If, immediately before the coming into force of an interim EDMO or final EDMO, an existing occupier had the right to occupy the dwelling under—

(a) a protected or statutory tenancy within the meaning of the Rent Act 1977,

(b) a protected or statutory tenancy within the meaning of the Rent (Agriculture) Act 1976, or

(c) an assured tenancy or assured agricultural occupancy within the meaning of Part 1 of the Housing Act 1988,

nothing in this Chapter (except an order under paragraph 22 determining a lease or licence) prevents the continuance of that tenancy or occupancy or affects the continued operation of any of those Acts in relation to the tenancy or occupancy after the coming into force of the order.

(8) In this paragraph "the commencement date" means the date on which the order came into force (or, if that order was preceded by one or more orders under this Chapter, the date when the first order came into force).

Effect of EDMOs: agreements and legal proceedings

19 (1) An agreement or instrument within sub-paragraph (2) has effect, while an interim EDMO or final EDMO is in force, as if any rights or liabilities of the relevant proprietor under the agreement or instrument were instead rights or liabilities of the local housing authority.

(2) An agreement or instrument is within this sub-paragraph if—

(a) it is effective on the commencement date,

(b) one of the parties to it is the relevant proprietor of the dwelling,

(c) it relates to the dwelling, whether in connection with any management activities with respect to it, or otherwise,

(d) it is specified for the purposes of this sub-paragraph in the order or falls within a description of agreements or instruments so specified, and

(e) the authority serve a notice in writing on all the parties to it stating that sub-paragraph (1) is to apply to it.

(3) An agreement or instrument is not within sub-paragraph (2) if—

(a) it is a lease or licence within paragraph 2(6) or 10(6), or

(b) it relates to any disposition by the relevant proprietor which is not precluded by paragraph 4(7) or 12(7).

(4) Proceedings in respect of any cause of action within sub-paragraph (5) may, while an interim EDMO or final EDMO is in force, be instituted or continued by or against the local housing authority instead of by or against the relevant proprietor.

(5) A cause of action is within this sub-paragraph if—

(a) it is a cause of action (of any nature) which accrued to or against the relevant proprietor of the dwelling before the commencement date,

(b) it relates to the dwelling as mentioned in sub-paragraph (2)(c),

(c) it is specified for the purposes of this sub-paragraph in the order or falls within a description of causes of action so specified, and

(d) the authority serve a notice in writing on all interested parties stating that sub-paragraph (4) is to apply to it.

(6) If, by virtue of this paragraph, the authority become subject to any liability to pay damages in respect of anything done (or omitted to be done) before the commencement date by or on behalf of the relevant proprietor of the dwelling, the relevant proprietor is liable to reimburse to the authority an amount equal to the amount of damages paid by them.

(7) In this paragraph—

"agreement" includes arrangement;

"the commencement date" means the date on which the order comes into force (or, if that order was preceded by one or more orders under this Chapter, the date when the first order came into force);

"management activities" includes repair, maintenance, improvement and insurance.

Effect of EDMOs: furniture

20 (1) Sub-paragraph (2) applies where, on the date on which an interim EDMO or final EDMO comes into force, there is furniture owned by the relevant proprietor in the dwelling.

(2) Subject to sub-paragraphs (3) and (4), the right to possession of the furniture against all persons vests in the local housing authority on that date and remains vested in the authority while the order is in force.

(3) The right of the local housing authority under sub-paragraph (2) to possession of the furniture is subject to the rights of any person who, on the date on which the interim EDMO or final EDMO comes into force, has the right to possession of the dwelling.

(4) Where—

(a) the local housing authority have the right to possession of the furniture under sub-paragraph (2), and

(b) they have not granted a right to possession of the furniture to any other person,

they must, on a request by the relevant proprietor, give up possession of the furniture to him.

(5) The local housing authority may renounce the right to possession of the furniture conferred by sub-paragraph (2) by serving notice on the relevant proprietor not less than two weeks before the renunciation is to have effect.

(6) Where the local housing authority renounce the right to possession of the furniture under sub-paragraph (5), they must make appropriate arrangements for storage of the furniture at their own cost.

(7) In this paragraph "furniture" includes fittings and other articles.

EDMOs: power to supply furniture

21 (1) The local housing authority may supply the dwelling to which an interim EDMO or final EDMO relates with such furniture as they consider to be required.

(2) For the purposes of paragraph 5 or paragraph 13, any expenditure incurred by the authority under this paragraph constitutes expenditure incurred by the authority in connection with performing their duties under section 135(1) to (3) or 137(1) to (3).

(3) In this paragraph "furniture" includes fittings and other articles.

Power of a residential property tribunal to determine certain leases and licences

22 (1) A residential property tribunal may make an order determining a lease or licence to which this paragraph applies if—

(a) the case falls within sub-paragraph (3) or (4), and

(b) the tribunal are satisfied that the dwelling is not being occupied and that the local housing authority need to have the right to possession of the dwelling in order to secure that the dwelling becomes occupied.

(2) This paragraph applies to the following leases and licences of a dwelling—

(a) a lease of the dwelling in respect of which the relevant proprietor is the lessor,

(b) a sub-lease of any such lease, and

(c) a licence of the dwelling.

(3) A case falls within this sub-paragraph if—

(a) an interim or final EDMO is in force in respect of the dwelling, and

(b) the local housing authority have applied under paragraph 2(3)(d) or 10(3)(d) for an order determining the lease or licence.

(4) A case falls within this sub-paragraph if—

(a) the local housing authority have applied to the residential property tribunal under section 133 for an order authorising them to make an interim EDMO in respect of the dwelling and an order determining the lease or licence, and

(b) the residential property tribunal has decided to authorise the authority to make an interim EDMO in respect of the dwelling.

(5) An order under this paragraph may include provision requiring the local housing authority to pay such amount or amounts to one or more of the lessor, lessee, licensor or licensee by way of compensation in respect of the determination of the lease or licence as the tribunal determines.

(6) Where—

(a) a final EDMO is in force in respect of a dwelling, and

(b) the tribunal makes an order requiring the local housing authority to pay an amount of compensation to a lessor, lessee, licensor or licensee in respect of the determination of a lease or licence of the dwelling,

the tribunal must make an order varying the management scheme contained in the final EDMO so as to make provision as to the payment of that compensation.

Termination of EDMOs: financial arrangements

23 (1) This paragraph applies where an interim EDMO or final EDMO ceases to have effect for any reason.

(2) If, on the termination date for an interim EDMO, the total amount of rent or other payments collected or recovered as mentioned in paragraph 5(3) exceeds the total amount of—

(a) the authority's relevant expenditure, and

(b) any amounts of compensation payable to third parties by virtue of orders under section 134(4) or 138(2) or decisions of the authority under section 136(4) or 138(3),

the authority must, as soon as possible after the termination date, pay the balance to the relevant proprietor.

(3) If, on the termination date for a final EDMO, any balance is payable to—

(a) a third party,

(b) a dispossessed landlord or tenant, or

(c) the relevant proprietor,

in accordance with the management scheme under paragraph 13, that amount must be paid to that person by the local housing authority in the manner provided by the scheme.

(4) Sub-paragraphs (5) and (6) apply where, on the termination date for an interim EDMO or final EDMO, the total amount of rent or other payments collected or recovered as mentioned in paragraph 5(3) is less than the total amount of the authority's relevant expenditure together with any such amounts of compensation as are mentioned in sub-paragraph (2)(b) above.

(5) The authority may recover from the relevant proprietor—

(a) the amount of any relevant expenditure (not exceeding the deficit mentioned in sub-paragraph (4)) which he has agreed in writing to pay either as a condition of revocation of the order or otherwise, and

(b) where the relevant proprietor is a tenant under a lease in respect of the dwelling, the amount of any outstanding service charges payable under the lease.

(6) In the case of an interim EDMO ceasing to have effect, the authority may recover the deficit mentioned in sub-paragraph (4) from the relevant proprietor if, in their opinion, he unreasonably refused to consent to the creation of an interest or right as mentioned in paragraph 2(3)(c) while the order was in force.

(7) The provisions of any of sub-paragraphs (2) to (6) do not, however, apply in relation to the order if—

(a) the order is followed by a final EDMO, and

(b) the management scheme contained in that final EDMO provides for those sub-paragraphs not to apply in relation to the order (see paragraph 13(4)(c) and (d)).

(8) Any sum recoverable by the authority under sub-paragraph (5) or (6) is, until recovered, a charge on the dwelling.

(9) The charge takes effect on the termination date for the order as a legal charge which is a local land charge.

(10) For the purpose of enforcing the charge the authority have the same powers and remedies under the Law of Property Act 1925 (c. 20) and otherwise as if they were mortgagees by deed having powers of sale and lease, of accepting surrenders of leases and of appointing a receiver.

(11) The power of appointing a receiver is exercisable at any time after the end of the period of one month beginning with the date on which the charge takes effect.

(12) In this paragraph—

"dispossessed landlord or tenant" means a person who was a lessor, lessee, licensor or licensee under a lease or licence determined by an order under paragraph 22;

"relevant expenditure" has the same meaning as in paragraph 5 (in relation to an interim EDMO) or paragraph 13 (in relation to a final EDMO);

"service charge" has the meaning given by section 18 of the Landlord and Tenant Act 1985 (c. 70);

"the termination date" means the date on which the order ceases to have effect.

Termination of EDMOs: leases, agreements and proceedings

24 (1) This paragraph applies where—

(a) an interim EDMO or final EDMO ceases to have effect for any reason, and

(b) the order is not immediately followed by a further order under this Chapter.

(2) As from the termination date, an agreement which (in accordance with paragraph 3 or 11) has effect as a lease or licence granted by the authority under paragraph 2 or 10 has effect with the substitution of the relevant proprietor for the authority.

(3) If the relevant proprietor is a lessee, nothing in a superior lease imposes liability on him or any superior lessee in respect of anything done before the termination date in pursuance of the terms of an agreement to which sub-paragraph (2) applies.

(4) If the condition in sub-paragraph (5) is met, any other agreement entered into by the authority in the performance of their duties under section 135(1) to (3) or 137(1) to (3) in respect of the dwelling has effect, as from the termination date, with the substitution of the relevant proprietor for the authority.

(5) The condition is that the authority serve a notice on the other party or parties to the agreement stating that sub-paragraph (4) applies to the agreement.

(6) If the condition in sub-paragraph (7) is met—

(a) any rights or liabilities that were rights or liabilities of the authority immediately before the termination date by virtue of any provision of this Chapter, or under any agreement to which sub-paragraph (4) applies, are rights or liabilities of the relevant proprietor instead, and

(b) any proceedings instituted or continued by or against the authority by virtue of any such provision or agreement may be continued by or against the relevant proprietor instead,

as from the termination date.

(7) The condition is that the authority serve a notice on all interested parties stating that sub-paragraph (6) applies to the rights or liabilities or (as the case may be) the proceedings.

(8) If by virtue of this paragraph a relevant proprietor becomes subject to any liability to pay damages in respect of anything done (or omitted to be done) before the termination date by or on behalf of the authority, the authority are liable to reimburse to the relevant proprietor an amount equal to the amount of the damages paid by him.

(9) This paragraph applies to instruments as it applies to agreements.

(10) In this paragraph—

"agreement" includes arrangement;

"the termination date" means the date on which the order ceases to have effect.

EDMOs: power of entry to carry out work

25 (1) The right mentioned in sub-paragraph (2) is exercisable by the local housing authority, or any person authorised in writing by them, at any time when an interim EDMO or final EDMO is in force.

(2) That right is the right at all reasonable times to enter any part of the dwelling for the purpose of carrying out works, and is exercisable as against any person having an estate or interest in the dwelling.

(3) If, after receiving reasonable notice of the intended action, any occupier of the dwelling prevents any officer, employee, agent or contractor of the local housing authority from carrying out work in the dwelling, a magistrates' court may order him to permit to be done on the premises anything which the authority consider to be necessary.

(4) A person who fails to comply with an order of the court under sub-paragraph (3) commits an offence.

(5) A person who commits an offence under sub-paragraph (4) is liable on summary conviction to a fine not exceeding level 5 on the standard scale.

PART 4

APPEALS

Appeals: decisions relating to EDMOs

26 (1) A relevant person may appeal to a residential property tribunal against—

(a) a decision of the local housing authority to make a final EDMO,

(b) the terms of a final EDMO (including the terms of the management scheme contained in it), or

(c) the terms of an interim EDMO on the grounds that they do not provide for one or both of the matters mentioned in paragraph 5(5)(a) and (b) (which relate to payments of surplus rent etc.).

(2) Where an appeal is made under sub-paragraph (1)(c)—

(a) the appeal may be brought at any time while the order is in force (with the result that nothing in sub-paragraph (3) or paragraph 27 applies in relation to the appeal); and

(b) the powers of the residential property tribunal under paragraph 28 are limited to determining whether the order should be varied by the tribunal so as to include a term providing for the matter or matters in question, and (if so) what provision should be made by the term.

(3) If no appeal is brought under this paragraph in respect of a final EDMO within the time allowed by paragraph 27 for making such an appeal, the order is final and conclusive as to the matters which could have been raised on appeal.

Appeals: time limits for appeals under paragraph 26

27 (1) This paragraph applies in relation to an appeal under paragraph 26 in respect of a final EDMO.

(2) Any such appeal must be made within the period of 28 days beginning with the date specified in the notice under paragraph 7(5) of Schedule 6 (as applied by section 136(5)) as the date on which the order was made.

(3) A residential property tribunal may allow an appeal to be made to it after the end of the period mentioned in sub-paragraph (2) if it is satisfied that there is a good reason for the failure to appeal before the end of that period (and for any delay since then in applying for permission to appeal out of time).

Appeals: powers of residential property tribunal on appeal under paragraph 26

28 (1) This paragraph applies to an appeal to a residential property tribunal under paragraph 26 in respect of an interim EDMO or a final EDMO.

(2) The appeal—

(a) is to be by way of a re-hearing, but

(b) may be determined having regard to matters of which the authority were unaware.

(3) The tribunal may—

(a) in the case of an interim EDMO, vary the order as mentioned in paragraph 26(2)(b), or

(b) in the case of a final EDMO, confirm or vary the order or revoke it as from the date of the tribunal's order.

"The operative time" for the purposes of paragraph 9(2)

29 (1) This paragraph defines "the operative time" for the purposes of paragraph 9(2).

(2) If no appeal is made under paragraph 26 before the end of the period of 28 days mentioned in paragraph 27(2), "the operative time" is the end of that period.

(3) If an appeal is made under paragraph 26 before the end of that period, and a decision is given on the appeal which confirms the order, "the operative time" is as follows—

(a) if the period within which an appeal to the Lands Tribunal may be brought expires without such an appeal having been brought, "the operative time" is the end of that period;

(b) if an appeal to the Lands Tribunal is brought, "the operative time" is the time when a decision is given on the appeal which confirms the order.

(4) For the purposes of sub-paragraph (3)—

(a) the withdrawal of an appeal has the same effect as a decision which confirms the order, and

(b) references to a decision which confirms the order are to a decision which confirms it with or without variation.

Right to appeal against decision or refusal to vary or revoke EDMO

30 A relevant person may appeal to a residential property tribunal against—

(a) a decision of a local housing authority to vary or revoke an interim EDMO or a final EDMO, or

(b) a refusal of a local housing authority to vary or revoke an interim EDMO or a final EDMO.

Time limits for appeals under paragraph 30

31 (1) This paragraph applies in relation to an appeal under paragraph 30 against a decision to vary or revoke, or (as the case may be) to refuse to vary or revoke, an interim EDMO or a final EDMO.

(2) Any such appeal must be made before the end of the period of 28 days beginning with the date specified in the notice under paragraph 11, 16, 19 or 22 of Schedule 6 (as applied by paragraph 8 or 17 of this Schedule (as the case may be)) as the date on which the decision concerned was made.

(3) A residential property tribunal may allow an appeal to be made to it after the end of the period mentioned in sub-paragraph (2) if it is satisfied that there is a good reason for the failure to appeal before the end of that period (and for any delay since then in applying for permission to appeal out of time).

Powers of residential property tribunal on appeal under paragraph 30

32 (1) This paragraph applies to an appeal to a residential property tribunal under paragraph 30 against a decision to vary or revoke, or (as the case may be) to refuse to vary or revoke, an interim EDMO or final EDMO.

(2) The appeal—

(a) is to be by way of a re-hearing, but

(b) may be determined having regard to matters of which the authority were unaware.

(3) The tribunal may confirm, reverse or vary the decision of the local housing authority.

(4) If the appeal is against a decision of the authority to refuse to revoke the order, the tribunal may make an order revoking the order as from a date specified in its order.

"The operative time" for the purposes of paragraphs 6, 7, 15 and 16

33 (1) This paragraph defines "the operative time" for the purposes of—

(a) paragraph 6(2) or 7(3) (variation or revocation of interim EDMO), or

(b) paragraph 15(2) or 16(3) (variation or revocation of final EDMO).

(2) If no appeal is made under paragraph 30 before the end of the period of 28 days mentioned in paragraph 31(2), "the operative time" is the end of that period.

(3) If an appeal is made under paragraph 30 before the end of that period, and a decision is given on the appeal which confirms the variation or revocation, "the operative time" is as follows—

(a) if the period within which an appeal to the Lands Tribunal may be brought expires without such an appeal having been brought, "the operative time" is the end of that period;

(b) if an appeal to the Lands Tribunal is brought, "the operative time" is the time when a decision is given on the appeal which confirms the variation or revocation.

(4) For the purposes of sub-paragraph (3)—

(a) the withdrawal of an appeal has the same effect as a decision which confirms the variation or revocation appealed against; and

(b) references to a decision which confirms a variation are to a decision which confirms it with or without variation.

Right to appeal against decision in respect of compensation payable to third parties

34 (1) This paragraph applies where a local housing authority have made a decision under section 136(4) or 138(3) as to whether compensation should be paid to a third party in respect of any interference with his rights in consequence of a final EDMO.

(2) The third party may appeal to a residential property tribunal against—

(a) a decision by the authority not to pay compensation to him, or

(b) a decision of the authority so far as relating to the amount of compensation that should be paid.

Time limits for appeals under paragraph 34

35 (1) This paragraph applies in relation to an appeal under paragraph 34 against a decision of a local housing authority not to pay compensation to a third party or as to the amount of compensation to be paid.

(2) Any such appeal must be made—

(a) where the decision is made before the final EDMO is made, within the period of 28 days beginning with the date specified in the notice under paragraph 7(5) of Schedule 6 (as applied by section 136(5)) as the date on which the order was made, or

(b) in any other case, within the period of 28 days beginning with the date the authority notifies the third party under section 138(4).

(3) A residential property tribunal may allow an appeal to be made to it after the end of the period mentioned in sub-paragraph (2) if it is satisfied that there is good reason for the failure to appeal before the end of that period (and for any delay since then in applying for permission to appeal out of time).

Powers of residential property tribunal on appeal under paragraph 34

36 (1) This paragraph applies in relation to an appeal under paragraph 34 against a decision of a local housing authority not to pay compensation to a third party or as to the amount of compensation to be paid.

(2) The appeal—

(a) is to be by way of re-hearing, but

(b) may be determined having regard to matters of which the authority were unaware.

(3) The tribunal may confirm, reverse or vary the decision of the local housing authority.

(4) Where the tribunal reverses or varies the decision of the authority, it must make an order varying the management scheme contained in the final EDMO accordingly.

Meaning of "relevant person" for the purposes of this Part

37 In this Part of this Schedule "relevant person" means any person who has an estate or interest in the dwelling (other than a person who is a tenant under a lease granted under paragraph 2(3)(c) or 10(3)(c)).

SCHEDULE 8

Section 168

PENALTY CHARGE NOTICES UNDER SECTION 168

1 A penalty charge notice given to a person under section 168 by an officer of an enforcement authority must—

(a) state the officer's belief that that person has committed a breach of duty;

(b) give such particulars of the circumstances as may be necessary to give reasonable notice of the breach of duty;

(c) require that person, within a period specified in the notice—

(i) to pay a penalty charge specified in the notice; or

(ii) to give notice to the enforcement authority that he wishes the authority to review the notice;

(d) state the effect of paragraph 8;

(e) specify the person to whom and the address at which the penalty charge may be paid and the method or methods by which payment may be made; and

(f) specify the person to whom and the address at which a notice requesting a review may be sent (and to which any representations relating to the review may be addressed).

2 The penalty charge specified in the notice shall be of such amount (not exceeding £500) as may be prescribed for the time being by regulations made by the Secretary of State.

3 (1) The period specified under paragraph 1(c) must not be less than 28 days beginning with the day after that on which the penalty charge notice was given.

(2) The enforcement authority may extend the period for complying with the requirement mentioned in paragraph 1(c) in any particular case if they consider it appropriate to do so.

4 The enforcement authority may, if they consider that the penalty charge notice ought not to have been given, give the recipient a notice withdrawing the penalty charge notice.

5 (1) If, within the period specified under paragraph 1(c) (or that period as extended under paragraph 3(2)), the recipient of the penalty charge notice gives notice to the enforcement authority requesting a review, the authority shall—

(a) consider any representations made by the recipient and all other circumstances of the case;

(b) decide whether to confirm or withdraw the notice; and

(c) give notice of their decision to the recipient.

(2) A notice under sub-paragraph (1)(c) confirming the penalty charge notice must also state the effect of paragraphs 6(1) to (3) and 8(1) and (3).

(3) If the authority are not satisfied—

(a) that the recipient committed the breach of duty specified in the notice;

(b) that the notice was given within the time allowed by section 168(2) and complies with the other requirements imposed by or under this Schedule; and

(c) that in the circumstances of the case it was appropriate for a penalty charge notice to be given to the recipient,

they shall withdraw the penalty charge notice.

6 (1) If after a review the penalty charge notice is confirmed by the enforcement authority, the recipient may, within the period of 28 days beginning with the day after that on which the notice under paragraph 5(1)(c) is given, appeal to the county court against the penalty charge notice.

(2) The county court may extend the period for appealing against the notice.

(3) Such an appeal must be on one (or more) of the following grounds—
- (a) that the recipient did not commit the breach of duty specified in the penalty charge notice;
- (b) that the notice was not given within the time allowed by section 168(2) or does not comply with any other requirement imposed by or under this Schedule; or
- (c) that in the circumstances of the case it was inappropriate for the notice to be given to the recipient.

(4) An appeal against a penalty charge notice shall be by way of a rehearing; and the court shall either uphold the notice or quash it.

7 If the penalty charge notice is withdrawn or quashed, the authority shall repay any amount previously paid as a penalty charge in pursuance of the notice.

8 (1) The amount of the penalty charge is recoverable from the recipient of the penalty charge notice as a debt owed to the authority unless—
- (a) the notice has been withdrawn or quashed, or
- (b) the charge has been paid.

(2) Proceedings for the recovery of the penalty charge may not be commenced before the end of the period mentioned in paragraph 5(1).

(3) And if within that period the recipient of the penalty charge notice gives notice to the authority that he wishes the authority to review the penalty charge notice, such proceedings may not be commenced—
- (a) before the end of the period mentioned in paragraph 6(1), and
- (b) where the recipient appeals against the penalty charge notice, before the end of the period of 28 days beginning with the day on which the appeal is withdrawn or determined.

9 In proceedings for the recovery of the penalty charge, a certificate which—
- (a) purports to be signed by or on behalf of the person having responsibility for the financial affairs of the enforcement authority; and
- (b) states that payment of the penalty charge was or was not received by a date specified in the certificate;

is evidence of the facts stated.

10 (1) A penalty charge notice and any other notice mentioned in this Schedule may be given by post.

(2) Any such notice may be given—
- (a) in the case of a body corporate, to the secretary or clerk of that body; and
- (b) in the case of a partnership, to any partner or to a person having control or management of the partnership business.

11 The Secretary of State may by regulations make provision supplementary or incidental to the preceding provisions of this Part, including in particular provision prescribing—

(a) the form of penalty charge notices or any other notice mentioned in this Schedule;

(b) circumstances in which penalty charge notices may not be given;

(c) the method or methods by which penalty charges may be paid.

SCHEDULE 9

Section 183

NEW SCHEDULE 5A TO THE HOUSING ACT 1985: INITIAL DEMOLITION NOTICES

"SCHEDULE 5A

Section 138A

INITIAL DEMOLITION NOTICES

1 Initial demolition notices

1 (1) For the purposes of this Schedule an "initial demolition notice" is a notice served on a secure tenant—

(a) stating that the landlord intends to demolish the dwelling-house or (as the case may be) the building containing it ("the relevant premises"),

(b) setting out the reasons why the landlord intends to demolish the relevant premises,

(c) specifying the period within which he intends to demolish those premises, and

(d) stating that, while the notice remains in force, he will not be under any obligation to make such a grant as is mentioned in section 138(1) in respect of any claim made by the tenant to exercise the right to buy in respect of the dwelling-house.

(2) An initial demolition notice must also state—

(a) that the notice does not prevent—

(i) the making by the tenant of any such claim, or

(ii) the taking of steps under this Part in connection with any such claim up to the point where section 138(1) would otherwise operate in relation to the claim, or

(iii) the operation of that provision in most circumstances where the notice ceases to be in force, but

(b) that, if the landlord subsequently serves a final demolition notice in respect of the dwelling-house, the right to buy will not arise in respect of it while that notice is in force and any existing claim will cease to be effective.

(3) If, at the time when an initial demolition notice is served, there is an existing claim to exercise the right to buy in respect of the dwelling-house, the notice shall—

(a) state that section 138C confers a right to compensation in respect of certain expenditure, and

(b) give details of that right to compensation and of how it may be exercised.

(4) The period specified in accordance with sub-paragraph (1)(c) must not—

(a) allow the landlord more than what is, in the circumstances, a reasonable period to carry out the proposed demolition of the relevant premises (whether on their own or as part of a scheme involving the demolition of other premises); or

(b) in any case expire more than five years after the date of service of the notice on the tenant.

2 Period of validity of initial demolition notice

2 (1) For the purposes of this Schedule an initial demolition notice—

(a) comes into force in respect of the dwelling-house concerned on the date of service of the notice on the tenant, and

(b) ceases to be so in force at the end of the period specified in accordance with paragraph 1(1)(c),

but this is subject to compliance with the conditions mentioned in sub-paragraph (2) (in a case to which they apply) and to paragraph 3.

(2) The conditions in sub-paragraphs (6) and (7) of paragraph 13 of Schedule 5 (publicity for final demolition notices) shall apply in relation to an initial demolition notice as they apply in relation to a final demolition notice.

(3) The notice mentioned in paragraph 13(7) (as it applies in accordance with sub-paragraph (2) above) must contain the following information—

(a) sufficient information to enable identification of the premises that the landlord intends to demolish,

(b) the reasons why the landlord intends to demolish those premises,

(c) the period within which the landlord intends to demolish those premises,

(d) the date when any initial demolition notice or notices relating to those premises will cease to be in force, unless revoked or otherwise terminated under or by virtue of paragraph 3 below,

(e) that, during the period of validity of any such notice or notices, the landlord will not be under any obligation to make such a grant as is mentioned in section 138(1) in respect of any claim to exercise the right to buy in respect of any dwelling-house contained in those premises,

(f) that there may be a right to compensation under section 138C in respect of certain expenditure incurred in respect of any existing claim.

3 Revocation or termination of initial demolition notices

3 (1) Paragraph 15(4) to (7) of Schedule 5 (revocation notices) shall apply in relation to an initial demolition notice as they apply in relation to a final demolition notice.

(2) If a compulsory purchase order has been made for the purpose of enabling the landlord to demolish the dwelling-house in respect of which he has served an initial demolition notice (whether or not it would enable him to demolish any other premises as well) and—

(a) a relevant decision within sub-paragraph (3)(a) becomes effective while the notice is in force, or

(b) a relevant decision within sub-paragraph (3)(b) becomes final while the notice is in force, the notice ceases to be in force as from the date when the decision becomes effective or final.

(3) A "relevant decision" is—

(a) a decision under Part 2 of the Acquisition of Land Act 1981 to confirm the order with modifications, or not to confirm the whole or part of the order, or

(b) a decision of the High Court to quash the whole or part of the order under section 24 of that Act,

where the effect of the decision is that the landlord will not be able, by virtue of that order, to carry out the demolition of the dwelling-house.

(4) A relevant decision within sub-paragraph (3)(a) becomes effective—

(a) at the end of the period of 16 weeks beginning with the date of the decision, if no application for judicial review is made in respect of the decision within that period, or

(b) if such an application is so made, at the time when—

(i) a decision on the application which upholds the relevant decision becomes final, or

(ii) the application is abandoned or otherwise ceases to have effect.

(5) A relevant decision within sub-paragraph (3)(b), or a decision within sub-paragraph (4)(b), becomes final—

(a) if not appealed against, at the end of the period for bringing an appeal, or

(b) if appealed against, at the time when the appeal (or any further appeal) is disposed of.

(6) An appeal is disposed of—

(a) if it is determined and the period for bringing any further appeal has ended, or

(b) if it is abandoned or otherwise ceases to have effect.

(7) Where an initial demolition notice ceases to be in force under sub-paragraph (2), the landlord must, as soon as is reasonably practicable, serve a notice on the tenant which informs him—

(a) that the notice has ceased to be in force as from the date in question, and

(b) of the reason why it has ceased to be in force.

(8) If, while an initial demolition notice is in force in respect of a dwelling-house, a final demolition notice comes into force under paragraph 13 of Schedule 5 in respect of that dwelling-house, the initial demolition notice ceases to be in force as from the date when the final demolition notice comes into force.

(9) In such a case the final demolition notice must state that it is replacing the initial demolition notice.

4 Restriction on serving further demolition notices

4 (1) This paragraph applies where an initial demolition notice ("the relevant notice") has (for any reason) ceased to be in force in respect of a dwelling-house without it being demolished.

(2) No further initial demolition notice may be served in respect of the dwelling-house during the period of 5 years following the time when the relevant notice ceases to be in force, unless—

(a) it is served with the consent of the Secretary of State, and

(b) it states that it is so served.

(3) Subject to sub-paragraph (4), no final demolition notice may be served in respect of the dwelling-house during the period of 5 years following the time when the relevant notice ceases to be in force, unless—

(a) it is served with the consent of the Secretary of State, and

(b) it states that it is so served.

(4) Sub-paragraph (3) does not apply to a final demolition notice which is served at a time when an initial demolition notice served in accordance with sub-paragraph (2) is in force.

(5) The Secretary of State's consent under sub-paragraph (2) or (3) may be given subject to compliance with such conditions as he may specify.

5 Service of notices

5 Paragraph 16 of Schedule 13 (service of notices) applies in relation to notices under this Schedule as it applies in relation to notices under paragraph 13 or 15 of that Schedule.

6 Interpretation

6 (1) In this Schedule any reference to the landlord, in the context of a reference to the demolition or intended demolition of any premises, includes a reference to a superior landlord.

(2) In this Schedule—

"final demolition notice" means a final demolition notice served under paragraph 13 of Schedule 5;

"premises" means premises of any description;

"scheme" includes arrangements of any description."

SCHEDULE 10

Section 212

PROVISIONS RELATING TO TENANCY DEPOSIT SCHEMES

Schemes to be custodial schemes or insurance schemes

1 (1) A tenancy deposit scheme must be either—

(a) a custodial scheme, or

(b) an insurance scheme.

(2) A "custodial scheme" is a scheme under which—

(a) tenancy deposits in connection with shorthold tenancies are paid to the landlords under the tenancies,

(b) amounts representing the deposits are then paid by the landlords into a designated account held by the scheme administrator, and
(c) those amounts are kept by the scheme administrator in that account until such time as, in accordance with the scheme, they fall to be paid (wholly or in part) to the landlords or tenants under the tenancies.

(3) An "insurance scheme" is a scheme under which—
(a) tenancy deposits in connection with shorthold tenancies are paid to the landlords under the tenancies,
(b) such deposits are retained by the landlords on the basis that, at the end of the tenancies—
(i) such amounts in respect of the deposits as are agreed between the tenants and the landlords will be repaid to the tenants, and
(ii) such amounts as the tenants request to be repaid to them and which are not so repaid will, in accordance with directions given by the scheme administrator, be paid into a designated account held by the scheme administrator,
(c) amounts paid into that account are kept by the scheme administrator in the account until such time as, in accordance with the scheme, they fall to be paid (wholly or in part) to the landlords or tenants under the tenancies,
(d) landlords undertake to reimburse the scheme administrator, in accordance with directions given by him, in respect of any amounts in respect of the deposits paid to the tenants by the scheme administrator (other than amounts paid to the tenants as mentioned in paragraph (c)), and
(e) insurance is maintained by the scheme administrator in respect of failures by landlords to comply with such directions.

Provisions applying to custodial and insurance schemes

2 (1) A custodial scheme must conform with the following provisions—
paragraphs 3 and 4, and
paragraphs 9 and 10.

(2) An insurance scheme must conform with the following provisions—
paragraphs 5 to 8, and
paragraphs 9 and 10.

Custodial schemes: general

3 (1) This paragraph applies to a custodial scheme.

(2) The scheme must provide for any landlord who receives a tenancy deposit in connection with a shorthold tenancy to pay an amount equal to the deposit into a designated account held by the scheme administrator.

(3) The designated account must not contain anything other than amounts paid into it as mentioned in sub-paragraph (2) and any interest accruing on such amounts.

(4) Subject to sub-paragraph (5), the scheme administrator may retain any interest accruing on such amounts.

(5) The relevant arrangements under section 212(1) may provide for any amount paid in accordance with paragraph 4 to be paid with interest—

(a) in respect of the period during which the relevant amount has remained in the designated account, and
(b) at such rate as the appropriate national authority may specify by order.

(6) With the exception of any interest retained in accordance with sub-paragraph (4), nothing contained in the designated account may be used to fund the administration of the scheme.

(7) In this paragraph "the relevant amount", in relation to a tenancy deposit, means the amount paid into the designated account in respect of the deposit.

Custodial schemes: termination of tenancies

4 (1) A custodial scheme must make provision—
(a) for enabling the tenant and the landlord under a shorthold tenancy in connection with which a tenancy deposit is held in accordance with the scheme to apply, at any time after the tenancy has ended, for the whole or part of the relevant amount to be paid to him, and
(b) for such an application to be dealt with by the scheme administrator in accordance with the following provisions of this paragraph.

(2) Sub-paragraph (3) applies where the tenant and the landlord notify the scheme administrator that they have agreed that the relevant amount should be paid—
(a) wholly to one of them, or
(b) partly to the one and partly to the other.

(3) If, having received such a notification, the scheme administrator is satisfied that the tenant and the landlord have so agreed, the scheme administrator must arrange for the relevant amount to be paid, in accordance with the agreement, within the period of 10 days beginning with the date on which the notification is received by the scheme administrator.

(4) Sub-paragraph (5) applies where the tenant or the landlord notifies the scheme administrator that—
(a) a court has decided that the relevant amount is payable either wholly to one of them or partly to the one and partly to the other, and
(b) that decision has become final.

(5) If, having received such a notification, the scheme administrator is satisfied as to the matters mentioned in sub-paragraph (4)(a) and (b), the scheme administrator must arrange for the relevant amount to be paid, in accordance with the decision, within the period of 10 days beginning with the date on which the notification is received by the scheme administrator.

(6) For the purposes of this Schedule a decision becomes final—
(a) if not appealed against, at the end of the period for bringing an appeal, or
(b) if appealed against, at the time when the appeal (or any further appeal) is disposed of.

(7) An appeal is disposed of—
(a) if it is determined and the period for bringing any further appeal has ended, or
(b) if it is abandoned or otherwise ceases to have effect.

(8) In this paragraph "the relevant amount" has the meaning given by paragraph 3(7).

Insurance schemes: general

5 (1) This paragraph applies to an insurance scheme.

(2) The scheme must provide that any landlord by whom a tenancy deposit is retained under the scheme must give the scheme administrator an undertaking that, if the scheme administrator directs the landlord to pay him any amount in respect of the deposit in accordance with paragraph 6(3) or (7), the landlord will comply with such a direction.

(3) The scheme must require the scheme administrator to effect, and maintain in force, adequate insurance in respect of failures by landlords by whom tenancy deposits are retained under the scheme to comply with such directions as are mentioned in sub-paragraph (2).

(4) If the scheme provides for landlords participating in the scheme to be members of the scheme, the scheme may provide for a landlord's membership to be terminated by the scheme administrator in the event of any such failure on the part of the landlord.

(5) The scheme may provide for landlords participating in the scheme to pay to the scheme administrator—

(a) fees in respect of the administration of the scheme, and

(b) contributions in respect of the cost of the insurance referred to in sub-paragraph (3).

Insurance schemes: termination of tenancies

6 (1) An insurance scheme must make provision in accordance with this paragraph and paragraphs 7 and 8 in relation to the respective obligations of the landlord and the scheme administrator where—

(a) a tenancy deposit has been retained by the landlord under the scheme, and

(b) the tenancy has ended.

(2) Sub-paragraphs (3) to (9) apply where the tenant notifies the scheme administrator that—

(a) the tenant has requested the landlord to repay to him the whole or any part of the deposit, and

(b) the amount in question ("the outstanding amount") has not been repaid to him within the period of 10 days beginning with the date on which the request was made.

(3) On receiving a notification in accordance with sub-paragraph (2), the scheme administrator must direct the landlord—

(a) to pay an amount equal to the outstanding amount into a designated account held by the scheme administrator, and

(b) to do so within the period of 10 days beginning with the date on which the direction is received by the landlord.

(4) The following sub-paragraphs apply where the tenant or the landlord notifies the scheme administrator—

(a) that a court has decided that the outstanding amount is payable either wholly to one of them or partly to the one and partly to the other and the decision has become final (see paragraph 4(6) and (7)), or

(b) that the tenant and landlord have agreed that such an amount is to be paid either wholly to one of them or partly to the one and partly to the other.

(5) If the scheme administrator is satisfied as to the matters mentioned in sub-paragraph (4)(a) or (b) (as the case may be), he must—

(a) pay to the tenant any amount due to him in accordance with the decision or agreement (and, to the extent possible, pay that amount out of any amount held by him by virtue of sub-paragraph (3)), and

(b) comply with sub-paragraph (6) or (7), as the case may be.

(6) Where any amount held by the scheme administrator by virtue of sub-paragraph (3) is more than any amount due to the tenant in accordance with the decision or agreement, the scheme administrator must pay the balance to the landlord.

(7) Where any amount so held by the scheme administrator is less than any amount so due to the tenant, the scheme administrator must direct the landlord to pay him the difference within the period of 10 days beginning with the date on which the direction is received by the landlord.

(8) The scheme administrator must pay any amounts required to be paid to the tenant or the landlord as mentioned in sub-paragraph (5)(a) or (6) within 10 days beginning with the date on which the notification is received by the scheme administrator.

(9) The landlord must comply with any direction given in accordance with sub-paragraph (3) or (7).

7 (1) The designated account held by the scheme administrator must not contain anything other than amounts paid into it as mentioned in paragraph 6(3) and any interest accruing on such amounts.

(2) Subject to sub-paragraph (3), the scheme administrator may retain any interest accruing on such amounts.

(3) The relevant arrangements under section 212(1) may provide for any amount paid in accordance with paragraph 6(5)(a) or (6) to be paid with interest—

(a) in respect of the period during which the relevant amount has remained in the designated account, and

(b) at such rate as the appropriate national authority may specify for the purposes of paragraph 3(5)(b).

(4) With the exception of any interest retained in accordance with sub-paragraph (2), nothing contained in the designated account may be used to fund the administration of the scheme.

(5) In this paragraph "the relevant amount", in relation to a tenancy deposit, means the amount, in respect of the deposit, paid into the designated account by virtue of a direction given in accordance with paragraph 6(3).

8 (1) The scheme must make provision for preventing double recovery by a tenant in respect of the whole or part of the deposit, and may in that connection make provision—

(a) for excluding or modifying any requirement imposed by the scheme in accordance with paragraph 6 or 7, and

(b) for requiring the repayment of amounts paid to the tenant by the scheme administrator.

(2) In this paragraph "double recovery", in relation to an amount of a tenancy deposit, means recovering that amount both from the scheme administrator and from the landlord.

Notifications to tenants

9 (1) Every custodial scheme or insurance scheme must provide for the scheme administrator to respond as soon as is practicable to any request within sub-paragraph (2) made by the tenant under a shorthold tenancy.

(2) A request is within this sub-paragraph if it is a request by the tenant to receive confirmation that a deposit paid in connection with the tenancy is being held in accordance with the scheme.

Dispute resolution procedures

10 (1) Every custodial scheme or insurance scheme must provide for facilities to be available for enabling disputes relating to tenancy deposits subject to the scheme to be resolved without recourse to litigation.

(2) The scheme must not, however, make the use of such facilities compulsory in the event of such a dispute.

Power to amend

11 The appropriate national authority may by order make such amendments of this Schedule as it considers appropriate.

Interpretation

12 In this Schedule references to tenants under shorthold tenancies include references to persons who, in accordance with arrangements made with such tenants, have paid tenancy deposits on behalf of the tenants.

SCHEDULE 11

Section 218

REGISTERED SOCIAL LANDLORDS

Housing Associations Act 1985 (c. 69)

1 In section 87 of the Housing Associations Act 1985 (financial assistance with respect to formation, management, etc. of certain housing associations) omit—

(a) in subsection (3), the words from ", acting" onwards, and

(b) subsection (6).

Housing Act 1988 (c. 50)

2 The Housing Act 1988 is amended as follows.

3 In section 50(2) (housing association grants) omit the words from ", acting" onwards.

4 In section 52(2) (recovery etc. of grants) omit the words from ", acting" to "determine,".

5 Omit section 55 (surplus rental income).

6 In section 59(1A) (interpretation) for "55" substitute "54".

Housing Act 1996 (c. 52)

7 The Housing Act 1996 is amended as follows.

8 In section 18(2) (social housing grants) omit the words from ", acting" to "determine,".

9 In section 20(3) (purchase grant where right to acquire exercised) omit the words from ", acting" to "determine,".

10 In section 21(3) (purchase grant in respect of other disposals) omit the words from ", acting" to "determine,".

11 In section 28 (grants under sections 50 to 55 of the Housing Act 1988), in the sidenote and in subsection (6), for "55" substitute "54".

12 (1) In section 31(2) (offence of intentionally altering etc. document required to be produced under section 30), for paragraph (b) substitute—

"(b) on conviction on indictment, to imprisonment for a term not exceeding two years or to a fine, or both."

(2) The amendment made by sub-paragraph (1) does not apply in relation to any offence committed before the day on which that sub-paragraph comes into force.

13 (1) Section 36 (issue of guidance by the Relevant Authority) is amended as follows.

(2) In subsection (2) (particular matters with respect to which guidance may be issued under the section) for "this section" substitute "subsection (1)".

(3) After subsection (2) insert—

"(2A) The Relevant Authority may also issue guidance with respect to—

(a) the governance of bodies that are registered social landlords;

(b) the effective management of such bodies;

(c) establishing and maintaining the financial viability of such bodies."

(4) In subsection (7) (guidance relevant to whether there has been mismanagement) after "there has been" insert "misconduct or".

14 In paragraph 1(2) of Schedule 1 (payments by way of gift, dividend or bonus) after paragraph (b) insert—

"(c) the payment of a sum, in accordance with the constitution or rules of the body, to a registered social landlord which is a subsidiary or associate of the body."

15 (1) Paragraph 15 of Schedule 1 (transfer of net assets on dissolution or winding up) is amended as follows.

(2) In sub-paragraph (1)(b), after "1985" insert "(including such a company which is also a registered charity)".

(3) At the end of sub-paragraph (4) insert—

"And in such a case any registered social landlord specified in a direction under sub-paragraph (2) must be one to which paragraphs (a) and (b) above apply."

16 After paragraph 15 insert—

"15A Transfer of net assets on termination of charity not within paragraph 15(1)

15A (1) The Secretary of State may by regulations provide for any provisions of paragraph 15(2) to (6) to apply in relation to a registered social landlord within sub-paragraph (2)—

(a) in such circumstances, and

(b) with such modifications,

as may be specified in the regulations.

(2) A registered social landlord is within this sub-paragraph if—

(a) it is a registered charity, and

(b) it does not fall within sub-paragraph (1) of paragraph 15.

(3) Regulations under this paragraph may in particular provide that any provision of the regulations requiring the transfer of any property of the charity is to have effect notwithstanding—

(a) anything in the terms of its trusts, or

(b) any resolution, order or other thing done for the purposes of, or in connection with, the termination of the charity in any manner specified in the regulations.

(4) Any regulations under this paragraph shall be made by statutory instrument which shall be subject to annulment in pursuance of a resolution of either House of Parliament."

17 (1) Paragraph 16 of Schedule 1 (general requirements as to accounts and audit) is amended as follows.

(2) Omit sub-paragraph (4) (auditor's report to state whether accounts comply with paragraph 16).

(3) For sub-paragraph (5) substitute—

"(5) Every registered social landlord shall furnish to the Relevant Authority—

(a) a copy of its accounts, and

(b) (subject to sub-paragraph (7)) a copy of the auditor's report in respect of them,

within six months of the end of the period to which they relate.

(6) The auditor's report shall state, in addition to any other matters which it is required to state, whether in the auditor's opinion the accounts comply with the requirements laid down under this paragraph.

(7) The provisions of sub-paragraphs (5)(b) and (6) do not apply where, by virtue of any enactment—

(a) any accounts of a registered social landlord are not required to be audited, and

(b) instead a report is required to be prepared in respect of them by a person appointed for the purpose ("the reporting accountant"), and sub-paragraph (8) shall apply in place of those provisions.

(8) In such a case—

(a) the registered social landlord shall furnish to the Relevant Authority a copy of the reporting accountant's report in respect of the accounts within six months of the end of the period to which they relate; and

(b) that report shall state, in addition to any other matters which it is required to state, whether in the reporting accountant's opinion the accounts comply with the requirements laid down under this paragraph."

18 After paragraph 16 of Schedule 1 insert—

"16A Companies exempt from audit requirements: accountant's report

16A (1) This paragraph applies to registered social landlords which are companies registered under the Companies Act 1985 ("RSL companies").

(2) In section 249A of the Companies Act 1985 (exemptions from audit)—

(a) subsection (2) shall apply in relation to an RSL company which meets the total exemption conditions in respect of a financial year (whether it is a charity or not), and

(b) that subsection shall apply in relation to such a company in the same way as it applies in relation to an RSL company which is a charity and meets the report conditions in relation to a financial year; and

(c) subsection (1) accordingly does not have effect in relation to an RSL company.

(3) In section 249C of that Act (report required for the purposes of section 249A(2)), subsection (3) shall apply in relation to an RSL company within sub-paragraph (2)(a) above as if the reference to satisfying the requirements of section 249A(4) were a reference to meeting the total exemption conditions.

(4) The Relevant Authority may, in respect of any relevant financial year of an RSL company, give a direction to the company requiring it—

(a) to appoint a qualified auditor to audit its accounts and balance sheet for that year, and

(b) to furnish to the Relevant Authority a copy of the auditor's report by such date as is specified in the direction.

(5) For the purposes of sub-paragraph (4), a financial year of an RSL company is a "relevant financial year" if—

(a) it precedes that in which the direction is given, and

(b) the company met either the total exemption conditions or the report conditions in respect of that year, and

(c) its accounts and balance sheet for that year were not audited in accordance with Part 7 of the Companies Act 1985.

(6) In this paragraph—

(a) "financial year" has the meaning given by section 223 of the Companies Act 1985;

(b) "qualified auditor" means a person who is eligible for appointment as auditor of the company under Part 2 of the Companies Act 1989;

(c) any reference to a company meeting the report conditions is to be read in accordance with section 249A(4) of the Companies Act 1985; and

(d) any reference to a company meeting the total exemption conditions is to be read in accordance with section 249A(3) or section 249A(3) and (3A) of that Act, depending on whether it is a charity."

19 For paragraph 17 of Schedule 1 (appointment of auditors by industrial and provident societies), together with the heading preceding it, substitute—

"17 Industrial and provident societies exempt from audit requirements: accountant's report

17 (1) This paragraph applies to registered social landlords which are industrial and provident societies.

(2) Section 9A of the Friendly and Industrial and Provident Societies Act 1968 (duty to obtain accountant's reports where section 4 applied) shall have effect, in its application to such a landlord, with the omission of subsection (1)(b) (accountant's report required only where turnover exceeds a specified sum).

(3) The Relevant Authority may, in respect of any relevant year of account of such a landlord, give a direction to the landlord requiring it—

(a) to appoint a qualified auditor to audit its accounts and balance sheet for that year, and

(b) to furnish to the Relevant Authority a copy of the auditor's report by such date as is specified in the direction.

(4) For the purposes of sub-paragraph (3), a year of account of a landlord is a "relevant year of account" if—

(a) it precedes that in which the direction is given, and

(b) at the end of it there is in force in relation to it a disapplication under section 4A(1) of the Friendly and Industrial and Provident Societies Act 1968.

(5) In this paragraph—

"qualified auditor" means a person who is a qualified auditor for the purposes of the Friendly and Industrial and Provident Societies Act 1968;

"year of account" has the meaning given by section 21(1) of that Act."

20 (1) Paragraph 18 of Schedule 1 (accounting and audit requirements for charities) is amended as follows.

(2) In the cross-heading preceding the paragraph, after "and audit" insert "or reporting".

(3) In sub-paragraph (1) (application of provisions to registered social landlord which is a registered charity) omit the words from "(which impose" onwards.

(4) For sub-paragraph (4) substitute—

"(4) The charity must appoint a qualified auditor ("the auditor") to audit the accounts prepared in accordance with sub-paragraph (3) in respect of each period of account in which—

(a) the charity's gross income (within the meaning of the Charities Act 1993) arising in connection with its housing activities, or

(b) its total expenditure arising in connection with those activities,

exceeds the sum for the time being specified in section 43(1) of the Charities Act 1993 (audit required for charities where gross income or total income exceeds the specified sum).

(4A) Where sub-paragraph (4) does not apply in respect of a period of account, the charity must appoint a qualified auditor ("the reporting accountant") to make such a report as is mentioned in paragraph 18A(1) in respect of the period of account.

(4B) In sub-paragraphs (4) and (4A) "qualified auditor" means a person who is eligible for appointment as auditor of the charity under Part 2 of the Companies Act 1989 or who would be so eligible if the charity were a company registered under the Companies Act 1985."

21 After paragraph 18 of Schedule 1 insert—

"18A Charities exempt from audit requirements: accountant's report

18A (1) The report referred to in paragraph 18(4A) is a report—

(a) relating to the charity's accounts prepared in accordance with paragraph 18(3) in respect of the period of account in question, and

(b) complying with sub-paragraphs (2) and (3) below.

(2) The report must state whether, in the opinion of the reporting accountant—

(a) the revenue account or accounts and the balance sheet are in agreement with the books of account kept by the charity under paragraph 18(2),

(b) on the basis of the information contained in those books of account, the revenue account or accounts and the balance sheet comply with the requirements of the Charities Act 1993, and

(c) on the basis of the information contained in those books of account, paragraph 18(4A) applied to the charity in respect of the period of account in question.

(3) The report must also state the name of the reporting accountant and be signed by him.

(4) Paragraph 18(7) applies to the reporting accountant and his functions under this paragraph as it applies to an auditor and his functions under paragraph 18.

(5) The Relevant Authority may, in respect of a relevant period of account of a charity, give a direction to the charity requiring it—

(a) to appoint a qualified auditor to audit its accounts for that period, and

(b) to furnish to the Relevant Authority a copy of the auditor's report by such date as is specified in the direction;

and paragraph 18(5) to (7) apply to an auditor so appointed as they apply to an auditor appointed under paragraph 18.

(6) For the purposes of sub-paragraph (5), a period of account of a charity is a relevant period of account if—

(a) it precedes that in which the direction is given; and

(b) paragraph 18(4A) applied in relation to it.

(7) In this paragraph "period of account" and "qualified auditor" have the same meaning as in paragraph 18(4A)."

22 (1) Paragraph 19 of Schedule 1 (responsibility for securing compliance with accounting requirements) is amended as follows.

(2) In sub-paragraph (2)—

(a) in paragraph (c), after "and audit" insert "or reporting";

(b) omit paragraph (d) (but not the "or" at the end); and

(c) for "level 3" substitute "level 5".

(3) The amendment made by sub-paragraph (2)(c) does not apply in relation to any offence committed before the day on which that sub-paragraph comes into force.

(4) After sub-paragraph (4) insert—

"(5) Where any of paragraphs (a) to (e) of sub-paragraph (2) applies in respect of any default on the part of a registered social landlord, the High Court may, on the application of the Relevant Authority, make such order as the court thinks fit for requiring the default to be made good.

Any such order may provide that all the costs or expenses of and incidental to the application shall be borne by the registered social landlord or by any of its officers who are responsible for the default."

23 After paragraph 19 of Schedule 1 insert—

"19A Disclosure of information by auditors etc. to the Relevant Authority

19A (1) A person who is, or has been, an auditor of a registered social landlord does not contravene any duty to which he is subject merely because he gives to the Relevant Authority —

(a) information on a matter of which he became aware in his capacity as auditor of the registered social landlord, or

(b) his opinion on such a matter,

if he is acting in good faith and he reasonably believes that the information or opinion is relevant to any functions of the Relevant Authority.

(2) Sub-paragraph (1) applies whether or not the person is responding to a request from the Relevant Authority.

(3) This paragraph applies to a person who is, or has been, a reporting accountant as it applies to a person who is, or has been, an auditor.

(4) A "reporting accountant" means a person appointed as mentioned in paragraph 16(7)(b)."

24 (1) Paragraph 20 of Schedule 1 (inquiry into affairs of registered social landlord) is amended as follows.

(2) After sub-paragraph (4) insert—

"(4A) The person or persons conducting the inquiry may determine the procedure to be followed in connection with the inquiry."

(3) At the end of sub-paragraph (7) add ", and the Relevant Authority may arrange for the whole or part of an interim or final report to be published in such manner as it considers appropriate."

(4) After sub-paragraph (7) insert—

"(8) A local authority may, if they think fit, contribute to the expenses of the Relevant Authority in connection with any inquiry under this paragraph."

25 After paragraph 20 of Schedule 1 insert—

"20A Evidence

20A (1) For the purposes of an inquiry the person or persons conducting it may serve a notice on an appropriate person directing him to attend at a specified time and place and do either or both of the following, namely—

(a) give evidence;

(b) produce any specified documents, or documents of a specified description, which are in his custody or under his control and relate to any matter relevant to the inquiry.

(2) The person or persons conducting such an inquiry—

(a) may take evidence on oath and for that purpose administer oaths, or

(b) instead of administering an oath, require the person examined to make and subscribe a declaration of the truth of the matters about which he is examined.

(3) In this paragraph—

"appropriate person" means a person listed in section 30(2);

"document" has the same meaning as in section 30;

"inquiry" means an inquiry under paragraph 20.

(4) A person may not be required under this paragraph to disclose anything that, by virtue of section 30(4), he could not be required to disclose under section 30.

(5) Section 31 (enforcement of notice to provide information, &c) applies in relation to a notice given under this paragraph by the person or persons

conducting an inquiry as it applies in relation to a notice given under section 30 by the Relevant Authority, but subject to sub-paragraph (6).

(6) A person guilty of an offence under section 31(1) as it applies in accordance with sub-paragraph (5) is liable—

(a) on summary conviction, to a fine not exceeding the statutory maximum;

(b) on conviction on indictment, to imprisonment for a term not exceeding two years or to a fine, or both.

(7) Any person who, in purported compliance with a notice given under this paragraph by the person or persons conducting an inquiry, knowingly or recklessly provides any information which is false or misleading in a material particular commits an offence and is liable to the penalties mentioned in sub-paragraph (6).

(8) Proceedings for an offence under sub-paragraph (7) may be brought only by or with the consent of the Relevant Authority or the Director of Public Prosecutions."

26 (1) Paragraph 21 of Schedule 1 (power of appointed person to obtain information) is amended as follows.

(2) At the end of sub-paragraph (3) (application of section 31 to notice under paragraph 20) add ", but subject to sub-paragraph (4)."

(3) After sub-paragraph (3) add—

"(4) A person guilty of an offence under section 31(1) as it applies in accordance with sub-paragraph (3) is liable—

(a) on summary conviction, to a fine not exceeding the statutory maximum;

(b) on conviction on indictment, to imprisonment for a term not exceeding two years or to a fine, or both.

(5) Any person who, in purported compliance with a notice given under this paragraph by an appointed person, knowingly or recklessly provides any information which is false or misleading in a material particular commits an offence and is liable to the penalties mentioned in sub-paragraph (4).

(6) Proceedings for an offence under sub-paragraph (5) may be brought only by or with the consent of the Relevant Authority or the Director of Public Prosecutions."

(4) The amendments made by this paragraph do not apply in relation to any offence committed or other thing done before the day on which this paragraph comes into force.

SCHEDULE 12

Section 228(3)

NEW SCHEDULE 2A TO THE HOUSING ACT 1996

"SCHEDULE 2A

Section 51A(7)

FURTHER PROVISION ABOUT THE SOCIAL HOUSING OMBUDSMAN FOR WALES

1 Status

1 The Social Housing Ombudsman for Wales ("the Ombudsman") shall be a corporation sole.

2 Remuneration, etc.

2 The National Assembly for Wales may pay to or in respect of the Ombudsman such amounts, by way of remuneration, pensions, allowances or gratuities or by way of provision for any such benefits, as it considers appropriate.

3 If a person ceases to be the Ombudsman and it appears to the National Assembly for Wales that there are special circumstances which make it right that the person should receive compensation, the National Assembly for Wales may pay to that person a sum of such amount as it considers appropriate.

4 Staff and advisers

4 (1) The Ombudsman may appoint such staff as he considers necessary for assisting him in the exercise of his functions.

(2) The Ombudsman shall include among his staff such persons having a command of the Welsh language as he considers are needed to enable him to investigate complaints in Welsh.

(3) To assist him in the exercise of his functions, the Ombudsman may obtain advice from any person who, in his opinion, is qualified to give it.

(4) The Ombudsman may pay to any person from whom he obtains advice under sub-paragraph (3) such fees or allowances as he may determine.

5 Delegation of functions

5 (1) Any function of the Ombudsman may be exercised by—

(a) a member of his staff, or

(b) a member of the staff of the Commission for Local Administration in Wales,

if authorised by the Ombudsman for that purpose.

(2) The Ombudsman may, with the approval of the National Assembly for Wales, make arrangements with persons under which they, or members of their staff, may perform functions of the Ombudsman.

(3) References in any provision made by or under an enactment to a member of staff of the Ombudsman include any person exercising any function of his by virtue of sub-paragraph (1)(b).

6 Reports and determinations

6 (1) The Ombudsman—

(a) shall annually prepare and lay before the National Assembly for Wales a general report on the performance of his functions; and

(b) may from time to time prepare and lay before the National Assembly for Wales such other reports with respect to his functions as he thinks fit.

(2) The National Assembly for Wales shall, and the Ombudsman may, publish reports laid before the National Assembly for Wales under sub-paragraph (1).

7 The Ombudsman may, subject to any provision made by regulations under section 51B, publish his determination on any complaint.

8 (1) The Ombudsman may include in any report or determination published under paragraph 6 or 7 statements, communications, reports, papers or other documentary evidence obtained in the exercise of his functions.

(2) In publishing any report or determination, the Ombudsman shall have regard to the need for excluding so far as practicable—

(a) any matter which relates to the private affairs of an individual, where publication would seriously and prejudicially affect the interests of that individual, and

(b) any matter which relates specifically to a social landlord in Wales, where publication would seriously and prejudicially affect its interests,

unless inclusion of the matter concerned is necessary for the purposes of the report or determination.

9 Expenses

9 (1) The expenses of the Ombudsman shall, so far as they cannot be met out of income received by him, be met by the National Assembly for Wales.

(2) Those expenses include any sums payable by the Ombudsman in consequence of a breach, in the course of the performance of any of his functions, of any contractual or other duty (whether that breach occurs by reason of his act or omission or that of a member of his staff or any other person assisting him in the exercise of his functions).

10 Absolute privilege for communications etc.

10 For the purposes of the law of defamation, absolute privilege attaches to—

(a) any communication between the Ombudsman and any person by or against whom a complaint is made to him;

(b) any determination by the Ombudsman; and

(c) the publication by him of any report or such a determination under paragraph 6, 7 or 8.

11 Disclosure of information

11 (1) Information obtained by the Ombudsman in the course of or for the purposes of an investigation of a complaint must not be disclosed except—

(a) for the purposes of the investigation, of any determination made in respect of the complaint or of the publication of a determination under paragraph 7;

(b) as provided in paragraph 12 or 17 or any regulations under section 51B;

(c) for the purposes of any proceedings for an offence of perjury alleged to have been committed in the course of an investigation of a complaint by the Ombudsman; or

(d) for the purposes of an inquiry with a view to the taking of any proceedings as mentioned in paragraph (c).

(2) The Ombudsman shall not be called upon to give evidence in any proceedings (other than proceedings within sub-paragraph (1)(c)) of matters coming to his knowledge in the course of an investigation of a complaint.

(3) Information obtained from the Information Commissioner by virtue of section 76 of the Freedom of Information Act 2000 shall be treated for the purposes of sub-paragraph (1) as obtained for the purposes of an investigation and, in relation to such information, the reference in paragraph (a) of that sub-paragraph to the investigation shall have effect as a reference to any investigation.

12 The Ombudsman may disclose to the Information Commissioner any information obtained by, or furnished to, the Ombudsman by virtue of or for the purposes of section 51A or 51B if the information appears to him to relate to—

(a) a matter in respect of which the Information Commissioner could exercise any power conferred by—

(i) Part V of the Data Protection Act 1998 (enforcement),

(ii) section 48 of the Freedom of Information Act 2000 (practice recommendations), or

(iii) Part IV of that Act (enforcement), or

(b) the commission of an offence under—

(i) any provision of the Data Protection Act 1998 other than paragraph 12 of Schedule 9 (obstruction of execution of warrant), or

(ii) section 77 of the Freedom of Information Act 2000 (offence of altering etc. records with intent to prevent disclosure).

13 Accounts and audit

13 (1) The Ombudsman shall keep proper accounting records.

(2) The Ombudsman shall, for each financial year, prepare accounts in accordance with directions given to him by the Treasury.

(3) The directions which the Treasury may give under sub-paragraph (2) include, in particular, directions as to—

(a) the information to be contained in the accounts and the manner in which it is to be presented,

(b) the methods and principles in accordance with which the accounts are to be prepared, and

(c) the additional information (if any) that is to accompany the accounts.

(4) In this paragraph and in paragraph 14, "financial year" means the twelve months ending with 31st March.

14 (1) The accounts prepared by the Ombudsman for any financial year shall be submitted by him to the Auditor General for Wales no later than the 30th November of the following year.

(2) The Auditor General for Wales shall—

(a) examine and certify any accounts submitted to him under this paragraph, and

(b) no later than four months after the accounts are submitted to him, lay before the National Assembly for Wales a copy of them as certified by him together with his report on them.

(3) In examining any accounts submitted to him under this paragraph, the Auditor General for Wales shall, in particular, satisfy himself that the expenditure to which the accounts relate has been incurred lawfully and in accordance with the authority which governs it.

15 Accounting officer

15 (1) The accounting officer for the Office of the Ombudsman shall be the Ombudsman.

(2) But where—

(a) the Ombudsman is incapable of discharging his responsibilities as accounting officer, or

(b) the office of the Ombudsman is vacant (and there is no acting Ombudsman),

the Treasury may designate a member of the Ombudsman's staff to be the accounting officer for so long as paragraph (a) or (b) applies.

(3) The accounting officer for the Office of the Ombudsman shall have, in relation to—

(a) the accounts of the Ombudsman, and

(b) the finances of the Office of the Ombudsman,

the responsibilities which are from time to time specified by the Treasury.

(4) In this paragraph references to responsibilities include in particular—

(a) responsibilities in relation to the signing of accounts,

(b) responsibilities for the propriety and regularity of the finances of the Office of the Ombudsman, and

(c) responsibilities for the economy, efficiency and effectiveness with which the resources of the Office of the Ombudsman are used.

(5) The responsibilities which may be specified under this paragraph include responsibilities owed to—

(a) the National Assembly for Wales, the executive committee or the Audit Committee, or

(b) the House of Commons or its Committee of Public Accounts.

(6) If requested to do so by the House of Commons Committee of Public Accounts, the Audit Committee may—

(a) on behalf of the Committee of Public Accounts take evidence from the accounting officer for the Office of the Ombudsman, and

(b) report to the Committee of Public Accounts and transmit to that Committee any evidence so taken.

(7) In this paragraph and paragraphs 16 and 17, "the Office of the Ombudsman" means the Ombudsman and the members of his staff.

(8) Section 13 of the National Audit Act 1983 (interpretation of references to the Committee of Public Accounts) applies for the purposes of this paragraph as for those of that Act.

16 Examinations into use of resources

16 (1) The Auditor General for Wales may carry out examinations into the economy, efficiency and effectiveness with which the Ombudsman has used the resources of the Office of the Ombudsman in discharging his functions.

(2) Sub-paragraph (1) shall not be construed as entitling the Auditor General for Wales to question the merits of the policy objectives of the Ombudsman.

(3) In determining how to exercise his functions under this paragraph, the Auditor General for Wales shall take into account the views of the Audit Committee as to the examinations which he should carry out under this paragraph.

(4) The Auditor General for Wales may lay before the National Assembly for Wales a report of the results of any examination carried out by him under this paragraph.

(5) Section 7 of the National Audit Act 1983 (economy, efficiency and effectiveness examinations by Comptroller and Auditor General) applies to the Ombudsman.

(6) The Auditor General for Wales and the Comptroller and Auditor General may co-operate with, and give assistance to, each other in connection with the carrying out of examinations in respect of the Ombudsman under this paragraph or section 7 of the National Audit Act 1983.

17 (1) For the purpose of enabling him to carry out examinations into, and report to Parliament on, the finances of the Office of the Ombudsman, the Comptroller and Auditor General—

(a) shall have a right of access at all reasonable times to all such documents in the custody or under the control of the Ombudsman, or of the Auditor General for Wales, as he may reasonably require for that purpose, and

(b) shall be entitled to require from any person holding or accountable for any of those documents any assistance, information or explanation which he reasonably thinks necessary for that purpose.

(2) The Comptroller and Auditor General shall—

(a) consult the Auditor General for Wales, and

(b) take into account any relevant work done or being done by the Auditor General for Wales,

before he acts in reliance on sub-paragraph (1) or carries out an examination in respect of the Ombudsman under section 7 of the National Audit Act 1983 (economy etc. examinations)."

SCHEDULE 13

Section 230

RESIDENTIAL PROPERTY TRIBUNALS: PROCEDURE

Procedure regulations

1 (1) The appropriate national authority may make regulations about the procedure of residential property tribunals.

(2) Nothing in the following provisions of this Schedule affects the generality of sub-paragraph (1).

(3) In those provisions—

"procedure regulations" means regulations under this paragraph;

"tribunal" means a residential property tribunal.

Appeals

2 (1) Procedure regulations may include provision, in relation to applications to tribunals—

(a) about the form of such applications and the particulars to be contained in them,

(b) requiring the service of notices of such applications, and

(c) in the case of applications under section 102(4) or (7) or 133(1), requiring the service of copies of the draft orders submitted with the applications.

(2) Procedure regulations may include provision, in relation to appeals to tribunals—

(a) about the form of notices of appeal and the particulars to be contained in them, and

(b) requiring the service of copies of such notices.

(3) Procedure regulations may include provision dispensing with the service of the notices or copies mentioned in sub-paragraph (1)(b) or (2)(b) in such cases of urgency as are specified in the regulations.

Transfers

3 (1) This paragraph applies where, in any proceedings before a court, there falls for determination a question which a tribunal would have jurisdiction to determine on an application or appeal to the tribunal.

(2) The court—

(a) may by order transfer to the tribunal so much of the proceedings as relate to the determination of that question, and

(b) may then dispose of all or any remaining proceedings, or adjourn the disposal of all or any remaining proceedings pending the determination of that question by the tribunal, as it thinks fit.

(3) When the tribunal has determined the question, the court may give effect to the determination in an order of the court.

(4) Rules of court may prescribe the procedure to be followed in a court in connection with or in consequence of a transfer under this paragraph.

(5) Procedure regulations may prescribe the procedure to be followed in a tribunal consequent on a transfer under this paragraph.

(6) Nothing in this Act affects any power of a court to make an order that could be made by a tribunal (such as an order quashing a licence granted or order made by a local housing authority) in a case where—

(a) the court has not made a transfer under this paragraph, and

(b) the order is made by the court in connection with disposing of any proceedings before it.

Parties etc.

4 (1) Procedure regulations may include provision enabling persons to be joined as parties to the proceedings.

(2) Procedure regulations may include provision enabling persons who are not parties to proceedings before a tribunal to make oral or written representations to the tribunal.

Information

5 (1) Procedure regulations may include—

(a) provision relating to the supply of information and documents by a party to the proceedings, and

(b) in particular any provision authorised by the following provisions of this paragraph.

(2) The regulations may include provision for requiring, or empowering the tribunal to require, a party to proceedings before a tribunal—

(a) to supply to the tribunal information or documents specified, or of a description specified, in the regulations or in an order made by the tribunal;

(b) to supply to any other party copies of any information or documents supplied to the tribunal;

(c) to supply any such information, documents or copies by such time as is specified in or determined in accordance with the regulations or order.

(3) The regulations may also include provision—

(a) for granting a party to the proceedings such disclosure or inspection of documents, or such right to further information, as might be granted by a county court;

(b) for requiring persons to attend to give evidence and produce documents;

(c) for authorising the administration of oaths to witnesses.

(4) The regulations may include provision empowering a tribunal to dismiss, or allow, the whole or part of an appeal or application in a case where a party to the proceedings has failed to comply with—

(a) a requirement imposed by regulations made by virtue of this paragraph, or

(b) an order of the tribunal made by virtue of any such regulations.

Pre-trial reviews etc.

6 (1) Procedure regulations may include provision for the holding of a pre-trial review (on the application of a party to the proceedings or on the tribunal's own initiative).

(2) Procedure regulations may provide for functions of a tribunal in relation to, or at, a pre-trial review to be exercised by a single qualified member of the panel.

(3) Procedure regulations may provide for other functions as to preliminary or incidental matters to be exercised by a single qualified member of the panel.

(4) For the purposes of this paragraph—

(a) a person is a qualified member of the panel if he was appointed to it by the Lord Chancellor; and

(b) "the panel" means the panel provided for in Schedule 10 to the Rent Act 1977 (c. 42).

Interim orders

7 Procedure regulations may include provision empowering tribunals to make orders, on an interim basis—

(a) suspending, in whole or in part, the effect of any decision, notice, order or licence which is the subject matter of proceedings before them;

(b) granting any remedy which they would have had power to grant in their final decisions.

Additional relief

8 (1) Procedure regulations may include provision as to—

(a) any additional relief which tribunals may grant in respect of proceedings before them; and

(b) the grounds on which such relief may be granted.

(2) In this paragraph "additional relief" means relief additional to any relief specifically authorised by any provision of Parts 1 to 4 of this Act.

Dismissal

9 Procedure regulations may include provision empowering tribunals to dismiss applications, appeals or transferred proceedings, in whole or in part, on the ground that they are—

(a) frivolous or vexatious, or

(b) otherwise an abuse of process.

Determination without hearing

10 (1) Procedure regulations may include provision for the determination of applications, appeals or transferred proceedings without an oral hearing.

(2) Procedure regulations may include provision enabling a single qualified member of the panel to decide whether an oral hearing is appropriate in a particular case.

(3) Procedure regulations may provide for a single qualified member of the panel to make determinations without an oral hearing.

(4) For the purposes of this paragraph—

(a) a person is a qualified member of the panel if he was appointed to it by the Lord Chancellor; and

(b) "the panel" means the panel provided for in Schedule 10 to the Rent Act 1977 (c. 42).

Fees

11 (1) Procedure regulations may include provision requiring the payment of fees in respect of applications, appeals or transfers of proceedings to, or oral hearings by, tribunals.

(2) The fees payable shall be such as are specified in or determined in accordance with procedure regulations.

(3) But the fee (or, where fees are payable in respect of both an application, appeal or transfer and an oral hearing, the aggregate of the fees) payable by a person in respect of any proceedings must not exceed—

(a) £500, or

(b) such other amount as may be specified in procedure regulations.

(4) Procedure regulations may empower a tribunal to require a party to proceedings before it to reimburse another party to the proceedings the whole or any part of any fees paid by him.

(5) Procedure regulations may provide for the reduction or waiver of fees by reference to the financial resources of the party by whom they are to be paid or met.

(6) If they do so they may apply, subject to such modifications as may be specified in the regulations, any other statutory means-testing regime as it has effect from time to time.

Costs

12 (1) A tribunal may determine that a party to proceedings before it is to pay the costs incurred by another party in connection with the proceedings in any circumstances falling within sub-paragraph (2).

(2) The circumstances are where—

(a) he has failed to comply with an order made by the tribunal;

(b) in accordance with regulations made by virtue of paragraph 5(4), the tribunal dismisses, or allows, the whole or part of an application or appeal by reason of his failure to comply with a requirement imposed by regulations made by virtue of paragraph 5;

(c) in accordance with regulations made by virtue of paragraph 9, the tribunal dismisses the whole or part of an application or appeal made by him to the tribunal; or

(d) he has, in the opinion of the tribunal, acted frivolously, vexatiously, abusively, disruptively or otherwise unreasonably in connection with the proceedings.

(3) The amount which a party to proceedings may be ordered to pay in the proceedings by a determination under this paragraph must not exceed—

(a) £500, or

(b) such other amount as may be specified in procedure regulations.

(4) A person may not be required to pay costs incurred by another person in connection with proceedings before a tribunal, except—

(a) by a determination under this paragraph, or

(b) in accordance with provision made by any enactment other than this paragraph.

Enforcement

13 Procedure regulations may provide for decisions of tribunals to be enforceable, with the permission of a county court, in the same way as orders of such a court.

SCHEDULE 14

Section 254

BUILDINGS WHICH ARE NOT HMOS FOR PURPOSES OF THIS ACT (EXCLUDING PART 1)

Introduction: buildings (or parts) which are not HMOs for purposes of this Act (excludingPart 1)

1 (1) The following paragraphs list buildings which are not houses in multiple occupation for any purposes of this Act other than those of Part 1.

(2) In this Schedule "building" includes a part of a building.

Buildings controlled or managed by public sector bodies etc.

2 (1) A building where the person managing or having control of it is—

(a) a local housing authority,

(b) a body which is registered as a social landlord under Part 1 of the Housing Act 1996 (c. 52),

(c) a police authority established under section 3 of the Police Act 1996 (c. 16),

(d) the Metropolitan Police Authority established under section 5B of that Act,

(e) a fire and rescue authority, or

(f) a health service body within the meaning of section 4 of the National Health Service and Community Care Act 1990 (c. 19).

(2) In sub-paragraph (1)(e) "fire and rescue authority" means a fire and rescue authority under the Fire and Rescue Services Act 2004 (c. 21).

Buildings regulated otherwise than under this Act

3 Any building whose occupation is regulated otherwise than by or under this Act and which is of a description specified for the purposes of this paragraph in regulations made by the appropriate national authority.

Buildings occupied by students

4 (1) Any building—

(a) which is occupied solely or principally by persons who occupy it for the purpose of undertaking a full-time course of further or higher education at a specified educational establishment or at an educational establishment of a specified description, and

(b) where the person managing or having control of it is the educational establishment in question or a specified person or a person of a specified description.

(2) In sub-paragraph (1) "specified" means specified for the purposes of this paragraph in regulations made by the appropriate national authority.

(3) Sub-paragraph (4) applies in connection with any decision by the appropriate national authority as to whether to make, or revoke, any regulations specifying—

(a) a particular educational establishment, or

(b) a particular description of educational establishments.

(4) The appropriate national authority may have regard to the extent to which, in its opinion—

(a) the management by or on behalf of the establishment in question of any building or buildings occupied for connected educational purposes is in conformity with any code of practice for the time being approved under section 233 which appears to the authority to be relevant, or

(b) the management of such buildings by or on behalf of establishments of the description in question is in general in conformity with any such code of practice,

as the case may be.

(5) In sub-paragraph (4) "occupied for connected educational purposes", in relation to a building managed by or on behalf of an educational establishment, means occupied solely or principally by persons who occupy it for the purpose of undertaking a full-time course of further or higher education at the establishment.

Buildings occupied by religious communities

5 (1) Any building which is occupied principally for the purposes of a religious community whose principal occupation is prayer, contemplation, education or the relief of suffering.

(2) This paragraph does not apply in the case of a converted block of flats to which section 257 applies.

Buildings occupied by owners

6 (1) Any building which is occupied only by persons within the following paragraphs—

(a) one or more persons who have, whether in the whole or any part of it, either the freehold estate or a leasehold interest granted for a term of more than 21 years;

(b) any member of the household of such a person or persons;

(c) no more than such number of other persons as is specified for the purposes of this paragraph in regulations made by the appropriate national authority.

(2) This paragraph does not apply in the case of a converted block of flats to which section 257 applies, except for the purpose of determining the status of any flat in the block.

Buildings occupied by two persons

7 Any building which is occupied only by two persons who form two households.

SCHEDULE 15

Section 265(1)

MINOR AND CONSEQUENTIAL AMENDMENTS

Parliamentary Commissioner Act 1967 (c. 13)

1 (1) Section 11A of the Parliamentary Commissioner Act 1967 (consultation between Parliamentary Commissioner and Welsh Administration Ombudsman or Health Service Commissioners) is amended as follows.

(2) In the sidenote for "Welsh Administration Ombudsman or Health Service Commissioners" substitute "other Commissioners or Ombudsmen".

(3) In subsection (1)—

(a) after "Ombudsman" insert ", of the Social Housing Ombudsman for Wales"; and

(b) in paragraph (b) for "or" substitute ", under regulations under section 51B of the Housing Act 1996 or under".

(4) In subsection (2) after "Ombudsman" insert ", the Social Housing Ombudsman for Wales".

Land Compensation Act 1973 (c. 26)

2 The Land Compensation Act 1973 has effect subject to the following amendments.

3 (1) Section 29 (right to home loss payment where person displaced from dwelling) is amended as follows.

(2) In subsection (1)—

(a) for paragraph (b) substitute—

"(b) the making of a housing order in respect of the dwelling;"; and

(b) in paragraph (ii) for the words from "the order" onwards substitute "the housing order;".

(3) In subsection (3A) for the words from "the acceptance" onwards substitute "the carrying out of any improvement to the dwelling unless he is permanently displaced from it in consequence of the carrying out of that improvement."

(4) For subsection (7) substitute—

"(7) In this section "a housing order" means—

(a) a prohibition order under section 20 or 21 of the Housing Act 2004, or

(b) a demolition order under section 265 of the Housing Act 1985."

4 (1) Section 33D (loss payments: exclusions) is amended as follows.

(2) In subsection (4) for paragraphs (b) and (c) substitute—

"(b) notice under section 11 of the Housing Act 2004 (improvement notice relating to category 1 hazard);

(c) notice under section 12 of that Act (improvement notice relating to category 2 hazard);".

(3) For subsection (5) substitute—

"(5) These are the orders—

(a) an order under section 20 of the Housing Act 2004 (prohibition order relating to category 1 hazard);

(b) an order under section 21 of that Act (prohibition order relating to category 2 hazard);

(c) an order under section 43 of that Act (emergency prohibition orders);

(d) an order under section 265 of the Housing Act 1985 (demolition order relating to category 1 or 2 hazard)."

5 (1) Section 37 (disturbance payments for persons with compensatable interests) is amended as follows.

(2) In subsection (1)—

(a) for paragraph (b) substitute—

"(b) the making of a housing order in respect of a house or building on the land;"; and

(b) in paragraph (ii) for the words from "the order" onwards substitute "the housing order;".

(3) In subsection (2)(c) for "closing" substitute "prohibition".

(4) In subsection (3) for the words from "any such order" onwards substitute "a housing order within paragraph (b) of that subsection unless he was in lawful possession as aforesaid at the time when the order was made."

(5) In subsection (3A) for the words from "the acceptance" onwards substitute "the carrying out of any improvement to a house or building unless he is permanently displaced in consequence of the carrying out of that improvement."

(6) In subsection (9) omit "or undertaking".

6 (1) Section 39 (duty to rehouse residential occupiers) is amended as follows.

(2) In subsection (1) for paragraph (b) substitute—

"(b) the making of a housing order in respect of a house or building on the land;".

(3) In subsection (6) for the words from "any such order" onwards substitute "a housing order within paragraph (b) of that subsection unless he was residing in the accommodation in question at the time when the order was made."

(4) In subsection (6A) for the words from "the acceptance" onwards substitute "the carrying out of any improvement to a house or building unless he is permanently displaced from the residential accommodation in question in consequence of the carrying out of that improvement."

(5) In subsection (9) omit "or undertaking".

Local Government Act 1974 (c. 7)

7 (1) Section 33 of the Local Government Act 1974 (consultation between the Local Commissioner, other commissioners and the Welsh Administration Ombudsman) is amended as follows.

(2) In the sidenote for "the Parliamentary Commissioner and the Health Service Commissioners" substitute "and other Commissioners and Ombudsmen".

(3) In subsection (1)—

(a) after paragraph (a) insert—

"(aza) by the Social Housing Ombudsman for Wales, in accordance with regulations under section 51B of the Housing Act 1996,";

(b) omit "the" after "appropriate Commissioner or"; and

(c) after "the Act of 1967" insert ", under the Housing Act 1996".

(4) In subsection (2)—

(a) after "Parliamentary Commissioner" insert ", the Social Housing Ombudsman for Wales"; and

(b) omit "the" after "that Commissioner or".

(5) In subsection (5) after "1967" insert ", in paragraph 13(1) of Schedule 2A to the Housing Act 1996".

Greater London Council (General Powers) Act 1981 (c. xvii)

8 In section 9(1) of the Greater London Council (General Powers) Act 1981—

(a) for the words from "a registration scheme" to "section 354 of that Act," substitute "a licence under Part 2 of the Housing Act 2004"; and

(b) for "358" substitute "134".

Mobile Homes Act 1983 (c. 34)

9 In section 2 of the Mobile Homes Act 1983 (terms of agreements) after subsection (4) insert—

"(5) The supplementary provisions in Part 3 of Schedule 1 to this Act have effect for the purposes of paragraphs 8 and 9 of Part 1 of that Schedule."

Housing Act 1985 (c. 68)

10 The Housing Act 1985 has effect subject to the following amendments.

11 In section 8(2) (periodical review of housing needs) for "section 605" substitute "section 3 of the Housing Act 2004".

12 For section 252(c) (definition of "house in multiple occupation" for purposes of Part 8) substitute—

"(c) "house in multiple occupation" means a house in multiple occupation as defined by sections 254 to 259 of the Housing Act 2004, as they have effect for the purposes of Part 1 of that Act (that is, without the exclusions contained in Schedule 14 to that Act), but does not include any part of such a house which is occupied as a separate dwelling by persons who form a single household."

13 For section 268 (service of notice of demolition and closing orders) substitute—

"Service of copies of demolition order

"Service of copies of demolition order

(1) A local housing authority who have made a demolition order must serve a copy of the order on every person who, to their knowledge, is—

(a) an owner or occupier of the whole or part of the premises to which the order relates,

(b) authorised to permit persons to occupy the whole or part of those premises, or

(c) a mortgagee of the whole or part of the premises.

(2) The copies required to be served under subsection (1) shall be served within the period of seven days beginning with the day on which the order is made.

(3) A copy of the order is to be regarded as having been served on every occupier in accordance with subsections (1) and (2) if a copy of the order is fixed to some conspicuous part of the premises within the period of seven days mentioned in subsection (2).

(4) A demolition order against which no appeal is brought under section 269 becomes operative at the end of the period of 28 days beginning with the day on which the order is made and is final and conclusive as to matters which could be raised on an appeal.

(5) Section 246 of the Housing Act 2004 (service of notices)—

(a) applies in relation to copies required to be served under this section (instead of section 617 below), and

(b) so applies as it applies in relation to documents required to be served under any provision of Parts 1 to 4 of that Act."

14 In section 269(1) (right of appeal against demolition or closing order) for the words from "demolition or closing order" to "the order," substitute "demolition order may, within the period of 28 days beginning with the day on which the order is made,".

15 After section 269 insert—

"Appeals suggesting certain other courses of action

"Appeals suggesting certain other courses of action

(1) One ground of appeal under section 269 in relation to a demolition order made under section 265 is that a course of action mentioned in subsection (2) is the best course of action in relation to the hazard concerned.

(2) The courses of action are—

(a) serving an improvement notice under section 11 or 12 of the Housing Act 2004;

(b) making a prohibition order under section 20 or 21 of that Act;

(c) serving a hazard awareness notice under section 28 or 29 of that Act; or

(d) declaring the area in which the premises concerned are situated to be a clearance area in accordance with section 289 of this Act.

(3) Subsection (4) applies where—

(a) a residential property tribunal is hearing an appeal under section 269 in relation to a demolition order made under section 265; and

(b) the grounds on which the appeal is brought are or include the ground that a course of action mentioned in subsection (2) is the best course of action in relation to each hazard concerned.

(4) The tribunal shall have regard to any guidance given to the local housing authority under section 9 of the Housing Act 2004.

(5) Subsection (6) applies where—

(a) an appeal under section 269 is allowed against a demolition order made under section 265; and

(b) the reason or one of the reasons for allowing the appeal is that a course of action mentioned in subsection (2) is the best course of action in relation to the hazard concerned.

(6) The tribunal shall, if requested to do so by the appellant or the local housing authority, include in its decision a finding to that effect and identifying the course of action concerned.

(7) Subsection (1) of this section is without prejudice to the generality of section 269."

16 In section 274 (demolition orders: power to permit reconstruction of condemned house) for subsections (2) to (5) substitute—

"(2) If the authority are satisfied that the result of the works will be—

(a) in the case of a demolition order made under section 265(1) or (2), that the hazard concerned ceases to be a category 1 hazard, or

(b) in the case of a demolition order made under section 265(3) or (4), that a prescribed state of affairs exists,

they may, in order that the person submitting the proposals may have an opportunity of carrying out the works, extend for such period as they may specify the time within which the owner of the premises is required under section 271 to demolish them.

(3) In subsection (2) "prescribed state of affairs" means such state of affairs as may be specified or described in an order made by the Secretary of State.

(4) An order under subsection (3)—

(a) may make different provision for different cases or descriptions of case (including different provision for different areas);

(b) may contain such incidental, supplementary, consequential, transitory, transitional or saving provision as the Secretary of State considers appropriate; and

(c) shall be made by statutory instrument which shall be subject to annulment in pursuance of a resolution of either House of Parliament.

(5) That time may be further extended by the authority, once or more often as the case may require, if—

(a) the works have begun and appear to the authority to be making satisfactory progress, or

(b) though they have not begun, the authority think there has been no unreasonable delay.

(6) Where the authority determine to extend, or further extend, the time within which the owner of any premises is required under section 271 to demolish them, notice of the determination shall be served by the authority on every person having an interest in the premises or part of the premises, whether as freeholder, mortgagee or otherwise.

(7) If the works are completed to the satisfaction of the authority they shall revoke the demolition order (but without prejudice to any subsequent proceedings under this Part or Part 1 of the Housing Act 2004)."

17 After section 274 insert—

"Effect of certain enforcement action under the Housing Act 2004

"Effect of certain enforcement action under the Housing Act 2004

A demolition order which has been made in respect of any premises shall cease to have effect if a management order under Chapter 1 or 2 of Part 4 of the Housing Act 2004 comes into force in relation to the premises."

18 For section 275 (demolition orders: substitution of closing orders) substitute—

"Demolition orders: substitution of prohibition order to permit use otherwise than for human habitation

"Demolition orders: substitution of prohibition order to permit use otherwise than for human habitation

(1) If—

(a) an owner of any premises in respect of which a demolition order has become operative, or

(b) any other person who has an interest in the premises,

submits proposals to the local housing authority for the use of the premises for a purpose other than human habitation, the authority may, if they think fit, determine the demolition order and make a prohibition order under section 20 or 21 of the Housing Act 2004 in respect of the hazard concerned.

(2) The authority shall serve notice that the demolition order has been determined, and a copy of the prohibition order, on every person on whom they are required by Part 1 of Schedule 2 to the Housing Act 2004 to serve a copy of the prohibition order."

19 (1) Section 289 (declaration of clearance area) is amended as follows.

(2) In subsection (2F)(b) for "are unfit for human habitation" substitute "contain category 1 or category 2 hazards".

(3) In subsection (3)—

(a) in sub-paragraph (i), for the words from "unfit" to "health" substitute "dangerous or harmful to health or safety"; and

(b) in sub-paragraph (ii), for "injurious to health" substitute "harmful to health or safety".

20 For section 300 (purchase of houses liable to be demolished or closed) substitute—

"Purchase of houses liable to be demolished or to be subject to a prohibition order

"Purchase of houses liable to be demolished or to be subject to a prohibition order

(1) Where—

(a) the local housing authority would be required under section 5 of the Housing Act 2004 to make a demolition order under section 265(1) or (2) of this Act in respect of a dwelling, a house in multiple occupation or a building containing one or more flats, and

(b) it appears to them that the dwelling, house in multiple occupation or, as the case may be, building is or can be rendered capable of providing accommodation of a standard which is adequate for the time being,

they may purchase it instead.

(2) Where—

(a) the local housing authority would be required under section 5 of the Housing Act 2004 to make a relevant prohibition order in respect of a dwelling, a house in multiple occupation or a building containing one or more flats, and

(b) it appears to them that the dwelling, house in multiple occupation or, as the case may be, building is or can be rendered capable of providing accommodation of a standard which is adequate for the time being,

they may purchase it instead.

(3) In subsection (2) "relevant prohibition order" means a prohibition order under section 20 of the Housing Act 2004 which imposes in relation to the whole of the dwelling, house in multiple occupation or building a prohibition on its use for all purposes other than any purpose approved by the authority.

(4) Where an authority have determined to purchase any premises under subsection (1)—

(a) they shall serve a notice of their determination on the persons on whom they would have been required by section 268(1) to serve a copy of a demolition order, and

(b) sections 268(4) and 269(1), (2), (3) and (6) (operative date and right of appeal) apply to such a notice as they apply to a demolition order.

(5) Where an authority have determined to purchase any premises under subsection (2)—

(a) they shall serve a notice of their determination on the persons on whom they would have been required by Part 1 of Schedule 2 to the

Housing Act 2004 (service of prohibition orders) to serve a copy of the relevant prohibition order; and

(b) section 24 of that Act and Parts 1 and 3 of that Schedule (operative date, right of appeal etc.) apply to such a notice as they apply to a prohibition order which is not suspended or to appeals against such an order (as the case may be).

(6) At any time after the notice has become operative the authority may purchase the dwelling, house in multiple occupation or building by agreement or be authorised by the Secretary of State to purchase it compulsorily.

(7) This section does not apply where section 304(1) applies (listed building or building protected pending listing)."

21 For section 304 (closing orders in relation to listed buildings) substitute—

"Demolition order not to be made in respect of listed building

"Demolition order not to be made in respect of listed building

(1) A local housing authority shall not make a demolition order under section 265 (power to make a demolition order) in respect of a listed building.

(2) Where a dwelling, house in multiple occupation or building in respect of which a demolition order has been made becomes a listed building, the local housing authority shall determine the order (whether or not it has become operative).

(3) The local housing authority shall serve notice that the demolition order has been determined on every person on whom they would be required by section 268 to serve a copy of a new demolition order in relation to the premises.

(4) The Secretary of State may give notice in respect of a dwelling, house in multiple occupation or building to the local housing authority stating that its architectural or historic interest is sufficient to render it inexpedient that it should be demolished pending determination of the question whether it should be a listed building; and the provisions of this section apply to a dwelling, house in multiple occupation or building in respect of which such a notice is in force as they apply to a listed building."

22 In section 307(1) (saving for rights arising from breach of covenant etc.) for the words from "relating to" to "prejudices" substitute "relating to the demolition or purchase of unfit premises prejudices".

23 In section 308(3) (approval of owner's proposals for re-development)—

(a) after "Part" insert "or Chapter 2 of Part 1 of the Housing Act 2004"; and

(b) for ", closing or purchase of unfit premises" substitute "or purchase of premises or the prohibition of uses of premises".

24 Omit section 310 (certificate of fitness for human habitation resulting from owner's improvements or alterations).

25 In section 318(1)(a) (power of court to authorise execution of works on unfit premises or for improvement)—

(a) for "dwelling-houses" substitute "dwellings"; and

(b) for "injurious to health or unfit for human habitation" substitute "harmful to health or safety".

26 For section 322 substitute—

"Minor definitions

"Minor definitions

(1) In this Part the following expressions have the same meaning as in Part 1 of the Housing Act 2004 (see sections 1(5) to (7) and 2(1) of that Act)—

"building containing one or more flats",
"category 1 hazard",
"category 2 hazard",
"common parts", in relation to a building containing one or more flats,
"dwelling",
"flat",
"hazard".

(2) In this Part—

"health" includes mental health;

"house in multiple occupation" means a house in multiple occupation as defined by sections 254 to 259 of the Housing Act 2004, as they have effect for the purposes of Part 1 of that Act (that is, without the exclusions contained in Schedule 14 to that Act);

"owner", in relation to premises—

(a) means a person (other than a mortgagee not in possession) who is for the time being entitled to dispose of the fee simple in premises, whether in possession or reversion, and

(b) includes also a person holding or entitled to the rents and profits of the premises under a lease of which the unexpired term exceeds three years;

"premises" in relation to a demolition order, means the dwelling, house in multiple occupation or building in respect of which the order is made.

(3) This Part applies to unoccupied HMO accommodation (as defined by section 1(5) of the Housing Act 2004) as it applies to a house in multiple occupation, and references to a house in multiple occupation in this Part are to be read accordingly."

27 In section 323 (index of defined expressions: Part 9) insert at the appropriate places—

"building containing one or more flats	section 322"

"category 1 hazard	section 322"

"category 2 hazard	section 322"

"common parts	section 322"

"dwelling	section 322"

"hazard	section 322"

"health	section 322"

"residential property tribunal	section 229 of the Housing Act 2004".

28 In section 439 (requirements as to fitness of premises before advancing money for certain purposes), omit subsections (1) and (2).

29 In section 582 (compulsory purchase orders: restriction on recovery of possession of houses in multiple occupation) for subsection (8) substitute—

"(8) In this section "house in multiple occupation" has the meaning given by sections 254 to 259 of the Housing Act 2004 for the purposes of that Act (other than Part 1)."

30 For section 584A (compensation payable in case of closing and demolition orders) substitute—

"Compensation payable in case of prohibition and demolition orders

"Compensation payable in case of prohibition and demolition orders

(1) Subject to subsection (3), where a relevant prohibition order becomes operative in respect of any premises or a demolition order under section 265 is made in respect of any premises, the local housing authority shall pay to every owner of the premises an amount determined in accordance with subsection (2).

(2) The amount referred to in subsection (1) is the diminution in the compulsory purchase value of the owner's interest in the premises as a result of the coming into operation of the relevant prohibition order or, as the case may be, the making of the demolition order; and that amount—

(a) shall be determined as at the date of the coming into operation or making of the order in question; and

(b) shall be determined (in default of agreement) as if it were compensation payable in respect of the compulsory purchase of the interest in question and shall be dealt with accordingly.

(3) In any case where—

(a) a relevant prohibition order has been made in respect of any premises, and

(b) that order is revoked and a demolition order is made in its place,

the amount payable to the owner under subsection (1) in connection with the demolition order shall be reduced by the amount (if any) paid to the owner or a previous owner under that subsection in connection with the relevant prohibition order.

(4) For the purposes of this section—

"compulsory purchase value", in relation to an owner's interest in premises, means the compensation which would be payable in respect of the compulsory purchase of that interest if it fell to be assessed in accordance with the Land Compensation Act 1961;

"premises", in relation to a demolition order, has the meaning given by section 322;

"premises", in relation to a prohibition order, means premises which are specified premises in relation to the order within the meaning of Part 1 of the Housing Act 2004;

"relevant prohibition order" means a prohibition order under section 20 or 21 of the Housing Act 2004 which imposes in relation to the whole of any premises a prohibition on their use for all purposes other than any purpose approved by the authority."

31 For section 584B (repayment on revocation of demolition or closing order) substitute—

"Repayment on revocation of demolition or prohibition order

"Repayment on revocation of demolition or prohibition order

(1) Where a payment in respect of any premises has been made by a local housing authority under section 584A(1) in connection with a demolition order or relevant prohibition order and—

(a) the demolition order is revoked under section 274 (revocation of demolition order to permit reconstruction of premises), or

(b) the relevant prohibition order is revoked under section 25(1) or (2) of the Housing Act 2004,

then, if at that time the person to whom the payment was made has the same interest in the premises as he had at the time the payment was made, he shall on demand repay to the authority the amount of the payment.

(2) In any case where—

(a) a payment in respect of any premises has been made by a local housing authority under section 584A(1) in connection with a relevant prohibition order, and

(b) by virtue of section 25(3) of the Housing Act 2004, the order is revoked as respects part of the premises and not varied, and

(c) the person to whom the payment was made (in this section referred to as "the recipient") had at the time the payment was made, an owner's interest in the part of the premises concerned (whether or not he had such an interest in the rest of the premises),

then, if at the time of the revocation of the relevant prohibition order the recipient has the same interest in the premises as he had at the time the payment was made, he shall on demand pay to the authority an amount determined in accordance with subsections (4), (5) and (6).

(3) In any case where—

(a) a payment in respect of any premises has been made by a local housing authority under section 584A(1) in connection with a relevant prohibition order, and

(b) by virtue of section 25(4) of the Housing Act 2004, the order is varied,

then, if at the time of the variation of the order the recipient has the same interest in the premises as he had at the time the payment was made, he shall on demand pay to the authority an amount determined in accordance with subsections (4), (5) and (6).

(4) The amount referred to in subsection (2) or (3) is whichever is the less of—

(a) the amount by which the value of the interest of the recipient in the premises increases as a result of the revocation or variation of the relevant prohibition order; and

(b) the amount paid to the recipient under section 584A(1) in respect of his interest in the premises;

and the amount referred to in paragraph (a) shall be determined as at the date of the revocation or variation of the relevant prohibition order.

(5) For the purpose of assessing the amount referred to in subsection (4)(a), the rules set out in section 5 of the Land Compensation Act 1961 shall, so far as applicable and subject to any necessary modifications, have effect as they have effect for the purpose of assessing compensation for the compulsory acquisition of an interest in land.

(6) Any dispute as to the amount referred to in subsection (4)(a) shall be referred to and determined by the Lands Tribunal; and section 2 and subsections (1)(a) and (4) to (6) of section 4 of the Land Compensation Act 1961 shall, subject to any necessary modifications, apply for the purposes of this section as they apply for the purposes of that Act.

(7) In this section "premises" and "relevant prohibition order" have the same meaning as in section 584A."

Landlord and Tenant Act 1985 (c. 70)

32 (1) Section 20C of the Landlord and Tenant Act 1985 (limitation of service charges: costs of proceedings) is amended as follows.

(2) In subsection (1) after "a court" insert ", residential property tribunal".

(3) In subsection (2) after paragraph (a) insert—

"(aa) in the case of proceedings before a residential property tribunal, to a leasehold valuation tribunal;".

Housing Act 1988 (c. 50)

33 In paragraph 47 of Schedule 17 to the Housing Act 1988 (amendments of Part 9 of Housing Act 1985) for "sections 264(5), 270(3), 276 and 286(3)" substitute "section 270(3)".

Local Government and Housing Act 1989 (c. 42)

34 In section 100 of the Local Government and Housing Act 1989 (interpretation of Part 7) for the definition of "house in multiple occupation" substitute—

> ""house in multiple occupation" means a house in multiple occupation as defined by sections 254 to 259 of the Housing Act 2004, as they have effect for the purposes of Part 1 of that Act (that is, without the exclusions contained in Schedule 14 to that Act), but does not include any part of such a house which is occupied as a separate dwelling by persons who form a single household;".

35 In section 195(2) of that Act (short title, commencement and extent) for "167" substitute "168".

Water Industry Act 1991 (c. 56)

36 For paragraph 2(2) of Schedule 4A to the Water Industry Act 1991 (premises that are not to be disconnected for non-payment of charges) substitute—

> "(2) In this paragraph "house in multiple occupation" means a house in multiple occupation as defined by sections 254 to 259 of the Housing Act 2004, as they have effect for the purposes of Part 1 of that Act (that is, without the exclusions contained in Schedule 14 to that Act)."

Health Service Commissioners Act 1993 (c. 46)

37 (1) Section 18 of the Health Service Commissioners Act 1993 (consultation during investigations) is amended as follows.

(2) In subsection (1)—

(a) omit "or" at the end of paragraph (c);

(b) at the end of paragraph (d) insert "or

> (e) by the Social Housing Ombudsman for Wales under regulations under section 51B of the Housing Act 1996,";

(c) omit "the" after "appropriate Commissioner or"; and

(d) omit "the" after "that Commissioner or".

(3) In subsection (2) omit "the Welsh Administration".

Home Energy Conservation Act 1995 (c. 10)

38 For paragraph (aa)(i) of the definition of "residential accommodation" in section 1(1) of the Home Energy Conservation Act 1995 (interpretation) substitute—

> "(i) in England and Wales, a house in multiple occupation as defined by sections 254 to 259 of the Housing Act 2004, as they have effect for the purposes of Part 1 of that Act (that is, without the exclusions contained in Schedule 14 to that Act),".

Gas Act 1995 (c. 45)

39 In paragraph 2 of Schedule 4 to the Gas Act 1995 (statutory undertakers), in sub-paragraph (1)(xxxvi) for "sections 283(2) and" substitute "section".

Housing Act 1996 (c. 52)

40 The Housing Act 1996 has effect subject to the following amendments.

41 In section 52(1) (general provisions as to orders) after "17," insert "27A,".

42 In section 54 (determinations requiring approval), at the end of paragraph (b) insert "or

(c) any determination under section 27B (transfer of property funded by grants under section 27A),".

43 In section 210 (homelessness: suitability of accommodation)—

(a) for "Parts IX, X and XI" substitute "Parts 9 and 10"; and

(b) for "; overcrowding; houses in multiple occupation)" substitute "and overcrowding) and Parts 1 to 4 of the Housing Act 2004".

Housing Grants, Construction and Regeneration Act 1996 (c. 53)

44 In section 24 of the Housing Grants, Construction and Regeneration Act 1996 (considerations of fitness before approving applications for certain grants), omit subsection (4).

Government of Wales Act 1998 (c. 38)

45 (1) Paragraph 27 of Schedule 9 to the Government of Wales Act 1998 (consultation by Welsh Administration Ombudsman with other Ombudsmen) is amended as follows.

(2) In sub-paragraph (1)—

(a) omit "or" at the end of paragraph (b);

(b) at the end of paragraph (c) insert "or

(d) by the Social Housing Ombudsman for Wales under regulations under section 51B of the Housing Act 1996,";

(c) after "appropriate Commissioner" insert "or Ombudsman"; and

(d) after "that Commissioner" insert "or Ombudsman".

(3) In sub-paragraph (2) after "Commissioner" insert "or Ombudsman".

Freedom of Information Act 2000 (c. 36)

46 In the table in section 76(1) of the Freedom of Information Act 2000, after the entry relating to the Welsh Administration Ombudsman, insert—

"The Social Housing Ombudsman for Wales	Part 1, Chapter 5 of the Housing Act 1996 (c. 52)."

Local Government Act 2003 (c. 26)

47 In section 87 of the Local Government Act 2003 (housing strategies and statements) for subsection (4) substitute—

"(4) In this section—

"housing" includes accommodation needs for gypsies and travellers within the meaning of section 225 of the Housing Act 2004;

"local housing authority" has the same meaning as in the Housing Act 1985 (c. 68)."

SCHEDULE 16

Section 266

REPEALS

Short title and chapter	*Extent of repeal*
London Building Acts (Amendment) Act 1939 (c. xcvii)	Section 35(1)(c)(i).
	In section 36(1), the words "or sleep".
Friendly and Industrial and Provident Societies Act 1968 (c. 55)	Section 4A(3)(b).
Land Compensation Act 1973 (c. 26)	In section 37(9), the words "or undertaking".
	In section 39(9), the words "or undertaking".
Local Government Act 1974 (c. 7)	In section 33, in subsection (1) the "the" after "appropriate Commissioner or", and in subsection (2) the "the" after "that Commissioner or".
County of Merseyside Act 1980 (c. x)	Section 48.
	Section 49(1) and (2).
	In section 132(2), the words "In section 48 (Means of escape from fire), subsection (5);".
	Section 139(3).
Civil Aviation Act 1982 (c. 16)	In Schedule 2, in the entry relating to the Housing Act 1985 in paragraph 4, "283,".
Mobile Homes Act 1983 (c. 34)	In Part 1 of Schedule 1, in paragraph 6(1), the words "age and".
Building Act 1984 (c. 55)	Section 72(6)(a).
Housing Act 1985 (c. 68)	In section 104(1)(b), the words "and Part V (the right to buy)".
	In section 157, in subsection (2) the words ", subject to subsection (4),", and subsections (4) and (5).
	Sections 189 to 208.
	Section 264.
	In section 267, in the sidenote the words "and closing orders", and subsections (2) and (3).

Short title and chapter	*Extent of repeal*
	Section 269(2A) and (3A).
	Sections 276 to 279.
	Sections 283 to 288.
	Section 289(5A).
	In section 305, subsection (5) and, in subsection (8), the words from "and" to the end of the subsection.
	Section 310.
	In section 311, in subsection (1) the words "or section 310 (owner's improvements or alterations)" and in subsection (3) the words "or 310, as the case may be".
	In section 316(1), the words ", or obstructive building order".
	In section 317, in the sidenote the words "or closed", and in subsection (1) the words "or closing".
	Section 318(4).
	In section 319(1)(b), the words "or closing" and ", or an obstructive building order,".
	In section 323, the entries relating to "closing order", "fit (or unfit) for human habitation", "house", "obstructive building", "obstructive building order" and "unfit (or fit) for human habitation".
	Sections 345 to 400.
	Section 439(1) and (2).
	Sections 604 to 606.
	In section 623(1), the words "and "flat", except in the expression "flat in multiple occupation"," and the definitions of "house in multiple occupation" and "flat in multiple occupation".
	In section 624, the entries relating to "flat", "flat in multiple occupation" and "house in multiple occupation".
	Schedule 10.
	Schedule 13.
Housing Associations Act 1985 (c. 69)	In section 87, in subsection (3) the words from ", acting" onwards, and subsection (6).

Short title and chapter	*Extent of repeal*
Housing (Consequential Provisions) Act 1985 (c. 71)	In Schedule 2, paragraph 24(2)(d).
Leicestershire Act 1985 (c. xvii)	Section 54(6)(a).
Airports Act 1986 (c. 31)	In Schedule 2, in the entry relating to the Housing Act 1985 in paragraph 1(1), "283,".
Housing Act 1988 (c. 50)	In section 50(2), the words from ", acting" onwards.
	In section 52(2), the words from ", acting" to "determine,".
	Section 55.
	In section 57(a), "or 55".
	Section 130.
	Schedule 15.
Electricity Act 1989 (c. 29)	In Schedule 16, paragraph 1(1)(xl).
Local Government and Housing Act 1989 (c. 42)	In section 165(1), paragraphs (a) and (c).
	Section 167.
	In Schedule 9, paragraphs 1 to 14, 16, 17(2) and (4), 20(2) and (3), 21 to 23, 25(1), 29, 32, 33(1), 36, 42, 43(b), 44 to 71, 75, 83, 84 and 86.
Health Service Commissioners Act 1993 (c. 46)	In section 18, in subsection (1), the "or" at the end of paragraph (c), the "the" after "appropriate Commissioner or" and the "the" after "that Commissioner or", and in subsection (2) the words "the Welsh Administration".
Housing Act 1996 (c. 52)	In section 18(2), the words from ", acting" to "determine,".
	In section 20(3), the words from ", acting" to "determine,".
	In section 21(3), the words from ", acting" to "determine,".
	Sections 65 to 79.
	In Schedule 1, paragraph 16(4), in paragraph 18(1) the words from "(which impose" onwards, and in paragraph 19(2) paragraph (d) (but not the "or" at the end).
Housing Grants, Construction and Regeneration Act 1996 (c. 53)	Section 24(4).
	In section 58, the definition of "qualifying park home".

Short title and chapter	Extent of repeal
	In section 59, the entries relating to "fit for human habitation" and "qualifying park home".
	Sections 81 to 91.
	Section 97.
	In Schedule 1, paragraph 10.
Government of Wales Act 1998 (c. 38)	In Schedule 9, in paragraph 27(1) the "or" at the end of paragraph (b).
Transport Act 2000 (c. 38)	In Schedule 5, in paragraph 1(2)(o), "283,".

GRANGIS - UK PUBLISHING 2022.

www.ingramcontent.com/pod-product-compliance
Lightning Source LLC
LaVergne TN
LVHW060210210926
848481LV00008B/2689

Adapted and published by GRANGIS under the OGL Licence 3.0.

www.nationalarchives.gov.uk/doc/open-government-licence/version/3/

GRANGIS - UK PUBLISHING 2022.

www.ingramcontent.com/pod-product-compliance
Lightning Source LLC
LaVergne TN
LVHW060211210926
848481LV00008B/2691
* 9 7 9 8 8 8 5 5 9 0 5 2 5 *

Licensing schemes and licensing bodies

References and applications with respect to licensing schemes

References and applications with respect to licensing by licensing bodies

Factors to be taken into account in certain classes of case

Implied indemnity in schemes or licences for reprographic copying

Reprographic copying by educational establishments

Royalty or other sum payable for rental of certain works

Certification of licensing schemes

Introductory

1 (1) The provisions of this Schedule specify acts which may...

Criticism, reviews and news reporting

2 (1) Fair dealing with a performance or recording—

Incidental inclusion of performance or recording

3 (1) The rights conferred by Part II are not infringed...

Things done for purposes of instruction or examination

4 (1) The rights conferred by Part II are not infringed...

Playing or showing sound recording, film, broadcast or cable programme at educational establishment

5 (1) The playing or showing of a sound recording, film,...

Recording of broadcasts and cable programmes by educational establishments

6 (1) A recording of a broadcast or cable programme, or...

Copy of work required to be made as condition of export

7 (1) If an article of cultural or historical importance or...

Parliamentary and judicial proceedings

8 (1) The rights conferred by Part II are not infringed...

Royal Commissions and statutory inquiries

9 (1) The rights conferred by Part II are not infringed...

Public records

10 (1) Material which is comprised in public records within the...

Acts done under statutory authority

11 (1) Where the doing of a particular act is specifically...

Transfer of copies of works in electronic form

12 (1) This paragraph applies where a recording of a performance...

Use of recordings of spoken works in certain cases

13 (1) Where a recording of the reading or recitation of...

Recordings of folksongs

14 (1) A recording of a performance of a song may...

Playing of sound recordings for purposes of club, society, &c

15 (1) It is not an infringement of any right conferred...

Incidental recording for purposes of broadcast or cable programme

16 (1) A person who proposes to broadcast a recording of...

Recordings for purposes of supervision and control of broadcasts and cable programmes

17 (1) The rights conferred by Part II are not infringed...

Free public showing or playing of broadcast or cable programme

18 (1) The showing or playing in public of a broadcast...

Reception and re-transmission of broadcast in cable programme service

19 (1) This paragraph applies where a broadcast made from a...

Provision of sub-titled copies of broadcast or cable programme

20 (1) A designated body may, for the purpose of providing...

Recording of broadcast or cable programme for archival purposes

21 (1) A recording of a broadcast or cable programme of...

SCHEDULE 3 — Registered designs: minor and consequential amendments of 1949 Act

Section 3: proceedings for registration

1 In section 3 of the Registered Designs Act 1949 (proceedings...

Section 4: registration of same design in respect of other articles, etc.

2 In section 4 of the Registered Designs Act 1949 (registration...

Section 5: provisions for secrecy of certain designs

3 (1) Section 5 of the Registered Designs Act 1949 is...

Section 6: provisions as to confidential disclosure, etc.

4 (1) Section 6 of the Registered Designs Act 1949 (provisions...

Section 9: exemption of innocent infringer from liability for damages

5 In section 9 of the Registered Designs Act 1949 (exemption...

Section 11: cancellation of registration

6 (1) Section 11 of the Registered Designs Act 1949 (cancellation...

Section 14: registration where application has been made in convention country

7 In section 14 of the Registered Designs Act 1949 (registration...

Section 15: extension of time for application under s.14 in certain cases

8 In section 15(1) of the Registered Designs Act 1949 (power...

Section 16: protection of designs communicated under international agreements

9 In section 16 of the Registered Designs Act 1949 (protection...

Section 19: registration of assignments, &c.

10 In section 19 of the Registered Designs Act 1949 (registration...

Section 20: rectification of the register

11 In section 20 of the Registered Designs Act 1949 (rectification...

Section 22: inspection of registered designs

12 (1) Section 22 of the Registered Designs Act 1949 (inspection...

Section 23: information as to existence of right in registered design

13 For section 23 of the Registered Designs Act 1949 (information...

Section 25: certificate of contested validity of registration

14 In section 25 of the Registered Designs Act 1949 (certificate...

Section 26: remedy for groundless threats of infringement proceedings

15 (1) Section 26 of the Registered Designs Act 1949 (remedy...

Section 27: the court

16 For section 27 of the Registered Designs Act 1949 (the...

Section 28: the Appeal Tribunal

17 (1) Section 28 of the Registered Designs Act 1949 (the...

Section 29: exercise of discretionary powers of registrar

18 In section 29 of the Registered Designs Act 1949 (exercise...

Section 30: costs and security for costs

19 For section 30 of the Registered Designs Act 1949 (costs...

Section 31: evidence before registrar

20 For section 31 of the Registered Designs Act 1949 (evidence...

Section 32: power of registrar to refuse to deal with certain agents

21 Section 32 of the Registered Designs Act 1949 (power of...

Section 33: offences under s.5 (secrecy of certain designs)

22 (1) Section 33 of the Registered Designs Act 1949 (offences...

Section 34: falsification of register, &c.

23 (1) In section 34 of the Registered Designs Act 1949...

Section 35: fine for falsely representing a design as registered

24 (1) Section 35 of the Registered Designs Act 1949 (fine...

Section 35A: offence by body corporate -liability of officers

25 (1) In the Registered Designs Act 1949 after section 35...

Section 36: general power to make rules, &c.

26 (1) Section 36 of the Registered Designs Act 1949 (general...

Section 37: provisions as to rules and Orders

27 (1) Section 37 of the Registered Designs Act 1949 (provisions...

Section 38: proceedings of the Board of Trade

28 Section 38 of the Registered Designs Act 1949 (proceedings of...

Section 39: hours of business and excluded days

29 In section 39 of the Registered Designs Act 1949 (hours...

Section 40: fees

30 In section 40 of the Registered Designs Act 1949 (fees)...

Section 44: interpretation

31 (1) In section 44 of the Registered Designs Act 1949...

Section 45: application to Scotland

32 In section 45 of the Registered Designs Act 1949 (application...

Section 46: application to Northern Ireland

33 (1) Section 46 of the Registered Designs Act 1949 (application...

Section 47: application to Isle of Man

34 For section 47 of the Registered Designs Act 1949 (application...

Section 47A: territorial waters and the continental shelf

35 In the Registered Designs Act 1949, after section 47 insert—...

Section 48: repeals, savings and transitional provisions

36 In section 48 of the Registered Designs Act 1949 (repeals,...

Schedule 1: provisions as to Crown use of registered designs

37 (1) The First Schedule to the Registered Designs Act 1949...

Schedule 2: enactments repealed

38 Schedule 2 to the Registered Designs Act 1949 (enactments repealed)...

Post Office Act 1969 (c. 48)

11 In Schedule 10 to the Post Office Act 1969 (special...

Merchant Shipping Act 1970 (c. 36)

12 In section 87 of the Merchant Shipping Act 1970 (merchant...

Taxes Management Act 1970 (c. 9)

13 In section 16 of the Taxes Management Act 1970 (returns...

Tribunals and Inquiries Act 1971 (c. 62)

14 In Part I of Schedule 1 to the Tribunals and...

Fair Trading Act 1973 (c. 41)

15 In Schedule 4 to the Fair Trading Act 1973 (excluded...

House of Commons Disqualification Act 1975 (c. 24)

16 In Part II of Schedule 1 to the House of...

Northern Ireland Assembly Disqualification Act 1975 (c. 25)

17 In Part II of Schedule 1 to the Northern Ireland...

Restrictive Trade Practices Act 1976 (c. 34)

18 (1) The Restrictive Trade Practices Act 1976 is amended as...

Resale Prices Act 1976 (c. 53)

19 In section 10(4) of the Resale Prices Act 1976 (patented...

Patents Act 1977 (c. 37)

20 In section 57 of the Patents Act 1977 (rights of...
21 In section 105 of the Patents Act 1977 (privilege in...
22 In section 123(7) of the Patents Act 1977 (publication of...
23 In section 130(1) of the Patents Act 1977 (interpretation), in...

Unfair Contract Terms Act 1977 (c. 50)

24 In paragraph 1 of Schedule 1 to the Unfair Contract...

Judicature (Northern Ireland) Act 1978 (c. 23)

25 In section 94A of the Judicature (Northern Ireland) Act 1978...

Capital Gains Tax Act 1979 (c. 14)

26 In section 18(4) of the Capital Gains Tax Act 1979...

British Telecommunications Act 1981 (c. 38)

27 In Schedule 5 to the British Telecommunications Act 1981 (special...

Supreme Court Act 1981 (c. 54)

28 (1) The Supreme Court Act 1981 is amended as follows....

Broadcasting Act 1981 (c. 68)

29 (1) The Broadcasting Act 1981 is amended as follows.

Cable and Broadcasting Act 1984 (c. 46)

30 (1) The Cable and Broadcasting Act 1984 is amended as...

Companies Act 1985 (c. 6)

31 (1) Part XII of the Companies Act 1985 (registration of...

Law Reform (Miscellaneous Provisions) (Scotland) Act 1985 (c. 73)

32 In section 15 of the Law Reform (Miscellaneous Provisions) (Scotland)...

Atomic Energy Authority Act 1986 (c. 3)

33 In section 8(2) of the Atomic Energy Authority Act 1986...

Education and Libraries (Northern Ireland) Order 1986 (S.I. 1986/594 (N.I.3))

34 In Article 77 of the Education and Libraries (Northern Ireland)...

Companies (Northern Ireland) Order 1986 (S.I. 1986/1032 (N.I.6))

35 In Article 403 of the Companies (Northern Ireland) Order 1986...

Income and Corporation Taxes Act 1988 (c. 1)

36 (1) The Income and Corporation Taxes Act 1988 is amended...

SCHEDULE 8 — Repeals

Copyright, Designs and Patents Act 1988

1988 CHAPTER 48

An Act to restate the law of copyright, with amendments; to make fresh provision as to the rights of performers and others in performances; to confer a design right in original designs; to amend the Registered Designs Act 1949; to make provision with respect to patent agents and trade mark agents; to confer patents and designs jurisdiction on certain county courts; to amend the law of patents; to make provision with respect to devices designed to circumvent copy-protection of works in electronic form; to make fresh provision penalising the fraudulent reception of transmissions; to make the fraudulent application or use of a trade mark an offence; to make provision for the benefit of the Hospital for Sick Children, Great Ormond Street, London; to enable financial assistance to be given to certain international bodies; and for connected purposes. [15th November 1988]

Be it enacted by the Queen's most Excellent Majesty, by and with the advice and consent of the Lords Spiritual and Temporal, and Commons, in this present Parliament assembled, and by the authority of the same, as follows:—

PART I

COPYRIGHT

CHAPTER I

SUBSISTENCE, OWNERSHIP AND DURATION OF COPYRIGHT

Introductory

1 Copyright and copyright works

(1) Copyright is a property right which subsists in accordance with this Part in the following descriptions of work—

(a) original literary, dramatic, musical or artistic works,

(b) sound recordings, films, broadcasts or cable programmes, and

(c) the typographical arrangement of published editions.

(2) In this Part "copyright work" means a work of any of those descriptions in which copyright subsists.

(3) Copyright does not subsist in a work unless the requirements of this Part with respect to qualification for copyright protection are met (see section 153 and the provisions referred to there).

2 Rights subsisting in copyright works

(1) The owner of the copyright in a work of any description has the exclusive right to do the acts specified in Chapter II as the acts restricted by the copyright in a work of that description.

(2) In relation to certain descriptions of copyright work the following rights conferred by Chapter IV (moral rights) subsist in favour of the author, director or commissioner of the work, whether or not he is the owner of the copyright—

(a) section 77 (right to be identified as author or director),

(b) section 80 (right to object to derogatory treatment of work), and

(c) section 85 (right to privacy of certain photographs and films).

Descriptions of work and related provisions

3 Literary, dramatic and musical works

(1) In this Part—

"literary work" means any work, other than a dramatic or musical work, which is written, spoken or sung, and accordingly includes—

(a) a table or compilation, and

(b) a computer program;

"dramatic work" includes a work of dance or mime; and

"musical work" means a work consisting of music, exclusive of any words or action intended to be sung, spoken or performed with the music.

(2) Copyright does not subsist in a literary, dramatic or musical work unless and until it is recorded, in writing or otherwise; and references in this Part to the time at which such a work is made are to the time at which it is so recorded.

(3) It is immaterial for the purposes of subsection (2) whether the work is recorded by or with the permission of the author; and where it is not recorded by the author, nothing in that subsection affects the question whether copyright subsists in the record as distinct from the work recorded.

4 Artistic works

(1) In this Part "artistic work" means—

(a) a graphic work, photograph, sculpture or collage, irrespective of artistic quality,
(b) a work of architecture being a building or a model for a building, or
(c) a work of artistic craftsmanship.

(2) In this Part—

"building" includes any fixed structure, and a part of a building or fixed structure;

"graphic work" includes—

(a) any painting, drawing, diagram, map, chart or plan, and
(b) any engraving, etching, lithograph, woodcut or similar work;

"photograph" means a recording of light or other radiation on any medium on which an image is produced or from which an image may by any means be produced, and which is not part of a film;

"sculpture" includes a cast or model made for purposes of sculpture.

5 Sound recordings and films

(1) In this Part—

"sound recording" means—

(a) a recording of sounds, from which the sounds may be reproduced, or
(b) a recording of the whole or any part of a literary, dramatic or musical work, from which sounds reproducing the work or part may be produced,

regardless of the medium on which the recording is made or the method by which the sounds are reproduced or produced; and

"film" means a recording on any medium from which a moving image may by any means be produced.

(2) Copyright does not subsist in a sound recording or film which is, or to the extent that it is, a copy taken from a previous sound recording or film.

6 Broadcasts

(1) In this Part a "broadcast" means a transmission by wireless telegraphy of visual images, sounds or other information which—

(a) is capable of being lawfully received by members of the public, or

(b) is transmitted for presentation to members of the public;

and references to broadcasting shall be construed accordingly.

(2) An encrypted transmission shall be regarded as capable of being lawfully received by members of the public only if decoding equipment has been made available to members of the public by or with the authority of the person making the transmission or the person providing the contents of the transmission.

(3) References in this Part to the person making a broadcast, broadcasting a work, or including a work in a broadcast are—

(a) to the person transmitting the programme, if he has responsibility to any extent for its contents, and

(b) to any person providing the programme who makes with the person transmitting it the arrangements necessary for its transmission;

and references in this Part to a programme, in the context of broadcasting, are to any item included in a broadcast.

(4) For the purposes of this Part the place from which a broadcast is made is, in the case of a satellite transmission, the place from which the signals carrying the broadcast are transmitted to the satellite.

(5) References in this Part to the reception of a broadcast include reception of a broadcast relayed by means of a telecommunications system.

(6) Copyright does not subsist in a broadcast which infringes, or to the extent that it infringes, the copyright in another broadcast or in a cable programme.

7 Cable programmes

(1) In this Part—

"cable programme" means any item included in a cable programme service; and

"cable programme service" means a service which consists wholly or mainly in sending visual images, sounds or other information by means of a telecommunications system, otherwise than by wireless telegraphy, for reception—

(a) at two or more places (whether for simultaneous reception or at different times in response to requests by different users), or

(b) for presentation to members of the public,

and which is not, or so far as it is not, excepted by or under the following provisions of this section.

(2) The following are excepted from the definition of "cable programme service"—

(a) a service or part of a service of which it is an essential feature that while visual images, sounds or other information are being conveyed by the person providing the service there will or may be sent from each place of reception, by means of the same system or (as the case may be) the same part of it, information (other than signals sent for the operation or control of the service) for reception by the person providing the service or other persons receiving it;

(b) a service run for the purposes of a business where—

(i) no person except the person carrying on the business is concerned in the control of the apparatus comprised in the system,

(ii) the visual images, sounds or other information are conveyed by the system solely for purposes internal to the running of the business and not by way of rendering a service or providing amenities for others, and

(iii) the system is not connected to any other telecommunications system;

(c) a service run by a single individual where—

(i) all the apparatus comprised in the system is under his control,

(ii) the visual images, sounds or other information conveyed by the system are conveyed solely for domestic purposes of his, and

(iii) the system is not connected to any other telecommunications system;

(d) services where—

(i) all the apparatus comprised in the system is situated in, or connects, premises which are in single occupation, and

(ii) the system is not connected to any other telecommunications system,

other than services operated as part of the amenities provided for residents or inmates of premises run as a business;

(e) services which are, or to the extent that they are, run for persons providing broadcasting or cable programme services or providing programmes for such services.

(3) The Secretary of State may by order amend subsection (2) so as to add or remove exceptions, subject to such transitional provision as appears to him to be appropriate.

(4) An order shall be made by statutory instrument; and no order shall be made unless a draft of it has been laid before and approved by resolution of each House of Parliament.

(5) References in this Part to the inclusion of a cable programme or work in a cable programme service are to its transmission as part of the service; and references to the person including it are to the person providing the service.

(6) Copyright does not subsist in a cable programme—

(a) if it is included in a cable programme service by reception and immediate re-transmission of a broadcast, or

(b) if it infringes, or to the extent that it infringes, the copyright in another cable programme or in a broadcast.

8 Published editions

(1) In this Part "published edition", in the context of copyright in the typographical arrangement of a published edition, means a published edition of the whole or any part of one or more literary, dramatic or musical works.

(2) Copyright does not subsist in the typographical arrangement of a published edition if, or to the extent that, it reproduces the typographical arrangement of a previous edition.

Authorship and ownership of copyright

9 Authorship of work

(1) In this Part "author", in relation to a work, means the person who creates it.

(2) That person shall be taken to be—

(a) in the case of a sound recording or film, the person by whom the arrangements necessary for the making of the recording or film are undertaken;
(b) in the case of a broadcast, the person making the broadcast (see section 6(3)) or, in the case of a broadcast which relays another broadcast by reception and immediate re-transmission, the person making that other broadcast;
(c) in the case of a cable programme, the person providing the cable programme service in which the programme is included;
(d) in the case of the typographical arrangement of a published edition, the publisher.

(3) In the case of a literary, dramatic, musical or artistic work which is computer-generated, the author shall be taken to be the person by whom the arrangements necessary for the creation of the work are undertaken.

(4) For the purposes of this Part a work is of "unknown authorship" if the identity of the author is unknown or, in the case of a work of joint authorship, if the identity of none of the authors is known.

(5) For the purposes of this Part the identity of an author shall be regarded as unknown if it is not possible for a person to ascertain his identity by reasonable inquiry; but if his identity is once known it shall not subsequently be regarded as unknown.

10 Works of joint authorship

(1) In this Part a "work of joint authorship" means a work produced by the collaboration of two or more authors in which the contribution of each author is not distinct from that of the other author or authors.

(2) A broadcast shall be treated as a work of joint authorship in any case where more than one person is to be taken as making the broadcast (see section 6(3)).

(3) References in this Part to the author of a work shall, except as otherwise provided, be construed in relation to a work of joint authorship as references to all the authors of the work.

11 First ownership of copyright

(1) The author of a work is the first owner of any copyright in it, subject to the following provisions.

(2) Where a literary, dramatic, musical or artistic work is made by an employee in the course of his employment, his employer is the first owner of any copyright in the work subject to any agreement to the contrary.

(3) This section does not apply to Crown copyright or Parliamentary copyright (see sections 163 and 165) or to copyright which subsists by virtue of section 168 (copyright of certain international organisations).

Duration of copyright

12 Duration of copyright in literary, dramatic, musical or artistic works

(1) Copyright in a literary, dramatic, musical or artistic work expires at the end of the period of 50 years from the end of the calendar year in which the author dies, subject to the following provisions of this section.

(2) If the work is of unknown authorship, copyright expires at the end of the period of 50 years from the end of the calendar year in which it is first made available to the public; and subsection (1) does not apply if the identity of the author becomes known after the end of that period.

For this purpose making available to the public includes—
(a)

in the case of a literary, dramatic or musical work—
(i) performance in public, or
(ii) being broadcast or included in a cable programme service;
(b) in the case of an artistic work—
(i) exhibition in public,
(ii) a film including the work being shown in public, or
(iii) being included in a broadcast or cable programme service;

but in determining generally for the purposes of this subsection whether a work has been made available to the public no account shall be taken of any unauthorised act.

(3) If the work is computer-generated neither of the above provisions applies and copyright expires at the end of the period of 50 years from the end of the calendar year in which the work was made.

(4) In relation to a work of joint authorship—
(a) the reference in subsection (1) to the death of the author shall be construed —
(i) if the identity of all the authors is known, as a reference to the death of the last of them to die, and
(ii) if the identity of one or more of the authors is known and the identity of one or more others is not, as a reference to the death of the last of the authors whose identity is known; and
(b) the reference in subsection (2) to the identity of the author becoming known shall be construed as a reference to the identity of any of the authors becoming known.

(5) This section does not apply to Crown copyright or Parliamentary copyright (see sections 163 to 166) or to copyright which subsists by virtue of section 168 (copyright of certain international organisations).

13 Duration of copyright in sound recordings and films

(1) Copyright in a sound recording or film expires—
(a) at the end of the period of 50 years from the end of the calendar year in which it is made, or

(b) if it is released before the end of that period, 50 years from the end of the calendar year in which it is released.

(2) A sound recording or film is "released" when—

(a) it is first published, broadcast or included in a cable programme service, or

(b) in the case of a film or film sound-track, the film is first shown in public;

but in determining whether a work has been released no account shall be taken of any unauthorised act.

14 Duration of copyright in broadcasts and cable programmes

(1) Copyright in a broadcast or cable programme expires at the end of the period of 50 years from the end of the calendar year in which the broadcast was made or the programme was included in a cable programme service.

(2) Copyright in a repeat broadcast or cable programme expires at the same time as the copyright in the original broadcast or cable programme; and accordingly no copyright arises in respect of a repeat broadcast or cable programme which is broadcast or included in a cable programme service after the expiry of the copyright in the original broadcast or cable programme.

(3) A repeat broadcast or cable programme means one which is a repeat either of a broadcast previously made or of a cable programme previously included in a cable programme service.

15 Duration of copyright in typographical arrangement of published editions

Copyright in the typographical arrangement of a published edition expires at the end of the period of 25 years from the end of the calendar year in which the edition was first published.

CHAPTER II

RIGHTS OF COPYRIGHT OWNER

The acts restricted by copyright

16 The acts restricted by copyright in a work

(1) The owner of the copyright in a work has, in accordance with the following provisions of this Chapter, the exclusive right to do the following acts in the United Kingdom—

(a) to copy the work (see section 17);

(b) to issue copies of the work to the public (see section 18);

(c) to perform, show or play the work in public (see section 19);

(d) to broadcast the work or include it in a cable programme service (see section 20);

(e) to make an adaptation of the work or do any of the above in relation to an adaptation (see section 21);

and those acts are referred to in this Part as the "acts restricted by the copyright".

(2) Copyright in a work is infringed by a person who without the licence of the copyright owner does, or authorises another to do, any of the acts restricted by the copyright.

(3) References in this Part to the doing of an act restricted by the copyright in a work are to the doing of it—

(a) in relation to the work as a whole or any substantial part of it, and

(b) either directly or indirectly;

and it is immaterial whether any intervening acts themselves infringe copyright.

(4) This Chapter has effect subject to—

(a) the provisions of Chapter III (acts permitted in relation to copyright works), and

(b) the provisions of Chapter VII (provisions with respect to copyright licensing).

17 Infringement of copyright by copying

(1) The copying of the work is an act restricted by the copyright in every description of copyright work; and references in this Part to copying and copies shall be construed as follows.

(2) Copying in relation to a literary, dramatic, musical or artistic work means reproducing the work in any material form.

This includes storing the work in any medium by electronic means.

(3) In relation to an artistic work copying includes the making of a copy in three dimensions of a two-dimensional work and the making of a copy in two dimensions of a three-dimensional work.

(4) Copying in relation to a film, television broadcast or cable programme includes making a photograph of the whole or any substantial part of any image forming part of the film, broadcast or cable programme.

(5) Copying in relation to the typographical arrangement of a published edition means making a facsimile copy of the arrangement.

(6) Copying in relation to any description of work includes the making of copies which are transient or are incidental to some other use of the work.

18 Infringement by issue of copies to the public

(1) The issue to the public of copies of the work is an act restricted by the copyright in every description of copyright work.

(2) References in this Part to the issue to the public of copies of a work are to the act of putting into circulation copies not previously put into circulation, in the United Kingdom or elsewhere, and not to—

(a) any subsequent distribution, sale, hiring or loan of those copies, or

(b) any subsequent importation of those copies into the United Kingdom;

except that in relation to sound recordings, films and computer programs the restricted act of issuing copies to the public includes any rental of copies to the public.

19 Infringement by performance, showing or playing of work in public

(1) The performance of the work in public is an act restricted by the copyright in a literary, dramatic or musical work.

(2) In this Part "performance", in relation to a work—

(a) includes delivery in the case of lectures, addresses, speeches and sermons, and

(b) in general, includes any mode of visual or acoustic presentation, including presentation by means of a sound recording, film, broadcast or cable programme of the work.

(3) The playing or showing of the work in public is an act restricted by the copyright in a sound recording, film, broadcast or cable programme.

(4) Where copyright in a work is infringed by its being performed, played or shown in public by means of apparatus for receiving visual images or sounds conveyed by electronic means, the person by whom the visual images or sounds are sent, and in the case of a performance the performers, shall not be regarded as responsible for the infringement.

20 Infringement by broadcasting or inclusion in a cable programme service

The broadcasting of the work or its inclusion in a cable programme service is an act restricted by the copyright in—

(a) a literary, dramatic, musical or artistic work,

(b) a sound recording or film, or

(c) a broadcast or cable programme.

21 Infringement by making adaptation or act done in relation to adaptation

(1) The making of an adaptation of the work is an act restricted by the copyright in a literary, dramatic or musical work.

For this purpose an adaptation is made when it is recorded, in writing or otherwise.

(2) The doing of any of the acts specified in sections 17 to 20, or subsection (1) above, in relation to an adaptation of the work is also an act restricted by the copyright in a literary, dramatic or musical work.

For this purpose it is immaterial whether the adaptation has been recorded, in writing or otherwise, at the time the act is done.

(3) In this Part "adaptation"—

(a) in relation to a literary or dramatic work, means—

(i) a translation of the work;

(ii) a version of a dramatic work in which it is converted into a non-dramatic work or, as the case may be, of a non-dramatic work in which it is converted into a dramatic work;

(iii) a version of the work in which the story or action is conveyed wholly or mainly by means of pictures in a form suitable for reproduction in a book, or in a newspaper, magazine or similar periodical;

(b) in relation to a musical work, means an arrangement or transcription of the work.

(4) In relation to a computer program a "translation" includes a version of the program in which it is converted into or out of a computer language or code or into a different computer language or code, otherwise than incidentally in the course of running the program.

(5) No inference shall be drawn from this section as to what does or does not amount to copying a work.

Secondary infringement of copyright

22 Secondary infringement: importing infringing copy

The copyright in a work is infringed by a person who, without the licence of the copyright owner, imports into the United Kingdom, otherwise than for his private and domestic use, an article which is, and which he knows or has reason to believe is, an infringing copy of the work.

23 Secondary infringement: possessing or dealing with infringing copy

The copyright in a work is infringed by a person who, without the licence of the copyright owner—

(a) possesses in the course of a business,
(b) sells or lets for hire, or offers or exposes for sale or hire,
(c) in the course of a business exhibits in public or distributes, or
(d) distributes otherwise than in the course of a business to such an extent as to affect prejudicially the owner of the copyright,

an article which is, and which he knows or has reason to believe is, an infringing copy of the work.

24 Secondary infringement: providing means for making infringing copies

(1) Copyright in a work is infringed by a person who, without the licence of the copyright owner—

(a) makes,
(b) imports into the United Kingdom,
(c) possesses in the course of a business, or
(d) sells or lets for hire, or offers or exposes for sale or hire,

an article specifically designed or adapted for making copies of that work, knowing or having reason to believe that it is to be used to make infringing copies.

(2) Copyright in a work is infringed by a person who without the licence of the copyright owner transmits the work by means of a telecommunications system (otherwise than by broadcasting or inclusion in a cable programme service), knowing or having reason to believe that infringing copies of the work will be made by means of the reception of the transmission in the United Kingdom or elsewhere.

25 Secondary infringement: permitting use of premises for infringing performance

(1) Where the copyright in a literary, dramatic or musical work is infringed by a performance at a place of public entertainment, any person who gave permission for

that place to be used for the performance is also liable for the infringement unless when he gave permission he believed on reasonable grounds that the performance would not infringe copyright.

(2) In this section "place of public entertainment" includes premises which are occupied mainly for other purposes but are from time to time made available for hire for the purposes of public entertainment.

26 Secondary infringement: provision of apparatus for infringing performance, &c

(1) Where copyright in a work is infringed by a public performance of the work, or by the playing or showing of the work in public, by means of apparatus for—

(a) playing sound recordings,

(b) showing films, or

(c) receiving visual images or sounds conveyed by electronic means,

the following persons are also liable for the infringement.

(2) A person who supplied the apparatus, or any substantial part of it, is liable for the infringement if when he supplied the apparatus or part—

(a) he knew or had reason to believe that the apparatus was likely to be so used as to infringe copyright, or

(b) in the case of apparatus whose normal use involves a public performance, playing or showing, he did not believe on reasonable grounds that it would not be so used as to infringe copyright.

(3) An occupier of premises who gave permission for the apparatus to be brought onto the premises is liable for the infringement if when he gave permission he knew or had reason to believe that the apparatus was likely to be so used as to infringe copyright.

(4) A person who supplied a copy of a sound recording or film used to infringe copyright is liable for the infringement if when he supplied it he knew or had reason to believe that what he supplied, or a copy made directly or indirectly from it, was likely to be so used as to infringe copyright.

Infringing copies

27 Meaning of "infringing copy"

(1) In this Part "infringing copy", in relation to a copyright work, shall be construed in accordance with this section.

(2) An article is an infringing copy if its making constituted an infringement of the copyright in the work in question.

(3) An article is also an infringing copy if—

(a) it has been or is proposed to be imported into the United Kingdom, and

(b) its making in the United Kingdom would have constituted an infringement of the copyright in the work in question, or a breach of an exclusive licence agreement relating to that work.

(4) Where in any proceedings the question arises whether an article is an infringing copy and it is shown—

(a) that the article is a copy of the work, and

(b) that copyright subsists in the work or has subsisted at any time,

it shall be presumed until the contrary is proved that the article was made at a time when copyright subsisted in the work.

(5) Nothing in subsection (3) shall be construed as applying to an article which may lawfully be imported into the United Kingdom by virtue of any enforceable Community right within the meaning of section 2(1) of the European Communities Act 1972.

(6) In this Part "infringing copy" includes a copy falling to be treated as an infringing copy by virtue of any of the following provisions—

section 32(5) (copies made for purposes of instruction or examination),

section 35(3) (recordings made by educational establishments for educational purposes),

section 36(5) (reprographic copying by educational establishments for purposes of instruction),

section 37(3)(b) (copies made by librarian or archivist in reliance on false declaration),

section 56(2) (further copies, adaptations, &c. of work in electronic form retained on transfer of principal copy),

section 63(2) (copies made for purpose of advertising artistic work for sale),

section 68(4) (copies made for purpose of broadcast or cable programme), or

any provision of an order under section 141 (statutory licence for certain reprographic copying by educational establishments).

CHAPTER III

ACTS PERMITTED IN RELATION TO COPYRIGHT WORKS

Introductory

28 Introductory provisions

(1) The provisions of this Chapter specify acts which may be done in relation to copyright works notwithstanding the subsistence of copyright; they relate only to the question of infringement of copyright and do not affect any other right or obligation restricting the doing of any of the specified acts.

(2) Where it is provided by this Chapter that an act does not infringe copyright, or may be done without infringing copyright, and no particular description of copyright work is mentioned, the act in question does not infringe the copyright in a work of any description.

(3) No inference shall be drawn from the description of any act which may by virtue of this Chapter be done without infringing copyright as to the scope of the acts restricted by the copyright in any description of work.

(4) The provisions of this Chapter are to be construed independently of each other, so that the fact that an act does not fall within one provision does not mean that it is not covered by another provision.

General

29 Research and private study

(1) Fair dealing with a literary, dramatic, musical or artistic work for the purposes of research or private study does not infringe any copyright in the work or, in the case of a published edition, in the typographical arrangement.

(2) Fair dealing with the typographical arrangement of a published edition for the purposes mentioned in subsection (1) does not infringe any copyright in the arrangement.

(3) Copying by a person other than the researcher or student himself is not fair dealing if—

(a) in the case of a librarian, or a person acting on behalf of a librarian, he does anything which regulations under section 40 would not permit to be done under section 38 or 39 (articles or parts of published works: restriction on multiple copies of same material), or

(b) in any other case, the person doing the copying knows or has reason to believe that it will result in copies of substantially the same material being provided to more than one person at substantially the same time and for substantially the same purpose.

30 Criticism, review and news reporting

(1) Fair dealing with a work for the purpose of criticism or review, of that or another work or of a performance of a work, does not infringe any copyright in the work provided that it is accompanied by a sufficient acknowledgement.

(2) Fair dealing with a work (other than a photograph) for the purpose of reporting current events does not infringe any copyright in the work provided that (subject to subsection (3)) it is accompanied by a sufficient acknowledgement.

(3) No acknowledgement is required in connection with the reporting of current events by means of a sound recording, film, broadcast or cable programme.

31 Incidental inclusion of copyright material

(1) Copyright in a work is not infringed by its incidental inclusion in an artistic work, sound recording, film, broadcast or cable programme.

(2) Nor is the copyright infringed by the issue to the public of copies, or the playing, showing, broadcasting or inclusion in a cable programme service, of anything whose making was, by virtue of subsection (1), not an infringement of the copyright.

(3) A musical work, words spoken or sung with music, or so much of a sound recording, broadcast or cable programme as includes a musical work or such words, shall not be regarded as incidentally included in another work if it is deliberately included.

Education

32 Things done for purposes of instruction or examination

(1) Copyright in a literary, dramatic, musical or artistic work is not infringed by its being copied in the course of instruction or of preparation for instruction, provided the copying—

(a) is done by a person giving or receiving instruction, and

(b) is not by means of a reprographic process.

(2) Copyright in a sound recording, film, broadcast or cable programme is not infringed by its being copied by making a film or film sound-track in the course of instruction, or of preparation for instruction, in the making of films or film sound-tracks, provided the copying is done by a person giving or receiving instruction.

(3) Copyright is not infringed by anything done for the purposes of an examination by way of setting the questions, communicating the questions to the candidates or answering the questions.

(4) Subsection (3) does not extend to the making of a reprographic copy of a musical work for use by an examination candidate in performing the work.

(5) Where a copy which would otherwise be an infringing copy is made in accordance with this section but is subsequently dealt with, it shall be treated as an infringing copy for the purpose of that dealing, and if that dealing infringes copyright for all subsequent purposes.

For this purpose "dealt with" means sold or let for hire or offered or exposed for sale or hire.

33 Anthologies for educational use

(1) The inclusion of a short passage from a published literary or dramatic work in a collection which—

(a) is intended for use in educational establishments and is so described in its title, and in any advertisements issued by or on behalf of the publisher, and

(b) consists mainly of material in which no copyright subsists,

does not infringe the copyright in the work if the work itself is not intended for use in such establishments and the inclusion is accompanied by a sufficient acknowledgement.

(2) Subsection (1) does not authorise the inclusion of more than two excerpts from copyright works by the same author in collections published by the same publisher over any period of five years.

(3) In relation to any given passage the reference in subsection (2) to excerpts from works by the same author—

(a) shall be taken to include excerpts from works by him in collaboration with another, and

(b) if the passage in question is from such a work, shall be taken to include excerpts from works by any of the authors, whether alone or in collaboration with another.

(4) References in this section to the use of a work in an educational establishment are to any use for the educational purposes of such an establishment.

34 Performing, playing or showing work in course of activities of educational establishment

(1) The performance of a literary, dramatic or musical work before an audience consisting of teachers and pupils at an educational establishment and other persons directly connected with the activities of the establishment—

(a) by a teacher or pupil in the course of the activities of the establishment, or

(b) at the establishment by any person for the purposes of instruction,

is not a public performance for the purposes of infringement of copyright.

(2) The playing or showing of a sound recording, film, broadcast or cable programme before such an audience at an educational establishment for the purposes of instruction is not a playing or showing of the work in public for the purposes of infringement of copyright.

(3) A person is not for this purpose directly connected with the activities of the educational establishment simply because he is the parent of a pupil at the establishment.

35 Recording by educational establishments of broadcasts and cable programmes

(1) A recording of a broadcast or cable programme, or a copy of such a recording, may be made by or on behalf of an educational establishment for the educational purposes of that establishment without thereby infringing the copyright in the broadcast or cable programme, or in any work included in it.

(2) This section does not apply if or to the extent that there is a licensing scheme certified for the purposes of this section under section 143 providing for the grant of licences.

(3) Where a copy which would otherwise be an infringing copy is made in accordance with this section but is subsequently dealt with, it shall be treated as an infringing copy for the purposes of that dealing, and if that dealing infringes copyright for all subsequent purposes.

For this purpose "dealt with" means sold or let for hire or offered or exposed for sale or hire.

36 Reprographic copying by educational establishments of passages from published works

(1) Reprographic copies of passages from published literary, dramatic or musical works may, to the extent permitted by this section, be made by or on behalf of an educational establishment for the purposes of instruction without infringing any copyright in the work, or in the typographical arrangement.

(2) Not more than one per cent. of any work may be copied by or on behalf of an establishment by virtue of this section in any quarter, that is, in any period 1st January to 31st March, 1st April to 30th June, 1st July to 30th September or 1st October to 31st December.

(3) Copying is not authorised by this section if, or to the extent that, licences are available authorising the copying in question and the person making the copies knew or ought to have been aware of that fact.

(4) The terms of a licence granted to an educational establishment authorising the reprographic copying for the purposes of instruction of passages from published literary, dramatic or musical works are of no effect so far as they purport to restrict the proportion of a work which may be copied (whether on payment or free of charge) to less than that which would be permitted under this section.

(5) Where a copy which would otherwise be an infringing copy is made in accordance with this section but is subsequently dealt with, it shall be treated as an infringing copy for the purposes of that dealing, and if that dealing infringes copyright for all subsequent purposes.

For this purpose "dealt with" means sold or let for hire or offered or exposed for sale or hire.

Libraries and archives

37 Libraries and archives: introductory

(1) In sections 38 to 43 (copying by librarians and archivists)—
- (a) references in any provision to a prescribed library or archive are to a library or archive of a description prescribed for the purposes of that provision by regulations made by the Secretary of State; and
- (b) references in any provision to the prescribed conditions are to the conditions so prescribed.

(2) The regulations may provide that, where a librarian or archivist is required to be satisfied as to any matter before making or supplying a copy of a work—
- (a) he may rely on a signed declaration as to that matter by the person requesting the copy, unless he is aware that it is false in a material particular, and
- (b) in such cases as may be prescribed, he shall not make or supply a copy in the absence of a signed declaration in such form as may be prescribed.

(3) Where a person requesting a copy makes a declaration which is false in a material particular and is supplied with a copy which would have been an infringing copy if made by him—
- (a) he is liable for infringement of copyright as if he had made the copy himself, and
- (b) the copy shall be treated as an infringing copy.

(4) The regulations may make different provision for different descriptions of libraries or archives and for different purposes.

(5) Regulations shall be made by statutory instrument which shall be subject to annulment in pursuance of a resolution of either House of Parliament.

(6) References in this section, and in sections 38 to 43, to the librarian or archivist include a person acting on his behalf.

38 Copying by librarians: articles in periodicals

(1) The librarian of a prescribed library may, if the prescribed conditions are complied with, make and supply a copy of an article in a periodical without infringing any copyright in the text, in any illustrations accompanying the text or in the typographical arrangement.

(2) The prescribed conditions shall include the following—

(a) that copies are supplied only to persons satisfying the librarian that they require them for purposes of research or private study, and will not use them for any other purpose;

(b) that no person is furnished with more than one copy of the same article or with copies of more than one article contained in the same issue of a periodical; and

(c) that persons to whom copies are supplied are required to pay for them a sum not less than the cost (including a contribution to the general expenses of the library) attributable to their production.

39 Copying by librarians: parts of published works

(1) The librarian of a prescribed library may, if the prescribed conditions are complied with, make and supply from a published edition a copy of part of a literary, dramatic or musical work (other than an article in a periodical) without infringing any copyright in the work, in any illustrations accompanying the work or in the typographical arrangement.

(2) The prescribed conditions shall include the following—

(a) that copies are supplied only to persons satisfying the librarian that they require them for purposes of research or private study, and will not use them for any other purpose;

(b) that no person is furnished with more than one copy of the same material or with a copy of more than a reasonable proportion of any work; and

(c) that persons to whom copies are supplied are required to pay for them a sum not less than the cost (including a contribution to the general expenses of the library) attributable to their production.

40 Restriction on production of multiple copies of the same material

(1) Regulations for the purposes of sections 38 and 39 (copying by librarian of article or part of published work) shall contain provision to the effect that a copy shall be supplied only to a person satisfying the librarian that his requirement is not related to any similar requirement of another person.

(2) The regulations may provide—

(a) that requirements shall be regarded as similar if the requirements are for copies of substantially the same material at substantially the same time and for substantially the same purpose; and

(b) that requirements of persons shall be regarded as related if those persons receive instruction to which the material is relevant at the same time and place.

41 Copying by librarians: supply of copies to other libraries

(1) The librarian of a prescribed library may, if the prescribed conditions are complied with, make and supply to another prescribed library a copy of—

(a) an article in a periodical, or

(b) the whole or part of a published edition of a literary, dramatic or musical work,

without infringing any copyright in the text of the article or, as the case may be, in the work, in any illustrations accompanying it or in the typographical arrangement.

(2) Subsection (1)(b) does not apply if at the time the copy is made the librarian making it knows, or could by reasonable inquiry ascertain, the name and address of a person entitled to authorise the making of the copy.

42 Copying by librarians or archivists: replacement copies of works

(1) The librarian or archivist of a prescribed library or archive may, if the prescribed conditions are complied with, make a copy from any item in the permanent collection of the library or archive—

(a) in order to preserve or replace that item by placing the copy in its permanent collection in addition to or in place of it, or

(b) in order to replace in the permanent collection of another prescribed library or archive an item which has been lost, destroyed or damaged,

without infringing the copyright in any literary, dramatic or musical work, in any illustrations accompanying such a work or, in the case of a published edition, in the typographical arrangement.

(2) The prescribed conditions shall include provision for restricting the making of copies to cases where it is not reasonably practicable to purchase a copy of the item in question to fulfil that purpose.

43 Copying by librarians or archivists: certain unpublished works

(1) The librarian or archivist of a prescribed library or archive may, if the prescribed conditions are complied with, make and supply a copy of the whole or part of a literary, dramatic or musical work from a document in the library or archive without infringing any copyright in the work or any illustrations accompanying it.

(2) This section does not apply if—

(a) the work had been published before the document was deposited in the library or archive, or

(b) the copyright owner has prohibited copying of the work,

and at the time the copy is made the librarian or archivist making it is, or ought to be, aware of that fact.

(3) The prescribed conditions shall include the following—

(a) that copies are supplied only to persons satisfying the librarian or archivist that they require them for purposes of research or private study and will not use them for any other purpose;

(b) that no person is furnished with more than one copy of the same material; and

(c) that persons to whom copies are supplied are required to pay for them a sum not less than the cost (including a contribution to the general expenses of the library or archive) attributable to their production.

44 Copy of work required to be made as condition of export

If an article of cultural or historical importance or interest cannot lawfully be exported from the United Kingdom unless a copy of it is made and deposited in an appropriate library or archive, it is not an infringement of copyright to make that copy.

Public administration

45 Parliamentary and judicial proceedings

(1) Copyright is not infringed by anything done for the purposes of parliamentary or judicial proceedings.

(2) Copyright is not infringed by anything done for the purposes of reporting such proceedings; but this shall not be construed as authorising the copying of a work which is itself a published report of the proceedings.

46 Royal Commissions and statutory inquiries

(1) Copyright is not infringed by anything done for the purposes of the proceedings of a Royal Commission or statutory inquiry.

(2) Copyright is not infringed by anything done for the purpose of reporting any such proceedings held in public; but this shall not be construed as authorising the copying of a work which is itself a published report of the proceedings.

(3) Copyright in a work is not infringed by the issue to the public of copies of the report of a Royal Commission or statutory inquiry containing the work or material from it.

(4) In this section—

"Royal Commission" includes a Commission appointed for Northern Ireland by the Secretary of State in pursuance of the prerogative powers of Her Majesty delegated to him under section 7(2) of the Northern Ireland Constitution Act 1973; and

"statutory inquiry" means an inquiry held or investigation conducted in pursuance of a duty imposed or power conferred by or under an enactment.

47 Material open to public inspection or on official register

(1) Where material is open to public inspection pursuant to a statutory requirement, or is on a statutory register, any copyright in the material as a literary work is not infringed by the copying of so much of the material as contains factual information of any description, by or with the authority of the appropriate person, for a purpose which does not involve the issuing of copies to the public.

(2) Where material is open to public inspection pursuant to a statutory requirement, copyright is not infringed by the copying or issuing to the public of copies of the material, by or with the authority of the appropriate person, for the purpose of enabling the material to be inspected at a more convenient time or place or otherwise facilitating the exercise of any right for the purpose of which the requirement is imposed.

(3) Where material which is open to public inspection pursuant to a statutory requirement, or which is on a statutory register, contains information about matters of general scientific, technical, commercial or economic interest, copyright is not infringed by

the copying or issuing to the public of copies of the material, by or with the authority of the appropriate person, for the purpose of disseminating that information.

(4) The Secretary of State may by order provide that subsection (1), (2) or (3) shall, in such cases as may be specified in the order, apply only to copies marked in such manner as may be so specified.

(5) The Secretary of State may by order provide that subsections (1) to (3) apply, to such extent and with such modifications as may be specified in the order—

(a) to material made open to public inspection by—

(i) an international organisation specified in the order, or

(ii) a person so specified who has functions in the United Kingdom under an international agreement to which the United Kingdom is party, or

(b) to a register maintained by an international organisation specified in the order,

as they apply in relation to material open to public inspection pursuant to a statutory requirement or to a statutory register.

(6) In this section—

"appropriate person" means the person required to make the material open to public inspection or, as the case may be, the person maintaining the register;

"statutory register" means a register maintained in pursuance of a statutory requirement; and

"statutory requirement" means a requirement imposed by provision made by or under an enactment.

(7) An order under this section shall be made by statutory instrument which shall be subject to annulment in pursuance of a resolution of either House of Parliament.

48 Material communicated to the Crown in the course of public business

(1) This section applies where a literary, dramatic, musical or artistic work has in the course of public business been communicated to the Crown for any purpose, by or with the licence of the copyright owner and a document or other material thing recording or embodying the work is owned by or in the custody or control of the Crown.

(2) The Crown may, for the purpose for which the work was communicated to it, or any related purpose which could reasonably have been anticipated by the copyright owner, copy the work and issue copies of the work to the public without infringing any copyright in the work.

(3) The Crown may not copy a work, or issue copies of a work to the public, by virtue of this section if the work has previously been published otherwise than by virtue of this section.

(4) In subsection (1) "public business" includes any activity carried on by the Crown.

(5) This section has effect subject to any agreement to the contrary between the Crown and the copyright owner.

49 Public records

Material which is comprised in public records within the meaning of the Public Records Act 1958, the Public Records (Scotland) Act 1937 or the Public Records Act (Northern Ireland) 1923 which are open to public inspection in pursuance of that Act, may be copied, and a copy may be supplied to any person, by or with the authority of any officer appointed under that Act, without infringement of copyright.

50 Acts done under statutory authority

(1) Where the doing of a particular act is specifically authorised by an Act of Parliament, whenever passed, then, unless the Act provides otherwise, the doing of that act does not infringe copyright.

(2) Subsection (1) applies in relation to an enactment contained in Northern Ireland legislation as it applies in relation to an Act of Parliament.

(3) Nothing in this section shall be construed as excluding any defence of statutory authority otherwise available under or by virtue of any enactment.

Designs

51 Design documents and models

(1) It is not an infringement of any copyright in a design document or model recording or embodying a design for anything other than an artistic work or a typeface to make an article to the design or to copy an article made to the design.

(2) Nor is it an infringement of the copyright to issue to the public, or include in a film, broadcast or cable programme service, anything the making of which was, by virtue of subsection (1), not an infringement of that copyright.

(3) In this section—

"design" means the design of any aspect of the shape or configuration (whether internal or external) of the whole or part of an article, other than surface decoration; and

"design document" means any record of a design, whether in the form of a drawing, a written description, a photograph, data stored in a computer or otherwise.

52 Effect of exploitation of design derived from artistic work

(1) This section applies where an artistic work has been exploited, by or with the licence of the copyright owner, by—

(a) making by an industrial process articles falling to be treated for the purposes of this Part as copies of the work, and

(b) marketing such articles, in the United Kingdom or elsewhere.

(2) After the end of the period of 25 years from the end of the calendar year in which such articles are first marketed, the work may be copied by making articles of any description, or doing anything for the purpose of making articles of any description, and anything may be done in relation to articles so made, without infringing copyright in the work.

(3) Where only part of an artistic work is exploited as mentioned in subsection (1), subsection (2) applies only in relation to that part.

(4) The Secretary of State may by order make provision—

(a) as to the circumstances in which an article, or any description of article, is to be regarded for the purposes of this section as made by an industrial process;

(b) excluding from the operation of this section such articles of a primarily literary or artistic character as he thinks fit.

(5) An order shall be made by statutory instrument which shall be subject to annulment in pursuance of a resolution of either House of Parliament.

(6) In this section—

(a) references to articles do not include films; and

(b) references to the marketing of an article are to its being sold or let for hire or offered or exposed for sale or hire.

53 Things done in reliance on registration of design

(1) The copyright in an artistic work is not infringed by anything done—

(a) in pursuance of an assignment or licence made or granted by a person registered under the Registered Designs Act 1949 as the proprietor of a corresponding design, and

(b) in good faith in reliance on the registration and without notice of any proceedings for the cancellation of the registration or for rectifying the relevant entry in the register of designs;

and this is so notwithstanding that the person registered as the proprietor was not the proprietor of the design for the purposes of the 1949 Act.

(2) In subsection (1) a "corresponding design", in relation to an artistic work, means a design within the meaning of the 1949 Act which if applied to an article would produce something which would be treated for the purposes of this Part as a copy of the artistic work.

Typefaces

54 Use of typeface in ordinary course of printing

(1) It is not an infringement of copyright in an artistic work consisting of the design of a typeface—

(a) to use the typeface in the ordinary course of typing, composing text, typesetting or printing,

(b) to possess an article for the purpose of such use, or

(c) to do anything in relation to material produced by such use;

and this is so notwithstanding that an article is used which is an infringing copy of the work.

(2) However, the following provisions of this Part apply in relation to persons making, importing or dealing with articles specifically designed or adapted for producing material in a particular typeface, or possessing such articles for the purpose of dealing with them, as if the production of material as mentioned in subsection (1) did infringe copyright in the artistic work consisting of the design of the typeface—

section 24 (secondary infringement: making, importing, possessing or dealing with article for making infringing copy),

sections 99 and 100 (order for delivery up and right of seizure),

section 107(2) (offence of making or possessing such an article), and
section 108 (order for delivery up in criminal proceedings).

(3) The references in subsection (2) to "dealing with" an article are to selling, letting for hire, or offering or exposing for sale or hire, exhibiting in public, or distributing.

55 Articles for producing material in particular typeface

(1) This section applies to the copyright in an artistic work consisting of the design of a typeface where articles specifically designed or adapted for producing material in that typeface have been marketed by or with the licence of the copyright owner.

(2) After the period of 25 years from the end of the calendar year in which the first such articles are marketed, the work may be copied by making further such articles, or doing anything for the purpose of making such articles, and anything may be done in relation to articles so made, without infringing copyright in the work.

(3) In subsection (1) "marketed" means sold, let for hire or offered or exposed for sale or hire, in the United Kingdom or elsewhere.

Works in electronic form

56 Transfers of copies of works in electronic form

(1) This section applies where a copy of a work in electronic form has been purchased on terms which, expressly or impliedly or by virtue of any rule of law, allow the purchaser to copy the work, or to adapt it or make copies of an adaptation, in connection with his use of it.

(2) If there are no express terms—

(a) prohibiting the transfer of the copy by the purchaser, imposing obligations which continue after a transfer, prohibiting the assignment of any licence or terminating any licence on a transfer, or

(b) providing for the terms on which a transferee may do the things which the purchaser was permitted to do,

anything which the purchaser was allowed to do may also be done without infringement of copyright by a transferee; but any copy, adaptation or copy of an adaptation made by the purchaser which is not also transferred shall be treated as an infringing copy for all purposes after the transfer.

(3) The same applies where the original purchased copy is no longer usable and what is transferred is a further copy used in its place.

(4) The above provisions also apply on a subsequent transfer, with the substitution for references in subsection (2) to the purchaser of references to the subsequent transferor.

Miscellaneous: literary, dramatic, musical and artistic works

57 Anonymous or pseudonymous works: acts permitted on assumptions as to expiry of copyright or death of author

(1) Copyright in a literary, dramatic, musical or artistic work is not infringed by an act done at a time when, or in pursuance of arrangements made at a time when—

(a) it is not possible by reasonable inquiry to ascertain the identity of the author, and

(b) it is reasonable to assume—

(i) that copyright has expired, or

(ii) that the author died 50 years or more before the beginning of the calendar year in which the act is done or the arrangements are made.

(2) Subsection (1)(b)(ii) does not apply in relation to—

(a) a work in which Crown copyright subsists, or

(b) a work in which copyright originally vested in an international organisation by virtue of section 168 and in respect of which an Order under that section specifies a copyright period longer than 50 years.

(3) In relation to a work of joint authorship—

(a) the reference in subsection (1) to its being possible to ascertain the identity of the author shall be construed as a reference to its being possible to ascertain the identity of any of the authors, and

(b) the reference in subsection (1)(b)(ii) to the author having died shall be construed as a reference to all the authors having died.

58 Use of notes or recordings of spoken words in certain cases

(1) Where a record of spoken words is made, in writing or otherwise, for the purpose—

(a) of reporting current events, or

(b) of broadcasting or including in a cable programme service the whole or part of the work,

it is not an infringement of any copyright in the words as a literary work to use the record or material taken from it (or to copy the record, or any such material, and use the copy) for that purpose, provided the following conditions are met.

(2) The conditions are that—

(a) the record is a direct record of the spoken words and is not taken from a previous record or from a broadcast or cable programme;

(b) the making of the record was not prohibited by the speaker and, where copyright already subsisted in the work, did not infringe copyright;

(c) the use made of the record or material taken from it is not of a kind prohibited by or on behalf of the speaker or copyright owner before the record was made; and

(d) the use is by or with the authority of a person who is lawfully in possession of the record.

59 Public reading or recitation

(1) The reading or recitation in public by one person of a reasonable extract from a published literary or dramatic work does not infringe any copyright in the work if it is accompanied by a sufficient acknowledgement.

(2) Copyright in a work is not infringed by the making of a sound recording, or the broadcasting or inclusion in a cable programme service, of a reading or recitation which by virtue of subsection (1) does not infringe copyright in the work, provided that the recording, broadcast or cable programme consists mainly of material in relation to which it is not necessary to rely on that subsection.

60 Abstracts of scientific or technical articles

(1) Where an article on a scientific or technical subject is published in a periodical accompanied by an abstract indicating the contents of the article, it is not an infringement of copyright in the abstract, or in the article, to copy the abstract or issue copies of it to the public.

(2) This section does not apply if or to the extent that there is a licensing scheme certified for the purposes of this section under section 143 providing for the grant of licences.

61 Recordings of folksongs

(1) A sound recording of a performance of a song may be made for the purpose of including it in an archive maintained by a designated body without infringing any copyright in the words as a literary work or in the accompanying musical work, provided the conditions in subsection (2) below are met.

(2) The conditions are that—
- (a) the words are unpublished and of unknown authorship at the time the recording is made,
- (b) the making of the recording does not infringe any other copyright, and
- (c) its making is not prohibited by any performer.

(3) Copies of a sound recording made in reliance on subsection (1) and included in an archive maintained by a designated body may, if the prescribed conditions are met, be made and supplied by the archivist without infringing copyright in the recording or the works included in it.

(4) The prescribed conditions shall include the following—
- (a) that copies are only supplied to persons satisfying the archivist that they require them for purposes of research or private study and will not use them for any other purpose, and
- (b) that no person is furnished with more than one copy of the same recording.

(5) In this section—
- (a) "designated" means designated for the purposes of this section by order of the Secretary of State, who shall not designate a body unless satisfied that it is not established or conducted for profit,
- (b) "prescribed" means prescribed for the purposes of this section by order of the Secretary of State, and
- (c) references to the archivist include a person acting on his behalf.

(6) An order under this section shall be made by statutory instrument which shall be subject to annulment in pursuance of a resolution of either House of Parliament.

62 Representation of certain artistic works on public display

(1) This section applies to—

(a) buildings, and

(b) sculptures, models for buildings and works of artistic craftsmanship, if permanently situated in a public place or in premises open to the public.

(2) The copyright in such a work is not infringed by—

(a) making a graphic work representing it,

(b) making a photograph or film of it, or

(c) broadcasting or including in a cable programme service a visual image of it.

(3) Nor is the copyright infringed by the issue to the public of copies, or the broadcasting or inclusion in a cable programme service, of anything whose making was, by virtue of this section, not an infringement of the copyright.

63 Advertisement of sale of artistic work

(1) It is not an infringement of copyright in an artistic work to copy it, or to issue copies to the public, for the purpose of advertising the sale of the work.

(2) Where a copy which would otherwise be an infringing copy is made in accordance with this section but is subsequently dealt with for any other purpose, it shall be treated as an infringing copy for the purposes of that dealing, and if that dealing infringes copyright for all subsequent purposes.

For this purpose "dealt with" means sold or let for hire, offered or exposed for sale or hire, exhibited in public or distributed.

64 Making of subsequent works by same artist

Where the author of an artistic work is not the copyright owner, he does not infringe the copyright by copying the work in making another artistic work, provided he does not repeat or imitate the main design of the earlier work.

65 Reconstruction of buildings

Anything done for the purposes of reconstructing a building does not infringe any copyright—

(a) in the building, or

(b) in any drawings or plans in accordance with which the building was, by or with the licence of the copyright owner, constructed.

Miscellaneous: sound recordings, films and computer programs

66 Rental of sound recordings, films and computer programs

(1) The Secretary of State may by order provide that in such cases as may be specified in the order the rental to the public of copies of sound recordings, films or computer programs shall be treated as licensed by the copyright owner subject only to the payment of such reasonable royalty or other payment as may be agreed or determined in default of agreement by the Copyright Tribunal.

(2) No such order shall apply if, or to the extent that, there is a licensing scheme certified for the purposes of this section under section 143 providing for the grant of licences.

(3) An order may make different provision for different cases and may specify cases by reference to any factor relating to the work, the copies rented, the renter or the circumstances of the rental.

(4) An order shall be made by statutory instrument; and no order shall be made unless a draft of it has been laid before and approved by a resolution of each House of Parliament.

(5) Copyright in a computer program is not infringed by the rental of copies to the public after the end of the period of 50 years from the end of the calendar year in which copies of it were first issued to the public in electronic form.

(6) Nothing in this section affects any liability under section 23 (secondary infringement) in respect of the rental of infringing copies.

67 Playing of sound recordings for purposes of club, society, &c

(1) It is not an infringement of the copyright in a sound recording to play it as part of the activities of, or for the benefit of, a club, society or other organisation if the following conditions are met.

(2) The conditions are—

- (a) that the organisation is not established or conducted for profit and its main objects are charitable or are otherwise concerned with the advancement of religion, education or social welfare, and
- (b) that the proceeds of any charge for admission to the place where the recording is to be heard are applied solely for the purposes of the organisation.

Miscellaneous: broadcasts and cable programmes

68 Incidental recording for purposes of broadcast or cable programme

(1) This section applies where by virtue of a licence or assignment of copyright a person is authorised to broadcast or include in a cable programme service—

- (a) a literary, dramatic or musical work, or an adaptation of such a work,
- (b) an artistic work, or
- (c) a sound recording or film.

(2) He shall by virtue of this section be treated as licensed by the owner of the copyright in the work to do or authorise any of the following for the purposes of the broadcast or cable programme—

(a) in the case of a literary, dramatic or musical work, or an adaptation of such a work, to make a sound recording or film of the work or adaptation;

(b) in the case of an artistic work, to take a photograph or make a film of the work;

(c) in the case of a sound recording or film, to make a copy of it.

(3) That licence is subject to the condition that the recording, film, photograph or copy in question—

(a) shall not be used for any other purpose, and

(b) shall be destroyed within 28 days of being first used for broadcasting the work or, as the case may be, including it in a cable programme service.

(4) A recording, film, photograph or copy made in accordance with this section shall be treated as an infringing copy—

(a) for the purposes of any use in breach of the condition mentioned in subsection (3)(a), and

(b) for all purposes after that condition or the condition mentioned in subsection (3)(b) is broken.

69 Recording for purposes of supervision and control of broadcasts and cable programmes

(1) Copyright is not infringed by the making or use by the British Broadcasting Corporation, for the purpose of maintaining supervision and control over programmes broadcast by them, of recordings of those programmes.

(2) Copyright is not infringed by—

(a) the making or use of recordings by the Independent Broadcasting Authority for the purposes mentioned in section 4(7) of the Broadcasting Act 1981 (maintenance of supervision and control over programmes and advertisements); or

(b) anything done under or in pursuance of provision included in a contract between a programme contractor and the Authority in accordance with section 21 of that Act.

(3) Copyright is not infringed by—

(a) the making by or with the authority of the Cable Authority, or the use by that Authority, for the purpose of maintaining supervision and control over programmes included in services licensed under Part I of the Cable and Broadcasting Act 1984, of recordings of those programmes; or

(b) anything done under or in pursuance of—

(i) a notice or direction given under section 16 of the Cable and Broadcasting Act 1984 (power of Cable Authority to require production of recordings); or

(ii) a condition included in a licence by virtue of section 35 of that Act (duty of Authority to secure that recordings are available for certain purposes).

70 Recording for purposes of time-shifting

The making for private and domestic use of a recording of a broadcast or cable programme solely for the purpose of enabling it to be viewed or listened to at a more convenient time does not infringe any copyright in the broadcast or cable programme or in any work included in it.

71 Photographs of television broadcasts or cable programmes

The making for private and domestic use of a photograph of the whole or any part of an image forming part of a television broadcast or cable programme, or a copy of such a photograph, does not infringe any copyright in the broadcast or cable programme or in any film included in it.

72 Free public showing or playing of broadcast or cable programme

(1) The showing or playing in public of a broadcast or cable programme to an audience who have not paid for admission to the place where the broadcast or programme is to be seen or heard does not infringe any copyright in—

(a) the broadcast or cable programme, or

(b) any sound recording or film included in it.

(2) The audience shall be treated as having paid for admission to a place—

(a) if they have paid for admission to a place of which that place forms part; or

(b) if goods or services are supplied at that place (or a place of which it forms part)—

(i) at prices which are substantially attributable to the facilities afforded for seeing or hearing the broadcast or programme, or

(ii) at prices exceeding those usually charged there and which are partly attributable to those facilities.

(3) The following shall not be regarded as having paid for admission to a place—

(a) persons admitted as residents or inmates of the place;

(b) persons admitted as members of a club or society where the payment is only for membership of the club or society and the provision of facilities for seeing or hearing broadcasts or programmes is only incidental to the main purposes of the club or society.

(4) Where the making of the broadcast or inclusion of the programme in a cable programme service was an infringement of the copyright in a sound recording or film, the fact that it was heard or seen in public by the reception of the broadcast or programme shall be taken into account in assessing the damages for that infringement.

73 Reception and re-transmission of broadcast in cable programme service

(1) This section applies where a broadcast made from a place in the United Kingdom is, by reception and immediate re-transmission, included in a cable programme service.

(2) The copyright in the broadcast is not infringed—

(a) if the inclusion is in pursuance of a requirement imposed under section 13(1) of the Cable and Broadcasting Act 1984 (duty of Cable Authority to secure inclusion in cable service of certain programmes), or

(b) if and to the extent that the broadcast is made for reception in the area in which the cable programme service is provided and is not a satellite transmission or an encrypted transmission.

(3) The copyright in any work included in the broadcast is not infringed—

(a) if the inclusion is in pursuance of a requirement imposed under section 13(1) of the Cable and Broadcasting Act 1984 (duty of Cable Authority to secure inclusion in cable service of certain programmes), or

(b) if and to the extent that the broadcast is made for reception in the area in which the cable programme service is provided;

but where the making of the broadcast was an infringement of the copyright in the work, the fact that the broadcast was re-transmitted as a programme in a cable programme service shall be taken into account in assessing the damages for that infringement.

74 Provision of sub-titled copies of broadcast or cable programme

(1) A designated body may, for the purpose of providing people who are deaf or hard of hearing, or physically or mentally handicapped in other ways, with copies which are sub-titled or otherwise modified for their special needs, make copies of television broadcasts or cable programmes and issue copies to the public, without infringing any copyright in the broadcasts or cable programmes or works included in them.

(2) A "designated body" means a body designated for the purposes of this section by order of the Secretary of State, who shall not designate a body unless he is satisfied that it is not established or conducted for profit.

(3) An order under this section shall be made by statutory instrument which shall be subject to annulment in pursuance of a resolution of either House of Parliament.

(4) This section does not apply if, or to the extent that, there is a licensing scheme certified for the purposes of this section under section 143 providing for the grant of licences.

75 Recording for archival purposes

(1) A recording of a broadcast or cable programme of a designated class, or a copy of such a recording, may be made for the purpose of being placed in an archive maintained by a designated body without thereby infringing any copyright in the broadcast or cable programme or in any work included in it.

(2) In subsection (1) "designated" means designated for the purposes of this section by order of the Secretary of State, who shall not designate a body unless he is satisfied that it is not established or conducted for profit.

(3) An order under this section shall be made by statutory instrument which shall be subject to annulment in pursuance of a resolution of either House of Parliament.

Adaptations

76 Adaptations

An act which by virtue of this Chapter may be done without infringing copyright in a literary, dramatic or musical work does not, where that work is an adaptation, infringe any copyright in the work from which the adaptation was made.

CHAPTER IV

MORAL RIGHTS

Right to be identified as author or director

77 Right to be identified as author or director

(1) The author of a copyright literary, dramatic, musical or artistic work, and the director of a copyright film, has the right to be identified as the author or director of the work in the circumstances mentioned in this section; but the right is not infringed unless it has been asserted in accordance with section 78.

(2) The author of a literary work (other than words intended to be sung or spoken with music) or a dramatic work has the right to be identified whenever—

(a) the work is published commercially, performed in public, broadcast or included in a cable programme service; or

(b) copies of a film or sound recording including the work are issued to the public;

and that right includes the right to be identified whenever any of those events occur in relation to an adaptation of the work as the author of the work from which the adaptation was made.

(3) The author of a musical work, or a literary work consisting of words intended to be sung or spoken with music, has the right to be identified whenever—

(a) the work is published commercially;

(b) copies of a sound recording of the work are issued to the public; or

(c) a film of which the sound-track includes the work is shown in public or copies of such a film are issued to the public;

and that right includes the right to be identified whenever any of those events occur in relation to an adaptation of the work as the author of the work from which the adaptation was made.

(4) The author of an artistic work has the right to be identified whenever—

(a) the work is published commercially or exhibited in public, or a visual image of it is broadcast or included in a cable programme service;

(b) a film including a visual image of the work is shown in public or copies of such a film are issued to the public; or

(c) in the case of a work of architecture in the form of a building or a model for a building, a sculpture or a work of artistic craftsmanship, copies of a graphic work representing it, or of a photograph of it, are issued to the public.

(5) The author of a work of architecture in the form of a building also has the right to be identified on the building as constructed or, where more than one building is constructed to the design, on the first to be constructed.

(6) The director of a film has the right to be identified whenever the film is shown in public, broadcast or included in a cable programme service or copies of the film are issued to the public.

(7) The right of the author or director under this section is—

- (a) in the case of commercial publication or the issue to the public of copies of a film or sound recording, to be identified in or on each copy or, if that is not appropriate, in some other manner likely to bring his identity to the notice of a person acquiring a copy,
- (b) in the case of identification on a building, to be identified by appropriate means visible to persons entering or approaching the building, and
- (c) in any other case, to be identified in a manner likely to bring his identity to the attention of a person seeing or hearing the performance, exhibition, showing, broadcast or cable programme in question;

and the identification must in each case be clear and reasonably prominent.

(8) If the author or director in asserting his right to be identified specifies a pseudonym, initials or some other particular form of identification, that form shall be used; otherwise any reasonable form of identification may be used.

(9) This section has effect subject to section 79 (exceptions to right).

78 Requirement that right be asserted

(1) A person does not infringe the right conferred by section 77 (right to be identified as author or director) by doing any of the acts mentioned in that section unless the right has been asserted in accordance with the following provisions so as to bind him in relation to that act.

(2) The right may be asserted generally, or in relation to any specified act or description of acts—

- (a) on an assignment of copyright in the work, by including in the instrument effecting the assignment a statement that the author or director asserts in relation to that work his right to be identified, or
- (b) by instrument in writing signed by the author or director.

(3) The right may also be asserted in relation to the public exhibition of an artistic work—

- (a) by securing that when the author or other first owner of copyright parts with possession of the original, or of a copy made by him or under his direction or control, the author is identified on the original or copy, or on a frame, mount or other thing to which it is attached, or
- (b) by including in a licence by which the author or other first owner of copyright authorises the making of copies of the work a statement signed by or on behalf of the person granting the licence that the author asserts his right to be identified in the event of the public exhibition of a copy made in pursuance of the licence.

(4) The persons bound by an assertion of the right under subsection (2) or (3) are—

(a) in the case of an assertion under subsection (2)(a), the assignee and anyone claiming through him, whether or not he has notice of the assertion;
(b) in the case of an assertion under subsection (2)(b), anyone to whose notice the assertion is brought;
(c) in the case of an assertion under subsection (3)(a), anyone into whose hands that original or copy comes, whether or not the identification is still present or visible;
(d) in the case of an assertion under subsection (3)(b), the licensee and anyone into whose hands a copy made in pursuance of the licence comes, whether or not he has notice of the assertion.

(5) In an action for infringement of the right the court shall, in considering remedies, take into account any delay in asserting the right.

79 Exceptions to right

(1) The right conferred by section 77 (right to be identified as author or director) is subject to the following exceptions.

(2) The right does not apply in relation to the following descriptions of work—
(a) a computer program;
(b) the design of a typeface;
(c) any computer-generated work.

(3) The right does not apply to anything done by or with the authority of the copyright owner where copyright in the work originally vested—
(a) in the author's employer by virtue of section 11(2) (works produced in course of employment), or
(b) in the director's employer by virtue of section 9(2)(a) (person to be treated as author of film).

(4) The right is not infringed by an act which by virtue of any of the following provisions would not infringe copyright in the work—
(a) section 30 (fair dealing for certain purposes), so far as it relates to the reporting of current events by means of a sound recording, film, broadcast or cable programme;
(b) section 31 (incidental inclusion of work in an artistic work, sound recording, film, broadcast or cable programme);
(c) section 32(3) (examination questions);
(d) section 45 (parliamentary and judicial proceedings);
(e) section 46(1) or (2) (Royal Commissions and statutory inquiries);
(f) section 51 (use of design documents and models);
(g) section 52 (effect of exploitation of design derived from artistic work);
(h) section 57 (anonymous or pseudonymous works: acts permitted on assumptions as to expiry of copyright or death of author).

(5) The right does not apply in relation to any work made for the purpose of reporting current events.

(6) The right does not apply in relation to the publication in—
(a) a newspaper, magazine or similar periodical, or

(b) an encyclopaedia, dictionary, yearbook or other collective work of reference,

of a literary, dramatic, musical or artistic work made for the purposes of such publication or made available with the consent of the author for the purposes of such publication.

(7) The right does not apply in relation to—

(a) a work in which Crown copyright or Parliamentary copyright subsists, or

(b) a work in which copyright originally vested in an international organisation by virtue of section 168,

unless the author or director has previously been identified as such in or on published copies of the work.

Right to object to derogatory treatment of work

80 Right to object to derogatory treatment of work

(1) The author of a copyright literary, dramatic, musical or artistic work, and the director of a copyright film, has the right in the circumstances mentioned in this section not to have his work subjected to derogatory treatment.

(2) For the purposes of this section—

(a) "treatment" of a work means any addition to, deletion from or alteration to or adaptation of the work, other than—

(i) a translation of a literary or dramatic work, or

(ii) an arrangement or transcription of a musical work involving no more than a change of key or register; and

(b) the treatment of a work is derogatory if it amounts to distortion or mutilation of the work or is otherwise prejudicial to the honour or reputation of the author or director;

and in the following provisions of this section references to a derogatory treatment of a work shall be construed accordingly.

(3) In the case of a literary, dramatic or musical work the right is infringed by a person who—

(a) publishes commercially, performs in public, broadcasts or includes in a cable programme service a derogatory treatment of the work; or

(b) issues to the public copies of a film or sound recording of, or including, a derogatory treatment of the work.

(4) In the case of an artistic work the right is infringed by a person who—

(a) publishes commercially or exhibits in public a derogatory treatment of the work, or broadcasts or includes in a cable programme service a visual image of a derogatory treatment of the work,

(b) shows in public a film including a visual image of a derogatory treatment of the work or issues to the public copies of such a film, or

(c) in the case of—

(i) a work of architecture in the form of a model for a building,

(ii) a sculpture, or

(iii) a work of artistic craftsmanship,

issues to the public copies of a graphic work representing, or of a photograph of, a derogatory treatment of the work.

(5) Subsection (4) does not apply to a work of architecture in the form of a building; but where the author of such a work is identified on the building and it is the subject of derogatory treatment he has the right to require the identification to be removed.

(6) In the case of a film, the right is infringed by a person who—

(a) shows in public, broadcasts or includes in a cable programme service a derogatory treatment of the film; or

(b) issues to the public copies of a derogatory treatment of the film,

or who, along with the film, plays in public, broadcasts or includes in a cable programme service, or issues to the public copies of, a derogatory treatment of the film sound-track.

(7) The right conferred by this section extends to the treatment of parts of a work resulting from a previous treatment by a person other than the author or director, if those parts are attributed to, or are likely to be regarded as the work of, the author or director.

(8) This section has effect subject to sections 81 and 82 (exceptions to and qualifications of right).

81 Exceptions to right

(1) The right conferred by section 80 (right to object to derogatory treatment of work) is subject to the following exceptions.

(2) The right does not apply to a computer program or to any computer-generated work.

(3) The right does not apply in relation to any work made for the purpose of reporting current events.

(4) The right does not apply in relation to the publication in—

(a) a newspaper, magazine or similar periodical, or

(b) an encyclopaedia, dictionary, yearbook or other collective work of reference,

of a literary, dramatic, musical or artistic work made for the purposes of such publication or made available with the consent of the author for the purposes of such publication.

Nor does the right apply in relation to any subsequent exploitation elsewhere of such a work without any modification of the published version.

(5) The right is not infringed by an act which by virtue of section 57 (anonymous or pseudonymous works: acts permitted on assumptions as to expiry of copyright or death of author) would not infringe copyright.

(6) The right is not infringed by anything done for the purpose of—

(a) avoiding the commission of an offence,

(b) complying with a duty imposed by or under an enactment, or

(c) in the case of the British Broadcasting Corporation, avoiding the inclusion in a programme broadcast by them of anything which offends against good taste or decency or which is likely to encourage or incite to crime or to lead to disorder or to be offensive to public feeling, provided, where the author or director is identified at the time of the relevant act or has previously been identified in or on published copies of the work, that there is a sufficient disclaimer.

82 Qualification of right in certain cases

(1) This section applies to—

(a) works in which copyright originally vested in the author's employer by virtue of section 11(2) (works produced in course of employment) or in the director's employer by virtue of section 9(2)(a) (person to be treated as author of film),

(b) works in which Crown copyright or Parliamentary copyright subsists, and

(c) works in which copyright originally vested in an international organisation by virtue of section 168.

(2) The right conferred by section 80 (right to object to derogatory treatment of work) does not apply to anything done in relation to such a work by or with the authority of the copyright owner unless the author or director—

(a) is identified at the time of the relevant act, or

(b) has previously been identified in or on published copies of the work;

and where in such a case the right does apply, it is not infringed if there is a sufficient disclaimer.

83 Infringement of right by possessing or dealing with infringing article

(1) The right conferred by section 80 (right to object to derogatory treatment of work) is also infringed by a person who—

(a) possesses in the course of a business, or

(b) sells or lets for hire, or offers or exposes for sale or hire, or

(c) in the course of a business exhibits in public or distributes, or

(d) distributes otherwise than in the course of a business so as to affect prejudicially the honour or reputation of the author or director,

an article which is, and which he knows or has reason to believe is, an infringing article.

(2) An "infringing article" means a work or a copy of a work which—

(a) has been subjected to derogatory treatment within the meaning of section 80, and

(b) has been or is likely to be the subject of any of the acts mentioned in that section in circumstances infringing that right.

False attribution of work

84 False attribution of work

(1) A person has the right in the circumstances mentioned in this section—

(a) not to have a literary, dramatic, musical or artistic work falsely attributed to him as author, and

(b) not to have a film falsely attributed to him as director;

and in this section an "attribution", in relation to such a work, means a statement (express or implied) as to who is the author or director.

(2) The right is infringed by a person who—

(a) issues to the public copies of a work of any of those descriptions in or on which there is a false attribution, or

(b) exhibits in public an artistic work, or a copy of an artistic work, in or on which there is a false attribution.

(3) The right is also infringed by a person who—

(a) in the case of a literary, dramatic or musical work, performs the work in public, broadcasts it or includes it in a cable programme service as being the work of a person, or

(b) in the case of a film, shows it in public, broadcasts it or includes it in a cable programme service as being directed by a person,

knowing or having reason to believe that the attribution is false.

(4) The right is also infringed by the issue to the public or public display of material containing a false attribution in connection with any of the acts mentioned in subsection (2) or (3).

(5) The right is also infringed by a person who in the course of a business—

(a) possesses or deals with a copy of a work of any of the descriptions mentioned in subsection (1) in or on which there is a false attribution, or

(b) in the case of an artistic work, possesses or deals with the work itself when there is a false attribution in or on it,

knowing or having reason to believe that there is such an attribution and that it is false.

(6) In the case of an artistic work the right is also infringed by a person who in the course of a business—

(a) deals with a work which has been altered after the author parted with possession of it as being the unaltered work of the author, or

(b) deals with a copy of such a work as being a copy of the unaltered work of the author,

knowing or having reason to believe that that is not the case.

(7) References in this section to dealing are to selling or letting for hire, offering or exposing for sale or hire, exhibiting in public, or distributing.

(8) This section applies where, contrary to the fact—

(a) a literary, dramatic or musical work is falsely represented as being an adaptation of the work of a person, or

(b) a copy of an artistic work is falsely represented as being a copy made by the author of the artistic work,

as it applies where the work is falsely attributed to a person as author.

Right to privacy of certain photographs and films

85 Right to privacy of certain photographs and films

(1) A person who for private and domestic purposes commissions the taking of a photograph or the making of a film has, where copyright subsists in the resulting work, the right not to have-

(a) copies of the work issued to the public,

(b) the work exhibited or shown in public, or
(c) the work broadcast or included in a cable programme service;

and, except as mentioned in subsection (2), a person who does or authorises the doing of any of those acts infringes that right.

(2) The right is not infringed by an act which by virtue of any of the following provisions would not infringe copyright in the work—
(a) section 31 (incidental inclusion of work in an artistic work, film, broadcast or cable programme);
(b) section 45 (parliamentary and judicial proceedings);
(c) section 46 (Royal Commissions and statutory inquiries);
(d) section 50 (acts done under statutory authority);
(e) section 57 (anonymous or pseudonymous works: acts permitted on assumptions as to expiry of copyright or death of author).

Supplementary

86 Duration of rights

(1) The rights conferred by section 77 (right to be identified as author or director), section 80 (right to object to derogatory treatment of work) and section 85 (right to privacy of certain photographs and films) continue to subsist so long as copyright subsists in the work.

(2) The right conferred by section 84 (false attribution) continues to subsist until 20 years after a person's death.

87 Consent and waiver of rights

(1) It is not an infringement of any of the rights conferred by this Chapter to do any act to which the person entitled to the right has consented.

(2) Any of those rights may be waived by instrument in writing signed by the person giving up the right.

(3) A waiver—
(a) may relate to a specific work, to works of a specified description or to works generally, and may relate to existing or future works, and
(b) may be conditional or unconditional and may be expressed to be subject to revocation;

and if made in favour of the owner or prospective owner of the copyright in the work or works to which it relates, it shall be presumed to extend to his licensees and successors in title unless a contrary intention is expressed.

(4) Nothing in this Chapter shall be construed as excluding the operation of the general law of contract or estoppel in relation to an informal waiver or other transaction in relation to any of the rights mentioned in subsection (1).

88 Application of provisions to joint works

(1) The right conferred by section 77 (right to be identified as author or director) is, in the case of a work of joint authorship, a right of each joint author to be identified as a joint author and must be asserted in accordance with section 78 by each joint author in relation to himself.

(2) The right conferred by section 80 (right to object to derogatory treatment of work) is, in the case of a work of joint authorship, a right of each joint author and his right is satisfied if he consents to the treatment in question.

(3) A waiver under section 87 of those rights by one joint author does not affect the rights of the other joint authors.

(4) The right conferred by section 84 (false attribution) is infringed, in the circumstances mentioned in that section—

(a) by any false statement as to the authorship of a work of joint authorship, and

(b) by the false attribution of joint authorship in relation to a work of sole authorship;

and such a false attribution infringes the right of every person to whom authorship of any description is, whether rightly or wrongly, attributed.

(5) The above provisions also apply (with any necessary adaptations) in relation to a film which was, or is alleged to have been, jointly directed, as they apply to a work which is, or is alleged to be, a work of joint authorship.

A film is "jointly directed" if it is made by the collaboration of two or more directors and the contribution of each director is not distinct from that of the other director or directors.

(6) The right conferred by section 85 (right to privacy of certain photographs and films) is, in the case of a work made in pursuance of a joint commission, a right of each person who commissioned the making of the work, so that—

(a) the right of each is satisfied if he consents to the act in question, and

(b) a waiver under section 87 by one of them does not affect the rights of the others.

89 Application of provisions to parts of works

(1) The rights conferred by section 77 (right to be identified as author or director) and section 85 (right to privacy of certain photographs and films) apply in relation to the whole or any substantial part of a work.

(2) The rights conferred by section 80 (right to object to derogatory treatment of work) and section 84 (false attribution) apply in relation to the whole or any part of a work.

CHAPTER V

DEALINGS WITH RIGHTS IN COPYRIGHT WORKS

Copyright

90 Assignment and licences

(1) Copyright is transmissible by assignment, by testamentary disposition or by operation of law, as personal or moveable property.

(2) An assignment or other transmission of copyright may be partial, that is, limited so as to apply—

(a) to one or more, but not all, of the things the copyright owner has the exclusive right to do;

(b) to part, but not the whole, of the period for which the copyright is to subsist.

(3) An assignment of copyright is not effective unless it is in writing signed by or on behalf of the assignor.

(4) A licence granted by a copyright owner is binding on every successor in title to his interest in the copyright, except a purchaser in good faith for valuable consideration and without notice (actual or constructive) of the licence or a person deriving title from such a purchaser; and references in this Part to doing anything with, or without, the licence of the copyright owner shall be construed accordingly.

91 Prospective ownership of copyright

(1) Where by an agreement made in relation to future copyright, and signed by or on behalf of the prospective owner of the copyright, the prospective owner purports to assign the future copyright (wholly or partially) to another person, then if, on the copyright coming into existence, the assignee or another person claiming under him would be entitled as against all other persons to require the copyright to be vested in him, the copyright shall vest in the assignee or his successor in title by virtue of this subsection.

(2) In this Part—

"future copyright" means copyright which will or may come into existence in respect of a future work or class of works or on the occurrence of a future event; and

"prospective owner" shall be construed accordingly, and includes a person who is prospectively entitled to copyright by virtue of such an agreement as is mentioned in subsection (1).

(3) A licence granted by a prospective owner of copyright is binding on every successor in title to his interest (or prospective interest) in the right, except a purchaser in good faith for valuable consideration and without notice (actual or constructive) of the licence or a person deriving title from such a purchaser; and references in this Part to doing anything with, or without, the licence of the copyright owner shall be construed accordingly.

92 Exclusive licences

(1) In this Part an "exclusive licence" means a licence in writing signed by or on behalf of the copyright owner authorising the licensee to the exclusion of all other persons, including the person granting the licence, to exercise a right which would otherwise be exercisable exclusively by the copyright owner.

(2) The licensee under an exclusive licence has the same rights against a successor in title who is bound by the licence as he has against the person granting the licence.

93 Copyright to pass under will with unpublished work

Where under a bequest (whether specific or general) a person is entitled, beneficially or otherwise, to—

- (a) an original document or other material thing recording or embodying a literary, dramatic, musical or artistic work which was not published before the death of the testator, or
- (b) an original material thing containing a sound recording or film which was not published before the death of the testator,

the bequest shall, unless a contrary intention is indicated in the testator's will or a codicil to it, be construed as including the copyright in the work in so far as the testator was the owner of the copyright immediately before his death.

Moral rights

94 Moral rights not assignable

The rights conferred by Chapter IV (moral rights) are not assignable.

95 Transmission of moral rights on death

(1) On the death of a person entitled to the right conferred by section 77 (right to identification of author or director), section 80 (right to object to derogatory treatment of work) or section 85 (right to privacy of certain photographs and films)—

- (a) the right passes to such person as he may by testamentary disposition specifically direct,
- (b) if there is no such direction but the copyright in the work in question forms part of his estate, the right passes to the person to whom the copyright passes, and
- (c) if or to the extent that the right does not pass under paragraph (a) or (b) it is exercisable by his personal representatives.

(2) Where copyright forming part of a person's estate passes in part to one person and in part to another, as for example where a bequest is limited so as to apply—

- (a) to one or more, but not all, of the things the copyright owner has the exclusive right to do or authorise, or
- (b) to part, but not the whole, of the period for which the copyright is to subsist,

any right which passes with the copyright by virtue of subsection (1) is correspondingly divided.

(3) Where by virtue of subsection (1)(a) or (b) a right becomes exercisable by more than one person—

(a) it may, in the case of the right conferred by section 77 (right to identification of author or director), be asserted by any of them;

(b) it is, in the case of the right conferred by section 80 (right to object to derogatory treatment of work) or section 85 (right to privacy of certain photographs and films), a right exercisable by each of them and is satisfied in relation to any of them if he consents to the treatment or act in question; and

(c) any waiver of the right in accordance with section 87 by one of them does not affect the rights of the others.

(4) A consent or waiver previously given or made binds any person to whom a right passes by virtue of subsection (1).

(5) Any infringement after a person's death of the right conferred by section 84 (false attribution) is actionable by his personal representatives.

(6) Any damages recovered by personal representatives by virtue of this section in respect of an infringement after a person's death shall devolve as part of his estate as if the right of action had subsisted and been vested in him immediately before his death.

CHAPTER VI

REMEDIES FOR INFRINGEMENT

Rights and remedies of copyright owner

96 Infringement actionable by copyright owner

(1) An infringement of copyright is actionable by the copyright owner.

(2) In an action for infringement of copyright all such relief by way of damages, injunctions, accounts or otherwise is available to the plaintiff as is available in respect of the infringement of any other property right.

(3) This section has effect subject to the following provisions of this Chapter.

97 Provisions as to damages in infringement action

(1) Where in an action for infringement of copyright it is shown that at the time of the infringement the defendant did not know, and had no reason to believe, that copyright subsisted in the work to which the action relates, the plaintiff is not entitled to damages against him, but without prejudice to any other remedy.

(2) The court may in an action for infringement of copyright having regard to all the circumstances, and in particular to—

(a) the flagrancy of the infringement, and

(b) any benefit accruing to the defendant by reason of the infringement,

award such additional damages as the justice of the case may require.

98 Undertaking to take licence of right in infringement proceedings

(1) If in proceedings for infringement of copyright in respect of which a licence is available as of right under section 144 (powers exercisable in consequence of report

of Monopolies and Mergers Commission) the defendant undertakes to take a licence on such terms as may be agreed or, in default of agreement, settled by the Copyright Tribunal under that section—

(a) no injunction shall be granted against him,

(b) no order for delivery up shall be made under section 99, and

(c) the amount recoverable against him by way of damages or on an account of profits shall not exceed double the amount which would have been payable by him as licensee if such a licence on those terms had been granted before the earliest infringement.

(2) An undertaking may be given at any time before final order in the proceedings, without any admission of liability.

(3) Nothing in this section affects the remedies available in respect of an infringement committed before licences of right were available.

99 Order for delivery up

(1) Where a person—

(a) has an infringing copy of a work in his possession, custody or control in the course of a business, or

(b) has in his possession, custody or control an article specifically designed or adapted for making copies of a particular copyright work, knowing or having reason to believe that it has been or is to be used to make infringing copies,

the owner of the copyright in the work may apply to the court for an order that the infringing copy or article be delivered up to him or to such other person as the court may direct.

(2) An application shall not be made after the end of the period specified in section 113 (period after which remedy of delivery up not available); and no order shall be made unless the court also makes, or it appears to the court that there are grounds for making, an order under section 114 (order as to disposal of infringing copy or other article).

(3) A person to whom an infringing copy or other article is delivered up in pursuance of an order under this section shall, if an order under section 114 is not made, retain it pending the making of an order, or the decision not to make an order, under that section.

(4) Nothing in this section affects any other power of the court.

100 Right to seize infringing copies and other articles

(1) An infringing copy of a work which is found exposed or otherwise immediately available for sale or hire, and in respect of which the copyright owner would be entitled to apply for an order under section 99, may be seized and detained by him or a person authorised by him.

The right to seize and detain is exercisable subject to the following conditions and is subject to any decision of the court under section 114.

(2) Before anything is seized under this section notice of the time and place of the proposed seizure must be given to a local police station.

(3) A person may for the purpose of exercising the right conferred by this section enter premises to which the public have access but may not seize anything in the possession, custody or control of a person at a permanent or regular place of business of his, and may not use any force.

(4) At the time when anything is seized under this section there shall be left at the place where it was seized a notice in the prescribed form containing the prescribed particulars as to the person by whom or on whose authority the seizure is made and the grounds on which it is made.

(5) In this section—

"premises" includes land, buildings, moveable structures, vehicles, vessels, aircraft and hovercraft; and "prescribed" means prescribed by order of the Secretary of State.

(6) An order of the Secretary of State under this section shall be made by statutory instrument which shall be subject to annulment in pursuance of a resolution of either House of Parliament.

Rights and remedies of exclusive licensee

101 Rights and remedies of exclusive licensee

(1) An exclusive licensee has, except against the copyright owner, the same rights and remedies in respect of matters occurring after the grant of the licence as if the licence had been an assignment.

(2) His rights and remedies are concurrent with those of the copyright owner; and references in the relevant provisions of this Part to the copyright owner shall be construed accordingly.

(3) In an action brought by an exclusive licensee by virtue of this section a defendant may avail himself of any defence which would have been available to him if the action had been brought by the copyright owner.

102 Exercise of concurrent rights

(1) Where an action for infringement of copyright brought by the copyright owner or an exclusive licensee relates (wholly or partly) to an infringement in respect of which they have concurrent rights of action, the copyright owner or, as the case may be, the exclusive licensee may not, without the leave of the court, proceed with the action unless the other is either joined as a plaintiff or added as a defendant.

(2) A copyright owner or exclusive licensee who is added as a defendant in pursuance of subsection (1) is not liable for any costs in the action unless he takes part in the proceedings.

(3) The above provisions do not affect the granting of interlocutory relief on an application by a copyright owner or exclusive licensee alone.

(4) Where an action for infringement of copyright is brought which relates (wholly or partly) to an infringement in respect of which the copyright owner and an exclusive licensee have or had concurrent rights of action—

(a) the court shall in assessing damages take into account—

(i) the terms of the licence, and

(ii) any pecuniary remedy already awarded or available to either of them in respect of the infringement;

(b) no account of profits shall be directed if an award of damages has been made, or an account of profits has been directed, in favour of the other of them in respect of the infringement; and

(c) the court shall if an account of profits is directed apportion the profits between them as the court considers just, subject to any agreement between them;

and these provisions apply whether or not the copyright owner and the exclusive licensee are both parties to the action.

(5) The copyright owner shall notify any exclusive licensee having concurrent rights before applying for an order under section 99 (order for delivery up) or exercising the right conferred by section 100 (right of seizure); and the court may on the application of the licensee make such order under section 99 or, as the case may be, prohibiting or permitting the exercise by the copyright owner of the right conferred by section 100, as it thinks fit having regard to the terms of the licence.

Remedies for infringement of moral rights

103 Remedies for infringement of moral rights

(1) An infringement of a right conferred by Chapter IV (moral rights) is actionable as a breach of statutory duty owed to the person entitled to the right.

(2) In proceedings for infringement of the right conferred by section 80 (right to object to derogatory treatment of work) the court may, if it thinks it is an adequate remedy in the circumstances, grant an injunction on terms prohibiting the doing of any act unless a disclaimer is made, in such terms and in such manner as may be approved by the court, dissociating the author or director from the treatment of the work.

Presumptions

104 Presumptions relevant to literary, dramatic, musical and artistic works

(1) The following presumptions apply in proceedings brought by virtue of this Chapter with respect to a literary, dramatic, musical or artistic work.

(2) Where a name purporting to be that of the author appeared on copies of the work as published or on the work when it was made, the person whose name appeared shall be presumed, until the contrary is proved—

(a) to be the author of the work;

(b) to have made it in circumstances not falling within section 11(2), 163, 165 or 168 (works produced in course of employment, Crown copyright, Parliamentary copyright or copyright of certain international organisations).

(3) In the case of a work alleged to be a work of joint authorship, subsection (2) applies in relation to each person alleged to be one of the authors.

(4) Where no name purporting to be that of the author appeared as mentioned in subsection (2) but—

(a) the work qualifies for copyright protection by virtue of section 155 (qualification by reference to country of first publication), and

(b) a name purporting to be that of the publisher appeared on copies of the work as first published,

the person whose name appeared shall be presumed, until the contrary is proved, to have been the owner of the copyright at the time of publication.

(5) If the author of the work is dead or the identity of the author cannot be ascertained by reasonable inquiry, it shall be presumed, in the absence of evidence to the contrary—

(a) that the work is an original work, and

(b) that the plaintiff's allegations as to what was the first publication of the work and as to the country of first publication are correct.

105 Presumptions relevant to sound recordings and films

(1) In proceedings brought by virtue of this Chapter with respect to a sound recording, where copies of the recording as issued to the public bear a label or other mark stating—

(a) that a named person was the owner of copyright in the recording at the date of issue of the copies, or

(b) that the recording was first published in a specified year or in a specified country,

the label or mark shall be admissible as evidence of the facts stated and shall be presumed to be correct until the contrary is proved.

(2) In proceedings brought by virtue of this Chapter with respect to a film, where copies of the film as issued to the public bear a statement—

(a) that a named person was the author or director of the film,

(b) that a named person was the owner of copyright in the film at the date of issue of the copies, or

(c) that the film was first published in a specified year or in a specified country,

the statement shall be admissible as evidence of the facts stated and shall be presumed to be correct until the contrary is proved.

(3) In proceedings brought by virtue of this Chapter with respect to a computer program, where copies of the program are issued to the public in electronic form bearing a statement—

(a) that a named person was the owner of copyright in the program at the date of issue of the copies, or

(b) that the program was first published in a specified country or that copies of it were first issued to the public in electronic form in a specified year,

the statement shall be admissible as evidence of the facts stated and shall be presumed to be correct until the contrary is proved.

(4) The above presumptions apply equally in proceedings relating to an infringement alleged to have occurred before the date on which the copies were issued to the public.

(5) In proceedings brought by virtue of this Chapter with respect to a film, where the film as shown in public, broadcast or included in a cable programme service bears a statement—

(a) that a named person was the author or director of the film, or

(b) that a named person was the owner of copyright in the film immediately after it was made,

the statement shall be admissible as evidence of the facts stated and shall be presumed to be correct until the contrary is proved.

This presumption applies equally in proceedings relating to an infringement alleged to have occurred before the date on which the film was shown in public, broadcast or included in a cable programme service.

106 Presumptions relevant to works subject to Crown copyright

In proceedings brought by virtue of this Chapter with respect to a literary, dramatic or musical work in which Crown copyright subsists, where there appears on printed copies of the work a statement of the year in which the work was first published commercially, that statement shall be admissible as evidence of the fact stated and shall be presumed to be correct in the absence of evidence to the contrary.

Offences

107 Criminal liability for making or dealing with infringing articles, &c

(1) A person commits an offence who, without the licence of the copyright owner—

(a) makes for sale or hire, or

(b) imports into the United Kingdom otherwise than for his private and domestic use, or

(c) possesses in the course of a business with a view to committing any act infringing the copyright, or

(d) in the course of a business —

(i) sells or lets for hire, or

(ii) offers or exposes for sale or hire, or

(iii) exhibits in public, or

(iv) distributes, or

(e) distributes otherwise than in the course of a business to such an extent as to affect prejudicially the owner of the copyright,

an article which is, and which he knows or has reason to believe is, an infringing copy of a copyright work.

(2) A person commits an offence who—

(a) makes an article specifically designed or adapted for making copies of a particular copyright work, or

(b) has such an article in his possession,

knowing or having reason to believe that it is to be used to make infringing copies for sale or hire or for use in the course of a business.

(3) Where copyright is infringed (otherwise than by reception of a broadcast or cable programme)—

(a) by the public performance of a literary, dramatic or musical work, or

(b) by the playing or showing in public of a sound recording or film,

any person who caused the work to be so performed, played or shown is guilty of an offence if he knew or had reason to believe that copyright would be infringed.

(4) A person guilty of an offence under subsection (1)(a), (b), (d)(iv) or (e) is liable—

(a) on summary conviction to imprisonment for a term not exceeding six months or a fine not exceeding the statutory maximum, or both;

(b) on conviction on indictment to a fine or imprisonment for a term not exceeding two years, or both.

(5) A person guilty of any other offence under this section is liable on summary conviction to imprisonment for a term not exceeding six months or a fine not exceeding level 5 on the standard scale, or both.

(6) Sections 104 to 106 (presumptions as to various matters connected with copyright) do not apply to proceedings for an offence under this section; but without prejudice to their application in proceedings for an order under section 108 below.

108 Order for delivery up in criminal proceedings

(1) The court before which proceedings are brought against a person for an offence under section 107 may, if satisfied that at the time of his arrest or charge—

(a) he had in his possession, custody or control in the course of a business an infringing copy of a copyright work, or

(b) he had in his possession, custody or control an article specifically designed or adapted for making copies of a particular copyright work, knowing or having reason to believe that it had been or was to be used to make infringing copies,

order that the infringing copy or article be delivered up to the copyright owner or to such other person as the court may direct.

(2) For this purpose a person shall be treated as charged with an offence—

(a) in England, Wales and Northern Ireland, when he is orally charged or is served with a summons or indictment;

(b) in Scotland, when he is cautioned, charged or served with a complaint or indictment.

(3) An order may be made by the court of its own motion or on the application of the prosecutor (or, in Scotland, the Lord Advocate or procurator-fiscal), and may be made whether or not the person is convicted of the offence, but shall not be made—

(a) after the end of the period specified in section 113 (period after which remedy of delivery up not available), or

(b) if it appears to the court unlikely that any order will be made under section 114 (order as to disposal of infringing copy or other article).

(4) An appeal lies from an order made under this section by a magistrates' court—

(a) in England and Wales, to the Crown Court, and

(b) in Northern Ireland, to the county court;

and in Scotland, where an order has been made under this section, the person from whose possession, custody or control the infringing copy or article has been removed may, without prejudice to any other form of appeal under any rule of law, appeal against that order in the same manner as against sentence.

(5) A person to whom an infringing copy or other article is delivered up in pursuance of an order under this section shall retain it pending the making of an order, or the decision not to make an order, under section 114.

(6) Nothing in this section affects the powers of the court under section 43 of the Powers of Criminal Courts Act 1973, section 223 or 436 of the Criminal Procedure (Scotland) Act 1975 or Article 7 of the Criminal Justice (Northern Ireland) Order 1980 (general provisions as to forfeiture in criminal proceedings).

109 Search warrants

(1) Where a justice of the peace (in Scotland, a sheriff or justice of the peace) is satisfied by information on oath given by a constable (in Scotland, by evidence on oath) that there are reasonable grounds for believing—

(a) that an offence under section 107(1)(a), (b), (d)(iv) or (e) has been or is about to be committed in any premises, and

(b) that evidence that such an offence has been or is about to be committed is in those premises,

he may issue a warrant authorising a constable to enter and search the premises, using such reasonable force as is necessary.

(2) The power conferred by subsection (1) does not, in England and Wales, extend to authorising a search for material of the kinds mentioned in section 9(2) of the Police and Criminal Evidence Act 1984 (certain classes of personal or confidential material).

(3) A warrant under this section—

(a) may authorise persons to accompany any constable executing the warrant, and

(b) remains in force for 28 days from the date of its issue.

(4) In executing a warrant issued under this section a constable may seize an article if he reasonably believes that it is evidence that any offence under section 107(1) has been or is about to be committed.

(5) In this section "premises" includes land, buildings, moveable structures, vehicles, vessels, aircraft and hovercraft.

110 Offence by body corporate: liability of officers

(1) Where an offence under section 107 committed by a body corporate is proved to have been committed with the consent or connivance of a director, manager, secretary or other similar officer of the body, or a person purporting to act in any such capacity, he as well as the body corporate is guilty of the offence and liable to be proceeded against and punished accordingly.

(2) In relation to a body corporate whose affairs are managed by its members "director" means a member of the body corporate.

Provision for preventing importation of infringing copies

111 Infringing copies may be treated as prohibited goods

(1) The owner of the copyright in a published literary, dramatic or musical work may give notice in writing to the Commissioners of Customs and Excise—

(a) that he is the owner of the copyright in the work, and

(b) that he requests the Commissioners, for a period specified in the notice, to treat as prohibited goods printed copies of the work which are infringing copies.

(2) The period specified in a notice under subsection (1) shall not exceed five years and shall not extend beyond the period for which copyright is to subsist.

(3) The owner of the copyright in a sound recording or film may give notice in writing to the Commissioners of Customs and Excise—

- (a) that he is the owner of the copyright in the work,
- (b) that infringing copies of the work are expected to arrive in the United Kingdom at a time and a place specified in the notice, and
- (c) that he requests the Commissioners to treat the copies as prohibited goods.

(4) When a notice is in force under this section the importation of goods to which the notice relates, otherwise than by a person for his private and domestic use, is prohibited; but a person is not by reason of the prohibition liable to any penalty other than forfeiture of the goods.

112 Power of Commissioners of Customs and Excise to make regulations

(1) The Commissioners of Customs and Excise may make regulations prescribing the form in which notice is to be given under section 111 and requiring a person giving notice—

- (a) to furnish the Commissioners with such evidence as may be specified in the regulations, either on giving notice or when the goods are imported, or at both those times, and
- (b) to comply with such other conditions as may be specified in the regulations.

(2) The regulations may, in particular, require a person giving such a notice—

- (a) to pay such fees in respect of the notice as may be specified by the regulations;
- (b) to give such security as may be so specified in respect of any liability or expense which the Commissioners may incur in consequence of the notice by reason of the detention of any article or anything done to an article detained;
- (c) to indemnify the Commissioners against any such liability or expense, whether security has been given or not.

(3) The regulations may make different provision as respects different classes of case to which they apply and may include such incidental and supplementary provisions as the Commissioners consider expedient.

(4) Regulations under this section shall be made by statutory instrument which shall be subject to annulment in pursuance of a resolution of either House of Parliament.

(5) Section 17 of the Customs and Excise Management Act 1979 (general provisions as to Commissioners' receipts) applies to fees paid in pursuance of regulations under this section as to receipts under the enactments relating to customs and excise.

Supplementary

113 Period after which remedy of delivery up not available

(1) An application for an order under section 99 (order for delivery up in civil proceedings) may not be made after the end of the period of six years from the date on which the infringing copy or article in question was made, subject to the following provisions.

(2) If during the whole or any part of that period the copyright owner—

(a) is under a disability, or

(b) is prevented by fraud or concealment from discovering the facts entitling him to apply for an order,

an application may be made at any time before the end of the period of six years from the date on which he ceased to be under a disability or, as the case may be, could with reasonable diligence have discovered those facts.

(3) In subsection (2) "disability"—

(a) in England and Wales, has the same meaning as in the Limitation Act 1980;

(b) in Scotland, means legal disability within the meaning of the Prescription and Limitation (Scotland) Act 1973;

(c) in Northern Ireland, has the same meaning as in the Statute of Limitations (Northern Ireland) 1958.

(4) An order under section 108 (order for delivery up in criminal proceedings) shall not, in any case, be made after the end of the period of six years from the date on which the infringing copy or article in question was made.

114 Order as to disposal of infringing copy or other article

(1) An application may be made to the court for an order that an infringing copy or other article delivered up in pursuance of an order under section 99 or 108, or seized and detained in pursuance of the right conferred by section 100, shall be—

(a) forfeited to the copyright owner, or

(b) destroyed or otherwise dealt with as the court may think fit,

or for a decision that no such order should be made.

(2) In considering what order (if any) should be made, the court shall consider whether other remedies available in an action for infringement of copyright would be adequate to compensate the copyright owner and to protect his interests.

(3) Provision shall be made by rules of court as to the service of notice on persons having an interest in the copy or other articles, and any such person is entitled—

(a) to appear in proceedings for an order under this section, whether or not he was served with notice, and

(b) to appeal against any order made, whether or not he appeared;

and an order shall not take effect until the end of the period within which notice of an appeal may be given or, if before the end of that period notice of appeal is duly given, until the final determination or abandonment of the proceedings on the appeal.

(4) Where there is more than one person interested in a copy or other article, the court shall make such order as it thinks just and may (in particular) direct that the article be sold, or otherwise dealt with, and the proceeds divided.

(5) If the court decides that no order should be made under this section, the person in whose possession, custody or control the copy or other article was before being delivered up or seized is entitled to its return.

(6) References in this section to a person having an interest in a copy or other article include any person in whose favour an order could be made in respect of it under this section or under section 204 or 231 of this Act or section 58C of the Trade

Marks Act 1938 (which make similar provision in relation to infringement of rights in performances, design right and trade marks).

115 Jurisdiction of county court and sheriff court

(1) In England, Wales and Northern Ireland a county court may entertain proceedings under—

section 99 (order for delivery up of infringing copy or other article),

section 102(5) (order as to exercise of rights by copyright owner where exclusive licensee has concurrent rights), or

section 114 (order as to disposal of infringing copy or other article),

where the value of the infringing copies and other articles in question does not exceed the county court limit for actions in tort.

(2) In Scotland proceedings for an order under any of those provisions may be brought in the sheriff court.

(3) Nothing in this section shall be construed as affecting the jurisdiction of the High Court or, in Scotland, the Court of Session.

CHAPTER VII

COPYRIGHT LICENSING

Licensing schemes and licensing bodies

116 Licensing schemes and licensing bodies

(1) In this Part a "licensing scheme" means a scheme setting out—

(a) the classes of case in which the operator of the scheme, or the person on whose behalf he acts, is willing to grant copyright licences, and

(b) the terms on which licences would be granted in those classes of case;

and for this purpose a "scheme" includes anything in the nature of a scheme, whether described as a scheme or as a tariff or by any other name.

(2) In this Chapter a "licensing body" means a society or other organisation which has as its main object, or one of its main objects, the negotiation or granting, either as owner or prospective owner of copyright or as agent for him, of copyright licences, and whose objects include the granting of licences covering works of more than one author.

(3) In this section "copyright licences" means licences to do, or authorise the doing of, any of the acts restricted by copyright.

(4) References in this Chapter to licences or licensing schemes covering works of more than one author do not include licences or schemes covering only—

(a) a single collective work or collective works of which the authors are the same, or

(b) works made by, or by employees of or commissioned by, a single individual, firm, company or group of companies.

For this purpose a group of companies means a holding company and its subsidiaries, within the meaning of section 736 of the Companies Act 1985.

References and applications with respect to licensing schemes

117 Licensing schemes to which ss. 118 to 123 apply

Sections 118 to 123 (references and applications with respect to licensing schemes) apply to—

(a) licensing schemes operated by licensing bodies in relation to the copyright in literary, dramatic, musical or artistic works or films (or film sound-tracks when accompanying a film) which cover works of more than one author, so far as they relate to licences for—

(i) copying the work,

(ii) performing, playing or showing the work in public, or

(iii) broadcasting the work or including it in a cable programme service;

(b) all licensing schemes in relation to the copyright in sound recordings (other than film sound-tracks when accompanying a film), broadcasts or cable programmes, or the typographical arrangement of published editions; and

(c) all licensing schemes in relation to the copyright in sound recordings, films or computer programs so far as they relate to licences for the rental of copies to the public;

and in those sections "licensing scheme" means a licensing scheme of any of those descriptions.

118 Reference of proposed licensing scheme to tribunal

(1) The terms of a licensing scheme proposed to be operated by a licensing body may be referred to the Copyright Tribunal by an organisation claiming to be representative of persons claiming that they require licences in cases of a description to which the scheme would apply, either generally or in relation to any description of case.

(2) The Tribunal shall first decide whether to entertain the reference, and may decline to do so on the ground that the reference is premature.

(3) If the Tribunal decides to entertain the reference it shall consider the matter referred and make such order, either confirming or varying the proposed scheme, either generally or so far as it relates to cases of the description to which the reference relates, as the Tribunal may determine to be reasonable in the circumstances.

(4) The order may be made so as to be in force indefinitely or for such period as the Tribunal may determine.

119 Reference of licensing scheme to tribunal

(1) If while a licensing scheme is in operation a dispute arises between the operator of the scheme and—

(a) a person claiming that he requires a licence in a case of a description to which the scheme applies, or

(b) an organisation claiming to be representative of such persons,

that person or organisation may refer the scheme to the Copyright Tribunal in so far as it relates to cases of that description.

(2) A scheme which has been referred to the Tribunal under this section shall remain in operation until proceedings on the reference are concluded.

(3) The Tribunal shall consider the matter in dispute and make such order, either confirming or varying the scheme so far as it relates to cases of the description to which the reference relates, as the Tribunal may determine to be reasonable in the circumstances.

(4) The order may be made so as to be in force indefinitely or for such period as the Tribunal may determine.

120 Further reference of scheme to tribunal

(1) Where the Copyright Tribunal has on a previous reference of a licensing scheme under section 118 or 119, or under this section, made an order with respect to the scheme, then, while the order remains in force—

(a) the operator of the scheme,

(b) a person claiming that he requires a licence in a case of the description to which the order applies, or

(c) an organisation claiming to be representative of such persons,

may refer the scheme again to the Tribunal so far as it relates to cases of that description.

(2) A licensing scheme shall not, except with the special leave of the Tribunal, be referred again to the Tribunal in respect of the same description of cases—

(a) within twelve months from the date of the order on the previous reference, or

(b) if the order was made so as to be in force for 15 months or less, until the last three months before the expiry of the order.

(3) A scheme which has been referred to the Tribunal under this section shall remain in operation until proceedings on the reference are concluded.

(4) The Tribunal shall consider the matter in dispute and make such order, either confirming, varying or further varying the scheme so far as it relates to cases of the description to which the reference relates, as the Tribunal may determine to be reasonable in the circumstances.

(5) The order may be made so as to be in force indefinitely or for such period as the Tribunal may determine.

121 Application for grant of licence in connection with licensing scheme

(1) A person who claims, in a case covered by a licensing scheme, that the operator of the scheme has refused to grant him or procure the grant to him of a licence in accordance with the scheme, or has failed to do so within a reasonable time after being asked, may apply to the Copyright Tribunal.

(2) A person who claims, in a case excluded from a licensing scheme, that the operator of the scheme either—

(a) has refused to grant him a licence or procure the grant to him of a licence, or has failed to do so within a reasonable time of being asked, and that in the circumstances it is unreasonable that a licence should not be granted, or

(b) proposes terms for a licence which are unreasonable,

may apply to the Copyright Tribunal.

(3) A case shall be regarded as excluded from a licensing scheme for the purposes of subsection (2) if—

(a) the scheme provides for the grant of licences subject to terms excepting matters from the licence and the case falls within such an exception, or

(b) the case is so similar to those in which licences are granted under the scheme that it is unreasonable that it should not be dealt with in the same way.

(4) If the Tribunal is satisfied that the claim is well-founded, it shall make an order declaring that, in respect of the matters specified in the order, the applicant is entitled to a licence on such terms as the Tribunal may determine to be applicable in accordance with the scheme or, as the case may be, to be reasonable in the circumstances.

(5) The order may be made so as to be in force indefinitely or for such period as the Tribunal may determine.

122 Application for review of order as to entitlement to licence

(1) Where the Copyright Tribunal has made an order under section 121 that a person is entitled to a licence under a licensing scheme, the operator of the scheme or the original applicant may apply to the Tribunal to review its order.

(2) An application shall not be made, except with the special leave of the Tribunal—

(a) within twelve months from the date of the order, or of the decision on a previous application under this section, or

(b) if the order was made so as to be in force for 15 months or less, or as a result of the decision on a previous application under this section is due to expire within 15 months of that decision, until the last three months before the expiry date.

(3) The Tribunal shall on an application for review confirm or vary its order as the Tribunal may determine to be reasonable having regard to the terms applicable in accordance with the licensing scheme or, as the case may be, the circumstances of the case.

123 Effect of order of tribunal as to licensing scheme

(1) A licensing scheme which has been confirmed or varied by the Copyright Tribunal—

(a) under section 118 (reference of terms of proposed scheme), or

(b) under section 119 or 120 (reference of existing scheme to Tribunal),

shall be in force or, as the case may be, remain in operation, so far as it relates to the description of case in respect of which the order was made, so long as the order remains in force.

(2) While the order is in force a person who in a case of a class to which the order applies—

(a) pays to the operator of the scheme any charges payable under the scheme in respect of a licence covering the case in question or, if the amount cannot be ascertained, gives an undertaking to the operator to pay them when ascertained, and

(b) complies with the other terms applicable to such a licence under the scheme,

shall be in the same position as regards infringement of copyright as if he had at all material times been the holder of a licence granted by the owner of the copyright in question in accordance with the scheme.

(3) The Tribunal may direct that the order, so far as it varies the amount of charges payable, has effect from a date before that on which it is made, but not earlier than the date on which the reference was made or, if later, on which the scheme came into operation.

If such a direction is made—
(a)

any necessary repayments, or further payments, shall be made in respect of charges already paid, and

(b) the reference in subsection (2)(a) to the charges payable under the scheme shall be construed as a reference to the charges so payable by virtue of the order.

No such direction may be made where subsection (4) below applies.

(4) An order of the Tribunal under section 119 or 120 made with respect to a scheme which is certified for any purpose under section 143 has effect, so far as it varies the scheme by reducing the charges payable for licences, from the date on which the reference was made to the Tribunal.

(5) Where the Tribunal has made an order under section 121 (order as to entitlement to licence under licensing scheme) and the order remains in force, the person in whose favour the order is made shall if he—

(a) pays to the operator of the scheme any charges payable in accordance with the order or, if the amount cannot be ascertained, gives an undertaking to pay the charges when ascertained, and
(b) complies with the other terms specified in the order,

be in the same position as regards infringement of copyright as if he had at all material times been the holder of a licence granted by the owner of the copyright in question on the terms specified in the order.

References and applications with respect to licensing by licensing bodies

124 Licences to which ss. 125 to 128 apply

Sections 125 to 128 (references and applications with respect to licensing by licensing bodies) apply to the following descriptions of licence granted by a licensing body otherwise than in pursuance of a licensing scheme—

(a) licences relating to the copyright in literary, dramatic, musical or artistic works or films (or film sound-tracks when accompanying a film) which cover works of more than one author, so far as they authorise—
  (i) copying the work,
  (ii) performing, playing or showing the work in public, or
  (iii) broadcasting the work or including it in a cable programme service;
(b) any licence relating to the copyright in a sound recording (other than a film sound-track when accompanying a film), broadcast or cable programme, or the typographical arrangement of a published edition; and
(c) all licences in relation to the copyright in sound recordings, films or computer programs so far as they relate to the rental of copies to the public;

and in those sections a "licence" means a licence of any of those descriptions.

125 Reference to tribunal of proposed licence

(1) The terms on which a licensing body proposes to grant a licence may be referred to the Copyright Tribunal by the prospective licensee.

(2) The Tribunal shall first decide whether to entertain the reference, and may decline to do so on the ground that the reference is premature.

(3) If the Tribunal decides to entertain the reference it shall consider the terms of the proposed licence and make such order, either confirming or varying the terms, as it may determine to be reasonable in the circumstances.

(4) The order may be made so as to be in force indefinitely or for such period as the Tribunal may determine.

126 Reference to tribunal of expiring licence

(1) A licensee under a licence which is due to expire, by effluxion of time or as a result of notice given by the licensing body, may apply to the Copyright Tribunal on the ground that it is unreasonable in the circumstances that the licence should cease to be in force.

(2) Such an application may not be made until the last three months before the licence is due to expire.

(3) A licence in respect of which a reference has been made to the Tribunal shall remain in operation until proceedings on the reference are concluded.

(4) If the Tribunal finds the application well-founded, it shall make an order declaring that the licensee shall continue to be entitled to the benefit of the licence on such terms as the Tribunal may determine to be reasonable in the circumstances.

(5) An order of the Tribunal under this section may be made so as to be in force indefinitely or for such period as the Tribunal may determine.

127 Application for review of order as to licence

(1) Where the Copyright Tribunal has made an order under section 125 or 126, the licensing body or the person entitled to the benefit of the order may apply to the Tribunal to review its order.

(2) An application shall not be made, except with the special leave of the Tribunal—

- (a) within twelve months from the date of the order or of the decision on a previous application under this section, or
- (b) if the order was made so as to be in force for 15 months or less, or as a result of the decision on a previous application under this section is due to expire within 15 months of that decision, until the last three months before the expiry date.

(3) The Tribunal shall on an application for review confirm or vary its order as the Tribunal may determine to be reasonable in the circumstances.

128 Effect of order of tribunal as to licence

(1) Where the Copyright Tribunal has made an order under section 125 or 126 and the order remains in force, the person entitled to the benefit of the order shall if he—

(a) pays to the licensing body any charges payable in accordance with the order or, if the amount cannot be ascertained, gives an undertaking to pay the charges when ascertained, and

(b) complies with the other terms specified in the order,

be in the same position as regards infringement of copyright as if he had at all material times been the holder of a licence granted by the owner of the copyright in question on the terms specified in the order.

(2) The benefit of the order may be assigned—

(a) in the case of an order under section 125, if assignment is not prohibited under the terms of the Tribunal's order; and

(b) in the case of an order under section 126, if assignment was not prohibited under the terms of the original licence.

(3) The Tribunal may direct that an order under section 125 or 126, or an order under section 127 varying such an order, so far as it varies the amount of charges payable, has effect from a date before that on which it is made, but not earlier than the date on which the reference or application was made or, if later, on which the licence was granted or, as the case may be, was due to expire.

If such a direction is made—
(a)

any necessary repayments, or further payments, shall be made in respect of charges already paid, and

(b) the reference in subsection (1)(a) to the charges payable in accordance with the order shall be construed, where the order is varied by a later order, as a reference to the charges so payable by virtue of the later order.

Factors to be taken into account in certain classes of case

129 General considerations: unreasonable discrimination

In determining what is reasonable on a reference or application under this Chapter relating to a licensing scheme or licence, the Copyright Tribunal shall have regard to—

(a) the availability of other schemes, or the granting of other licences, to other persons in similar circumstances, and

(b) the terms of those schemes or licences,

and shall exercise its powers so as to secure that there is no unreasonable discrimination between licensees, or prospective licensees, under the scheme or licence to which the reference or application relates and licensees under other schemes operated by, or other licences granted by, the same person.

130 Licences for reprographic copying

Where a reference or application is made to the Copyright Tribunal under this Chapter relating to the licensing of reprographic copying of published literary, dramatic, musical or artistic works, or the typographical arrangement of published editions, the Tribunal shall have regard to—

(a) the extent to which published editions of the works in question are otherwise available,

(b) the proportion of the work to be copied, and

(c) the nature of the use to which the copies are likely to be put.

131 Licences for educational establishments in respect of works included in broadcasts or cable programmes

(1) This section applies to references or applications under this Chapter relating to licences for the recording by or on behalf of educational establishments of broadcasts or cable programmes which include copyright works, or the making of copies of such recordings, for educational purposes.

(2) The Copyright Tribunal shall, in considering what charges (if any) should be paid for a licence, have regard to the extent to which the owners of copyright in the works included in the broadcast or cable programme have already received, or are entitled to receive, payment in respect of their inclusion.

132 Licences to reflect conditions imposed by promoters of events

(1) This section applies to references or applications under this Chapter in respect of licences relating to sound recordings, films, broadcasts or cable programmes which include, or are to include, any entertainment or other event.

(2) The Copyright Tribunal shall have regard to any conditions imposed by the promoters of the entertainment or other event; and, in particular, the Tribunal shall not hold a refusal or failure to grant a licence to be unreasonable if it could not have been granted consistently with those conditions.

(3) Nothing in this section shall require the Tribunal to have regard to any such conditions in so far as they—

(a) purport to regulate the charges to be imposed in respect of the grant of licences, or

(b) relate to payments to be made to the promoters of any event in consideration of the grant of facilities for making the recording, film, broadcast or cable programme.

133 Licences to reflect payments in respect of underlying rights

(1) In considering what charges should be paid for a licence—

(a) on a reference or application under this Chapter relating to licences for the rental to the public of copies of sound recordings, films or computer programs, or

(b) on an application under section 142 (settlement of royalty or other sum payable for deemed licence),

the Copyright Tribunal shall take into account any reasonable payments which the owner of the copyright in the sound recording, film or computer program is liable to make in consequence of the granting of the licence, or of the acts authorised by the licence, to owners of copyright in works included in that work.

(2) On any reference or application under this Chapter relating to licensing in respect of the copyright in sound recordings, films, broadcasts or cable programmes, the Copyright Tribunal shall take into account, in considering what charges should be paid for a licence, any reasonable payments which the copyright owner is liable to

make in consequence of the granting of the licence, or of the acts authorised by the licence, in respect of any performance included in the recording, film, broadcast or cable programme.

134 Licences in respect of works included in re-transmissions

(1) This section applies to references or applications under this Chapter relating to licences to include in a broadcast or cable programme service—

(a) literary, dramatic, musical or artistic works, or,

(b) sound recordings or films,

where one broadcast or cable programme ("the first transmission") is, by reception and immediate re-transmission, to be further broadcast or included in a cable programme service ("the further transmission").

(2) So far as the further transmission is to the same area as the first transmission, the Copyright Tribunal shall, in considering what charges (if any) should be paid for licences for either transmission, have regard to the extent to which the copyright owner has already received, or is entitled to receive, payment for the other transmission which adequately remunerates him in respect of transmissions to that area.

(3) So far as the further transmission is to an area outside that to which the first transmission was made, the Tribunal shall (except where subsection (4) applies) leave the further transmission out of account in considering what charges (if any) should be paid for licences for the first transmission.

(4) If the Tribunal is satisfied that requirements imposed under section 13(1) of the Cable and Broadcasting Act 1984 (duty of Cable Authority to secure inclusion of certain broadcasts in cable programme services) will result in the further transmission being to areas part of which fall outside the area to which the first transmission is made, the Tribunal shall exercise its powers so as to secure that the charges payable for licences for the first transmission adequately reflect that fact.

135 Mention of specific matters not to exclude other relevant considerations

The mention in sections 129 to 134 of specific matters to which the Copyright Tribunal is to have regard in certain classes of case does not affect the Tribunal's general obligation in any case to have regard to all relevant considerations.

Implied indemnity in schemes or licences for reprographic copying

136 Implied indemnity in certain schemes and licences for reprographic copying

(1) This section applies to—

(a) schemes for licensing reprographic copying of published literary, dramatic, musical or artistic works, or the typographical arrangement of published editions, and

(b) licences granted by licensing bodies for such copying,

where the scheme or licence does not specify the works to which it applies with such particularity as to enable licensees to determine whether a work falls within the scheme or licence by inspection of the scheme or licence and the work.

(2) There is implied—

(a) in every scheme to which this section applies an undertaking by the operator of the scheme to indemnify a person granted a licence under the scheme, and

(b) in every licence to which this section applies an undertaking by the licensing body to indemnify the licensee,

against any liability incurred by him by reason of his having infringed copyright by making or authorising the making of reprographic copies of a work in circumstances within the apparent scope of his licence.

(3) The circumstances of a case are within the apparent scope of a licence if—

(a) it is not apparent from inspection of the licence and the work that it does not fall within the description of works to which the licence applies; and

(b) the licence does not expressly provide that it does not extend to copyright of the description infringed.

(4) In this section "liability" includes liability to pay costs; and this section applies in relation to costs reasonably incurred by a licensee in connection with actual or contemplated proceedings against him for infringement of copyright as it applies to sums which he is liable to pay in respect of such infringement.

(5) A scheme or licence to which this section applies may contain reasonable provision—

(a) with respect to the manner in which, and time within which, claims under the undertaking implied by this section are to be made;

(b) enabling the operator of the scheme or, as the case may be, the licensing body to take over the conduct of any proceedings affecting the amount of his liability to indemnify.

Reprographic copying by educational establishments

137 Power to extend coverage of scheme or licence

(1) This section applies to—

(a) a licensing scheme to which sections 118 to 123 apply (see section 117) and which is operated by a licensing body, or

(b) a licence to which sections 125 to 128 apply (see section 124),

so far as it provides for the grant of licences, or is a licence, authorising the making by or on behalf of educational establishments for the purposes of instruction of reprographic copies of published literary, dramatic, musical or artistic works, or of the typographical arrangement of published editions.

(2) If it appears to the Secretary of State with respect to a scheme or licence to which this section applies that—

(a) works of a description similar to those covered by the scheme or licence are unreasonably excluded from it, and

(b) making them subject to the scheme or licence would not conflict with the normal exploitation of the works or unreasonably prejudice the legitimate interests of the copyright owners,

he may by order provide that the scheme or licence shall extend to those works.

(3) Where he proposes to make such an order, the Secretary of State shall give notice of the proposal to—

(a) the copyright owners,

(b) the licensing body in question, and

(c) such persons or organisations representative of educational establishments, and such other persons or organisations, as the Secretary of State thinks fit.

(4) The notice shall inform those persons of their right to make written or oral representations to the Secretary of State about the proposal within six months from the date of the notice; and if any of them wishes to make oral representations, the Secretary of State shall appoint a person to hear the representations and report to him.

(5) In considering whether to make an order the Secretary of State shall take into account any representations made to him in accordance with subsection (4), and such other matters as appear to him to be relevant.

138 Variation or discharge of order extending scheme or licence

(1) The owner of the copyright in a work in respect of which an order is in force under section 137 may apply to the Secretary of State for the variation or discharge of the order, stating his reasons for making the application.

(2) The Secretary of State shall not entertain an application made within two years of the making of the original order, or of the making of an order on a previous application under this section, unless it appears to him that the circumstances are exceptional.

(3) On considering the reasons for the application the Secretary of State may confirm the order forthwith; if he does not do so, he shall give notice of the application to—

(a) the licensing body in question, and

(b) such persons or organisations representative of educational establishments, and such other persons or organisations, as he thinks fit.

(4) The notice shall inform those persons of their right to make written or oral representations to the Secretary of State about the application within the period of two months from the date of the notice; and if any of them wishes to make oral representations, the Secretary of State shall appoint a person to hear the representations and report to him.

(5) In considering the application the Secretary of State shall take into account the reasons for the application, any representations made to him in accordance with subsection (4), and such other matters as appear to him to be relevant.

(6) The Secretary of State may make such order as he thinks fit confirming or discharging the order (or, as the case may be, the order as previously varied), or varying (or further varying) it so as to exclude works from it.

139 Appeals against orders

(1) The owner of the copyright in a work which is the subject of an order under section 137 (order extending coverage of scheme or licence) may appeal to the Copyright Tribunal which may confirm or discharge the order, or vary it so as to exclude works from it, as it thinks fit having regard to the considerations mentioned in subsection (2) of that section.

(2) Where the Secretary of State has made an order under section 138 (order confirming, varying or discharging order extending coverage of scheme or licence)—

(a) the person who applied for the order, or

(b) any person or organisation representative of educational establishments who was given notice of the application for the order and made representations in accordance with subsection (4) of that section,

may appeal to the Tribunal which may confirm or discharge the order or make any other order which the Secretary of State might have made.

(3) An appeal under this section shall be brought within six weeks of the making of the order or such further period as the Tribunal may allow.

(4) An order under section 137 or 138 shall not come into effect until the end of the period of six weeks from the making of the order or, if an appeal is brought before the end of that period, until the appeal proceedings are disposed of or withdrawn.

(5) If an appeal is brought after the end of that period, any decision of the Tribunal on the appeal does not affect the validity of anything done in reliance on the order appealed against before that decision takes effect.

140 Inquiry whether new scheme or general licence required

(1) The Secretary of State may appoint a person to inquire into the question whether new provision is required (whether by way of a licensing scheme or general licence) to authorise the making by or on behalf of educational establishments for the purposes of instruction of reprographic copies of—

(a) published literary, dramatic, musical or artistic works, or

(b) the typographical arrangement of published editions,

of a description which appears to the Secretary of State not to be covered by an existing licensing scheme or general licence and not to fall within the power conferred by section 137 (power to extend existing schemes and licences to similar works).

(2) The procedure to be followed in relation to an inquiry shall be such as may be prescribed by regulations made by the Secretary of State.

(3) The regulations shall, in particular, provide for notice to be given to—

(a) persons or organisations appearing to the Secretary of State to represent the owners of copyright in works of that description, and

(b) persons or organisations appearing to the Secretary of State to represent educational establishments,

and for the making of written or oral representations by such persons; but without prejudice to the giving of notice to, and the making of representations by, other persons and organisations.

(4) The person appointed to hold the inquiry shall not recommend the making of new provision unless he is satisfied—

(a) that it would be of advantage to educational establishments to be authorised to make reprographic copies of the works in question, and

(b) that making those works subject to a licensing scheme or general licence would not conflict with the normal exploitation of the works or unreasonably prejudice the legitimate interests of the copyright owners.

(5) If he does recommend the making of new provision he shall specify any terms, other than terms as to charges payable, on which authorisation under the new provision should be available.

(6) Regulations under this section shall be made by statutory instrument which shall be subject to annulment in pursuance of a resolution of either House of Parliament.

(7) In this section (and section 141) a "general licence" means a licence granted by a licensing body which covers all works of the description to which it applies.

141 Statutory licence where recommendation not implemented

(1) The Secretary of State may, within one year of the making of a recommendation under section 140 by order provide that if, or to the extent that, provision has not been made in accordance with the recommendation, the making by or on behalf of an educational establishment, for the purposes of instruction, of reprographic copies of the works to which the recommendation relates shall be treated as licensed by the owners of the copyright in the works.

(2) For that purpose provision shall be regarded as having been made in accordance with the recommendation if—

- (a) a certified licensing scheme has been established under which a licence is available to the establishment in question, or
- (b) a general licence has been—
  - (i) granted to or for the benefit of that establishment, or
  - (ii) referred by or on behalf of that establishment to the Copyright Tribunal under section 125 (reference of terms of proposed licence), or
  - (iii) offered to or for the benefit of that establishment and refused without such a reference,

and the terms of the scheme or licence accord with the recommendation.

(3) The order shall also provide that any existing licence authorising the making of such copies (not being a licence granted under a certified licensing scheme or a general licence) shall cease to have effect to the extent that it is more restricted or more onerous than the licence provided for by the order.

(4) The order shall provide for the licence to be free of royalty but, as respects other matters, subject to any terms specified in the recommendation and to such other terms as the Secretary of State may think fit.

(5) The order may provide that where a copy which would otherwise be an infringing copy is made in accordance with the licence provided by the order but is subsequently dealt with, it shall be treated as an infringing copy for the purposes of that dealing, and if that dealing infringes copyright for all subsequent purposes.

In this subsection "dealt with" means sold or let for hire, offered or exposed for sale or hire, or exhibited in public.

(6) The order shall not come into force until at least six months after it is made.

(7) An order may be varied from time to time, but not so as to include works other than those to which the recommendation relates or remove any terms specified in the recommendation, and may be revoked.

(8) An order under this section shall be made by statutory instrument which shall be subject to annulment in pursuance of a resolution of either House of Parliament.

(9) In this section a "certified licensing scheme" means a licensing scheme certified for the purposes of this section under section 143.

Royalty or other sum payable for rental of certain works

142 Royalty or other sum payable for rental of sound recording, film or computer program

(1) An application to settle the royalty or other sum payable in pursuance of section 66 (rental of sound recordings, films and computer programs) may be made to the Copyright Tribunal by the copyright owner or the person claiming to be treated as licensed by him.

(2) The Tribunal shall consider the matter and make such order as it may determine to be reasonable in the circumstances.

(3) Either party may subsequently apply to the Tribunal to vary the order, and the Tribunal shall consider the matter and make such order confirming or varying the original order as it may determine to be reasonable in the circumstances.

(4) An application under subsection (3) shall not, except with the special leave of the Tribunal, be made within twelve months from the date of the original order or of the order on a previous application under that subsection.

(5) An order under subsection (3) has effect from the date on which it is made or such later date as may be specified by the Tribunal.

Certification of licensing schemes

143 Certification of licensing schemes

(1) A person operating or proposing to operate a licensing scheme may apply to the Secretary of State to certify the scheme for the purposes of—

(a) section 35 (educational recording of broadcasts or cable programmes),

(b) section 60 (abstracts of scientific or technical articles),

(c) section 66 (rental of sound recordings, films and computer programs),

(d) section 74 (sub-titled copies of broadcasts or cable programmes for people who are deaf or hard of hearing), or

(e) section 141 (reprographic copying of published works by educational establishments).

(2) The Secretary of State shall by order made by statutory instrument certify the scheme if he is satisfied that it—

(a) enables the works to which it relates to be identified with sufficient certainty by persons likely to require licences, and

(b) sets out clearly the charges (if any) payable and the other terms on which licences will be granted.

(3) The scheme shall be scheduled to the order and the certification shall come into operation for the purposes of section 35, 60, 66, 74 or 141, as the case may be—

(a) on such date, not less than eight weeks after the order is made, as may be specified in the order, or

(b) if the scheme is the subject of a reference under section 118 (reference of proposed scheme), any later date on which the order of the Copyright Tribunal under that section comes into force or the reference is withdrawn.

(4) A variation of the scheme is not effective unless a corresponding amendment of the order is made; and the Secretary of State shall make such an amendment in the case of a variation ordered by the Copyright Tribunal on a reference under section 118, 119 or 120, and may do so in any other case if he thinks fit.

(5) The order shall be revoked if the scheme ceases to be operated and may be revoked if it appears to the Secretary of State that it is no longer being operated according to its terms.

Powers exercisable in consequence of competition report

144 Powers exercisable in consequence of report of Monopolies and Mergers Commission

(1) Where the matters specified in a report of the Monopolies and Mergers Commission as being those which in the Commission's opinion operate, may be expected to operate or have operated against the public interest include—

(a) conditions in licences granted by the owner of copyright in a work restricting the use of the work by the licensee or the right of the copyright owner to grant other licences, or

(b) a refusal of a copyright owner to grant licences on reasonable terms,

the powers conferred by Part I of Schedule 8 to the Fair Trading Act 1973 (powers exercisable for purpose of remedying or preventing adverse effects specified in report of Commission) include power to cancel or modify those conditions and, instead or in addition, to provide that licences in respect of the copyright shall be available as of right.

(2) The references in sections 56(2) and 73(2) of that Act, and sections 10(2)(b) and 12(5) of the Competition Act 1980, to the powers specified in that Part of that Schedule shall be construed accordingly.

(3) A Minister shall only exercise the powers available by virtue of this section if he is satisfied that to do so does not contravene any Convention relating to copyright to which the United Kingdom is a party.

(4) The terms of a licence available by virtue of this section shall, in default of agreement, be settled by the Copyright Tribunal on an application by the person requiring the licence; and terms so settled shall authorise the licensee to do everything in respect of which a licence is so available.

(5) Where the terms of a licence are settled by the Tribunal, the licence has effect from the date on which the application to the Tribunal was made.

CHAPTER VIII

THE COPYRIGHT TRIBUNAL

The Tribunal

145 The Copyright Tribunal

(1) The Tribunal established under section 23 of the Copyright Act 1956 is renamed the Copyright Tribunal.

(2) The Tribunal shall consist of a chairman and two deputy chairmen appointed by the Lord Chancellor, after consultation with the Lord Advocate, and not less than two or more than eight ordinary members appointed by the Secretary of State.

(3) A person is not eligible for appointment as chairman or deputy chairman unless he is a barrister, advocate or solicitor of not less than seven years' standing or has held judicial office.

146 Membership of the Tribunal

(1) The members of the Copyright Tribunal shall hold and vacate office in accordance with their terms of appointment, subject to the following provisions.

(2) A member of the Tribunal may resign his office by notice in writing to the Secretary of State or, in the case of the chairman or a deputy chairman, to the Lord Chancellor.

(3) The Secretary of State or, in the case of the chairman or a deputy chairman, the Lord Chancellor may by notice in writing to the member concerned remove him from office if—

- (a) he has become bankrupt or made an arrangement with his creditors or, in Scotland, his estate has been sequestrated or he has executed a trust deed for his creditors or entered into a composition contract, or
- (b) he is incapacitated by physical or mental illness,

or if he is in the opinion of the Secretary of State or, as the case may be, the Lord Chancellor otherwise unable or unfit to perform his duties as member.

(4) If a member of the Tribunal is by reason of illness, absence or other reasonable cause for the time being unable to perform the duties of his office, either generally or in relation to particular proceedings, a person may be appointed to discharge his duties for a period not exceeding six months at one time or, as the case may be, in relation to those proceedings.

(5) The appointment shall be made—

- (a) in the case of the chairman or deputy chairman, by the Lord Chancellor, who shall appoint a person who would be eligible for appointment to that office, and
- (b) in the case of an ordinary member, by the Secretary of State;

and a person so appointed shall have during the period of his appointment, or in relation to the proceedings in question, the same powers as the person in whose place he is appointed.

(6) The Lord Chancellor shall consult the Lord Advocate before exercising his powers under this section.

147 Financial provisions

(1) There shall be paid to the members of the Copyright Tribunal such remuneration (whether by way of salaries or fees), and such allowances, as the Secretary of State with the approval of the Treasury may determine.

(2) The Secretary of State may appoint such staff for the Tribunal as, with the approval of the Treasury as to numbers and remuneration, he may determine.

(3) The remuneration and allowances of members of the Tribunal, the remuneration of any staff and such other expenses of the Tribunal as the Secretary of State with the approval of the Treasury may determine shall be paid out of money provided by Parliament.

148 Constitution for purposes of proceedings

(1) For the purposes of any proceedings the Copyright Tribunal shall consist of—

(a) a chairman, who shall be either the chairman or a deputy chairman of the Tribunal, and

(b) two or more ordinary members.

(2) If the members of the Tribunal dealing with any matter are not unanimous, the decision shall be taken by majority vote; and if, in such a case, the votes are equal the chairman shall have a further, casting vote.

(3) Where part of any proceedings before the Tribunal has been heard and one or more members of the Tribunal are unable to continue, the Tribunal shall remain duly constituted for the purpose of those proceedings so long as the number of members is not reduced to less than three.

(4) If the chairman is unable to continue, the chairman of the Tribunal shall—

(a) appoint one of the remaining members to act as chairman, and

(b) appoint a suitably qualified person to attend the proceedings and advise the members on any questions of law arising.

(5) A person is "suitably qualified" for the purposes of subsection (4)(b) if he is, or is eligible for appointment as, a deputy chairman of the Tribunal.

Jurisdiction and procedure

149 Jurisdiction of the Tribunal

The function of the Copyright Tribunal is to hear and determine proceedings under—

(a) section 118, 119, or 120 (reference of licensing scheme);

(b) section 121 or 122 (application with respect to entitlement to licence under licensing scheme);

(c) section 125, 126 or 127 (reference or application with respect to licensing by licensing body);

(d) section 139 (appeal against order as to coverage of licensing scheme or licence);

(e) section 142 (application to settle royalty or other sum payable for rental of sound recording, film or computer program);
(f) section 144(4) (application to settle terms of copyright licence available as of right);
(g) section 190 (application to give consent for purposes of Part II on behalf of performer);
(h) paragraph 5 of Schedule 6 (determination of royalty or other remuneration to be paid to trustees for the Hospital for Sick Children).

150 General power to make rules

(1) The Lord Chancellor may, after consultation with the Lord Advocate, make rules for regulating proceedings before the Copyright Tribunal and, subject to the approval of the Treasury, as to the fees chargeable in respect of such proceedings.

(2) The rules may apply in relation to the Tribunal—
(a) as respects proceedings in England and Wales, any of the provisions of the Arbitration Act 1950;
(b) as respects proceedings in Northern Ireland, any of the provisions of the Arbitration Act (Northern Ireland) 1937;

and any provisions so applied shall be set out in or scheduled to the rules.

(3) Provision shall be made by the rules—
(a) prohibiting the Tribunal from entertaining a reference under section 118, 119 or 120 by a representative organisation unless the Tribunal is satisfied that the organisation is reasonably representative of the class of persons which it claims to represent;
(b) specifying the parties to any proceedings and enabling the Tribunal to make a party to the proceedings any person or organisation satisfying the Tribunal that they have a substantial interest in the matter; and
(c) requiring the Tribunal to give the parties to proceedings an opportunity to state their case, in writing or orally as the rules may provide.

(4) The rules may make provision for regulating or prescribing any matters incidental to or consequential upon any appeal from the Tribunal under section 152 (appeal to the court on point of law).

(5) Rules under this section shall be made by statutory instrument which shall be subject to annulment in pursuance of a resolution of either House of Parliament.

151 Costs, proof of orders, &c

(1) The Copyright Tribunal may order that the costs of a party to proceedings before it shall be paid by such other party as the Tribunal may direct; and the Tribunal may tax or settle the amount of the costs, or direct in what manner they are to be taxed.

(2) A document purporting to be a copy of an order of the Tribunal and to be certified by the chairman to be a true copy shall, in any proceedings, be sufficient evidence of the order unless the contrary is proved.

(3) As respect proceedings in Scotland, the Tribunal has the like powers for securing the attendance of witnesses and the production of documents, and with regard to the examination of witnesses on oath, as an arbiter under a submission.

Appeals

152 Appeal to the court on point of law

(1) An appeal lies on any point of law arising from a decision of the Copyright Tribunal to the High Court or, in the case of proceedings of the Tribunal in Scotland, to the Court of Session.

(2) Provision shall be made by rules under section 150 limiting the time within which an appeal may be brought.

(3) Provision may be made by rules under that section—
- (a) for suspending, or authorising or requiring the Tribunal to suspend, the operation of orders of the Tribunal in cases where its decision is appealed against;
- (b) for modifying in relation to an order of the Tribunal whose operation is suspended the operation of any provision of this Act as to the effect of the order;
- (c) for the publication of notices or the taking of other steps for securing that persons affected by the suspension of an order of the Tribunal will be informed of its suspension.

CHAPTER IX

QUALIFICATION FOR AND EXTENT OF COPYRIGHT PROTECTION

Qualification for copyright protection

153 Qualification for copyright protection

(1) Copyright does not subsist in a work unless the qualification requirements of this Chapter are satisfied as regards—
- (a) the author (see section 154), or
- (b) the country in which the work was first published (see section 155), or
- (c) in the case of a broadcast or cable programme, the country from which the broadcast was made or the cable programme was sent (see section 156).

(2) Subsection (1) does not apply in relation to Crown copyright or Parliamentary copyright (see sections 163 to 166) or to copyright subsisting by virtue of section 168 (copyright of certain international organisations).

(3) If the qualification requirements of this Chapter, or section 163, 165 or 168, are once satisfied in respect of a work, copyright does not cease to subsist by reason of any subsequent event.

154 Qualification by reference to author

(1) A work qualifies for copyright protection if the author was at the material time a qualifying person, that is—

(a) a British citizen, a British Dependent Territories citizen, a British National (Overseas), a British Overseas citizen, a British subject or a British protected person within the meaning of the British Nationality Act 1981, or

(b) an individual domiciled or resident in the United Kingdom or another country to which the relevant provisions of this Part extend, or

(c) a body incorporated under the law of a part of the United Kingdom or of another country to which the relevant provisions of this Part extend.

(2) Where, or so far as, provision is made by Order under section 159 (application of this Part to countries to which it does not extend), a work also qualifies for copyright protection if at the material time the author was a citizen or subject of, an individual domiciled or resident in, or a body incorporated under the law of, a country to which the Order relates.

(3) A work of joint authorship qualifies for copyright protection if at the material time any of the authors satisfies the requirements of subsection (1) or (2); but where a work qualifies for copyright protection only under this section, only those authors who satisfy those requirements shall be taken into account for the purposes of—

section 11(1) and (2) (first ownership of copyright; entitlement of author or author's employer),

section 12(1) and (2) (duration of copyright; dependent on life of author unless work of unknown authorship), and section 9(4) (meaning of "unknown authorship") so far as it applies for the purposes of section 12(2), and

section 57 (anonymous or pseudonymous works: acts permitted on assumptions as to expiry of copyright or death of author).

(4) The material time in relation to a literary, dramatic, musical or artistic work is—

(a) in the case of an unpublished work, when the work was made or, if the making of the work extended over a period, a substantial part of that period;

(b) in the case of a published work, when the work was first published or, if the author had died before that time, immediately before his death.

(5) The material time in relation to other descriptions of work is as follows—

(a) in the case of a sound recording or film, when it was made;

(b) in the case of a broadcast, when the broadcast was made;

(c) in the case of a cable programme, when the programme was included in a cable programme service;

(d) in the case of the typographical arrangement of a published edition, when the edition was first published.

155 Qualification by reference to country of first publication

(1) A literary, dramatic, musical or artistic work, a sound recording or film, or the typographical arrangement of a published edition, qualifies for copyright protection if it is first published—

(a) in the United Kingdom, or

(b) in another country to which the relevant provisions of this Part extend.

(2) Where, or so far as, provision is made by Order under section 159 (application of this Part to countries to which it does not extend), such a work also qualifies for copyright protection if it is first published in a country to which the Order relates.

(3) For the purposes of this section, publication in one country shall not be regarded as other than the first publication by reason of simultaneous publication elsewhere; and for this purpose publication elsewhere within the previous 30 days shall be treated as simultaneous.

156 Qualification by reference to place of transmission

(1) A broadcast qualifies for copyright protection if it is made from, and a cable programme qualifies for copyright protection if it is sent from, a place in—

(a) the United Kingdom, or

(b) another country to which the relevant provisions of this Part extend.

(2) Where, or so far as, provision is made by Order under section 159 (application of this Part to countries to which it does not extend), a broadcast or cable programme also qualifies for copyright protection if it is made from or, as the case may be, sent from a place in a country to which the Order relates.

Extent and application of this Part

157 Countries to which this Part extends

(1) This Part extends to England and Wales, Scotland and Northern Ireland.

(2) Her Majesty may by Order in Council direct that this Part shall extend, subject to such exceptions and modifications as may be specified in the Order, to—

(a) any of the Channel Islands,

(b) the Isle of Man, or

(c) any colony.

(3) That power includes power to extend, subject to such exceptions and modifications as may be specified in the Order, any Order in Council made under the following provisions of this Chapter.

(4) The legislature of a country to which this Part has been extended may modify or add to the provisions of this Part, in their operation as part of the law of that country, as the legislature may consider necessary to adapt the provisions to the circumstances of that country—

(a) as regards procedure and remedies, or

(b) as regards works qualifying for copyright protection by virtue of a connection with that country.

(5) Nothing in this section shall be construed as restricting the extent of paragraph 36 of Schedule 1 (transitional provisions: dependent territories where the Copyright Act 1956 or the Copyright Act 1911 remains in force) in relation to the law of a dependent territory to which this Part does not extend.

158 Countries ceasing to be colonies

(1) The following provisions apply where a country to which this Part has been extended ceases to be a colony of the United Kingdom.

(2) As from the date on which it ceases to be a colony it shall cease to be regarded as a country to which this Part extends for the purposes of—

- (a) section 160(2)(a) (denial of copyright protection to citizens of countries not giving adequate protection to British works), and
- (b) sections 163 and 165 (Crown and Parliamentary copyright).

(3) But it shall continue to be treated as a country to which this Part extends for the purposes of sections 154 to 156 (qualification for copyright protection) until—

- (a) an Order in Council is made in respect of that country under section 159 (application of this Part to countries to which it does not extend), or
- (b) an Order in Council is made declaring that it shall cease to be so treated by reason of the fact that the provisions of this Part as part of the law of that country have been repealed or amended.

(4) A statutory instrument containing an Order in Council under subsection (3)(b) shall be subject to annulment in pursuance of a resolution of either House of Parliament.

159 Application of this Part to countries to which it does not extend

(1) Her Majesty may by Order in Council make provision for applying in relation to a country to which this Part does not extend any of the provisions of this Part specified in the Order, so as to secure that those provisions—

- (a) apply in relation to persons who are citizens or subjects of that country or are domiciled or resident there, as they apply to persons who are British citizens or are domiciled or resident in the United Kingdom, or
- (b) apply in relation to bodies incorporated under the law of that country as they apply in relation to bodies incorporated under the law of a part of the United Kingdom, or
- (c) apply in relation to works first published in that country as they apply in relation to works first published in the United Kingdom, or
- (d) apply in relation to broadcasts made from or cable programmes sent from that country as they apply in relation to broadcasts made from or cable programmes sent from the United Kingdom.

(2) An Order may make provision for all or any of the matters mentioned in subsection (1) and may—

- (a) apply any provisions of this Part subject to such exceptions and modifications as are specified in the Order; and
- (b) direct that any provisions of this Part apply either generally or in relation to such classes of works, or other classes of case, as are specified in the Order.

(3) Except in the case of a Convention country or another member State of the European Economic Community, Her Majesty shall not make an Order in Council under this section in relation to a country unless satisfied that provision has been or will be made under the law of that country, in respect of the class of works to which the Order relates, giving adequate protection to the owners of copyright under this Part.

(4) In subsection (3) "Convention country" means a country which is a party to a Convention relating to copyright to which the United Kingdom is also a party.

(5) A statutory instrument containing an Order in Council under this section shall be subject to annulment in pursuance of a resolution of either House of Parliament.

160 Denial of copyright protection to citizens of countries not giving adequate protection to British works

(1) If it appears to Her Majesty that the law of a country fails to give adequate protection to British works to which this section applies, or to one or more classes of such works, Her Majesty may make provision by Order in Council in accordance with this section restricting the rights conferred by this Part in relation to works of authors connected with that country.

(2) An Order in Council under this section shall designate the country concerned and provide that, for the purposes specified in the Order, works first published after a date specified in the Order shall not be treated as qualifying for copyright protection by virtue of such publication if at that time the authors are—

(a) citizens or subjects of that country (not domiciled or resident in the United Kingdom or another country to which the relevant provisions of this Part extend), or

(b) bodies incorporated under the law of that country;

and the Order may make such provision for all the purposes of this Part or for such purposes as are specified in the Order, and either generally or in relation to such class of cases as are specified in the Order, having regard to the nature and extent of that failure referred to in subsection (1).

(3) This section applies to literary, dramatic, musical and artistic works, sound recordings and films; and "British works" means works of which the author was a qualifying person at the material time within the meaning of section 154.

(4) A statutory instrument containing an Order in Council under this section shall be subject to annulment in pursuance of a resolution of either House of Parliament.

Supplementary

161 Territorial waters and the continental shelf

(1) For the purposes of this Part the territorial waters of the United Kingdom shall be treated as part of the United Kingdom.

(2) This Part applies to things done in the United Kingdom sector of the continental shelf on a structure or vessel which is present there for purposes directly connected with the exploration of the sea bed or subsoil or the exploitation of their natural resources as it applies to things done in the United Kingdom.

(3) The United Kingdom sector of the continental shelf means the areas designated by order under section 1(7) of the Continental Shelf Act 1964.

162 British ships, aircraft and hovercraft

(1) This Part applies to things done on a British ship, aircraft or hovercraft as it applies to things done in the United Kingdom.

(2) In this section—

"British ship" means a ship which is a British ship for the purposes of the Merchant Shipping Acts (see section 2 of the Merchant Shipping Act 1988) otherwise than by virtue of registration in a country outside the United Kingdom; and

"British aircraft" and "British hovercraft" mean an aircraft or hovercraft registered in the United Kingdom.

CHAPTER X

MISCELLANEOUS AND GENERAL

Crown and Parliamentary copyright

163 Crown copyright

(1) Where a work is made by Her Majesty or by an officer or servant of the Crown in the course of his duties—

(a) the work qualifies for copyright protection notwithstanding section 153(1) (ordinary requirement as to qualification for copyright protection), and

(b) Her Majesty is the first owner of any copyright in the work.

(2) Copyright in such a work is referred to in this Part as "Crown copyright", notwithstanding that it may be, or have been, assigned to another person.

(3) Crown copyright in a literary, dramatic, musical or artistic work continues to subsist—

(a) until the end of the period of 125 years from the end of the calendar year in which the work was made, or

(b) if the work is published commercially before the end of the period of 75 years from the end of the calendar year in which it was made, until the end of the period of 50 years from the end of the calendar year in which it was first so published.

(4) In the case of a work of joint authorship where one or more but not all of the authors are persons falling within subsection (1), this section applies only in relation to those authors and the copyright subsisting by virtue of their contribution to the work.

(5) Except as mentioned above, and subject to any express exclusion elsewhere in this Part, the provisions of this Part apply in relation to Crown copyright as to other copyright.

(6) This section does not apply to a work if, or to the extent that, Parliamentary copyright subsists in the work (see sections 165 and 166).

164 Copyright in Acts and Measures

(1) Her Majesty is entitled to copyright in every Act of Parliament or Measure of the General Synod of the Church of England.

(2) The copyright subsists from Royal Assent until the end of the period of 50 years from the end of the calendar year in which Royal Assent was given.

(3) References in this Part to Crown copyright (except in section 163) include copyright under this section; and, except as mentioned above, the provisions of this Part apply in relation to copyright under this section as to other Crown copyright.

(4) No other copyright, or right in the nature of copyright, subsists in an Act or Measure.

165 Parliamentary copyright

(1) Where a work is made by or under the direction or control of the House of Commons or the House of Lords—

(a) the work qualifies for copyright protection notwithstanding section 153(1) (ordinary requirement as to qualification for copyright protection), and

(b) the House by whom, or under whose direction or control, the work is made is the first owner of any copyright in the work, and if the work is made by or under the direction or control of both Houses, the two Houses are joint first owners of copyright.

(2) Copyright in such a work is referred to in this Part as "Parliamentary copyright", notwithstanding that it may be, or have been, assigned to another person.

(3) Parliamentary copyright in a literary, dramatic, musical or artistic work continues to subsist until the end of the period of 50 years from the end of the calendar year in which the work was made.

(4) For the purposes of this section, works made by or under the direction or control of the House of Commons or the House of Lords include—

(a) any work made by an officer or employee of that House in the course of his duties, and

(b) any sound recording, film, live broadcast or live cable programme of the proceedings of that House;

but a work shall not be regarded as made by or under the direction or control of either House by reason only of its being commissioned by or on behalf of that House.

(5) In the case of a work of joint authorship where one or more but not all of the authors are acting on behalf of, or under the direction or control of, the House of Commons or the House of Lords, this section applies only in relation to those authors and the copyright subsisting by virtue of their contribution to the work.

(6) Except as mentioned above, and subject to any express exclusion elsewhere in this Part, the provisions of this Part apply in relation to Parliamentary copyright as to other copyright.

(7) The provisions of this section also apply, subject to any exceptions or modifications specified by Order in Council, to works made by or under the direction or control of any other legislative body of a country to which this Part extends; and references in this Part to "Parliamentary copyright" shall be construed accordingly.

(8) A statutory instrument containing an Order in Council under subsection (7) shall be subject to annulment in pursuance of a resolution of either House of Parliament.

166 Copyright in Parliamentary Bills

(1) Copyright in every Bill introduced into Parliament belongs, in accordance with the following provisions, to one or both of the Houses of Parliament.

(2) Copyright in a public Bill belongs in the first instance to the House into which the Bill is introduced, and after the Bill has been carried to the second House to both Houses jointly, and subsists from the time when the text of the Bill is handed in to the House in which it is introduced.

(3) Copyright in a private Bill belongs to both Houses jointly and subsists from the time when a copy of the Bill is first deposited in either House.

(4) Copyright in a personal Bill belongs in the first instance to the House of Lords, and after the Bill has been carried to the House of Commons to both Houses jointly, and subsists from the time when it is given a First Reading in the House of Lords.

(5) Copyright under this section ceases—

(a) on Royal Assent, or

(b) if the Bill does not receive Royal Assent, on the withdrawal or rejection of the Bill or the end of the Session:

Provided that, copyright in a Bill continues to subsist notwithstanding its rejection in any Session by the House of Lords if, by virtue of the Parliament Acts 1911 and 1949, it remains possible for it to be presented for Royal Assent in that Session.

(6) References in this Part to Parliamentary copyright (except in section 165) include copyright under this section; and, except as mentioned above, the provisions of this Part apply in relation to copyright under this section as to other Parliamentary copyright.

(7) No other copyright, or right in the nature of copyright, subsists in a Bill after copyright has once subsisted under this section; but without prejudice to the subsequent operation of this section in relation to a Bill which, not having passed in one Session, is reintroduced in a subsequent Session.

167 Houses of Parliament: supplementary provisions with respect to copyright

(1) For the purposes of holding, dealing with and enforcing copyright, and in connection with all legal proceedings relating to copyright, each House of Parliament shall be treated as having the legal capacities of a body corporate, which shall not be affected by a prorogation or dissolution.

(2) The functions of the House of Commons as owner of copyright shall be exercised by the Speaker on behalf of the House; and if so authorised by the Speaker, or in case of a vacancy in the office of Speaker, those functions may be discharged by the Chairman of Ways and Means or a Deputy Chairman.

(3) For this purpose a person who on the dissolution of Parliament was Speaker of the House of Commons, Chairman of Ways and Means or a Deputy Chairman may continue to act until the corresponding appointment is made in the next Session of Parliament.

(4) The functions of the House of Lords as owner of copyright shall be exercised by the Clerk of the Parliaments on behalf of the House; and if so authorised by him, or in case of a vacancy in the office of Clerk of the Parliaments, those functions may be discharged by the Clerk Assistant or the Reading Clerk.

(5) Legal proceedings relating to copyright—

(a) shall be brought by or against the House of Commons in the name of "The Speaker of the House of Commons"; and

(b) shall be brought by or against the House of Lords in the name of "The Clerk of the Parliaments".

Other miscellaneous provisions

168 Copyright vesting in certain international organisations

(1) Where an original literary, dramatic, musical or artistic work—

(a) is made by an officer or employee of, or is published by, an international organisation to which this section applies, and

(b) does not qualify for copyright protection under section 154 (qualification by reference to author) or section 155 (qualification by reference to country of first publication),

copyright nevertheless subsists in the work by virtue of this section and the organisation is first owner of that copyright.

(2) The international organisations to which this section applies are those as to which Her Majesty has by Order in Council declared that it is expedient that this section should apply.

(3) Copyright of which an international organisation is first owner by virtue of this section continues to subsist until the end of the period of 50 years from the end of the calendar year in which the work was made or such longer period as may be specified by Her Majesty by Order in Council for the purpose of complying with the international obligations of the United Kingdom.

(4) An international organisation to which this section applies shall be deemed to have, and to have had at all material times, the legal capacities of a body corporate for the purpose of holding, dealing with and enforcing copyright and in connection with all legal proceedings relating to copyright.

(5) A statutory instrument containing an Order in Council under this section shall be subject to annulment in pursuance of a resolution of either House of Parliament.

169 Folklore, &c.: anonymous unpublished works

(1) Where in the case of an unpublished literary, dramatic, musical or artistic work of unknown authorship there is evidence that the author (or, in the case of a joint work, any of the authors) was a qualifying individual by connection with a country outside the United Kingdom, it shall be presumed until the contrary is proved that he was such a qualifying individual and that copyright accordingly subsists in the work, subject to the provisions of this Part.

(2) If under the law of that country a body is appointed to protect and enforce copyright in such works, Her Majesty may by Order in Council designate that body for the purposes of this section.

(3) A body so designated shall be recognised in the United Kingdom as having authority to do in place of the copyright owner anything, other than assign copyright, which it is empowered to do under the law of that country; and it may, in particular, bring proceedings in its own name.

(4) A statutory instrument containing an Order in Council under this section shall be subject to annulment in pursuance of a resolution of either House of Parliament.

(5) In subsection (1) a "qualifying individual" means an individual who at the material time (within the meaning of section 154) was a person whose works qualified under that section for copyright protection.

(6) This section does not apply if there has been an assignment of copyright in the work by the author of which notice has been given to the designated body; and nothing in this section affects the validity of an assignment of copyright made, or licence granted, by the author or a person lawfully claiming under him.

Transitional provisions and savings

170 Transitional provisions and savings

Schedule 1 contains transitional provisions and savings relating to works made, and acts or events occurring, before the commencement of this Part, and otherwise with respect to the operation of the provisions of this Part.

171 Rights and privileges under other enactments or the common law

(1) Nothing in this Part affects—

(a) any right or privilege of any person under any enactment (except where the enactment is expressly repealed, amended or modified by this Act);

(b) any right or privilege of the Crown subsisting otherwise than under an enactment;

(c) any right or privilege of either House of Parliament;

(d) the right of the Crown or any person deriving title from the Crown to sell, use or otherwise deal with articles forfeited under the laws relating to customs and excise;

(e) the operation of any rule of equity relating to breaches of trust or confidence.

(2) Subject to those savings, no copyright or right in the nature of copyright shall subsist otherwise than by virtue of this Part or some other enactment in that behalf.

(3) Nothing in this Part affects any rule of law preventing or restricting the enforcement of copyright, on grounds of public interest or otherwise.

(4) Nothing in this Part affects any right of action or other remedy, whether civil or criminal, available otherwise than under this Part in respect of acts infringing any of the rights conferred by Chapter IV (moral rights).

(5) The savings in subsection (1) have effect subject to section 164(4) and section 166(7) (copyright in Acts, Measures and Bills: exclusion of other rights in the nature of copyright).

Interpretation

172 General provisions as to construction

(1) This Part restates and amends the law of copyright, that is, the provisions of the Copyright Act 1956, as amended.

(2) A provision of this Part which corresponds to a provision of the previous law shall not be construed as departing from the previous law merely because of a change of expression.

(3) Decisions under the previous law may be referred to for the purpose of establishing whether a provision of this Part departs from the previous law, or otherwise for establishing the true construction of this Part.

173 Construction of references to copyright owner

(1) Where different persons are (whether in consequence of a partial assignment or otherwise) entitled to different aspects of copyright in a work, the copyright owner for any purpose of this Part is the person who is entitled to the aspect of copyright relevant for that purpose.

(2) Where copyright (or any aspect of copyright) is owned by more than one person jointly, references in this Part to the copyright owner are to all the owners, so that, in particular, any requirement of the licence of the copyright owner requires the licence of all of them.

174 Meaning of "educational establishment" and related expressions

(1) The expression "educational establishment" in a provision of this Part means—
   (a) any school, and
   (b) any other description of educational establishment specified for the purposes of this Part, or that provision, by order of the Secretary of State.

(2) The Secretary of State may by order provide that the provisions of this Part relating to educational establishments shall apply, with such modifications and adaptations as may be specified in the order, in relation to teachers who are employed by a local education authority to give instruction elsewhere to pupils who are unable to attend an educational establishment.

(3) In subsection (1)(a) "school"—
   (a) in relation to England and Wales, has the same meaning as in the Education Act 1944;
   (b) in relation to Scotland, has the same meaning as in the Education (Scotland) Act 1962, except that it includes an approved school within the meaning of the Social Work (Scotland) Act 1968; and
   (c) in relation to Northern Ireland, has the same meaning as in the Education and Libraries (Northern Ireland) Order 1986.

(4) An order under subsection (1)(b) may specify a description of educational establishment by reference to the instruments from time to time in force under any enactment specified in the order.

(5) In relation to an educational establishment the expressions "teacher" and "pupil" in this Part include, respectively, any person who gives and any person who receives instruction.

(6) References in this Part to anything being done "on behalf of" an educational establishment are to its being done for the purposes of that establishment by any person.

(7) An order under this section shall be made by statutory instrument which shall be subject to annulment in pursuance of a resolution of either House of Parliament.

175 Meaning of publication and commercial publication

(1) In this Part "publication", in relation to a work—

(a) means the issue of copies to the public, and

(b) includes, in the case of a literary, dramatic, musical or artistic work, making it available to the public by means of an electronic retrieval system;

and related expressions shall be construed accordingly.

(2) In this Part "commercial publication", in relation to a literary, dramatic, musical or artistic work means—

(a) issuing copies of the work to the public at a time when copies made in advance of the receipt of orders are generally available to the public, or

(b) making the work available to the public by means of an electronic retrieval system;

and related expressions shall be construed accordingly.

(3) In the case of a work of architecture in the form of a building, or an artistic work incorporated in a building, construction of the building shall be treated as equivalent to publication of the work.

(4) The following do not constitute publication for the purposes of this Part and references to commercial publication shall be construed accordingly—

(a) in the case of a literary, dramatic or musical work—

(i) the performance of the work, or

(ii) the broadcasting of the work or its inclusion in a cable programme service (otherwise than for the purposes of an electronic retrieval system);

(b) in the case of an artistic work—

(i) the exhibition of the work,

(ii) the issue to the public of copies of a graphic work representing, or of photographs of, a work of architecture in the form of a building or a model for a building, a sculpture or a work of artistic craftsmanship,

(iii) the issue to the public of copies of a film including the work, or

(iv) the broadcasting of the work or its inclusion in a cable programme service (otherwise than for the purposes of an electronic retrieval system);

(c) in the case of a sound recording or film—

(i) the work being played or shown in public, or

(ii) the broadcasting of the work or its inclusion in a cable programme service.

(5) References in this Part to publication or commercial publication do not include publication which is merely colourable and not intended to satisfy the reasonable requirements of the public.

(6) No account shall be taken for the purposes of this section of any unauthorised act.

176 Requirement of signature: application in relation to body corporate

(1) The requirement in the following provisions that an instrument be signed by or on behalf of a person is also satisfied in the case of a body corporate by the affixing of its seal—

section 78(3)(b) (assertion by licensor of right to identification of author in case of public exhibition of copy made in pursuance of the licence),

section 90(3) (assignment of copyright),

section 91(1) (assignment of future copyright),

section 92(1) (grant of exclusive licence).

(2) The requirement in the following provisions that an instrument be signed by a person is satisfied in the case of a body corporate by signature on behalf of the body or by the affixing of its seal—

section 78(2)(b) (assertion by instrument in writing of right to have author identified),

section 87(2) (waiver of moral rights).

177 Adaptation of expressions for Scotland

In the application of this Part to Scotland—

"account of profits" means accounting and payment of profits;

"accounts" means count, reckoning and payment;

"assignment" means assignation;

"costs" means expenses;

"defendant" means defender;

"delivery up" means delivery;

"estoppel" means personal bar;

"injunction" means interdict;

"interlocutory relief" means interim remedy; and

"plaintiff" means pursuer.

178 Minor definitions

In this Part—

"article", in the context of an article in a periodical, includes an item of any description;

"business" includes a trade or profession;

"collective work" means—

(a) a work of joint authorship, or

(b) a work in which there are distinct contributions by different authors or in which works or parts of works of different authors are incorporated;

"computer-generated", in relation to a work, means that the work is generated by computer in circumstances such that there is no human author of the work;

"country" includes any territory;

"the Crown" includes the Crown in right of Her Majesty's Government in Northern Ireland or in any country outside the United Kingdom to which this Part extends;

"electronic" means actuated by electric, magnetic, electro-magnetic, electro-chemical or electro-mechanical energy, and "in electronic form" means in a form usable only by electronic means;

"employed", "employee", "employer" and "employment" refer to employment under a contract of service or of apprenticeship;

"facsimile copy" includes a copy which is reduced or enlarged in scale;

"international organisation" means an organisation the members of which include one or more states;

"judicial proceedings" includes proceedings before any court, tribunal or person having authority to decide any matter affecting a person's legal rights or liabilities;

"parliamentary proceedings" includes proceedings of the Northern Ireland Assembly or of the European Parliament;

"rental" means any arrangement under whch a copy of a work is made available—

(a) for payment (in money or money's worth), or

(b) in the course of a business as part of services or amenities for whch payment is made,

on terms that it will or may be returned;

"reprographic copy" and "reprographic copying" refer to copying by means of a reprographic process;

"reprographic process" means a process—

(a) for making facsimile copies, or

(b) involving the use of an appliance for making multiple copies,

and includes, in relation to a work held in electronic form, any copying by electronic means, but does not include the making of a film or sound recording;

"sufficient acknowledgement" means an acknowledgement identifying the work in question by its title or other description, and identifying the author unless—

(a) in the case of a published work, it is published anonymously;

(b) in the case of an unpublished work, it is not possible for a person to ascertain the identity of the author by reasonable inquiry;

"sufficient disclaimer", in relation to an act capable of infringing the right conferred by section 80 (right to object to derogatory treatment of work), means a clear and reasonably prominent indication—

(a) given at the time of the act, and

(b) if the author or director is then identified, appearing along with the identification,

that the work has been subjected to treatment to which the author or director has not consented;

"telecommunications system" means a system for conveying visual images, sounds or other information by electronic means;

"typeface" includes an ornamental motif used in printing;

"unauthorised", as regards anything done in relation to a work, means done otherwise than—

(a) by or with the licence of the copyright owner, or

(b) if copyright does not subsist in the work, by or with the licence of the author or, in a case where section 11(2) would have applied, the author's employer or, in either case, persons lawfully claiming under him, or

(c) in pursuance of section 48 (copying, &c. of certain material by the Crown);

"wireless telegraphy" means the sending of electro-magnetic energy over paths not provided by a material substance constructed or arranged for that purpose;

"writing" includes any form of notation or code, whether by hand or otherwise and regardless of the method by which, or medium in or on which, it is recorded, and "written" shall be construed accordingly.

179 Index of defined expressions

The following Table shows provisions defining or otherwise explaining expressions used in this Part (other than provisions defining or explaining an expression used only in the same section)—

account of profits and accounts (in Scotland)	section 177
acts restricted by copyright	section 16(1)
adaptation	section 21(3)
archivist (in sections 37 to 43)	section 37(6)
article (in a periodical)	sectio 178
artistic work	section 4(1)
assignment (in Scotland)	section 177
author	sections 9 and 10(3)
broadcast (and related expressions)	section 6
building	section 4(2)
business	section 178
cable programme, cable programme service (and related expressions)	section 7
collective work	section 178
commencement (in Schedule 1)	paragraph 1(2) of that Schedule
commercial publication	section 175
computer-generated	section 178
copy and copying	section 17
copyright (generally)	section 1
copyright (in Schedule 1)	paragraph 2(2) of that Schedule
copyright owner	section 101(2) and 173
Copyright Tribunal	section 145
copyright work	section 1(2)
costs (in Scotland)	section 177
country	section 178
the Crown	section 178

Crown copyright	sections 163(2) and 164(3)
defendant (in Scotland)	section 177
delivery up (in Scotland)	section 177
dramatic work	section 3(1)
educational establishment	sections 174(1) to (4)
electronic and electronic form	section 178
employed, employee, employer and employment	section 178
exclusive licence	section 92(1)
existing works (in Schedule 1)	paragraph 1(3) of that Schedule
facsimile copy	section 178
film	section 5
future copyright	section 91(2)
general licence (in sections 140 and 141)	section 140(7)
graphic work	section 4(2)
infringing copy	section 27
injunction (in Scotland)	section 177
interlocutory relief (in Scotland)	section 177
international organisation	section 178
issue of copies to the public	section 18(2)
joint authorship (work of)	sections 10(1) and (2)
judicial proceedings	section 178
librarian (in sections 37 and 43)	section 37(6)
licence (in sections 125 to 128)	section 124
licence of copyright owner	sections 90(4), 91(3) and 173
licensing body (in Chapter VII)	section 116(2)
licensing scheme (generally)	section 116(1)
licensing scheme (in sections 118 to 121)	section 117
literary work	section 3(1)
made (in relation to a literary, dramatic or musical work)	section 3(2)
musical work	section 3(1)
the new copyright provisions (in Schedule 1)	paragraph 1(1) of that Schedjule
the 1911 Act (in Schedule 1)	paragraph 1(1) of that Schedule
the 1956 Act (in Schedule 1)	paragraph 1(1) of that Schedule

on behalf of (in relation to an educational establishment)	section 174(5)
Parliamentary copyright	sections 165(2) and (7) and 166(6)
parliamentary proceedings	section 178
performance	section 19(2)
photograph	section 4(2)
plaintiff (in Scotland)	section 177
prescribed conditions (in sections 38 to 43)	section 37(1)(b)
prescribed library or archive (in sections 38 to 43)	section 37(1)(a)
programme (in the context of broadcasting)	section 6(3)
prospective owner (of copyright)	section 91(2)
publication and related expressions	section 175
published edition (in the context of copyright in the typographical arrangement)	section 8
pupil	section 174(5)
rental	section 178
reprographic copies and reprographic copying	section 178
reprographic process	section 178
sculpture	section 4(2)
signed	section 176
sound recording	section 5
sufficient acknowledgement	section 178
sufficient disclaimer	section 178
teacher	section 174(5)
telecommunications system	section 178
typeface	section 178
unauthorised (as regards things done in relation to a work)	section 178
unknown (in relation to the author of a work)	section 9(5)
unknown authorship (work of)	section 9(4)
wireless telegraphy	section 178
work (in Schedule 1)	paragraph 2(1) of that Schedule

work of more than one author (in Chapter VII)	section 116(4)
writing and written	section 178

PART II

RIGHTS IN PERFORMANCES

Introductory

180 Rights conferred on performersw and persons having recording rights

(1) This Part confers rights—

(a) on a performer, by requiring his consent to the exploitation of his performances (see section 181 to 184), and

(b) on a person having recording rights in relation to a performance, in relation to recordings made without his consent or that of the performer (see sections 185 to 188),

and creates offences in relation to dealing with or using illicit recordings and certain other related acts (see sections 198 and 201).

(2) In this part—

"performance" means—

(a) a dramatic performance (which includes dance and mime),

(b) a musical performance,

(c) a reading or recitation of a literary work, or

(d) a performance of a variety act or any similar presentation,

which is, or so far as it is, a live performance given by one or more individuals; and

"recording", in relation to a performance, means a film or sound recording—

(a) made directly from the live perfornmance,

(b) made from a broadcast of, or cable programme including, the performance, or

(c) made, directly or indirectly, from another recording of the performance.

(3) The rights conferred by this Part apply in relation to performances taking place before the commencement of this Part; but no act done before commencement, or in pursuance of arrangements made before commencement, shall be regarded as infringing those rights.

(4) The rights conferred by this Part are independent of—

(a) any copyright in, or moral rights relating to, any work performed or any film or sound recording of, or broadcast or cable programme including, the performance, and

(b) any other right or obligation arising otherwise than under this Part.

Performers' rights

181 Qualifying performances

A performance is a qualifying performance for the purposes of the provisions of this Part relating to performers' rights if it is given by a qualifying individual (as defined in section 206) or takes place in a qualifying country (as so defined).

182 Consent required for recording or live transmission of performance

(1) A performer's rights are infringed by a person who, without his consent—

(a) makes, otherwise than for his private and domestic use, a recording of the whole or any substantial part of a qualifying performance, or

(b) broadcast live, or includes live in a cable programme service, the whole or any substantial part of a qualifying performance.

(2) In an action for infringement of a performer's rights brought by virtue of this section damages shall not be awarded against a defendant who shows that at the time of the infringement he believed on reasonable grounds that consent had been given.

183 Infringement of performer's rights by use of recording made without consent

A performer's rights are infringed by a person who, without his consent—

(a) shows or plays in public the whole or any substantial part of a qualifying performance, or

(b) broadcasts or includes in a cable programme service the whole or any substantial part of a qualifying performance,

by means of a recording which was, and which that person knows or has reason to believe was, made without the performer's consent.

184 Infringement of performer's rights by importing, possessing or dealing with illicit recording

(1) A performer's rights are infringed by a person who, without his consent—

(a) imports into the United Kingdom otherwise than for his private and domestic use, or

(b) in the course of a business possesses, sells or lets for hire, offers or exposes for sale or hire, or distributes,

a recording of a qualifying performance which is, and which that person knows or has reason to believe is, an illicit recording.

(2) Where in an action for infringement of a performer's rights brought by virtue of this section a defendant shows that the illicit recording was innocently acquired by him or a predecessor in title of his, the only remedy available against him in respect of the infringement is damages not exceeding a reasonable payment in respect of the act complained of.

(3) In subsection (2) "innocently acquired" means that the person acquiring the recording did not know and had no reason to believe that it was an illicit recording.

Rights of person having recording rights

185 Exclusive recording contracts and persons having recording rights

(1) In this Part an "exclusive recording contract" means a contract between a performer and another person under which that person is entitled to the exclusion of all other persons (including the performer) to make recordings of one or more of his performances with a view to their commercial exploitation.

(2) References in this Part to a "person having recording rights", in relation to a performance, are (subject to subsection (3)) to a person—

(a) who is party to and has the benefit of an exclusive recording contract to which the performance is subject, or

(b) to whom the benefit of such a contract has been assigned,

and who is a qualifying person.

(3) If a performance is subject to an exclusive recording contract but the person mentioned in subsection (2) is not a qualifying person, references in this Part to a "person having recording rights" in relation to the performance are to any person—

(a) who is licensed by such a person to make recordings of the performance with a view to their commercial exploitation, or

(b) to whom the benefit of such a licence has been assigned,

and who is a qualifying person.

(4) In this section "with a view to commercial exploitation" means with a view to the recordings being sold or let for hire, or shown or played in public.

186 Consent required for recording of performance subject to exclusive contract

(1) A person infringes the rights of a person having recording rights in relation to a performance who, without his consent or that of the performer, makes a recording of the whole or any substantial part of the performance, otherwise than for his private and domestic use.

(2) In an action for infringement of those rights brought by virtue of this section damages shall not be awarded against a defendant who shows that at the time of the infringement he believed on reasonable grounds that consent had been given.

187 Infringement of recording rights by use of recording made without consent

(1) A person infringes the rights of a person having recording rights in relation to a performance who, without his consent or, in the case of a qualifying performance, that of the performer—

(a) shows or plays in public the whole or any substantial part of the performance, or

(b) broadcasts or includes in a cable programme service the whole or any substantial part of the performance,

by means of a recording which was, and which that person knows or has reason to believe was, made without the appropriate consent.

(2) The reference in subsection (1) to "the appropriate consent" is to the consent of—

(a) the performer, or

(b) the person who at the time the consent was given had recording rights in relation to the performance (or, if there was more than one such person, of all of them).

188 Infringement of recording rights by importing, possessing or dealing with illicit recording

(1) A person infringes the rights of a person having recording rights in relation to a performance who, without his consent or, in the case of a qualifying performance, that of the performer—

(a) imports into the United Kingdom otherwise than for his private and domestic use, or

(b) in the course of a business possesses, sells or lets for hire, offers or exposes for sale or hire, or distributes,

a recording of the performance which is, and which that person knows or has reason to believe is, an illicit recording.

(2) Where in an action for infringement of those rights brought by virtue of this section a defendant shows that the illicit recording was innocently acquired by him or a predecessor in title of his, the only remedy available against him in respect of the infringement is damages not exceeding a reasonable payment in respect of the act complained of.

(3) In subsection (2) "innocently acquired" means that the person acquiring the recording did not know and had no reason to believe that it was an illicit recording.

Exceptions to rights conferred

189 Acts permitted notwithstanding rights conferred by this Part

The provisions of Schedule 2 specify acts which may be done notwithstanding the rights conferred by this Part, being acts which correspond broadly to certain of those specified in Chapter III of Part I (acts permitted notwithstanding copyright).

190 Power of tribunal to give consent on behalf of performer in certain cases

(1) The Copyright Tribunal may, on the application of a person wishing to make a recording from a previous recording of a performance, give consent in a case where—

(a) the identity or whereabouts of a performer cannot be ascertained by reasonable inquiry, or

(b) a performer unreasonably withholds his consent.

(2) Consent given by the Tribunal has effect as consent of the performer for the purposes of—

(a) the provisions of this Part relating to performers' rights, and

(b) section 198(3)(a) (criminal liability: sufficient consent in relation to qualifying performances),

and may be given subject to any conditions specified in the Tribunal's order.

(3) The Tribunal shall not give consent under subsection (1)(a) except after the service or publication of such notices as may be required by rules made under section 150 (general procedural rules) or as the Tribunal may in any particular case direct.

(4) The Tribunal shall not give consent under subsection (1)(b) unless satisfied that the performer's reasons for withholding consent do not include the protection of any legitimate interest of his; but it shall be for the performer to show what his reasons are for withholding consent, and in default of evidence as to his reasons the Tribunal may draw such inferences as it thinks fit.

(5) In any case the Tribunal shall take into account the following factors—

(a) whether the original recording was made with the performer's consent and is lawfully in the possession or control of the person proposing to make the further recording;

(b) whether the making of the further recording is consistent with the obligations of the parties to the arrangements under which, or is otherwise consistent with the purposes for which, the original recording was made.

(6) Where the Tribunal gives consent under this section it shall, in default of agreement between the applicant and the performer, make such order as it thinks fit as to the payment to be made to the performer in consideration of consent being given.

Duration and transmission of rights; consent

191 Duration of rights

The rights conferred by this Part continue to subsist in relation to a performance until the end of the period of 50 years from the end of the calendar year in which the performance takes place.

192 Transmission of rights

(1) The rights conferred by this Part are not assignable or transmissible, except to the extent that performers' rights are transmissible in accordance with the following provisions.

(2) On the death of a person entitled to performer's rights—

(a) the rights pass to such person as he may by testamentary disposition specifically direct, and

(b) if or to the extent that there is no such direction, the rights are exercisable by his personal representatives;

and references in this Part to the performer, in the context of the person having performers' rights, shall be construed as references to the person for the time being entitled to exercise those rights.

(3) Where by virtue of subsection (2)(a) a right becomes exercisable by more than one person, it is exercisable by each of them independently of the other or others.

(4) The above provisions do not affect section 185(2)(b) or (3)(b), so far as those provisions confer rights under this Part on a person to whom the benefit of a contract or licence is assigned.

(5) Any damages recovered by personal representatives by virtue of this section in respect of an infringement after a person's death shall devolve as part of his estate as if the right of action had subsisted and been vested in him immediately before his death.

193 Consent

(1) Consent for the purposes of this Part may be given in relation to a specific performance, a specified description of performances or performances generally, and may relate to past or future performances.

(2) A person having recording rights in a performance is bound by any consent given by a person through whom he derives his rights under the exclusive recording contract or licence in question, in the same way as if the consent had been given by him.

(3) Where a right conferred by this Part passes to another person, any consent binding on the person previously entitled binds the person to whom the right passes in the same way as if the consent had been given by him.

Remedies for infringement

194 Infringement actionable as breach of statutory duty

An infringement of any of the rights conferred by this Part is actionable by the person entitled to the right as a breach of statutory duty.

195 Order for delivery up

(1) Where a person has in his possession, custody or control in the course of a business an illicit recording of a performance, a person having performer's rights or recording rights in relation to the performance under this Part may apply to the court for an order that the recording be delivered up to him or to such other person as the court may direct.

(2) An application shall not be made after the end of the period specified in section 203; and no order shall be made unless the court also makes, or it appears to the court that there are grounds for making, an order under section 204 (order as to disposal of illicit recording).

(3) A person to whom a recording is delivered up in pursuance of an order under this section shall, if an order under section 204 is not made, retain it pending the making of an order, or the decision not to make an order, under that section.

(4) Nothing in this section affects any other power of the court.

196 Right to seize illicit recordings

(1) An illicit recording of a performance which is found exposed or otherwise immediately available for sale or hire, and in respect of which a person would be entitled to apply for an order under section 195, may be seized and detained by him or a person authorised by him.

The right to seize and detain is exercisable subject to the following conditions and is subject to any decision of the court under section 204 (order as to disposal of illicit recording).

(2) Before anything is seized under this section notice of the time and place of the proposed seizure must be given to a local police station.

(3) A person may for the purpose of exercising the right conferred by this section enter premises to which the public have access but may not seize anything in the possession, custody or control of a person at a permanent or regular place of business of his and may not use any force.

(4) At the time when anything is seized under this section there shall be left at the place where it was seized a notice in the prescribed form containing the prescribed particulars as to the person by whom or on whose authority the seizure is made and the grounds on which it is made.

(5) In this section—

"premises" includes land, buildings, fixed or moveable structures, vehicles, vessels, aircraft and hovercraft; and

"prescribed" means prescribed by order of the Secretary of State.

(6) An order of the Secretary of State under this section shall be made by statutory instrument which shall be subject to annulment in pursuance of a resolution of either House of Parliament.

197 Meaning of "illicit recording"

(1) In this Part "illicit recording", in relation to a performance, shall be construed in accordance with this section.

(2) For the purposes of a performer's rights, a recording of the whole or any substantial part of a performance of his is an illicit recording if it is made, otherwise than for private purposes, without his consent.

(3) For the purposes of the rights of a person having recording rights, a recording of the whole or any substantial part of a performance subject to the exclusive recording contract is an illicit recording if it is made, otherwise than for private purposes, without his consent or that of the performer.

(4) For the purposes of sections 198 and 199 (offences and orders for delivery up in criminal proceedings), a recording is an illicit recording if it is an illicit recording for the purposes mentioned in subsection (2) or subsection (3).

(5) In this Part "illicit recording" includes a recording falling to be treated as an illicit recording by virtue of any of the following provisions of Schedule 2—

paragraph 4(3) (recordings made for purposes of instruction or examination),

paragraph 6(2) (recordings made by educational establishments for educational purposes),

paragraph 12(2) (recordings of performance in electronic form retained on transfer of principal recording), or

paragraph 16(3) (recordings made for purposes of broadcast or cable programme), but otherwise does not include a recording made in accordance with any of the provisions of that Schedule.

(6) It is immaterial for the purposes of this section where the recording was made.

Offences

198 Criminal liability for making, dealing with or using illicit recordings

(1) A person commits an offence who without sufficient consent—

(a) makes for sale or hire, or

(b) imports into the United Kingdom otherwise than for his private and domestic use, or

(c) possesses in the course of a business with a view to committing any act infringing the rights conferred by this Part, or

(d) in the course of a business—

(i) sells or lets for hire, or

(ii) offers or exposes for sale or hire, or

(iii) distributes,

a recording which is, and which he knows or has reason to believe is, an illicit recording.

(2) A person commits an offence who causes a recording of a performance made without sufficient consent to be—

(a) shown or played in public, or

(b) broadcast or included in a cable programme service,

thereby infringing any of the rights conferred by this Part, if he knows or has reason to believe that those rights are thereby infringed.

(3) In subsections (1) and (2) "sufficient consent" means—

(a) in the case of a qualifying performance, the consent of the performer, and

(b) in the case of a non-qualifying performance subject to an exclusive recording contract—

(i) for the purposes of subsection (1)(a) (making of recording), the consent of the performer or the person having recording rights, and

(ii) for the purposes of subsection (1)(b), (c) and (d) and subsection (2) (dealing with or using recording), the consent of the person having recording rights.

The references in this subsection to the person having recording rights are to the person having those rights at the time the consent is given or, if there is more than one such person, to all of them.

(4) No offence is committed under subsection (1) or (2) by the commission of an act which by virtue of any provision of Schedule 2 may be done without infringing the rights conferred by this Part.

(5) A person guilty of an offence under subsection (1)(a), (b) or (d)(iii) is liable—

(a) on summary conviction to imprisonment for a term not exceeding six months or a fine not exceeding the statutory maximum, or both;

(b) on conviction on indictment to a fine or imprisonment for a term not exceeding two years, or both.

(6) A person guilty of any other offence under this section is liable on summary conviction to a fine not exceeding level 5 on the standard scale or imprisonment for a term not exceeding six months, or both.

199 Order for delivery up in criminal proceedings

(1) The court before which proceedings are brought against a person for an offence under section 198 may, if satisfied that at the time of his arrest or charge he had in his possession, custody or control in the course of a business an illicit recording of a performance, order that it be delivered up to a person having performers' rights or recording rights in relation to the performance or to such other person as the court may direct.

(2) For this purpose a person shall be treated as charged with an offence—

(a) in England, Wales and Northern Ireland, when he is orally charged or is served with a summons or indictment;

(b) in Scotland, when he is cautioned, charged or served with a complaint or indictment.

(3) An order may be made by the court of its own motion or on the application of the prosecutor (or, in Scotland, the Lord Advocate or procurator-fiscal), and may be made whether or not the person is convicted of the offence, but shall not be made—

(a) after the end of the period specified in section 203 (period after which remedy of delivery up not available), or

(b) if it appears to the court unlikely that any order will be made under section 204 (order as to disposal of illicit recording).

(4) An appeal lies from an order made under this section by a magistrates' court—

(a) in England and Wales, to the Crown Court, and

(b) in Northern Ireland, to the county court;

and in Scotland, where an order has been made under this section, the person from whose possession, custody or control the illicit recording has been been removed may, without predudice to any other form of appeal under any rule of law, appeal against that order in the same manner as against sentence.

(5) A person to whom an illicit recording is delivered up in pursuance of an order under this section shall retain it pending the making of an order, or the decision not to make an order, under section 204.

(6) Nothing in in this section affects the powers of the court under section 43 of the Powers of Criminal Courts Act 1973, section 223 or 436 of the Criminal Procedure (Scotland) Act 1975 or Article 7 of the Criminal Justice (Northern Ireland) Order 1980 (general provisions as to forfeiture in criminal proceedings).

200 Search warrants

(1) Where a justice of the peace (in Scotland, a sheriff or justice of the peace) is satisfied by information on oath given by a constable (in Scotland, by evidence on oath) that there are reasonable grounds for believing—

(a) that an offence under section 198(1)(a), (b) or (d)(iii) (offences of making, importing or distributing illicit recordings) has been or is about to be committed in any premises, and

(b) that evidence that such an offence has been or is about to be committed is in those premises,

he may issue a warrant authorising a constable to enter and search the premises, using such reasonable force as is necessary.

(2) The power conferred by subsection (1) does not, in England and Wales, extend to authorising a search for material of the kinds mentioned in section 9(2) of the Police and Criminal Evidence Act 1984 (certain classes of personal or confidential material).

(3) A warrant under subsection (1)—

(a) may authorise persons to accompany any constable executing the warrant, and

(b) remains in force for 28 days from the date of its issue.

(4) In this section "premises" includes land, buildings, fixed or moveable structures, vehicles, vessels, aircraft and hovercraft.

201 False representation of authority to give consent

(1) It is an offence for a person to represent falsely that he is authorised by any person to give consent for the purposes of this Part in relation to a performance, unless he believes on reasonable grounds that he is so authorised.

(2) A person guilty of an offence under this section is liable on summary conviction to imprisonment for a term not exceeding six months or a fine not exceeding level 5 on the standard scale or both.

202 Offence by body corporate: liability of officers

(1) Where an offence under this Part committed by a body corporate is proved to have been committed with the consent or connivance of a director, manager, secretary or other similar officer of the body, or a person purporting to act in any such capacity, he as well as the body corporate is guilty of the offence and liable to be proceeded against and punished accordingly.

(2) In relation to a body corporate whose affairs are managed by its members "director" means a member of the body corporate.

Supplementary provisions with respect to delivery up and seizure

203 Period after which remedy of delivery up not available

(1) An application for an order under section 195 (order for delivery up in civil proceedings) may not be made after the end of the period of six years from the date on which the illicit recording in question was made, subject to the following provisions.

(2) If during the whole or any part of that period a person entitled to apply for an order—

(a) is under a disability, or

(b) is prevented by fraud or concealment from discovering the facts entitling him to apply, an application may be made by him at any time before the end of the period of six years from the date on which he ceased to be under a disability or, as the case may be, could with reasonable diligence have discovered those facts.

(3) In subsection (2) "disability"—

(a) in England and Wales, has the same meaning as in the Limitation Act 1980;

(b) in Scotland, means legal disability within the meaning of the Prescription and Limitations (Scotland) Act 1973;

(c) in Northern Ireland, has the same meaning as in the Statute of Limitation (Northern Ireland) 1958.

(4) An order under section 199 (order for delivery up in criminal proceedings) shall not, in any case, be made after the end of the period of six years from the date on which the illicit recording in question was made.

204 Order as to disposal of illicit recording

(1) An application may be made to the court for an order that an illicit recording of a performance delivered up in pursuance of an order under section 195 or 199, or seized and detained in pursuance of the right conferred by section 196, shall be—

(a) forfeited to such person having performer's rights or recording rights in relation to the performance as the court may direct, or

(b) destroyed or otherwise dealt with as the court may think fit,

or for a decision that no such order should be made.

(2) In considering what order (if any) should be made, the court shall consider whether other remedies available in an action for infringement of the rights conferred by this Part would be adequate to compensate the person or persons entitled to the rights and to protect their interests.

(3) Provision shall be made by rules of court as to the service of notice on persons having an interest in the recording, and any such person is entitled—

(a) to appear in proceedings for an order under this section, whether or not he was served with notice, and

(b) to appeal against any order made, whether or not he appeared;

and an order shall not take effect until the end of the period within which notice of an appeal may be given or, if before the end of that period notice of appeal is duly given, until the final determination or abandonment of the proceedings on the appeal.

(4) Where there is more than one person interested in a recording, the court shall make such order as it thinks just and may (in particular) direct that the recording be sold, or otherwise dealt with, and the proceeds divided.

(5) If the court decides that no order should be made under this section, the person in whose possession, custody or control the recording was before being delivered up or seized is entitled to its return.

(6) References in this section to a person having an interest in a recording include any person in whose favour an order could be made in respect of the recording under this section or under section 114 or 231 of this Act or section 58C of the Trade Marks Act 1938 (which make similar provision in relation to infringement of copyright, design right and trade marks).

205 Jurisdiction of county court and sheriff court

(1) In England, Wales and Northern Ireland a county court may entertain proceedings under—

section 195 (order for delivery up of illicit recording), or

section 204 (order as to disposal of illicit recording),

where the value of the illicit recordings in question does not exceed the county court limit for actions in tort.

(2) In Scotland proceedings for an order under either of those provisions may be brought in the sheriff court.

(3) Nothing in this section shall be construed as affecting the jurisdiction of the High Court or, in Scotland, the Court of Session.

Qualification for protection and extent

206 Qualifying countries, individuals and persons

(1) In this Part—

"qualifying country" means—

(a) the United Kingdom,

(b) another member State of the European Economic Community, or

(c) to the extent that an Order under section 208 so provides, a country designated under that section as enjoying reciprocal protection;

"qualifying individual" means a citizen or subject of, or an individual resident in, a qualifying country; and

"qualifying person" means a qualifying individual or a body corporate or other body having legal personality which—

(a) is formed under the law of a part of the United Kingdom or another qualifying country, and

(b) has in any qualifying country a place of business at which substantial business activity is carried on.

(2) The reference in the definition of "qualifying individual" to a person's being a citizen or subject of a qualifying country shall be construed—

(a) in relation to the United Kingdom, as a reference to his being a British citizen, and

(b) in relation to a colony of the United Kingdom, as a reference to his being a British Dependent Territories' citizen by connection with that colony.

(3) In determining for the purpose of the definition of "qualifying person" whether substantial business activity is carried on at a place of business in any country, no account shall be taken of dealings in goods which are at all material times outside that country.

207 Countries to which this Part extends

This Part extends to England and Wales, Scotland and Northern Ireland.

208 Countries enjoying reciprocal protection

(1) Her Majesty may by Order in Council designate as enjoying reciprocal protection under this Part—

(a) a Convention country, or

(b) a country as to which Her Majesty is satisfied that provision has been or will be made under its law giving adequate protection for British performances.

(2) A "Convention country" means a country which is a party to a Convention relating to performers' rights to which the United Kingdom is also a party.

(3) A "British performance" means a performance—

(a) given by an individual who is a British citizen or resident in the United Kingdom, or

(b) taking place in the United Kingdom.

(4) If the law of that country provides adequate protection only for certain descriptions of performance, an Order under subsection (1)(b) designating that country shall contain provision limiting to a corresponding extent the protection afforded by this Part in relation to performances connected with that country.

(5) The power conferred by subsection (1)(b) is exercisable in relation to any of the Channel Islands, the Isle of Man or any colony of the United Kingdom, as in relation to a foreign country.

(6) A statutory instrument containing an Order in Council under this section shall be subject to annulment in pursuance of a resolution of either House of Parliament.

209 Territorial waters and the continental shelf

(1) For the purposes of this Part the territorial waters of the United Kingdom shall be treated as part of the United Kingdom.

(2) This Part applies to things done in the United Kingdom sector of the continental shelf on a structure or vessel which is present there for purposes directly connected with the exploration of the sea bed or subsoil or the exploitation of their natural resources as it applies to things done in the United Kingdom.

(3) The United Kingdom sector of the continental shelf means the areas designated by order under section 1(7) of the Continental Shelf Act 1964.

210 British ships, aircraft and hovercraft

(1) This Part applies to things done on a British ship, aircraft or hovercraft as it applies to things done in the United Kingdom.

(2) In this section—

"British ship" means a ship which is a British ship for the purposes of the Merchant Shipping Acts (see section 2 of the Merchant Shipping Act 1988) otherwise than by virtue of registration in a country outside the United Kingdom; and

"British aircraft" and "British hovercraft" mean an aircraft or hovercraft registered in the United Kingdom.

Interpretation

211 Expressions having same meaning as in copyright provisions

(1) The following expressions have the same meaning in this Part as in Part I (copyright) —

broadcast,
business,
cable programme,
cable programme service,
country,
defendant (in Scotland),
delivery up (in Scotland),
film,
literary work,
published, and
sound recording.

(2) The provisions of section 6(3) to (5), section 7(5) and 19(4) (supplementary provisions relating to broadcasting and cable programme services) apply for the purposes of this Part, and in relation to an infringement of the rights conferred by this Part, as they apply for the purposes of Part I and in relation to an infringement of copyright.

212 Index of defined expressions

The following Table shows provisions defining or otherwise explaining expressions used in this Part (other than provisions defining or explaining an expression used only in the same section)—

broadcast (and related expressions)	section 211 (and section 6)
business	section 211(1) (and section 178)
cable programme, cable programme service (and related expressions)	section 211 (and section 7)
country	section 211(1) (and section 178)
defendant (in Scotland)	section 211(1) (and section 177)
delivery up (in Scotland)	section 211(1) (and section 177)
exclusive recording contract	section 185(1)
film	section 211(1) (and section 5)
illicit recording	section 197
literary work	section 211(1) (and section 3(1))
performance	section 180(2)
published	section 211(1) (and section 175)
qualifying country	section 206(1)
qualifying individual	section 206(1) and (2)

qualifying performance	section 181
qualifying person	section 206(1) and (3)
recording (of a performance)	section 180(2)
recording rights (person having)	section 185(2) and (3)
sound recording	section 211(1) (and section 5).

PART III

DESIGN RIGHT

CHAPTER I

DESIGN RIGHT IN ORIGINAL DESIGNS

Introductory

213 Design right

(1) Design right is a property right which subsists in accordance with this Part in an original design.

(2) In this Part "design" means the design of any aspect of the shape or configuration (whether internal or external) of the whole or part of an article.

(3) Design right does not subsist in—

- (a) a method or principle of construction,
- (b) features of shape or configuration of an article which—
  - (i) enable the article to be connected to, or placed in, around or against, another article so that either article may perform its function, or
  - (ii) are dependent upon the appearance of another article of which the article is intended by the designer to form an integral part, or
- (c) surface decoration.

(4) A design is not "original" for the purposes of this Part if it is commonplace in the design field in question at the time of its creation.

(5) Design right subsists in a design only if the design qualifies for design right protection by reference to—

- (a) the designer or the person by whom the design was commissioned or the designer employed (see sections 218 and 219), or
- (b) the person by whom and country in which articles made to the design were first marketed (see section 220),

or in accordance with any Order under section 221 (power to make further provision with respect to qualification).

(6) Design right does not subsist unless and until the design has been recorded in a design document or an article has been made to the design.

(7) Design right does not subsist in a design which was so recorded, or to which an article was made, before the commencement of this Part.

214 The designer

(1) In this Part the "designer", in relation to a design, means the person who creates it.

(2) In the case of a computer-generated design the person by whom the arrangements necessary for the creation of the design are undertaken shall be taken to be the designer.

215 Ownership of design right

(1) The designer is the first owner of any design right in a design which is not created in pursuance of a commission or in the course of employment.

(2) Where a design is created in pursuance of a commission, the person commissioning the design is the first owner of any design right in it.

(3) Where, in a case not falling within subsection (2) a design is created by an employee in the course of his employment, his employer is the first owner of any design right in the design.

(4) If a design qualifies for design right protection by virtue of section 220 (qualification by reference to first marketing of articles made to the design), the above rules do not apply and the person by whom the articles in question are marketed is the first owner of the design right.

216 Duration of design right

(1) Design right expires—

(a) fifteen years from the end of the calendar year in which the design was first recorded in a design document or an article was first made to the design, whichever first occurred, or

(b) if articles made to the design are made available for sale or hire within five years from the end of that calendar year, ten years from the end of the calendar year in which that first occurred.

(2) The reference in subsection (1) to articles being made available for sale or hire is to their being made so available anywhere in the world by or with the licence of the design right owner.

Qualification for design right protection

217 Qualifying individuals and qualifying persons

(1) In this Part—

"qualifying individual" means a citizen or subject of, or an individual habitually resident in, a qualifying country; and

"qualifying person" means a qualifying individual or a body corporate or other body having legal personality which—

(a) is formed under the law of a part of the United Kingdom or another qualifying country, and

(b) has in any qualifying country a place of business at which substantial business activity is carried on.

(2) References in this Part to a qualifying person include the Crown and the government of any other qualifying country.

(3) In this section "qualifying country" means—

(a) the United Kingdom,

(b) a country to which this Part extends by virtue of an Order under section 255,

(c) another member State of the European Economic Community, or

(d) to the extent that an Order under section 256 so provides, a country designated under that section as enjoying reciprocal protection.

(4) The reference in the definition of "qualifying individual" to a person's being a citizen or subject of a qualifying country shall be construed—

(a) in relation to the United Kingdom, as a reference to his being a British citizen, and

(b) in relation to a colony of the United Kingdom, as a reference to his being a British Dependent Territories' citizen by connection with that colony.

(5) In determining for the purpose of the definition of "qualifying person" whether substantial business activity is carried on at a place of business in any country, no account shall be taken of dealings in goods which are at all material times outside that country.

218 Qualification by reference to designer

(1) This section applies to a design which is not created in pursuance of a commission or in the course of employment.

(2) A design to which this section applies qualifies for design right protection if the designer is a qualifying individual or, in the case of a computer-generated design, a qualifying person.

(3) A joint design to which this section applies qualifies for design right protection if any of the designers is a qualifying individual or, as the case may be, a qualifying person.

(4) Where a joint design qualifies for design right protection under this section, only those designers who are qualifying individuals or qualifying persons are entitled to design right under section 215(1) (first ownership of design right: entitlement of designer).

219 Qualification by reference to commissioner or employer

(1) A design qualifies for design right protection if it is created in pursuance of a commission from, or in the course of employment with, a qualifying person.

(2) In the case of a joint commission or joint employment a design qualifies for design right protection if any of the commissioners or employers is a qualifying person.

(3) Where a design which is jointly commissioned or created in the course of joint employment qualifies for design right protection under this section, only those commissioners or employers who are qualifying persons are entitled to design right under section 215(2) or (3) (first ownership of design right: entitlement of commissioner or employer).

220 Qualification by reference to first marketing

(1) A design which does not qualify for design right protection under section 218 or 219 (qualification by reference to designer, commissioner or employer) qualifies for design right protection if the first marketing of articles made to the design—

(a) is by a qualifying person who is exclusively authorised to put such articles on the market in the United Kingdom, and

(b) takes place in the United Kingdom, another country to which this Part extends by virtue of an Order under section 255, or another member State of the European Economic Community.

(2) If the first marketing of articles made to the design is done jointly by two or more persons, the design qualifies for design right protection if any of those persons meets the requirements specified in subsection (1)(a).

(3) In such a case only the persons who meet those requirements are entitled to design right under section 215(4) (first ownership of design right: entitlement of first marketer of articles made to the design).

(4) In subsection (1)(a) "exclusively authorised" refers—

(a) to authorisation by the person who would have been first owner of design right as designer, commissioner of the design or employer of the designer if he had been a qualifying person, or by a person lawfully claiming under such a person, and

(b) to exclusivity capable of being enforced by legal proceedings in the United Kingdom.

221 Power to make further provision as to qualification

(1) Her Majesty may, with a view to fulfilling an international obligation of the United Kingdom, by Order in Council provide that a design qualifies for design right protection if such requirements as are specified in the Order are met.

(2) An Order may make different provision for different descriptions of design or article; and may make such consequential modifications of the operation of sections 215 (ownership of design right) and sections 218 to 220 (other means of qualification) as appear to Her Majesty to be appropriate.

(3) A statutory instrument containing an Order in Council under this section shall be subject to annulment in pursuance of a resolution of either House of Parliament.

Dealings with design right

222 Assignment and licences

(1) Design right is transmissible by assignment, by testamentary disposition or by operation of law, as personal or moveable property.

(2) An assignment or other transmission of design right may be partial, that is, limited so as to apply—

(a) to one or more, but not all, of the things the design right owner has the exclusive right to do;

(b) to part, but not the whole, of the period for which the right is to subsist.

(3) An assignment of design right is not effective unless it is in writing signed by or on behalf of the assignor.

(4) A licence granted by the owner of design right is binding on every successor in title to his interest in the right, except a purchaser in good faith for valuable consideration and without notice (actual or constructive) of the licence or a person deriving title from such a purchaser; and references in this Part to doing anything with, or without, the licence of the design right owner shall be construed accordingly.

223 Prospective ownership of design right

(1) Where by an agreement made in relation to future design right, and signed by or on behalf of the prospective owner of the design right, the prospective owner purports to assign the future design right (wholly or partially) to another person, then if, on the right coming into existence, the assignee or another person claiming under him would be entitled as against all other persons to require the right to be vested in him, the right shall vest in him by virtue of this section.

(2) In this section—

"future design right" means design right which will or may come into existence in respect of a future design or class of designs or on the occurrence of a future event; and

"prospective owner" shall be construed accordingly, and includes a person who is prospectively entitled to design right by virtue of such an agreement as is mentioned in subsection (1).

(3) A licence granted by a prospective owner of design right is binding on every successor in title to his interest (or prospective interest) in the right, except a purchaser in good faith for valuable consideration and without notice (actual or constructive) of the licence or a person deriving title from such a purchaser; and references in this Part to doing anything with, or without, the licence of the design right owner shall be construed accordingly.

224 Assignment of right in registered design presumed to carry with it design right

Where a design consisting of a design in which design right subsists is registered under the Registered Designs Act 1949 and the proprietor of the registered design is also the design right owner, an assignment of the right in the registered design shall be taken to be also an assignment of the design right, unless a contrary intention appears.

225 Exclusive licences

(1) In this Part an "exclusive licence" means a licence in writing signed by or on behalf of the design right owner authorising the licensee to the exclusion of all other persons, including the person granting the licence, to exercise a right which would otherwise be exercisable exclusively by the design right owner.

(2) The licensee under an exclusive licence has the same rights against any successor in title who is bound by the licence as he has against the person granting the licence.

CHAPTER II

RIGHTS OF DESIGN RIGHT OWNER AND REMEDIES

Infringement of design right

226 Primary infringement of design right

(1) The owner of design right in a design has the exclusive right to reproduce the design for commercial purposes—

(a) by making articles to that design, or

(b) by making a design document recording the design for the purpose of enabling such articles to be made.

(2) Reproduction of a design by making articles to the design means copying the design so as to produce articles exactly or substantially to that design, and references in this Part to making articles to a design shall be construed accordingly.

(3) Design right is infringed by a person who without the licence of the design right owner does, or authorises another to do, anything which by virtue of this section is the exclusive right of the design right owner.

(4) For the purposes of this section reproduction may be direct or indirect, and it is immaterial whether any intervening acts themselves infringe the design right.

(5) This section has effect subject to the provisions of Chapter III (exceptions to rights of design right owner).

227 Secondary infringement: importing or dealing with infringing article

(1) Design right is infringed by a person who, without the licence of the design right owner—

(a) imports into the United Kingdom for commercial purposes, or

(b) has in his possession for commercial purposes, or

(c) sells, lets for hire, or offers or exposes for sale or hire, in the course of a business,

an article which is, and which he knows or has reason to believe is, an infringing article.

(2) This section has effect subject to the provisions of Chapter III (exceptions to rights of design right owner).

228 Meaning of "infringing article"

(1) In this Part "infringing article", in relation to a design, shall be construed in accordance with this section.

(2) An article is an infringing article if its making to that design was an infringement of design right in the design.

(3) An article is also an infringing article if—

(a) it has been or is proposed to be imported into the United Kingdom, and

(b) its making to that design in the United Kingdom would have been an infringement of design right in the design or a breach of an exclusive licence agreement relating to the design.

(4) Where it is shown that an article is made to a design in which design right subsists or has subsisted at any time, it shall be presumed until the contrary is proved that the article was made at a time when design right subsisted.

(5) Nothing in subsection (3) shall be construed as applying to an article which may lawfully be imported into the United Kingdom by virtue of any enforceable Community right within the meaning of section 2(1) of the European Communities Act 1972.

(6) The expression "infringing article" does not include a design document, notwithstanding that its making was or would have been an infringement of design right.

Remedies for infringement

229 Rights and remedies of design right owner

(1) An infringement of design right is actionable by the design right owner.

(2) In an action for infringement of design right all such relief by way of damages, injunctions, accounts or otherwise is available to the plaintiff as is available in respect of the infringement of any other property right.

(3) The court may in an action for infringement of design right, having regard to all the circumstances and in particular to—

(a) the flagrancy of the infringement, and

(b) any benefit accruing to the defendant by reason of the infringement,

award such additional damages as the justice of the case may require.

(4) This section has effect subject to section 233 (innocent infringement).

230 Order for delivery up

(1) Where a person—

(a) has in his possession, custody or control for commercial purposes an infringing article, or

(b) has in his possession, custody or control anything specifically designed or adapted for making articles to a particular design, knowing or having reason to believe that it has been or is to be used to make an infringing article,

the owner of the design right in the design in question may apply to the court for an order that the infringing article or other thing be delivered up to him or to such other person as the court may direct.

(2) An application shall not be made after the end of the period specified in the following provisions of this section; and no order shall be made unless the court also makes, or it appears to the court that there are grounds for making, an order under section 231 (order as to disposal of infringing article, &c.).

(3) An application for an order under this section may not be made after the end of the period of six years from the date on which the article or thing in question was made, subject to subsection (4).

(4) If during the whole or any part of that period the design right owner—

(a) is under a disability, or

(b) is prevented by fraud or concealment from discovering the facts entitling him to apply for an order,

an application may be made at any time before the end of the period of six years from the date on which he ceased to be under a disability or, as the case may be, could with reasonable diligence have discovered those facts.

(5) In subsection (4) "disability"—

(a) in England and Wales, has the same meaning as in the Limitation Act 1980;

(b) in Scotland, means legal disability within the meaning of the Prescription and Limitation (Scotland) Act 1973;

(c) in Northern Ireland, has the same meaning as in the Statute of Limitations (Northern Ireland) 1958.

(6) A person to whom an infringing article or other thing is delivered up in pursuance of an order under this section shall, if an order under section 231 is not made, retain it pending the making of an order, or the decision not to make an order, under that section.

(7) Nothing in this section affects any other power of the court.

231 Order as to disposal of infringing articles, &c

(1) An application may be made to the court for an order that an infringing article or other thing delivered up in pursuance of an order under section 230 shall be—

(a) forfeited to the design right owner, or

(b) destroyed or otherwise dealt with as the court may think fit,

or for a decision that no such order should be made.

(2) In considering what order (if any) should be made, the court shall consider whether other remedies available in an action for infringement of design right would be adequate to compensate the design right owner and to protect his interests.

(3) Provision shall be made by rules of court as to the service of notice on persons having an interest in the article or other thing, and any such person is entitled—

(a) to appear in proceedings for an order under this section, whether or not he was served with notice, and

(b) to appeal against any order made, whether or not he appeared;

and an order shall not take effect until the end of the period within which notice of an appeal may be given or, if before the end of that period notice of appeal is duly given, until the final determination or abandonment of the proceedings on the appeal.

(4) Where there is more than one person interested in an article or other thing, the court shall make such order as it thinks just and may (in particular) direct that the thing be sold, or otherwise dealt with, and the proceeds divided.

(5) If the court decides that no order should be made under this section, the person in whose possession, custody or control the article or other thing was before being delivered up or seized is entitled to its return.

(6) References in this section to a person having an interest in an article or other thing include any person in whose favour an order could be made in respect of it under this section or under section 114 or 204 of this Act or section 58C of the Trade Marks Act 1938 (which make similar provision in relation to infringement of copyright, rights in performances and trade marks).

232 Jurisdiction of county court and sheriff court

(1) In England, Wales and Northern Ireland a county court may entertain proceedings under—

section 230 (order for delivery up of infringing article, &c.),

section 231 (order as to disposal of infringing article, &c.), or

section 235(5) (application by exclusive licensee having concurrent rights),

where the value of the infringing articles and other things in question does not exceed the county court limit for actions in tort.

(2) In Scotland proceedings for an order under any of those provisions may be brought in the sheriff court.

(3) Nothing in this section shall be construed as affecting the jurisdiction of the High Court or, in Scotland, the Court of Session.

233 Innocent infringement

(1) Where in an action for infringement of design right brought by virtue of section 226 (primary infringement) it is shown that at the time of the infringement the defendant did not know, and had no reason to believe, that design right subsisted in the design to which the action relates, the plaintiff is not entitled to damages against him, but without prejudice to any other remedy.

(2) Where in an action for infringement of design right brought by virtue of section 227 (secondary infringement) a defendant shows that the infringing article was innocently acquired by him or a predecessor in title of his, the only remedy available against him in respect of the infringement is damages not exceeding a reasonable royalty in respect of the act complained of.

(3) In subsection (2) "innocently acquired" means that the person acquiring the article did not know and had no reason to believe that it was an infringing article.

234 Rights and remedies of exclusive licensee

(1) An exclusive licensee has, except against the design right owner, the same rights and remedies in respect of matters occurring after the grant of the licence as if the licence had been an assignment.

(2) His rights and remedies are concurrent with those of the design right owner; and references in the relevant provisions of this Part to the design right owner shall be construed accordingly.

(3) In an action brought by an exclusive licensee by virtue of this section a defendant may avail himself of any defence which would have been available to him if the action had been brought by the design right owner.

235 Exercise of concurrent rights

(1) Where an action for infringement of design right brought by the design right owner or an exclusive licensee relates (wholly or partly) to an infringement in respect of which they have concurrent rights of action, the design right owner or, as the case may be, the exclusive licensee may not, without the leave of the court, proceed with the action unless the other is either joined as a plaintiff or added as a defendant.

(2) A design right owner or exclusive licensee who is added as a defendant in pursuance of subsection (1) is not liable for any costs in the action unless he takes part in the proceedings.

(3) The above provisions do not affect the granting of interlocutory relief on the application of the design right owner or an exclusive licensee.

(4) Where an action for infringement of design right is brought which relates (wholly or partly) to an infringement in respect of which the design right owner and an exclusive licensee have concurrent rights of action—

- (a) the court shall, in assessing damages, take into account—
  - (i) the terms of the licence, and
  - (ii) any pecuniary remedy already awarded or available to either of them in respect of the infringement;
- (b) no account of profits shall be directed if an award of damages has been made, or an account of profits has been directed, in favour of the other of them in respect of the infringement; and
- (c) the court shall if an account of profits is directed apportion the profits between them as the court considers just, subject to any agreement between them;

and these provisions apply whether or not the design right owner and the exclusive licensee are both parties to the action.

(5) The design right owner shall notify any exclusive licensee having concurrent rights before applying for an order under section 230 (order for delivery up of infringing article, &c.); and the court may on the application of the licensee make such order under that section as it thinks fit having regard to the terms of the licence.

CHAPTER III

EXCEPTIONS TO RIGHTS OF DESIGN RIGHT OWNERS

Infringement of copyright

236 Infringement of copyright

Where copyright subsists in a work which consists of or includes a design in which design right subsists, it is not an infringement of design right in the design to do anything which is an infringement of the copyright in that work.

Availability of licences of right

237 Licences available in last five years of design right

(1) Any person is entitled as of right to a licence to do in the last five years of the design right term anything which would otherwise infringe the design right.

(2) The terms of the licence shall, in default of agreement, be settled by the comptroller.

(3) The Secretary of State may if it appears to him necessary in order to—

(a) comply with an international obligation of the United Kingdom, or

(b) secure or maintain reciprocal protection for British designs in other countries,

by order exclude from the operation of subsection (1) designs of a description specified in the order or designs applied to articles of a description so specified.

(4) An order shall be made by statutory instrument; and no order shall be made unless a draft of it has been laid before and approved by a resolution of each House of Parliament.

238 Powers exercisable for protection of the public interest

(1) Where the matters specified in a report of the Monopolies and Mergers Commission as being those which in the Commission's opinion operate, may be expected to operate or have operated against the public interest include—

(a) conditions in licences granted by a design right owner restricting the use of the design by the licensee or the right of the design right owner to grant other licences, or

(b) a refusal of a design right owner to grant licences on reasonable terms,

the powers conferred by Part I of Schedule 8 to the Fair Trading Act 1973 (powers exercisable for purpose of remedying or preventing adverse effects specified in report of Commission) include power to cancel or modify those conditions and, instead or in addition, to provide that licences in respect of the design right shall be available as of right.

(2) The references in sections 56(2) and 73(2) of that Act, and sections 10(2)(b) and 12(5) of the Competition Act 1980, to the powers specified in that Part of that Schedule shall be construed accordingly.

(3) The terms of a licence available by virtue of this section shall, in default of agreement, be settled by the comptroller.

239 Undertaking to take licence of right in infringement proceedings

(1) If in proceedings for infringement of design right in a design in respect of which a licence is available as of right under section 237 or 238 the defendant undertakes to take a licence on such terms as may be agreed or, in default of agreement, settled by the comptroller under that section—

(a) no injunction shall be granted against him,

(b) no order for delivery up shall be made under section 230, and

(c) the amount recoverable against him by way of damages or on an account of profits shall not exceed double the amount which would have been payable by him as licensee if such a licence on those terms had been granted before the earliest infringement.

(2) An undertaking may be given at any time before final order in the proceedings, without any admission of liability.

(3) Nothing in this section affects the remedies available in respect of an infringement committed before licences of right were available.

Crown use of designs

240 Crown use of designs

(1) A government department, or a person authorised in writing by a government department, may without the licence of the design right owner—

(a) do anything for the purpose of supplying articles for the services of the Crown, or

(b) dispose of articles no longer required for the services of the Crown;

and nothing done by virtue of this section infringes the design right.

(2) References in this Part to "the services of the Crown" are to—

(a) the defence of the realm,

(b) foreign defence purposes, and

(c) health service purposes.

(3) The reference to the supply of articles for "foreign defence purposes" is to their supply—

(a) for the defence of a country outside the realm in pursuance of an agreement or arrangement to which the government of that country and Her Majesty's Government in the United Kingdom are parties; or

(b) for use by armed forces operating in pursuance of a resolution of the United Nations or one of its organs.

(4) The reference to the supply of articles for "health service purposes" are to their supply for the purpose of providing—

(a) pharmaceutical services,

(b) general medical services, or

(c) general dental services,

that is, services of those kinds under Part II of the National Health Service Act 1977, Part II of the National Health Service (Scotland) Act 1978 or the corresponding provisions of the law in force in Northern Ireland.

(5) In this Part—

"Crown use", in relation to a design, means the doing of anything by virtue of this section which would otherwise be an infringement of design right in the design; and

"the government department concerned", in relation to such use, means the government department by whom or on whose authority the act was done.

(6) The authority of a government department in respect of Crown use of a design may be given to a person either before or after the use and whether or not he is authorised, directly or indirectly, by the design right owner to do anything in relation to the design.

(7) A person acquiring anything sold in the exercise of powers conferred by this section, and any person claiming under him, may deal with it in the same manner as if the design right were held on behalf of the Crown.

241 Settlement of terms for Crown use

(1) Where Crown use is made of a design, the government department concerned shall—

(a) notify the design right owner as soon as practicable, and

(b) give him such information as to the extent of the use as he may from time to time require,

unless it appears to the department that it would be contrary to the public interest to do so or the identity of the design right owner cannot be ascertained on reasonable inquiry.

(2) Crown use of a design shall be on such terms as, either before or after the use, are agreed between the government department concerned and the design right owner with the approval of the Treasury or, in default of agreement, are determined by the court.

In the application of this subsection to Northern Ireland the reference to the Treasury shall, where the government department referred to in that subsection is a Northern Ireland department, be construed as a reference to the Department of Finance and Personnel.

(3) Where the identity of the design right owner cannot be ascertained on reasonable inquiry, the government department concerned may apply to the court who may order that no royalty or other sum shall be payable in respect of Crown use of the design until the owner agrees terms with the department or refers the matter to the court for determination.

242 Rights of third parties in case of Crown use

(1) The provisions of any licence, assignment or agreement made between the design right owner (or anyone deriving title from him or from whom he derives title) and any person other than a government department are of no effect in relation to Crown use of a design, or any act incidental to Crown use, so far as they—

(a) restrict or regulate anything done in relation to the design, or the use of any model, document or other information relating to it, or

(b) provide for the making of payments in respect of, or calculated by reference to such use;

and the copying or issuing to the public of copies of any such model or document in connection with the thing done, or any such use, shall be deemed not to be an infringement of any copyright in the model or document.

(2) Subsection (1) shall not be construed as authorising the disclosure of any such model, document or information in contravention of the licence, assignment or agreement.

(3) Where an exclusive licence is in force in respect of the design—

(a) if the licence was granted for royalties—

(i) any agreement between the design right owner and a government department under section 241 (settlement of terms for Crown use) requires the consent of the licensee, and

(ii) the licensee is entitled to recover from the design right owner such part of the payment for Crown use as may be agreed between them or, in default of agreement, determined by the court;

(b) if the licence was granted otherwise than for royalties—

(i) section 241 applies in relation to anything done which but for section 240 (Crown use) and subsection (1) above would be an infringement of the rights of the licensee with the substitution for references to the design right owner of references to the licensee, and

(ii) section 241 does not apply in relation to anything done by the licensee by virtue of an authority given under section 240.

(4) Where the design right has been assigned to the design right owner in consideration of royalties—

(a) section 241 applies in relation to Crown use of the design as if the references to the design right owner included the assignor, and any payment for Crown use shall be divided between them in such proportion as may be agreed or, in default of agreement, determined by the court; and

(b) section 241 applies in relation to any act incidental to Crown use as it applies in relation to Crown use of the design.

(5) Where any model, document or other information relating to a design is used in connection with Crown use of the design, or any act incidental to Crown use, section 241 applies to the use of the model, document or other information with the substitution for the references to the design right owner of references to the person entitled to the benefit of any provision of an agreement rendered inoperative by subsection (1) above.

(6) In this section—

"act incidental to Crown use" means anything done for the services of the Crown to the order of a government department by the design right owner in respect of a design;

"payment for Crown use" means such amount as is payable by the government department concerned by virtue of section 241; and

"royalties" includes any benefit determined by reference to the use of the design.

243 Crown use: compensation for loss of profit

(1) Where Crown use is made of a design, the government department concerned shall pay—

(a) to the design right owner, or

(b) if there is an exclusive licence in force in respect of the design, to the exclusive licensee,

compensation for any loss resulting from his not being awarded a contract to supply the articles made to the design.

(2) Compensation is payable only to the extent that such a contract could have been fulfilled from his existing manufacturing capacity; but is payable notwithstanding the existence of circumstances rendering him ineligible for the award of such a contract.

(3) In determining the loss, regard shall be had to the profit which would have been made on such a contract and to the extent to which any manufacturing capacity was under-used.

(4) No compensation is payable in respect of any failure to secure contracts for the supply of articles made to the design otherwise than for the services of the Crown.

(5) The amount payable shall, if not agreed between the design right owner or licensee and the government department concerned with the approval of the Treasury, be determined by the court on a reference under section 252; and it is in addition to any amount payable under section 241 or 242.

(6) In the application of this section to Northern Ireland, the reference in subsection (5) to the Treasury shall, where the government department concerned is a Northern Ireland department, be construed as a reference to the Department of Finance and Personnel.

244 Special provision for Crown use during emergency

(1) During a period of emergency the powers exercisable in relation to a design by virtue of section 240 (Crown use) include power to do any act which would otherwise be an infringement of design right for any purpose which appears to the government department concerned necessary or expedient—

(a) for the efficient prosecution of any war in which Her Majesty may be engaged;

(b) for the maintenance of supplies and services essential to the life of the community;

(c) for securing a sufficiency of supplies and services essential to the well-being of the community;

(d) for promoting the productivity of industry, commerce and agriculture;

(e) for fostering and directing exports and reducing imports, or imports of any classes, from all or any countries and for redressing the balance of trade;

(f) generally for ensuring that the whole resources of the community are available for use, and are used, in a manner best calculated to serve the interests of the community; or

(g) for assisting the relief of suffering and the restoration and distribution of essential supplies and services in any country outside the United Kingdom which is in grave distress as the result of war.

(2) References in this Part to the services of the Crown include, as respects a period of emergency, those purposes; and references to "Crown use" include any act which would apart from this section be an infringement of design right.

(3) In this section "period of emergency" means a period beginning with such date as may be declared by Order in Council to be the beginning, and ending with such date as may be so declared to be the end, of a period of emergency for the purposes of this section.

(4) No Order in Council under this section shall be submitted to Her Majesty unless a draft of it has been laid before and approved by a resolution of each House of Parliament.

General

245 Power to provide for further exceptions

(1) The Secretary of State may if it appears to him necessary in order to—

(a) comply with an international obligation of the United Kingdom, or

(b) secure or maintain reciprocal protection for British designs in other countries,

by order provide that acts of a description specified in the order do not infringe design right.

(2) An order may make different provision for different descriptions of design or article.

(3) An order shall be made by statutory instrument and no order shall be made unless a draft of it has been laid before and approved by a resolution of each House of Parliament.

CHAPTER IV

JURISDICTION OF THE COMPTROLLER AND THE COURT

Jurisdiction of the comptroller

246 Jurisdiction to decide matters relating to design right

(1) A party to a dispute as to any of the following matters may refer the dispute to the comptroller for his decision—

(a) the subsistence of design right,

(b) the term of design right, or

(c) the identity of the person in whom design right first vested;

and the comptroller's decision on the reference is binding on the parties to the dispute.

(2) No other court or tribunal shall decide any such matter except—

(a) on a reference or appeal from the comptroller,

(b) in infringement or other proceedings in which the issue arises incidentally, or

(c) in proceedings brought with the agreement of the parties or the leave of the comptroller.

(3) The comptroller has jurisdiction to decide any incidental question of fact or law arising in the course of a reference under this section.

247 Application to settle terms of licence of right

(1) A person requiring a licence which is available as of right by virtue of—

(a) section 237 (licences available in last five years of design right), or

(b) an order under section 238 (licences made available in the public interest),

may apply to the comptroller to settle the terms of the licence.

(2) No application for the settlement of the terms of a licence available by virtue of section 237 may be made earlier than one year before the earliest date on which the licence may take effect under that section.

(3) The terms of a licence settled by the comptroller shall authorise the licensee to do—

(a) in the case of licence available by virtue of section 237, everything which would be an infringement of the design right in the absence of a licence;

(b) in the case of a licence available by virtue of section 238, everything in respect of which a licence is so available.

(4) In settling the terms of a licence the comptroller shall have regard to such factors as may be prescribed by the Secretary of State by order made by statutory instrument.

(5) No such order shall be made unless a draft of it has been laid before and approved by a resolution of each House of Parliament.

(6) Where the terms of a licence are settled by the comptroller, the licence has effect—

(a) in the case of an application in respect of a licence available by virtue of section 237 made before the earliest date on which the licence may take effect under that section, from that date;

(b) in any other case, from the date on which the application to the comptroller was made.

248 Settlement of terms where design right owner unknown

(1) This section applies where a person making an application under section 247 (settlement of terms of licence of right) is unable on reasonable inquiry to discover the identity of the design right owner.

(2) The comptroller may in settling the terms of the licence order that the licence shall be free of any obligation as to royalties or other payments.

(3) If such an order is made the design right owner may apply to the comptroller to vary the terms of the licence with effect from the date on which his application is made.

(4) If the terms of a licence are settled by the comptroller and it is subsequently established that a licence was not available as of right, the licensee shall not be liable in damages for, or for an account of profits in respect of, anything done before he was aware of any claim by the design right owner that a licence was not available.

249 Appeals as to terms of licence of right

(1) An appeal lies from any decision of the comptroller under section 247 or 248 (settlement of terms of licence of right) to the Appeal Tribunal constituted under section 28 of the Registered Designs Act 1949.

(2) Section 28 of that Act applies to appeals from the comptroller under this section as it applies to appeals from the registrar under that Act; but rules made under that section may make different provision for appeals under this section.

250 Rules

(1) The Secretary of State may make rules for regulating the procedure to be followed in connection with any proceeding before the comptroller under this Part.

(2) Rules may, in particular, make provision—

(a) prescribing forms;

(b) requiring fees to be paid;
(c) authorising the rectification of irregularities of procedure;
(d) regulating the mode of giving evidence and empowering the comptroller to compel the attendance of witnesses and the discovery of and production of documents;
(e) providing for the appointment of advisers to assist the comptroller in proceedings before him;
(f) prescribing time limits for doing anything required to be done (and providing for the alteration of any such limit); and
(g) empowering the comptroller to award costs and to direct how, to what party and from what parties, costs are to be paid.

(3) Rules prescribing fees require the consent of the Treasury.

(4) The remuneration of an adviser appointed to assist the comptroller shall be determined by the Secretary of State with the consent of the Treasury and shall be defrayed out of money provided by Parliament.

(5) Rules shall be made by statutory instrument which shall be subject to annulment in pursuance of a resolution of either House of Parliament.

Jurisdiction of the court

251 References and appeals on design right matters

(1) In any proceedings before him under section 246 (reference of matter relating to design right), the comptroller may at any time order the whole proceedings or any question or issue (whether of fact or law) to be referred, on such terms as he may direct, to the High Court or, in Scotland, the Court of Session.

(2) The comptroller shall make such an order if the parties to the proceedings agree that he should do so.

(3) On a reference under this section the court may exercise any power available to the comptroller by virtue of this Part as respects the matter referred to it and, following its determination, may refer any matter back to the comptroller.

(4) An appeal lies from any decision of the comptroller in proceedings before him under section 246 (decisions on matters relating to design right) to the High Court or, in Scotland, the Court of Session.

252 Reference of disputes relating to Crown use

(1) A dispute as to any matter which falls to be determined by the court in default of agreement under—
(a) section 241 (settlement of terms for Crown use),
(b) section 242 (rights of third parties in case of Crown use), or
(c) section 243 (Crown use: compensation for loss of profit),
may be referred to the court by any party to the dispute.

(2) In determining a dispute between a government department and any person as to the terms for Crown use of a design the court shall have regard to—

(a) any sums which that person or a person from whom he derives title has received or is entitled to receive, directly or indirectly, from any government department in respect of the design; and

(b) whether that person or a person from whom he derives title has in the court's opinion without reasonable cause failed to comply with a request of the department for the use of the design on reasonable terms.

(3) One of two or more joint owners of design right may, without the concurrence of the others, refer a dispute to the court under this section, but shall not do so unless the others are made parties; and none of those others is liable for any costs unless he takes part in the proceedings.

(4) Where the consent of an exclusive licensee is required by section 242(3)(a)(i) to the settlement by agreement of the terms for Crown use of a design, a determination by the court of the amount of any payment to be made for such use is of no effect unless the licensee has been notified of the reference and given an opportunity to be heard.

(5) On the reference of a dispute as to the amount recoverable as mentioned in section 242(3)(a)(ii) (right of exclusive licensee to recover part of amount payable to design right owner) the court shall determine what is just having regard to any expenditure incurred by the licensee—

(a) in developing the design, or

(b) in making payments to the design right owner in consideration of the licence (other than royalties or other payments determined by reference to the use of the design).

(6) In this section "the court" means—

(a) in England and Wales, the High Court or any patents county court having jurisdiction by virtue of an order under section 287 of this Act,

(b) in Scotland, the Court of Session, and

(c) in Northern Ireland, the High Court.

CHAPTER V

MISCELLANEOUS AND GENERAL

Miscellaneous

253 Remedy for groundless threats of infringement proceedings

(1) Where a person threatens another person with proceedings for infringement of design right, a person aggrieved by the threats may bring an action against him claiming—

(a) a declaration to the effect that the threats are unjustifiable;

(b) an injunction against the continuance of the threats;

(c) damages in respect of any loss which he has sustained by the threats.

(2) If the plaintiff proves that the threats were made and that he is a person aggrieved by them, he is entitled to the relief claimed unless the defendant shows that the acts in respect of which proceedings were threatened did constitute, or if done would have constituted, an infringement of the design right concerned.

(3) Proceedings may not be brought under this section in respect of a threat to bring proceedings for an infringement alleged to consist of making or importing anything.

(4) Mere notification that a design is protected by design right does not constitute a threat of proceedings for the purposes of this section.

254 Licensee under licence of right not to claim connection with design right owner

(1) A person who has a licence in respect of a design by virtue of section 237 or 238 (licences of right) shall not, without the consent of the design right owner—

(a) apply to goods which he is marketing, or proposes to market, in reliance on that licence a trade description indicating that he is the licensee of the design right owner, or

(b) use any such trade description in an advertisement in relation to such goods.

(2) A contravention of subsection (1) is actionable by the design right owner.

(3) In this section "trade description", the reference to applying a trade description to goods and "advertisement" have the same meaning as in the Trade Descriptions Act 1968.

Extent of operation of this Part

255 Countries to which this Part extends

(1) This Part extends to England and Wales, Scotland and Northern Ireland.

(2) Her Majesty may by Order in Council direct that this Part shall extend, subject to such exceptions and modifications as may be specified in the Order, to—

(a) any of the Channel Islands,

(b) the Isle of Man, or

(c) any colony.

(3) That power includes power to extend, subject to such exceptions and modifications as may be specified in the Order, any Order in Council made under section 221 (further provision as to qualification for design right protection) or section 256 (countries enjoying reciprocal protection).

(4) The legislature of a country to which this Part has been extended may modify or add to the provisions of this Part, in their operation as part of the law of that country, as the legislature may consider necessary to adapt the provisions to the circumstances of that country; but not so as to deny design right protection in a case where it would otherwise exist.

(5) Where a country to which this Part extends ceases to be a colony of the United Kingdom, it shall continue to be treated as such a country for the purposes of this Part until—

(a) an Order in Council is made under section 256 designating it as a country enjoying reciprocal protection, or

(b) an Order in Council is made declaring that it shall cease to be so treated by reason of the fact that the provisions of this Part as part of the law of that country have been amended or repealed.

(6) A statutory instrument containing an Order in Council under subsection (5)(b) shall be subject to annulment in pursuance of a resolution of either House of Parliament.

256 Countries enjoying reciprocal protection

(1) Her Majesty may, if it appears to Her that the law of a country provides adequate protection for British designs, by Order in Council designate that country as one enjoying reciprocal protection under this Part.

(2) If the law of a country provides adequate protection only for certain classes of British design, or only for designs applied to certain classes of article, any Order designating that country shall contain provision limiting, to a corresponding extent, the protection afforded by this Part in relation to designs connected with that country.

(3) An Order under this section shall be subject to annulment in pursuance of a resolution of either House of Parliament.

257 Territorial waters and the continental shelf

(1) For the purposes of this Part the territorial waters of the United Kingdom shall be treated as part of the United Kingdom.

(2) This Part applies to things done in the United Kingdom sector of the continental shelf on a structure or vessel which is present there for purposes directly connected with the exploration of the sea bed or subsoil or the exploitation of their natural resources as it applies to things done in the United Kingdom.

(3) The United Kingdom sector of the continental shelf means the areas designated by order under section 1(7) of the Continental Shelf Act 1964.

Interpretation

258 Construction of references to design right owner

(1) Where different persons are (whether in consequence of a partial assignment or otherwise) entitled to different aspects of design right in a work, the design right owner for any purpose of this Part is the person who is entitled to the right in the respect relevant for that purpose.

(2) Where design right (or any aspect of design right) is owned by more than one person jointly, references in this Part to the design right owner are to all the owners, so that, in particular, any requirement of the licence of the design right owner requires the licence of all of them.

259 Joint designs

(1) In this Part a "joint design" means a design produced by the collaboration of two or more designers in which the contribution of each is not distinct from that of the other or others.

(2) References in this Part to the designer of a design shall, except as otherwise provided, be construed in relation to a joint design as references to all the designers of the design.

260 Application of provisions to articles in kit form

(1) The provisions of this Part apply in relation to a kit, that is, a complete or substantially complete set of components intended to be assembled into an article, as they apply in relation to the assembled article.

(2) Subsection (1) does not affect the question whether design right subsists in any aspect of the design of the components of a kit as opposed to the design of the assembled article.

261 Requirement of signature: application in relation to body corporate

The requirement in the following provisions that an instrument be signed by or on behalf of a person is also satisfied in the case of a body corporate by the affixing of its seal—

section 222(3) (assignment of design right),

section 223(1) (assignment of future design right),

section 225(1) (grant of exclusive licence).

262 Adaptation of expressions in relation to Scotland

In the application of this Part to Scotland—

"account of profits" means accounting and payment of profits;

"accounts" means count, reckoning and payment;

"assignment" means assignation;

"costs" means expenses;

"defendant" means defender;

"delivery up" means delivery;

"injunction" means interdict;

"interlocutory relief" means interim remedy; and

"plaintiff" means pursuer.

263 Minor definitions

(1) In this Part—

"British design" means a design which qualifies for design right protection by reason of a connection with the United Kingdom of the designer or the person by whom the design is commissioned or the designer is employed;

"business" includes a trade or profession;

"commission" means a commission for money or money's worth;

"the comptroller" means the Comptroller-General of Patents, Designs and Trade Marks;

"computer-generated", in relation to a design, means that the design is generated by computer in circumstances such that there is no human designer,

"country" includes any territory;

"the Crown" includes the Crown in right of Her Majesty's Government in Northern Ireland;

"design document" means any record of a design, whether in the form of a drawing, a written description, a photograph, data stored in a computer or otherwise;

"employee", "employment" and "employer" refer to employment under a contract of service or of apprenticeship;

"government department" includes a Northern Ireland department.

(2) References in this Part to "marketing", in relation to an article, are to its being sold or let for hire, or offered or exposed for sale or hire, in the course of a business, and related expressions shall be construed accordingly; but no account shall be taken for the purposes of this Part of marketing which is merely colourable and not intended to satisfy the reasonable requirements of the public.

(3) References in this Part to an act being done in relation to an article for "commercial purposes" are to its being done with a view to the article in question being sold or hired in the course of a business.

264 Index of defined expressions

The following Table shows provisions defining or otherwise explaining expressions used in this Part (other than provisions defining or explaining an expression used only in the same section)—

account of profits and accounts (in Scotland)	section 262
assignment (in Scotland)	section 262
British designs	section 263(1)
business	section 263(1)
commercial purposes	section 263(3)
commission	section 263(1)
the comptroller	section 263(1)
computer-generated	section 263(1)
costs (in Scotland)	section 262
country	section 263(1)
the Crown	section 263(1)
Crown use	sections 240(5) and 244(2)
defendant (in Scotland)	section 262
delivery up (in Scotland)	section 262
design	section 213(2)
design document	section 263(1)
designer	sections 214 and 259(2)
design right	section 213(1)
design right owner	sections 234(2) and 258
employee, employment and employer	section 263(1)
exclusive licence	section 225(1)

government department	section 263(1)
government department concerned (in relation to Crown use)	section 240(5)
infringing article	section 228
injunction (in Scotland)	section 262
interlocutory relief (in Scotland)	section 262
joint design	section 259(1)
licence (of the design right owner)	sections 222(4), 223(3) and 258
making articles to a design	section 226(2)
marketing (and related expressions)	section 263(2)
original	section 213(4)
plaintiff (in Scotland)	section 262
qualifying individual	section 217(1)
qualifying person	sections 217(1) and (2)
signed	section 261

PART IV

REGISTERED DESIGNS

Amendments of the Registered Designs Act 1949

265 Registrable designs

(1) For section 1 of the Registered Designs Act 1949 (designs registrable under that Act) substitute—

"1 Designs registrable under Act

(1) In this Act "design" means features of shape, configuration, pattern or ornament applied to an article by any industrial process, being features which in the finished article appeal to and are judged by the eye, but does not include—

(a) a method or principle of construction, or

(b) features of shape or configuration of an article which—

(i) are dictated solely by the function which the article has to perform, or

(ii) are dependent upon the appearance of another article of which the article is intended by the author of the design to form an integral part.

(2) A design which is new may, upon application by the person claiming to be the proprietor, be registered under this Act in respect of any article, or set of articles, specified in the application.

(3) A design shall not be registered in respect of an article if the appearance of the article is not material, that is, if aesthetic considerations are not normally taken into account to a material extent by persons acquiring or using articles of that description, and would not be so taken into account if the design were to be applied to the article.

(4) A design shall not be regarded as new for the purposes of this Act if it is the same as a design—

(a) registered in respect of the same or any other article in pursuance of a prior application, or

(b) published in the United Kingdom in respect of the same or any other article before the date of the application,

or if it differs from such a design only in immaterial details or in features which are variants commonly used in the trade.

This subsection has effect subject to the provisions of sections 4, 6 and 16 of this Act.

(5) The Secretary of State may by rules provide for excluding from registration under this Act designs for such articles of a primarily literary or artistic character as the Secretary of State thinks fit.".

(2) The above amendment does not apply in relation to applications for registration made before the commencement of this Part; but the provisions of section 266 apply with respect to the right in certain designs registered in pursuance of such an application.

266 Provisions with respect to certain designs registered in pursuance of application made before commencement

(1) Where a design is registered under the Registered Designs Act 1949 in pursuance of an application made after 12th January 1988 and before the commencement of this Part which could not have been registered under section 1 of that Act as substituted by section 265 above—

(a) the right in the registered design expires ten years after the commencement of this Part, if it does not expire earlier in accordance with the 1949 Act, and

(b) any person is, after the commencement of this Part, entitled as of right to a licence to do anything which would otherwise infringe the right in the registered design.

(2) The terms of licence available by virtue of this section shall, in default of agreement, be settled by the registrar of an application by the person requiring the licence; and the terms so settled shall authorise the licensee to do everything which would be an infringement of the right in the registered design in the absence of a licence.

(3) In settling the terms of a licence the registrar shall have regard to such factors as may be prescribed by the Secretary of State by order made by statutory instrument.

No such order shall be made unless a draft of it has been laid before and approved by a resolution of each House of Parliament.

(4) Where the terms of a licence are settled by the registrar, the licence has effect from the date on which the application to the registrar was made.

(5) Section 11B of the 1949 Act (undertaking to take licence of right in infringement proceedings), as inserted by section 270 below, applies where a licence is available as of right under this section, as it applies where a licence is available as of right under section 11A of that Act.

(6) Where a licence is available as of right under this section, a person to whom a licence was granted before the commencement of this Part may apply to the registrar for an order adjusting the terms of that licence.

(7) An appeal lies from any decision of the registrar under this section.

(8) This section shall be construed as one with the Registered Designs Act 1949.

267 Authorship and first ownership of designs

(1) Section 2 of the Registered Designs Act 1949 (proprietorship of designs) is amended as follows.

(2) For subsection (1) substitute—

"(1) The author of a design shall be treated for the purposes of this Act as the original proprietor of the design, subject to the following provisions.

(1A) Where a design is created in pursuance of a commission for money or money's worth, the person commissioning the design shall be treated as the original proprietor of the design.

(1B) Where, in a case not falling within subsection (1A), a design is created by an employee in the course of his employment, his employer shall be treated as the original proprietor of the design.".

(3) After subsection (2) insert—

"(3) In this Act the "author" of a design means the person who creates it.

(4) In the case of a design generated by computer in circumstance such that there is no human author, the person by whom the arrangements necessary for the creation of the design are made shall be taken to be the author.".

(4) The amendments made by this section do not apply in relation to an application for registration made before the commencement of this Part.

268 Right given by registration of design

(1) For section 7 of the Registered Designs Act 1949 (right given by registration) substitute—

"7 Right given by registration

(1) The registration of a design under this Act gives the registered proprietor the exclusive right—

(a) to make or import—

(i) for sale or hire, or

(ii) for use for the purposes of a trade or business, or

(b) to sell, hire or offer or expose for sale or hire,

an article in respect of which the design is registered and to which that design or a design not substantially different from it has been applied.

(2) The right in the registered design is infringed by a person who without the licence of the registered proprietor does anything which by virtue of subsection (1) is the exclusive right of the proprietor.

(3) The right in the registered design is also infringed by a person who without the licence of the registered proprietor makes anything for enabling any such article to be made, in the United Kingdom or elsewhere, as mentioned in subsection (1).

(4) The right in the registered design is also infringed by a person who without the licence of the registered proprietor—

(a) does anything in relation to a kit that would be an infringement if done in relation to the assembled article (see subsection (1)), or

(b) makes anything for enabling a kit to be made or assembled, in the United Kingdom or elsewhere, if the assembled article would be such an article as is mentioned in subsection (1);

and for this purpose a "kit" means a complete or substantially complete set of components intended to be assembled into an article.

(5) No proceedings shall be taken in respect of an infringement committed before the date on which the certificate of registration of the design under this Act is granted.

(6) The right in a registered design is not infringed by the reproduction of a feature of the design which, by virtue of section 1(1)(b), is left out of account in determining whether the design is registrable.".

(2) The above amendment does not apply in relation to a design registered in pursuance of an application made before the commencement of this Part.

269 Duration of right in registered design

(1) For section 8 of the Registered Designs Act 1949 (period of right) substitute—

"8 Duration of right in registered design

(1) The right in a registered design subsists in the first instance for a period of five years from the date of the registration of the design.

(2) The period for which the right subsists may be extended for a second, third, fourth and fifth period of five years, by applying to the registrar for an extension and paying the prescribed renewal fee.

(3) If the first, second, third or fourth period expires without such application and payment being made, the right shall cease to have effect; and the registrar shall, in accordance with rules made by the Secretary of State, notify the proprietor of that fact.

(4) If during the period of six months immediately following the end of that period an application for extension is made and the prescribed renewal fee and any prescribed additional fee is paid, the right shall be treated as if it had never expired, with the result that—

(a) anything done under or in relation to the right during that further period shall be treated as valid,

(b) an act which would have constituted an infringement of the right if it had not expired shall be treated as an infringement, and

(c) an act which would have constituted use of the design for the services of the Crown if the right had not expired shall be treated as such use.

(5) Where it is shown that a registered design—

(a) was at the time it was registered a corresponding design in relation to an artistic work in which copyright subsists, and

(b) by reason of a previous use of that work would not have been registrable but for section 6(4) of this Act (registration despite certain prior applications of design),

the right in the registered design expires when the copyright in that work expires, if that is earlier than the time at which it would otherwise expire, and it may not thereafter be renewed.

(6) The above provisions have effect subject to the proviso to section 4(1) (registration of same design in respect of other articles, &c.).

8A Restoration of lapsed right in design

(1) Where the right in a registered design has expired by reason of a failure to extend, in accordance with section 8(2) or (4), the period for which the right subsists, an application for the restoration of the right in the design may be made to the registrar within the prescribed period.

(2) The application may be made by the person who was the registered proprietor of the design or by any other person who would have been entitled to the right in the design if it had not expired; and where the design was held by two or more persons jointly, the application may, with the leave of the registrar, be made by one or more of them without joining the others.

(3) Notice of the application shall be published by the registrar in the prescribed manner.

(4) If the registrar is satisfied that the proprietor took reasonable care to see that the period for which the right subsisted was extended in accordance with section 8(2) or (4), he shall, on payment of any unpaid renewal fee and any prescribed additional fee, order the restoration of the right in the design.

(5) The order may be made subject to such conditions as the registrar thinks fit, and if the proprietor of the design does not comply with any condition the registrar may revoke the order and give such consequential directions as he thinks fit.

(6) Rules altering the period prescribed for the purposes of subsection (1) may contain such transitional provisions and savings as appear to the Secretary of State to be necessary or expedient.

8B Effect of order for restoration of right

(1) The effect of an order under section 8A for the restoration of the right in a registered design is as follows.

(2) Anything done under or in relation to the right during the period between expiry and restoration shall be treated as valid.

(3) Anything done during that period which would have constituted an infringement if the right had not expired shall be treated as an infringement—

(a) if done at a time when it was possible for an application for extension to be made under section 8(4); or

(b) if it was a continuation or repetition of an earlier infringing act.

(4) If, after it was no longer possible for such an application for extension to be made and before publication of notice of the application for restoration, a person—

(a) began in good faith to do an act which would have constituted an infringement of the right in the design if it had not expired, or

(b) made in good faith effective and serious preparations to do such an act,

he has the right to continue to do the act or, as the case may be, to do the act, notwithstanding the restoration of the right in the design; but this does not extend to granting a licence to another person to do the act.

(5) If the act was done, or the preparations were made, in the course of a business, the person entitled to the right conferred by subsection (4) may—

(a) authorise the doing of that act by any partners of his for the time being in that business, and

(b) assign that right, or transmit it on death (or in the case of a body corporate on its dissolution), to any person who acquires that part of the business in the course of which the act was done or the preparations were made.

(6) Where an article is disposed of to another in exercise of the rights conferred by subsection (4) or subsection (5), that other and any person claiming through him may deal with the article in the same way as if it had been disposed of by the registered proprietor of the design.

(7) The above provisions apply in relation to the use of a registered design for the services of the Crown as they apply in relation to infringement of the right in the design.".

(2) The above amendment does not apply in relation to the right in a design registered in pursuance of an application made before the commencement of this Part.

270 Powers exercisable for protection of the public interest

In the Registered Designs Act 1949 after section 11 insert—

"11A Powers exercisable for protection of the public interest

(1) Where a report of the Monopolies and Mergers Commission has been laid before Parliament containing conclusions to the effect—

(a) on a monopoly reference, that a monopoly situation exists and facts found by the Commission operate or may be expected to operate against the public interest,

(b) on a merger reference, that a merger situation qualifying for investigation has been created and the creation of the situation, or particular elements in or consequences of it specified in the report, operate or may be expected to operate against the public interest,

(c) on a competition reference, that a person was engaged in an anti-competitive practice which operated or may be expected to operate against the public interest, or

(d) on a reference under section 11 of the Competition Act 1980 (reference of public bodies and certain other persons), that a person is pursuing a course of conduct which operates against the public interest,

the appropriate Minister or Ministers may apply to the registrar to take action under this section.

(2) Before making an application the appropriate Minister or Ministers shall publish, in such a manner as he or they think appropriate, a notice describing the nature of the proposed application and shall consider any representations which may be made within 30 days of such publication by persons whose interests appear to him or them to be affected.

(3) If on an application under this section it appears to the registrar that the matters specified in the Commission's report as being those which in the Commission's opinion operate or operated or may be expected to operate against the public interest include—

(a) conditions in licences granted in respect of a registered design by its proprietor restricting the use of the design by the licensee or the right of the proprietor to grant other licences, or

(b) a refusal by the proprietor of a registered design to grant licences on reasonable terms,

he may by order cancel or modify any such condition or may, instead or in addition, make an entry in the register to the effect that licences in respect of the design are to be available as of right.

(4) The terms of a licence available by virtue of this section shall, in default of agreement, be settled by the registrar on an application by the person requiring the licence; and terms so settled shall authorise the licensee to do everything which would be an infringement of the right in the registered design in the absence of a licence.

(5) Where the terms of a licence are settled by the registrar the licence has effect from the date on which the application to him was made.

(6) An appeal lies from any order of the registrar under this section.

(7) In this section "the appropriate Minister or Ministers" means the Minister or Ministers to whom the report of the Monopolies and Mergers Commission was made.

11B Undertaking to take licence of right in infringement proceedings

(1) If in proceedings for infringement of the right in a registered design in respect of which a licence is available as of right under section 11A of this Act the defendant undertakes to take a licence on such terms as may be agreed or, in default of agreement, settled by the registrar under that section—

(a) no injunction shall be granted against him, and

(b) the amount recoverable against him by way of damages or on an account of profits shall not exceed double the amount which would have been payable by him as licensee if such a licence on those terms had been granted before the earliest infringement.

(2) An undertaking may be given at any time before final order in the proceedings, without any admission of liability.

(3) Nothing in this section affects the remedies available in respect of an infringement committed before licences of right were available.".

271 Crown use: compensation for loss of profit

(1) In Schedule 1 to the Registered Designs Act 1949 (Crown use), after paragraph 2 insert—

"2A Compensation for loss of profit

2A (1) Where Crown use is made of a registered design, the government department concerned shall pay—

(a) to the registered proprietor, or

(b) if there is an exclusive licence in force in respect of the design, to the exclusive licensee,

compensation for any loss resulting from his not being awarded a contract to supply the articles to which the design is applied.

(2) Compensation is payable only to the extent that such a contract could have been fulfilled from his existing manufacturing capacity; but is payable notwithstanding the existence of circumstances rendering him ineligible for the award of such a contract.

(3) In determining the loss, regard shall be had to the profit which would have been made on such a contract and to the extent to which any manufacturing capacity was underused.

(4) No compensation is payable in respect of any failure to secure contracts for the supply of articles to which the design is applied otherwise than for the services of the Crown.

(5) The amount payable under this paragraph shall, if not agreed between the registered proprietor or licensee and the government department concerned with the approval of the Treasury, be determined by the court on a reference under paragraph 3; and it is in addition to any amount payable under paragraph 1 or 2 of this Schedule.

(6) In this paragraph—

"Crown use", in relation to a design, means the doing of anything by virtue of paragraph 1 which would otherwise be an infringement of the right in the design; and

"the government department concerned", in relation to such use, means the government department by whom or on whose authority the act was done.".

(2) In paragraph 3 of that Schedule (reference of disputes as to Crown use), for sub-paragraph (1) substitute—

"(1) Any dispute as to—

(a) the exercise by a Government department, or a person authorised by a Government department, of the powers conferred by paragraph 1 of this Schedule,

(b) terms for the use of a design for the services of the Crown under that paragraph,

(c) the right of any person to receive any part of a payment made under paragraph 1(3), or

(d) the right of any person to receive a payment under paragraph 2A,

may be referred to the court by either party to the dispute.".

(3) The above amendments apply in relation to any Crown use of a registered design after the commencement of this section, even if the terms for such use were settled before commencement.

272 Minor and consequential amendments

The Registered Designs Act 1949 is further amended in accordance with Schedule 3 which contains minor amendments and amendments consequential upon the provisions of this Act.

Supplementary

273 Text of Registered Designs Act 1949 as amended

Schedule 4 contains the text of the Registered Designs Act 1949 as amended.

PART V

PATENT AGENTS AND TRADE MARK AGENTS

Patent agents

274 Persons permitted to carry on business of a patent agent

(1) Any individual, partnership or body corporate may, subject to the following provisions of this Part, carry on the business of acting as agent for others for the purpose of—

(a) applying for or obtaining patents, in the United Kingdom or elsewhere, or

(b) conducting proceedings before the comptroller relating to applications for, or otherwise in connection with, patents.

(2) This does not affect any restriction under the European Patent Convention as to who may act on behalf of another for any purpose relating to European patents.

275 The register of patent agents

(1) The Secretary of State may make rules requiring the keeping of a register of persons who act as agent for others for the purposes of applying for or obtaining patents; and in this Part a "registered patent agent" means a person whose name is entered in the register kept under this section.

(2) The rules may contain such provision as the Secretary of State thinks fit regulating the registration of persons, and may in particular—

(a) require the payment of such fees as may be prescribed, and

(b) authorise in prescribed cases the erasure from the register of the name of any person registered in it, or the suspension of a person's registration.

(3) The rules may delegate the keeping of the register to another person, and may confer on that person—

(a) power to make regulations—

(i) with respect to the payment of fees, in the cases and subject to the limits prescribed by rules, and

(ii) with respect to any other matter which could be regulated by rules, and

(b) such other functions, including disciplinary functions, as may be prescribed by rules.

(4) Rules under this section shall be made by statutory instrument which shall be subject to annulment in pursuance of a resolution of either House of Parliament.

276 Persons entitled to describe themselves as patent agents

(1) An individual who is not a registered patent agent shall not—

(a) carry on a business (otherwise than in partnership) under any name or other description which contains the words "patent agent" or "patent attorney"; or

(b) in the course of a business otherwise describe himself, or permit himself to be described, as a "patent agent" or "patent attorney".

(2) A partnership shall not—

(a) carry on a business under any name or other description which contains the words "patent agent" or "patent attorney"; or

(b) in the course of a business otherwise describe itself, or permit itself to be described as, a firm of "patent agents" or "patent attorneys",

unless all the partners are registered patent agents or the partnership satisfies such conditions as may be prescribed for the purposes of this section.

(3) A body corporate shall not—

(a) carry on a business (otherwise than in partnership) under any name or other description which contains the words "patent agent" or "patent attorney"; or

(b) in the course of a business otherwise describe itself, or permit itself to be described as, a "patent agent" or "patent attorney",

unless all the directors of the body corporate are registered patent agents or the body satisfies such conditions as may be prescribed for the purposes of this section.

(4) Subsection (3) does not apply to a company which began to carry on business as a patent agent before 17th November 1917 if the name of a director or the manager of

the company who is a registered patent agent is mentioned as being so registered in all professional advertisements, circulars or letters issued by or with the company's consent on which its name appears.

(5) Where this section would be contravened by the use of the words "patent agent" or "patent attorney" in reference to an individual, partnership or body corporate, it is equally contravened by the use of other expressions in reference to that person, or his business or place of business, which are likely to be understood as indicating that he is entitled to be described as a "patent agent" or "patent attorney".

(6) A person who contravenes this section commits an offence and is liable on summary conviction to a fine not exceeding level 5 on the standard scale; and proceedings for such an offence may be begun at any time within a year from the date of the offence.

(7) This section has effect subject to—

(a) section 277 (persons entitled to describe themselves as European patent attorneys, &c.), and

(b) section 278(1) (use of term "patent attorney" in reference to solicitors).

277 Persons entitled to describe themselves as European patent attorneys, &c

(1) The term "European patent attorney" or "European patent agent" may be used in the following cases without any contravention of section 276.

(2) An individual who is on the European list may—

(a) carry on business under a name or other description which contains the words "European patent attorney" or "European patent agent", or

(b) otherwise describe himself, or permit himself to be described, as a "European patent attorney" or "European patent agent".

(3) A partnership of which not less than the prescribed number or proportion of partners is on the European list may—

(a) carry on a business under a name or other description which contains the words "European patent attorneys" or "European patent agents", or

(b) otherwise describe itself, or permit itself to be described, as a firm which carries on the business of a "European patent attorney" or "European patent agent".

(4) A body corporate of which not less than the prescribed number or proportion of directors is on the European list may—

(a) carry on a business under a name or other description which contains the words "European patent attorney" or "European patent agent", or

(b) otherwise describe itself, or permit itself to be described as, a company which carries on the business of a "European patent attorney" or "European patent agent".

(5) Where the term "European patent attorney" or "European patent agent" may, in accordance with this section, be used in reference to an individual, partnership or body corporate, it is equally permissible to use other expressions in reference to that person, or to his business or place of business, which are likely to be understood as indicating that he is entitled to be described as a "European patent attorney" or "European patent agent."

278 Use of the term "patent attorney": supplementary provisions

(1) The term "patent attorney" may be used in reference to a solicitor, and a firm of solicitors may be described as a firm of "patent attorneys", without any contravention of section 276.

(2) No offence is committed under the enactments restricting the use of certain expressions in reference to persons not qualified to act as solicitors—

(a) by the use of the term "patent attorney" in reference to a registered patent agent, or

(b) by the use of the term "European patent attorney" in reference to a person on the European list.

(3) The enactments referred to in subsection (2) are section 21 of the Solicitors Act 1974, section 31 of the Solicitors (Scotland) Act 1980 and Article 22 of the Solicitors (Northern Ireland) Order 1976.

279 Power to prescribe conditions, &c. for mixed partnerships and bodies corporate

(1) The Secretary of State may make rules—

(a) prescribing the conditions to be satisfied for the purposes of section 276 (persons entitled to describe themselves as patent agents) in relation to a partnership where not all the partners are qualified persons or a body corporate where not all the directors are qualified persons, and

(b) imposing requirements to be complied with by such partnerships and bodies corporate.

(2) The rules may, in particular—

(a) prescribe conditions as to the number or proportion of partners or directors who must be qualified persons;

(b) impose requirements as to—

(i) the identification of qualified and unqualified persons in professional advertisements, circulars or letters issued by or with the consent of the partnership or body corporate and which relate to it or to its business; and

(ii) the manner in which a partnership or body corporate is to organise its affairs so as to secure that qualified persons exercise a sufficient degree of control over the activities of unqualified persons.

(3) Contravention of a requirement imposed by the rules is an offence for which a person is liable on summary conviction to a fine not exceeding level 5 on the standard scale.

(4) The Secretary of State may make rules prescribing for the purposes of section 277 the number or proportion of partners of a partnership or directors of a body corporate who must be qualified persons in order for the partnership or body to take advantage of that section.

(5) In this section "qualified person"—

(a) in subsections (1) and (2), means a person who is a registered patent agent, and

(b) in subsection (4), means a person who is on the European list.

(6) Rules under this section shall be made by statutory instrument which shall be subject to annulment in pursuance of a resolution of either House of Parliament.

280 Privilege for communications with patent agents

(1) This section applies to communications as to any matter relating to the protection of any invention, design, technical information, trade mark or service mark, or as to any matter involving passing off.

(2) Any such communication—

(a) between a person and his patent agent, or

(b) for the purpose of obtaining, or in response to a request for, information which a person is seeking for the purpose of instructing his patent agent,

is privileged from disclosure in legal proceedings in England, Wales or Northern Ireland in the same way as a communication between a person and his solicitor or, as the case may be, a communication for the purpose of obtaining, or in response to a request for, information which a person seeks for the purpose of instructing his solicitor.

(3) In subsection (2) "patent agent" means—

(a) a registered patent agent or a person who is on the European list,

(b) a partnership entitled to describe itself as a firm of patent agents or as a firm carrying on the business of a European patent attorney, or

(c) a body corporate entitled to describe itself as a patent agent or as a company carrying on the business of a European patent attorney.

(4) It is hereby declared that in Scotland the rules of law which confer privilege from disclosure in legal proceedings in respect of communications extend to such communications as are mentioned in this section.

281 Power of comptroller to refuse to deal with certain agents

(1) This section applies to business under the Patents Act 1949, the Registered Designs Act 1949 or the Patents Act 1977.

(2) The Secretary of State may make rules authorising the comptroller to refuse to recognise as agent in respect of any business to which this section applies—

(a) a person who has been convicted of an offence under section 88 of the Patents Act 1949, section 114 of the Patents Act 1977 or section 276 of this Act;

(b) an individual whose name has been erased from and not restored to, or who is suspended from, the register of patent agents on the ground of misconduct;

(c) a person who is found by the Secretary of State to have been guilty of such conduct as would, in the case of an individual registered in the register of patent agents, render him liable to have his name erased from the register on the ground of misconduct;

(d) a partnership or body corporate of which one of the partners or directors is a person whom the comptroller could refuse to recognise under paragraph (a), (b) or (c) above.

(3) The rules may contain such incidental and supplementary provisions as appear to the Secretary of State to be appropriate and may, in particular, prescribe circumstances in which a person is or is not to be taken to have been guilty of misconduct.

(4) Rules made under this section shall be made by statutory instrument which shall be subject to annulment in pursuance of a resolution of either House of Parliament.

(5) The comptroller shall refuse to recognise as agent in respect of any business to which this section applies a person who neither resides nor has a place of business in the United Kingdom, the Isle of Man or another member State of the European Economic Community.

Trade mark agents

282 The register of trade mark agents

(1) The Secretary of State may make rules requiring the keeping of a register of persons who act as agent for others for the purpose of applying for or obtaining the registration of trade marks; and in this Part a "registered trade mark agent" means a person whose name is entered in the register kept under this section.

(2) The rules may contain such provision as the Secretary of State thinks fit regulating the registration of persons, and may in particular—

(a) require the payment of such fees as may be prescribed, and

(b) authorise in prescribed cases the erasure from the register of the name of any person registered in it, or the suspension of a person's registration.

(3) The rules may delegate the keeping of the register to another person, and may confer on that person—

(a) power to make regulations—

(i) with respect to the payment of fees, in the cases and subject to the limits prescribed by rules, and

(ii) with respect to any other matter which could be regulated by rules, and

(b) such other functions, including disciplinary functions, as may be prescribed by rules.

(4) Rules under this section shall be made by statutory instrument which shall be subject to annulment in pursuance of a resolution of either House of Parliament.

283 Unregistered persons not to be described as registered trade mark agents

(1) An individual who is not a registered trade mark agent shall not—

(a) carry on a business (otherwise than in partnership) under any name or other description which contains the words "registered trade mark agent"; or

(b) in the course of a business otherwise describe or hold himself out, or permit himself to be described or held out, as a registered trade mark agent.

(2) A partnership shall not—

(a) carry on a business under any name or other description which contains the words "registered trade mark agent"; or

(b) in the course of a business otherwise describe or hold itself out, or permit itself to be described or held out, as a firm of registered trade mark agents,

unless all the partners are registered trade mark agents or the partnership satisfies such conditions as may be prescribed for the purposes of this section.

(3) A body corporate shall not—

(a) carry on a business (otherwise than in partnership) under any name or other description which contains the words "registered trade mark agent"; or

(b) in the course of a business otherwise describe or hold itself out, or permit itself to be described or held out, as a registered trade mark agent,

unless all the directors of the body corporate are registered trade mark agents or the body satisfies such conditions as may be prescribed for the purposes of this section.

(4) The Secretary of State may make rules prescribing the conditions to be satisfied for the purposes of this section in relation to a partnership where not all the partners are registered trade mark agents or a body corporate where not all the directors are registered trade mark agents; and the rules may, in particular, prescribe conditions as to the number or proportion of partners or directors who must be registered trade mark agents.

(5) Rules under this section shall be made by statutory instrument which shall be subject to annulment in pursuance of a resolution of either House of Parliament.

(6) A person who contravenes this section commits an offence and is liable on summary conviction to a fine not exceeding level 5 on the standard scale; and proceedings for such an offence may be begun at any time within a year from the date of the offence.

284 Privilege for communications with registered trade mark agents

(1) This section applies to communications as to any matter relating to the protection of any design, trade mark or service mark, or as to any matter involving passing off.

(2) Any such communication—

(a) between a person and his trade mark agent, or

(b) for the purpose of obtaining, or in response to a request for, information which a person is seeking for the purpose of instructing his trade mark agent,

is privileged from disclosure in legal proceedings in England, Wales or Northern Ireland in the same way as a communication between a person and his solicitor or, as the case may be, a communication for the purpose of obtaining, or in response to a request for, information which a person seeks for the purpose of instructing his solicitor.

(3) In subsection (1) "trade mark agent" means—

(a) a registered trade mark agent, or

(b) a partnership entitled to describe itself as a firm of registered trade mark agents, or

(c) a body corporate entitled to describe itself as a registered trade mark agent.

(4) It is hereby declared that in Scotland the rules of law which confer privilege from disclosure in legal proceedings in respect of communications extend to such communications as are mentioned in subsection (1).

Supplementary

285 Offences committed by partnerships and bodies corporate

(1) Proceedings for an offence under this Part alleged to have been committed by a partnership shall be brought in the name of the partnership and not in that of the partners; but without prejudice to any liability of theirs under subsection (4) below.

(2) The following provisions apply for the purposes of such proceedings as in relation to a body corporate—

(a) any rules of court relating to the service of documents;

(b) in England, Wales or Northern Ireland, Schedule 3 to the Magistrates' Courts Act 1980 or Schedule 4 to the Magistrates' Courts (Northern Ireland) Order 1981 (procedure on charge of offence).

(3) A fine imposed on a partnership on its conviction in such proceedings shall be paid out of the partnership assets.

(4) Where a partnership is guilty of an offence under this Part, every partner, other than a partner who is proved to have been ignorant of or to have attempted to prevent the commission of the offence, is also guilty of the offence and liable to be proceeded against and punished accordingly.

(5) Where an offence under this Part committed by a body corporate is proved to have been committed with the consent or connivance of a director, manager, secretary or other similar officer of the body, or a person purporting to act in any such capacity, he as well as the body corporate is guilty of the offence and liable to be proceeded against and punished accordingly.

286 Interpretation

In this Part—

"the comptroller" means the Comptroller-General of Patents, Designs and Trade Marks;

"director", in relation to a body corporate whose affairs are managed by its members, means any member of the body corporate;

"the European list" means the list of professional representatives maintained by the European Patent Office in pursuance of the European Patent Convention;

"registered patent agent" has the meaning given by section 275(1);

"registered trade mark agent" has the meaning given by section 282(1).

PART VI

PATENTS

Patents county courts

287 Patents county courts: special jurisdiction

(1) The Lord Chancellor may by order made by statutory instrument designate any county court as a patents county court and confer on it jurisdiction (its "special jurisdiction") to hear and determine such descriptions of proceedings—

(a) relating to patents or designs, or

(b) ancillary to, or arising out of the same subject matter as, proceedings relating to patents or designs,

as may be specified in the order.

(2) The special jurisdiction of a patents county court is exercisable throughout England and Wales, but rules of court may provide for a matter pending in one such court to be heard and determined in another or partly in that and partly in another.

(3) A patents county court may entertain proceedings within its special jurisdiction notwithstanding that no pecuniary remedy is sought.

(4) An order under this section providing for the discontinuance of any of the special jurisdiction of a patents county court may make provision as to proceedings pending in the court when the order comes into operation.

(5) Nothing in this section shall be construed as affecting the ordinary jurisdiction of a county court.

288 Financial limits in relation to proceedings within special jurisdiction of patents county court

(1) Her Majesty may by Order in Council provide for limits of amount or value in relation to any description of proceedings within the special jurisdiction of a patents county court.

(2) If a limit is imposed on the amount of a claim of any description and the plaintiff has a cause of action for more than that amount, he may abandon the excess; in which case a patents county court shall have jurisdiction to hear and determine the action, but the plaintiff may not recover more than that amount.

(3) Where the court has jurisdiction to hear and determine an action by virtue of subsection (2), the judgment of the court in the action is in full discharge of all demands in respect of the cause of action, and entry of the judgment shall be made accordingly.

(4) If the parties agree, by a memorandum signed by them or by their respective solicitors or other agents, that a patents county court shall have jurisdiction in any proceedings, that court shall have jurisdiction to hear and determine the proceedings notwithstanding any limit imposed under this section.

(5) No recommendation shall be made to Her Majesty to make an Order under this section unless a draft of the Order has been laid before and approved by a resolution of each House of Parliament.

289 Transfer of proceedings between High Court and patents county court

(1) No order shall be made under section 41 of the County Courts Act 1984 (power of High Court to order proceedings to be transferred from the county court) in respect of proceedings within the special jurisdiction of a patents county court.

(2) In considering in relation to proceedings within the special jurisdiction of a patents county court whether an order should be made under section 40 or 42 of the County Courts Act 1984 (transfer of proceedings from or to the High Court), the court shall have regard to the financial position of the parties and may order the transfer of the proceedings to a patents county court or, as the case may be, refrain from ordering their transfer to the High Court notwithstanding that the proceedings are likely to raise an important question of fact or law.

290 Limitation of costs where pecuniary claim could have been brought in patents county court

(1) Where an action is commenced in the High Court which could have been commenced in a patents county court and in which a claim for a pecuniary remedy is made, then, subject to the provisions of this section, if the plaintiff recovers less than the prescribed amount, he is not entitled to recover any more costs than those to which he would have been entitled if the action had been brought in the county court.

(2) For this purpose a plaintiff shall be treated as recovering the full amount recoverable in respect of his claim without regard to any deduction made in respect of matters not falling to be taken into account in determining whether the action could have been commenced in a patents county court.

(3) This section does not affect any question as to costs if it appears to the High Court that there was reasonable ground for supposing the amount recoverable in respect of the plaintiff's claim to be in excess of the prescribed amount.

(4) The High Court, if satisfied that there was sufficient reason for bringing the action in the High Court, may make an order allowing the costs or any part of the costs on the High Court scale or on such one of the county court scales as it may direct.

(5) This section does not apply to proceedings brought by the Crown.

(6) In this section "the prescribed amount" means such amount as may be prescribed by Her Majesty for the purposes of this section by Order in Council.

(7) No recommendation shall be made to Her Majesty to make an Order under this section unless a draft of the Order has been laid before and approved by a resolution of each House of Parliament.

291 Proceedings in patents county court

(1) Where a county court is designated a patents county court, the Lord Chancellor shall nominate a person entitled to sit as a judge of that court as the patents judge.

(2) County court rules shall make provision for securing that, so far as is practicable and appropriate—

(a) proceedings within the special jurisdiction of a patents county court are dealt with by the patents judge, and

(b) the judge, rather than a registrar or other officer of the court, deals with interlocutory matters in the proceedings.

(3) County court rules shall make provision empowering a patents county court in proceedings within its special jurisdiction, on or without the application of any party—

(a) to appoint scientific advisers or assessors to assist the court, or

(b) to order the Patent Office to inquire into and report on any question of fact or opinion.

(4) Where the court exercises either of those powers on the application of a party, the remuneration or fees payable to the Patent Office shall be at such rate as may be determined in accordance with county court rules and shall be costs of the proceedings unless otherwise ordered by the judge.

(5) Where the court exercises either of those powers of its own motion, the remuneration or fees payable to the Patent Office shall be at such rate as may be determined by the Lord Chancellor with the approval of the Treasury and shall be paid out of money provided by Parliament.

292 Rights and duties of registered patent agents in relation to proceedings in patents county court

(1) A registered patent agent may do, in or in connection with proceedings in a patents county court which are within the special jurisdiction of that court, anything which a solicitor of the Supreme Court might do, other than prepare a deed.

(2) The Lord Chancellor may by regulations provide that the right conferred by subsection (1) shall be subject to such conditions and restrictions as appear to the Lord Chancellor to be necessary or expedient; and different provision may be made for different descriptions of proceedings.

(3) A patents county court has the same power to enforce an undertaking given by a registered patent agent acting in pursuance of this section as it has, by virtue of section 142 of the County Courts Act 1984, in relation to a solicitor.

(4) Nothing in section 143 of the County Courts Act 1984 (prohibition on persons other than solicitors receiving remuneration) applies to a registered patent agent acting in pursuance of this section.

(5) The provisions of county court rules prescribing scales of costs to be paid to solicitors apply in relation to registered patent agents acting in pursuance of this section.

(6) Regulations under this section shall be made by statutory instrument which shall be subject to annulment in pursuance of a resolution of either House of Parliament.

Licences of right in respect of certain patents

293 Restriction of acts authorised by certain licences

In paragraph 4(2)(c) of Schedule 1 to the Patents Act 1977 (licences to be available as of right where term of existing patent extended), at the end insert ", but subject to paragraph 4A below", and after that paragraph insert—

"4A (1) If the proprietor of a patent for an invention which is a product files a declaration with the Patent Office in accordance with this paragraph, the licences to which persons are entitled by virtue of paragraph 4(2)(c) above shall not extend to a use of the product which is excepted by or under this paragraph.

(2) Pharmaceutical use is excepted, that is—

(a) use as a medicinal product within the meaning of the Medicines Act 1968, and

(b) the doing of any other act mentioned in section 60(1)(a) above with a view to such use.

(3) The Secretary of State may by order except such other uses as he thinks fit; and an order may—

(a) specify as an excepted use any act mentioned in section 60(1)(a) above, and

(b) make different provision with respect to acts done in different circumstances or for different purposes.

(4) For the purposes of this paragraph the question what uses are excepted, so far as that depends on—

(a) orders under section 130 of the Medicines Act 1968 (meaning of "medicinal product"), or

(b) orders under sub-paragraph (3) above,

shall be determined in relation to a patent at the beginning of the sixteenth year of the patent.

(5) A declaration under this paragraph shall be in the prescribed form and shall be filed in the prescribed manner and within the prescribed time limits.

(6) A declaration may not be filed—

(a) in respect of a patent which has at the commencement of section 293 of the Copyright, Designs and Patents Act 1988 passed the end of its fifteenth year; or

(b) if at the date of filing there is—

(i) an existing licence for any description of excepted use of the product, or

(ii) an outstanding application under section 46(3)(a) or (b) above for the settlement by the comptroller of the terms of a licence for any description of excepted use of the product,

and, in either case, the licence took or is to take effect at or after the end of the sixteenth year of the patent.

(7) Where a declaration has been filed under this paragraph in respect of a patent—

(a) section 46(3)(c) above (restriction of remedies for infringement where licences available as of right) does not apply to an infringement of the patent in so far as it consists of the excepted use of the product after the filing of the declaration; and

(b) section 46(3)(d) above (abatement of renewal fee if licences available as of right) does not apply to the patent.".

294 When application may be made for settlement of terms of licence

In Schedule 1 to the Patents Act 1977, after the paragraph inserted by section 293 above, insert—

"4B (1) An application under section 46(3)(a) or (b) above for the settlement by the comptroller of the terms on which a person is entitled to a licence by virtue of paragraph 4(2)(c) above is ineffective if made before the beginning of the sixteenth year of the patent.

(2) This paragraph applies to applications made after the commencement of section 294 of the Copyright, Designs and Patents Act 1988 and to any application made before the commencement of that section in respect of a patent which has not at the commencement of that section passed the end of its fifteenth year.".

Patents: miscellaneous amendments

295 Patents: miscellaneous amendments

The Patents Act 1949 and the Patents Act 1977 are amended in accordance with Schedule 5.

PART VII

MISCELLANEOUS AND GENERAL

Devices designed to circumvent copy-protection

296 Devices designed to circumvent copy-protection

(1) This section applies where copies of a copyright work are issued to the public, by or with the licence of the copyright owner, in an electronic form which is copy-protected.

(2) The person issuing the copies to the public has the same rights against a person who, knowing or having reason to believe that it will be used to make infringing copies—

(a) makes, imports, sells or lets for hire, offers or exposes for sale or hire, or advertises for sale or hire, any device or means specifically designed or adapted to circumvent the form of copy-protection employed, or

(b) publishes information intended to enable or assist persons to circumvent that form of copy-protection,

as a copyright owner has in respect of an infringement of copyright.

(3) Further, he has the same rights under section 99 or 100 (delivery up or seizure of certain articles) in relation to any such device or means which a person has in his possession, custody or control with the intention that it should be used to make infringing copies of copyright works, as a copyright owner has in relation to an infringing copy.

(4) References in this section to copy-protection include any device or means intended to prevent or restrict copying of a work or to impair the quality of copies made.

(5) Expressions used in this section which are defined for the purposes of Part I of this Act (copyright) have the same meaning as in that Part.

(6) The following provisions apply in relation to proceedings under this section as in relation to proceedings under Part I (copyright)—

(a) sections 104 to 106 of this Act (presumptions as to certain matters relating to copyright), and

(b) section 72 of the Supreme Court Act 1981, section 15 of the Law Reform (Miscellaneous Provisions) (Scotland) Act 1985 and section 94A of the Judicature (Northern Ireland) Act 1978 (withdrawal of privilege against self-incrimination in certain proceedings relating to intellectual property);

and section 114 of this Act applies, with the necessary modifications, in relation to the disposal of anything delivered up or seized by virtue of subsection (3) above.

Fraudulent reception of transmissions

297 Offence of fraudulently receiving programmes

(1) A person who dishonestly receives a programme included in a broadcasting or cable programme service provided from a place in the United Kingdom with intent to avoid payment of any charge applicable to the reception of the programme commits an offence and is liable on summary conviction to a fine not exceeding level 5 on the standard scale.

(2) Where an offence under this section committed by a body corporate is proved to have been committed with the consent or connivance of a director, manager, secretary or other similar officer of the body, or a person purporting to act in any such capacity, he as well as the body corporate is guilty of the offence and liable to be proceeded against and punished accordingly.

In relation to a body corporate whose affairs are managed by its members "director" means a member of the body corporate.

298 Rights and remedies in respect of apparatus, &c. for unauthorised reception of transmissions

(1) A person who—

(a) makes charges for the reception of programmes included in a broadcasting or cable programme service provided from a place in the United Kingdom, or

(b) sends encrypted transmissions of any other description from a place in the United Kingdom,

is entitled to the following rights and remedies.

(2) He has the same rights and remedies against a person who—

(a) makes, imports or sells or lets for hire any apparatus or device designed or adapted to enable or assist persons to receive the programmes or other transmissions when they are not entitled to do so, or

(b) publishes any information which is calculated to enable or assist persons to receive the programmes or other transmissions when they are not entitled to do so,

as a copyright owner has in respect of an infringement of copyright.

(3) Further, he has the same rights under section 99 or 100 (delivery up or seizure of certain articles) in relation to any such apparatus or device as a copyright owner has in relation to an infringing copy.

(4) Section 72 of the Supreme Court Act 1981, section 15 of the Law Reform (Miscellaneous Provisions) (Scotland) Act 1985 and section 94A of the Judicature (Northern Ireland) Act 1978 (withdrawal of privilege against self-incrimination in certain proceedings relating to intellectual property) apply to proceedings under this section as to proceedings under Part I of this Act (copyright).

(5) In section 97(1) (innocent infringement of copyright) as it applies to proceedings for infringement of the rights conferred by this section, the reference to the defendant not knowing or having reason to believe that copyright subsisted in the work shall be construed as a reference to his not knowing or having reason to believe that his acts infringed the rights conferred by this section.

(6) Section 114 of this Act applies, with the necessary modifications, in relation to the disposal of anything delivered up or seized by virtue of subsection (3) above.

299 Supplementary provisions as to fraudulent reception

(1) Her Majesty may by Order in Council—

(a) provide that section 297 applies in relation to programmes included in services provided from a country or territory outside the United Kingdom, and

(b) provide that section 298 applies in relation to such programmes and to encrypted transmissions sent from such a country or territory.

(2) No such Order shall be made unless it appears to Her Majesty that provision has been or will be made under the laws of that country or territory giving adequate protection to persons making charges for programmes included in broadcasting or cable programme services provided from the United Kingdom or, as the case may be, for encrypted transmissions sent from the United Kingdom.

(3) A statutory instrument containing an Order in Council under subsection (1) shall be subject to annulment in pursuance of a resolution of either House of Parliament.

(4) Where sections 297 and 298 apply in relation to a broadcasting service or cable programme service, they also apply to any service run for the person providing that service, or a person providing programmes for that service, which consists wholly or mainly in the sending by means of a telecommunications system of sounds or visual images, or both.

(5) In sections 297 and 298, and this section, "programme", "broadcasting" and "cable programme service", and related expressions, have the same meaning as in Part I (copyright).

Fraudulent application or use of trade mark

300 Fraudulent application or use of trade mark an offence

In the Trade Marks Act 1938 the following sections are inserted before section 59, after the heading "*Offences and restraint of use of Royal Arms*"—

"58A Fraudulent application or use of trade mark an offence

(1) It is an offence, subject to subsection (3) below, for a person—
   (a) to apply a mark identical to or nearly resembling a registered trade mark to goods, or to material used or intended to be used for labelling, packaging or advertising goods, or
   (b) to sell, let for hire, or offer or expose for sale or hire, or distribute—
      (i) goods bearing such a mark, or
      (ii) material bearing such a mark which is used or intended to be used for labelling, packaging or advertising goods, or
   (c) to use material bearing such a mark in the course of a business for labelling, packaging or advertising goods, or
   (d) to possess in the course of a business goods or material bearing such a mark with a view to doing any of the things mentioned in paragraphs (a) to (c),

when he is not entitled to use the mark in relation to the goods in question and the goods are not connected in the course of trade with a person who is so entitled.

(2) It is also an offence, subject to subsection (3) below, for a person to possess in the course of a business goods or material bearing a mark identical to or nearly resembling a registered trade mark with a view to enabling or assisting another person to do any of the things mentioned in subsection (1)(a) to (c), knowing or having reason to believe that the other person is not entitled to use the mark in relation to the goods in question and that the goods are not connected in the course of trade with a person who is so entitled.

(3) A person commits an offence under subsection (1) or (2) only if—
   (a) he acts with a view to gain for himself or another, or with intent to cause loss to another, and
   (b) he intends that the goods in question should be accepted as connected in the course of trade with a person entitled to use the mark in question;

and it is a defence for a person charged with an offence under subsection (1) to show that he believed on reasonable grounds that he was entitled to use the mark in relation to the goods in question.

(4) A person guilty of an offence under this section is liable—
   (a) on summary conviction to imprisonment for a term not exceeding six months or a fine not exceeding the statutory maximum, or both;
   (b) on conviction on indictment to a fine or imprisonment for a term not exceeding ten years, or both.

(5) Where an offence under this section committed by a body corporate is proved to have been committed with the consent or connivance of a director, manager, secretary or other similar officer of the body, or a person purporting to act in any such capacity, he as well as the body corporate is guilty of the offence and liable to be proceeded against and punished accordingly.

In relation to a body corporate whose affairs are managed by its members "director" means a member of the body corporate.

(6) In this section "business" includes a trade or profession."

58B Delivery up of offending goods and material

(1) The court by which a person is convicted of an offence under section 58A may, if satisfied that at the time of his arrest or charge he had in his possession, custody or control—

(a) goods or material in respect of which the offence was committed, or

(b) goods of the same description as those in respect of which the offence was committed, or material similar to that in respect of which the offence was committed, bearing a mark identical to or nearly resembling that in relation to which the offence was committed,

order that the goods or material be delivered up to such person as the court may direct.

(2) For this purpose a person shall be treated as charged with an offence—

(a) in England, Wales and Northern Ireland, when he is orally charged or is served with a summons or indictment;

(b) in Scotland, when he is cautioned, charged or served with a complaint or indictment.

(3) An order may be made by the court of its own motion or on the application of the prosecutor (or, in Scotland, the Lord Advocate or procurator-fiscal), but shall not be made if it appears to the court unlikely that any order will be made under section 58C (order as to disposal of offending goods or material).

(4) An appeal lies from an order made under this section by a magistrates' court—

(a) in England and Wales, to the Crown Court, and

(b) in Northern Ireland, to the county court;

and in Scotland, where an order has been made under this section, the person from whose possession, custody or control the goods or material have been removed may, without prejudice to any other form of appeal under any rule of law, appeal against that order in the same manner as against sentence.

(5) A person to whom goods or material are delivered up in pursuance of an order under this section shall retain it pending the making of an order under section 58C.

(6) Nothing in this section affects the powers of the court under section 43 of the Powers of Criminal Courts Act 1973, section 223 or 436 of the Criminal Procedure (Scotland) Act 1975 or Article 7 of the Criminal Justice (Northern Ireland) Order 1980 (general provisions as to forfeiture in criminal proceedings).

58C Order as to disposal of offending goods or material

(1) Where goods or material have been delivered up in pursuance of an order under section 58B, an application may be made to the court for an order that they be destroyed or forfeited to such person as the court may think fit.

(2) Provision shall be made by rules of court as to the service of notice on persons having an interest in the goods or material, and any such person is entitled—

(a) to appear in proceedings for an order under this section, whether or not he was served with notice, and

(b) to appeal against any order made, whether or not he appeared;

and an order shall not take effect until the end of the period within which notice of an appeal may be given or, if before the end of that period notice of appeal is duly given, until the final determination or abandonment of the proceedings on the appeal.

(3) Where there is more than one person interested in goods or material, the court shall make such order as it thinks just.

(4) References in this section to a person having an interest in goods or material include any person in whose favour an order could be made under this section or under sections 114, 204 or 231 of the Copyright, Designs and Patents Act 1988 (which make similar provision in relation to infringement of copyright, rights in performances and design right).

(5) Proceedings for an order under this section may be brought—

(a) in a county court in England, Wales and Northern Ireland, provided the value of the goods or material in question does not exceed the county court limit for actions in tort, and

(b) in a sheriff court in Scotland;

but this shall not be construed as affecting the jurisdiction of the High Court or, in Scotland, the Court of Session.

58D Enforcement of section 58A

(1) The functions of a local weights and measures authority include the enforcement in their area of section 58A.

(2) The following provisions of the Trade Descriptions Act 1968 apply in relation to the enforcement of that section as in relation to the enforcement of that Act—

section 27 (power to make test purchases),

section 28 (power to enter premises and inspect and seize goods and documents),

section 29 (obstruction of authorised officers), and

section 33 (compensation for loss, &c. of goods seized under s.28).

(3) Subsection (1) above does not apply in relation to the enforcement of section 58A in Northern Ireland, but the functions of the Department of Economic Development include the enforcement of that section in Northern Ireland.

For that purpose the provisions of the Trade Descriptions Act 1968 specified in subsection (2) apply as if for the references to a local weights and measures authority and any officer of such an authority there were substituted references to that Department and any of its officers.

(4) Any enactment which authorises the disclosure of information for the purpose of facilitating the enforcement of the Trade Descriptions Act 1968 shall apply as if section 58A above were contained in that Act and as if the functions of any person in relation to the enforcement of that section were functions under that Act.”.

Provisions for the benefit of the Hospital for Sick Children

301 Provisions for the benefit of the Hospital for Sick Children

The provisions of Schedule 6 have effect for conferring on trustees for the benefit of the Hospital for Sick Children, Great Ormond Street, London, a right to a royalty in respect of the public performance, commercial publication, broadcasting or inclusion in a cable programme service of the play "Peter Pan" by Sir James Matthew Barrie, or of any adaptation of that work, notwithstanding that copyright in the work expired on 31st December 1987.

Financial assistance for certain international bodies

302 Financial assistance for certain international bodies

(1) The Secretary of State may give financial assistance, in the form of grants, loans or guarantees to—

(a) any international organisation having functions relating to trade marks or other intellectual property, or

(b) any Community institution or other body established under any of the Community Treaties having any such functions,

with a view to the establishment or maintenance by that organisation, institution or body of premises in the United Kingdom.

(2) Any expenditure of the Secretary of State under this section shall be defrayed out of money provided by Parliament; and any sums received by the Secretary of State in consequence of this section shall be paid into the Consolidated Fund.

General

303 Consequential amendments and repeals

(1) The enactments specified in Schedule 7 are amended in accordance with that Schedule, the amendments being consequential on the provisions of this Act.

(2) The enactments specified in Schedule 8 are repealed to the extent specified.

304 Extent

(1) Provision as to the extent of Part I (copyright), Part II (rights in performances) and Part III (design right) is to be found in sections 157, 207 and 255 respectively; the extent of the other provisions of this Act is as follows.

(2) Parts IV to VII extend to England and Wales, Scotland and Northern Ireland, except that—

(a) sections 287 to 292 (patents county courts) extend to England and Wales only,

(b) the proper law of the trust created by Schedule 6 (provisions for the benefit of the Hospital for Sick Children) is the law of England and Wales, and

(c) the amendments and repeals in Schedules 7 and 8 have the same extent as the enactments amended or repealed.

(3) The following provisions extend to the Isle of Man subject to any modifications contained in an Order made by Her Majesty in Council—

(a) sections 293 and 294 (patents: licences of right), and

(b) paragraphs 24 and 29 of Schedule 5 (patents: effect of filing international application for patent and power to extend time limits).

(4) Her Majesty may by Order in Council direct that the following provisions extend to the Isle of Man, with such exceptions and modifications as may be specified in the Order—

(a) Part IV (registered designs),

(b) Part V (patent agents),

(c) the provisions of Schedule 5 (patents: miscellaneous amendments) not mentioned in subsection (3) above,

(d) sections 297 to 299 (fraudulent reception of transmissions), and

(e) section 300 (fraudulent application or use of trade mark).

(5) Her Majesty may by Order in Council direct that sections 297 to 299 (fraudulent reception of transmissions) extend to any of the Channel Islands, with such exceptions and modifications as may be specified in the Order.

(6) Any power conferred by this Act to make provision by Order in Council for or in connection with the extent of provisions of this Act to a country outside the United Kingdom includes power to extend to that country, subject to any modifications specified in the Order, any provision of this Act which amends or repeals an enactment extending to that country.

305 Commencement

(1) The following provisions of this Act come into force on Royal Assent—

paragraphs 24 and 29 of Schedule 5 (patents: effect of filing international application for patent and power to extend time limits);

section 301 and Schedule 6 (provisions for the benefit of the Hospital for Sick Children).

(2) Sections 293 and 294 (licences of right) come into force at the end of the period of two months beginning with the passing of this Act.

(3) The other provisions of this Act come into force on such day as the Secretary of State may appoint by order made by statutory instrument, and different days may be appointed for different provisions and different purposes.

306 Short title

This Act may be cited as the Copyright, Designs and Patents Act 1988.

SCHEDULES

SCHEDULE 1

Section 170.

COPYRIGHT: TRANSITIONAL PROVISIONS AND SAVINGS

Introductory

1 (1) In this Schedule—

"the 1911 Act" means the Copyright Act 1911,

"the 1956 Act" means the Copyright Act 1956, and

"the new copyright provisions" means the provisions of this Act relating to copyright, that is, Part I (including this Schedule) and Schedules 3, 7 and 8 so far as they make amendments or repeals consequential on the provisions of Part I.

(2) References in this Schedule to "commencement", without more, are to the date on which the new copyright provisions come into force.

(3) References in this Schedule to "existing works" are to works made before commencement; and for this purpose a work of which the making extended over a period shall be taken to have been made when its making was completed.

2 (1) In relation to the 1956 Act, references in this Schedule to a work include any work or other subject-matter within the meaning of that Act.

(2) In relation to the 1911 Act—

(a) references in this Schedule to copyright include the right conferred by section 24 of that Act in substitution for a right subsisting immediately before the commencement of that Act;

(b) references in this Schedule to copyright in a sound recording are to the copyright under that Act in records embodying the recording; and

(c) references in this Schedule to copyright in a film are to any copyright under that Act in the film (so far as it constituted a dramatic work for the purposes of that Act) or in photographs forming part of the film.

General principles: continuity of the law

3 The new copyright provisions apply in relation to things existing at commencement as they apply in relation to things coming into existence after commencement, subject to any express provision to the contrary.

4 (1) The provisions of this paragraph have effect for securing the continuity of the law so far as the new copyright provisions re-enact (with or without modification) earlier provisions.

(2) A reference in an enactment, instrument or other document to copyright, or to a work or other subject-matter in which copyright subsists, which apart from this Act would be construed as referring to copyright under the 1956 Act shall be construed, so far

as may be required for continuing its effect, as being, or as the case may require, including, a reference to copyright under this Act or to works in which copyright subsists under this Act.

(3) Anything done (including subordinate legislation made), or having effect as done, under or for the purposes of a provision repealed by this Act has effect as if done under or for the purposes of the corresponding provision of the new copyright provisions.

(4) References (expressed or implied) in this Act or any other enactment, instrument or document to any of the new copyright provisions shall, so far as the context permits, be construed as including, in relation to times, circumstances and purposes before commencement, a reference to corresponding earlier provisions.

(5) A reference (express or implied) in an enactment, instrument or other document to a provision repealed by this Act shall be construed, so far as may be required for continuing its effect, as a reference to the corresponding provision of this Act.

(6) The provisions of this paragraph have effect subject to any specific transitional provision or saving and to any express amendment made by this Act.

Subsistence of copyright

5 (1) Copyright subsists in an existing work after commencement only if copyright subsisted in it immediately before commencement.

(2) Sub-paragraph (1) does not prevent an existing work qualifying for copyright protection after commencement—

(a) under section 155 (qualification by virtue of first publication), or

(b) by virtue of an Order under section 159 (application of Part I to countries to which it does not extend).

6 (1) Copyright shall not subsist by virtue of this Act in an artistic work made before 1st June 1957 which at the time when the work was made constituted a design capable of registration under the Registered Designs Act 1949 or under the enactments repealed by that Act, and was used, or intended to be used, as a model or pattern to be multiplied by an industrial process.

(2) For this purpose a design shall be deemed to be used as a model or pattern to be multiplied by any industrial process—

(a) when the design is reproduced or is intended to be reproduced on more than 50 single articles, unless all the articles in which the design is reproduced or is intended to be reproduced together form only a single set of articles as defined in section 44(1) of the Registered Designs Act 1949, or

(b) when the design is to be applied to—

(i) printed paper hangings,

(ii) carpets, floor cloths or oil cloths, manufactured or sold in lengths or pieces,

(iii) textile piece goods, or textile goods manufactured or sold in lengths or pieces, or

(iv) lace, not made by hand.

7 (1) No copyright subsists in a film, as such, made before 1st June 1957.

(2) Where a film made before that date was an original dramatic work within the meaning of the 1911 Act, the new copyright provisions have effect in relation to the film as if it was an original dramatic work within the meaning of Part I.

(3) The new copyright provisions have effect in relation to photographs forming part of a film made before 1st June 1957 as they have effect in relation to photographs not forming part of a film.

8 (1) A film sound-track to which section 13(9) of the 1956 Act applied before commencement (film to be taken to include sounds in associated sound-track) shall be treated for the purposes of the new copyright provisions not as part of the film, but as a sound recording.

(2) However—

(a) copyright subsists in the sound recording only if copyright subsisted in the film immediately before commencement, and it continues to subsist until copyright in the film expires;

(b) the author and first owner of copyright in the film shall be treated as having been author and first owner of the copyright in the sound recording; and

(c) anything done before commencement under or in relation to the copyright in the film continues to have effect in relation to the sound recording as in relation to the film.

9 No copyright subsists in—

(a) a broadcast made before 1st June 1957, or

(b) a cable programme included in a cable programme service before 1st January 1985;

and any such broadcast or cable programme shall be disregarded for the purposes of section 14(2) (duration of copyright in repeats).

Authorship of work

10 The question who was the author of an existing work shall be determined in accordance with the new copyright provisions for the purposes of the rights conferred by Chapter IV of Part I (moral rights), and for all other purposes shall be determined in accordance with the law in force at the time the work was made.

First ownership of copyright

11 (1) The question who was first owner of copyright in an existing work shall be determined in accordance with the law in force at the time the work was made.

(2) Where before commencement a person commissioned the making of a work in circumstances falling within—

(a) section 4(3) of the 1956 Act or paragraph (a) of the proviso to section 5(1) of the 1911 Act (photographs, portraits and engravings), or

(b) the proviso to section 12(4) of the 1956 Act (sound recordings),

those provisions apply to determine first ownership of copyright in any work made in pursuance of the commission after commencement.

Duration of copyright in existing works

12 (1) The following provisions have effect with respect to the duration of copyright in existing works.

The question which provision applies to a work shall be determined by reference to the facts immediately before commencement; and expressions used in this paragraph which were defined for the purposes of the 1956 Act have the same meaning as in that Act.

(2) Copyright in the following descriptions of work continues to subsist until the date on which it would have expired under the 1956 Act—

(a) literary, dramatic or musical works in relation to which the period of 50 years mentioned in the proviso to section 2(3) of the 1956 Act (duration of copyright in works made available to the public after the death of the author) has begun to run;

(b) engravings in relation to which the period of 50 years mentioned in the proviso to section 3(4) of the 1956 Act (duration of copyright in works published after the death of the author) has begun to run;

(c) published photographs and photographs taken before 1st June 1957;

(d) published sound recordings and sound recordings made before 1st June 1957;

(e) published films and films falling within section 13(3)(a) of the 1956 Act (films registered under former enactments relating to registration of films).

(3) Copyright in anonymous or pseudonymous literary, dramatic, musical or artistic works (other than photographs) continues to subsist—

(a) if the work is published, until the date on which it would have expired in accordance with the 1956 Act, and

(b) if the work is unpublished, until the end of the period of 50 years from the end of the calendar year in which the new copyright provisions come into force or, if during that period the work is first made available to the public within the meaning of section 12(2) (duration of copyright in works of unknown authorship), the date on which copyright expires in accordance with that provision;

unless, in any case, the identity of the author becomes known before that date, in which case section 12(1) applies (general rule: life of the author plus 50 years).

(4) Copyright in the following descriptions of work continues to subsist until the end of the period of 50 years from the end of the calendar year in which the new copyright provisions come into force—

(a) literary, dramatic and musical works of which the author has died and in relation to which none of the acts mentioned in paragraphs (a) to (e) of the proviso to section 2(3) of the 1956 Act has been done;

(b) unpublished engravings of which the author has died;

(c) unpublished photographs taken on or after 1st June 1957.

(5) Copyright in the following descriptions of work continues to subsist until the end of the period of 50 years from the end of the calendar year in which the new copyright provisions come into force—

(a) unpublished sound recordings made on or after 1st June 1957;

(b) films not falling within sub-paragraph (2)(e) above,

unless the recording or film is published before the end of that period in which case copyright in it shall continue until the end of the period of 50 years from the end of the calendar year in which the recording or film is published.

(6) Copyright in any other description of existing work continues to subsist until the date on which copyright in that description of work expires in accordance with sections 12 to 15 of this Act.

(7) The above provisions do not apply to works subject to Crown or Parliamentary copyright (see paragraphs 41 to 43 below).

Perpetual copyright under the Copyright Act 1775

13 (1) The rights conferred on universities and colleges by the Copyright Act 1775 shall continue to subsist until the end of the period of 50 years from the end of the calendar year in which the new copyright provisions come into force and shall then expire.

(2) The provisions of the following Chapters of Part I—

Chapter III (acts permitted in relation to copyright works),

Chapter VI (remedies for infringement),

Chapter VII (provisions with respect to copyright licensing), and

Chapter VIII (the Copyright Tribunal),

apply in relation to those rights as they apply in relation to copyright under this Act.

Acts infringing copyright

14 (1) The provisions of Chapters II and III of Part I as to the acts constituting an infringement of copyright apply only in relation to acts done after commencement; the provisions of the 1956 Act continue to apply in relation to acts done before commencement.

(2) So much of section 18(2) as extends the restricted act of issuing copies to the public to include the rental to the public of copies of sound recordings, films or computer programs does not apply in relation to a copy of a sound recording, film or computer program acquired by any person before commencement for the purpose of renting it to the public.

(3) For the purposes of section 27 (meaning of "infringing copy") the question whether the making of an article constituted an infringement of copyright, or would have done if the article had been made in the United Kingdom, shall be determined—

(a) in relation to an article made on or after 1st June 1957 and before commencement, by reference to the 1956 Act, and

(b) in relation to an article made before 1st June 1957, by reference to the 1911 Act.

(4) For the purposes of the application of sections 31(2), 51(2) and 62(3) (subsequent exploitation of things whose making was, by virtue of an earlier provision of the section, not an infringement of copyright) to things made before commencement, it shall be assumed that the new copyright provisions were in force at all material times.

(5) Section 55 (articles for producing material in a particular typeface) applies where articles have been marketed as mentioned in subsection (1) before commencement with the substitution for the period mentioned in subsection (3) of the period of 25

years from the end of the calendar year in which the new copyright provisions come into force.

(6) Section 56 (transfer of copies, adaptations, &c. of work in electronic form) does not apply in relation to a copy purchased before commencement.

(7) In section 65 (reconstruction of buildings) the reference to the owner of the copyright in the drawings or plans is, in relation to buildings constructed before commencement, to the person who at the time of the construction was the owner of the copyright in the drawings or plans under the 1956 Act, the 1911 Act or any enactment repealed by the 1911 Act.

15 (1) Section 57 (anonymous or pseudonymous works: acts permitted on assumptions as to expiry of copyright or death of author) has effect in relation to existing works subject to the following provisions.

(2) Subsection (1)(b)(i) (assumption as to expiry of copyright) does not apply in relation to—

(a) photographs, or

(b) the rights mentioned in paragraph 13 above (rights conferred by the Copyright Act 1775).

(3) Subsection (1)(b)(ii) (assumption as to death of author) applies only—

(a) where paragraph 12(3)(b) above applies (unpublished anonymous or pseudonymous works), after the end of the period of 50 years from the end of the calendar year in which the new copyright provisions come into force, or

(b) where paragraph 12(6) above applies (cases in which the duration of copyright is the same under the new copyright provisions as under the previous law).

16 The following provisions of section 7 of the 1956 Act continue to apply in relation to existing works—

(a) subsection (6) (copying of unpublished works from manuscript or copy in library, museum or other institution);

(b) subsection (7) (publication of work containing material to which subsection (6) applies), except paragraph (a) (duty to give notice of intended publication);

(c) subsection (8) (subsequent broadcasting, performance, &c. of material published in accordance with subsection (7));

and subsection (9)(d) (illustrations) continues to apply for the purposes of those provisions.

17 Where in the case of a dramatic or musical work made before 1st July 1912, the right conferred by the 1911 Act did not include the sole right to perform the work in public, the acts restricted by the copyright shall be treated as not including—

(a) performing the work in public,

(b) broadcasting the work or including it in a cable programme service, or

(c) doing any of the above in relation to an adaptation of the work;

and where the right conferred by the 1911 Act consisted only of the sole right to perform the work in public, the acts restricted by the copyright shall be treated as consisting only of those acts.

18 Where a work made before 1st July 1912 consists of an essay, article or portion forming part of and first published in a review, magazine or other periodical or work

of a like nature, the copyright is subject to any right of publishing the essay, article, or portion in a separate form to which the author was entitled at the commencement of the 1911 Act, or would if that Act had not been passed, have become entitled under section 18 of the Copyright Act 1842.

Designs

19 (1) Section 51 (exclusion of copyright protection in relation to works recorded or embodied in design document or models) does not apply for ten years after commencement in relation to a design recorded or embodied in a design document or model before commencement.

(2) During those ten years the following provisions of Part III (design right) apply to any relevant copyright as in relation to design right—

(a) sections 237 to 239 (availability of licences of right), and

(b) sections 247 and 248 (application to comptroller to settle terms of licence of right).

(3) In section 237 as it applies by virtue of this paragraph, for the reference in subsection (1) to the last five years of the design right term there shall be substituted a reference to the last five years of the period of ten years referred to in sub-paragraph (1) above, or to so much of those last five years during which copyright subsists.

(4) In section 239 as it applies by virtue of this paragraph, for the reference in subsection (1)(b) to section 230 there shall be substituted a reference to section 99.

(5) Where a licence of right is available by virtue of this paragraph, a person to whom a licence was granted before commencement may apply to the comptroller for an order adjusting the terms of that licence.

(6) The provisions of sections 249 and 250 (appeals and rules) apply in relation to proceedings brought under or by virtue of this paragraph as to proceedings under Part III.

(7) A licence granted by virtue of this paragraph shall relate only to acts which would be permitted by section 51 if the design document or model had been made after commencement.

(8) Section 100 (right to seize infringing copies, &c.) does not apply during the period of ten years referred to in sub-paragraph (1) in relation to anything to which it would not apply if the design in question had been first recorded or embodied in a design document or model after commencement.

(9) Nothing in this paragraph affects the operation of any rule of law preventing or restricting the enforcement of copyright in relation to a design.

20 (1) Where section 10 of the 1956 Act (effect of industrial application of design corresponding to artistic work) applied in relation to an artistic work at any time before commencement, section 52(2) of this Act applies with the substitution for the period of 25 years mentioned there of the relevant period of 15 years as defined in section 10(3) of the 1956 Act.

(2) Except as provided in sub-paragraph (1), section 52 applies only where articles are marketed as mentioned in subsection (1)(b) after commencement.

Abolition of statutory recording licence

21 Section 8 of the 1956 Act (statutory licence to copy records sold by retail) continues to apply where notice under subsection (1)(b) of that section was given before the repeal of that section by this Act, but only in respect of the making of records—

(a) within one year of the repeal coming into force, and

(b) up to the number stated in the notice as intended to be sold.

Moral rights

22 (1) No act done before commencement is actionable by virtue of any provision of Chapter IV of Part I (moral rights).

(2) Section 43 of the 1956 Act (false attribution of authorship) continues to apply in relation to acts done before commencement.

23 (1) The following provisions have effect with respect to the rights conferred by—

(a) section 77 (right to be identified as author or director), and

(b) section 80 (right to object to derogatory treatment of work).

(2) The rights do not apply—

(a) in relation to a literary, dramatic, musical and artistic work of which the author died before commencement; or

(b) in relation to a film made before commencement.

(3) The rights in relation to an existing literary, dramatic, musical or artistic work do not apply—

(a) where copyright first vested in the author, to anything which by virtue of an assignment of copyright made or licence granted before commencement may be done without infringing copyright;

(b) where copyright first vested in a person other than the author, to anything done by or with the licence of the copyright owner.

(4) The rights do not apply to anything done in relation to a record made in pursuance of section 8 of the 1956 Act (statutory recording licence).

24 The right conferred by section 85 (right to privacy of certain photographs and films) does not apply to photographs taken or films made before commencement.

Assignments and licences

25 (1) Any document made or event occurring before commencement which had any operation—

(a) affecting the ownership of the copyright in an existing work, or

(b) creating, transferring or terminating an interest, right or licence in respect of the copyright in an existing work,

has the corresponding operation in relation to copyright in the work under this Act.

(2) Expressions used in such a document shall be construed in accordance with their effect immediately before commencement.

26 (1) Section 91(1) of this Act (assignment of future copyright: statutory vesting of legal interest on copyright coming into existence) does not apply in relation to an agreement made before 1st June 1957.

(2) The repeal by this Act of section 37(2) of the 1956 Act (assignment of future copyright: devolution of right where assignee dies before copyright comes into existence) does not affect the operation of that provision in relation to an agreement made before commencement.

27 (1) Where the author of a literary, dramatic, musical or artistic work was the first owner of the copyright in it, no assignment of the copyright and no grant of any interest in it, made by him (otherwise than by will) after the passing of the 1911 Act and before 1st June 1957, shall be operative to vest in the assignee or grantee any rights with respect to the copyright in the work beyond the expiration of 25 years from the death of the author.

(2) The reversionary interest in the copyright expectant on the termination of that period may after commencement be assigned by the author during his life but in the absence of any assignment shall, on his death, devolve on his legal personal representatives as part of his estate.

(3) Nothing in this paragraph affects—

(a) an assignment of the reversionary interest by a person to whom it has been assigned,

(b) an assignment of the reversionary interest after the death of the author by his personal representatives or any person becoming entitled to it, or

(c) any assignment of the copyright after the reversionary interest has fallen in.

(4) Nothing in this paragraph applies to the assignment of the copyright in a collective work or a licence to publish a work or part of a work as part of a collective work.

(5) In sub-paragraph (4) "collective work" means—

(a) any encyclopaedia, dictionary, yearbook, or similar work;

(b) a newspaper, review, magazine, or similar periodical; and

(c) any work written in distinct parts by different authors, or in which works or parts of works of different authors are incorporated.

28 (1) This paragraph applies where copyright subsists in a literary, dramatic, musical or artistic work made before 1st July 1912 in relation to which the author, before the commencement of the 1911 Act, made such an assignment or grant as was mentioned in paragraph (a) of the proviso to section 24(1) of that Act (assignment or grant of copyright or performing right for full term of the right under the previous law).

(2) If before commencement any event has occurred or notice has been given which by virtue of paragraph 38 of Schedule 7 to the 1956 Act had any operation in relation to copyright in the work under that Act, the event or notice has the corresponding operation in relation to copyright under this Act.

(3) Any right which immediately before commencement would by virtue of paragraph 38(3) of that Schedule have been exercisable in relation to the work, or copyright in it, is exercisable in relation to the work or copyright in it under this Act.

(4) If in accordance with paragraph 38(4) of that Schedule copyright would, on a date after the commencement of the 1956 Act, have reverted to the author or his personal representatives and that date falls after the commencement of the new copyright provisions—

(a) the copyright in the work shall revert to the author or his personal representatives, as the case may be, and

(b) any interest of any other person in the copyright which subsists on that date by virtue of any document made before the commencement of the 1911 Act shall thereupon determine.

29 Section 92(2) of this Act (rights of exclusive licensee against successors in title of person granting licence) does not apply in relation to an exclusive licence granted before commencement.

Bequests

30 (1) Section 93 of this Act (copyright to pass under will with original document or other material thing embodying unpublished work)—

(a) does not apply where the testator died before 1st June 1957, and

(b) where the testator died on or after that date and before commencement, applies only in relation to an original document embodying a work.

(2) In the case of an author who died before 1st June 1957, the ownership after his death of a manuscript of his, where such ownership has been acquired under a testamentary disposition made by him and the manuscript is of a work which has not been published or performed in public, is prima facie proof of the copyright being with the owner of the manuscript.

Remedies for infringement

31 (1) Sections 96 and 97 of this Act (remedies for infringement) apply only in relation to an infringement of copyright committed after commencement; section 17 of the 1956 Act continues to apply in relation to infringements committed before commencement.

(2) Sections 99 and 100 of this Act (delivery up or seizure of infringing copies, &c.) apply to infringing copies and other articles made before or after commencement; section 18 of the 1956 Act, and section 7 of the 1911 Act, (conversion damages, &c.), do not apply after commencement except for the purposes of proceedings begun before commencement.

(3) Sections 101 to 102 of this Act (rights and remedies of exclusive licensee) apply where sections 96 to 100 of this Act apply; section 19 of the 1956 Act continues to apply where section 17 or 18 of that Act applies.

(4) Sections 104 to 106 of this Act (presumptions) apply only in proceedings brought by virtue of this Act; section 20 of the 1956 Act continues to apply in proceedings brought by virtue of that Act.

32 Sections 101 and 102 of this Act (rights and remedies of exclusive licensee) do not apply to a licence granted before 1st June 1957.

33 (1) The provisions of section 107 of this Act (criminal liability for making or dealing with infringing articles, &c.) apply only in relation to acts done after commencement; section 21 of the 1956 Act (penalties and summary proceedings in respect of dealings which infringe copyright) continues to apply in relation to acts done before commencement.

(2) Section 109 of this Act (search warrants) applies in relation to offences committed before commencement in relation to which section 21A or 21B of the 1956 Act

applied; sections 21A and 21B continue to apply in relation to warrants issued before commencement.

Copyright Tribunal: proceedings pending on commencement

34 (1) The Lord Chancellor may, after consultation with the Lord Advocate, by rules make such provision as he considers necessary or expedient with respect to proceedings pending under Part IV of the 1956 Act immediately before commencement.

(2) Rules under this paragraph shall be made by statutory instrument which shall be subject to annulment in pursuance of a resolution of either House of Parliament.

Qualification for copyright protection

35 Every work in which copyright subsisted under the 1956 Act immediately before commencement shall be deemed to satisfy the requirements of Part I of this Act as to qualification for copyright protection.

Dependent territories

36 (1) The 1911 Act shall remain in force as part of the law of any dependent territory in which it was in force immediately before commencement until—

(a) the new copyright provisions come into force in that territory by virtue of an Order under section 157 of this Act (power to extend new copyright provisions), or

(b) in the case of any of the Channel Islands, the Act is repealed by Order under sub-paragraph (3) below.

(2) An Order in Council in force immediately before commencement which extends to any dependent territory any provisions of the 1956 Act shall remain in force as part of the law of that territory until—

(a) the new copyright provisions come into force in that territory by virtue of an Order under section 157 of this Act (power to extend new copyright provisions), or

(b) in the case of the Isle of Man, the Order is revoked by Order under sub-paragraph (3) below;

and while it remains in force such an Order may be varied under the provisions of the 1956 Act under which it was made.

(3) If it appears to Her Majesty that provision with respect to copyright has been made in the law of any of the Channel Islands or the Isle of Man otherwise than by extending the provisions of Part I of this Act, Her Majesty may by Order in Council repeal the 1911 Act as it has effect as part of the law of that territory or, as the case may be, revoke the Order extending the 1956 Act there.

(4) A dependent territory in which the 1911 or 1956 Act remains in force shall be treated, in the law of the countries to which Part I extends, as a country to which that Part extends; and those countries shall be treated in the law of such a territory as countries to which the 1911 Act or, as the case may be, the 1956 Act extends.

(5) If a country in which the 1911 or 1956 Act is in force ceases to be a colony of the United Kingdom, section 158 of this Act (consequences of country ceasing to be colony) applies with the substitution for the reference in subsection (3)(b) to the

provisions of Part I of this Act of a reference to the provisions of the 1911 or 1956 Act, as the case may be.

(6) In this paragraph "dependent territory" means any of the Channel Islands, the Isle of Man or any colony.

37 (1) This paragraph applies to a country which immediately before commencement was not a dependent territory within the meaning of paragraph 36 above but—

(a) was a country to which the 1956 Act extended, or

(b) was treated as such a country by virtue of paragraph 39(2) of Schedule 7 to that Act (countries to which the 1911 Act extended or was treated as extending);

and Her Majesty may by Order in Council conclusively declare for the purposes of this paragraph whether a country was such a country or was so treated.

(2) A country to which this paragraph applies shall be treated as a country to which Part I extends for the purposes of sections 154 to 156 (qualification for copyright protection) until—

(a) an Order in Council is made in respect of that country under section 159 (application of Part I to countries to which it does not extend), or

(b) an Order in Council is made declaring that it shall cease to be so treated by reason of the fact that the provisions of the 1956 Act or, as the case may be, the 1911 Act, which extended there as part of the law of that country have been repealed or amended.

(3) A statutory instrument containing an Order in Council under this paragraph shall be subject to annulment in pursuance of a resolution of either House of Parliament.

Territorial waters and the continental shelf

38 Section 161 of this Act (application of Part I to things done in territorial waters or the United Kingdom sector of the continental shelf) does not apply in relation to anything done before commencement.

British ships, aircraft and hovercraft

39 Section 162 (British ships, aircraft and hovercraft) does not apply in relation to anything done before commencement.

Crown copyright

40 (1) Section 163 of this Act (general provisions as to Crown copyright) applies to an existing work if—

(a) section 39 of the 1956 Act applied to the work immediately before commencement, and

(b) the work is not one to which section 164, 165 or 166 applies (copyright in Acts, Measures and Bills and Parliamentary copyright: see paragraphs 42 and 43 below).

(2) Section 163 (1)(b) (first ownership of copyright) has effect subject to any agreement entered into before commencement under section 39(6) of the 1956 Act.

41 (1) The following provisions have effect with respect to the duration of copyright in existing works to which section 163 (Crown copyright) applies.

The question which provision applies to a work shall be determined by reference to the facts immediately before commencement; and expressions used in this paragraph which were defined for the purposes of the 1956 Act have the same meaning as in that Act.

(2) Copyright in the following descriptions of work continues to subsist until the date on which it would have expired in accordance with the 1956 Act—

(a) published literary, dramatic or musical works;

(b) artistic works other than engravings or photographs;

(c) published engravings;

(d) published photographs and photographs taken before 1st June 1957;

(e) published sound recordings and sound recordings made before 1st June 1957;

(f) published films and films falling within section 13(3)(a) of the 1956 Act (films registered under former enactments relating to registration of films).

(3) Copyright in unpublished literary, dramatic or musical works continues to subsist until—

(a) the date on which copyright expires in accordance with section 163(3), or

(b) the end of the period of 50 years from the end of the calendar year in which the new copyright provisions come into force,

whichever is the later.

(4) Copyright in the following descriptions of work continues to subsist until the end of the period of 50 years from the end of the calendar year in which the new copyright provisions come into force—

(a) unpublished engravings;

(b) unpublished photographs taken on or after 1st June 1957.

(5) Copyright in a film or sound recording not falling within sub-paragraph (2) above continues to subsist until the end of the period of 50 years from the end of the calendar year in which the new copyright provisions come into force, unless the film or recording is published before the end of that period, in which case copyright expires 50 years from the end of the calendar year in which it is published.

42 (1) Section 164 (copyright in Acts and Measures) applies to existing Acts of Parliament and Measures of the General Synod of the Church of England.

(2) References in that section to Measures of the General Synod of the Church of England include Church Assembly Measures.

Parliamentary copyright

43 (1) Section 165 of this Act (general provisions as to Parliamentary copyright) applies to existing unpublished literary, dramatic, musical or artistic works, but does not otherwise apply to existing works.

(2) Section 166 (copyright in Parliamentary Bills) does not apply—

(a) to a public Bill which was introduced into Parliament and published before commencement,

(b) to a private Bill of which a copy was deposited in either House before commencement, or

(c) to a personal Bill which was given a First Reading in the House of Lords before commencement.

Copyright vesting in certain international organisations

44 (1) Any work in which immediately before commencement copyright subsisted by virtue of section 33 of the 1956 Act shall be deemed to satisfy the requirements of section 168(1); but otherwise section 168 does not apply to works made or, as the case may be, published before commencement.

(2) Copyright in any such work which is unpublished continues to subsist until the date on which it would have expired in accordance with the 1956 Act, or the end of the period of 50 years from the end of the calendar year in which the new copyright provisions come into force, whichever is the earlier.

Meaning of "publication"

45 Section 175(3) (construction of building treated as equivalent to publication) applies only where the construction of the building began after commencement.

Meaning of "unauthorised"

46 For the purposes of the application of the definition in section 178 (minor definitions) of the expression "unauthorised" in relation to things done before commencement—

(a) paragraph (a) applies in relation to things done before 1st June 1957 as if the reference to the licence of the copyright owner were a reference to his consent or acquiescence;

(b) paragraph (b) applies with the substitution for the words from "or, in a case" to the end of the words "or any person lawfully claiming under him"; and

(c) paragraph (c) shall be disregarded.

SCHEDULE 2

Section 189.

Rights in performances: permitted acts

Introductory

1 (1) The provisions of this Schedule specify acts which may be done in relation to a performance or recording notwithstanding the rights conferred by Part II; they relate only to the question of infringement of those rights and do not affect any other right or obligation restricting the doing of any of the specified acts.

(2) No inference shall be drawn from the description of any act which may by virtue of this Schedule be done without infringing the rights conferred by Part II as to the scope of those rights.

(3) The provisions of this Schedule are to be construed independently of each other, so that the fact that an act does not fall within one provision does not mean that it is not covered by another provision.

Criticism, reviews and news reporting

2 (1) Fair dealing with a performance or recording—

(a) for the purpose of criticism or review, of that or another performance or recording, or of a work, or

(b) for the purpose of reporting current events,

does not infringe any of the rights conferred by Part II.

(2) Expressions used in this paragraph have the same meaning as in section 30.

Incidental inclusion of performance or recording

3 (1) The rights conferred by Part II are not infringed by the incidental inclusion of a performance or recording in a sound recording, film, broadcast or cable programme.

(2) Nor are those rights infringed by anything done in relation to copies of, or the playing, showing, broadcasting or inclusion in a cable programme service of, anything whose making was, by virtue of sub-paragraph (1), not an infringement of those rights.

(3) A performance or recording so far as it consists of music, or words spoken or sung with music, shall not be regarded as incidentally included in a sound recording, broadcast or cable programme if it is deliberately included.

(4) Expressions used in this paragraph have the same meaning as in section 31.

Things done for purposes of instruction or examination

4 (1) The rights conferred by Part II are not infringed by the copying of a recording of a performance in the course of instruction, or of preparation for instruction, in the making of films or film sound-tracks, provided the copying is done by a person giving or receiving instruction.

(2) The rights conferred by Part II are not infringed—

(a) by the copying of a recording of a performance for the purposes of setting or answering the questions in an examination, or

(b) by anything done for the purposes of an examination by way of communicating the questions to the candidates.

(3) Where a recording which would otherwise be an illicit recording is made in accordance with this paragraph but is subsequently dealt with, it shall be treated as an illicit recording for the purposes of that dealing, and if that dealing infringes any right conferred by Part II for all subsequent purposes.

For this purpose "dealt with" means sold or let for hire, or offered or exposed for sale or hire.

(4) Expressions used in this paragraph have the same meaning as in section 32.

Playing or showing sound recording, film, broadcast or cable programme at educational establishment

5 (1) The playing or showing of a sound recording, film, broadcast or cable programme at an educational establishment for the purposes of instruction before an audience consisting of teachers and pupils at the establishment and other persons directly connected with the activities of the establishment is not a playing or showing of a

performance in public for the purposes of infringement of the rights conferred by Part II.

(2) A person is not for this purpose directly connected with the activities of the educational establishment simply because he is the parent of a pupil at the establishment.

(3) Expressions used in this paragraph have the same meaning as in section 34 and any provision made under section 174(2) with respect to the application of that section also applies for the purposes of this paragraph.

Recording of broadcasts and cable programmes by educational establishments

6 (1) A recording of a broadcast or cable programme, or a copy of such a recording, may be made by or on behalf of an educational establishment for the educational purposes of that establishment without thereby infringing any of the rights conferred by Part II in relation to any performance or recording included in it.

(2) Where a recording which would otherwise be an illicit recording is made in accordance with this paragraph but is subsequently dealt with, it shall be treated as an illicit recording for the purposes of that dealing, and if that dealing infringes any right conferred by Part II for all subsequent purposes.

For this purpose "dealt with" means sold or let for hire, or offered or exposed for sale or hire.

(3) Expressions used in this paragraph have the same meaning as in section 35 and any provision made under section 174(2) with respect to the application of that section also applies for the purposes of this paragraph.

Copy of work required to be made as condition of export

7 (1) If an article of cultural or historical importance or interest cannot lawfully be exported from the United Kingdom unless a copy of it is made and deposited in an appropriate library or archive, it is not an infringement of any right conferred by Part II to make that copy.

(2) Expressions used in this paragraph have the same meaning as in section 44.

Parliamentary and judicial proceedings

8 (1) The rights conferred by Part II are not infringed by anything done for the purposes of parliamentary or judicial proceedings or for the purpose of reporting such proceedings.

(2) Expressions used in this paragraph have the same meaning as in section 45.

Royal Commissions and statutory inquiries

9 (1) The rights conferred by Part II are not infringed by anything done for the purposes of the proceedings of a Royal Commission or statutory inquiry or for the purpose of reporting any such proceedings held in public.

(2) Expressions used in this paragraph have the same meaning as in section 46.

Public records

10 (1) Material which is comprised in public records within the meaning of the Public Records Act 1958, the Public Records (Scotland) Act 1937 or the Public Records Act (Northern Ireland) 1923 which are open to public inspection in pursuance of that Act, may be copied, and a copy may be supplied to any person, by or with the authority of any officer appointed under that Act, without infringing any right conferred by Part II.

(2) Expressions used in this paragraph have the same meaning as in section 49.

Acts done under statutory authority

11 (1) Where the doing of a particular act is specifically authorised by an Act of Parliament, whenever passed, then, unless the Act provides otherwise, the doing of that act does not infringe the rights conferred by Part II.

(2) Sub-paragraph (1) applies in relation to an enactment contained in Northern Ireland legislation as it applies to an Act of Parliament.

(3) Nothing in this paragraph shall be construed as excluding any defence of statutory authority otherwise available under or by virtue of any enactment.

(4) Expressions used in this paragraph have the same meaning as in section 50.

Transfer of copies of works in electronic form

12 (1) This paragraph applies where a recording of a performance in electronic form has been purchased on terms which, expressly or impliedly or by virtue of any rule of law, allow the purchaser to make further recordings in connection with his use of the recording.

(2) If there are no express terms—

- (a) prohibiting the transfer of the recording by the purchaser, imposing obligations which continue after a transfer, prohibiting the assignment of any consent or terminating any consent on a transfer, or
- (b) providing for the terms on which a transferee may do the things which the purchaser was permitted to do,

anything which the purchaser was allowed to do may also be done by a transferee without infringement of the rights conferred by this Part, but any recording made by the purchaser which is not also transferred shall be treated as an illicit recording for all purposes after the transfer.

(3) The same applies where the original purchased recording is no longer usable and what is transferred is a further copy used in its place.

(4) The above provisions also apply on a subsequent transfer, with the substitution for references in sub-paragraph (2) to the purchaser of references to the subsequent transferor.

(5) This paragraph does not apply in relation to a recording purchased before the commencement of Part II.

(6) Expressions used in this paragraph have the same meaning as in section 56.

Use of recordings of spoken works in certain cases

13 (1) Where a recording of the reading or recitation of a literary work is made for the purpose—

(a) of reporting current events, or

(b) of broadcasting or including in a cable programme service the whole or part of the reading or recitation,

it is not an infringement of the rights conferred by Part II to use the recording (or to copy the recording and use the copy) for that purpose, provided the following conditions are met.

(2) The conditions are that—

(a) the recording is a direct recording of the reading or recitation and is not taken from a previous recording or from a broadcast or cable programme;

(b) the making of the recording was not prohibited by or on behalf of the person giving the reading or recitation;

(c) the use made of the recording is not of a kind prohibited by or on behalf of that person before the recording was made; and

(d) the use is by or with the authority of a person who is lawfully in possession of the recording.

(3) Expressions used in this paragraph have the same meaning as in section 58.

Recordings of folksongs

14 (1) A recording of a performance of a song may be made for the purpose of including it in an archive maintained by a designated body without infringing any of the rights conferred by Part II, provided the conditions in sub-paragraph (2) below are met.

(2) The conditions are that—

(a) the words are unpublished and of unknown authorship at the time the recording is made,

(b) the making of the recording does not infringe any copyright, and

(c) its making is not prohibited by any performer.

(3) Copies of a recording made in reliance on sub-paragraph (1) and included in an archive maintained by a designated body may, if the prescribed conditions are met, be made and supplied by the archivist without infringing any of the rights conferred by Part II.

(4) In this paragraph—

"designated body" means a body designated for the purposes of section 61, and

"the prescribed conditions" means the conditions prescribed for the purposes of subsection (3) of that section;

and other expressions used in this paragraph have the same meaning as in that section.

Playing of sound recordings for purposes of club, society, &c

15 (1) It is not an infringement of any right conferred by Part II to play a sound recording as part of the activities of, or for the benefit of, a club, society or other organisation if the following conditions are met.

(2) The conditions are—

(a) that the organisation is not established or conducted for profit and its main objects are charitable or are otherwise concerned with the advancement of religion, education or social welfare, and

(b) that the proceeds of any charge for admission to the place where the recording is to be heard are applied solely for the purposes of the organisation.

(3) Expressions used in this paragraph have the same meaning as in section 67.

Incidental recording for purposes of broadcast or cable programme

16 (1) A person who proposes to broadcast a recording of a performance, or include a recording of a performance in a cable programme service, in circumstances not infringing the rights conferred by Part II shall be treated as having consent for the purposes of that Part for the making of a further recording for the purposes of the broadcast or cable programme.

(2) That consent is subject to the condition that the further recording—

(a) shall not be used for any other purpose, and

(b) shall be destroyed within 28 days of being first used for broadcasting the performance or including it in a cable programme service.

(3) A recording made in accordance with this paragraph shall be treated as an illicit recording—

(a) for the purposes of any use in breach of the condition mentioned in sub-paragraph (2)(a), and

(b) for all purposes after that condition or the condition mentioned in sub-paragraph (2)(b) is broken.

(4) Expressions used in this paragraph have the same meaning as in section 68.

Recordings for purposes of supervision and control of broadcasts and cable programmes

17 (1) The rights conferred by Part II are not infringed by the making or use by the British Broadcasting Corporation, for the purpose of maintaining supervision and control over programmes broadcast by them, of recordings of those programmes.

(2) The rights conferred by Part II are not infringed by—

(a) the making or use of recordings by the Independent Broadcasting Authority for the purposes mentioned in section 4(7) of the Broadcasting Act 1981 (maintenance of supervision and control over programmes and advertisements); or

(b) anything done under or in pursuance of provision included in a contract between a programme contractor and the Authority in accordance with section 21 of that Act.

(3) The rights conferred by Part II are not infringed by—

(a) the making by or with the authority of the Cable Authority, or the use by that Authority, for the purpose of maintaining supervision and control over programmes included in services licensed under Part I of the Cable and Broadcasting Act 1984, of recordings of those programmes; or

(b) anything done under or in pursuance of—

(i) a notice or direction given under section 16 of the Cable and Broadcasting Act 1984 (power of Cable Authority to require production of recordings); or

(ii) a condition included in a licence by virtue of section 35 of that Act (duty of Authority to secure that recordings are available for certain purposes).

(4) Expressions used in this paragraph have the same meaning as in section 69.

Free public showing or playing of broadcast or cable programme

18 (1) The showing or playing in public of a broadcast or cable programme to an audience who have not paid for admission to the place where the broadcast or programme is to be seen or heard does not infringe any right conferred by Part II in relation to a performance or recording included in—

(a) the broadcast or cable programme, or

(b) any sound recording or film which is played or shown in public by reception of the broadcast or cable programme.

(2) The audience shall be treated as having paid for admission to a place—

(a) if they have paid for admission to a place of which that place forms part; or

(b) if goods or services are supplied at that place (or a place of which it forms part)—

(i) at prices which are substantially attributable to the facilities afforded for seeing or hearing the broadcast or programme, or

(ii) at prices exceeding those usually charged there and which are partly attributable to those facilities.

(3) The following shall not be regarded as having paid for admission to a place—

(a) persons admitted as residents or inmates of the place;

(b) persons admitted as members of a club or society where the payment is only for membership of the club or society and the provision of facilities for seeing or hearing broadcasts or programmes is only incidental to the main purposes of the club or society.

(4) Where the making of the broadcast or inclusion of the programme in a cable programme service was an infringement of the rights conferred by Part II in relation to a performance or recording, the fact that it was heard or seen in public by the reception of the broadcast or programme shall be taken into account in assessing the damages for that infringement.

(5) Expressions used in this paragraph have the same meaning as in section 72.

Reception and re-transmission of broadcast in cable programme service

19 (1) This paragraph applies where a broadcast made from a place in the United Kingdom is, by reception and immediate re-transmission, included in a cable programme service.

(2) The rights conferred by Part II in relation to a performance or recording included in the broadcast are not infringed—

(a) if the inclusion of the broadcast in the cable programme service is in pursuance of a requirement imposed under section 13(1) of the Cable and Broadcasting Act 1984 (duty of Cable Authority to secure inclusion in cable service of certain programmes), or

(b) if and to the extent that the broadcast is made for reception in the area in which the cable programme service is provided;

but where the making of the broadcast was an infringement of those rights, the fact that the broadcast was re-transmitted as a programme in a cable programme service shall be taken into account in assessing the damages for that infringement.

(3) Expressions used in this paragraph have the same meaning as in section 73.

Provision of sub-titled copies of broadcast or cable programme

20 (1) A designated body may, for the purpose of providing people who are deaf or hard of hearing, or physically or mentally handicapped in other ways, with copies which are sub-titled or otherwise modified for their special needs, make recordings of television broadcasts or cable programmes without infringing any right conferred by Part II in relation to a performance or recording included in the broadcast or cable programme.

(2) In this paragraph "designated body" means a body designated for the purposes of section 74 and other expressions used in this paragraph have the same meaning as in that section.

Recording of broadcast or cable programme for archival purposes

21 (1) A recording of a broadcast or cable programme of a designated class, or a copy of such a recording, may be made for the purpose of being placed in an archive maintained by a designated body without thereby infringing any right conferred by Part II in relation to a performance or recording included in the broadcast or cable programme.

(2) In this paragraph "designated class" and "designated body" means a class or body designated for the purposes of section 75 and other expressions used in this paragraph have the same meaning as in that section.

SCHEDULE 3

Section 272.

REGISTERED DESIGNS: MINOR AND CONSEQUENTIAL AMENDMENTS OF 1949 ACT

Section 3: proceedings for registration

1 In section 3 of the Registered Designs Act 1949 (proceedings for registration) for subsections (2) to (6) substitute—

"(2) An application for the registration of a design in which design right subsists shall not be entertained unless made by the person claiming to be the design right owner.

(3) For the purpose of deciding whether a design is new, the registrar may make such searches, if any, as he thinks fit.

(4) The registrar may, in such cases as may be prescribed, direct that for the purpose of deciding whether a design is new an application shall be treated as made on a date earlier or later than that on which it was in fact made.

(5) The registrar may refuse an application for the registration of a design or may register the design in pursuance of the application subject to such modifications, if any, as he thinks fit; and a design when registered shall be registered as of the date on which the application was made or is treated as having been made.

(6) An application which, owing to any default or neglect on the part of the applicant, has not been completed so as to enable registration to be effected within such time as may be prescribed shall be deemed to be abandoned.

(7) An appeal lies from any decision of the registrar under this section.".

Section 4: registration of same design in respect of other articles, etc.

2 In section 4 of the Registered Designs Act 1949 (registration of same design in respect of other articles, etc.), in subsection (1), for the proviso substitute—

"Provided that the right in a design registered by virtue of this section shall not extend beyond the end of the period, and any extended period, for which the right subsists in the original registered design.".

Section 5: provisions for secrecy of certain designs

3 (1) Section 5 of the Registered Designs Act 1949 is amended as follows.

(2) For "a competent authority" or "the competent authority", wherever occurring, substitute "the Secretary of State"; and in subsection (3)(c) for "that authority" substitute "he".

(3) For subsection (2) substitute—

"(2) The Secretary of State shall by rules make provision for securing that where such directions are given—

(a) the representation or specimen of the design, and

(b) any evidence filed in support of the applicant's contention that the appearance of an article is material (for the purposes of section 1(3) of this Act),

shall not be open to public inspection at the Patent Office during the continuance in force of the directions."

(4) In subsection (3)(b) after "representation or specimen of the design" insert ", or any such evidence as is mentioned in subsection (2)(b) above,".

(5) Omit subsection (5).

Section 6: provisions as to confidential disclosure, etc.

4 (1) Section 6 of the Registered Designs Act 1949 (provisions as to confidential disclosure, etc.) is amended as follows.

(2) In subsection (2) (display of design at certified exhibition), in paragraph (a) for "certified by the Board of Trade" substitute "certified by the Secretary of State".

(3) For subsections (4) and (5) (registration of designs corresponding to copyright artistic works) substitute—

"(4) Where an application is made by or with the consent of the owner of copyright in an artistic work for the registration of a corresponding design, the design shall not be treated for the purposes of this Act as being other than new by reason only of any use previously made of the artistic work, subject to subsection (5).

(5) Subsection (4) does not apply if the previous use consisted of or included the sale, letting for hire or offer or exposure for sale or hire of articles to which had been applied industrially—

(a) the design in question, or

(b) a design differing from it only in immaterial details or in features which are variants commonly used in the trade,

and that previous use was made by or with the consent of the copyright owner.

(6) The Secretary of State may make provision by rules as to the circumstances in which a design is to be regarded for the purposes of this section as "applied industrially" to articles, or any description of articles.".

Section 9: exemption of innocent infringer from liability for damages

5 In section 9 of the Registered Designs Act 1949 (exemption of innocent infringer from liability for damages), in subsections (1) and (2) for "copyright in a registered design" substitute "the right in a registered design".

Section 11: cancellation of registration

6 (1) Section 11 of the Registered Designs Act 1949 (cancellation of registration) is amended as follows.

(2) In subsection (2) omit "or original".

(3) For subsections (2A) and (3) substitute—

"(3) At any time after a design has been registered, any person interested may apply to the registrar for the cancellation of the registration on the ground that—

(a) the design was at the time it was registered a corresponding design in relation to an artistic work in which copyright subsisted, and

(b) the right in the registered design has expired in accordance with section 8(4) of this Act (expiry of right in registered design on expiry of copyright in artistic work);

and the registrar may make such order on the application as he thinks fit.

(4) A cancellation under this section takes effect—

(a) in the case of cancellation under subsection (1), from the date of the registrar's decision,

(b) in the case of cancellation under subsection (2), from the date of registration,

(c) in the case of cancellation under subsection (3), from the date on which the right in the registered design expired, or, in any case, from such other date as the registrar may direct.

(5) An appeal lies from any order of the registrar under this section.".

Section 14: registration where application has been made in convention country

7 In section 14 of the Registered Designs Act 1949 (registration where application has been made in convention country), for subsections (2) and (3) substitute—

"(2) Where an application for registration of a design is made by virtue of this section, the application shall be treated, for the purpose of determining whether that or any other design is new, as made on the date of the application for protection in the convention country or, if more than one such application was made, on the date of the first such application.

(3) Subsection (2) shall not be construed as excluding the power to give directions under section 3(4) of this Act in relation to an application made by virtue of this section.".

Section 15: extension of time for application under s.14 in certain cases

8 In section 15(1) of the Registered Designs Act 1949 (power to make rules empowering registrar to extend time for applications under s.14) for "the Board of Trade are satisfied" substitute "the Secretary of State is satisfied" and for "they" substitute "he".

Section 16: protection of designs communicated under international agreements

9 In section 16 of the Registered Designs Act 1949 (protection of designs communicated under international agreements)—

(a) in subsection (1) for "the Board of Trade" substitute "the Secretary of State", and

(b) in subsection (3) for "the Board of Trade" substitute "the Secretary of State" and for "the Board are satisfied" substitute "the Secretary of State is satisfied".

Section 19: registration of assignments, &c.

10 In section 19 of the Registered Designs Act 1949 (registration of assignments, &c.), after subsection (3) insert—

"(3A) Where design right subsists in a registered design, the registrar shall not register an interest under subsection (3) unless he is satisfied that the person entitled to that interest is also entitled to a corresponding interest in the design right.

(3B) Where design right subsists in a registered design and the proprietor of the registered design is also the design right owner, an assignment of the design right shall be taken to be also an assignment of the right in the registered design, unless a contrary intention appears.".

Section 20: rectification of the register

11 In section 20 of the Registered Designs Act 1949 (rectification of the register), after subsection (4) add—

"(5) A rectification of the register under this section has effect as follows—

(a) an entry made has effect from the date on which it should have been made,

(b) an entry varied has effect as if it had originally been made in its varied form, and

(c) an entry deleted shall be deemed never to have had effect, unless, in any case, the court directs otherwise.".

Section 22: inspection of registered designs

12 (1) Section 22 of the Registered Designs Act 1949 (inspection of registered designs) is amended as follows.

(2) For subsection (1) substitute—

"(1) Where a design has been registered under this Act, there shall be open to inspection at the Patent Office on and after the day on which the certificate of registration is issued—

(a) the representation or specimen of the design, and

(b) any evidence filed in support of the applicant's contention that the appearance of an article is material (for the purposes of section 1(3) of this Act).

This subsection has effect subject to the following provisions of this section and to any rules made under section 5(2) of this Act.".

(3) In subsection (2), subsection (3) (twice) and subsection (4) for "representation or specimen of the design" substitute "representation, specimen or evidence".

Section 23: information as to existence of right in registered design

13 For section 23 of the Registered Designs Act 1949 (information as to existence of right in registered design) substitute—

"23 Information as to existence of right in registered design

"23 "23 Information as to existence of right in registered design

On the request of a person furnishing such information as may enable the registrar to identify the design, and on payment of the prescribed fee, the registrar shall inform him—

(a) whether the design is registered and, if so, in respect of what articles, and

(b) whether any extension of the period of the right in the registered design has been granted,

and shall state the date of registration and the name and address of the registered proprietor.".

Section 25: certificate of contested validity of registration

14 In section 25 of the Registered Designs Act 1949 (certificate of contested validity of registration), in subsection (2) for "the copyright in the registered design"substitute "the right in the registered design".

Section 26: remedy for groundless threats of infringement proceedings

15 (1) Section 26 of the Registered Designs Act 1949 (remedy for groundless threats of infringement proceedings) is amended as follows.

(2) In subsections (1) and (2) for "the copyright in a registered design" substitute "the right in a registered design".

(3) After subsection (2) insert—

"(2A) Proceedings may not be brought under this section in respect of a threat to bring proceedings for an infringement alleged to consist of the making or importing of anything.".

Section 27: the court

16 For section 27 of the Registered Designs Act 1949 (the court) substitute—

"27 The court

"27 "27 The court

(1) In this Act "the court" means—

(a) in England and Wales the High Court or any patents county court having jurisdiction by virtue of an order under section 287 of the Copyright, Designs and Patents Act 1988,

(b) in Scotland, the Court of Session, and

(c) in Northern Ireland, the High Court.

(2) Provision may be made by rules of court with respect to proceedings in the High Court in England and Wales for references and applications under this Act to be dealt with by such judge of that court as the Lord Chancellor may select for the purpose.".

Section 28: the Appeal Tribunal

17 (1) Section 28 of the Registered Designs Act 1949 (the Appeal Tribunal) is amended as follows.

(2) For subsection (2) (members of Tribunal) substitute—

"(2) The Appeal Tribunal shall consist of—

(a) one or more judges of the High Court nominated by the Lord Chancellor, and

(b) one judge of the Court of Session nominated by the Lord President of that Court.".

(3) In subsection (5) (costs), after "costs" (twice) insert "or expenses", and for the words from "and any such order" to the end substitute—

"and any such order may be enforced—

(a) in England and Wales or Northern Ireland, in the same way as an order of the High Court;

(b) in Scotland, in the same way as a decree for expenses granted by the Court of Session.".

(4) For subsection (10) (seniority of judges) substitute—

"(10) In this section "the High Court" means the High Court in England and Wales; and for the purposes of this section the seniority of judges shall be reckoned by reference to the dates on which they were appointed judges of that court or the Court of Session.".

(5) The amendments to section 28 made by section 10(5) of the Administration of Justice Act 1970 (power to make rules as to right of audience) shall be deemed always to have extended to Northern Ireland.

Section 29: exercise of discretionary powers of registrar

18 In section 29 of the Registered Designs Act 1949 (exercise of discretionary powers of registrar) for "the registrar shall give" substitute "rules made by the Secretary of State under this Act shall require the registrar to give".

Section 30: costs and security for costs

19 For section 30 of the Registered Designs Act 1949 (costs and security for costs) substitute—

"30 Costs and security for costs

"30 "30 Costs and security for costs

(1) Rules made by the Secretary of State under this Act may make provision empowering the registrar, in any proceedings before him under this Act—

(a) to award any party such costs as he may consider reasonable, and

(b) to direct how and by what parties they are to be paid.

(2) Any such order of the registrar may be enforced—

(a) in England and Wales or Northern Ireland, in the same way as an order of the High Court;

(b) in Scotland, in the same way as a decree for expenses granted by the Court of Session.

(3) Rules made by the Secretary of State under this Act may make provision empowering the registrar to require a person, in such cases as may be prescribed, to give security for the costs of—

(a) an application for cancellation of the registration of a design,

(b) an application for the grant of a licence in respect of a registered design, or

(c) an appeal from any decision of the registrar under this Act,

and enabling the application or appeal to be treated as abandoned in default of such security being given.".

Section 31: evidence before registrar

20 For section 31 of the Registered Designs Act 1949 (evidence before registrar) substitute—

"31 Evidence before registrar

"31 "31 Evidence before registrar

Rules made by the Secretary of State under this Act may make provision—

(a) as to the giving of evidence in proceedings before the registrar under this Act by affidavit or statutory declaration;

(b) conferring on the registrar the powers of an official referee of the Supreme Court as regards the examination of witnesses on oath and the discovery and production of documents; and

(c) applying in relation to the attendance of witnesses in proceedings before the registrar the rules applicable to the attendance of witnesses in proceedings before such a referee.".

Section 32: power of registrar to refuse to deal with certain agents

21 Section 32 of the Registered Designs Act 1949 (power of registrar to refuse to deal with certain agents) is repealed.

Section 33: offences under s.5 (secrecy of certain designs)

22 (1) Section 33 of the Registered Designs Act 1949 (offences under s.5 (secrecy of certain designs)) is amended as follows.

(2) In subsection (1), for paragraphs (a) and (b) substitute—

"(a) on conviction on indictment to imprisonment for a term not exceeding two years or a fine, or both;

(b) on summary conviction to imprisonment for a term not exceeding six months or a fine not exceeding the statutory maximum, or both.".

(3) Omit subsection (2).

(4) The above amendments do not apply in relation to offences committed before the commencement of Part IV.

Section 34: falsification of register, &c.

23 (1) In section 34 of the Registered Designs Act 1949 (falsification of register, &c.) for "shall be guilty of a misdemeanour" substitute—

"shall be guilty of an offence and liable—

(a) on conviction on indictment to imprisonment for a term not exceeding two years or a fine, or both;

(b) on summary conviction to imprisonment for a term not exceeding six months or a fine not exceeding the statutory maximum, or both.".

(2) The above amendment does not apply in relation to offences committed before the commencement of Part IV.

Section 35: fine for falsely representing a design as registered

24 (1) Section 35 of the Registered Designs Act 1949 (fine for falsely representing a design as registered) is amended as follows.

(2) In subsection (1) for the words from "a fine not exceeding £50" substitute "a fine not exceeding level 3 on the standard scale".

(3) In subsection (2)—

(a) for "the copyright in a registered design" substitute "the right in a registered design";

(b) for "subsisting copyright in the design" substitute "subsisting right in the design under this Act"; and

(c) for the words from "a fine" to the end substitute "a fine not exceeding level 1 on the standard scale".

(4) The amendment in sub-paragraph (2) does not apply in relation to offences committed before the commencement of Part IV.

Section 35A: offence by body corporate -liability of officers

25 (1) In the Registered Designs Act 1949 after section 35 insert—

"35A Offence by body corporate: liability of officers

"35A "35A Offence by body corporate: liability of officers

(1) Where an offence under this Act committed by a body corporate is proved to have been committed with the consent or connivance of a director, manager, secretary or other similar officer of the body, or a person purporting to act in any such capacity, he as well as the body corporate is guilty of the offence and liable to be proceeded against and punished accordingly.

(2) In relation to a body corporate whose affairs are managed by its members "director" means a member of the body corporate.".

(2) The above amendment does not apply in relation to offences committed before the commencement of Part IV.

Section 36: general power to make rules, &c.

26 (1) Section 36 of the Registered Designs Act 1949 (general power to make rules, &c.) is amended as follows.

(2) In subsection (1) for "the Board of Trade" and "the Board" substitute "the Secretary of State", and for "as they think expedient" substitute "as he thinks expedient".

(3) For the words in subsection (1) from "and in particular" to the end substitute the following subsections—

"(1A) Rules may, in particular, make provision—

(a) prescribing the form of applications for registration of designs and of any representations or specimens of designs or other documents which may be filed at the Patent Office, and requiring copies to be furnished of any such representations, specimens or documents;

(b) regulating the procedure to be followed in connection with any application or request to the registrar or in connection with any proceeding before him, and authorising the rectification of irregularities of procedure;

(c) providing for the appointment of advisers to assist the registrar in proceedings before him;

(d) regulating the keeping of the register of designs;

(e) authorising the publication and sale of copies of representations of designs and other documents in the Patent Office;

(f) prescribing anything authorised or required by this Act to be prescribed by rules.

(1B) The remuneration of an adviser appointed to assist the registrar shall be determined by the Secretary of State with the consent of the Treasury and shall be defrayed out of money provided by Parliament.".

Section 37: provisions as to rules and Orders

27 (1) Section 37 of the Registered Designs Act 1949 (provisions as to rules and orders) is amended as follows.

(2) Omit subsection (1) (duty to advertise making of rules).

(3) In subsections (2), (3) and (4) for "the Board of Trade" substitute "the Secretary of State".

Section 38: proceedings of the Board of Trade

28 Section 38 of the Registered Designs Act 1949 (proceedings of the Board of Trade) is repealed.

Section 39: hours of business and excluded days

29 In section 39 of the Registered Designs Act 1949 (hours of business and excluded days), in subsection (1) for "the Board of Trade" substitute "the Secretary of State".

Section 40: fees

30 In section 40 of the Registered Designs Act 1949 (fees) for "the Board of Trade" substitute "the Secretary of State".

Section 44: interpretation

31 (1) In section 44 of the Registered Designs Act 1949 (interpretation), subsection (1) is amended as follows.

(2) In the definition of "artistic work" for "the Copyright Act 1956" substitute "Part I of the Copyright, Designs and Patents Act 1988".

(3) At the appropriate place insert—

""author" in relation to a design, has the meaning given by section 2(3) and (4);".

(4) Omit the definition of "copyright".

(5) In the definition of "corresponding design", for the words from "has the same meaning" to the end substitute ", in relation to an artistic work, means a design which if applied to an article would produce something which would be treated for the purposes of Part I of the Copyright, Designs and Patents Act 1988 as a copy of that work;".

(6) For the definition of "court" substitute—

""the court" shall be construed in accordance with section 27 of this Act;".

(7) In the definition of "design" for "subsection (3) of section one of this Act" substitute "section 1(1) of this Act".

(8) At the appropriate place insert—

""employee", "employment" and "employer" refer to employment under a contract of service or of apprenticeship,".

(9) Omit the definition of "Journal".

(10) In the definition of "prescribed" for "the Board of Trade" substitute "the Secretary of State".

Section 45: application to Scotland

32 In section 45 of the Registered Designs Act 1949 (application to Scotland), omit paragraphs (1) and (2).

Section 46: application to Northern Ireland

33 (1) Section 46 of the Registered Designs Act 1949 (application to Northern Ireland) is amended as follows.

(2) Omit paragraphs (1) and (2).

(3) For paragraph (3) substitute—

"(3) References to enactments include enactments comprised in Northern Ireland legislation:".

(4) After paragraph (3) insert—

"(3A) References to the Crown include the Crown in right of Her Majesty's Government in Northern Ireland:".

(5) In paragraph (4) for "a department of the Government of Northern Ireland" substitute "a Northern Ireland department", and at the end add "and in relation to a Northern Ireland department references to the Treasury shall be construed as references to the Department of Finance and Personnel".

Section 47: application to Isle of Man

34 For section 47 of the Registered Designs Act 1949 (application to Isle of Man) substitute—

"47 Application to Isle of Man

"47 "47 Application to Isle of Man

This Act extends to the Isle of Man, subject to any modifications contained in an Order made by Her Majesty in Council, and accordingly, subject to any such Order, references in this Act to the United Kingdom shall be construed as including the Isle of Man.".

Section 47A: territorial waters and the continental shelf

35 In the Registered Designs Act 1949, after section 47 insert—

"47A Territorial waters and the continental shelf

"47A "47A Territorial waters and the continental shelf

(1) For the purposes of this Act the territorial waters of the United Kingdom shall be treated as part of the United Kingdom.

(2) This Act applies to things done in the United Kingdom sector of the continental shelf on a structure or vessel which is present there for purposes directly connected with the exploration of the sea bed or subsoil or the exploitation of their natural resources as it applies to things done in the United Kingdom.

(3) The United Kingdom sector of the continental shelf means the areas designated by order under section 1(7) of the Continental Shelf Act 1964.".

Section 48: repeals, savings and transitional provisions

36 In section 48 of the Registered Designs Act 1949 (repeals, savings and transitional provisions), omit subsection (1) (repeals).

Schedule 1: provisions as to Crown use of registered designs

37 (1) The First Schedule to the Registered Designs Act 1949 (provisions as to Crown use of registered designs) is amended as follows.

(2) In paragraph 2(1) after "copyright" insert "or design right".

(3) In paragraph 3(1) omit "in such manner as may be prescribed by rules of court".

(4) In paragraph 4(2) (definition of "period of emergency") for the words from "the period ending" to "any other period" substitute "a period".

(5) For paragraph 4(3) substitute—

"(3) No Order in Council under this paragraph shall be submitted to Her Majesty unless a draft of it has been laid before and approved by a resolution of each House of Parliament.".

Schedule 2: enactments repealed

38 Schedule 2 to the Registered Designs Act 1949 (enactments repealed) is repealed.

SCHEDULE 4

Section 273.

THE REGISTERED DESIGNS ACT 1949 AS AMENDED ARRANGEMENT OF SECTIONS

SCHEDULE 5

Section 295.

PATENTS: MISCELLANEOUS AMENDMENTS

Withdrawal of application before publication of specification

1 In section 13(2) of the Patents Act 1949 (duty of comptroller to advertise acceptance of and publish complete specification) after the word "and", in the first place where it occurs, insert ", unless the application is withdrawn,".

Correction of clerical errors

2 (1) In section 15 of the Patents Act 1977 (filing of application), after subsection (3) insert—

"(3A) Nothing in subsection (2) or (3) above shall be construed as affecting the power of the comptroller under section 117(1) below to correct errors or mistakes with respect to the filing of drawings.".

(2) The above amendment applies only in relation to applications filed after the commencement of this paragraph.

Supplementary searches

3 (1) Section 17 of the Patents Act 1977 (preliminary examination and search) is amended as follows.

(2) In subsection (7) (supplementary searches) for "subsection (4) above" substitute "subsections (4) and (5) above" and for "it applies" substitute "they apply".

(3) After that subsection add—

"(8) A reference for a supplementary search in consequence of—

(a) an amendment of the application made by the applicant under section 18(3) or 19(1) below, or

(b) a correction of the application, or of a document filed in connection with the application, under section 117 below,

shall be made only on payment of the prescribed fee, unless the comptroller directs otherwise.".

4 In section 18 of the Patents Act 1977 (substantive examination and grant or refusal of patent), after subsection (1) insert—

"(1A) If the examiner forms the view that a supplementary search under section 17 above is required for which a fee is payable, he shall inform the comptroller, who may decide that the substantive examination should not proceed until the fee is paid; and if he so decides, then unless within such period as he may allow—

(a) the fee is paid, or

(b) the application is amended so as to render the supplementary search unnecessary,

he may refuse the application.".

5 In section 130(1) of the Patents Act 1977 (interpretation), in the definition of "search fee", for "section 17 above" substitute "section 17(1) above".

Application for restoration of lapsed patent

6 (1) Section 28 of the Patents Act 1977 (restoration of lapsed patents) is amended as follows.

(2) For subsection (1) (application for restoration within period of one year) substitute—

"(1) Where a patent has ceased to have effect by reason of a failure to pay any renewal fee, an application for the restoration of the patent may be made to the comptroller within the prescribed period.

(1A) Rules prescribing that period may contain such transitional provisions and savings as appear to the Secretary of State to be necessary or expedient.".

(3) After subsection (2) insert—

"(2A) Notice of the application shall be published by the comptroller in the prescribed manner.".

(4) In subsection (3), omit paragraph (b) (requirement that failure to renew is due to circumstances beyond proprietor's control) and the word "and" preceding it.

This amendment does not apply to a patent which has ceased to have effect in accordance with section 25(3) of the Patents Act 1977 (failure to renew within prescribed period) and in respect of which the period referred to in subsection (4) of that section (six months' period of grace for renewal) has expired before commencement.

(5) Omit subsections (5) to (9) (effect of order for restoration).

7 After that section insert—

"28A Effect of order for restoration of patent

"28A "28A Effect of order for restoration of patent

(1) The effect of an order for the restoration of a patent is as follows.

(2) Anything done under or in relation to the patent during the period between expiry and restoration shall be treated as valid.

(3) Anything done during that period which would have constituted an infringement if the patent had not expired shall be treated as an infringement—

(a) if done at a time when it was possible for the patent to be renewed under section 25(4), or

(b) if it was a continuation or repetition of an earlier infringing act.

(4) If after it was no longer possible for the patent to be so renewed, and before publication of notice of the application for restoration, a person—

(a) began in good faith to do an act which would have constituted an infringement of the patent if it had not expired, or

(b) made in good faith effective and serious preparations to do such an act,

he has the right to continue to do the act or, as the case may be, to do the act, notwithstanding the restoration of the patent; but this right does not extend to granting a licence to another person to do the act.

(5) If the act was done, or the preparations were made, in the course of a business, the person entitled to the right conferred by subsection (4) may—

(a) authorise the doing of that act by any partners of his for the time being in that business, and

(b) assign that right, or transmit it on death (or in the case of a body corporate on its dissolution), to any person who acquires that part of the business in the course of which the act was done or the preparations were made.

(6) Where a product is disposed of to another in exercise of the rights conferred by subsection (4) or (5), that other and any person claiming through him may deal with the product in the same way as if it had been disposed of by the registered proprietor of the patent.

(7) The above provisions apply in relation to the use of a patent for the services of the Crown as they apply in relation to infringement of the patent.".

8 In consequence of the above amendments—

(a) in section 60(6)(b) of the Patents Act 1977, for "section 28(6)" substitute "section 28A(4) or (5)"; and

(b) in sections 77(5), 78(6) and 80(4) of that Act, for the words from "section 28(6)" to the end substitute "section 28A(4) and (5) above, and subsections (6) and (7) of that section shall apply accordingly.".

Determination of right to patent after grant

9 (1) Section 37 of the Patents Act 1977 (determination of right to patent after grant) is amended as follows.

(2) For subsection (1) substitute—

"(1) After a patent has been granted for an invention any person having or claiming a proprietary interest in or under the patent may refer to the comptroller the question—

(a) who is or are the true proprietor or proprietors of the patent,

(b) whether the patent should have been granted to the person or persons to whom it was granted, or

(c) whether any right in or under the patent should be transferred or granted to any other person or persons;

and the comptroller shall determine the question and make such order as he thinks fit to give effect to the determination.".

(3) Substitute "this section"—

(a) in subsections (4) and (7) for "subsection (1)(a) above", and

(b) in subsection (8) for "subsection (1) above".

10 In section 74(6) (meaning of "entitlement proceedings"), for "section 37(1)(a) above" substitute "section 37(1) above".

Employees' inventions

11 (1) In section 39 of the Patents Act 1977 (right to employees' inventions), after subsection (2) add—

"(3) Where by virtue of this section an invention belongs, as between him and his employer, to an employee, nothing done—

(a) by or on behalf of the employee or any person claiming under him for the purposes of pursuing an application for a patent, or

(b) by any person for the purpose of performing or working the invention,

shall be taken to infringe any copyright or design right to which, as between him and his employer, his employer is entitled in any model or document relating to the invention.".

(2) In section 43 of the Patents Act 1977 (supplementary provisions with respect to employees' inventions), in subsection (4) (references to patents to include other forms of protection, whether in UK or elsewhere) for "in sections 40 to 42" substitute "in sections 39 to 42.".

Undertaking to take licence in infringement proceedings

12 (1) Section 46 of the Patents Act 1977 (licences of right) is amended as follows.

(2) In subsection (3)(c) (undertaking to take licence in infringement proceedings) after the words "(otherwise than by the importation of any article" insert "from a country which is not a member State of the European Economic Community".

(3) After subsection (3) insert—

"(3A) An undertaking under subsection (3)(c) above may be given at any time before final order in the proceedings, without any admission of liability.".

Power of comptroller on grant of compulsory licence

13 In section 49 of the Patents Act 1977 (supplementary provisions with respect to compulsory licences), omit subsection (3) (power to order that licence has effect to revoke existing licences and deprive proprietor of power to work invention or grant licences).

Powers exercisable in consequence of report of Monopolies and Mergers Commission

14 For section 51 of the Patents Act 1977 (licences of right: application by Crown in consequence of report of Monopolies and Mergers Commission) substitute—

"51 Powers exercisable in consequence of report of Monopolies and Mergers Commission

"51 "51 Powers exercisable in consequence of report of Monopolies and Mergers Commission

(1) Where a report of the Monopolies and Mergers Commission has been laid before Parliament containing conclusions to the effect—

(a) on a monopoly reference, that a monopoly situation exists and facts found by the Commission operate or may be expected to operate against the public interest,

(b) on a merger reference, that a merger situation qualifying for investigation has been created and the creation of the situation, or particular elements in or consequences of it specified in the report, operate or may be expected to operate against the public interest,

(c) on a competition reference, that a person was engaged in an anti-competitive practice which operated or may be expected to operate against the public interest, or

(d) on a reference under section 11 of the Competition Act 1980 (reference of public bodies and certain other persons), that a person is pursuing a course of conduct which operates against the public interest,

the appropriate Minister or Ministers may apply to the comptroller to take action under this section.

(2) Before making an application the appropriate Minister or Ministers shall publish, in such manner as he or they think appropriate, a notice describing the nature of the proposed application and shall consider any representations which may be made within 30 days of such publication by persons whose interests appear to him or them to be affected.

(3) If on an application under this section it appears to the comptroller that the matters specified in the Commission's report as being those which in the Commission's opinion operate, or operated or may be expected to operate, against the public interest include—

(a) conditions in licences granted under a patent by its proprietor restricting the use of the invention by the licensee or the right of the proprietor to grant other licences, or

(b) a refusal by the proprietor of a patent to grant licences on reasonable terms

he may by order cancel or modify any such condition or may, instead or in addition, make an entry in the register to the effect that licences under the patent are to be available as of right.

(4) In this section "the appropriate Minister or Ministers" means the Minister or Ministers to whom the report of the Commission was made.".

Compulsory licensing: reliance on statements in competition report

15 In section 53(2) of the Patents Act 1977 (compulsory licensing: reliance on statements in reports of Monopolies and Mergers Commission)—

(a) for "application made in relation to a patent under sections 48 to 51 above" substitute "application made under section 48 above in respect of a patent"; and

(b) after "Part VIII of the Fair Trading Act 1973" insert "or section 17 of the Competition Act 1980".

Crown use: compensation for loss of profit

16 (1) In the Patents Act 1977, after section 57 insert—

"57A Compensation for loss of profit

"57A "57A Compensation for loss of profit

(1) Where use is made of an invention for the services of the Crown, the government department concerned shall pay—

(a) to the proprietor of the patent, or

(b) if there is an exclusive licence in force in respect of the patent, to the exclusive licensee,

compensation for any loss resulting from his not being awarded a contract to supply the patented product or, as the case may be, to perform the patented process or supply a thing made by means of the patented process.

(2) Compensation is payable only to the extent that such a contract could have been fulfilled from his existing manufacturing or other capacity; but is payable notwithstanding the existence of circumstances rendering him ineligible for the award of such a contract.

(3) In determining the loss, regard shall be had to the profit which would have been made on such a contract and to the extent to which any manufacturing or other capacity was under-used.

(4) No compensation is payable in respect of any failure to secure contracts to supply the patented product or, as the case may be, to perform the patented process or supply a thing made by means of the patented process, otherwise than for the services of the Crown.

(5) The amount payable shall, if not agreed between the proprietor or licensee and the government department concerned with the approval of the Treasury, be determined by the court on a reference under section 58, and is in addition to any amount payable under section 55 or 57.

(6) In this section "the government department concerned", in relation to any use of an invention for the services of the Crown, means the government department by whom or on whose authority the use was made.

(7) In the application of this section to Northern Ireland, the reference in subsection (5) above to the Treasury shall, where the government department concerned is a department of the Government of Northern Ireland, be construed as a reference to the Department of Finance and Personnel.".

(2) In section 58 of the Patents Act 1977 (reference of disputes as to Crown use), for subsection (1) substitute—

"(1) Any dispute as to—

(a) the exercise by a government department, or a person authorised by a government department, of the powers conferred by section 55 above,

(b) terms for the use of an invention for the services of the Crown under that section,

(c) the right of any person to receive any part of a payment made in pursuance of subsection (4) of that section, or

(d) the right of any person to receive a payment under section 57A,

may be referred to the court by either party to the dispute after a patent has been granted for the invention.";

and in subsection (4) for "under this section" substitute "under subsection (1)(a), (b) or (c) above".

(3) In section 58(11) of the Patents Act 1977 (exclusion of right to compensation for Crown use if relevant transaction, instrument or event not registered), after "section 57(3) above)" insert ", or to any compensation under section 57A above,".

(4) The above amendments apply in relation to any use of an invention for the services of the Crown after the commencement of this section, even if the terms for such use were settled before commencement.

Right to continue use begun before priority date

17 For section 64 of the Patents Act 1977 (right to continue use begun before priority date) substitute—

"64 Right to continue use begun before priority date

"64 "64 Right to continue use begun before priority date

(1) Where a patent is granted for an invention, a person who in the United Kingdom before the priority date of the invention—

(a) does in good faith an act which would constitute an infringement of the patent if it were in force, or

(b) makes in good faith effective and serious preparations to do such an act,

has the right to continue to do the act or, as the case may be, to do the act, notwithstanding the grant of the patent; but this right does not extend to granting a licence to another person to do the act.

(2) If the act was done, or the preparations were made, in the course of a business, the person entitled to the right conferred by subsection (1) may—

(a) authorise the doing of that act by any partners of his for the time being in that business, and

(b) assign that right, or transmit it on death (or in the case of a body corporate on its dissolution), to any person who acquires that part of the business in the course of which the act was done or the preparations were made.

(3) Where a product is disposed of to another in exercise of the rights conferred by subsection (1) or (2), that other and any person claiming through him may

deal with the product in the same way as if it had been disposed of by the registered proprietor of the patent.".

Revocation on grounds of grant to wrong person

18 In section 72(1) of the Patents Act 1977 (grounds for revocation of patent), for paragraph (b) substitute—

"(b) that the patent was granted to a person who was not entitled to be granted that patent;".

Revocation where two patents granted for same invention

19 In section 73 of the Patents Act 1977 (revocation on initiative of comptroller), for subsections (2) and (3) (revocation of patent where European patent (UK) granted in respect of same invention) substitute—

"(2) If it appears to the comptroller that a patent under this Act and a European patent (UK) have been granted for the same invention having the same priority date, and that the applications for the patents were filed by the same applicant or his successor in title, he shall give the proprietor of the patent under this Act an opportunity of making observations and of amending the specification of the patent, and if the proprietor fails to satisfy the comptroller that there are not two patents in respect of the same invention, or to amend the specification so as to prevent there being two patents in respect of the same invention, the comptroller shall revoke the patent.

(3) The comptroller shall not take action under subsection (2) above before—

(a) the end of the period for filing an opposition to the European patent (UK) under the European Patent Convention, or

(b) if later, the date on which opposition proceedings are finally disposed of;

and he shall not then take any action if the decision is not to maintain the European patent or if it is amended so that there are not two patents in respect of the same invention.

(4) The comptroller shall not take action under subsection (2) above if the European patent (UK) has been surrendered under section 29(1) above before the date on which by virtue of section 25(1) above the patent under this Act is to be treated as having been granted or, if proceedings for the surrender of the European patent (UK) have been begun before that date, until those proceedings are finally disposed of; and he shall not then take any action if the decision is to accept the surrender of the European patent.".

Applications and amendments not to include additional matter

20 For section 76 of the Patents Act 1977 (amendments of applications and patents not to include added matter) substitute—

"76 Amendments of applications and patents not to include added matter

"76 "76 Amendments of applications and patents not to include added matter

(1) An application for a patent which—

(a) is made in respect of matter disclosed in an earlier application, or in the specification of a patent which has been granted, and

(b) discloses additional matter, that is, matter extending beyond that disclosed in the earlier application, as filed, or the application for the patent, as filed,

may be filed under section 8(3), 12 or 37(4) above, or as mentioned in section 15(4) above, but shall not be allowed to proceed unless it is amended so as to exclude the additional matter.

(2) No amendment of an application for a patent shall be allowed under section 17(3), 18(3) or 19(1) if it results in the application disclosing matter extending beyond that disclosed in the application as filed.

(3) No amendment of the specification of a patent shall be allowed under section 27(1), 73 or 75 if it—

(a) results in the specification disclosing additional matter, or

(b) extends the protection conferred by the patent.".

Effect of European patent (UK)

21 (1) Section 77 of the Patents Act 1977 (effect of European patent (UK)) is amended as follows.

(2) For subsection (3) (effect of finding of partial validity on pending proceedings) substitute—

"(3) Where in the case of a European patent (UK)—

(a) proceedings for infringement, or proceedings under section 58 above, have been commenced before the court or the comptroller and have not been finally disposed of, and

(b) it is established in proceedings before the European Patent Office that the patent is only partially valid,

the provisions of section 63 or, as the case may be, of subsections (7) to (9) of section 58 apply as they apply to proceedings in which the validity of a patent is put in issue and in which it is found that the patent is only partially valid.".

(3) For subsection (4) (effect of amendment or revocation under European Patent Convention) substitute—

"(4) Where a European patent (UK) is amended in accordance with the European Patent Convention, the amendment shall have effect for the purposes of Parts I and III of this Act as if the specification of the patent had been amended under this Act; but subject to subsection (6)(b) below.

(4A) Where a European patent (UK) is revoked in accordance with the European Patent Convention, the patent shall be treated for the purposes of Parts I and III of this Act as having been revoked under this Act.".

(4) In subsection (6) (filing of English translation), in paragraph (b) (amendments) for "a translation of the amendment into English" substitute "a translation into English of the specification as amended".

(5) In subsection (7) (effect of failure to file translation) for the words from "a translation" to "above" substitute "such a translation is not filed".

The state of the art: material contained in patent applications

22 In section 78 of the Patents Act 1977 (effect of filing an application for a European patent (UK)), for subsection (5) (effect of withdrawal of application, &c.) substitute—

"(5) Subsections (1) to (3) above shall cease to apply to an application for a European patent (UK), except as mentioned in subsection (5A) below, if—

(a) the application is refused or withdrawn or deemed to be withdrawn, or

(b) the designation of the United Kingdom in the application is withdrawn or deemed to be withdrawn,

but shall apply again if the rights of the applicant are re-established under the European Patent Convention, as from their re-establishment.

(5A) The occurrence of any of the events mentioned in subsection (5)(a) or (b) shall not affect the continued operation of section 2(3) above in relation to matter contained in an application for a European patent (UK) which by virtue of that provision has become part of the state of the art as regards other inventions.".

Jurisdiction in certain proceedings

23 Section 88 of the Patents Act 1977 (jurisdiction in legal proceedings in connection with Community Patent Convention) is repealed.

Effect of filing international application for patent

24 (1) Section 89 of the Patents Act 1977 (effect of filing international application for patent) is amended as follows.

(2) After subsection (3) insert—

"(3A) If the relevant conditions are satisfied with respect to an application which is amended in accordance with the Treaty and the relevant conditions are not satisfied with respect to any amendment, that amendment shall be disregarded.".

(3) After subsection (4) insert—

"(4A) In subsection (4)(a) "a copy of the application" includes a copy of the application published in accordance with the Treaty in a language other than that in which it was filed.".

(4) For subsection (10) (exclusion of certain applications subject to European Patent Convention) substitute—

"(10) The foregoing provisions of this section do not apply to an application which falls to be treated as an international application for a patent (UK) by reason only of its containing an indication that the applicant wishes to obtain a European patent (UK); but without prejudice to the application of those provisions to an application which also separately designates the United Kingdom.".

(5) The amendments in this paragraph shall be deemed always to have had effect.

(6) This paragraph shall be repealed by the order bringing the following paragraph into force.

25 For section 89 of the Patents Act 1977 (effect of filing international application for patent) substitute—

"89 Effect of international application for patent

"89 "89 Effect of international application for patent

(1) An international application for a patent (UK) for which a date of filing has been accorded under the Patent Co-operation Treaty shall, subject to—

section 89A (international and national phases of application), and

section 89B (adaptation of provisions in relation to international application),

be treated for the purposes of Parts I and III of this Act as an application for a patent under this Act.

(2) If the application, or the designation of the United Kingdom in it, is withdrawn or (except as mentioned in subsection (3)) deemed to be withdrawn under the Treaty, it shall be treated as withdrawn under this Act.

(3) An application shall not be treated as withdrawn under this Act if it, or the designation of the United Kingdom in it, is deemed to be withdrawn under the Treaty—

(a) because of an error or omission in an institution having functions under the Treaty, or

(b) because, owing to circumstances outside the applicant's control, a copy of the application was not received by the International Bureau before the end of the time limited for that purpose under the Treaty,

or in such other circumstances as may be prescribed.

(4) For the purposes of the above provisions an application shall not be treated as an international application for a patent (UK) by reason only of its containing an indication that the applicant wishes to obtain a European patent (UK), but an application shall be so treated if it also separately designates the United Kingdom.

(5) If an international application for a patent which designates the United Kingdom is refused a filing date under the Treaty and the comptroller determines that the refusal was caused by an error or omission in an institution having functions under the Treaty, he may direct that the

application shall be treated as an application under this Act, having such date of filing as he may direct.

89A International and national phases of application

89A 89A International and national phases of application

(1) The provisions of the Patent Co-operation Treaty relating to publication, search, examination and amendment, and not those of this Act, apply to an international application for a patent (UK) during the international phase of the application.

(2) The international phase of the application means the period from the filing of the application in accordance with the Treaty until the national phase of the application begins.

(3) The national phase of the application begins—

(a) when the prescribed period expires, provided any necessary translation of the application into English has been filed at the Patent Office and the prescribed fee has been paid by the applicant; or

(b) on the applicant expressly requesting the comptroller to proceed earlier with the national phase of the application, filing at the Patent Office—

(i) a copy of the application, if none has yet been sent to the Patent Office in accordance with the Treaty, and

(ii) any necessary translation of the application into English,

and paying the prescribed fee.

For this purpose a "copy of the application" includes a copy published in accordance with the Treaty in a language other than that in which it was originally filed.

(4) If the prescribed period expires without the conditions mentioned in subsection (3)(a) being satisfied, the application shall be taken to be withdrawn.

(5) Where during the international phase the application is amended in accordance with the Treaty, the amendment shall be treated as made under this Act if—

(a) when the prescribed period expires, any necessary translation of the amendment into English has been filed at the Patent Office, or

(b) where the applicant expressly requests the comptroller to proceed earlier with the national phase of the application, there is then filed at the Patent Office—

(i) a copy of the amendment, if none has yet been sent to the Patent Office in accordance with the Treaty, and

(ii) any necessary translation of the amendment into English;

otherwise the amendment shall be disregarded.

(6) The comptroller shall on payment of the prescribed fee publish any translation filed at the Patent Office under subsection (3) or (5) above.

89B Adaptation of provisions in relation to international application

89B 89B Adaptation of provisions in relation to international application

(1) Where an international application for a patent (UK) is accorded a filing date under the Patent Co-operation Treaty—

(a) that date, or if the application is re-dated under the Treaty to a later date that later date, shall be treated as the date of filing the application under this Act,

(b) any declaration of priority made under the Treaty shall be treated as made under section 5(2) above, and where in accordance with the Treaty any extra days are allowed, the period of 12 months specified in section 5(2) shall be treated as altered accordingly, and

(c) any statement of the name of the inventor under the Treaty shall be treated as a statement filed under section 13(2) above.

(2) If the application, not having been published under this Act, is published in accordance with the Treaty it shall be treated, for purposes other than those mentioned in subsection (3), as published under section 16 above when the conditions mentioned in section 89A(3)(a) are complied with.

(3) For the purposes of section 55 (use of invention for service of the Crown) and section 69 (infringement of rights conferred by publication) the application, not having been published under this Act, shall be treated as published under section 16 above—

(a) if it is published in accordance with the Treaty in English, on its being so published; and

(b) if it is so published in a language other than English—

(i) on the publication of a translation of the application in accordance with section 89A(6) above, or

(ii) on the service by the applicant of a translation into English of the specification of the application on the government department concerned or, as the case may be, on the person committing the infringing act.

The reference in paragraph (b)(ii) to the service of a translation on a government department or other person is to its being sent by post or delivered to that department or person.

(4) During the international phase of the application, section 8 above does not apply (determination of questions of entitlement in relation to application under this Act) and section 12 above (determination of entitlement in relation to foreign and convention patents) applies notwithstanding the application; but after the end of the international phase, section 8 applies and section 12 does not.

(5) When the national phase begins the comptroller shall refer the application for so much of the examination and search under section 17 and 18 above as he considers appropriate in view of any examination or search carried out under the Treaty.".

Proceedings before the court or the comptroller

26 In the Patents Act 1977, after section 99 (general powers of the court) insert—

"99A Power of Patents Court to order report

"99A "99A Power of Patents Court to order report

(1) Rules of court shall make provision empowering the Patents Court in any proceedings before it under this Act, on or without the application of any party, to order the Patent Office to inquire into and report on any question of fact or opinion.

(2) Where the court makes such an order on the application of a party, the fee payable to the Patent Office shall be at such rate as may be determined in accordance with rules of court and shall be costs of the proceedings unless otherwise ordered by the court.

(3) Where the court makes such an order of its own motion, the fee payable to the Patent Office shall be at such rate as may be determined by the Lord Chancellor with the approval of the Treasury and shall be paid out of money provided by Parliament.

99B Power of Court of Session to order report

99B 99B Power of Court of Session to order report

(1) In any proceedings before the Court of Session under this Act the court may, either of its own volition or on the application of any party, order the Patent Office to inquire into and report on any question of fact or opinion.

(2) Where the court makes an order under subsection (1) above of its own volition the fee payable to the Patent Office shall be at such rate as may be determined by the Lord President of the Court of Session with the consent of the Treasury and shall be defrayed out of moneys provided by Parliament.

(3) Where the court makes an order under subsection (1) above on the application of a party, the fee payable to the Patent Office shall be at such rate as may be provided for in rules of court and shall be treated as expenses in the cause.".

27 For section 102 of the Patents Act 1977 (right of audience in patent proceedings) substitute—

"102 Right of audience, &c. in proceedings before comptroller

"102 "102 Right of audience, &c. in proceedings before comptroller

(1) A party to proceedings before the comptroller under this Act, or under any treaty or international convention to which the United Kingdom is a party, may appear before the comptroller in person or be represented by any person whom he desires to represent him.

(2) No offence is committed under the enactments relating to the preparation of documents by persons not legally qualified by reason only of the preparation by any person of a document, other than a deed, for use in such proceedings.

(3) Subsection (1) has effect subject to rules made under section 281 of the Copyright, Designs and Patents Act 1988 (power of comptroller to refuse to recognise certain agents).

(4) In its application to proceedings in relation to applications for, or otherwise in connection with, European patents, this section has effect subject to any restrictions imposed by or under the European Patent Convention.

102A Right of audience, &c. in proceedings on appeal from the comptroller

102A 102A Right of audience, &c. in proceedings on appeal from the comptroller

(1) A solicitor of the Supreme Court may appear and be heard on behalf of any party to an appeal under this Act from the comptroller to the Patents Court.

(2) A registered patent agent or a member of the Bar not in actual practice may do, in or in connection with proceedings on an appeal under this Act from the comptroller to the Patents Court, anything which a solicitor of the Supreme Court might do, other than prepare a deed.

(3) The Lord Chancellor may by regulations—

(a) provide that the right conferred by subsection (2) shall be subject to such conditions and restrictions as appear to the Lord Chancellor to be necessary or expedient, and

(b) apply to persons exercising that right such statutory provisions, rules of court and other rules of law and practice applying to solicitors as may be specified in the regulations;

and different provision may be made for different descriptions of proceedings.

(4) Regulations under this section shall be made by statutory instrument which shall be subject to annulment in pursuance of a resolution of either House of Parliament.

(5) This section is without prejudice to the right of counsel to appear before the High Court.".

Provision of information

28 In section 118 of the Patents Act 1977 (information about patent applications, &c.), in subsection (3) (restriction on disclosure before publication of application: exceptions) for "section 22(6)(a) above" substitute "section 22(6) above".

Power to extend time limits

29 In section 123 of the Patents Act 1977 (rules), after subsection (3) insert—

"(3A) It is hereby declared that rules—

(a) authorising the rectification of irregularities of procedure, or

(b) providing for the alteration of any period of time,

may authorise the comptroller to extend or further extend any period notwithstanding that the period has already expired.".

Availability of samples of micro-organisms

30 In the Patents Act 1977 after section 125 insert—

"125A Disclosure of invention by specification: availability of samples of micro-organisms

"125A "125A Disclosure of invention by specification: availability of samples of micro-organisms

(1) Provision may be made by rules prescribing the circumstances in which the specification of an application for a patent, or of a patent, for an invention which requires for its performance the use of a micro-organism is to be treated as disclosing the invention in a manner which is clear enough and complete enough for the invention to be performed by a person skilled in the art.

(2) The rules may in particular require the applicant or patentee—

(a) to take such steps as may be prescribed for the purposes of making available to the public samples of the micro-organism, and

(b) not to impose or maintain restrictions on the uses to which such samples may be put, except as may be prescribed.

(3) The rules may provide that, in such cases as may be prescribed, samples need only be made available to such persons or descriptions of persons as may be prescribed; and the rules may identify a description of persons by reference to whether the comptroller has given his certificate as to any matter.

(4) An application for revocation of the patent under section 72(1)(c) above may be made if any of the requirements of the rules cease to be complied with.".

SCHEDULE 6

Section 301.

PROVISIONS FOR THE BENEFIT OF THE HOSPITAL FOR SICK CHILDREN

Interpretation

1 (1) In this Schedule—

"the Hospital" means The Hospital for Sick Children, Great Ormond Street, London,

"the trustees" means the special trustees appointed for the Hospital under the National Health Service Act 1977; and

"the work" means the play "Peter Pan" by Sir James Matthew Barrie.

(2) Expressions used in this Schedule which are defined for the purposes of Part I of this Act (copyright) have the same meaning as in that Part.

Entitlement to royalty

2 (1) The trustees are entitled, subject to the following provisions of this Schedule, to a royalty in respect of any public performance, commercial publication, broadcasting

or inclusion in a cable programme service of the whole or any substantial part of the work or an adaptation of it.

(2) Where the trustees are or would be entitled to a royalty, another form of remuneration may be agreed.

Exceptions

3 No royalty is payable in respect of—

(a) anything which immediately before copyright in the work expired on 31st December 1987 could lawfully have been done without the licence, or further licence, of the trustees as copyright owners; or

(b) anything which if copyright still subsisted in the work could, by virtue of any provision of Chapter III of Part I of this Act (acts permitted notwithstanding copyright), be done without infringing copyright.

Saving

4 No royalty is payable in respect of anything done in pursuance of arrangements made before the passing of this Act.

Procedure for determining amount payable

5 (1) In default of agreement application may be made to the Copyright Tribunal which shall consider the matter and make such order regarding the royalty or other remuneration to be paid as it may determine to be reasonable in the circumstances.

(2) Application may subsequently be made to the Tribunal to vary its order, and the Tribunal shall consider the matter and make such order confirming or varying the original order as it may determine to be reasonable in the circumstances.

(3) An application for variation shall not, except with the special leave of the Tribunal, be made within twelve months from the date of the original order or of the order on a previous application for variation.

(4) A variation order has effect from the date on which it is made or such later date as may be specified by the Tribunal.

Sums received to be held on trust

6 The sums received by the trustees by virtue of this Schedule, after deduction of any relevant expenses, shall be held by them on trust for the purposes of the Hospital.

Right only for the benefit of the Hospital

7 (1) The right of the trustees under this Schedule may not be assigned and shall cease if the trustees purport to assign or charge it.

(2) The right may not be the subject of an order under section 92 of the National Health Service Act 1977 (transfers of trust property by order of the Secretary of State) and shall cease if the Hospital ceases to have a separate identity or ceases to have purposes which include the care of sick children.

(3) Any power of Her Majesty, the court (within the meaning of the Charities Act 1960) or any other person to alter the trusts of a charity is not exercisable in relation to the trust created by this Schedule.

SCHEDULE 7

Section 303(1).

CONSEQUENTIAL AMENDMENTS: GENERAL

British Mercantile Marine Uniform Act 1919 (c. 62)

1 For section 2 of the British Mercantile Marine Uniform Act 1919 (copyright in distinctive marks of uniform) substitute—

"2 Right in registered design of distinctive marks of uniform

"2 "2 Right in registered design of distinctive marks of uniform

The right of the Secretary of State in any design forming part of the British mercantile marine uniform which is registered under the Registered Designs Act 1949 is not limited to the period prescribed by section 8 of that Act but shall continue to subsist so long as the design remains on the register.".

Chartered Associations (Protection of Names and Uniforms) Act 1926 (c. 26)

2 In section 1(5) of the Chartered Associations (Protection of Names and Uniforms) Act 1926 for "the copyright in respect thereof" substitute "the right in the registered design".

Patents, Designs, Copyright and Trade Marks (Emergency) Act 1939 (c. 107)

3 (1) The Patents, Designs, Copyright and Trade Marks (Emergency) Act 1939 is amended as follows.

(2) In section 1 (effect of licence where owner is enemy or enemy subject)—
- (a) in subsection (1) after "a copyright" and "the copyright" insert "or design right";
- (b) in subsection (2) after "the copyright" insert "or design right" and for "or copyright" substitute ", copyright or design right".

(3) In section 2 (power of comptroller to grant licences)—
- (a) in subsection (1) after "a copyright", "the copyright" (twice) and "the said copyright" insert "or design right" and for "or copyright" (twice) substitute ", copyright or design right";
- (b) in subsections (2) and (3) for ", or copyright" substitute ", copyright or design right";
- (c) in subsection (4) and in subsection (5) (twice), after "the copyright" insert "or design right";
- (d) in subsection (8)(c) for "or work in which copyright subsists" substitute "work in which copyright subsists or design in which design right subsists".

(4) In section 5 (effect of war on international arrangements)—

(a) in subsection (1) for "section twenty-nine of the Copyright Act 1911" substitute "section 159 or 256 of the Copyright, Designs and Patents Act 1988 (countries enjoying reciprocal copyright or design right protection)";

(b) in subsection (2) after "copyright" (four times) insert "or design right" and for "the Copyright Act 1911" (twice) substitute "Part I or III of the Copyright, Designs and Patents Act 1988".

(5) In section 10(1) (interpretation) omit the definition of "copyright", and for the definitions of "design", "invention", "patent" and "patentee" substitute—

""design" has in reference to a registered design the same meaning as in the Registered Designs Act 1949, and in reference to design right the same meaning as in Part III of the Copyright, Designs and Patents Act 1988;

"invention" and "patent" have the same meaning as in the Patents Act 1977.".

Crown Proceedings Act 1947 (c. 44)

4 (1) In the Crown Proceedings Act 1947 for section 3 (provisions as to industrial property) substitute—

"3 Infringement of intellectual property rights

"3 "3 Infringement of intellectual property rights

(1) Civil proceedings lie against the Crown for an infringement committed by a servant or agent of the Crown, with the authority of the Crown, of—

(a) a patent,
(b) a registered trade mark or registered service mark,
(c) the right in a registered design,
(d) design right, or
(e) copyright;

but save as provided by this subsection no proceedings lie against the Crown by virtue of this Act in respect of an infringement of any of those rights.

(2) Nothing in this section, or any other provision of this Act, shall be construed as affecting—

(a) the rights of a government department under section 55 of the Patents Act 1977, Schedule 1 to the Registered Designs Act 1949 or section 240 of the Copyright, Designs and Patents Act 1988 (Crown use of patents and designs), or

(b) the rights of the Secretary of State under section 22 of the Patents Act 1977 or section 5 of the Registered Designs Act 1949 (security of information prejudicial to defence or public safety).".

(2) In the application of sub-paragraph (1) to Northern Ireland—

(a) the reference to the Crown Proceedings Act 1947 is to that Act as it applies to the Crown in right of Her Majesty's Government in Northern Ireland, as well as to the Crown in right of Her Majesty's Government in the United Kingdom, and

(b) in the substituted section 3 as it applies in relation to the Crown in right of Her Majesty's Government in Northern Ireland, subsection (2)(b) shall be omitted.

Patents Act 1949 (c. 87)

5 In section 47 of the Patents Act 1949 (rights of third parties in respect of Crown use of patent), in the closing words of subsection (1) (which relate to the use of models or documents), after "copyright" insert "or design right".

Public Libraries (Scotland) Act 1955 (c. 27)

6 In section 4 of the Public Libraries (Scotland) Act 1955 (extension of lending power of public libraries), make the existing provision subsection (1) and after it add—

"(2) The provisions of Part I of the Copyright, Designs and Patents Act 1988 (copyright) relating to the rental of copies of sound recordings, films and computer programs apply to any lending by a statutory library authority of copies of such works, whether or not a charge is made for that facility.".

London County Council (General Powers) Act 1958 (c.xxi)

7 In section 36 of the London County Council (General Powers) Act 1958 (power as to libraries: provision and repair of things other than books) for subsection (5) substitute—

"(5) Nothing in this section shall be construed as authorising an infringement of copyright.".

Public Libraries and Museums Act 1964 (c. 75)

8 In section 8 of the Public Libraries and Museums Act 1964 (restrictions on charges for library facilities), after subsection (5) add—

"(6) The provisions of Part I of the Copyright, Designs and Patents Act 1988 (copyright) relating to the rental of copies of sound recordings, films and computer programs apply to any lending by a library authority of copies of such works, whether or not a charge is made for that facility.".

Marine, &c., Broadcasting (Offences) Act 1967 (c. 41)

9 In section 5 of the Marine, &c., Broadcasting (Offences) Act 1967 (provision of material for broadcasting by pirate radio stations)—

(a) in subsection (3)(a) for the words from "cinematograph film" to "in the record" substitute "film or sound recording with intent that a broadcast of it"; and

(b) in subsection (6) for the words from "and references" to the end substitute "and "film", "sound recording", "literary, dramatic or musical work" and "artistic work" have the same meaning as in Part I of the Copyright, Designs and Patents Act 1988 (copyright)".

Medicines Act 1968 (c. 67)

10 (1) Section 92 of the Medicines Act 1968 (scope of provisions restricting promotion of sales of medicinal products) is amended as follows.

(2) In subsection (1) (meaning of "advertisement") for the words from "or by the exhibition" to "service" substitute "or by means of a photograph, film, sound recording, broadcast or cable programme,".

(3) In subsection (2) (exception for the spoken word)—

(a) in paragraph (a) omit the words from "or embodied" to "film"; and

(b) in paragraph (b) for the words from "by way of" to the end substitute "or included in a cable programme service".

(4) For subsection (6) substitute—

"(6) In this section "film", "sound recording", "broadcast", "cable programme", "cable programme service", and related expressions, have the same meaning as in Part I of the Copyright, Designs and Patents Act 1988 (copyright).".

Post Office Act 1969 (c. 48)

11 In Schedule 10 to the Post Office Act 1969 (special transitional provisions relating to use of patents and registered designs), in the closing words of paragraphs 8(1) and 18(1) (which relate to the use of models and documents), after "copyright" insert "or design right".

Merchant Shipping Act 1970 (c. 36)

12 In section 87 of the Merchant Shipping Act 1970 (merchant navy uniform), for subsection (4) substitute—

"(4) Where any design forming part of the merchant navy uniform has been registered under the Registered Designs Act 1949 and the Secretary of State is the proprietor of the design, his right in the design is not limited to the period prescribed by section 8 of that Act but shall continue to subsist so long as the design remains registered.".

Taxes Management Act 1970 (c. 9)

13 In section 16 of the Taxes Management Act 1970 (returns to be made in respect of certain payments)—

(a) in subsection (1)(c), and

(b) in subsection (2)(b),

for "or public lending right" substitute ", public lending right, right in a registered design or design right".

Tribunals and Inquiries Act 1971 (c. 62)

14 In Part I of Schedule 1 to the Tribunals and Inquiries Act 1971 (tribunals under direct supervision of Council on Tribunals) renumber the entry inserted by the Data Protection Act 1984 as "5B" and before it insert—

"5A Copyright

5A The Copyright Tribunal."

Fair Trading Act 1973 (c. 41)

15 In Schedule 4 to the Fair Trading Act 1973 (excluded services), for paragraph 10 (services of patent agents) substitute—

"10 The services of registered patent agents (within the meaning of Part V of the Copyright, Designs and Patents Act 1988) in their capacity as such.";

and in paragraph 10A (services of European patent attorneys) for "section 84(7) of the Patents Act 1977" substitute "Part V of the Copyright, Designs and Patents Act 1988".

House of Commons Disqualification Act 1975 (c. 24)

16 In Part II of Schedule 1 to the House of Commons Disqualification Act 1975 (bodies of which all members are disqualified), at the appropriate place insert "The Copyright Tribunal".

Northern Ireland Assembly Disqualification Act 1975 (c. 25)

17 In Part II of Schedule 1 to the Northern Ireland Assembly Disqualification Act 1975 (bodies of which all members are disqualified), at the appropriate place insert "The Copyright Tribunal".

Restrictive Trade Practices Act 1976 (c. 34)

18 (1) The Restrictive Trade Practices Act 1976 is amended as follows.

(2) In Schedule 1 (excluded services) for paragraph 10 (services of patent agents) substitute—

"10 The services of registered patent agents (within the meaning of Part V of the Copyright, Designs and Patents Act 1988) in their capacity as such.";

and in paragraph 10A (services of European patent attorneys) for "section 84(7) of the Patents Act 1977" substitute "Part V of the Copyright, Designs and Patents Act 1988".

(3) In Schedule 3 (excepted agreements), after paragraph 5A insert—

"Design right

5B (1) This Act does not apply to—

(a) a licence granted by the owner or a licensee of any design right,

(b) an assignment of design right, or

(c) an agreement for such a licence or assignment,

if the licence, assignment or agreement is one under which no such restrictions as are described in section 6(1) above are accepted, or no such information provisions as are described in section 7(1) above are made, except in respect of articles made to the design; but subject to the following provisions.

(2) Sub-paragraph (1) does not exclude a licence, assignment or agreement which is a design pooling agreement or is granted or made (directly or indirectly) in pursuance of a design pooling agreement.

(3) In this paragraph a "design pooling agreement" means an agreement—

(a) to which the parties are or include at least three persons (the "principal parties") each of whom has an interest in one or more design rights, and

(b) by which each principal party agrees, in respect of design right in which he has, or may during the currency of the agreement acquire, an interest to grant an interest (directly or indirectly) to one or more of the other principal parties, or to one or more of those parties and to other persons.

(4) In this paragraph—

"assignment", in Scotland, means assignation; and

"interest" means an interest as owner or licensee of design right.

(5) This paragraph applies to an interest held by or granted to more than one person jointly as if they were one person.

(6) References in this paragraph to the granting of an interest to a person indirectly are to its being granted to a third person for the purpose of enabling him to make a grant to the person in question.".

Resale Prices Act 1976 (c. 53)

19 In section 10(4) of the Resale Prices Act 1976 (patented articles: articles to be treated in same way), in paragraph (a) after "protected" insert "by design right or".

Patents Act 1977 (c. 37)

20 In section 57 of the Patents Act 1977 (rights of third parties in respect of Crown use of patent), in the closing words of subsection (1) (which relate to the use of models or documents), after "copyright" insert "or design right".

21 In section 105 of the Patents Act 1977 (privilege in Scotland for communications relating to patent proceedings), omit "within the meaning of section 104 above", make the existing text subsection (1) and after it insert—

"(2) In this section—

"patent proceedings" means proceedings under this Act or any of the relevant conventions, before the court, the comptroller or the relevant convention court, whether contested or uncontested and including an application for a patent; and

"the relevant conventions" means the European Patent Convention, the Community Patent Convention and the Patent Co-operation Treaty.".

22 In section 123(7) of the Patents Act 1977 (publication of case reports by the comptroller)—

(a) for "and registered designs" substitute "registered designs or design right",

(b) for "and copyright" substitute ", copyright and design right".

23 In section 130(1) of the Patents Act 1977 (interpretation), in the definition of "court", for paragraph (a) substitute—

"(a) as respects England and Wales, the High Court or any patents county court having jurisdiction by virtue of an order under section 287 of the Copyright, Designs and Patents Act 1988;".

Unfair Contract Terms Act 1977 (c. 50)

24 In paragraph 1 of Schedule 1 to the Unfair Contract Terms Act 1977 (scope of main provisions: excluded contracts), in paragraph (c) (contracts relating to grant or transfer of interest in intellectual property) after "copyright" insert "or design right".

Judicature (Northern Ireland) Act 1978 (c. 23)

25 In section 94A of the Judicature (Northern Ireland) Act 1978 (withdrawal of privilege against self-incrimination in certain proceedings relating to intellectual property), in subsection (5) (meaning of "intellectual property") after "copyright" insert "or design right".

Capital Gains Tax Act 1979 (c. 14)

26 In section 18(4) of the Capital Gains Tax Act 1979 (situation of certain assets for purposes of Act), for paragraph (h) (intellectual property) substitute—

"(ha) patents, trade marks, service marks and registered designs are situated where they are registered, and if registered in more than one register, where each register is situated, and rights or licences to use a patent, trade mark, service mark or registered design are situated in the United Kingdom if they or any right derived from them are exercisable in the United Kingdom,

(hb) copyright, design right and franchises, and rights or licences to use any copyright work or design in which design right subsists, are situated in the United Kingdom if they or any right derived from them are exercisable in the United Kingdom,".

British Telecommunications Act 1981 (c. 38)

27 In Schedule 5 to the British Telecommunications Act 1981 (special transitional provisions relating to use of patents and registered designs), in the closing words of paragraphs 9(1) and 19(1) (which relate to the use of models and documents), after "copyright" insert "or design right".

Supreme Court Act 1981 (c. 54)

28 (1) The Supreme Court Act 1981 is amended as follows.

(2) In section 72 (withdrawal of privilege against self-incrimination in certain proceedings relating to intellectual property), in subsection (5) (meaning of "intellectual property") after "copyright" insert ", design right".

(3) In Schedule 1 (distribution of business in the High Court), in paragraph 1(i) (business assigned to the Chancery Division: causes and matters relating to certain intellectual property) for "or copyright" substitute ", copyright or design right".

Broadcasting Act 1981 (c. 68)

29 (1) The Broadcasting Act 1981 is amended as follows.

(2) In section 4 (general duties of IBA as regards programmes) for subsection (7) substitute—

"(7) For the purpose of maintaining supervision and control over the programmes (including advertisements) broadcast by them the Authority may make and use recordings of those programmes or any part of them.".

(3) In section 20(9), omit paragraph (a).

Cable and Broadcasting Act 1984 (c. 46)

30 (1) The Cable and Broadcasting Act 1984 is amended as follows.

(2) In section 8, omit subsection (8).

(3) In section 49 (power of Secretary of State to give directions in the public interest), for subsection (7) substitute—

"(7) For the purposes of this section the place from which a broadcast is made is, in the case of a satellite transmission, the place from which the signals carrying the broadcast are transmitted to the satellite.".

(4) In section 56(2) (interpretation) omit the definition of "the 1956 Act".

Companies Act 1985 (c. 6)

31 (1) Part XII of the Companies Act 1985 (registration of charges) is amended as follows.

(2) In section 396 (registration of charges in England and Wales: charges which must be registered), in subsection (1)(j) for the words from "on a patent" to the end substitute "or on any intellectual property", and after subsection (3) insert—

"(3A) The following are "intellectual property" for the purposes of this section—
(a) any patent, trade mark, service mark, registered design, copyright or design right;
(b) any licence under or in respect of any such right.".

(3) In section 410 (registration of charges in Scotland: charges which must be registered), in subsection (3)(c) (incorporeal moveable property) after subparagraph (vi) insert—
"(vii) a registered design or a licence in respect of such a design,
(viii) a design right or a licence under a design right,".

Law Reform (Miscellaneous Provisions) (Scotland) Act 1985 (c. 73)

32 In section 15 of the Law Reform (Miscellaneous Provisions) (Scotland) Act 1985 (withdrawal of privilege against self-incrimination in certain proceedings relating

to intellectual property), in subsection (5) (meaning of "intellectual property") after "copyright" insert "or design right".

Atomic Energy Authority Act 1986 (c. 3)

33 In section 8(2) of the Atomic Energy Authority Act 1986 (powers of Authority as to exploitation of research: meaning of "intellectual property"), after "copyrights" insert ", design rights".

Education and Libraries (Northern Ireland) Order 1986 (S.I. 1986/594 (N.I.3))

34 In Article 77 of the Education and Libraries (Northern Ireland) Order 1986 (charges for library services), after paragraph (2) add—

"(3) The provisions of Part I of the Copyright, Designs and Patents Act 1988 (copyright) relating to the rental of copies of sound recordings, films and computer programs apply to any lending by a board of copies of such works, whether or not a charge is made for that facility.".

Companies (Northern Ireland) Order 1986 (S.I. 1986/1032 (N.I.6))

35 In Article 403 of the Companies (Northern Ireland) Order 1986 (registration of charges: charges which must be registered), in paragraph (1)(j) for the words from "on a patent" to the end substitute "or on any intellectual property", and after paragraph (3) insert—

"(3A) The following are "intellectual property" for the purposes of this Article—

(a) any patent, trade mark, service mark, registered design, copyright or design right;

(b) any licence under or in respect of any such right.".

Income and Corporation Taxes Act 1988 (c. 1)

36 (1) The Income and Corporation Taxes Act 1988 is amended as follows.

(2) In section 83 (fees and expenses deductible in computing profits and gains of trade) for "the extension of the period of copyright in a design" substitute "an extension of the period for which the right in a registered design subsists".

(3) In section 103 (charge on receipts after discontinuance of trade, profession or vocation), in subsection (3) (sums to which the section does not apply), after paragraph (b) insert—

"(bb) a lump sum paid to the personal representatives of the designer of a design in which design right subsists as consideration for the assignment by them, wholly or partially, of that right,".

(4) In section 387 (carry forward as losses of certain payments made under deduction of tax), in subsection (3) (payments to which the section does not apply), in paragraph (e) (copyright royalties) after "applies" insert "or royalties in respect of a right in a design to which section 537B applies".

(5) In section 536 (taxation of copyright royalties where owner abroad), for the definition of "copyright" in subsection (2) substitute—

""copyright" does not include copyright in—

(i) a cinematograph film or video recording, or

(ii) the sound-track of such a film or recording, so far as it is not separately exploited; and".

(6) In Chapter I of Part XIII (miscellaneous special provisions: intellectual property), after section 537 insert—

"Designs

537A Relief for payments in respect of designs

537A 537A Relief for payments in respect of designs

(1) Where the designer of a design in which design right subsists assigns that right, or the author of a registered design assigns the right in the design, wholly or partially, or grants an interest in it by licence, and—

(a) the consideration for the assignment or grant consists, in whole or in part, of a payment to which this section applies, the whole amount of which would otherwise be included in computing the amount of his profits or gains for a single year of assessment, and

(b) he was engaged in the creation of the design for a period of more than 12 months,

he may, on making a claim, require that effect shall be given to the following provisions in connection with that payment.

(2) If the period for which he was engaged in the creation of the design does not exceed 24 months, then, for all income tax purposes, one-half only of the amount of the payment shall be treated as having become receivable on the date on which it actually became receivable and the remaining half shall be treated as having become receivable 12 months before that date.

(3) If the period for which he was engaged in the creation of the design exceeds 24 months, then, for all income tax purposes, one-third only of the amount of the payment shall be treated as having become receivable on the date on which it actually became receivable, and one-third shall be treated as having become receivable 12 months, and one-third 24 months, before that date.

(4) This section applies to—

(a) a lump sum payment, including an advance on account of royalties which is not returnable, and

(b) any other payment of or on account of royalties or sums payable periodically which does not only become receivable more than two years after articles made to the design or, as the case may be, articles to which the design is applied are first made available for sale or hire.

(5) A claim under this section with respect to any payment to which it applies by virtue only of subsection (4)(b) above shall have effect as a claim with respect to all such payments in respect of rights in the design in question which are receivable by the claimant, whether before or after the claim; and such a claim may be made at any time not later than 5th April next following the expiration of eight years after articles made to the design or, as the case may be, articles to which the design is applied were first made available for sale or hire.

(6) In this section—

(a) "designer" includes a joint designer, and

(b) any reference to articles being made available for sale or hire is to their being so made available anywhere in the world by or with the licence of the design right owner or, as the case may be, the proprietor of the registered design.

537B Taxation of design royalties where owner abroad

537B 537B Taxation of design royalties where owner abroad

(1) Where the usual place of abode of the owner of a right in a design is not within the United Kingdom, section 349(1) shall apply to any payment of or on account of any royalties or sums paid periodically for or in respect of that right as it applies to annual payments not payable out of profits or gains brought into charge to income tax.

(2) In subsection (1) above—

(a) "right in a design" means design right or the right in a registered design,

(b) the reference to the owner of a right includes a person who, notwithstanding that he has assigned the right to some other person, is entitled to receive periodical payments in respect of the right, and

(c) the reference to royalties or other sums paid periodically for or in respect of a right does not include royalties or sums paid in respect of articles which are shown on a claim to have been exported from the United Kingdom for distribution outside the United Kingdom.

(3) Where a payment to which subsection (1) above applies is made through an agent resident in the United Kingdom and that agent is entitled as against the owner of the right to deduct any sum by way of commission in respect of services rendered, the amount of the payment shall for the purposes of section 349(1) be taken to be diminished by the sum which the agent is entitled to deduct.

(4) Where the person by or through whom the payment is made does not know that any such commission is payable or does not know the amount of any such commission, any income tax deducted by or assessed and charged on him shall be computed in the first instance on, and the account to be delivered of the payment shall be an account of, the total amount of the payment without regard being had to any diminution thereof, and in that case, on proof of the facts on a claim, there shall be made to the agent on behalf of the owner of the right such repayment of income tax as is proper in respect of the sum deducted by way of commission.

(5) The time of the making of a payment to which subsection (1) above applies shall, for all tax purposes, be taken to be the time when it is made by the person by whom it is first made and not the time when it is made by or through any other person.

(6) Any agreement for the making of any payment to which subsection (1) above applies in full and without deduction of income tax shall be void.".

(7) In section 821 (payments made under deduction of tax before passing of Act imposing income tax for that year), in subsection (3) (payments subject to adjustment) after paragraph (a) insert—

"(aa) any payment for or in respect of a right in a design to which section 537B applies; and".

(8) In Schedule 19 (apportionment of income of close companies), in paragraph 10(4) (cessation or liquidation: debts taken into account although creditor is participator or associate), in paragraph (c) (payments for use of certain property) for the words from "tangible property" to "extend)" substitute—

"(i) tangible property,

(ii) copyright in a literary, dramatic, musical or artistic work within the meaning of Part I of the Copyright, Designs and Patents Act 1988 (or any similar right under the law of a country to which that Part does not extend), or

(iii) design right,".

(9) In Schedule 25 (taxation of UK-controlled foreign companies: exempt activities), in paragraph 9(1)(a) (investment business: holding of property) for "patents or copyrights" substitute "or intellectual property" and after that subparagraph insert—

"(1A) In sub-paragraph (1)(a) above "intellectual property" means patents, registered designs, copyright and design right (or any similar rights under the law of a country outside the United Kingdom).".

SCHEDULE 8

Section 303(2).

Repeals

1939 c. 107.	Patents, Designs, Copyright and Trade Marks (Emergency) Act 1939.	In section 10(1), the definition of "copyright".
1945 c. 16.	Limitation (Enemies and War Prisoners) Act 1945.	In sections 2(1) and 4(a), the reference to section 10 of the Copyright Act 1911.
1949 c. 88.	Registered Designs Act 1949.	In section 3(2), the words "or original".
		Section 5(5).
		In section 11(2), the words "or original".
		In section 14(3), the words "or the Isle of Man".
		Section 32.
		Section 33(2).
		Section 37(1).

		Section 38.
		In section 44(1), the definitions of "copyright" and "Journal".
		In section 45, paragraphs (1) and (2).
		In section 46, paragraphs (1) and (2).
		Section 48(1).
		In Schedule 1, in paragraph 3(1), the words "in such manner as may be prescribed by rules of court".
		Schedule 2.
1956 c. 74.	Copyright Act 1956.	The whole Act.
1957 c. 6.	Ghana Independence Act 1957.	In Schedule 2, paragraph 12.
1957 c. 60.	Federation of Malaya Independence Act 1957.	In Schedule 1, paragraphs 14 and 15.
1958 c. 44.	Dramatic and Musical Performers' Protection Act 1958.	The whole Act.
1958 c. 51.	Public Records Act 1958.	Section 11.
		Schedule 3.
1960 c. 52.	Cyprus Independence Act 1960.	In the Schedule, paragraph 13.
1960 c. 55.	Nigeria Independence Act 1960.	In Schedule 2, paragraphs 12 and 13.
1961 c. 1.	Tanganyika Independence Act 1961.	In Schedule 2, paragraphs 13 and 14.
1961 c. 16.	Sierra Leone Independence Act 1961.	In Schedule 3, paragraphs 13 and 14.
1961 c. 25.	Patents and Designs (Renewals, Extensions and Fees) Act 1961.	The whole Act.
1962 c. 40.	Jamaica Independence Act 1962.	In Schedule 2, paragraph 13.
1962 c. 54.	Trinidad and Tobago Independence Act 1962.	In Schedule 2, paragraph 13.
1963 c. 53.	Performers' Protection Act 1963.	The whole Act.

1964 c. 46.	Malawi Independence Act 1964.	In Schedule 2, paragraph 13.
1964 c. 65.	Zambia Independence Act 1964.	In Schedule 1, paragraph 9.
1964 c. 86.	Malta Independence Act 1964.	In Schedule 1, paragraph 11.
1964 c. 93.	Gambia Independence Act 1964.	In Schedule 2, paragraph 12.
1966 c. 24.	Lesotho Independence Act 1966.	In the Schedule, paragraph 9.
1966 c. 37.	Barbados Independence Act 1966.	In Schedule 2, paragraph 12.
1967 c. 80.	Criminal Justice Act 1967.	In Parts I and IV of Schedule 3, the entries relating to the Registered Designs Act 1949.
1968 c. 56.	Swaziland Independence Act 1968.	In the Schedule, paragraph 9.
1968 c. 67.	Medicines Act 1968.	In section 92(2)(a), the words from "or embodied" to "film".
		Section 98.
1968 c. 68.	Design Copyright Act 1968.	The whole Act.
1971 c. 4.	Copyright (Amendment) Act 1971.	The whole Act.
1971 c. 23.	Courts Act 1971.	In Schedule 9, the entry relating to the Copyright Act 1956.
1971 c. 62.	Tribunals and Inquiries Act 1971.	In Schedule 1, paragraph 24.
1972 c. 32.	Performers' Protection Act 1972.	The whole Act.
1975 c. 24.	House of Commons Disqualification Act 1975.	In Part II of Schedule 1, the entry relating to the Performing Right Tribunal.
1975 c. 25.	Northern Ireland Assembly Disqualification Act 1975.	In Part II of Schedule 1, the entry relating to the Performing Right Tribunal.
1977 c. 37.	Patents Act 1977.	Section 14(4) and (8).
		In section 28(3), paragraph (b) and the word "and" preceding it.
		Section 28(5) to (9).

Status: This is the original version (as it was originally enacted).

		Section 49(3).
		Sections 72(3).
		Sections 84 and 85.
		Section 88.
		Section 104.
		In section 105, the words "within the meaning of section 104 above".
		Sections 114 and 115.
		Section 123(2)(k).
		In section 130(1), the definition of "patent agent".
		In section 130(7), the words "88(6) and (7),".
		In Schedule 5, paragraphs 1 and 2, in paragraph 3 the words "and 44(1)" and "in each case", and paragraphs 7 and 8.
1979 c. 2.	Customs and Excise Management Act 1979.	In Schedule 4, the entry relating to the Copyright Act 1956.
1980 c. 21.	Competition Act 1980.	Section 14.
1981 c. 68.	Broadcasting Act 1981.	Section 20(9)(a).
1982 c. 35.	Copyright Act 1956 (Amendment) Act 1982.	The whole Act.
1983 c. 42.	Copyright (Amendment) Act 1983.	The whole Act.
1984 c. 46.	Cable and Broadcasting Act 1984.	Section 8(8).
		Section 16(4) and (5).
		Sections 22 to 24.
		Section 35(2) and (3).
		Sections 53 and 54.
		In section 56(2), the definition of "the 1956 Act".
		In Schedule 5, paragraphs 6, 7, 13 and 23.
1985 c. 21.	Films Act 1985.	Section 7(2).

1985 c. 41.	Copyright (Computer Software) Amendment Act 1985.	The whole Act.
1985 c. 61.	Administration of Justice Act 1985.	Section 60.
1986 c. 39.	Patents, Designs and Marks Act 1986.	In Schedule 2, paragraph 1(2)(a), in paragraph 1(2)(k) the words "subsection (1)(j) of section 396 and" and in paragraph 1(2)(1) the words "subsection (2)(i) of section 93".
1988 c. 1.	Income and Corporation Taxes Act 1988.	In Schedule 29, paragraph 5.

ARRANGEMENT OF SECTIONS

Registrable designs and proceedings for registration

Effect of registration, &c.

International arrangements

Register of designs, &c.

17 Register of designs.
18 Certificate of registration.
19 Registration of assignments, &c.
20 Rectification of register.
21 Power to correct clerical errors.
22 Inspection of registered designs.
23 Information as to existence of right in registered design.
24 … … … … … … …

Legal proceedings and appeals

25 Certificate of contested validity of registration.
26 Remedy for groundless threats of infringement proceedings.
27 The court.
28 The Appeal Tribunal.

Powers and duties of registrar

29 Exercise of discretionary powers of registrar.
30 Costs and security for costs.
31 Evidence before registrar.
32 … … … … … … …
33 Offences under s.5.
34 Falsification of register, &c.
35 Fine for falsely representing a design as registered.
35A Offence by body corporate: liability of officers.

Rules, &c.

36 General power of Secretary of State to make rules, &c.
37 Provisions as to rules and Orders.
38 … … … … … … …

Supplemental

39 Hours of business and excluded days.
40 Fees.
41 Service of notices, &c., by post.
42 Annual report of registrar.
43 Savings.
44 Interpretation.
45 Application to Scotland.
46 Application to Northern Ireland.
47 Application to Isle of Man.
47A Territorial waters and the continental shelf.
48 Repeals, savings and transitional provisions.
49 Short title and commencement.

Schedules:
Schedule 1 — Provisions as to the use of registered designs for the services of the Crown and as to rights of third parties in respect of such use.

Schedule 2 — … … … … … … …

An Act to consolidate certain enactments relating to registered designs.

[16th December 1949]

Registrable designs and proceedings for registration

1 Designs registrable under Act

(1) In this Act "design" means features of shape, configuration, pattern or ornament applied to an article by any industrial process, being features which in the finished article appeal to and are judged by the eye, but does not include—

(a) a method or principle of construction, or

(b) features of shape or configuration of an article which—

(i) are dictated solely by the function which the article has to perform, or

(ii) are dependent upon the appearance of another article of which the article is intended by the author of the design to form an integral part.

(2) A design which is new may, upon application by the person claiming to be the proprietor, be registered under this Act in respect of any article, or set of articles, specified in the application.

(3) A design shall not be registered in respect of an article if the appearance of the article is not material, that is, if aesthetic considerations are not normally taken into account to a material extent by persons acquiring or using articles of that description, and would not be so taken into account if the design were to be applied to the article.

(4) A design shall not be regarded as new for the purposes of this Act if it is the same as a design—

(a) registered in respect of the same or any other article in pursuance of a prior application, or

(b) published in the United Kingdom in respect of the same or any other article before the date of the application,

or if it differs from such a design only in immaterial details or in features which are variants commonly used in the trade.

This subsection has effect subject to the provisions of sections 4, 6 and 16 of this Act.

(5) The Secretary of State may by rules provide for excluding from registration under this Act designs for such articles of a primarily literary or artistic character as the Secretary of State thinks fit.

2 Proprietorship of designs

(1) The author of a design shall be treated for the purposes of this Act as the original proprietor of the design, subject to the following provisions.

(1A) Where a design is created in pursuance of a commission for money or money's worth, the person commissioning the design shall be treated as the original proprietor of the design.

(1B) Where, in a case not falling within subsection (1A), a design is created by an employee in the course of his employment, his employer shall be treated as the original proprietor of the design.

(2) Where a design, or the right to apply a design to any article, becomes vested, whether by assignment, transmission or operation of law, in any person other than the original proprietor, either alone or jointly with the original proprietor, that other person, or as the case may be the original proprietor and that other person, shall be treated for the purposes of this Act as the proprietor of the design or as the proprietor of the design in relation to that article.

(3) In this Act the "author" of a design means the person who creates it.

(4) In the case of a design generated by computer in circumstances such that there is no human author, the person by whom the arrangements necessary for the creation of the design are made shall be taken to be the author.

3 Proceedings for registration

(1) An application for the registration of a design shall be made in the prescribed form and shall be filed at the Patent Office in the prescribed manner.

(2) An application for the registration of a design in which design right subsists shall not be entertained unless made by the person claiming to be the design right owner.

(3) For the purpose of deciding whether a design is new, the registrar may make such searches, if any, as he thinks fit.

(4) The registrar may, in such cases as may be prescribed, direct that for the purpose of deciding whether a design is new an application shall be treated as made on a date earlier or later than that on which it was in fact made.

(5) The registrar may refuse an application for the registration of a design or may register the design in pursuance of the application subject to such modifications, if any, as he thinks fit; and a design when registered shall be registered as of the date on which the application was made or is treated as having been made.

(6) An application which, owing to any default or neglect on the part of the applicant, has not been completed so as to enable registration to be effected within such time as may be prescribed shall be deemed to be abandoned.

(7) An appeal lies from any decision of the registrar under this section.

4 Registration of same design in respect of other articles, etc

(1) Where the registered proprietor of a design registered in respect of any article makes an application—

(a) for registration in respect of one or more other articles, of the registered design, or

(b) for registration in respect of the same or one or more other articles, of a design consisting of the registered design with modifications or variations not sufficient to alter the character or substantially to affect the identity thereof,

the application shall not be refused and the registration made on that application shall not be invalidated by reason only of the previous registration or publication of the registered design:

Provided that the right in a design registered by virtue of this section shall not extend beyond the end of the period, and any extended period, for which the right subsists in the original registered design.

(2) Where any person makes an application for the registration of a design in respect of any article and either—

(a) that design has been previously registered by another person in respect of some other article; or

(b) the design to which the application relates consists of a design previously registered by another person in respect of the same or some other article with modifications or variations not sufficient to alter the character or substantially to affect the identity thereof,

then, if at any time while the application is pending the applicant becomes the registered proprietor of the design previously registered, the foregoing provisions of this section shall apply as if at the time of making the application the applicant had been the registered proprietor of that design.

5 Provisions for secrecy of certain designs

(1) Where, either before or after the commencement of this Act, an application for the registration of a design has been made, and it appears to the registrar that the design is one of a class notified to him by the Secretary of State as relevant for defence purposes, he may give directions for prohibiting or restricting the publication of information with respect to the design, or the communication of such information to any person or class of persons specified in the directions.

(2) The Secretary of State shall by rules make provision for securing that where such directions are given—

(a) the representation or specimen of the design, and

(b) any evidence filed in support of the applicant's contention that the appearance of an article is material (for the purposes of section 1(3) of this Act),

shall not be open to public inspection at the Patent Office during the continuance in force of the directions.

(3) Where the registrar gives any such directions as aforesaid, he shall give notice of the application and of the directions to the Secretary of State, and thereupon the following provisions shall have effect, that is to say:—

(a) the Secretary of State shall, upon receipt of such notice, consider whether the publication of the design would be prejudicial to the defence of the realm and unless a notice under paragraph (c) of this subsection has previously been given by that authority to the registrar, shall reconsider that question before the expiration of nine months from the date of filing of the application for registration of the design and at least once in every subsequent year;

(b) for the purpose aforesaid, the Secretary of State may, at any time after the design has been registered or, with the consent of the applicant, at any time before the design has been registered, inspect the representation or specimen of the design, or any such evidence as is mentioned in subsection (2)(b) above, filed in pursuance of the application;

(c) if upon consideration of the design at any time it appears to the Secretary of State that the publication of the design would not, or would no longer, be prejudicial to the defence of the realm, he shall give notice to the registrar to that effect;

(d) on the receipt of any such notice the registrar shall revoke the directions and may, subject to such conditions, if any, as he thinks fit, extend the time for doing anything required or authorised to be done by or under this Act in connection with the application or registration, whether or not that time has previously expired.

(4) No person resident in the United Kingdom shall, except under the authority of a written permit granted by or on behalf of the registrar, make or cause to be made any application outside the United Kingdom for the registration of a design of any class prescribed for the purposes of this subsection unless—

(a) an application for registration of the same design has been made in the United Kingdom not less than six weeks before the application outside the United Kingdom; and

(b) either no directions have been given under subsection (1) of this section in relation to the application in the United Kingdom or all such directions have been revoked:

Provided that this subsection shall not apply in relation to a design for which an application for protection has first been filed in a country outside the United Kingdom by a person resident outside the United Kingdom.

… … … …

6 Provisions as to confidential disclosure, etc

(1) An application for the registration of a design shall not be refused, and the registration of a design shall not be invalidated, by reason only of—

(a) the disclosure of the design by the proprietor to any other person in such circumstances as would make it contrary to good faith for that other person to use or publish the design;

(b) the disclosure of the design in breach of good faith by any person other than the proprietor of the design; or

(c) in the case of a new or original textile design intended for registration, the acceptance of a first and confidential order for goods bearing the design.

(2) An application for the registration of a design shall not be refused and the registration of a design shall not be invalidated by reason only—

(a) that a representation of the design, or any article to which the design has been applied, has been displayed, with the consent of the proprietor of the design, at an exhibition certified by the Secretary of State for the purposes of this subsection;

(b) that after any such display as aforesaid, and during the period of the exhibition, a representation of the design or any such article as aforesaid has been displayed by any person without the consent of the proprietor; or

(c) that a representation of the design has been published in consequence of any such display as is mentioned in paragraph (a) of this subsection,

if the application for registration of the design is made not later than six months after the opening of the exhibition.

(3) An application for the registration of a design shall not be refused, and the registration of a design shall not be invalidated, by reason only of the communication of the design

by the proprietor thereof to a government department or to any person authorised by a government department to consider the merits of the design, or of anything done in consequence of such a communication.

(4) Where an application is made by or with the consent of the owner of copyright in an artistic work for the registration of a corresponding design, the design shall not be treated for the purposes of this Act as being other than new by reason only of any use previously made of the artistic work, subject to subsection (5).

(5) Subsection (4) does not apply if the previous use consisted of or included the sale, letting for hire or offer or exposure for sale or hire of articles to which had been applied industrially—

(a) the design in question, or

(b) a design differing from it only in immaterial details or in features which are variants commonly used in the trade,

and that previous use was made by or with the consent of the copyright owner.

(6) The Secretary of State may make provision by rules as to the circumstances in which a design is to be regarded for the purposes of this section as "applied industrially" to articles, or any description of articles.

Effect of registration, &c.

7 Right given by registration

(1) The registration of a design under this Act gives the registered proprietor the exclusive right—

(a) to make or import—

(i) for sale or hire, or

(ii) for use for the purposes of a trade or business, or

(b) to sell, hire or offer or expose for sale or hire,

an article in respect of which the design is registered and to which that design or a design not substantially different from it has been applied.

(2) The right in the registered design is infringed by a person who without the licence of the registered proprietor does anything which by virtue of subsection (1) is the exclusive right of the proprietor.

(3) The right in the registered design is also infringed by a person who, without the licence of the registered proprietor makes anything for enabling any such article to be made, in the United Kingdom or elsewhere, as mentioned in subsection (1).

(4) The right in the registered design is also infringed by a person who without the licence of the registered proprietor—

(a) does anything in relation to a kit that would be an infringement if done in relation to the assembled article (see subsection (1)), or

(b) makes anything for enabling a kit to be made or assembled, in the United Kingdom or elsewhere, if the assembled article would be such an article as is mentioned in subsection (1);

and for this purpose a "kit" means a complete or substantially complete set of components intended to be assembled into an article.

(5) No proceedings shall be taken in respect of an infringement committed before the date on which the certificate of registration of the design under this Act is granted.

(6) The right in a registered design is not infringed by the reproduction of a feature of the design which, by virtue of section 1(1)(b), is left out of account in determining whether the design is registrable.

8 Duration of right in registered design

(1) The right in a registered design subsists in the first instance for a period of five years from the date of the registration of the design.

(2) The period for which the right subsists may be extended for a second, third, fourth and fifth period of five years, by applying to the registrar for an extension and paying the prescribed renewal fee.

(3) If the first, second, third or fourth period expires without such application and payment being made, the right shall cease to have effect; and the registrar shall, in accordance with rules made by the Secretary of State, notify the proprietor of that fact.

(4) If during the period of six months immediately following the end of that period an application for extension is made and the prescribed renewal fee and any prescribed additional fee is paid, the right shall be treated as if it had never expired, with the result that—

(a) anything done under or in relation to the right during that further period shall be treated as valid,

(b) an act which would have constituted an infringement of the right if it had not expired shall be treated as an infringement, and

(c) an act which would have constituted use of the design for the services of the Crown if the right had not expired shall be treated as such use.

(5) Where it is shown that a registered design—

(a) was at the time it was registered a corresponding design in relation to an artistic work in which copyright subsists, and

(b) by reason of a previous use of that work would not have been registrable but for section 6(4) of this Act (registration despite certain prior applications of design),

the right in the registered design expires when the copyright in that work expires, if that is earlier than the time at which it would otherwise expire, and it may not thereafter be renewed.

(6) The above provisions have effect subject to the proviso to section 4(1) (registration of same design in respect of other articles, &c.).

8A Restoration of lapsed right in design

(1) Where the right in a registered design has expired by reason of a failure to extend, in accordance with section 8(2) or (4), the period for which the right subsists, an application for the restoration of the right in the design may be made to the registrar within the prescribed period.

(2) The application may be made by the person who was the registered proprietor of the design or by any other person who would have been entitled to the right in the design

if it had not expired; and where the design was held by two or more persons jointly, the application may, with the leave of the registrar, be made by one or more of them without joining the others.

(3) Notice of the application shall be published by the registrar in the prescribed manner.

(4) If the registrar is satisfied that the proprietor took reasonable care to see that the period for which the right subsisted was extended in accordance with section 8(2) or (4), he shall, on payment of any unpaid renewal fee and any prescribed additional fee, order the restoration of the right in the design.

(5) The order may be made subject to such conditions as the registrar thinks fit, and if the proprietor of the design does not comply with any condition the registrar may revoke the order and give such consequential directions as he thinks fit.

(6) Rules altering the period prescribed for the purposes of subsection (1) may contain such transitional provisions and savings as appear to the Secretary of State to be necessary or expedient.

8B Effect of order for restoration of right

(1) The effect of an order under section 8A for the restoration of the right in a registered design is as follows.

(2) Anything done under or in relation to the right during the period between expiry and restoration shall be treated as valid.

(3) Anything done during that period which would have constituted an infringement if the right had not expired shall be treated as an infringement—

(a) if done at a time when it was possible for an application for extension to be made under section 8(4); or

(b) if it was a continuation or repetition of an earlier infringing act.

(4) If after it was no longer possible for such an application for extension to be made, and before publication of notice of the application for restoration, a person—

(a) began in good faith to do an act which would have constituted an infringement of the right in the design if it had not expired, or

(b) made in good faith effective and serious preparations to do such an act,

he has the right to continue to do the act or, as the case may be, to do the act, notwithstanding the restoration of the right in the design; but this does not extend to granting a licence to another person to do the act.

(5) If the act was done, or the preparations were made, in the course of a business, the person entitled to the right conferred by subsection (4) may—

(a) authorise the doing of that act by any partners of his for the time being in that business, and

(b) assign that right, or transmit it on death (or in the case of a body corporate on its dissolution), to any person who acquires that part of the business in the course of which the act was done or the preparations were made.

(6) Where an article is disposed of to another in exercise of the rights conferred by subsection (4) or subsection (5), that other and any person claiming through him may deal with the article in the same way as if it had been disposed of by the registered proprietor of the design.

(7) The above provisions apply in relation to the use of a registered design for the services of the Crown as they apply in relation to infringement of the right in the design.

9 Exemption of innocent infringer from liability for damages

(1) In proceedings for the infringement of the right in a registered design damages shall not be awarded against a defendant who proves that at the date of the infringement he was not aware, and had no reasonable ground for supposing, that the design was registered; and a person shall not be deemed to have been aware or to have had reasonable grounds for supposing as aforesaid by reason only of the marking of an article with the word "registered" or any abbreviation thereof, or any word or words expressing or implying that the design applied to the article has been registered, unless the number of the design accompanied the word or words or the abbreviation in question.

(2) Nothing in this section shall affect the power of the court to grant an injunction in any proceedings for infringement of the right in a registered design.

10 Compulsory licence in respect of registered design

(1) At any time after a design has been registered any person interested may apply to the registrar for the grant of a compulsory licence in respect of the design on the ground that the design is not applied in the United Kingdom by any industrial process or means to the article in respect of which it is registered to such an extent as is reasonable in the circumstances of the case; and the registrar may make such order on the application as he thinks fit.

(2) An order for the grant of a licence shall, without prejudice to any other method of enforcement, have effect as if it were a deed executed by the registered proprietor and all other necessary parties, granting a licence in accordance with the order.

(3) No order shall be made under this section which would be at variance with any treaty, convention, arrangement or engagement applying to the United Kingdom and any convention country.

(4) An appeal shall lie from any order of the registrar under this section.

11 Cancellation of registration

(1) The registrar may, upon a request made in the prescribed manner by the registered proprietor, cancel the registration of a design.

(2) At any time after a design has been registered any person interested may apply to the registrar for the cancellation of the registration of the design on the ground that the design was not, at the date of the registration thereof, new…, or on any other ground on which the registrar could have refused to register the design; and the registrar may make such order on the application as he thinks fit.

(3) At any time after a design has been registered, any person interested may apply to the registrar for the cancellation of the registration on the ground that—

(a) the design was at the time it was registered a corresponding design in relation to an artistic work in which copyright subsisted, and

(b) the right in the registered design has expired in accordance with section 8(4) of this Act (expiry of right in registered design on expiry of copyright in artistic work);

and the registrar may make such order on the application as he thinks fit.

(4) A cancellation under this section takes effect—

(a) in the case of cancellation under subsection (1), from the date of the registrar's decision,

(b) in the case of cancellation under subsection (2), from the date of registration,

(c) in the case of cancellation under subsection (3), from the date on which the right in the registered design expired,

or, in any case, from such other date as the registrar may direct.

(5) An appeal lies from any order of the registrar under this section.

11A Powers exercisable for protection of the public interest

(1) Where a report of the Monopolies and Mergers Commission has been laid before Parliament containing conclusions to the effect—

(a) on a monopoly reference, that a monopoly situation exists and facts found by the Commission operate or may be expected to operate against the public interest,

(b) on a merger reference, that a merger situation qualifying for investigation has been created and the creation of the situation, or particular elements in or consequences of it specified in the report, operate or may be expected to operate against the public interest,

(c) on a competition reference, that a person was engaged in an anti-competitive practice which operated or may be expected to operate against the public interest, or

(d) on a reference under section 11 of the Competition Act 1980 (reference of public bodies and certain other persons), that a person is pursuing a course of conduct which operates against the public interest,

the appropriate Minister or Ministers may apply to the registrar to take action under this section.

(2) Before making an application the appropriate Minister or Ministers shall publish, in such manner as he or they think appropriate, a notice describing the nature of the proposed application and shall consider any representations which may be made within 30 days of such publication by persons whose interests appear to him or them to be affected.

(3) If on an application under this section it appears to the registrar that the matters specified in the Commission's report as being those which in the Commission's opinion operate, or operated or may be expected to operate, against the public interest include—

(a) conditions in licences granted in respect of a registered design by its proprietor restricting the use of the design by the licensee or the right of the proprietor to grant other licences, or

(b) a refusal by the proprietor of a registered design to grant licences on reasonable terms, he may by order cancel or modify any such condition or may, instead or in addition, make an entry in the register to the effect that licences in respect of the design are to be available as of right.

(4) The terms of a licence available by virtue of this section shall, in default of agreement, be settled by the registrar on an application by the person requiring the licence; and terms so settled shall authorise the licensee to do everything which would be an infringement of the right in the registered design in the absence of a licence.

(5) Where the terms of a licence are settled by the registrar, the licence has effect from the date on which the application to him was made.

(6) An appeal lies from any order of the registrar under this section.

(7) In this section "the appropriate Minister or Ministers" means the Minister or Ministers to whom the report of the Monopolies and Mergers Commission was made.

11B Undertaking to take licence of right in infringement proceedings

(1) If in proceedings for infringement of the right in a registered design in respect of which a licence is available as of right under section 11A of this Act the defendant undertakes to take a licence on such terms as may be agreed or, in default of agreement, settled by the registrar under that section—

(a) no injunction shall be granted against him, and

(b) the amount recoverable against him by way of damages or on an account of profits shall not exceed double the amount which would have been payable by him as licensee if such a licence on those terms had been granted before the earliest infringement.

(2) An undertaking may be given at any time before final order in the proceedings, without any admission of liability.

(3) Nothing in this section affects the remedies available in respect of an infringement committed before licences of right were available.

12 Use for services of the Crown

The provisions of the First Schedule to this Act shall have effect with respect to the use of registered designs for the services of the Crown and the rights of third parties in respect of such use.

International Arrangements

13 Orders in Council as to convention countries

(1) His Majesty may, with a view to the fulfilment of a treaty, convention, arrangement or engagement, by Order in Council declare that any country specified in the Order is a convention country for the purposes of this Act:

Provided that a declaration may be made as aforesaid for the purposes either of all or of some only of the provisions of this Act, and a country in the case of which a declaration made for the purposes of some only of the provisions of this Act is in force shall be deemed to be a convention country for the purposes of those provisions only.

(2) His Majesty may by Order in Council direct that any of the Channel Islands, any colony,... shall be deemed to be a convention country for the purposes of all or any of the provisions of this Act; and an Order made under this subsection may direct that any such provisions shall have effect, in relation to the territory in question, subject to such conditions or limitations, if any, as may be specified in the Order.

(3) For the purposes of subsection (1) of this section, every colony, protectorate, territory subject to the authority or under the suzerainty of another country, and territory administered by another country... under the trusteeship system of the United Nations, shall be deemed to be a country in the case of which a declaration may be made under that subsection.

14 Registration of design where application for protection in convention country has been made

(1) An application for registration of a design in respect of which protection has been applied for in a convention country may be made in accordance with the provisions of this Act by the person by whom the application for protection was made or his personal representative or assignee:

Provided that no application shall be made by virtue of this section after the expiration of six months from the date of the application for protection in a convention country or, where more than one such application for protection has been made, from the date of the first application.

(2) Where an application for registration of a design is made by virtue of this section, the application shall be treated, for the purpose of determining whether that or any other design is new, as made on the date of the application for protection in the convention country or, if more than one such application was made, on the date of the first such application.

(3) Subsection (2) shall not be construed as excluding the power to give directions under section 3(4) of this Act in relation to an application made by virtue of this section.

(4) Where a person has applied for protection for a design by an application which—

(a) in accordance with the terms of a treaty subsisting between two or more convention countries, is equivalent to an application duly made in any one of those convention countries; or

(b) in accordance with the law of any convention country, is equivalent to an application duly made in that convention country,

he shall be deemed for the purposes of this section to have applied in that convention country.

15 Extension of time for applications under s.14 in certain cases

(1) If the Secretary of State is satisfied that provision substantially equivalent to the provision to be made by or under this section has been or will be made under the law of any convention country, he may make rules empowering the registrar to extend the time for making application under subsection (1) of section 14 of this Act for registration of a design in respect of which protection has been applied for in that country in any case where the period specified in the proviso to that subsection expires during a period prescribed by the rules.

(2) Rules made under this section—

(a) may, where any agreement or arrangement has been made between His Majesty's Government in the United Kingdom and the government of the convention country for the supply or mutual exchange of information or articles, provide, either generally or in any class of case specified in the rules, that an extension of time shall not be granted under this section unless the design has been communicated in accordance with the agreement or arrangement;

(b) may, either generally or in any class of case specified in the rules, fix the maximum extension which may be granted under this section;

(c) may prescribe or allow any special procedure in connection with applications made by virtue of this section;

(d) may empower the registrar to extend, in relation to an application made by virtue of this section, the time limited by or under the foregoing provisions of this Act for doing any act, subject to such conditions, if any, as may be imposed by or under the rules;

(e) may provide for securing that the rights conferred by registration on an application made by virtue of this section shall be subject to such restrictions or conditions as may be specified by or under the rules and in particular to restrictions and conditions for the protection of persons (including persons acting on behalf of His Majesty) who, otherwise than as the result of a communication made in accordance with such an agreement or arrangement as is mentioned in paragraph (a) of this subsection, and before the date of the application in question or such later date as may be allowed by the rules, may have imported or made articles to which the design is applied or may have made any application for registration of the design.

16 Protection of designs communicated under international agreements

(1) Subject to the provisions of this section, the Secretary of State may make rules for securing that, where a design has been communicated in accordance with an agreement or arrangement made between His Majesty's Government in the United Kingdom and the government of any other country for the supply or mutual exchange of information or articles,—

(a) an application for the registration of the design made by the person from whom the design was communicated or his personal representative or assignee shall not be prejudiced, and the registration of the design in pursuance of such an application shall not be invalidated, by reason only that the design has been communicated as aforesaid or that in consequence thereof—

(i) the design has been published or applied, or

(ii) an application for registration of the design has been made by any other person, or the design has been registered on such an application;

(b) any application for the registration of a design made in consequence of such a communication as aforesaid may be refused and any registration of a design made on such an application may be cancelled.

(2) Rules made under subsection (1) of this section may provide that the publication or application of a design, or the making of any application for registration thereof shall, in such circumstances and subject to such conditions or exceptions as may be prescribed by the rules, be presumed to have been in consequence of such a communication as is mentioned in that subsection.

(3) The powers of the Secretary of State under this section, so far as they are exercisable for the benefit of persons from whom designs have been communicated to His Majesty's Government in the United Kingdom by the government of any other country, shall only be exercised if and to the extent that the Secretary of State is satisfied that substantially equivalent provision has been or will be made under the law of that country for the benefit of persons from whom designs have been communicated by His Majesty's Government in the United Kingdom to the government of that country.

(4) References in the last foregoing subsection to the communication of a design to or by His Majesty's Government or the government of any other country shall be construed as including references to the communication of the design by or to any person authorised in that behalf by the government in question.

Register of designs, etc.

17 Register of designs

(1) The registrar shall maintain the register of designs, in which shall be entered—
 (a) the names and addresses of proprietors of registered designs;
 (b) notices of assignments and of transmissions of registered designs; and
 (c) such other matters as may be prescribed or as the registrar may think fit.

(2) No notice of any trust, whether express, implied or constructive, shall be entered in the register of designs, and the registrar shall not be affected by any such notice.

(3) The register need not be kept in documentary form.

(4) Subject to the provisions of this Act and to rules made by the Secretary of State under it, the public shall have a right to inspect the register at the Patent Office at all convenient times.

(5) Any person who applies for a certified copy of an entry in the register or a certified extract from the register shall be entitled to obtain such a copy or extract on payment of a fee prescribed in relation to certified copies and extracts; and rules made by the Secretary of State under this Act may provide that any person who applies for an uncertified copy or extract shall be entitled to such a copy or extract on payment of a fee prescribed in relation to uncertified copies and extracts.

(6) Applications under subsection (5) above or rules made by virtue of that subsection shall be made in such manner as may be prescribed.

(7) In relation to any portion of the register kept otherwise than in documentary form—
 (a) the right of inspection conferred by subsection (4) above is a right to inspect the material on the register; and
 (b) the right to a copy or extract conferred by subsection (5) above or rules is a right to a copy or extract in a form in which it can be taken away and in which it is visible and legible.

(8) Subject to subsection (11) below, the register shall be prima facie evidence of anything required or authorised to be entered in it and in Scotland shall be sufficient evidence of any such thing.

(9) A certificate purporting to be signed by the registrar and certifying that any entry which he is authorised by or under this Act to make has or has not been made, or that any

other thing which he is so authorised to do has or has not been done, shall be prima facie evidence, and in Scotland shall be sufficient evidence, of the matters so certified.

(10) Each of the following—

(a) a copy of an entry in the register or an extract from the register which is supplied under subsection (5) above;

(b) a copy or any representation, specimen or document kept in the Patent Office or an extract from any such document,

which purports to be a certified copy or certified extract shall, subject to subsection (11) below, be admitted in evidence without further proof and without production of any original; and in Scotland such evidence shall be sufficient evidence.

(11) In the application of this section to England and Wales nothing in it shall be taken as detracting from section 69 or 70 of the Police and Criminal Evidence Act 1984 or any provision made by virtue of either of them.

(12) In this section "certified copy" and "certified extract" means a copy and extract certified by the registrar and sealed with the seal of the Patent Office.

18 Certificate of registration

(1) The registrar shall grant a certificate of registration in the prescribed form to the registered proprietor of a design when the design is registered.

(2) The registrar may, in a case where he is satisfied that the certificate of registration has been lost or destroyed, or in any other case in which he thinks it expedient, furnish one or more copies of the certificate.

19 Registration of assignments, etc

(1) Where any person becomes entitled by assignment, transmission or operation of law to a registered design or to a share in a registered design, or becomes entitled as mortgagee, licensee or otherwise to any other interest in a registered design, he shall apply to the registrar in the prescribed manner for the registration of his title as proprietor or co-proprietor or, as the case may be, of notice of his interest, in the register of designs.

(2) Without prejudice to the provisions of the foregoing subsection, an application for the registration of the title of any person becoming entitled by assignment to a registered design or a share in a registered design, or becoming entitled by virtue of a mortgage, licence or other instrument to any other interest in a registered design, may be made in the prescribed manner by the assignor, mortgagor, licensor or other party to that instrument, as the case may be.

(3) Where application is made under this section for the registration of the title of any person, the registrar shall, upon proof of title to his satisfaction—

(a) where that person is entitled to a registered design or a share in a registered design, register him in the register of designs as proprietor or co-proprietor of the design, and enter in that register particulars of the instrument or event by which he derives title; or

(b) where that person is entitled to any other interest in the registered design, enter in that register notice of his interest, with particulars of the instrument (if any) creating it.

(3A) Where design right subsists in a registered design, the registrar shall not register an interest under subsection (3) unless he is satisfied that the person entitled to that interest is also entitled to a corresponding interest in the design right.

(3B) Where design right subsists in a registered design and the proprietor of the registered design is also the design right owner, an assignment of the design right shall be taken to be also an assignment of the right in the registered design, unless a contrary intention appears.

(4) Subject to any rights vested in any other person of which notice is entered in the register of designs, the person or persons registered as proprietor of a registered design shall have power to assign, grant licences under, or otherwise deal with the design, and to give effectual receipts for any consideration for any such assignment, licence or dealing.

Provided that any equities in respect of the design may be enforced in like manner as in respect of any other personal property.

(5) Except for the purposes of an application to rectify the register under the following provisions of this Act, a document in respect of which no entry has been made in the register of designs under subsection (3) of this section shall not be admitted in any court as evidence of the title of any person to a registered design or share of or interest in a registered design unless the court otherwise directs.

20 Rectification of register

(1) The court may, on the application of any person aggrieved, order the register of designs to be rectified by the making of any entry therein or the variation or deletion of any entry therein.

(2) In proceedings under this section the court may determine any question which it may be necessary or expedient to decide in connection with the rectification of the register.

(3) Notice of any application to the court under this section shall be given in the prescribed manner to the registrar, who shall be entitled to appear and be heard on the application, and shall appear if so directed by the court.

(4) Any order made by the court under this section shall direct that notice of the order shall be served on the registrar in the prescribed manner; and the registrar shall, on receipt of the notice, rectify the register accordingly.

(5) A rectification of the register under this section has effect as follows—

(a) an entry made has effect from the date on which it should have been made,

(b) an entry varied has effect as if it had originally been made in its varied form, and

(c) an entry deleted shall be deemed never to have had effect,

unless, in any case, the court directs otherwise.

21 Power to correct clerical errors

(1) The registrar may, in accordance with the provisions of this section, correct any error in an application for the registration or in the representation of a design, or any error in the register of designs.

(2) A correction may be made in pursuance of this section either upon a request in writing made by any person interested and accompanied by the prescribed fee, or without such a request.

(3) Where the registrar proposes to make any such correction as aforesaid otherwise than in pursuance of a request made under this section, he shall give notice of the proposal to the registered proprietor or the applicant for registration of the design, as the case may be, and to any other person who appears to him to be concerned, and shall give them an opportunity to be heard before making the correction.

22 Inspection of registered designs

(1) Where a design has been registered under this Act, there shall be open to inspection at the Patent Office on and after the day on which the certificate of registration is issued—

(a) the representation or specimen of the design, and

(b) any evidence filed in support of the applicant's contention that the appearance of an article is material (for the purposes of section 1(3) of this Act).

This subsection has effect subject to the following provisions of this section and to any rules made under section 5(2) of this Act.

(2) In the case of a design registered in respect of an article of any class prescribed for the purposes of this subsection, no representation, specimen or evidence filed in pursuance of the application shall, until the expiration of such period after the day on which the certificate of registration is issued as may be prescribed in relation to articles of that class, be open to inspection at the Patent Office except by the registered proprietor, a person authorised in writing by the registered proprietor, or a person authorised by the registrar or by the court:

Provided that where the registrar proposes to refuse an application for the registration of any other design on the ground that it is the same as the first-mentioned design or differs from that design only in immaterial details or in features which are variants commonly used in the trade, the applicant shall be entitled to inspect the representation or specimen of the first-mentioned design filed in pursuance of the application for registration of that design.

(3) In the case of a design registered in respect of an article of any class prescribed for the purposes of the last foregoing subsection, the representation, specimen or evidence shall not, during the period prescribed as aforesaid, be inspected by any person by virtue of this section except in the presence of the registrar or of an officer acting under him; and except in the case of an inspection authorised by the proviso to that subsection, the person making the inspection shall not be entitled to take a copy of the representation, specimen or evidence or any part thereof.

(4) Where an application for the registration of a design has been abandoned or refused, neither the application for registration nor any representation, specimen or evidence filed in pursuance thereof shall at any time be open to inspection at the Patent Office or be published by the registrar.

23 Information as to existence of right in registered design

On the request of a person furnishing such information as may enable the registrar to identify the design, and on payment of the prescribed fee, the registrar shall inform him—

(a) whether the design is registered and, if so, in respect of what articles, and
(b) whether any extension of the period of the right in the registered design has been granted,

and shall state the date of registration and the name and address of the registered proprietor.

… … … … … … …

Legal proceedings and appeals

25 Certificate of contested validity of registration

(1) If in any proceedings before the court the validity of the registration of a design is contested, and it is found by the court that the design is validly registered, the court may certify that the validity of the registration of the design was contested in those proceedings.

(2) Where any such certificate has been granted, then if in any subsequent proceedings before the court for infringement of the right in the registered design or for cancellation of the registration of the design, a final order or judgment is made or given in favour of the registered proprietor, he shall, unless the court otherwise directs, be entitled to his costs as between solicitor and client:

Provided that this subsection shall not apply to the costs of any appeal in any such proceedings as aforesaid.

26 Remedy for groundless threats of infringement proceedings

(1) Where any person (whether entitled to or interested in a registered design or an application for registration of a design or not) by circulars, advertisements or otherwise threatens any other person with proceedings for infringement of the right in a registered design, any person aggrieved thereby may bring an action against him for any such relief as is mentioned in the next following subsection.

(2) Unless in any action brought by virtue of this section the defendant proves that the acts in respect of which proceedings were threatened constitute or, if done, would constitute, an infringement of the right in a registered design the registration of which is not shown by the plaintiff to be invalid, the plaintiff shall be entitled to the following relief, that is to say:—
(a) a declaration to the effect that the threats are unjustifiable;
(b) an injunction against the continuance of the threats; and
(c) such damages, if any, as he has sustained thereby.

(2A) Proceedings may not be brought under this section in respect of a threat to bring proceedings for an infringement alleged to consist of the making or importing of anything.

(3) For the avoidance of doubt it is hereby declared that a mere notification that a design is registered does not constitute a threat of proceedings within the meaning of this section.

27 The court

(1) In this Act "the court" means—

(a) in England and Wales, the High Court or any patents county court having jurisdiction by virtue of an order under section 287 of the Copyright, Designs and Patents Act 1988,

(b) in Scotland, the Court of Session, and

(c) in Northern Ireland, the High Court.

(2) Provision may be made by rules of court with respect to proceedings in the High Court in England and Wales for references and applications under this Act to be dealt with by such judge of that court as the Lord Chancellor may select for the purpose.

28 The Appeal Tribunal

(1) Any appeal from the registrar under this Act shall lie to the Appeal Tribunal.

(2) The Appeal Tribunal shall consist of—

(a) one or more judges of the High Court nominated by the Lord Chancellor, and

(b) one judge of the Court of Session nominated by the Lord President of that Court.

(2A) At any time when it consists of two or more judges, the jurisdiction of the Appeal Tribunal—

(a) where in the case of any particular appeal the senior of those judges so directs, shall be exercised in relation to that appeal by both of the judges, or (if there are more than two) by two of them, sitting together, and

(b) in relation to any appeal in respect of which no such direction is given, may be exercised by any one of the judges;

and, in the exercise of that jurisdiction, different appeals may be heard at the same time by different judges.

(3) The expenses of the Appeal Tribunal shall be defrayed and the fees to be taken therein may be fixed as if the Tribunal were a court of the High Court.

(4) The Appeal Tribunal may examine witnesses on oath and administer oaths for that purpose.

(5) Upon any appeal under this Act the Appeal Tribunal may by order award to any party such costs or expenses as the Tribunal may consider reasonable and direct how and by what parties the costs or expenses are to be paid; and any such order may be enforced—

(a) in England and Wales or Northern Ireland, in the same way as an order of the High Court;

(b) in Scotland, in the same way as a decree for expenses granted by the Court of Session.

… … … … … … …

(7) Upon any appeal under this Act the Appeal Tribunal may exercise any power which could have been exercised by the registrar in the proceeding from which the appeal is brought.

(8) Subject to the foregoing provisions of this section the Appeal Tribunal may make rules for regulating all matters relating to proceedings before it under this Act, including right of audience.

(8A) At any time when the Appeal Tribunal consists of two or more judges, the power to make rules under subsection (8) of this section shall be exercisable by the senior of those judges:

Provided that another of those judges may exercise that power if it appears to him that it is necessary for rules to be made and that the judge (or, if more than one, each of the judges) senior to him is for the time being prevented by illness, absence or otherwise from making them.

(9) An appeal to the Appeal Tribunal under this Act shall not be deemed to be a proceeding in the High Court.

(10) In this section "the High Court" means the High Court in England and Wales; and for the purposes of this section the seniority of judges shall be reckoned by reference to the dates on which they were appointed judges of that court or the Court of Session.

Powers and duties of Registrar

29 Exercise of discretionary powers of registrar

Without prejudice to any provisions of this Act requiring the registrar to hear any party to proceedings thereunder, or to give to any such party an opportunity to be heard, rules made by the Secretary of State under this Act shall require the registrar to give to any applicant for registration of a design an opportunity to be heard before exercising adversely to the applicant any discretion vested in the registrar by or under this Act.

30 Costs and security for costs

(1) Rules made by the Secretary of State under this Act may make provision empowering the registrar, in any proceedings before him under this Act—
- (a) to award any party such costs as he may consider reasonable, and
- (b) to direct how and by what parties they are to be paid.

(2) Any such order of the registrar may be enforced—
- (a) in England and Wales or Northern Ireland, in the same way as an order of the High Court;
- (b) in Scotland, in the same way as a decree for expenses granted by the Court of Session.

(3) Rules made by the Secretary of State under this Act may make provision empowering the registrar to require a person, in such cases as may be prescribed, to give security for the costs of—
- (a) an application for cancellation of the registration of a design,
- (b) an application for the grant of a licence in respect of a registered design, or
- (c) an appeal from any decision of the registrar under this Act,

and enabling the application or appeal to be treated as abandoned in default of such security being given.

31 Evidence before registrar

Rules made by the Secretary of State under this Act may make provision—

(a) as to the giving of evidence in proceedings before the registrar under this Act by affidavit or statutory declaration;
(b) conferring on the registrar the powers of an official referee of the Supreme Court as regards the examination of witnesses on oath and the discovery and production of documents; and
(c) applying in relation to the attendance of witnesses in proceedings before the registrar the rules applicable to the attendance of witnesses in proceedings before such a referee.

… … … … … … …

Offences

33 Offences under s.5

(1) If any person fails to comply with any direction given under section five of this Act or makes or causes to be made an application for the registration of a design in contravention of that section, he shall be guilty of an offence and liable—
(a) on conviction on indictment to imprisonment for a term not exceeding two years or a fine, or both;
(b) on summary conviction to imprisonment for a term not exceeding six months or a fine not exceeding the statutory maximum, or both.

… … … … … … …

34 Falsification of register, etc

If any person makes or causes to be made a false entry in the register of designs, or a writing falsely purporting to be a copy of an entry in that register, or produces or tenders or causes to be produced or tendered in evidence any such writing, knowing the entry or writing to be false, he shall be guilty of an offence and liable—
(a) on conviction on indictment to imprisonment for a term not exceeding two years or a fine, or both;
(b) on summary conviction to imprisonment for a term not exceeding six months or a fine not exceeding the statutory maximum, or both.

35 Fine for falsely representing a design as registered

(1) If any person falsely represents that a design applied to any article sold by him is registered in respect of that article, he shall be liable on summary conviction to a fine not exceeding level 3 on the standard scale; and for the purposes of this provision a person who sells an article having stamped, engraved or impressed thereon or otherwise applied thereto the word "registered", or any other word expressing or implying that the design applied to the article is registered, shall be deemed to represent that the design applied to the article is registered in respect of that article.

(2) If any person, after the right in a registered design has expired, marks any article to which the design has been applied with the word "registered", or any word or words implying that there is a subsisting right in the design under this Act, or causes any such article to be so marked, he shall be liable on summary conviction to a fine not exceeding level 1 on the standard scale.

35A Offence by body corporate: liability of officers

(1) Where an offence under this Act committed by a body corporate is proved to have been committed with the consent or connivance of a director, manager, secretary or other similar officer of the body, or a person purporting to act in any such capacity, he as well as the body corporate is guilty of the offence and liable to be proceeded against and punished accordingly.

(2) In relation to a body corporate whose affairs are managed by its members "director" means a member of the body corporate.

Rules, etc.

36 General power of Secretary of State to make rules, etc

(1) Subject to the provisions of this Act, the Secretary of State may make such rules as he thinks expedient for regulating the business of the Patent Office in relation to designs and for regulating all matters by this Act placed under the direction or control of the registrar or the Secretary of State.

(1A) Rules may, in particular, make provision—

(a) prescribing the form of applications for registration of designs and of any representations or specimens of designs or other documents which may be filed at the Patent Office, and requiring copies to be furnished of any such representations, specimens or documents;

(b) regulating the procedure to be followed in connection with any application or request to the registrar or in connection with any proceeding before him, and authorising the rectification of irregularities of procedure;

(c) providing for the appointment of advisers to assist the registrar in proceedings before him;

(d) regulating the keeping of the register of designs;

(e) authorising the publication and sale of copies of representations of designs and other documents in the Patent Office;

(f) prescribing anything authorised or required by this Act to be prescribed by rules.

(1B) The remuneration of an adviser appointed to assist the registrar shall be determined by the Secretary of State with the consent of the Treasury and shall be defrayed out of money provided by Parliament.

(2) Rules made under this section may provide for the establishment of branch offices for designs and may authorise any document or thing required by or under this Act to be filed or done at the Patent Office to be filed or done at the branch office at Manchester or any other branch office established in pursuance of the rules.

37 Provisions as to rules and Orders

(1) … … … … … … …

(2) Any rules made by the Secretary of State in pursuance of section 15 or section 16 of this Act, and any order made, direction given, or other action taken under the rules by the registrar, may be made, given or taken so as to have effect as respects things done

or omitted to be done on or after such date, whether before or after the coming into operation of the rules or of this Act, as may be specified in the rules.

(3) Any power to make rules conferred by this Act on the Secretary of State or on the Appeal Tribunal shall be exercisable by statutory instrument; and the Statutory Instruments Act 1946 shall apply to a statutory instrument containing rules made by the Appeal Tribunal in like manner as if the rules had been made by a Minister of the Crown.

(4) Any statutory instrument containing rules made by the Secretary of State under this Act shall be subject to annulment in pursuance of a resolution of either House of Parliament.

(5) Any Order in Council made under this Act may be revoked or varied by a subsequent Order in Council.

… … … … … … …

Supplemental

39 Hours of business and excluded days

(1) Rules made by the Secretary of State under this Act may specify the hour at which the Patent Office shall be deemed to be closed on any day for purposes of the transaction by the public of business under this Act or of any class of such business, and may specify days as excluded days for any such purposes.

(2) Any business done under this Act on any day after the hour specified as aforesaid in relation to business of that class, or on a day which is an excluded day in relation to business of that class, shall be deemed to have been done on the next following day not being an excluded day; and where the time for doing anything under this Act expires on an excluded day, that time shall be extended to the next following day not being an excluded day.

40 Fees

There shall be paid in respect of the registration of designs and applications therefor, and in respect of other matters relating to designs arising under this Act, such fees as may be prescribed by rules made by the Secretary of State with the consent of the Treasury.

41 Service of notices, &c., by post

Any notice required or authorised to be given by or under this Act, and any application or other document so authorised or required to be made or filed, may be given, made or filed by post.

42 Annual report of registrar

The Comptroller-General of Patents, Designs and Trade Marks shall, in his annual report with respect to the execution of the Patents Act 1977, include a report with respect to the execution of this Act as if it formed a part of or was included in that Act.

43 Savings

(1) Nothing in this Act shall be construed as authorising or requiring the registrar to register a design the use of which would, in his opinion, be contrary to law or morality.

(2) Nothing in this Act shall affect the right of the Crown or of any person deriving title directly or indirectly from the Crown to sell or use articles forfeited under the laws relating to customs or excise.

44 Interpretation

(1) In this Act, except where the context otherwise requires, the following expressions have the meanings hereby respectively assigned by them, that is to say—

"Appeal Tribunal" means the Appeal Tribunal constituted and acting in accordance with section 28 of this Act as amended by the Administration of Justice Act 1969;

"article" means any article of manufacture and includes any part of an article if that part is made and sold separately;

"artistic work" has the same meaning as in Part I of the Copyright, Designs and Patents Act 1988;

"assignee" includes the personal representative of a deceased assignee, and references to the assignee of any person include references to the assignee of the personal representative or assignee of that person;

"author", in relation to a design, has the meaning given by section 2(3) and (4);

… … … … … … …

"corresponding design", in relation to an artistic work, means a design which if applied to an article would produce something which would be treated for the purposes of Part I of the Copyright, Designs and Patents Act 1988 as a copy of that work;

"the court" shall be construed in accordance with section 27 of this Act;

"design" has the meaning assigned to it by section 1(1) of this Act;

"employee", "employment" and "employer" refer to employment under a contract of service or of apprenticeship;

… … … … … … …

"prescribed" means prescribed by rules made by the Secretary of State under this Act;

"proprietor" has the meaning assigned to it by section two of this Act;

"registered proprietor" means the person or persons for the time being entered in the register of designs as proprietor of the design;

"registrar" means the Comptroller-General of Patents Designs and Trade Marks;

"set of articles" means a number of articles of the same general character ordinarily on sale or intended to be used together, to each of which the same design, or the same design with modifications or variations not sufficient to alter the character or substantially to affect the identity thereof, is applied.

(2) Any reference in this Act to an article in respect of which a design is registered shall, in the case of a design registered in respect of a set of articles, be construed as a reference to any article of that set.

(3) Any question arising under this Act whether a number of articles constitute a set of articles shall be determined by the registrar; and notwithstanding anything in this Act any determination of the registrar under this subsection shall be final.

(4) For the purposes of subsection (1) of section 14 and of section 16 of this Act, the expression "personal representative", in relation to a deceased person, includes the legal representative of the deceased appointed in any country outside the United Kingdom.

45 Application to Scotland

In the application of this Act to Scotland—

… … … … … … …

(3) The expression "injunction" means "interdict"; the expression " arbitrator" means " arbiter";

the expression "plaintiff" means "pursuer"; the expression "defendant" means "defender".

46 Application to Northern Ireland

In the application of this Act to Northern Ireland—

… … … … … … …

(3) References to enactments include enactments comprised in Northern Ireland legislation:

(3A) References to the Crown include the Crown in right of Her Majesty's Government in Northern Ireland:

(4) References to a government department shall be construed as including references to a Northern Ireland department, and in relation to a Northern Ireland department references to the Treasury shall be construed as references to the Department of Finance and Personnel.

… … … … … … …

47 Application to Isle of Man

This Act extends to the Isle of Man, subject to any modifications contained in an Order made by Her Majesty in Council, and accordingly, subject to any such Order, references in this Act to the United Kingdom shall be construed as including the Isle of Man.

47A Territorial waters and the continental shelf

(1) For the purposes of this Act the territorial waters of the United Kingdom shall be treated as part of the United Kingdom.

(2) This Act applies to things done in the United Kingdom sector of the continental shelf on a structure or vessel which is present there for purposes directly connected with the exploration of the sea bed or subsoil or the exploitation of their natural resources as it applies to things done in the United Kingdom.

(3) The United Kingdom sector of the continental shelf means the areas designated by order under section 1(7) of the Continental Shelf Act 1964.

48 Repeals, savings, and transitional provisions

(1) … … … … … … …

(2) Subject to the provisions of this section, any Order in Council, rule, order, requirement, certificate, notice, decision, direction, authorisation, consent, application, request or thing made, issued, given or done under any enactment repealed by this Act shall, if in force at the commencement of this Act, and so far as it could have been made, issued, given or done under this Act, continue in force and have effect as if made, issued, given or done under the corresponding enactment of this Act.

(3) Any register kept under the Patents and Designs Act 1907 shall be deemed to form part of the corresponding register under this Act.

(4) Any design registered before the commencement of this Act shall be deemed to be registered under this Act in respect of articles of the class in which it is registered.

(5) Where, in relation to any design, the time for giving notice to the registrar under section 59 of the Patents and Designs Act 1907 expired before the commencement of this Act and the notice was not given, subsection (2) of section 6 of this Act shall not apply in relation to that design or any registration of that design.

(6) Any document referring to any enactment repealed by this Act shall be construed as referring to the corresponding enactment of this Act.

(7) Nothing in the foregoing provisions of this section shall be taken as prejudicing the operation of section 38 of the Interpretation Act 1889 (which relates to the effect of repeals).

49 Short title and commencement

(1) This Act may be cited as the Registered Designs Act 1949.

(2) This Act shall come into operation on the first day of January, nineteen hundred and fifty, immediately after the coming into operation of the Patents and Designs Act 1949.

FIRST SCHEDULE

PROVISIONS AS TO THE USE OF REGISTERED DESIGNS FOR THE SERVICES OF THE CROWN AND AS TO THE RIGHTS OF THIRD PARTIES IN RESPECT OF SUCH USE

Use of registered designs for services of the Crown

1 (1) Notwithstanding anything in this Act, any Government department, and any person authorised in writing by a Government department, may use any registered design for the services of the Crown in accordance with the following provisions of this paragraph.

(2) If and so far as the design has before the date of registration thereof been duly recorded by or applied by or on behalf of a Government department otherwise than in consequence of the communication of the design directly or indirectly by the registered proprietor or any person from whom he derives title, any use of the design by virtue of this paragraph may be made free of any royalty or other payment to the registered proprietor.

(3) If and so far as the design has not been so recorded or applied as aforesaid, any use of the design made by virtue of this paragraph at any time after the date of registration thereof, or in consequence of any such communication as aforesaid, shall be made upon such terms as may be agreed upon, either before or after the use, between the Government department and the registered proprietor with the approval of the Treasury, or as may in default of agreement be determined by the court on a reference under paragraph 3 of this Schedule.

(4) The authority of a Government department in respect of a design may be given under this paragraph either before or after the design is registered and either before or after the acts in respect of which the authority is given are done, and may be given to any person whether or not he is authorised directly or indirectly by the registered proprietor to use the design.

(5) Where any use of a design is made by or with the authority of a Government department under this paragraph, then, unless it appears to the department that it would be contrary to the public interest so to do, the department shall notify the registered proprietor as soon as practicable after the use is begun, and furnish him with such information as to the extent of the use as he may from time to time require.

(6) For the purposes of this and the next following paragraph "the services of the Crown" shall be deemed to include—

(a) the supply to the government of any country outside the United Kingdom, in pursuance of an agreement or arrangement between Her Majesty's Government in the United Kingdom and the government of that country, of articles required—

(i) for the defence of that country; or

(ii) for the defence of any other country whose government is party to any agreement or arrangement with Her Majesty's said Government in respect of defence matters;

(b) the supply to the United Nations, or the government of any country belonging to that organisation, in pursuance of an agreement or arrangement between Her Majesty's Government and that organisation or government, of articles required for any armed forces operating in pursuance of a resolution of that organisation or any organ of that organisation;

and the power of a Government department or a person authorised by a Government department under this paragraph to use a design shall include power to sell to any such government or to the said organisation any articles the supply of which is authorised by this sub-paragraph, and to sell to any person any articles made in the exercise of the powers conferred by this paragraph which are no longer required for the purpose for which they were made.

(7) The purchaser of any articles sold in the exercise of powers conferred by this paragraph, and any person claiming through him, shall have power to deal with them in the same manner as if the rights in the registered design were held on behalf of His Majesty.

Rights of third parties in respect of Crown use

2 (1) In relation to any use of a registered design, or a design in respect of which an application for registration is pending, made for the services of the Crown—

(a) by a Government department or a person authorised by a Government department under the last foregoing paragraph; or

(b) by the registered proprietor or applicant for registration to the order of a Government department,

the provisions of any licence, assignment or agreement made, whether before or after the commencement of this Act, between the registered proprietor or applicant for registration or any person who derives title from him or from whom he derives title and any person other than a Government department shall be of no effect so far as those provisions restrict or regulate the use of the design, or any model, document or information relating thereto, or provide for the making of payments in respect of any such use, or calculated by reference thereto; and the reproduction or publication of any model or document in connection with the said use shall not be deemed to be an infringement of any copyright or design right subsisting in the model or document.

(2) Where an exclusive licence granted otherwise than for royalties or other benefits determined by reference to the use of the design is in force under the registered design then—

(a) in relation to any use of the design which, but for the provisions of this and the last foregoing paragraph, would constitute an infringement of the rights of the licensee, sub-paragraph (3) of the last foregoing paragraph shall have effect as if for the reference to the registered proprietor there were substituted a reference to the licensee; and

(b) in relation to any use of the design by the licensee by virtue of an authority given under the last foregoing paragraph, that paragraph shall have effect as if the said sub-paragraph (3) were omitted.

(3) Subject to the provisions of the last foregoing sub-paragraph, where the registered design or the right to apply for or obtain registration of the design has been assigned to the registered proprietor in consideration of royalties or other benefits determined by reference to the use of the design, then—

(a) in relation to any use of the design by virtue of paragraph 1 of this Schedule, sub-paragraph (3) of that paragraph shall have effect as if the reference to the registered proprietor included a reference to the assignor, and any sum payable by virtue of that sub-paragraph shall be divided between the registered proprietor and the assignor in such proportion as may be agreed upon between them or as may in default of agreement be determined by the court on a reference under the next following paragraph; and

(b) in relation to any use of the design made for the services of the Crown by the registered proprietor to the order of a Government department, sub-paragraph (3) of paragraph 1 of this Schedule shall have effect as if that use were made by virtue of an authority given under that paragraph.

(4) Where, under sub-paragraph (3) of paragraph 1 of this Schedule, payments are required to be made by a Government department to a registered proprietor in respect of any use of a design, any person being the holder of an exclusive licence under the registered design (not being such a licence as is mentioned in sub-paragraph (2) of this paragraph) authorising him to make that use of the design shall be entitled to recover from the registered proprietor such part (if any) of those payments as may be agreed upon between that person and the registered proprietor, or as may in default

of agreement be determined by the court under the next following paragraph to be just having regard to any expenditure incurred by that person—

(a) in developing the said design; or

(b) in making payments to the registered proprietor, other than royalties or other payments determined by reference to the use of the design, in consideration of the licence;

and if, at any time before the amount of any such payment has been agreed upon between the Government department and the registered proprietor, that person gives notice in writing of his interest to the department, any agreement as to the amount of that payment shall be of no effect unless it is made with his consent.

(5) In this paragraph "exclusive licence" means a licence from a registered proprietor which confers on the licensee, or on the licensee and persons authorised by him, to the exclusion of all other persons (including the registered proprietor), any right in respect of the registered design.

Compensation for loss of profit

2A (1) Where Crown use is made of a registered design, the government department concerned shall pay—

(a) to the registered proprietor, or

(b) if there is an exclusive licence in force in respect of the design, to the exclusive licensee,

compensation for any loss resulting from his not being awarded a contract to supply the articles to which the design is applied.

(2) Compensation is payable only to the extent that such a contract could have been fulfilled from his existing manufacturing capacity; but is payable notwithstanding the existence of circumstances rendering him ineligible for the award of such a contract.

(3) In determining the loss, regard shall be had to the profit which would have been made on such a contract and to the extent to which any manufacturing capacity was under-used.

(4) No compensation is payable in respect of any failure to secure contracts for the supply of articles to which the design is applied otherwise than for the services of the Crown.

(5) The amount payable under this paragraph shall, if not agreed between the registered proprietor or licensee and the government department concerned with the approval of the Treasury, be determined by the court on a reference under paragraph 3; and it is in addition to any amount payable under paragraph 1 or 2 of this schedule.

(6) In this paragraph—

"Crown use", in relation to a design, means the doing of anything by virtue of paragraph 1 which would otherwise be an infringement of the right in the design; and

"the government department concerned", in relation to such use, means the government department by whom or on whose authority the act was done.

Reference of disputes as to Crown use

3 (1) Any dispute as to—

(a) the exercise by a Government department, or a person authorised by a Government department, of the powers conferred by paragraph 1 of this Schedule,

(b) terms for the use of a design for the services of the Crown under that paragraph,

(c) the right of any person to receive any part of a payment made under paragraph 1(3), or

(d) the right of any person to receive a payment under paragraph 2A,

may be referred to the court by either party to the dispute.

(2) In any proceedings under this paragraph to which a Government department are a party, the department may—

(a) if the registered proprietor is a party to the proceedings, apply for cancellation of the registration of the design upon any ground upon which the registration of a design may be cancelled on an application to the court under section twenty of this Act;

(b) in any case, put in issue the validity of the registration of the design without applying for its cancellation.

(3) If in such proceedings as aforesaid any question arises whether a design has been recorded or applied as mentioned in paragraph 1 of this Schedule, and the disclosure of any document recording the design, or of any evidence of the application thereof, would in the opinion of the department be prejudicial to the public interest, the disclosure may be made confidentially to counsel for the other party or to an independent expert mutually agreed upon.

(4) In determining under this paragraph any dispute between a Government department and any person as to terms for the use of a design for the services of the Crown, the court shall have regard to any benefit or compensation which that person or any person from whom he derives title may have received, or may be entitled to receive, directly or indirectly from any Government department in respect of the design in question.

(5) In any proceedings under this paragraph the court may at any time order the whole proceedings or any question or issue of fact arising therein to be referred to a special or official referee or an arbitrator on such terms as the court may direct; and references to the court in the foregoing provisions of this paragraph shall be construed accordingly.

Special provisions as to Crown use during emergency

4 (1) During any period of emergency within the meaning of this paragraph, the powers exercisable in relation to a design by a Government department, or a person authorised by a Government department under paragraph 1 of this Schedule shall include power to use the design for any purpose which appears to the department necessary or expedient—

(a) for the efficient prosecution of any war in which His Majesty may be engaged;

(b) for the maintenance of supplies and services essential to the life of the community;

(c) for securing a sufficiency of supplies and services essential to the well-being of the community;

(d) for promoting the productivity of industry, commerce and agriculture;

(e) for fostering and directing exports and reducing imports, or imports of any classes, from all or any countries and for redressing the balance of trade;

(f) generally for ensuring that the whole resources of the community are available for use, and are used, in a manner best calculated to serve the interests of the community; or

(g) for assisting the relief of suffering and the restoration and distribution of essential supplies and services in any part of His Majesty's dominions or any foreign countries that are in grave distress as the result of war;

and any reference in this Schedule to the services of the Crown shall be construed as including a reference to the purposes aforesaid.

(2) In this paragraph the expression "period of emergency" means a period beginning on such date as may be declared by Order in Council to be the commencement, and ending on such date as may be so declared to be the termination, of a period of emergency for the purposes of this paragraph.

(3) No Order in Council under this paragraph shall be submitted to Her Majesty unless a draft of it has been laid before and approved by a resolution of each House of Parliament.

… … … … … … …